Programming Flash
Communication Server

Other resources from O'Reilly

Related titles

Essential ActionScript 2.0

ActionScript for Flash MX:
The Definitive Guide

ActionScript for Flash MX
Pocket Reference

Programming ColdFusion MX

Flash Remoting: The
Definitive Guide

ActionScript Cookbook

Flash Out of the Box

Flash Hacks

oreilly.com

oreilly.com is more than a complete catalog of O'Reilly books. You'll also find links to news, events, articles, weblogs, sample chapters, and code examples.

oreillynet.com is the essential portal for developers interested in open and emerging technologies, including new platforms, programming languages, and operating systems.

Conferences

O'Reilly brings diverse innovators together to nurture the ideas that spark revolutionary industries. We specialize in documenting the latest tools and systems, translating the innovator's knowledge into useful skills for those in the trenches. Visit *conferences.oreilly.com* for our upcoming events.

Safari Bookshelf (*safari.oreilly.com*) is the premier online reference library for programmers and IT professionals. Conduct searches across more than 1,000 books. Subscribers can zero in on answers to time-critical questions in a matter of seconds. Read the books on your Bookshelf from cover to cover or simply flip to the page you need. Try it today with a free trial.

Programming Flash
Communication Server

*Brian Lesser, Giacomo Guilizzoni, Joey Lott,
Robert Reinhardt, and Justin Watkins*

O'REILLY®

Beijing · Cambridge · Farnham · Köln · Sebastopol · Tokyo

Programming Flash Communication Server

Brian Lesser, Giacomo Guilizzoni, Joey Lott, Robert Reinhardt, and Justin Watkins

Published by O'Reilly Media, Inc., 1005 Gravenstein Highway North, Sebastopol, CA 95472.

O'Reilly books may be purchased for educational, business, or sales promotional use. Online editions are also available for most titles (*safari.oreilly.com*). For more information, contact our corporate/institutional sales department: (800) 998-9938 or *corporate@oreilly.com*.

Editor:	Bruce Epstein
Production Editor:	Adam Witwer
Cover Designer:	Emma Colby
Interior Designer:	David Futato

Printing History:

February 2005:	First Edition.

ISBN: 978-0-596-00504-7
[LSI]

Table of Contents

Part I.   FlashCom Foundation

Foreword

Although Flash Communication Server MX has many groundbreaking features, it has roots in much of the work that preceded it.

Five things allowed Flash Communication Server to be realized:

- The body of knowledge of real-time, collaborative communication software
- The ubiquity of the Flash Player on the client
- The growing availability of broadband
- Adoption of digital devices like web cams and digital cameras
- Macromedia's investment in server-side technologies

Looking back at the path that led us here, it is hard to believe that my interest in creating multiuser software already spans 10 years.

In 1994, I was working for Novell, developing a toolkit that allowed application programmers to write once and compile and deploy anywhere (similar to Java, Director, and Flash). In October of 1994, Novell decided to get out of this business. I had an opportunity to work for a different group or take a fat severance check and find another job. I decided to take the layoff and the check!

Dan Greening, who was the director of engineering for my group at Novell, asked me if I would be interested in starting a company. At that time, there was a lot of buzz about the Internet and I felt the timing was perfect to take some risks. Dan and I, along with two other Novell alumni, Ron Lussier and Glenn Crocker, started Chaco Communications, Inc., in November 1994. We spent the next couple of months exploring multiuser role-playing games.

During the next year, we developed a Chaco client that used VRML to represent the virtual world. The VRML client didn't succeed, but I learned many lessons from its failures. We had developed a client that could be customized using HTML and VRML, but there was no authoring tool. The product was a standalone client, not integrated with the browser, so it required a separate installation. Server-side extension was difficult, limiting its customizability. Creating content was not easy, and that was a big problem. VRML as a technology was ahead of the hardware, which wasn't yet capable of an immersive 3D experience, and broadband was not yet widely available.

In 1996, NTT of Japan noticed Chaco's MUD (multiuser domain/dungeon/dimension) client and approached us to build a Java-based client and server for children, based on the Hello Kitty theme. We delivered this product in 1997, and it was very popular in Japan. The requirement for this project was to create an extensible client that ran inside a browser with a seamless install. We picked Java, which was the most ubiquitous client at the time. This proved very successful and showed me the importance of a ubiquitous client and an easy-to-customize application with the right authoring and development tools.

In 1997, Chaco merged with Songline Studios (owned by O'Reilly) to form Like-Minds. We changed direction, and I started work on a personalization server, intended to customize the web experience for repeat visitors to a given site. For the next 3 years, I was deep in the world of real-time data mining. This product was used by companies like NetFlix, Columbia House, and a bunch of dot-com retailers, many of which are no longer in business. Working on the LikeMinds personalization server, I learned a lot about building highly scalable servers in terms of moving large amounts of data in and out, managing large numbers of connections, interfacing with other systems, and so on.

While working on the LikeMinds social server, which was a chat server that we developed for NTT, we needed a data synchronization scheme, and I came up with something called distributed buckets. This was little more than name/value pairs plus a mechanism to replicate the name/value on all clients when any client added to a distributed bucket. I later used a similar design in the Flash Communication Server, and we called it shared objects.

LikeMinds was acquired by Andromedia, which was in turn acquired by Macromedia in 1999. Toward the end of 2000, Macromedia sold LikeMinds' technology to IBM, and it is now part of the IBM WebSphere personalization engine. I was still working for Macromedia when they decided to get out of personalization technology. I started exploring other opportunities, but I wanted to stick with server-side development. At that time, Macromedia did not have a lot of server-side technology; one product I considered was Generator. Before I had made a decision, I got a call from Jonathan Gay (the Father of Flash) who asked me if I would be interested in exploring a new project.

Jon had this idea of building real-time communication capabilities into the client-side Flash Player and wanted to know if I could help him build a server product to provide the server-side functionality. This brought back memories of my Chaco days. I felt that the time was right to again venture into the world of multiuser collaboration. Given my earlier experience of building multiuser communication products and knowing the reasons for its failures, I felt that with the combination of Flash Player, broadband, and the adoption of communication technologies like IM, there was a huge opportunity to move the technology to the next level by introducing audio and video. Combined with the multimedia capabilities of Flash, we had a realistic chance of succeeding, and I felt I could make a significant contribution in making this a reality.

For the next 4 months, we did an extensive study of the market, technologies, and trends to see what we should build. Our vision was to build a real-time communication infrastructure to take Flash and Macromedia into a new, profitable business in the telecommunications world. Flash's adoption as the standard for web animation was made possible by providing a lightweight Player and a rich, easy-to-use authoring system that provides a set of high-level APIs approachable by a large audience. We wanted to continue this vision by providing a platform for real-time communications that was easy to develop for and deploy. To better understand what this platform had to provide, we put together ideas for 10 real-time applications—classroom, company meeting, front door cam, customer service, car race, remote presence, and so on—and collected all the requirements to come up with the base features. All applications required some combination of audio, video, or data as streams (some real-time and some on-demand) and data synchronization. They all required an application model to create and control groups, which resulted in the server-side application model defined by Flash Communication Server.

This resulted in the following features the platform needed to provide:

- An easy-to-install, ubiquitous client supporting multimedia devices such as microphones and cameras
- A low-overhead protocol with support for real-time delivery of media, data, and control messages
- Real-time or stored (on-demand) data
- Software applications that add intelligence and support communication
- An easy way to blend content and communication
- Support for remote presence

The first two items on the list describe the Flash Player and the RTMP protocol. But to succeed, we also needed to provide a simple, reliable, and flexible model for communications and application development, with a high-level API for developers. Furthermore, we needed to set application development standards and help the developer community understand how to build communication applications.

Despite the misperception that Flash Communication Server (FlashCom) was based on Shockwave Multiuser Server (SMUS), a multiuser server once provided with Macromedia Director, FlashCom was built from the ground up. FlashCom provides features never available in SMUS, such as shared objects and the publish-subscribe model for audio, video, and data streams. That is not to say FlashCom didn't borrow from my past projects in real-time collaborative software. As I said, the distributed buckets in LikeMinds' social server became FlashCom shared objects. And I had developed a high-performance socket I/O architecture for the LikeMinds server that became the core I/O architecture for FlashCom. Of course, FlashCom provided new challenges, for which I developed the RTMP protocol (with help from Jon Gay and Brad Edelman), its server-side object model, on-demand streaming, the FlashCom application model, and the configuration model.

After nearly 2 years of development, Macromedia released Flash Communication Server MX 1.0 in September 2002. FlashCom version 1.5 followed in March 2003, and the latest update, version 1.5.2, was released in May 2004. We succeeded in defining a new application development platform for real-time communication applications. Looking back at the vision and value we pursued, I am very proud to say that we delivered on our promise. We may have had some unrealistic optimism about its instant success, but over the last year, we have seen Flash Communication Server establish a toehold in the market, and now we are seeing our dreams realized.

One of the challenges with any new technology is finding early adopters who can invest in an unproven technology. This problem was compounded by the fact that the Internet bubble burst, and developing a collaboration application requires a new skill set and significant resources. Given this slow adoption, we decided it was time for us to eat our own dog food and show what could be done with FlashCom, so we built Breeze Live atop the FlashCom platform. Breeze Live is probably one of the most complex FlashCom applications ever developed and has greatly benefited me in evolving the core FlashCom platform. And Breeze Live is one of Macromedia's fastest-growing products, proving that there is a market for compelling, media-rich, real-time communication applications.

Another key to the success of any platform is teaching developers how to build applications beyond "hello world." I am confident that *Programming Flash Communication Server* will go a long way in making this adoption possible. It is a must-read book for anyone serious about writing communication applications using Flash Communication Server.

—Pritham Shetty
Principal Architect
Flash Communication Server
Macromedia

Preface

This book is intended to show you how to design and build applications that use Macromedia's Flash Communication Server MX. Together, Flash and the Flash Communication Server (FlashCom) can be used to create a dizzying array of applications including virtual classrooms, real-time multiplayer games, media-on-demand services, instant messaging applications, interactive live event broadcasts, video conferencing systems, and more. Macromedia designed FlashCom to simplify developing these types of communication applications. This book covers everything you need to know to program for FlashCom, whether creating simple standalone applications or more complex applications that work with web application servers, databases, and directory servers.

What Does FlashCom Offer?

FlashCom is a real-time communication server. It provides an extensible and customizable platform for developing real-time, media-rich, web-based communication applications. As described in the Foreword, FlashCom takes care of the plumbing required to create networked applications, allowing you to focus on your unique application rather than write code to support network protocols.

A Flash movie running in Flash Player 6 or later can connect to a FlashCom Server and through it exchange audio, video, and ActionScript data with other Flash movies. Creating communication applications involves scripting using ActionScript on the client side and its close relative, Server-Side ActionScript, on the server side. Macromedia provides ActionScript classes that make managing real-time multiuser communications much simpler than in other platforms. The NetConnection class used to connect a Flash movie to the server, and the NetStream class used to stream audio, video, and data between them are just two examples.

FlashCom Server runs on Windows or Linux, but the Flash client runs on multiple platforms, including Windows and Macintosh. Authoring is often performed in Flash MX 2004 or Flash MX Professional 2004 on Windows or Macintosh.

Macromedia also provides higher-level communication components that can be used with a minimum of coding to create a variety of basic applications. Examples include the PeopleList component that shows who is online and the Chat, WhiteBoard, and VideoConference components. It is a remarkable experience to create a communication application by simply dragging some of these components onto Flash's Stage, creating a directory and a little code on the server, and then participate in a video conference complete with text chat, whiteboard, and people list. Applications created this way are not really complete—for example, they are usually single room applications with minimal security—but communication components are powerful tools that make developing even full-fledged applications much easier. Macromedia also provides administrative tools to manage, monitor, and log server activity.

What does FlashCom Server offer that you can't get with the Flash client alone? FlashCom's features include:

- Streaming video if the user has Flash Player 6 or higher
- Real-time video, audio, text, and data exchange
- Uploading of video and audio from the user's Camera and Microphone objects

So how do you know if you need FlashCom?

If you want to stream live video to the Flash Player, you need FlashCom. If you just want to play back a recorded stream, you can do so without FlashCom, but performance might suffer.

For many more details on other advantages of FlashCom, see "Streaming Video with FlashCom" later in this Preface.

Also refer to the comparison that Macromedia provides at:

http://www.macromedia.com/devnet/mx/flash/articles/video_primer_03.html

The Flash Communication Server is also evolving. The first release was quickly followed with the version 1.5 release that runs on Linux or Windows and included new features such as HTTP tunneling and MP3 support. Since then, two updaters have been released that went beyond fixing bugs by extending features or improving performance. The most recent release is FlashCom Version 1.5.2 and is covered in this book. Regardless of future updates to the software, this book provides a rich understanding of FlashCom development. The foundation it provides will help you to design and build whatever types of applications you decide to create.

For a sneak peek at the next version of FlashCom, see:

http://www.peldi.com/blog/archives/2004/11/recording_of_th.html

An extensive review of the proposed feature set for FlashCom 2.0 can be found at:

http://flash-communications.net/news/max2004SneakPeek/

Robert Reinhardt also wrote a critique of FlashCom 2.0's proposed feature set at:

http://www.communitymx.com/abstract.cfm?cid=0F44C

What's in This Book?

As with any technology, as you move away from creating simple applications to creating larger-scale, robust, and secure applications, design and development increase in difficulty. This is especially true in an environment in which events are occurring in multiple Flash movies and on the server at the same time. Coordinating concurrent events introduces an extra level of complexity that many Flash and web developers may not be used to. This book addresses these and other problems directly. It describes in detail how to:

- Avoid conflicts when multiple users update data in real time
- Manage contention for the same resources—for example, multiple users trying to add text to the same shared text area
- Minimize the effects of network latency
- Adapt to differences in client bandwidth
- Use and extend Macromedia's communication classes
- Design and develop components that work well within Macromedia's component framework
- Design applications without Macromedia's framework using your own set of components
- Create applications that can scale from a few simultaneous users to many thousands
- Create secure applications

The book also includes numerous samples files—especially in the later chapters—that I hope you will find useful, including:

- A collection of components such as PeopleGrid, OnlineStatus, TextChat, SharedText, VideoConference, Authentication, and PersonalCursor
- An alternative, lightweight component framework
- A recording framework for recording and playing back events, audio, video, and data

The book also includes numerous useful ColdFusion examples to perform operations beyond the capabilities of FlashCom Server, such as FTP file copying and database access. All sample code is available on the book's web site.

How to Use This Book

To get the most out of the book, you should have FlashCom Server 1.5.2 installed and running on your server (or a hosting company's server). The trial version is freely available from Macromedia's site. If you are using an older version, obtain and install the updater.

You also should have Flash MX 2004 or Flash MX Professional 2004 available for client-side development, although you can write server-side scripts in any text editor. Again, trial versions are freely available on Macromedia's site.

Depending on your application, it also is beneficial to have:

- A microphone, for audio input
- A web cam, for video input
- ColdFusion Server MX 2004 or later, for Chapters 11, 12, 14, and 18, which all make use of CFML code examples

The book is divided into four parts:

Part I: FlashCom Foundation

The first four chapters of the book introduce the Flash Communication Server and the client-side components available to construct applications, such as a video chat. Chapters 3 and 4 go into detail about creating applications and connecting to them.

Chapter 1, Introducing the Flash Communication Server
 Introduces the communication classes by using them to build a simple video conferencing application

Chapter 2, Communication Components
 Shows how to assemble applications using Macromedia's communication components

Chapter 3, Managing Connections
 Covers all aspects of establishing and managing client connection requests and the server response

Chapter 4, Applications, Instances, and Server-Side ActionScript
 Covers server-side application development in detail

Part II: Audio, Video, and Data Streams

Chapters 5 through 7 focus on the media and data that can be transmitted to and from FlashCom applications and their clients.

Chapter 5, Managing Streams
 Offers extensive details on publishing and playing live and recorded streams, including audio, video, and data

Chapter 6, Camera and Microphone
 Provides detailed coverage of the Camera and Microphone classes for managing video and audio input

Chapter 7, Media Preparation and Delivery
 Addresses issues revolving around audio and video preparation to ensure the best user experience

Part III: Remote Connectivity and Communication

Chapters 8 through 12 cover communication between FlashCom applications and their clients or communicating with other application servers using Flash Remoting.

Chapter 8, Shared Objects
> Offers extensive details on communicating between clients and applications using temporary and persistent remote shared objects

Chapter 9, Remote Methods
> Describes how to use the *NetConnection* and *Client* classes to implement remote method invocation

Chapter 10, Server Management API
> Covers the powerful API available to monitor and control FlashCom Server operations

Chapter 11, Flash Remoting
> Explains how to communicate with other applications, such as ColdFusion, to implement features not available to FlashCom directly

Chapter 12, ColdFusion MX and FlashCom
> Builds on the previous chapter and gives practical examples of ColdFusion and FlashCom integration

Part IV: Design and Deployment

Chapters 13 through 18 cover building and extending components, application design, scalability, managing latency and bandwidth limitations, and creating secure applications.

Chapter 13, Building Communication Components
> Introduces communication component development using the Flash UI components and client-side ActionScript 2.0

Chapter 14, Understanding the Macromedia Component Framework
> Describes how to write components that work with Macromedia's communication component framework

Chapter 15, Application Design Patterns and Best Practices
> Offers advice on application design, improving component performance, and best practices

Chapter 16, Building Scalable Applications
> Looks at multi-instance applications and how components can support scalable designs

Chapter 17, Network Performance, Latency, Concurrency
> Covers performance tuning to deal with latency and bandwidth limitations, plus addresses concurrency issues and solutions in a networked environment

Chapter 18, Securing Applications
> Looks at integrating authentication and role-based authorization into components, including a ticketing mechanism

Although later chapters assume you have read and understood earlier material, you can jump around the book to suit your experience level and needs.

 Read Chapters 10 and 18 before making your server publicly available on the Internet.

Audience

My coauthors and I assume you have some experience with scripting in either Flash ActionScript, ECMAScript, or JavaScript, but the book is designed to meet the needs of a wide variety of readers with varying backgrounds and interests. Where Action-Script is discussed, familiarity with the Flash development environment is assumed. If you're new to the Flash authoring tool, you'll want to read *Flash Out of the Box* (O'Reilly). This book is not designed as an introductory step-by-step tutorial to programming in Flash. There is a wonderful and growing variety of books and sources on Flash programming. If you have little or no experience with ActionScript programming, you should consult *ActionScript for Flash MX: The Definitive Guide* and *Essential ActionScript 2.0* (both from O'Reilly).

If you are looking for a step-by-step introduction to programming FlashCom, have a look at the introductory chapters of this book. If you feel they are over your head, consult the resources cited in the previous paragraph before returning to this book. Also consider books such as *Flash Remoting: The Definitive Guide* and the *Action-Script Cookbook* (also from O'Reilly) for targeted coverage of other areas of interest.

The book is not a printed version of the online documentation, nor does it attempt to reproduce materials on widely available topics, such as how to install FlashCom. Instead, it is designed to clarify and extend the information provided by Macromedia's documentation and web site. See in particular the documentation available at:

> *http://www.macromedia.com/support/documentation/en/flashcom/index.htm*

This book was written by people who have used FlashCom and Macromedia's documentation from the earliest days of the product. We all had to struggle to understand just what Macromedia had given us and hope to help you avoid having to repeat all our early tests and experiments. The book is designed to be read and reread as your experience developing Flash communication applications increases.

The changes in Flash from versions 4 to 5 were revolutionary, and the changes from version 5 to MX—among them components and video support—were also very dramatic. Flash MX 2004 introduced ActionScript 2.0 and added an entire new set of user interface components. ActionScript 2.0 added some features familiar to C++ and Java programmers, such as strong typing and formal classes.

In Chapters 1 through 12, the book's client-side ActionScript examples are written in both ActionScript 1.0 and ActionScript 2.0. From Chapter 13 onward, the client-side samples are written almost exclusively in ActionScript 2.0 and use the newer v2 Flash UI components. All server-side FlashCom code is written in Server-Side ActionScript, which uses ActionScript 1.0 syntax, because that is the only supported version.

Among the reasons for the mixture of ActionScript 1.0 (AS 1.0) and ActionScript 2.0 (AS 2.0) throughout the book:

- The communication classes provided for client-side scripting, such as SharedObject, NetStream, and NetConnection, were all designed to use AS 1.0–style dynamic methods and properties. In Chapter 13, I show how to wrap shared objects up so that you can use AS 2.0, but that is an extra step and not something provided by Macromedia. Macromedia's communication components are available only in AS 1.0 and require the Flash UI client-side v1 components. For example, the Chat component's client-side code is written in AS 1.0 because the communication components were originally built for Flash MX and have not been updated to AS 2.0.

- Server-Side ActionScript (SSAS) is JavaScript 1.5, which is very close to AS 1.0. The client-side classes such as SharedObject and NetConnection also exist on the server where AS 1.0 must be used to do the same sort of work you must do on the client such as setting up *onStatus( )* or *onSync( )* event handlers. That is, it is much easier to port client-side AS 1.0 code than AS 2.0 code to SSAS.

- ActionScript 2.0 is a superset of ActionScript 1.0. I think this is something people coming from the Java world or just discovering the discipline of strong typing, formal class and interface definitions, and so on often forget. AS 2.0 code compiles down to the same bytecode as AS 1.0, allowing AS 2.0 code to be exported for use in Flash Player 6 (although Flash Player 6 doesn't support all the latest AS 2.0 classes). Regardless, ActionScript provides all the benefits of a simple scripting language, such as loose typing and dynamic objects, while offering the option of stronger typing and formal classes. AS 2.0 simply provides new options that are particularly valuable for larger-scale projects.

- ActionScript 2.0 means different things to different developers. On the syntactic level, it means support for strict typing and different commands (such as import instead of #include). On the architectural level, it includes support for formal classes, packages, and interfaces. In the end, the purpose of the book is to teach FlashCom programming, not ActionScript 1.0 or 2.0. We didn't want to obscure the basics of FlashCom programming with a heavy reliance on object-oriented programming (OOP) and formal classes. This allows scripters of all levels to focus on the new FlashCom material.

- Robust, deployment-ready code is not conducive to learning a topic. The book often presents pared-down examples, but the web site has full-blown code examples in both AS 1.0 and AS 2.0 format, when appropriate.

ActionScript 1.0 Versus ActionScript 2.0

The ActionScript 2.0 examples must be compiled in the Flash MX 2004 or Flash MX Professional 2004 authoring environment. To make sure the AS 2.0 examples compile, you should set the ActionScript version to ActionScript 2.0 under File → Publish Settings → Flash. All examples have been tested in Flash Player 7.

In ActionScript 2.0, all custom class definitions must be placed in external *.as* files. For example, the custom Whatever class must be placed in an external plain text file named *Whatever.as* (both the capitalization of the name and the *.as* extension are mandatory). You can create and edit such a file in Flash MX Professional 2004 if you select File → New → ActionScript File. If using Flash MX 2004, you'll need an external text editor.

We can't give a full course on OOP and ActionScript 2.0 here, although we do try to provide pointers throughout the book. For many more details on ActionScript 2.0 classes and object-oriented development, see *Essential ActionScript 2.0* (O'Reilly).

Most examples can also be exported in Flash Player 6 format from Flash MX 2004 (standard or Professional edition), by setting the Export format to Flash Player 6 under File → Publish Settings → Flash.

However, methods that are new to Flash MX 2004 and Flash Player 7 won't work if you are exporting to Flash Player 6 format.

The previous version of the Flash authoring tool, Flash MX, does not support ActionScript 2.0. However, many of the AS 1.0 code examples will work in Flash MX.

In some cases, this book uses timeline-based code, which, although it is not necessarily a best practice, is supported for both ActionScript 1.0 and ActionScript 2.0. We made this choice when an example didn't benefit markedly from using ActionScript 2.0 classes. This makes the examples easier to follow and implement in both Flash MX and Flash MX 2004.

Some of the class-based OOP examples written in ActionScript 2.0 won't compile in ActionScript 1.0 and require Flash MX 2004 (standard or Professional edition). If you are still using ActionScript 1.0 in Flash MX 2004, consider this an opportunity to broaden your horizons and use AS 2.0.

Server-Side ActionScript

There are two distinct types of ActionScript: client-side ActionScript—which includes both ActionScript 1.0 and ActionScript 2.0—and the server-side version, known as Server-Side ActionScript (SSAS). Client-side ActionScript is used to create .swf moves that run in the Flash Player on the user's machine. Server-Side Action-Script is stored in .asc files that run on the FlashCom Server. As you'll see, Server-Side ActionScript does not support the OOP features of AS 2.0. Instead, Server-Side ActionScript is like JavaScript 1.5, which is very similar to AS 1.0 (all are based on ECMAScript 3). For more on the differences between client-side and server-side scripting, see "Differences Between Flash ActionScript and Server-Side ActionScript" in Chapter 4. FlashCom SSAS is not the same as the Server-Side ActionScript that can be used to script Flash Remoting applications in ColdFusion and JRun. For more information on that topic, see *Flash Remoting: The Definitive Guide* (O'Reilly).

The flash-communications.net Site

As FlashCom evolves, you will find new information on the companion site to this book:

> *http://flash-communications.net*

You can also find the examples from the book, additional tutorials and tech notes, news, additional sample files, and errata.

As people use and adapt code from the book—especially the communication components —you'll find bug fixes and enhancements on the site as well.

Director, Breeze, and Other Options

In addition to creating Flash movies that connect to a FlashCom Server, you can also connect using Director movies. Working with Director is not covered in this book. However, the same communication classes used in Flash can be accessed from Director, so Director developers will find a lot of useful information here. Additional resources are available at:

> *http://www.macromedia.com/devnet/mx/director/cross_product_integration.html*

After releasing FlashCom, Macromedia purchased a company named Presedia, Inc. Presedia's products included:

- A PowerPoint-to-Flash converter that has the ability to record audio for each PowerPoint slide in order to make self-running presentations
- A server product that stores, organizes, and plays presentations created with the converter and that can host standards-compliant tests and quizzes as well as track user progress through them

Macromedia renamed the Presedia product Breeze and used FlashCom to add a new module named Breeze Live. The Breeze Live module is possibly the most complex and feature-rich FlashCom-based product on the market. It provides an extensible online meeting environment that includes the ability to play converted PowerPoint presentations, share each user's video screen, upload and download files, use a whiteboard, conduct instant polls, load web pages into users' browsers and more. The Breeze Live user interface is composed of "pods." For example, the Whiteboard and PeopleList components in Breeze are both pods. Macromedia makes available a software development kit for Breeze pods so developers can extend Breeze Live to include custom features. Information on Breeze is available here:

http://www.macromedia.com/software/breeze

This book does not cover Breeze development, but Breeze developers will find much of the book lays the foundation they need for developing Breeze pods, because Breeze is built atop the FlashCom Server platform. Pods rely on the communication classes described in Chapters 3 through 9 and are similar in many respects to the communication components described in Chapters 13 through 15. More information on developing with Breeze is available here:

http://www.macromedia.com/devnet/breeze

Breeze is a large and full-featured application for conducting corporate training, holding meetings, and hosting presentations. Macromedia acts as a Breeze hosting provider and provides pay-per-use and monthly fee plans. The Breeze software can also be licensed from Macromedia. Should you be using Breeze? That depends. It is certainly a well-engineered and capable product, but it is also fairly expensive. If you want to create custom applications or have simpler requirements, FlashCom may be more cost-effective for your needs.

After Breeze Live was announced, some people were concerned that it would replace FlashCom. However, Breeze's reliance on the FlashCom platform has spurred further development of the Flash Communication Server by Macromedia.

Another product built on top of FlashCom is ASAP from Convoq. ASAP supports ad hoc and scheduled meetings. The user interface is similar to instant messaging systems but includes video conferencing and other features. Information on ASAP, including subscription pricing, is available at:

http://www.convoq.com

Chris Hock maintains a site that lists many of the other applications built using FlashCom:

http://flashcommunicationserver.net

I can't offer detailed advice on when to buy and extend an existing communication application and when to develop your own. However, you may want to consider the following things:

- How closely the application meets your requirements
- The cost of development and maintenance versus the licensing cost of an existing application
- Whether an existing application can be customized to meet your needs and the cost of extending it
- The cost of integrating another application with your existing systems

Flash XML Socket servers provide an interesting alternative to some of the features available with the FlashCom Server. While they do not provide streaming audio or video, they do provide real-time data sharing services. In some cases, socket servers have been used in partnership with FlashCom. The socket server provides a less expensive alternative for real-time messaging while FlashCom manages audio and video streaming. Information on two well-known socket servers is available here:

http://moock.org/unity
http://www.electrotank.com/electroserver

There are other alternatives to using Flash and FlashCom to develop rich real-time communication applications. However, few have all the following features:

- The Flash Player is pervasive, meaning that almost all web users can play Flash-Com content. Users will resist downloading another plugin and that limits the reach of other competing technologies. Flash Player's ubiquity far outstrips alternatives such as Windows Media Player, QuickTime, and the Real Player.
- Extending and customizing Flash clients in the Flash authoring environment makes rapid development of highly customized interfaces relatively simple. In particular, the seamless integration of video with other visible elements in a Flash movie is a compelling advantage. Systems based on Java and other clients are more difficult to develop and much less flexible.
- FlashCom was designed from the beginning to be a flexible platform capable of delivering a wide range of applications. It did not start life as an instant messaging server or media server with additional features bolted on later. It has an excellent and well-thought-out application programming interface that lowers the cost of application development.
- Together, Flash and FlashCom can be used to develop an amazing range of compelling applications such as multiuser games with live audio, online help and counseling systems, and video and educational applications where teams can collaborate while working through a simulation. It provides the resources needed to build traditional applications such as instant messaging systems, streaming media systems, video email, and other systems in one package.

Flash Video Options

Whether you need FlashCom for an application requiring video depends on how you are trying to serve your video, which depends on your application's requirements. For assistance in choosing the right technology based on the length of video clips, number of viewers, and so on, see the chart at:

http://www.macromedia.com/devnet/mx/flash/articles/video_primer.html

 Currently, FlashCom is the only way to collect and redistribute live video from Flash movies as well as to stream recorded video to Flash movies.

This book assumes you've made the decision to use FlashCom (whether for video or other applications, such as chat).

However, there are other ways to play prerecorded video in Flash as described next.

For a feature comparison of FlashCom versus other Flash video alternatives, see:

http://www.macromedia.com/devnet/mx/flash/articles/video_primer_03.html

Embedded Video

Flash MX and later versions of the Flash authoring tool make it possible to import video files directly into a Flash movie. A Flash movie containing embedded video can be played in Flash Player 4 and later. Unfortunately, embedded video has severe limitations. The video is incorporated into the *.fla* file before it is converted to a *.swf*, meaning that the developer must republish the *.swf* whenever the video changes. Furthermore, the video makes the *.swf* very large and slow to download. Embedded video must be played at the same rate as the timeline and is limited to 16,000 frames. Furthermore, sound synchronization problems occur after about 2 minutes of video playback.

Progressive Download

Flash Player 7 added the ability to play FLV video files as they were downloaded from a web server. The feature is usually referred to as progressive download in order to distinguish it from streaming. All that is required to make an FLV available for progressive download is to post it on a web server and create a Flash movie that downloads and plays it. When a Flash movie requests an FLV file, the web server sends the file starting from the beginning of the file until either the entire file is downloaded or the browser and player disconnect. The file is held in cache so that the Player can seek to different parts of the video that have already been downloaded. The Player cannot seek ahead to sections of the video that have not been downloaded from the web server.

Although video starts playing immediately with progressive download, this approach doesn't support live video nor does it support all the features of FlashCom such as total control over seeking. Another limitation is that the entire video is downloaded to the user's cache, which is undesirable when dealing with copyrighted material.

The new Macromedia Video Kit is a utility for Dreamweaver developers that includes Squeeze Lite to compress video in FLV format. The utility allows HTML developers to easily embed Flash video in a web page by automatically creating the *.swf* file to play the video without the need for the Flash authoring environment. The Flash video plays using progressive download, as can also be accomplished using Flash MX 2004 or Flash Pro. For full details, see:

> *http://www.macromedia.com/software/studio/flashvideokit*

For streaming video from Dreamweaver, see the Flash Video Streaming Service Lite as described at:

> *http://www.macromedia.com/software/flashcom/fvss*
> *http://www.macromedia.com/devnet/mx/flash/articles/video_primer_04.*
> *html#authordwfl*

Streaming Video with FlashCom

Unlike embedded video and progressive download, a Flash movie can ask the Flash-Com Server to stream any part of a prerecorded video at any time. FlashCom will locate the video file, find the part of the video to send, and start streaming from that point. Whenever it is important to be able to quickly seek to any portion of a large video file, FlashCom provides an important advantage over progressive download and embedded video.

FlashCom also makes it possible to seamlessly adapt to each client's bandwidth. You can script a bandwidth test that will estimate the bandwidth available to the client and then select an appropriate size video to stream. See Chapter 17 for more on bandwidth detection.

Macromedia maintains a video section on its DevNet site:

> *http://www.macromedia.com/devnet/mx/flash/video.html*

Macromedia has also published a video primer that provides a good summary comparing different ways to deliver prerecorded video using Flash:

> *http://www.macromedia.com/devnet/mx/flash/articles/video_primer_print.html*

FlashCom offers a persistent connection, allowing you to implement many features with streaming not supported by progressive download. It also offers the most robust and consistent delivery platform, especially for large videos and large numbers of users. Most notably, FlashCom streaming video allows you to:

- Deliver live video and audio, whether from a web cam or digital video camera

- Enable multiuser video conferencing and similar applications
- Start video playing as soon as possible
- Implement bandwidth detection to optimize video serving
- Monitor quality of service and provide logging, tracking, and reporting statistics
- Maintain full scripting control of streams for detailed interactive control of the video experience
- Easily change content by updating external videos (this also applies to progressive download)
- Use less client memory and disk space (especially true for large videos)
- Minimize the network load because only the portion of the video that is viewed needs to be downloaded
- Securely deliver copyrighted material without its being saved to the user's cache

See also Chapters 5 and 7 in this book for details on streaming.

Licensing and Hosting Options

This book does not focus on the numerous server configuration details, nor does it offer networking hardware advice. If you don't want to run FlashCom Server from your own hardware, many different options are available for hosting communication applications. You can load FlashCom on a server you control. In that case, you, your organization, or your customers will have to pay for the FlashCom license, server, and bandwidth necessary to support your applications. FlashCom includes a license manager that monitors the number of simultaneous client connections and the bandwidth being consumed by the server. The license manager ensures that FlashCom will refuse connections after the number of clients or the allowed bandwidth has been exceeded. Information on FlashCom licensing options is available here:

http://www.macromedia.com/software/flashcom/productinfo/editions

If you do not want to host the server yourself, a number of companies specialize in FlashCom hosting.

The Flash Video Streaming Service is a load-balanced, redundant deployment of FlashCom Server, hosted by a Macromedia-authorized Content Delivery Network partner. For details, see:

http://www.macromedia.com/software/flashcom/fvss

Speedera offers FlashCom video-on-demand hosting. For details, see:

http://www.speedera.com

VitalStream focuses on live event and on-demand applications. VitalStream provides prebuilt applications and services but will not (as of this writing) host custom applications. For details, see:

http://www.vitalstream.com
http://www.macromedia.com/devnet/mx/flash/articles/fvss.html

Other hosting providers will host your custom applications for you. A short list of providers is available from Macromedia on their partners' page (scroll down to the ISP/Hosting Partners section):

http://www.macromedia.com/partners/flashcom

You can find many other providers with different hosting and service plans via a web search. There are other related products for which you might consider hosted options. Macromedia offers Breeze Live hosting. The third-party HostMySite.com (*http://www.hostmysite.com*) offers ColdFusion hosting, including the latest Blackstone version of ColdFusion.

Conventions Used in This Book

The following typographical conventions are used in this book:

Plain text
> Indicates menu titles, menu options, menu buttons, and keyboard accelerators (such as Alt and Ctrl). Submenu options are also indicated with an arrow, such as File → Open.

Italic
> Indicates application names, new terms, library symbol names, function names, method names, class names, package names, layer names, URLs, URIs, stream names, email addresses, filenames, file extensions, pathnames, and directories. In addition to being italicized in the body text, method and function names are also followed by parentheses, such as *setInterval( )*.

`Constant width`
> Indicates code samples, application instance names, clip instance names, symbol linkage identifiers, frame labels, commands, variables, attributes, properties, parameters, values, objects, XML tags, HTML tags, the contents of files, or the output from commands.

`Constant width bold`
> Shows commands or other text that should be entered literally by the user. It is also used within code examples for emphasis, such as to highlight an important line of code in a larger example.

Constant width italic

Shows text that should be replaced with user-supplied values. *Constant width italic* is also used to emphasize variable, property, method, and function names referenced in comments within code examples.

 This icon signifies a tip, suggestion, or general note.

 This icon indicates a warning or caution.

In the interest of brevity, we expect you to understand the following conventions used throughout all O'Reilly books on Flash and ActionScript. For so-called instance-level methods, such as *connect( )*, which are invoked on an instance of a class, such as *NetConnection*, we refer to it in the prose as *NetConnection.connect( )*. However, in the code examples, you don't use the class name but rather an instance of the *NetConnection* class, such as:

```
my_connection.connect( )
```

On the other hand, so-called class methods (a.k.a. static methods) are invoked on the class itself, in which case the class name is used verbatim, such as:

```
Classname.methodname( )
```

The analogous issue applies when referring to instance or class (static) properties. The difference should be clear from context or the Macromedia documentation for a particular class.

Once a concept, component, or class has been introduced, we often simplify the language for readability. For example, instead of writing "establish a network connection using an instance of the NetConnection class," we might simply write "create a NetConnection to access the FlashCom application."

When there are multiple names for an item, or nuances as to its meaning, we choose the most appropriate or convenient one. The meaning should always be clear from context. Most notably:

- The `client` object is technically an instance of the server-side Client class stored in a variable named `client`.

- The `application` object is technically an instance of the server-side *Application* class.

- Shared objects have two names. One of the names matches the external shared object file, but without the extension. For example, `people` can refer to the *people.sol* or *people.lso* file. The variable that holds a reference to the shared object usually includes the _so suffix, such as people_so. Regardless, constant-width text can become distracting, so we also refer to it informally as "the people shared object." Again, let your context be your guide.

- Many items have related names that take different formatting or use different capitalization. For example, an instance of the DataProvider class might be used to populate the dataProvider property of a DataGrid component. Likewise, the PeopleList component might be supported by the *PeopleList* class.

Voice

This book is the combined effort of five authors. While every effort has been made to ensure uniformity, some differences in voice, writing style, and coding style are inevitable. In places, "we" refers to the collective authors, such as in, "We hope you enjoy this book." In other places, "we" refers to the reader and the author together, such as in, "We'll see how to create a chat application shortly." In places, the author uses first-person singular, such as in, "When I test the speed of the Internet connection at my house, it isn't as fast as my computer at work."

This book also follows the O'Reilly convention of alternating gender occasionally throughout the chapters. "He," "her," and "the user" generally refer to the human participant interacting with a Flash-based UI to access a FlashCom application. The term "client" usually refers to the Flash Player running in a desktop PC's browser. Exceptions are noted when applicable.

Using Code Examples

Keep in mind that there is a difference between the teaching examples shown in the book and robust, deployment-ready code. Always consult the web site for the latest and greatest version of a given example.

 Source files (including many that don't appear in the book) can be downloaded from the book's web site at *http://www.flash-communications.net*.
Package names begin with the path *com.oreilly.pfcs*.

This book is here to help you get your job done. In general, you may use the code in this book in your programs and documentation. You do not need to contact O'Reilly for permission unless you're reproducing a significant portion of the code. For example, writing a program that uses several chunks of code from this book does not require permission. Selling or distributing a CD-ROM of examples from O'Reilly books *does* require permission. Answering a question by citing this book and quoting example code does not require permission. Incorporating a significant amount of example code from this book into your product's documentation *does* require permission.

We appreciate, but do not require, attribution. An attribution usually includes the title, author, publisher, and ISBN. For example: "*Programming Flash Communication Server*, by Brian Lesser et al. Copyright 2005 O'Reilly Media, Inc., 0-596-00504-0."

If you feel your use of code examples falls outside fair use or the preceding permission, feel free to contact us at *permissions@oreilly.com*.

Getting the Code Examples Working

The most common reason for being unable to get a code example to work (assuming you haven't made any typos) is a failure to set up the Flash file according to the instructions. Reread the surrounding text and follow the steps carefully. Be sure to place the code where it belongs (usually in the first frame of a layer named *Scripts* or *Actions* or in an external *.as* or *.asc* file). When compiling AS 2.0 code, be sure you've set the compiler version to ActionScript 2.0 under File → Publish Settings → Flash → ActionScript Version.

Any code example that accesses movie clips, buttons, or text fields via ActionScript won't work unless you set the item's instance name properly. To set the instance name for a movie clip, button, or text field, select it on stage and enter the instance name on the left side of the Properties panel (Window → Properties) where you see the placeholder "<Instance Name>".

Another common source of problems is failure to set a symbol's linkage identifier properly, as is necessary when accessing Library symbols from ActionScript. To set the linkage identifier for a symbol, check the Export for ActionScript and Export in First Frame checkboxes in the Symbol Properties or Linkage Properties dialog box. (These are accessible by selecting a symbol in the Library (Window → Library) and choosing either Properties or Linkage from the Library panel's pop-up Options menu.) Then enter the identifier in the field labeled Identifier (which isn't active until Export for ActionScript is checked).

Read the instructions carefully to make sure you haven't confused a movie clip instance name with a symbol linkage identifier.

If you still can't get it working, download the examples from the book's web site, contact O'Reilly book support, or check the book's errata page. If all else fails, get a tutorial book on Flash or ask an experienced Flasher for help.

Safari Enabled

 When you see a Safari® Enabled icon on the cover of your favorite technology book, that means the book is available online through the O'Reilly Network Safari Bookshelf.

Safari offers a solution that's better than e-books. It's a virtual library that lets you easily search thousands of top tech books, cut and paste code samples, download chapters, and find quick answers when you need the most accurate, current information. Try it for free at *http://safari.oreilly.com*.

Comments and Questions

Please address comments and questions concerning this book to the publisher:

O'Reilly Media, Inc.
1005 Gravenstein Highway North
Sebastopol, CA 95472
(800) 998-9938 (in the United States or Canada)
(707) 829-0515 (international or local)
(707) 829-0104 (fax)

We have a web page for this book, where we list errata, examples, and any additional information. You can access this page at:

http://www.oreilly.com/catalog/progflashcs/

To comment or ask technical questions about this book, send email to:

bookquestions@oreilly.com

For more information about our books, conferences, Resource Centers, and the O'Reilly Network, see our web site at:

http://www.oreilly.com

Acknowledgments

Pritham Shetty and his colleagues at Macromedia have helped create a unique and powerful new way to develop richer and more compelling Internet applications. Working with their creation has been a wonderful opportunity for me to rediscover the value of the Internet and how it can facilitate communications between people. Looking back through the emails I've filed away from many engineers and others, I'm surprised by how many Macromedians have so patiently answered questions and been so generous with information since FlashCom was released. My thanks to Pritham Shetty, Srinivas Manapragada, Giacomo "Peldi" Guilizzoni, Brad Edelman, Brian Payne, Manish Anand, Slavik Lozben, Jonathan Gay, David Simmons, Chris Hock, Sarah Allen, Edward Chan, Peter Ryce, Elliot Winard, Colin Cherot, Asa Whillock, Rick Jashnani, Damian Burns, Peter Santangeli, Hava Edelstein, Jim Whitfield, Mike Chambers, and Stephen Cheng.

This book took a long time to write. When I first read that Bruce Epstein was interested in receiving proposals for an O'Reilly book on the FlashCom Server, I knew there was no way I could write the book alone. I worked with a few other people to produce a proposal and start work. Some of the original coauthors had to drop out of the project because of other commitments. So I am especially appreciative of the efforts of my coauthors: Giacomo Guilizzoni, Joey Lott, Robert Reinhardt, and Justin Watkins, who saw this project through with me. All of them, like me, worked many long hours trying to balance work, family, and the extra effort of writing a book about a new technology for O'Reilly. See the *About the Authors* section in the back of the book for each author's biography and a list of the chapters each contributed.

My coauthors and I are all indebted to the people who took time to carefully review chapters in the book: Srinivas Manapragada, David Simmons, Asa Whillock, Edward Chan, Brian Robbins, Nigel Pegg, Will Law, and Brad Edelman. The book is so much better because of their efforts. The book also benefited from reviews, comments, or short contributions from Craig Moehl, Graeme Bull, and Chafic Kazoun.

The FlashComm mailing list available at *http://chattyfig.figleaf.com* has been an excellent resource for developers using the Flash Communication Server. Contributions to the list by Pritham Shetty, Srinivas Manapragada, Giacomo Guilizzoni, Jonathan Gay, David Simmons, Chris Hock, Edward Chan, Mike Chambers, and Asa Whillock at Macromedia have been tremendously helpful. But the list has also seen valuable questions, experiments, sample code postings, and other contributions from Samuel Wan, Justin Watkins, Branden Hall, Brian Hogg, Robert Reinhardt, Joey Lott, Aral Balkan, aYo Binitie, Jesse Warden, John Robinson, Jorge Maiquez, Peter Hall, Greg Burch, Marc Vezina, Nick Kuh, Phillip Kerman, Fernando Flórez, Chris Harper, Bill Sanders, and many others. I am thankful for being able to correspond with so many interesting people with so many different perspectives. The archives of the FlashComm mailing list can be searched at *http://chattyfig.figleaf.com/ mailman/private/flashcomm*.

Thanks to Ryuichi Matsuse for inspiring me to look more seriously at remote objects that are also locally persistent.

Bruce Epstein made this book possible. From his original request for proposals, through his guidance in shaping our work, to his tireless work as the editor of the book itself, he never failed to astonish me with his knowledge, attention to detail, and energy. Bruce is always working for the reader so if you enjoy reading this book it is partly because of his hard work.

Thanks to the entire O'Reilly staff who contributed to this book's publication, including the production editor, Adam Witwer; the copyeditor, Norma Emory; the proofreader, Sada Preisch; as well as Rob Romano, Bill Takacs, and Julie Hawks.

I have the privilege to work with many talented and hardworking people at Ryerson University who were quite understanding when my work on this book took me away from spending extra hours on other projects. My thanks to Renee Lemieux, Larry

Lemieux, Grace Chan, Robin Whittamore, Wendy Freeman, Ken Woo, and Ira Levine, and to everyone in CCS and my students.

Thank you so much, Norma and Emma.

—Brian Lesser
Toronto, Canada
December 2004

FlashCom Foundation

Part I introduces the Flash Communication Server and the client-side components available to construct applications, such as a video chat. Chapters 3 and 4 go into detail about creating applications and connecting to them.

- Chapter 1, *Introducing the Flash Communication Server*
- Chapter 2, *Communication Components*
- Chapter 3, *Managing Connections*
- Chapter 4, *Applications, Instances, and Server-Side ActionScript*

Introducing the Flash Communication Server

Macromedia Flash has evolved from a way to easily create and distribute lightweight animated graphics on the Web to a rich application platform. Macromedia reported that Flash Player 6 was available on more than 94% of Internet-accessible workstations in Canada, the United States, and Europe as of June 2004. Availability in Asia exceeded 92%. Flash Player 7 penetration ranged from 67% in the U.S. to 81% in Europe. (For the latest statistics, see *http://www.macromedia.com/software/player_census/flashplayer/version_penetration.html*.) Flash Player 6 and 7 provide some remarkable capabilities to the hundreds of millions of machines on which they are already installed. With the user's consent, a Flash movie can capture real-time audio and video from the machine's microphone or web cam and stream it to Flash Communication Server MX. (Here we use the term *movie* to refer to *.swf* files. We use the term *video* for visual content streamed from the server.) The server can redistribute the streams to other users who have the Flash Player. The resulting real-time communications make it possible to develop a remarkable range of compelling applications. The Flash authoring tool and the Flash Communication Server MX can be used to create:

- Highly customized video conferences, team meetings, and web chats with shareable components such as versioned text areas, whiteboards, and instant polls
- Video- and data-on-demand applications with rich user interfaces that can include closed captions and skinnable controls
- Live event broadcasting with customizable user interaction such as moderated chat and question/answer components
- Multiplayer games, simulations, and other applications with the added value of audio and video if required

Flash and the Flash Communication Server MX (FlashCom) provide a rich development environment in which applications that clearly match requirements can be created without an outrageous investment in development time. The Flash Player and FlashCom support a rich set of objects that make sharing real-time audio, video, and data remarkably simple. In addition, Flash provides a set of user interface components such as the DataGrid, Tree, ComboBox, Accordion, and MenuBar, among others. The Flash authoring tool includes a full complement of tools for manually or programmatically generating vector graphics and animations, making it possible to create unique and rich custom user interfaces that can present and update data including audio and video. See the Preface for additional important details about the video delivery options made available by Flash and the FlashCom Server.

Clients and Servers

FlashCom is a server-side application that is installed on a host machine much like a web server; however, FlashCom works very differently than a web server. Instead of accepting many brief connections from browsers requesting a web page or other resource, FlashCom accepts persistent connections from Flash movies running in a Flash Player. Each Flash movie can share data with other Flash movies via the server using Macromedia's proprietary Real-Time Messaging Protocol (RTMP). Unlike the HTTP request/response model used by browsers to communicate with web servers, the Flash Player's RTMP connection to the FlashCom Server is persistent, so no special steps are needed to maintain session information. Once the server accepts a client connection, the connection can be used to exchange audio, video, and ActionScript data until either the client or server disconnects.

The Flash Player may be running within the Standalone Player or within a web browser. The Flash Player (and any movie playing within it) is considered the client. FlashCom cannot initiate a connection to a movie; the connection must be initiated from the Flash Player running on the client. Let's review the architecture briefly so you can understand all the pieces to the puzzle. The client/server architecture for FlashCom applications is shown in Figure 1-1.

Web browsers load Flash movie files (.*swf* files), load the Flash Player, and pass the .*swf* file to the Player to execute. The Flash movie provides the user interface and can attempt to connect via the Player to any FlashCom Server. Once connected, the Flash movie can communicate with the server. Furthermore, it can communicate— via the server—with movies playing on other Flash clients. A Flash movie can stream audio and video to the FlashCom Server so that other Flash clients with access to the same server can play recorded streams stored on the server and live streams from other clients.

A live stream is usually one that is published to the server by one client so that other clients can receive it. As the client's data arrives at the server, the server duplicates it and forwards it to each client, where it is seen and heard. In contrast, recorded streams are stored on the server and can be played from any point within the stream, paused, and restarted. It is also possible to stop a recorded stream, seek to any point within it, and begin playing again.

If multiple FlashCom Servers are connected to one another, clients connected to one server may be able to communicate with clients connected to another server. The ability to communicate between servers and the clients connected to them makes possible large-scale applications, such as live event streaming to many thousands of viewers.

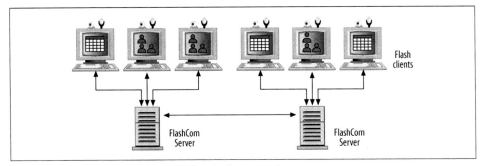

Figure 1-1. Client/server architecture for FlashCom applications

FlashCom can host many different applications. More than one *instance* of an application can be run at the same time. Each instance is given its own unique name. When a client connects to the server, it always connects to an instance of an application by name. For example, many separate instances of an application named *chatRoom* may be available. Each instance has its own unique name and may provide unique resources for the client. Figure 1-2 illustrates three clients connected to the same instance of the *chatRoom* application.

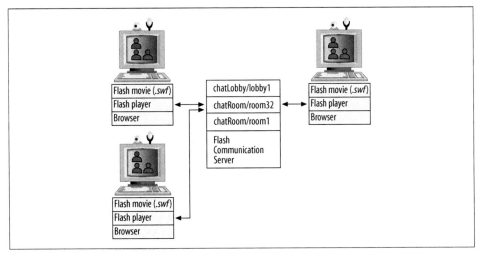

Figure 1-2. Three Flash movies connected to a FlashCom application instance via the Flash Player

Creating an Application

Due to the client/server nature of communication applications, the developer ordinarily creates a client-side Flash movie to handle the user interaction and a separate server-side FlashCom application to which it connects. Client-side Flash movies can be written in ActionScript 1.0 or 2.0.

The server-side FlashCom application is written in Server-Side ActionScript (SSAS), which is very similar to the well-known client-side ActionScript. Throughout the book, the code examples identify whether they are client-side or server-side code. To create a FlashCom application, first create a home directory for it on the server. This registers the application with the server and makes it available to movies that attempt to connect to it. Server-Side ActionScript source code files placed in an application's home directory give each application its unique server-side behavior. The Flash authoring tool or *integrated development environment* (IDE) is used to develop the movie and optionally code the HTML page into which the movie is embedded. During authoring, a Flash movie is saved as a *.fla* file. When the Flash movie is ready for distribution, it is compiled into a *.swf* file using Flash's File → Publish command. After the HTML page and *.swf* file are posted on a web server, they can be downloaded by a browser, allowing the Flash movie to connect to the application on the FlashCom Server.

Developing a Flash movie almost always involves programming with ActionScript, Flash's scripting language based on the ECMA standard (similar to JavaScript). The book assumes an intermediate familiarity with ActionScript. To learn ActionScript, see *ActionScript for Flash MX: The Definitive Guide* and *Essential ActionScript 2.0*, both from O'Reilly. In addition to typical objects, ActionScript supports a special *MovieClip* datatype. Movie clips are the essential building blocks for Flash animations and are the basis for higher-level components such as the Button, DataGrid, and Tree.

The Flash movie can be hardcoded to connect to a particular instance of a FlashCom application or it can load the instance's address at runtime. For example, the movie could load an XML file with connection information or load address information from the HTML page.

For many video-on-demand applications, you can use the prebuilt FLVPlayer, which doesn't require any Flash authoring, available from:

> *http://www.peldi.com/blog/FLVPlayer.html*

The FLVPlayer's behavior can be customized to connect to any application instance and includes automatic bandwidth detection and stream selection. A video player is also available as part of the Macromedia Video Kit:

> *http://www.macromedia.com/software/studio/flashvideokit*

Creating an application to do anything more complex than video-on-demand requires some level of Flash authoring. Unless stated otherwise, when I refer to *Flash*, I mean the Flash authoring tool, such as Flash MX 2004 or Flash MX Professional 2004 (Flash Pro). If you are not familiar with authoring in Flash, see *Flash Out of the Box* (O'Reilly), which is an excellent introduction to the authoring tool.

You can create simple communication applications—such as a video conferencing application—using prebuilt components such as the SimpleConnect, PeopleList, and VideoConference components supplied by Macromedia. You can drag the components from Flash's Components panel to the Stage to construct the user interface. Using Flash's Properties panel, you can configure the components to work together and supply them with the address of the application instance on a FlashCom Server to connect to. Chapter 2 describes working with Macromedia's communication components in this way.

For more diverse applications, you must use ActionScript to create or customize components and build unique user interfaces. Chapters 13 through 15 describe how to extend the existing components or roll your own. Existing communication-related ActionScript classes make developing custom components and applications much easier. On the client side, they include the *NetConnection*, *NetStream*, *Camera*, *SharedObject*, and *Microphone* classes. Server-Side ActionScript classes include the *Application*, *Client*, *Stream*, and *SharedObject* classes. We'll cover these classes and their methods throughout the remainder of the book.

Real-Time Messaging Protocol

The Flash Player communicates with FlashCom using Macromedia's proprietary Real-Time Messaging Protocol (RTMP). RTMP uses TCP (transmission control protocol) for transmission of packets between the Flash Player and the server. TCP is a reliable protocol that guarantees delivery of every packet of information. RTMP can transport audio encoded in MP3 and Nellymoser (*http://www.nellymoser.com*) formats, video encoded in the Flash Video format (FLV), and data encoded using Macromedia's Action Message Format (AMF). AMF provides an efficient way to serialize/deserialize data so that both primitive and complex ActionScript data can be transferred between client and server without needing to manually encode or decode the data. AMF is briefly described in Chapter 11, but for full details, see *Flash Remoting: The Definitive Guide* (O'Reilly).

FlashCom Versus Traditional Media Servers

Using TCP as the foundation protocol for Flash communications simplifies managing the transfer of audio, video, and ActionScript data flowing between the client and server. However, TCP is a point-to-point protocol, which means each client requires a separate client/server TCP connection; consequently, it cannot broadcast or multicast packets from the server to multiple clients at the network level. If a live audio stream must be sent simultaneously to multiple clients, the server must send duplicate copies of the audio data to each client over discrete connections. Traditional media servers, designed primarily to distribute media streams from server to client, normally provide the option to send the stream using UDP (user datagram protocol) as well as TCP. UDP can be used to multicast or unicast a stream. When multicast is enabled, a single copy of the stream is transmitted, and any client that subscribes to the multicast can receive it. Multicasting has two tremendous advantages: it reduces the load on the server and the bandwidth required to send streams to large numbers of clients. Unfortunately, the vast majority of Internet service providers (ISPs) have disabled multicast on their networks because of security concerns. Consequently, media servers provide a fallback to unicast streaming over UDP. Unicasting means the server must duplicate the stream data and send it in a separate stream to every client. If for some reason the client does not accept the unicast stream, UDP media servers typically fall back to sending duplicate stream data to each client over TCP in much the same way FlashCom does.

Even without multicast, UDP has some advantages for traditional media servers. UDP is not a "reliable" protocol. It does not guarantee that every packet sent from the server to the client will arrive. For audio and video streams, some missing packets may not make any noticeable difference in perceived quality. The network overhead of sending UDP is lower than TCP, so UDP often delivers data faster than TCP. The more congested a network, the more packets will be dropped, so that the stream quality may degrade without dramatically slowing down delivery of the stream. In contrast, TCP will adjust to network congestion and bandwidth limits by slowing the transfer of data and by resending lost packets. To support the streaming of media data over TCP, the amount of data being sent must be dynamically adjusted in response to network bandwidth and congestion. RTMP is designed to adjust the amount of video and audio being transmitted by dropping audio messages and video frames in response to inadequate network bandwidth. On congested networks, it is not as effective as UDP-based protocols for delivering streaming media, but on modern networks it delivers very good performance.

RTMP supports more than the streaming media protocols of traditional media servers. It supports dynamic transmission of multiple streams that can contain audio, video, and ActionScript data both from server to client and from client to server. RTMP manages sending audio, video, and ActionScript data separately. ActionScript data is never dropped, because any loss could have catastrophic effects on an application. Audio and video data is buffered separately on the server. If audio data in the audio buffer grows to a certain threshold, all the data in the buffer is dropped, and newly arrived data is allowed to start collecting in the buffer to be sent on to each client. Video data is managed in a similar manner except that the data in the buffer is dropped when a new keyframe arrives. Dropping video data when a keyframe arrives ensures that the client never receives partial frame updates for the wrong keyframe. If the client did, the video image would be made up of a mosaic of 8 x 8 pixel blocks from two different frames. RTMP also prioritizes data. Audio is given the highest priority because it is so essential for real-time conversations. Video is given the lowest priority, and ActionScript is given a priority in between audio and video.

The Communication Classes

While RTMP conveniently manages the flow of multiple streams of data across a network, the real power of Flash and FlashCom for developers is realized in the high-level classes that make connecting to the server, sharing information, and streaming audio and video so easy and flexible. I'll briefly review the major classes, which will be explored in more detail and used in examples throughout the remainder of the book.

Connecting to the Server

The *NetConnection* class connects a client to an application instance on a server. In the simplest case, you can create a connection by invoking *NetConnection.connect( )* with the URI of the remote application:

```
nc = new NetConnection( );
nc.connect("rtmp://echo.ryerson.ca/campusCameras/connector");
```

To determine if the connection was established successfully, define an *onStatus( )* method on the *NetConnection* object before invoking *connect( )*:

```
nc = new NetConnection( );
nc.onStatus = function (info) {
  trace("The connection code is: " + info.code);
};
nc.connect("rtmp://echo.ryerson.ca/campusCameras/connector");
```

In this example, the RTMP address includes the host (*echo.ryerson.ca*), the application name (*campusCameras*), and the instance name (connector). If you've ever developed network applications using other application programming interfaces, you'll likely agree that creating a network connection between Flash and FlashCom is ridiculously easy. Chapter 3 goes into greater detail on the *NetConnection* class and how to use *NetConnection* objects.

Streaming Audio, Video, and ActionScript Data

Once you establish a connection using a *NetConnection* object in the client, you can use it to send or receive a stream containing audio and/or video. Suppose you know that a recorded Flash video file named *Ryerson_High_Speed.flv* is available in the instance's *public* directory. You can attach the video stream to a video object, here named videoArea, using *Video.attachVideo( )* and play it using *NetStream.play( )*. The

NetStream object, in_ns, is created by passing the *NetConnection* object, nc, from the preceding example to the *NetStream( )* constructor function:

```
in_ns = new NetStream(nc);
videoArea.attachVideo(in_ns);
in_ns.play("public/Ryerson_High_Speed");
```

In this case, the video appears in a video object that was placed on the Stage during authoring and given the instance name videoArea; the audio within the video stream is heard automatically. Note that the *.flv* extension is not included in the stream URI passed into the *play( )* method.

Publishing a stream in a Flash movie is also easy. Here, we create a new *NetStream* object, out_ns, and attach the audio and video streams from the user's microphone and camera before publishing the stream using *NetStream.publish( )*:

```
out_ns = new NetStream(nc);
out_ns.attachAudio(Microphone.get( ));
out_ns.attachVideo(Camera.get( ));
out_ns.publish(userName);   // Name the stream after the user's name.
```

The *Camera* class can get a video stream from a web camera or other video source, and the *Microphone* class can get an audio stream from a microphone or other source.

You can create multiple streams (*NetStream* objects) for a single *NetConnection*, as shown in Figure 1-3. Each stream can publish or play a stream to or from the server, but data within a stream travels in only one direction. If each user must publish a single stream, it is easiest to name the stream after his unique username or unique ID number.

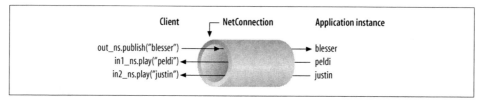

Figure 1-3. A client publishing a stream and receiving two streams over one NetConnection

On the server, the *Stream* class can be used to create playlists of streams and even to play and publish streams across multiple servers. A playlist defines a sequence of streams to be played one after the other. The server buffers them so they play seamlessly without interruption; when one stream ends, another begins. Chapter 5 covers the *NetStream* and *Stream* classes in depth.

Camera, Microphone, and Video

The *Camera* and *Microphone* classes, covered in depth in Chapter 6, provide access to video and audio sources (typically cameras and microphones) on the client system. Multiple cameras and microphones can be accessed by the same Flash movie. Only one video and audio stream can be published or played within a single *NetStream*; however, there can be multiple *NetStreams* within a single *NetConnection*, as shown in Figure 1-4. The Flash Player is responsible for encoding all audio and video data. Video encoding from each video source is currently limited to constant bit rate encoding at a single resolution. The *Camera* and *Microphone* classes can be used to control the amount of audio and video data being sent to the server and can be dynamically adjusted to match the bandwidth limitations of the clients connected to an application. No real-time hardware encoding options are currently available, though that may have changed by the time you read this. Some video cards can present different resolution video streams from the same input as separate video sources so that multiple *NetStream* objects carrying different resolution video from the same source can be published simultaneously. Otherwise, the only way to provide different streams matched to the bandwidth of each client is to use multiple video sources.

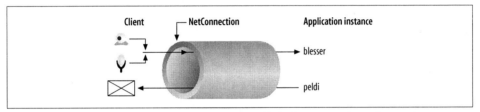

Figure 1-4. Attaching audio and video sources to a published stream and attaching a playing stream to an embedded Video object to view incoming video

The *Camera* class provides a convenient way to change the resolution, frame rate, and quality settings for each video source. The *Microphone* class allows setting the sampling rate, gain, and silence level, among others. A Video object is used to display video within a Flash movie and can be dynamically resized and moved as video is played. See Chapter 6 for working examples.

Sharing Data in Real Time

Real-time applications often require data to be shared among or transmitted between multiple movies. The *SharedObject* class is familiar to many Flash programmers as a way to create a kind of supercookie; a *local shared object* (LSO) can store ActionScript data on the client between sessions. Flash communication applications can use *remote shared objects* (RSOs) to share information in real time between movies running on different clients. If a movie updates a property of a remote shared object, the same property is updated in every other movie connected to it. When a shared object changes, each client is notified of the changes. Shared objects can be used to:

- Notify all the movies connected to a video conference application of the name of every available live stream
- Update the position of elements in a game

- Hold the position, shape, and color information of each graphical element in a shared whiteboard
- Hold the data for each form element in a shared form

In object-oriented programming (OOP), the data within all the objects in an application defines the current state of the application.

 Shared objects provide a convenient mechanism to hold the state of a communication application distributed across multiple clients and servers.

Remote shared objects can be temporary or persistent. Temporary shared objects last only while they are being used. Persistent shared objects are saved on the server when they are not in use, allowing clients to pick up where they left off as soon as they reconnect to the server. *Proxied shared objects* are a mechanism for making shared objects available across multiple application instances; one application instance always owns the shared object but others can create a network connection to the master instance and create proxies (essentially an alias) of the shared object. That way, clients connected to any instance can connect to the same shared object. The feature is often important for creating large scale applications.

The code to work with shared objects on the client is a little different from that required on the server. Working with shared objects is also a little more complicated than working with streams or managing network connections. You need to do four basic things when working with shared objects:

1. Get a remote shared object using *SharedObject.getRemote( )*.
2. Customize the shared object so your program can respond to changes made to the shared object by each movie or by the server.
3. Connect to the shared object.
4. Once connected, update the shared object's properties as necessary.

Chapter 8 provides complete coverage of using shared objects, but let's have a quick look at what some client-side code looks like. On the client, the *SharedObject. getRemote( )* method returns a remote shared object. However, the shared object usually needs to be set up with an *onSync( )* method and then connected using a *Net-Connection* object before it can be used. Here we get a shared object named users to which each movie will connect. Then, an *onSync( )* method is defined that, for demonstration purposes, displays information about changes made to the shared object as soon as they occur. Then the shared object is connected to the server:

```
users_so = SharedObject.getRemote("users", nc.uri);
users_so.onSync = function (infoList) {
  for (var i in infoList) {
    var info = infoList[i];
    switch (info.code) {
```

```
        case "change":
          var id = info.name;
          trace("User connected with id: " + id);
          trace("and name: " + users_so.data[id]);
          break;
        case "delete":
          var id = info.name;
          trace("User disconnected with id: " + id);
          break;
      }
    }
  };
  users_so.connect(nc);
```

The *onSync( )* method is often the most interesting part of shared object coding. When the local copy of the shared object is synchronized with the server and whenever any *slots* (properties) in the shared object change, the *onSync( )* method is invoked automatically. The *onSync( )* method is passed an array of information objects. Each object contains information about the shared object or about what has happened to a slot (property) in the shared object. Chapter 8 describes shared objects and the *onSync( )* method in detail. Each information object has a code property, which describes what happened ("clear" if every slot is deleted, "change" if a slot is added or updated remotely, or "delete" if a slot is deleted). The name of the slot that has been updated or deleted is always found in the information object's name property. To add or update data to a shared object slot within Flash, use the data property of the shared object:

```
  users_so.data["guest_4"] = "brian";
```

Likewise, you can retrieve the value in a slot using the data property:

```
  trace("The user's name is: " + users_so.data["guest_4"]);
```

Client and Application Objects

Whenever a client connects to an application instance on the server, a *Client* object is created on the server side to represent the remote client. The *Client* object can be used by server-side scripts to send and receive data messages to and from each individual remote Flash client. Every application instance also has a single application object that provides a convenient way to manage the instance's life cycle. The application is a singleton instance of the server-side *Application* class.

Scripting *Client* objects and the application object is covered in Chapter 4. The *Client* and application objects, in concert with the ability to query web application servers, provide the core features needed to authenticate clients as they connect. Authentication is covered in detail in Chapter 18.

Remote Methods

In a typical application, an individual client may need to ask the server to perform some action on its behalf. For example, it may need to ask the server for the length of a recorded stream before playing it. The server may also have to ask the client to do something. For example, the server may need to have the client use a unique string provided by the server to name the streams the client will publish. Remote method calls are a way that the client and server can invoke methods on each other.

An application instance can invoke a method on a client using the *Client.call( )* method. A client can invoke a method on an application instance using the *NetConnection.call( )* method. For example, a server-side script can invoke a method on an individual client in order to let the client know its unique ID number:

```
client.call("setID", null, id);
```

If a client method named *setID( )* is invoked using *Client.call( )* from the server, the method must be defined on the client's *NetConnection* object or nothing will happen. For example, the client-side script might look like this:

```
nc = new NetConnection();
nc.setID = function (id) {
  myID = id;
};
```

Conversely, the client can call a method on the server using a *NetConnection* object:

```
nc.call("getStreamLength", streamInfoResponder, streamName);
```

For a result to be returned by the remote method, the second parameter passed to *NetConnection.call( )* must be a object with an *onResult( )* method.

FlashCom also supports mechanisms to send a remote method request to multiple clients at the same time. Clients connected to the same shared object or playing the same stream can all receive a remote method call at the same time. For example, a popular way to update a text chat area is to use the *send( )* method of a shared object to send a text message to every client:

```
chat_so.send("showMessage", "Welcome to the chat.");
```

In this case, a *showMessage( )* method must be defined on the shared object or nothing will happen:

```
chat_so.showMessage = function (msg) {
  chatTextArea.text += msg + '\n';
  chatTextArea.vPosition = chatTextArea.maxVPosition;
};
```

Chapter 9 describes calling and defining remote methods in detail.

Communicating with Application Servers, Databases, and Directory Servers

Flash and the Flash Communication Server often must work with other existing applications and resources. For example, users may have to log in against an existing directory service or database before being allowed to chat or view streams. Database systems can be used to store large amounts of information that FlashCom cannot easily manage, such as millions of records that represent the location of video messages in a video email system. Each record might contain the email text and the location of the recorded video message within a FlashCom application.

Both the Flash Player and FlashCom can interact with web application servers and, through them, database and directory servers. The Flash client can call any server-side script available on a web server, send and receive XML data, access web services, and use the Flash Remoting gateway to more efficiently access application servers. In contrast, the Flash Communication Server (as of the latest version, 1.5.2) supports only Flash Remoting to connect to other servers. It cannot directly consume web services, send or receive XML, or call a CGI script, which often complicates designing applications that need to access a database or other service already available via a web server. However, Flash Remoting is a powerful and efficient technology that can be used with J2EE, ColdFusion, and .NET servers to provide access to databases or other services. Macromedia sells the Flash Remoting gateway separately for J2EE and .NET servers and bundles it with ColdFusion. There are also open source implementations of Flash Remoting for Perl, PHP, and Java. See Chapter 11 for more details on Remoting, and see *http://opensource.org* for information on open source code.

Flash Remoting is a request/response technology that allows scripts in the Flash client or FlashCom to call remote methods on an application server. It uses HTTP to send and receive data in the AMF. Those remote methods can retrieve information from a database, directory server, or web server and return the information to FlashCom. From a developer's point of view, Flash Remoting is easy to work with because complex ActionScript data is serialized and deserialized automatically. Flash Remoting can be used with or without FlashCom. The point is that Flash Remoting is flexible enough that it allows FlashCom to communicate effectively despite FlashCom's lack of direct support for XML or server-side script access.

Figure 1-5 illustrates some of the communication options for Flash and FlashCom. A Flash client can access a web application directly, as can FlashCom.

In some cases, clients may connect to both an application server and FlashCom. In other cases, FlashCom may connect to the application server and provide information from or to its clients. When many clients need access to the same data, FlashCom should be used as an intermediary between application servers. Application performance will be improved by reducing the number of queries from each Flash

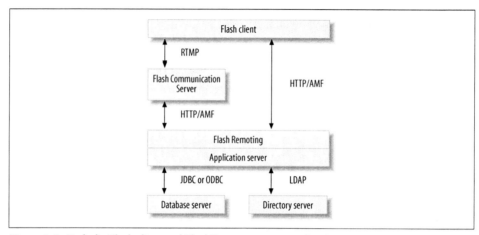

Figure 1-5. Both the Flash client and FlashCom can access application servers

movie. When each movie needs to look up information unique to it, a direct connection to an application server is usually a better approach.

Firewalls and Security

Some corporate firewalls and proxy servers with restrictive access rules make it impossible to establish a persistent TCP/RTMP connection to a FlashCom Server. Some corporate IT staffs may open access to remote FlashCom Servers, but others will not. When corporate web access is permitted but TCP/RTMP connections are not allowed, FlashCom provides a tunneling feature that allows Flash and FlashCom to send and receive RTMP over HTTP. When tunneling is employed, the Flash Player works with the user's browser to poll the communication server instead of establishing a direct Player-to-server TCP connection. When RTMP is tunneled, it is known as RTMPT. As of this writing, neither the Flash Player nor FlashCom directly supports SSL. However, encryption is an option when using tunneling, because browsers support SSL and an SSL proxy can be used with the server. For more information, see the article *Tunneling Flash Communications Through Firewalls and Proxy Servers* at:

> *http://www.macromedia.com/devnet/mx/flashcom/articles/firewalls_proxy.html*

Getting Started

A free development edition of the Flash Communication Server is available from Macromedia. You can find more information on downloading it along with other licensing options at Macromedia's web site:

> *http://www.macromedia.com/software/flashcom*

To install FlashCom:

1. Follow the link from the preceding URL to download the free developer edition or go directly to:

    http://www.macromedia.com/cfusion/tdrc/index.cfm?product=flashcom

2. Once you install FlashCom, you should download the most recent updater from *http://www.macromedia.com/support/flashcom/downloads_updaters.html*   and install it. (Updaters are not normally added to the installation files of the most recent release, so if an updater is available for the most recent release, you should download and install it.)

3. Finally, download the most recent Flash communication components and run the installation program to install them in the Flash authoring environment. Separate Windows or Macintosh component updates are also available at:

    http://www.macromedia.com/support/flashcom/downloads_updaters.html

FlashCom runs on Windows Server 2003, Windows Server 2000, Windows NT Server SP6 or later, and RedHat Linux. The complete system requirements and supported servers are listed at:

http://www.macromedia.com/software/flashcom/productinfo/systemreqs

Detailed documentation about the server including installation instructions is available from Macromedia at:

http://www.macromedia.com/support/flashcom/documentation.html

See the *Installing Flash Communication Server* and *Managing Flash Communication Server* documents at the preceding URL. However, for a simple test and development server, you can simply run the installer, supply an initial administrative username and password, and then run the samples to make sure the server is working. You do not need to provide a serial number. On Windows, the installer is named *FlashComInstaller.exe* and you can simply run it. Under Linux, you must unzip and then untar the installation file, *cd*, to the *installation_directory* and type:

./installFCS

The default installation includes applications that can be used by anyone who can connect to your computer. It is a good idea to protect a test development server behind some type of firewall. See Chapters 10 and 18 for important information about securing your FlashCom Server installation.

By default, the FlashCom Server listens for TCP connections on port 1935. Ideally, you should allow access to that port only from other machines under your control. If the machine is not behind a firewall, you should at least make sure the server accepts connection requests only from *.swf* files originating in your own domain. See Macromedia's *Managing Flash Communication Server* document for more details or see:

http://www.macromedia.com/devnet/mx/flashcom/articles/firewalls_proxy06.html

Finally, make sure you can run some of Macromedia's sample applications. On my Windows machine, the default installation places the sample files in:

C:\Program Files\Macromedia\Flash Communication Server MX\samples

You can test that the server is working by going into the *tutorial_sharedball* subdirectory and starting up two copies of the *tutorial_sharedball.swf* file. You should be able to drag the ball around in one window and watch it move in the other movie. If it doesn't work, you may have to manually start the server. On Windows, select Start → Programs → Macromedia → Flash Communication Server → Start Server. Detailed instructions for both Windows and Linux systems are available in Macromedia's *Installing Flash Communication Server*.

Macromedia provides different editions and licensing schemes for the FlashCom Server. The developer edition is not licensed for production. The FlashCom Server includes a license manager that controls the number of simultaneous clients that are allowed to connect at one time and the total bandwidth the server is permitted to consume. There are also restrictions on the server editions than can be used to create virtual hosts. A complete description of product editions and licensing can be found here:

http://www.macromedia.com/software/flashcom/productinfo/editions

Chris Hock has also written a valuable white paper, *Calculating your Bandwidth and Software License Needs for the Macromedia Flash Communication Server MX*. You can find it here:

http://www.macromedia.com/software/flashcom/productinfo/editions/fcs_whitepaper_bandwidth.pdf

For the purposes of the rest of the book, I assume you are developing on a test system using a default installation and not on a specially configured production system. You should read Macromedia's *Managing Flash Communication Server* document for details on configuring production systems.

 To get the most out of the book, you should also have a microphone and web cam. For some exercises, you'll need ColdFusion Server.

Admin Service, Administration Console, and App Inspector

The FlashCom installer also includes a secondary application known variously as the Admin Service or Administration Controller. On Windows, the Admin Service is installed as *FlashComAdmin.exe*, and on Linux as the *fcadmin* file. By default, the

Admin Service is started whenever FlashCom is started and provides both administrative services and application monitoring, control, and debugging services. You can connect directly to the Admin Service using one of two Flash movies provided with FlashCom. In the FlashCom 1.5.2 release, you'll find them in the *flashcom_help\ html\admin* subdirectory of the installation directory. The Administration Console (*admin.swf*) movie can be used to update license information, start and stop application instances, and review server diagnostic information. The Communication Application Inspector (*app_inspector.swf*) can be used to start and stop application instances, monitor application instance resources, and display *trace( )* statement output. To use either movie, start the movie and log in to the Admin Service using the administrator username and password that you defined when you installed the server. Macromedia provides information on using the Administration Console and Communication App Inspector in *Managing Flash Communication Server* and *Developing Communication Applications*, both available from:

> *http://www.macromedia.com/support/flashcom/documentation.html*

The Communication Application Inspector is particularly useful while developing and debugging applications as covered in Chapter 4 under "Using the App Inspector to Run Scripts." You can also create your own Flash movies and communication applications that connect to the Admin Service. Chapter 10 describes the services that are available via the Admin Service and how to use the Server Management API.

Hello Video!

I'd like to dive in and take you through building a very simple video conference application. The application is designed to demonstrate many of the different things described in this chapter, such as publishing and playing streams and updating and responding to changes in a shared object. If you don't understand all the code as I walk through it, don't worry. The idea is to provide a quick tour to building a communication application. The rest of the book explains everything in much greater detail. Although a premade video chat application already exists, this is good exposure to the concepts and operations you'll need when you build your own applications.

Setting Up helloVideo on the Server

Creating the *helloVideo* application on the server requires you find the *applications* directory and add a subdirectory named *helloVideo*. After the default installation on my system, the *applications* directory is located at:

> *C:\Program Files\Macromedia\Flash Communication Server MX\applications*

Once you create the *helloVideo* subdirectory, you have created a FlashCom application. Now you need to provide the application with its unique server-side behavior.

Create a plain text file named *main.asc* and save it into the *helloVideo* directory. You can use any plain text editor such as the one included with Flash MX Professional 2004 or Dreamweaver MX 2004. Example 1-1 shows the source code you should add to the *main.asc* file.

Example 1-1. The main.asc file for the helloVideo application

```
idPool = ["guest_1", "guest_2", "guest_3", "guest_4"];

application.onAppStart = function () {
  users_so = SharedObject.get("users");
};

application.onConnect = function (client, name) {
  if (idPool.length <= 0) {
    application.rejectConnection(client, {msg:"Too many users."});
  }
  client.id = idPool.pop();
  application.acceptConnection(client);
  client.call("setID", null, client.id);
  users_so.setProperty(client.id, name);
};

application.onDisconnect = function (client) {
  idPool.push(client.id);
  users_so.setProperty(client.id, null);
};
```

You can also download the source files for the *helloVideo* example from the book's web site (*http://www.flash-communications.net*). The *main.asc* file will be loaded, compiled, and run by the server when the first client attempts to connect to a *helloVideo* instance. The *application.onAppStart( )* method will be called once after the file is executed. From then on, whenever a movie tries to connect, the *application.onConnect( )* method will be called, and when a movie disconnects, *application. onDisconnect( )* will be called.

The *main.asc* file listed in Example 1-1 is designed to do three things:

- Only four clients are allowed to connect at any time. So the application creates four unique user ID values, assigns one to each client when it connects, and reclaims the ID when the client leaves.

- It notifies each client of its ID by calling a remote method of the client after the connection succeeds.

- It updates a shared object when a client arrives or leaves so that all the other clients know who is connected and the name of each client's stream to play.

The application does not use Flash Remoting to connect to an authentication database or directory server. It is a simple demonstration program and is not designed for security. See Chapter 18 for information on designing and building secure applications. In the *helloVideo* application, any four users are allowed to connect and each is given a unique user ID string. The global `idPool` array contains the four available ID strings. It is created as soon as the *main.asc* file is loaded by the server—usually when the first client attempts to connect. The *application.onAppStart( )* method is called immediately after the *main.asc* file is loaded and executed. The *onAppStart( )* method uses *SharedObject.get( )* to create a temporary shared object that holds an optional name provided by each user. For example, if four users with the names "justin", "peldi", "robert", and "brian" are connected, the shared object would have the slot names and values illustrated in Table 1-1.

Table 1-1. Slot names and values for the users_so shared object

Slot name	Slot value
"guest_1"	"justin"
"guest_2"	"peldi"
"guest_3"	"robert"
"guest_4"	"brian"

The following statement gets a shared object named users and assigns it to the variable users_so:

```
users_so = SharedObject.get("users");
```

Thereafter, we can use users_so to access the methods and properties of the users shared object.

Whenever a client attempts to connect, the *application.onConnect( )* method is called with a client object passed in by FlashCom that represents the client trying to connect. Any other information supplied about the client is also passed into *onConnect( )* as additional parameters. In Example 1-1, the name a user enters is the second parameter, name.

When *onConnect( )* is called, we have the option of rejecting or accepting the connection or leaving it pending. In this example, if there are no user ID strings left in the idPool, the application rejects the connection and passes a message back to the client to say why:

```
if (idPool.length <= 0) {
    application.rejectConnection(client, {msg:"Too many users."});
}
```

If there is an available ID string, it is removed from the end of the idPool array and assigned to an id property of the client object (id is not a built-in property of a *Client* object; we chose it to suit our own needs):

```
client.id = idPool.pop( );
```

If an ID is available, the application will accept the client's request to connect and send the client its user ID by invoking *setID( )*, which was introduced earlier under "Remote Methods," on the client:

```
application.acceptConnection(client);
client.call("setID", null, client.id);
```

We'll look at the client-side *setID( )* method again later. Finally, the application lets all the other clients know that a new client has connected, so they can subscribe to the video and audio stream the client will publish:

```
users_so.setProperty(client.id, name);
```

The *setProperty( )* method saves the name parameter in a slot named after the client's ID string.

Later, when the client disconnects by clicking the Disconnect button or by visiting a different page with her browser, the *application.onDisconnect( )* method will be called on the server and passed the client object representing the client that has disconnected. When a client disconnects, we need to reclaim her ID string for use with other clients, and we need to delete her slot in the users shared object to indicate she is no long connected:

```
application.onDisconnect = function (client) {
  idPool.push(client.id);
  users_so.setProperty(client.id, null);
};
```

The application pushes the ID back into the idPool array and sets its slot in the shared object to null.

Building the helloVideo Client in Flash

The Flash movie we are going to walk through building will automatically publish audio and video for the person using it and will play any audio and video being streamed from the other clients. When it connects to the server, it receives its own unique user ID string in return. It will publish a stream named after its user ID while monitoring changes in the users shared object to discover the unique ID of each user who connects. It uses the user IDs in the users shared object to play each remote user's stream.

Building the user interface

Figure 1-6 shows the user interface for the *helloVideo* client. Each user's video is displayed above the name he chose when he connected. The example shows the screen Robert used to connect.

The interface is made using four movie clips and a few components. There is one movie clip for each user. The movie clip contains an embedded Video object and a Label and TextInput component. The TextInput component in each movie clip will

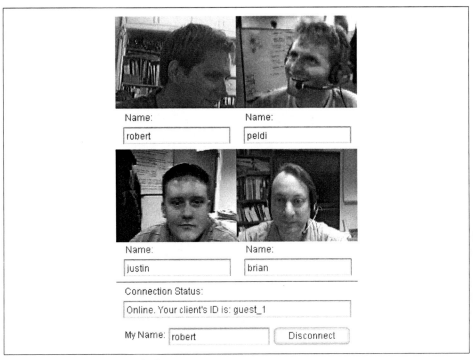

Name:
robert

Name:
peldi

Name:
justin

Name:
brian

Connection Status:
Online. Your client's ID is: guest_1

My Name: robert   Disconnect

Figure 1-6. The helloVideo Flash movie

display the name each user enters in the My Name field. Note the TextInput component at the bottom of the screen containing the text "robert." I also use a TextInput component to display the current connection status of the application. The button also indicates that the user is connected by displaying the Disconnect label. If the user is not connected, it toggles to Connect.

To build the interface:

1. Start with an empty Flash movie and set its dimensions to 320 x 480 using the Properties panel.

2. Create a new library symbol using the Insert → New Symbol (Ctrl-F8) command.

3. In the Create New Symbol dialog box, enter the symbol name **GuestVideo** and set the Behavior type to MovieClip. Enable the Export for ActionScript option, (click the Advanced button to display this option if it isn't already visible). Set the Identifier field to **GuestVideo** as well.

4. When the symbol is created in the Library, the Stage displays the empty symbol and its registration point. We want to place an embedded Video object within the symbol so that the video's upper-left corner is at the symbol's registration point.

5. To add a Video object to the Library, open the Library panel (Ctrl-L or Cmd-L), and choose New Video from the Library panel's Options menu, as shown in Figure 1-7.

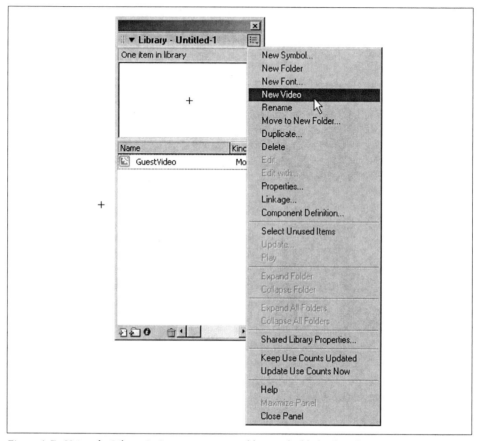

Figure 1-7. Using the Library's Options menu to add an embedded video object

To place the embedded Video object within the symbol so that the video's upper-left corner is at the symbol's registration point:

1. Drag the Video object from the Library to the Stage and position it at the *GuestVideo* symbol's registration point. Use the X and Y fields in the Properties panel as illustrated in Figure 1-8 to position it at exactly (0, 0), and give it the instance name video.

2. Drag one Label and one TextInput component from the Components panel to the Stage. Arrange them as illustrated in Figure 1-8 and give the TextInput component the instance name nameInput.

3. Set the Text parameter of the Label to the text **Name:** using the Properties panel.

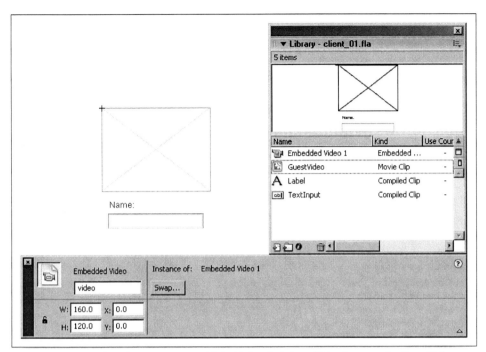

Figure 1-8. Using the Library menu to add the Video, Label, and TextInput to the GuestVideo symbol

Now that you're done creating the *GuestVideo* symbol with the embedded Video object, we want four instances on stage (to display the four possible simultaneous clients):

1. To return to the main movie's Stage, click the *Scene 1* link in the Timeline panel's Edit bar.

2. Drag the *GuestVideo* symbol from the Library to the Stage four times and arrange the four instances as shown in Figure 1-6. Select each one in turn and set its name to guest_1, guest_2, guest_3, or guest_4 using Flash's Properties panel.

3. Finally, at the bottom of the movie, add the two Label components, two TextInput components, and one Button component. Position and resize them as illustrated in Figure 1-6. Name the large TextInput instance statusInput, the small TextField instance userNameInput, and the Button instance connectButton.

With the main Stage of the movie laid out, it's time to start coding.

Setting up the NetConnection and showing its status

Example 1-2 shows how to create the *NetConnection* object and add methods to it dynamically. This client-side script, like the code in the following examples, should be placed in the first frame on a separate *Scripts* layer in the movie's timeline. Have a look at the sample *helloVideo.fla* file from the book's web site and you'll find the code from Examples 1-2, 1-3, and 1-4 attached to the first frame of the *Scripts* layer.

After the nc variable is assigned a new *NetConnection*, the code adds two methods. The *setID( )* method is invoked by the server to notify the client of its unique user ID. The *onStatus( )* method is called whenever a change in connection status occurs. Have a look at Example 1-2 and see if you can figure out what the two methods do. I'll discuss it in more detail later.

Example 1-2. Setting up the NetConnection

```
myID = "";
nc = new NetConnection( );
/* setID( ) is a remote method that will be called by the server
 * after the client connects. Once we get our unique ID from the
 * server we can use it to publish our stream.
 */
nc.setID = function (id) {
  myID = id;
  statusInput.text = "Online. Your client's ID is: " + myID;
  ns = new NetStream(nc);
  ns.attachAudio(Microphone.get( ));
  var cam = Camera.get( );
  ns.attachVideo(cam);
  ns.publish(id);
  _root[id].video.attachVideo(cam);
  initUsers( );
};

// onStatus( ) is called whenever the status of the network
// connection changes. It is how we know whether we are connected.
nc.onStatus = function (info) {
  connectButton.label = "Connect";
  connectButton.enabled = true;
  switch (info.code) {
    case "NetConnection.Connect.Success":
      connectButton.label = "Disconnect";
      statusInput.text = "Online";
      break;
    case "NetConnection.Connect.Failed":
      statusInput.text = "Cannot reach server. Possible network error.";
      break;
    case "NetConnection.Connect.Rejected":
      statusInput.text = info.application.msg;
      break;
    case "NetConnection.Connect.Closed":
      statusInput.text += " Connection closed.";
      break;
  }
};
```

Some time after a connection to the server is made, the *setID( )* method is called by the server and its id parameter is passed as one of four strings: "guest_1", "guest_2", "guest_3", or "guest_4". The *setID( )* method saves the name in the myID variable and displays it for the user in the TextInput field statusInput. Then it uses its ID string to publish a stream containing audio and video by creating a *NetStream* object on the nc net connection. It attaches a microphone and camera object to the stream and publishes it using the id as the stream name. Finally, it displays the stream it is sending in one of the *GuestVideo* movie clips on the Stage. Since each clip is named after the user IDs the server provides, there will be one clip on the Stage with the same name as the user who has just been assigned. The _root property, which holds a reference to the movie's main timeline, is used to get a reference to the movie clip. _root[id] returns a reference to one of the *GuestVideo* clips. The statement _root[id].video returns a reference to the embedded Video object in the clip, and _root[id].video. attachVideo(cam) displays what the camera sees in the Video object. The *setID( )* method also calls the *initUsers( )* method to set up the users' shared object. We'll have a look at *initUsers( )* later.

The *onStatus( )* method receives an information object that contains information about the most recent connection-related event. The code property of the object is a string in dot-delimited format, such as "NetConnection.Connect.Success". Depending on the string in the code property, a message indicating the network connection status is displayed in the statusInput text field. As we'll see shortly, in order to connect to the server, the user must click the Connect button (connectButton). At that time, the button is disabled so the user can't attempt a second connection while waiting for the result of the first attempt. The *onStatus( )* method therefore reenables the button and sets its label to Connect unless the connection has been established.

Making the connection

In Example 1-3, connectButton is set to deliver click events to the *click( )* function whenever it is clicked. The button displays one of three labels—Connect, Wait..., or Disconnect—depending on the state of the connection. If the button label is Connect, the *click( )* function tries to make a connection using *nc.connect( )*. If the button label is Disconnect, clicking the button closes the current connection by calling *nc.close( )*.

Example 1-3. Making or breaking a connection when the Connect button is clicked

```
connectButton.addEventListener("click", this);
function click (ev) {
  var button = ev.target;
  var command = button.label;
  switch (command) {
    case "Connect":
      nc.connect("rtmp:/helloVideo", userNameInput.text);
      button.label = "Wait...";
      button.enabled = false;
```

Example 1-3. Making or breaking a connection when the Connect button is clicked (continued)

```
      break;
    case "Disconnect":
      nc.close( );
      button.label = "Connect";
      break;
  }
}
```

Attempting to connect displays the Wait... button until the *nc.onStatus( )* method from Example 1-2 is called and the results of the attempt are known.

Showing remote users

So far we've seen how a connection is established and how shortly afterward the client knows its own ID, which it uses to publish a stream by the same name. Let's have a look at how the client knows what streams to subscribe to and how to display their video along with the name of each user.

When the server calls the client's *setID( )* method, *setID( )* calls the *initUsers( )* method shown in Example 1-4 to set up a shared object and connect it to the users shared object. Example 1-4 does three things: it gets a shared object, dynamically defines an *onSync( )* method for it, and then connects it using the nc net connection. When the shared object is first synchronized with the server, any data in the server's version of the shared object is copied to the client's version of the shared object, and then *onSync( )* will be called to notify the client of the changes. After that, any changes made in the server's version result in the client's version being updated and *onSync( )* being called again. The *onSync( )* method in Example 1-4 does all the work of reacting to changes in the shared object. When invoked, it receives an array of information objects. Each object has a code property, which indicates what kind of change the object represents. There are numerous possible codes as discussed in Chapter 8, but we are interested in only two of them: "change" and "delete". We can ignore the rest because all of the updates and deletions of the shared object are done by the server-side code in *main.asc*. A "change" code indicates that the server has added or updated a slot in the shared object.

Besides the built-in code property, the contents of the information object depend on the type of change reported by the shared object. In this example, the information object's name property contains the name of the slot that has changed. For example, if a user has logged in and been given the ID "guest_2", then an information object with a code value of "change" will also have a name property of "guest_2". If a user disconnects, the server will delete a slot of the shared object so the code value will be "delete" and the name property will identify the deleted slot. The *onSync( )* code in Example 1-4 loops through the array of information objects passed into *onSync( )* and examines each object's code property. If the code property is "change", the *initUsers( )* method plays the user's stream and shows her name in one of the

GuestVideo movie clips. If the code property is "delete," the example stops playing the stream associated with the user who has disconnected.

Example 1-4. Setting up the users SharedObject

```
function initUsers () {
  users_so = SharedObject.getRemote("users", nc.uri);
  users_so.onSync = function (infoList) {
    for (var i in infoList) {
      var info = infoList[i];
      switch (info.code) {
        case "change":
          var id = info.name;
          var mc = _root[id];
          mc.nameInput.text = users_so.data[id];
          if (myID != id) {
            var ns = new NetStream(nc);
            mc.video.attachVideo(ns);
            ns.play(id);
            mc.ns = ns;
          }
          break;
        case "delete":
          var id = info.name;
          var mc = _root[id];
          mc.ns.close( );
          mc.nameInput.text = "";
          mc.video.clear( );
          break;
      }
    }
  };
  users_so.connect(nc);
}
```

I'd like to look more closely at the code that starts playing a remote user's stream and shows her name:

```
      case "change":
        var id = info.name;
        var mc = _root[id];
        mc.nameInput.text = users_so.data[id];
        if (myID != id) {
          var ns = new NetStream(nc);
          mc.video.attachVideo(ns);
          ns.play(id);
          mc.ns = ns;
        }
        break;
```

The name property is the remote user's ID. For example, if it is "guest_2", _root[id] equates to the *GuestVideo* movie clip of the same name. Once we know what clip represents the user, we can show the name the user selected when she logged in by setting the text of the nameInput TextInput component inside the movie clip:

```
mc.nameInput.text = users_so.data[id];
```

Unlike the server-side code that used *users_so.setProperty( )* and *users_so.getProperty( )* to set and get values in a shared object slot, in the client a special data object is available to read and write slot values. For example, to get or set the guest_2 slot of the shared object, use the expression: users_so.data["guest_2"].

Because the server-side code changes a slot each time a user connects, the client will receive notification that a slot has changed when other remote users connect as well as when it connects. However, we want to play only the streams of remote users because there is no point in wasting bandwidth to play the local user's own stream. Fortunately, the *setID( )* method was called before the shared object was set up and connected, so we already know the local user's ID. If id is different from the value in the myID variable, id represents a remote user and we can safely play it. To play it, the code creates a new *NetStream* object and attaches it as a dynamic property of the movie clip:

```
var ns = new NetStream(nc);
mc.video.attachVideo(ns);
ns.play(id);
mc.ns = ns;
```

If a remote user disconnects, the *NetStream* object playing her stream can be safely closed, her video cleared, and the nameInput field set to an empty string:

```
case "delete":
  var id = info.name;
  var mc = _root[id];
  mc.ns.close( );
  mc.nameInput.text = "";
  mc.video.clear( );
  break;
```

Hello Video! Summary

If you've read through the code and commentary on the *helloVideo* application, you've seen most of the communication classes working together to create a very simple video conference application. And, while there is a lot more we can do with Flash and FlashCom, you've already seen many of the essential techniques for building a communication application.

Conclusion

While writing this book, I met online with the other authors to discuss our project. I used some of the sample applications I wrote for the book and another Macromedia application built on top of Flash and FlashCom: Breeze Live. One of the earliest conferences I had was with Robert Reinhardt. I was at home in Toronto, on eastern standard time, and he was in Los Angeles on Pacific time. It was dark in Toronto and the sun was about to start setting in L.A. Aside from the immediacy of our conversation—something more akin to being in the same room than being on the phone or using text messaging—there was something compelling about seeing the light gradually change on the other side of the continent as we spoke. In later conferences with Giacomo Guilizzoni, I was impressed with how helpful it was to be able to share code and make notes that we could both see and edit while we discussed what parts of this book each of us should work on. Communication applications that include live video, audio, and data make collaboration at a distance more immediate and effective. Flash and FlashCom together provide a platform that can be used to build a wide range of compelling communication applications. Whether you need to build a shared simulation to enhance an online course or a simple video conference, text chat, or video-on-demand application, you'll find a rich toolbox of classes and components to create it described in detail in the chapters that follow.

CHAPTER 2
Communication Components

Macromedia introduced components with the release of Flash MX. Components allow a Flash designer or developer to quickly add interface elements or interactive behaviors to a Flash movie. The default installation of Flash MX 2004 enables the UI components, which are basic GUI enhancements, such as scrollbars, list boxes, and push buttons. Macromedia has continued to release additional component packages for Flash MX 2004, especially those to complement Macromedia MX server products such as Flash Remoting MX and Flash Communication Server MX. In this chapter, you will learn about the communication components and how the essential components can be used to create basic FlashCom applications.

Before you begin this chapter, make sure you have downloaded and installed the latest communication components.

If using Flash MX, obtain the communication components here:

http://www.macromedia.com/software/flashcom/download/components

If using Flash MX 2004 or Flash MX Pro 2004, download the updated components here:

http://www.macromedia.com/support/flashcom/downloads_updaters.html

You don't have to rely solely on Macromedia's components. You can download third-party components from the Flash Communication Server category of the Exchange (*http://www.macromedia.com/cfusion/exchange*) and install them with the Macromedia Extension Manager. You can also create your own custom components as described in Chapter 13.

The original communication components released for Flash MX featured the Flash MX UI Components with new skins, decorating push buttons with rounded bluish rectangles. The communication components for Flash MX 2004 still use the older Flash MX UI Components, except that these versions use the original gray themed skins. The newer v2 UI components of Flash MX 2004 are not used by either version of the communication components. While the look-and-feel of the older components is not as refreshing as the newer ones, keep in mind that the older UI components are compatible with all minor releases of Flash Player 6, while the new UI components are compatible only with the last releases of Flash Player 6 and higher.

This chapter and its figures show the look-and-feel of the communication components for Flash MX 2004.

Overview of Communication Components

There are 16 components in the communication components set. Like all Macromedia components, each contains several built-in ActionScript methods and properties, and you can change the look-and-feel (or *skin*) of each component to suit your particular tastes.

Some developers report difficulty creating custom skins (it may involve writing extra drawing code, changing hard-to-find assets, or dealing with components that implement the skinning API only partially). Search the FlashCoders archive or Wiki at *http://chattyfig.figleaf.com* for some of the discussion.

Chafic Kazoun wrote the following guide to skinning the Flash MX 2004 Components:

http://www.macromedia.com/devnet/mx/flash/articles/skinning_2004_print.html

You can use the communication components to quickly set up a proof-of-concept FlashCom application that connects one or more users to an application instance and enables live real-time interactivity between the participants. Many of the components can publish audio/video streams to a FlashCom application, while others focus on text or data sharing.

After you have installed the communication components, you can view the components in Flash:

1. If you just installed the components and Flash was running, quit and restart Flash.

2. Open the Components panel by choosing Window → Development Panels → Components.

3. In the Components panel, expand the Communication Components node as shown in Figure 2-1.

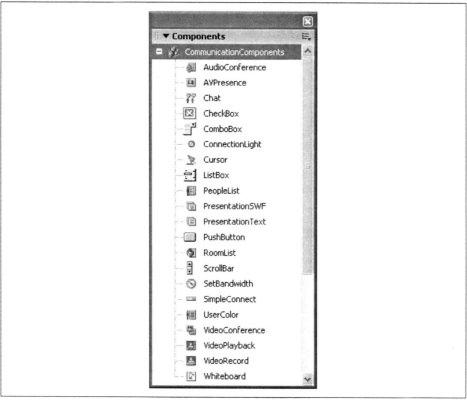

Figure 2-1. The communication components in the Components panel

You will likely find that most of these components have limited appeal for final pro-duction-quality Flash movies that you'll make available on a public web site.

> By themselves (and unaltered), the communication components oper-ate in an unrestricted manner on your FlashCom Server; anyone can connect to the Flash movie and start using the FlashCom application to which the movie is tied. For that reason, we strongly suggest that you restrict your development of this chapter's examples to a test server located within a private network.

The components are summarized briefly in Table 2-1. After describing each of the components, we'll show you how to create some simple FlashCom applications using them.

Table 2-1. Communication components

Component name	Description	Notes
AudioConference	Enables two or more users to communicate with each other	Nests CheckBox, ListBox, PushButton, and ScrollBar
AVPresence	Allows a user to send an audio and/or video stream to other users	Nests no other components; see VideoConference and SetBandwidth
Chat	Creates a text-based messaging interface for a Flash movie	Nests PushButton and ScrollBar; see UserColor
ConnectionLight	Displays a colored circle indicating the connection status	Nests no other components; see SimpleConnect
Cursor	Displays the positions and login names of users' cursors	Nests no other components; see UserColor
PeopleList	Displays the names of all users connected to a FlashCom application	Nests ListBox and ScrollBar
PresentationSWF	Displays a synchronized slideshow under speaker control to multiple users	Nests PushButton
PresentationText	Displays synchronized text slides under speaker control to multiple users	Nests ListBox, PushButton, and ScrollBar
RoomList	Enables a developer to create a gateway to other applications running on your FlashCom Server	Nests ListBox, PushButton, and ScrollBar
SetBandwidth	Allows a user to control how much bandwidth can be used by Camera and Microphone objects	Nests ComboBox, PushButton, and ScrollBar
SimpleConnect	Establishes the primary connection to a FlashCom application from a Flash movie client	Nests PushButton
UserColor	Allows each user to choose a color to represent her identity within the Chat and Cursor components	Nests ComboBox and ScrollBar; affects Chat and Cursor
VideoConference	Creates a Flash client capable of displaying multiple instances of the AVPresence component	Automatically includes AVPresence
VideoPlayback	Provides a quick user interface to play back recorded streams	Nests no other components
VideoRecord	Records and publishes audio and video streams from a Flash movie to a FlashCom application	Nests no other components
Whiteboard	Displays a shared whiteboard with drawing and text tools	Nests no other components

Server-Side Requirements

Every communication component requires one or more Server-Side ActionScript (SSAS) files, which use the *.asc* extension. These files exist within the *scriptlib* folder of the installation directory for FlashCom and are automatically installed with Flash Communication Server MX. Fortunately, you can quickly enable communication components (i.e., make them available for use by your client-side applications) by loading the *components.asc* file into the *main.asc* document of any FlashCom application. The *components.asc* file loads other *.asc* files into the application instance to enable all of the communication components. Alternatively, you can load each component's *.asc* file individually to minimize the memory requirements of your Flash-Com application.

Every communication component requires a client-side and server-side interaction. When you use a communication component instance in a Flash movie (the client), the component makes calls to a server-side component of the same name. For example, if you have a Chat component in your Flash movie, the component automatically creates a class named *FCChatClass*. When the Chat instance connects to the FlashCom application, the server-side application creates an *FCChat* class designed to communicate with the client-side *FCChatClass* instances.

You'll learn more about the component framework in Chapter 14. For the purposes of this chapter and its examples, we'll explore the basic functionality of the component framework with respect to the communication components.

To load the component framework, which enables client-side movies to use the communication components:

1. Create a directory, such as *myApplication*, for your FlashCom application in the *applications* directory of your FlashCom installation.

2. Use a text editor such as the one in Flash MX Pro 2004 to create a text document containing the following code:

   ```
   load("components.asc");
   ```

3. Save this document as *main.asc*, in the directory you created in Step 1.

You can continue to add Server-Side ActionScript code to the *main.asc* to implement functionality beyond that of the communication components. Later in this chapter, we'll create basic applications that use the code shown in the previous steps.

 If you don't want to load the server-side code for all communication components into your FlashCom application, you can load just the server-side code for the specific components you use in your Flash movie. For example, to load the server-side Chat component file, use:

```
load("framework.asc");
load("components/chat.asc");
```

in the first lines of your *main.asc* document.

Common Methods of the Communication Components

If you edit any of the communication component symbols in Flash MX 2004, you will find several methods that are common to all components.

In the following exercises, we place all ActionScript in frame 1 of the *Actions* layer of a document. Create a new layer named *Actions* for the purpose of holding scripts, and place it at the top of the timeline.

To follow along with a sample component, place an instance of the Connection-Light component onto the Stage of a Flash document, right-click (Windows) or Ctrl-click (Mac) the instance, and choose Edit. Select frame 1 of the *Actions* layer and open the Actions panel (F9).

init( )

The *init( )* method prepares, or initializes, each component instance with `name` and `prefix` properties as well as other properties specific to the component type. The `prefix` is a string used to help identify each component instance within the server-side component framework of the FlashCom application. Each instance is assigned a `prefix` property using the following convention:

```
class name + "." + instance name + "."
```

For example, an instance of the ConnectionLight component named `connLight_mc` using the Properties panel would have the `prefix` string value:

```
FCConnectionLightClass.connLight_mc.
```

Each component instance is also given a `name` property, which is exactly the same as the _name property of the movie clip instance for that component. If a component instance was not named in the Properties panel, the `name` property is set to the string value "_DEFAULT_".

connect( )

The *connect( )* method of each communication component establishes a connection for the component instance to the FlashCom application. This method requires one argument: a *NetConnection* object that has already successfully connected to a Flash-Com application. That is, the component piggybacks onto the previously established connection. For a component specified within the list of communication components for a SimpleConnect instance, its *connect( )* method is called automatically. See "Forgoing the SimpleConnect Component" later in this chapter for details on calling *connect( )* manually.

The *connect( )* method uses the `prefix` property established in the *init( )* method (discussed earlier) to invoke the server-side *connect( )* method for the same component class. The server-side code is invoked from the client with a *NetConnection.call( )* method, passing the `prefix` value and the "connect" method name as a string, along with any other necessary parameters for the communication component. Each component requires its *connect( )* method to be called in order to initialize the new component within the FlashCom application.

We don't use the term *connection* here to imply an actual *NetConnection* instance connection or a user connection to the FlashCom application. Even though you may have several communication component instances in a Flash movie, all of the components can be connected to the FlashCom application via one *NetConnection* instance. A communication component's connection simply establishes one or more remote shared objects (RSOs) or streams associated with the component's functionality.

close( )

Each communication component's connection to the FlashCom application can be terminated with the *close( )* method. This method invokes the server-side *close( )* method for the component's class, using the same *NetConnection.call( )* methodology discussed for the *connect( )* method. Note that the communication component's *close( )* method does *not* invoke the *NetConnection.close( )* method from the Flash client; a connection to the FlashCom application is still maintained even though the component instance has closed its connection.

onUnload( )

The *onUnload( )* method of each communication component simply invokes the same *close( )* method discussed in the previous section. The *onUnload( )* handler is invoked when a component instance is removed from the Stage of the Flash movie. An instance can be removed by the act of the playhead going to a frame where the instance does not exist or by client-side ActionScript code using the *MovieClip. removeMovieClip( )* method.

setUsername( )

Many of the communication components, such as AVPresence and PeopleList, contain a *setUsername( )* method. This method specifies the user's name as a string and is usually displayed somewhere in the user interface of the component. For example, if an AVPresence component instance named user_1_mc invokes the *setUsername( )* method with a string of "Alan", the name appears at the top left of the AVPresence instance when the user begins to stream audio and video. The following syntax demonstrates this functionality:

```
user_1_mc.setUsername("Alan");
```

Summary of Communication Components

Now that we've discussed the methods common to all components, let's look at the specifics of the individual components (in alphabetical order). You may want to take a quick peak at the SimpleConnect component discussed later in the chapter, as many other components rely on the connection it establishes. See "Forgoing the SimpleConnect Component" at the end of the chapter for how to notify other components of a connection without using the SimpleConnect component.

Here are some guidelines to help you understand the following sections on the individual components:

- The corresponding client-side ActionScript class for a FlashCom communication component has a name of the form *FCComponentNameClass*; for example, the class name of the AudioConference component is *FCAudioConferenceClass*.

- Most of the communication components have parameters that can be configured in the Properties panel or the Component Inspector panel. If there are parameters that are configurable through the UI for a component, we cover them in the description of each component. All component parameters can also be configured using ActionScript properties of the component as noted. For example, the LatencyThreshold parameter of the ConnectionLight component is configurable using the component's threshold property. Some component parameters are configurable only via ActionScript, such as the username property of the Chat component. It is up to the component developer to determine which properties of a component are exposed in the Properties panel or the Component Inspector panel. The communication components' parameters can be exposed in the Component Definition dialog box (available by right-clicking or Cmd-clicking the component symbol in the Library). For any component written in ActionScript 2.0 (AS 2.0), such as the Flash MX 2004 UI Components, parameters can also be exposed by defining inspectable properties in its *.as* class file. The Macromedia communication components are not written in AS 2.0; therefore, configurable parameters can't be exposed to the UI via their *.as* files.

- Unless otherwise specified, the component does not include (nest) any other Flash UI components (see Table 2-1). If a component does require other components, they will be included with the Flash movie automatically.

AudioConference

The AudioConference component enables two or more users to communicate with each other by subscribing to one or more audio-only streams. Each user who wants to publish an audio stream must have a microphone that is compatible with Flash Player 6 or higher. The interface of the component (see Figure 2-2) displays all the connected users. It allows each user to click a Talk button to start sending the audio stream, or the user can select an Auto checkbox wherein the component automatically starts and stops an audio stream when the user begins or stops talking. When a user is talking, a light to the left of the user's name turns green. When the user stops talking, the light reverts to gray.

Figure 2-2. The AudioConference component

Nested Flash UI components

The AudioConference component uses four Flash MX UI components: CheckBox, ListBox, PushButton, and ScrollBar.

Component process overview

When the AudioConference component loads into a Flash movie, the component uses an existing *NetConnection* object (which can be provided by a SimpleConnect component) to create or connect to a non-persistent RSO named FCAudioConference. audio.

 Whenever a communication component instance uses an RSO, any changes made to the RSO are broadcast to all connected users (or participants) of the same application instance. The communication components do not prohibit or exclude users of the same application instance from sharing data with one another.

This RSO keeps track of each connected user. When a user clicks the Talk button, the component attaches his microphone output to a *NetStream* instance and sets a property within the RSO to true. This property's name is based on the user's ID, which is provided by the server-side component framework. When other clients receive this updated value in the *SharedObject.onSync( )* handler, the audio stream from the other user is played. When the user releases the Talk button, the component sets the RSO's property to false, and the user's microphone output detaches from the stream.

AVPresence

The AVPresence component, by far one of the more popular communication components, allows a user connected to a FlashCom application to send an audio and/or video stream to other users. An AVPresence instance presents a masked area of the user's camera output as shown in Figure 2-3. The user can selectively mute the audio and/or video output. The component displays the microphone's activity level along the right border.

Figure 2-3. The AVPresence component

One of the special attributes of the AVPresence component is that it can be used to either send a user's audio/video stream or receive another user's audio/video stream. The AVPresence instance name establishes a unique identifier within the FlashCom application. If you place an AVPresence component instance named user_1_mc within a Flash movie (a *.swf* file), anyone who loads the Flash movie and connects to the FlashCom application can engage the user_1_mc instance to begin streaming audio/video. Once a user has started to publish a stream with the user_1_mc instance, any other users who have loaded the same Flash movie will start to see that user's stream in their instance of user_1_mc. If you want to provide multiple users simultaneous access to the functionality of the AVPresence component, you will need to create a unique instance of the AVPresence component for each user.

Once a user relinquishes control of an AVPresence instance, another user can use that same instance to start publishing her audio/video stream.

In order for a user to gain access to the AVPresence component, the following events must occur:

1. The AVPresence component must be connected to the active *NetConnection* instance of the FlashCom application. This connection can be created with the SimpleConnect component (discussed later in this chapter) or with custom ActionScript.

2. The user must specify a preferred login name in the SimpleConnect component, or *AVPresence.setUsername( )* must be invoked with a string value. If a user's name is not set, the AVPresence instance displays the text "Login to Send Audio/Video."

3. Once a username has been established, the user can click the Send Audio/Video link within the AVPresence instance to begin publishing an audio/video stream to the FlashCom application. Any other user viewing the same AVPresence instance will receive the streaming audio and video.

4. To stop sending an audio/video stream, the user must roll over the instance's video area and click the button depicting a red X in a circle, in the lower-left corner of the component as seen in Figure 2-3. Once the stream stops publishing, another user can begin using the same AVPresence instance.

Client-side component parameters

An instance of the AVPresence component has six unique settings in the Properties panel or the Parameters tab of the Component Inspector (aka the Component Parameters panel). These settings control the quality and data rates of the streams utilized by the component:

Sync Speed

Controls the frequency (in frames per second) at which data is updated from the client to the server. It controls the update frequency of the RSO used by the AVPresence component. Higher values consume more data bandwidth and update the microphone-level display more quickly. The default value is 3 fps. The ActionScript equivalent for this property is updateFps.

Video Width

Sets the capture area width, in pixels, of the camera source used by the AVPresence component. This width should not be confused with scale; the Video Width value establishes the cropping area of the local camera's video. For example, if the native capture area of a camera is 640 x 480 pixels, a Video Width setting of 320 would crop 160 pixels from the left and right margins of the capture frame. The default value for this setting is 120 pixels. The ActionScript equivalent for this property is vidWidth.

Video Height

Sets the capture area height, in pixels, of the local camera source. Like Video Width, Video Height establishes the cropping border of the capture frame. The default value is 120 pixels. The ActionScript equivalent for this property is vidHeight.

Video Bandwidth

Limits the amount of data, in bits per second, that can be consumed by the video portion of the *NetStream* object used by the AVPresence component. A value of 0 allows the video portion to use the maximum bandwidth available over the Flash movie's connection to the FlashCom Server. The default value is 12,000 bps, equivalent to 11.7 Kbps. The ActionScript equivalent of this property is vidBandwidth.

Video Quality

Sets the quality (0 to 100) of the video portion of the *NetStream* object used by the AVPresence component. Higher values yield better quality but increase the bandwidth required per frame of video. If you exceed the available bandwidth, the camera source will drop video frames as they are sent over the *NetStream* object. The default value is 0, which allows the stream to use the maximum quality for the bandwidth allocated to the stream. The ActionScript equivalent for this property is vidQuality.

Video FPS

This value controls the frame rate of the video portion of the *NetStream* object used by the AVPresence component. Faster frame rates yield smoother motion captured from the user's camera but increase the amount of bandwidth required for the stream. The default value is 10 fps. The ActionScript equivalent for this property is `vidFps`.

The Video Width, Video Height, Video Bandwidth, Video Quality, and Video FPS settings in the Properties panel for an AVPresence instance are ignored if the Set-Bandwidth component is also used in the Flash movie. In that case, the SetBandwidth instance's settings override those of the AVPresence instance.

Component process overview

The AVPresence component's client-side ActionScript creates several objects within the *connect( )* method. These objects allow multiple instances of the AVPresence component to communicate with one another, provided they are connected to the same FlashCom application.

The *connect( )* method creates a *NetStream* instance named `ns`, which is used to either publish or subscribe to an audio/video stream.

Like most communication components, the AVPresence instance creates an RSO whose name is formed from the `prefix` value of the component. For an AVPresence instance, the `prefix` value is of the form:

```
"FCAVPresence." + instance name + "."
```

This value is then concatenated to the prototype's `soName` value, "av". For example, if you place an instance of the AVPresence component on stage and named it `speaker_mc` in the Properties panel, the name of the RSO created by the AVPresence instance is `FCAVPresence.speaker_mc.av`.

This RSO tracks two primary properties: `broadcast` and `speakerID`. The `broadcast` property is a Boolean (either `true` or `false`). If the AVPresence instance is publishing a stream, `broadcast` is set to `true`. If the stream is open (that is, no one is publishing on the stream), `broadcast` is set to `false`. The `speakerID` property keeps track of an identification string, indicating which user is publishing on the stream. The ID string for each user is stored within the client-side AVPresence instance, and named `userID`. The string is determined by the Server-Side ActionScript code built for the AVPresence component.

Chat

The Chat component creates a text-based messaging interface for a Flash movie. The interface of the component, as shown in Figure 2-4, provides a text history area with a scrollbar, a user input text field, and a Send button. You can use the Chat component in combination with the PeopleList component to create a basic chat application as discussed later under "Building a Simple Chat Room." The UserColor component can also be used in conjunction with the Chat component, to assign a color to each user's text in the text history area.

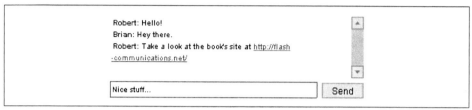

Figure 2-4. The Chat component

Nested Flash UI components

The Chat component uses variations of two Flash UI components: PushButton and ScrollBar. You can alter the look of these components by changing the appropriate skin symbols in the Component Skins folder within the Flash document's Library panel.

Component process overview

When you place an instance of the Chat component into a Flash movie, the instance needs to be connected to your FlashCom application. As with all communication components, this connection can be made by a SimpleConnect instance, or you can create your own *NetConnection* object and invoke the *Chat.connect( )* method directly.

If you elect to create your own custom connection, you must set up a global client object within the Server-Side ActionScript of your FlashCom application. If you use the SimpleConnect component, this client object is already created for your application. The Server-Side ActionScript code contained with the *chat.asc* document retrieves each user's name with the *Component.getClientGlobalStorage( )* method. The name of each user is stored within a property named username. The value of username is appended to each message that is transferred to each connected client. For more information on *getClientGlobalStorage( )*, see Chapter 14.

Two RSOs are created by the Server-Side ActionScript of the Chat component: message and history. The full names of these RSOs are created using the same type of formula discussed for the AVPresence component. The prefix value of each shared object begins with "FCChat.", followed by the client-side instance name of the component.

Whenever a user enters a message into the input text field of the Chat component and clicks the Send button, a *call( )* method from the client-side Chat instance sends the text of the message to the server-side *FCChat.sendMessage( )* method. The Send button of the Chat component is already set up to listen for Enter key events when the input text field has focus. If the user enters a message into the input text field, pressing the Enter (or Return) key automatically sends the message to the FlashCom application.

Once the *sendMessage( )* method receives the message text, the server-side code processes the message, inserting the sender's username value and converting any text beginning with "http:" or "www." to HTML-enabled links. The complete message text is then sent to the *message( )* method of the message shared object. This shared object carries the message text to each connected client.

The history remote shared object is also instantiated by the server-side *FCChat* component class. This shared object has one property, also named history, which stores an array wherein each index is a message that has been sent by a client. Whenever a new message is sent over the Chat instance, the message text is pushed into the history array.

Configurable server-side attributes

Unlike other communication components, the Chat component has a few features that can be controlled by settings in the server-side *chat.asc* document. You can find this document in the *scriptlib/components* folder of your FlashCom installation. The following code appears between lines 33 and 35 of *scriptlib/components/chat.asc*:

```
FCChat.prototype.histlen   = 250;    // Maximum history length.
FCChat.prototype.persist   = true;   // Whether to save history.
FCChat.prototype.allowClear = true;  // Allow clients to clear history.
```

The histlen property controls the maximum length of the history array, which represents the maximum number of messages stored (the default is 250). Increase this number to allow a longer chat history to be stored.

The persist property, as the code comment indicates, determines whether to save the state of the history shared object. If persist is set to true (the default), the history of the chat session is saved from one session to the next. Even after an application instance using the Chat component unloads, the history is saved. The history is then reloaded whenever a new application instance starts. If the persist property is set to false, each chat session starts with a blank slate—no past messages are loaded into the client-side Chat instance when it starts up.

The allowClear property determines whether the server-side *FCChat.clearHistory( )* method can be invoked by client-side ActionScript. By default, the value is true, allowing client-side ActionScript to clear the history. To prevent client-side code from clearing the history, set allowClear to false.

ConnectionLight

The ConnectionLight component provides a visual aid to indicate the status of the connection to the server-side FlashCom application.

The status is shown as a colored circle with one of four color states:

Gray

   Indicates a connection has yet to be attempted or a prior connection is closed.

Green

   Indicates a stable connection (via a *NetConnection* instance) to the FlashCom application.

Red

   Indicates an attempt to connect to the FlashCom application failed or was rejected. This color can also indicate that the current connection was unexpectedly lost or intentionally closed.

Yellow

   After making a successful connection to the FlashCom application, the client movie may experience delays with packet submissions. If the delay period exceeds the specified threshold, the light turns yellow.

The ConnectionLight component rechecks the connection's status (connected or disconnected) every half second (500 milliseconds).

If the user clicks the ConnectionLight instance (the colored circle), Flash displays the information overlay shown in Figure 2-5.

Figure 2-5. The information overlay of the ConnectionLight component

The overlay contains more detailed information about the connection status:

Latency

   Average time, in milliseconds (ms), for packets to be transmitted from the client movie to the FlashCom Server. Higher latency values can indicate a slow connection (usually on the client side), temporary network congestion, or an overtaxed FlashCom Server.

Up

   The bit rate of data sent from the client movie to the FlashCom Server. Use this to monitor bandwidth consumed by shared object connections and when publishing audio and video over a *NetStream* instance.

Down

> The bit rate of data received by the client from the FlashCom Server. Synchronization operations with shared object data and subscribed streams contribute to the overall value.

The Up and Down values are automatically displayed in units of bit/s (bits per second), kbit/s (kilobits per second), or mbit/s (megabits per second) based on the connection speed.

Client-side component parameters

The ConnectionLight component has two settings that can be configured at an instance level in the Properties panel or Component Parameters panel:

Measurement Interval

> This parameter, corresponding to the `interval` property, specifies the time, in seconds, that the instance waits to poll the FlashCom Server for updated connection statistics. The default value is 2 seconds. If you set a higher value, such as 5 or 10 seconds, the component will not consume as much bandwidth for data transfers as a lower interval such as 1 second. If you do not want to add to the bandwidth overhead for your application, use higher values.

Latency Threshold

> If a packet's travel time between the Flash movie and FlashCom Server exceeds this value, in seconds, the ConnectionLight instance's icon changes from green to yellow. This parameter corresponds to the `threshold` property; the default value is 0.1 second (100 milliseconds). This value adequately lets you know if audio/video streaming will have noticeable delays to other participants subscribing to the stream or if text messages between users in a chat will be delayed.

 Any time a Flash movie connects to a FlashCom application, data packets are sent back and forth to the client in order for the FlashCom Server to know that a client still exists. As such, the FlashCom Server always knows how much latency is present between itself and any connected client.

How the component works

In order for the ConnectionLight component to function properly, an instance of it must be connected to the *NetConnection* object used by the Flash movie using *ConnectionLight.connect( )*. Using a SimpleConnect instance and specifying the ConnectionLight instance in its list of communication components invokes *ConnectionLight.connect( )* automatically. Otherwise, you need to invoke *connect( )* on the ConnectionLight instance manually in your client-side ActionScript code.

Unlike other communication components, the ConnectionLight component does not use any remote shared objects or *NetStream* objects. It uses only *call( )* to invoke methods between client-side and server-side ActionScript. The client-side *Connec-tionLight.connect( )* method issues a *call( )* method to the server-side *FCConnection-Light.connect( )* method. The server-side *connect( )* method uses the measurement interval passed in to calculate a ping interval between the FlashCom application and the Flash movie client. Based on the ping interval, *Client.getStats( )* periodically cal-culates the bandwidth statistic data and sends it to the Flash client via a server-side *Client.call( )* method. This continues until the client disconnects or until the client-side *ConnectionLight.close( )* method is invoked.

Enabling ConnectionLight without SimpleConnect

To use the ConnectionLight component without the help of the SimpleConnect component, invoke *ConnectionLight.connect( )* in your client-side ActionScript. The following code example invokes the *connect( )* method of the ConnectionLight instance named connLight_mc when the first *onStatus( )* message is received over a *NetConnection* object named app_nc:

```
var app_nc:NetConnection = new NetConnection( );
app_nc.onStatus = function (info) {
  if (info.code == "NetConnection.Connect.Success") {
    trace("--successful connection");
  }
  if (!initConnLight) {
    initConnLight = true;
    connLight_mc.connect(this);
  }
};
app_nc.connect("rtmp:/my_app");
```

For more on this technique, see "Forgoing the SimpleConnect Component" at the end of this chapter.

Cursor

The Cursor component provides a visual representation of each connected user's mouse position within the Flash movie. The component displays each user's login name below a cursor indicating the position of the user's mouse on stage, as seen in Figure 2-6. The cursor is also shown in the user's preferred color when used in con-junction with the UserColor component, discussed later in this chapter.

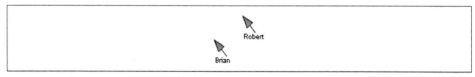

Figure 2-6. The Cursor component displays cursor positions for each user

How the component works

When a Cursor instance initializes, it creates two RSOs, cursors and mov, to add the client's cursor to the FlashCom application and to track its movements. When a new client loads the Flash movie and connects to the same FlashCom application, the cursors shared object is updated with the username and color of the earlier Flash client(s). FlashCom broadcasts this update to all subscribers of the cursors shared object, enabling each client to add a new cursor for every participant. Likewise, if a participant moves his mouse cursor, the mov shared object is updated and each subscriber receives the new coordinates of that participant's mouse cursor.

PeopleList

The PeopleList component displays the name of each user connected to a given FlashCom application, as shown in Figure 2-7. When a new user joins the application, her name is added to the PeopleList instance. When a user leaves, his name is removed from the list. If this component is used in conjunction with the SimpleConnect component, the displayed name of the user is the same as the text she entered into the text field of the SimpleConnect component when logging in.

If you want to enable actions for specific users, you can add a change handler for the ListBox instance, named people_lb, within the PeopleList component. For an example of this functionality, see Chapter 13.

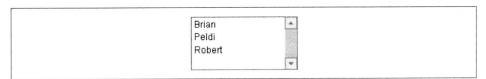

Figure 2-7. The PeopleList component lists participants

Nested Flash UI components

The PeopleList component uses two Flash UI components: ListBox and ScrollBar. ScrollBar is used within the ListBox component, just as the regular Flash MX UI ScrollBar component is nested within the ListBox component (or the UIScrollBar component within the List component in Flash MX 2004). You can alter the look of these components by changing the appropriate skin symbols in the Component Skins folder within the Flash document's Library panel.

Component process overview

The PeopleList component adheres to a similar server-side initiation process as the Chat component. Like the Chat component, the PeopleList component uses the server-side *Component.getClientGlobalStorage( )* method to retrieve the name of each connected user. When a client-side PeopleList instance is loaded into a Flash movie, a users RSO is created. The users RSO stores the user ID value, created by the Server-Side ActionScript in *scriptlib/components/people.asc*, along with the corresponding username. When an update occurs to this shared object, the people_lb instance within the PeopleList component removes the existing set of displayed usernames and adds the new list of usernames. By default, the label and data value of each item in the people_lb instance is the name (as a string value) of a given user.

To store the user ID value of each connected user as the data value of each item in the people_lb instance, you can modify line 46 of the client-side ActionScript code found on the *actions* layers of the PeopleList component to read:

```
this.owner.people_lb.addItem(this.data[i], i);
```

The new code applies the user ID string, i, as the data value to the new ListBox item.

What Is Lurker Mode?

If you look through the PeopleList component's client-side and server-side Action-Script code, you'll notice references to " fc_lurker" (note the leading space). The PeopleList component supports a *lurker mode*, allowing a user to hide his presence from the PeopleList component if a username is not returned in the result object from *Component.getClientGlobalStorage( )*. In that case, the PeopleList component assigns the value " fc_lurker" to that user's slot in the users RSO. When the client-side *onSync( )* method of the users RSO processes updates, a user's name will not be added to the people_lb instance if its value is " fc_lurker".

PresentationSWF

The PresentationSWF component allows you to create a live slideshow environment for multiple users to watch. The component synchronizes the playback of a secondary Flash movie (a *.swf* file) between a speaker's version and that of the viewers' version, as indicated in Figure 2-8. The Flash movie containing the slideshow will be loaded into the speaker's and viewers' primary Flash movie by the PresentationSWF component.

Nested Flash UI components

The PresentationSWF component uses the PushButton Flash UI component. The PushButton component is used as the Sync button within the user interface of the PresentationSWF component. You can alter the look of the PushButton component by changing the appropriate skin symbol in the Component Skins folder within the Flash document's Library panel.

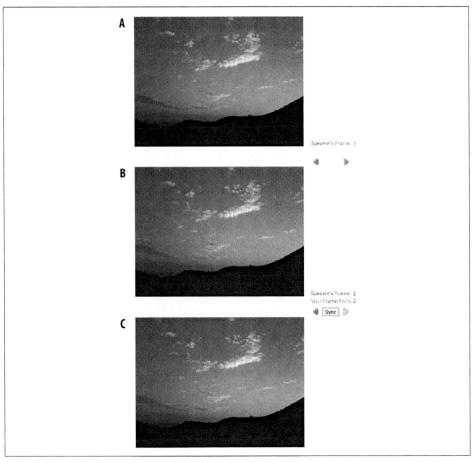

Figure 2-8. The PresentationSWF component in its two modes: (a) speaker and (b) viewer; both modes load the same (c) content movie

Client-side component parameters

An instance of the PresentationSWF component has two settings in the Properties panel or Component Parameters panel:

PresentationSWF

The filename of the content Flash movie to be loaded by the PresentationSWF component. This parameter, corresponding to the swfFile property, should be identical in the speaker and viewer versions of the component. You can use a relative or absolute path to the location of the content movie. The default value is *simple_preso.swf* (a sample movie included with FlashCom).

Viewer Buttons Enabled

This value, corresponding to the viewerButtons property, determines whether viewers can navigate the already-viewed frames of the slideshow with Forward,

Back, and Sync buttons. The default value is true, which displays these buttons to the viewer. Viewers can jump to the speaker's current frame using the Sync button, but they cannot move past it. If false, viewers cannot independently navigate frames of the slideshow, and they always see the same slide as the speaker.

Component process overview

The typical usage of this component requires the following assets:

Content Movie
> The movie containing the slideshow. Its main timeline must have one slide per frame and a *stop( )* action on the first frame. For example, a presentation with 10 slides should have 10 frames in its timeline.

Speaker Movie
> The person controlling the slideshow must have _global.speakerMode set to true in her version of the primary Flash movie holding the PresentationSWF component. There can be only one controller (or speaker) per application using the PresentationSWF component.

Viewer Movie
> Everyone else who is watching the slideshow needs to use a Flash movie with _global.speakerMode set to false.

You don't need two separate Flash movies for the speaker and viewer versions. You can create one Flash movie with a login interface that allows a specific user to have control over the presentation, while other users are set in viewer mode.

Regardless of whether you use the SimpleConnect component or create your own custom *NetConnection* object to connect to a FlashCom application, you need to set a global variable named speakerMode to true or false within the Flash movie(s) containing the PresentationSWF component. In the speaker version, the following code should be invoked before or at the same time the PresentationSWF instance is loaded onto the Stage:

```
_global.speakerMode = true;
```

For the viewer version, the variable needs to be set to false:

```
_global.speakerMode = false;
```

The PresentationSWF instance looks for this value to determine which controls are displayed within the component's user interface.

When the PresentationSWF component initializes, it creates an RSO named presentation. When the speaker moves forward or backward in the slideshow, a data slot named frameNum is updated within the presentation RSO. Then, the *onSync( )* method of the client-side shared object instance named so instructs any connected Flash movies to respond accordingly.

PresentationText

The PresentationText component is very similar to the PresentationSWF component discussed in the previous section. With the PresentationText component, you can create a FlashCom application wherein a set of text slides is controlled by a speaker and is synchronized with all other connected viewers. Unlike the PresentationSWF component, however, the PresentationText component does not require a secondary Flash movie to provide the context of the slideshow, nor does it provide a Viewer Buttons Enabled parameter. The Forward and Back buttons are visible only if the user is a presenter, and not to non-presenter participants. The PresentationText component is actually a text slide creator and editor. Like the PresentationSWF component, the speaker version can create and edit the text, while the viewer version can only watch and navigate already-viewed slides within the presentation. The speaker version of the component also provides a list of slide titles within a navigation listbox, as seen in Figure 2-9.

Figure 2-9. The PresentationText component in its two modes: (a) speaker and (b) viewer

Nested Flash UI Components

The PresentationText component uses three Flash MX UI components: ListBox, PushButton, and ScrollBar. You can alter the look of the PushButton component by changing the appropriate skin symbol in the Component Skins folder within the Flash document's Library panel. If you want to change the look of the forward and back arrows, you can alter the graphics within the movie clip symbols found in the Communication Components → Core Assets - Developer Only → PresentationText Assets → fc_presentationtext_arrow_elements folder.

Client-side component parameters

An instance of the PresentationText component has only one setting in the Properties panel or Component Parameters panel.

Speaker Mode

Whereas the PresentationSWF component uses a global variable named speakerMode, the PresentationText component provides the speaker/viewer toggle value at the instance level. For the speaker version of the PresentationText component, set the parameter to true. For the viewer version, set the parameter to false. This parameter corresponds to the speakerMode property of the PresentationText component, not the global variable of the same name.

How the component works

The PresentationText component uses the same overall structure as the Presentation-SWF component, in that both of them use an RSO to synchronize slide information among connected users. However, the presentation RSO created by the PresentationText component is persistent—the data used for the slides, once created by a user in speaker mode, can exist in perpetuity. This feature allows the speaker to create the outline and text slides of a presentation before the live presentation. For example, a professor could create the headings and text for each slide days in advance; each text slide's information would be stored within the persistent presentation RSO. When the professor is ready to conduct his online course, the speaker-enabled PresentationText component automatically loads the existing slide information and displays it to the viewers.

RoomList

The RoomList component is perhaps the most advanced communication component. Of all the communication components, it requires the most manual coding—you can't simply drag and drop this component onto the Stage, even with the use of SimpleConnect, and be on your way. The RoomList component enables you to create a gateway to other application instances running on your FlashCom Server. Remember, when you create a FlashCom application, a Flash movie can connect to the default instance or a specific named instance of the application. For a chat application, you can equate an application instance with a room within the chat application. The RoomList component enables a Flash movie to show each of these instances. The movie containing the RoomList component, however, must connect to an application entirely separate from the chat application. As shown in Figure 2-10, the user interface of the RoomList component displays a list of running FlashCom applications and allows a Flash client to join, create, or delete instances of those applications.

Unlike other communication components, the RoomList component is used with an entirely separate FlashCom application instance than the one to which the clients will ultimately connect.

Figure 2-10. The RoomList component provides a lobby

The following steps outline a standard user experience with an application using the RoomList component:

1. The user loads an HTML page containing a Flash movie (SWF file #1) with an instance of the RoomList component. The RoomList instance connects to a FlashCom application (application A) that monitors one or more instances of another FlashCom application (application B).

2. The user logs into application A from SWF file #1, using the SimpleConnect component.

3. In SWF file #1, the user chooses one of the application instances from the UI of the RoomList component and clicks the Create Room or Join Room button.

4. The RoomList component opens a new browser window, containing a different HTML page with another Flash movie (SWF file #2). The HTML code of this document passes parameters from the original Flash movie (SWF file #1); SWF file #2 connects to a new FlashCom application (application B), which receives the parameters. A custom server-side script must be written for application B to process the parameters and notify application A that a user has now connected to application B.

See the *Developing Communication Applications* documentation that accompanies Flash Communication Server MX 1.5 (available in both LiveDocs and PDF format from *http://www.macromedia.com/support/documentation/en/flashcom/index.html*) for more information about the specific server-side event handlers that are necessary for two FlashCom applications to use the RoomList component.

Nested Flash UI components

The RoomList component uses three Flash MX UI components: ListBox, PushButton, and ScrollBar. You can alter the look of these component by changing the appropriate skin symbol in the Component Skins folder within the Flash document's Library panel.

Client-side component parameters

An instance of the RoomList component has one setting in the Properties panel or Component Parameters panel:

Room Application Path
> Using the previous example as a guide, this parameter specifies the URL of the HTML document containing the second Flash movie (SWF file #2), which connects to FlashCom application B. This HTML document receives two parameters from the Flash movie hosting the RoomList component: the user's name and the application instance path used to connect to application A. The HTML document must use either client-side scripting, such as JavaScript or VBScript, or server-side scripting, such as ColdFusion, to process the passed parameters in the URL string and append them to the <OBJECT> and <EMBED> tags for the second Flash movie connecting to application B.

Component process overview

As mentioned earlier, the RoomList component is designed to work in a scenario of two FlashCom applications, with separate HTML and SWF files for each application. A more detailed explanation of utilizing the RoomList component follows.

This is intended to be a technical overview of the requirements and steps necessary to use the RoomList component. See *Developing Communication Applications* for an introductory exercise to using the RoomList component:

1. An application folder (application A) is created on the FlashCom Server for the Flash movie displaying the RoomList component. This application keeps track of all application instances created by users connecting to a second application (application B) managed by the RoomList component.

2. Another application folder (application B) is created on the FlashCom Server. This application will connect to application A via the *Application.call( )* server-side method to update application A's information, which is displayed in the RoomList component.

3. Both applications load the server-side *components.asc* code at startup, in order for the applications to access and store client and component instance variables.

4. A Flash document (*.fla* file), which we use to create SWF #1, is created with an instance of the SimpleConnect component and an instance of the RoomList component. The SimpleConnect component's Application Directory parameter uses the *rtmp://* URI to application A discussed in Step 1. The RoomList component's instance name is specified in the Communication Components value list parameter of the SimpleConnect component (discussed later in this chapter). The RoomList component's Room Application Path parameter is set to the URL of the HTML document hosting the Flash movie connecting to application B (discussed in Step 5). Note that this URL is an *http://* URL, not an *rtmp://* URI.

This Flash movie and HTML document are published and put on your web server.

5. A Flash document (*.fla* file), which we'll use to create SWF #2, is made for the second application (application B). This document contains the managed application monitored by the RoomList component and application A. The Flash movie (*.swf*) for this document is embedded in the HTML document specified in the Room Application Path parameter of the RoomList component as well. For example, you can create a Flash document that uses the SimpleConnect, Chat, and PeopleList components for a basic chat room. This document needs to process parameters passed by the RoomList component in the URL of the HTML document hosting the Flash movie (SWF #2). If you use the SimpleConnect component in SWF #2 that connects to application B, the parameters will be processed automatically. Otherwise, you'll need to use client-side ActionScript to process two _root variables, username and appInstance, which are passed by the RoomList component (username is the string value entered by the user in the SimpleConnect component of SWF #1, and appInstance is the name of the "room" instance specified in the Create Room dialog box or an existing instance name displayed in the RoomList component).

6. Finally, the *application.onConnect( )* method of the Server-Side ActionScript code for application B must pass the username and appInstance values to the Server-Side ActionScript code of application A. There, an RSO used by the server-side RoomList component stores, updates, and broadcasts the new information. In turn, any users connected to SWF #1 will see an updated user count and new "room" (or application instance) displayed in the UI of the client-side RoomList component.

SetBandwidth

The SetBandwidth component allows a user to control how much bandwidth can be used by *Camera* and *Microphone* objects utilized by other communication components, such as the AVPresence and AudioConference components. The SetBandwidth component limits the byte throughput of a client Flash movie to a FlashCom application. The component's UI consists of a combo box with labels—Modem, DSL, LAN, and Custom—as shown in Figure 2-11, indicating four connection types. These labels are associated with preset bandwidth caps (typical connection speeds), which can be set in the Properties panel or in client-side ActionScript.

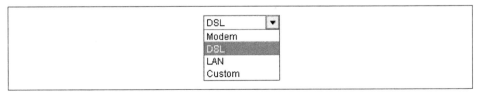

Figure 2-11. The SetBandwidth component menu

Selecting Custom opens a separate window, shown in Figure 2-12, in which the user can customize the Up and Down bandwidth limits.

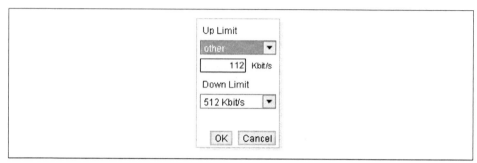

Figure 2-12. The Custom options for the SetBandwidth component

Whenever a user chooses an item in the SetBandwidth component, the quality and attributes of *Camera* and *Microphone* objects managed by other communication components will change. As more bandwidth is allocated to the movie, the quality of the audio/video output improves.

Nested Flash UI components

The SetBandwidth component uses three Flash MX UI components: ComboBox, PushButton, and ScrollBar. You can alter the look of these components by changing the appropriate skin symbol in the Component Skins folder within the Flash document's Library panel.

Client-side component parameters

An instance of the SetBandwidth component has six settings in the Properties panel or Component Parameters panel, as listed in Table 2-2.

These parameters establish the preferred bandwidth limit for the incoming and outgoing connection when the user chooses the specified connection type (Modem, DSL, or LAN) in the SetBandwidth component. The connection type also affects the capture attributes of the Camera object (as used by the AVPresence component) and the sampling rate of the Microphone object (as used by the AVPresence or Audio-Conference component).

Note that:

- The practical throughput for a typical 56 Kbps dial-up modem is only 33 Kbps.
- The DSL options reflect the typical upper limit of household ADSL (asymmetric DSL) connections. The default DSL Down value is greater than DSL Up; therefore, the quality of incoming streams to the Flash movie client can be more than twice the quality of the user's outgoing stream.

- The default value for the LAN option is 10,000 Kbps, which reflects a typical 10 Mbps network.
- You can change the values to be more restrictive or lax. For example, if you'd prefer the DSL rates to be higher and identical, you could use a value of 512 Kbps for DSL Up and DSL Down.

Table 2-2. SetBandwidth defaults for each connection parameter

Parameter name	Default	Camera settings	Microphone sampling rate	Property
Modem Up	33 Kbps	120 x 90 capture area, 6 fps, 60 quality, keyframe interval of 12	5 kHz	modemUp
Modem Down	33 Kbps	Same as Modem Up	5 kHz	modemDown
DSL Up	128 Kbps	160 x 120 capture area, 12 fps, 80 quality, keyframe interval of 7	11 kHz	dslUp
DSL Down	384 Kbps	Same as DSL Up	11 kHz	dslDown
LAN Up	10,000 Kbps	320 x 240 capture area, 15 fps, 90 quality, keyframe interval of 5	22 kHz	lanUp
LAN Down	10,000 Kbps	Same as LAN Up	22 kHz	lanDown

Keep in mind that the limits established by the SetBandwidth component are secondary to the limits of the practical speed available by a user's Internet (or network) connection. For example, if a user chooses the LAN option but is transmitting over a DSL connection, the outgoing stream will transmit only at the quality limit dictated by the actual connection. The degradation of the quality may not affect the user experience markedly. However, if a user chooses the LAN option despite the fact that she's using a dial-up modem connection, the bandwidth won't support the increased video capture area and frame rate. In that case, FlashCom will drop video frames, causing the image to stutter noticeably. The audio stream will use 22 kHz, and that's just too much data to push over a dial-up connection. Therefore, the audio will stutter as well, resulting in a fairly incomprehensible stream of audio and video to other participants.

Component process overview

The SetBandwidth component performs two overall functions within a Flash movie. It creates a *Notifier* instance within a gFlashCom object that broadcasts changes to other components that are subscribed. The gFlashCom object is simply an object created in the _global namespace for the explicit purpose of sharing parameters, such as bandwidth preferences, between client-side communication components. For example, when you add an AVPresence component or AudioConference room component, each instance is added as a listener to the *Notifier* instance. At runtime, when a user chooses an option in the SetBandwidth component, any subscribers will receive the new updates, instructing them to change capture attributes of the Camera and/or Microphone object.

The SetBandwidth component also sends these changes to the FlashCom application. When the server-side FCSetBandwidth component receives updates, it invokes *Client.setBandwidthLimit( )* to restrict the bandwidth for streams managed by the server. Note that this method controls both the bandwidth to the client from the server and the bandwidth from the client to the server. The server changes override any settings established by client-side ActionScript code.

SimpleConnect

The SimpleConnect component establishes the primary connection to a FlashCom application from a Flash movie client. As you have undoubtedly gathered, other communication components often use the connection established by the SimpleConnect component to communicate with a FlashCom application. As its name implies, this component is very simple to use from both authoring and runtime viewpoints. At runtime, this component displays a username field and a Login button, as shown in Figure 2-13.

Figure 2-13. The SimpleConnect component interface

The user types his name into the text field and clicks the Login button. When the component successfully establishes a connection to the FlashCom application, it passes its *NetConnection* object to other communication components (or your own custom objects).

Nested Flash UI components

The SimpleConnect component uses the Flash MX UI component PushButton. You can alter the look of this component by changing the appropriate skin symbol in the Component Skins folder within the Flash document's Library panel.

Client-side component parameters

An instance of the SimpleConnect component has two settings in the Properties panel or Component Parameters panel:

Application Directory
>   The path of the FlashCom Server and application to which the component connects. This value is an RTMP URI, starting with the string "rtmp:". You can use a relative RTMP URI that omits the server's domain name if the FlashCom Server coexists on the same IP address or domain as your web server. For example, *rtmp:/chat* tells the SimpleConnect component to connect to the *chat*

application on the FlashCom Server. For production-ready applications, though, you should use a full RTMP URI, such as *rtmp://fcs.mydomain.com/app*, where *fcs.mydomain.com* is the name of the server where FlashCom is running, and *app* is the name of the application folder. This parameter corresponds to the appDirectory property.

Communication Components

A list of other communication component instance names. If you double-click this parameter in the Properties panel, you can enter multiple instance names of other communication components that coexist on stage with the SimpleConnect component. When the SimpleConnect instance connects to a FlashCom application, it shares its connection with the objects specified in the Communication Components list. You can directly manipulate this listener list using the fcComponents property (an array).

You can create your own custom objects that can be recognized by the SimpleConnect component. Simply create a *connect( )* method for your object, and specify the object's name in the Communication Components list. Your object should be instantiated on the parent timeline of the SimpleConnect instance.

How the component works

The SimpleConnect component connects a Flash movie to a FlashCom application by invoking a client-side *NetConnection.connect( )* method as soon as the instance loads in the movie. The SimpleConnect component actually tries to connect with both a standard RTMP and a tunneling RTMPT connection. Whichever connection type responds first becomes the active URI of the connection. The connection is then shared with the objects specified in the Communication Components parameter (fcComponents property) of the SimpleConnect instance.

When the user enters a name and clicks the Login button (or presses the Enter key), the SimpleConnect component issues a *NetConnection.call( )* method to the server-side *FCSimpleConnect.changeName( )* method. This method keeps track of the user's name, as entered in the SimpleConnect's text field, and shares that data with other communication components.

Because the SimpleConnect component doesn't support common features, such as entering a password in addition to a username, you may want to create a connection manually as part of a custom login. The manual approach requires you to notify other components of the connection's status as discussed under "Forgoing the SimpleConnect Component" at the end of this chapter.

UserColor

The UserColor component is a UI element that allows each user to choose a color to represent her identity within the Chat and Cursor components. The UI of the

UserColor component is a combo box with 10 preselected colors, as shown in Figure 2-14. When the user selects a color within the UserColor component, her text appears in that color within the history window of the Chat component. If the Cursor component is used with the Flash movie, the user's cursor will be displayed to other users in the chosen color as well.

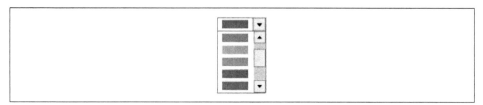

Figure 2-14. The UserColor component

Nested Flash UI components

The UserColor component uses the Flash MX UI components ComboBox and ScrollBar. You can alter the look of this component by changing the appropriate skin symbol in the Component Skins folder within the Flash document's Library panel.

How the component works

The UserColor component, like the SetBandwidth component, uses a *gFlashCom. Notifier* object in client-side ActionScript to notify other color-aware communication components of changes made to the user's color preference. When the user loads a Flash movie that contains a UserColor component, the UserColor component connects to the FlashCom application specified by a SimpleConnect component or a custom connection that passed its *NetConnection* object to the UserColor's *connect( )* method. In order for the UserColor component to work properly, the *setUsername( )* method of the component must be invoked and passed a string value for the user's name. If you use the SimpleConnect component, this happens automatically. The UserColor component also stores its selected color value within the usercolor property of the client's global storage object within Server-Side ActionScript for the duration of the application session.

VideoConference

The VideoConference component enables you to create a Flash client capable of displaying multiple instances of the AVPresence component. As each user connects to the FlashCom application, a new AVPresence instance is added to the Stage, displaying her audio/video stream as shown in Figure 2-15.

This component can be particularly bandwidth-intensive for both client-side and server-side connections. As each user is added to the AV chat, the stream must manage multiple additional streams depending on the number of users—the new user

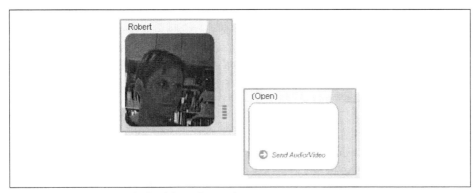

Figure 2-15. The runtime look of the VideoConference component

has one outgoing stream, plus one incoming stream for each existing user. Likewise, the new user's stream must be sent to existing users (in addition to the streams they already have). For example, if you have three users connected to an application using the VideoConference component, the server is managing nine streams; the server and each user's bandwidth must be capable of handling three streams for each user: his own stream (outgoing) and the two from the other participants (incoming). You can quickly determine how many streams a server must handle by squaring the number of participants. For example, five participants will require the server to handle 25 streams (five for each participant).

Nested Flash UI components

The VideoConference component does not use any Flash UI components. It does however automatically include the AVPresence component symbol. The skin assets of the VideoConference component are located in the Communication Components → Core Assets - Developer Only → VideoConference Assets folder of your document's Library. You can also change the look of the AVPresence component by modifying the graphics in the AVPresence Assets → fc_av_icons folder.

Client-side component parameters

The VideoConference component has four parameters that can be set in the Properties panel or Component Parameters panel:

Show Boundary

This Boolean parameter, corresponding to the showBoundary property, determines if the border of the VideoConference instance is displayed. The default value is false. You can use Flash's Transform tool to stretch the dimensions of the instance without distorting the physical appearance of the AVPresence instances that will be attached for each user.

Show Background

This Boolean parameter, corresponding to the showBackground property, controls the display of the background fill color in the VideoConference component. The background graphic can be modified in the *VideoConfBackground* symbol of the VideoConference Assets folder in the Library. By default, this value is set to false.

Clip Mask

This Boolean parameter, corresponding to the clipMask property, controls whether instances of AVPresence appear when dragged outside the VideoConference object's boundary area. If this parameter is true (the default), AVPresence instances appear only within the VideoConference instance's boundary area. Otherwise, AVPresence instances appear even if outside the VideoConference instance's boundary area.

Drag Sharing

This parameter, corresponding to the dragSharing property, controls dragging of AVPresence instances to a new position on the Stage. If true (the default), when one user moves an instance, all users see it in the new position. If set to false, each user can configure the instance positions without affecting the positions of the same instances in other users' movies. This parameter is set per user; if there are three users (A, B, and C) and users A and B have Drag Sharing set to true while user C's value is set to false, users A and B will see each other's changes. Meanwhile, user C is free to drag the AV instances within her application to any position without those changes being broadcast to users A and B.

Component process overview

When the VideoConference instance's *connect( )* method is invoked by a SimpleConnect instance or a custom client-side *NetConnection* object, the VideoConference instance invokes a *NetConnection.call( )* method to the server-side *FCVideoConference.connect( )* method, as defined in the *videoconference.asc* code (located in the *scriptlib/components* folder of your FlashCom Server installation). The server-side *connect( )* method creates a unique ID for the Flash client and stores the ID in a users RSO. The server-side *connect( )* method also calls the client-side *VideoConference. setID( )* method. This method sets everything else in motion, wherein the VideoConference component attaches an instance of the Video Window (whose linkage ID is FCVideoWindowSymbol) to its Stage. This symbol in turn attaches an instance of the AVPresence component to its timeline. Any time a user connects to the FlashCom application, the user's ID is added to the users RSO, forcing the *onSync( )* handler of the VideoConference's reference to the shared object to update the Stage with a new Video Window instance for the new user.

VideoPlayback

The VideoPlayback component provides a quick user interface to play back recorded streams that reside in a FlashCom application. You can play streams recorded by FlashCom from a user's web cam, or you can play *.flv* files that you created from Macromedia's FLV Exporter tool or a third-party utility, such as Sorenson Squeeze or Wildform Flix. The VideoPlayback component includes a control bar, as shown in Figure 2-16. You can play, pause, and seek the stream, as well as control its volume. The edges of the video are masked by rounded corners.

Figure 2-16. The runtime look of the VideoPlayback component

Nested Flash UI components

This component does not use any Flash UI components. If you wish to change the appearance of this component, you can modify the graphics found in the Communication Components → Core Assets - Developer Only → VideoPlayback Assets folder of your Flash document's Library.

Client-side component parameters

The VideoPlayback component has two settings that can be modified in the Properties panel or the Component Parameters panel:

Default Stream Name

This parameter, corresponding to the streamName property, specifies the name of the stream to play from the FlashCom application. You do not need to include the *.flv* extension in the stream name. For example, if you want to play a file named *recording.flv* that is stored in the application's *streams/_definst_* folder, specify **recording** in this field in the Properties panel. If you have created a virtual directory to store streams on your FlashCom Server, you can specify the alias name in front of the stream's name. For example, if you created an alias named *common*, you can play a file named *recording.flv* located there by specifying `common/recording`.

Buffer Time

> This parameter, corresponding to the `bufferTime` property, controls how much of the stream will be buffered, in seconds, before playback begins. The default value is 2 seconds. While longer times will add to the wait time users experience before playback begins, overall playback performance may be improved because there is less chance of video pausing due to network congestion.

Component process overview

When a VideoPlayback instance is initialized in a Flash movie and its *connect( )* method is invoked by a SimpleConnect instance or a custom *NetConnection* object that you have created, the VideoPlayback instance creates a new instance of *FCPlayStreamClass*, a class that is defined in the *FCPlayStream_Class* symbol (linkage ID *FCPlayStreamSymbol*) of the component. This class inherits from the *NetStream* class and augments its functionality by creating methods and properties that allow streams to work smoothly with the control bar interface of the VideoPlayback component.

VideoRecord

The VideoRecord component can publish and record an audio/video stream from a Flash movie to a FlashCom application. The UI of the VideoRecord component, shown in Figure 2-17, is similar to that of the VideoPlayback component. When the component instance loads, the output from your local camera source is automatically displayed in the video window. The leftmost button in the control interface is a record start/stop toggle. The button to its right is a play/stop toggle, which allows you to review your recorded stream. To its right is a buffering status display. While a user records a stream, the buffering area is empty. When a user previews his stream, the buffering area displays a progress bar indicating how much of the stream's buffer has been filled. A record/playback status indicator is shown to the right of the buffering display. When a stream is recording, the status indicator is a blinking red dot. When a stream is being reviewed, the status indicator is a blinking blue dot.

You can use the VideoPlayback component in tandem with the VideoRecord component. The VideoPlayback component offers more playback control of the recorded stream than the play/stop button in the VideoRecord component. After you have recorded a stream with the VideoRecord component, you can use an instance of the VideoPlayback component to play the recorded stream.

Nested Flash UI components

The VideoRecord component does not use any nested Flash UI components. You can find the skin symbols for the component in the Communication Components →

Figure 2-17. The runtime look of the VideoRecord component

Core Assets - Developer Only → VideoRecord Assets folder of your document's Library.

Client-side component parameters

The VideoRecord component has six settings in the Properties panel or Component Parameters panel:

Default Stream Name

This parameter, corresponding to the streamName property, specifies the name of the stream that is recorded to the FlashCom application. You can use the same conventions described earlier for the VideoPlayback component's Default Stream Name parameter.

Default Settings

This parameter controls which quality setting is applied to the Camera and Microphone objects during recording. The quality setting properties are discussed later in this list. The default value is setHigh, which is a reference to the object specified by the High Quality Settings parameter. You can create your own custom quality object and use it as the value of the defaultSetting property of a VideoRecord instance. Alternatively, you can pass this custom object to *VideoRecord.adjustSettings( )*.

Buffer Time

This parameter, corresponding to the bufferTime property, establishes the amount of time, in seconds, that both the recording stream and the replay stream use for buffering. The default is 10.

Low Quality Settings, Medium Quality Settings, and High Quality Settings

These parameters are used to adjust the quality of the Camera and Microphone objects' output to the recording stream. These settings control the default values for low, medium, and high bit rate Internet connections. (The settings used depend on the value of the Default Settings parameter or the defaultSetting property.) Each setting uses an object with the following properties to adjust the Camera object's output: width (in pixels), height (in pixels), fps, bandwidth (in Kbps), and key (for keyframe interval). The object also has a rate property that controls the sampling rate of the Microphone object. You can override these settings in client-side ActionScript by writing a new value to the setLow, setMed, and setHigh properties of the VideoRecord component.

The SetBandwidth component does not apply any changes to the VideoRecord component. You can, however, use a ComboBox instance to let the user choose which quality setting should be applied to a VideoRecord instance.

Component process overview

When the *connect( )* method of a VideoRecord instance is invoked and passed a reference to a *NetConnection* object, the component creates two streams: an outgoing stream (out_ns) for the recording stream and an incoming stream (in_ns) for the replay stream. Unlike the VideoPlayback component, the VideoRecord component does not utilize *FCPlayStreamClass* to create a custom *NetStream* class. Rather, the component uses the existing methods of the *NetStream* class. The component also invokes a *cameraOn( )* method upon connection, which grabs the output from the Camera and Microphone objects. The *cameraOn( )* method invokes the *adjustSettings( )* method to control the quality of output captured by the Camera and Microphone objects. You can invoke *VideoRecord.adjustSettings( )* from your own custom UI elements, such as a combo box, to change the quality of recorded output on the fly.

Whiteboard

The Whiteboard component is, as the name implies, a component that shows the UI of a whiteboard with drawing and text tools, as shown in Figure 2-18. The menu has the following options (from top to bottom):

Move/Transform tool
> Selects and moves objects on the whiteboard. You can delete an item by clicking it with the Move/Transform tool and pressing the Delete key. You can use this tool to resize arrow lines, but you cannot resize text or text boxes with this tool.

Text tool
> Creates standard text, in a _serif device font.

Text Box tool
> Draws a black-outlined box, using the selected color in the color menu as its fill. The text in this box uses the _sans device font.

End Arrow Line tool

Draws a line with an arrow point at the end of the line (as determined by the location of the second click).

Start Arrow Line tool

Works the same as the End Arrow Line tool, except that the arrow point is placed at the first click point and not the second.

Dual Arrow Line tool

Creates a line with arrow points at both ends.

Color menu

Features eight colors that you can use as fill colors for the Text or Text Box tool or as line colors for the line tools.

Expand/Collapse button

Expands and collapses the UI of the tools palette.

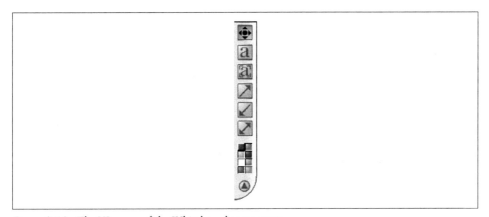

Figure 2-18. The UI menu of the Whiteboard component

 If you're looking for a full-featured whiteboard component, check out Fig Leaf Software's WYSIdraw at *http://products.figleaf.com*. This whiteboard features more drawing tools and can layer JPEG images with other artwork in a collaborative environment. This component is priced for enterprise use, starting at $995.

Nested Flash UI components

The Whiteboard component does not use any nested Flash UI components. You can adjust the look-and-feel of the component by adjusting its skin symbols in the Communication Components → Core Assets - Developer Only → Whiteboard Assets folder of the document's Library.

How the component works

When the Whiteboard component's *connect( )* method is called by a SimpleConnect instance or a custom *NetConnection* object, the component creates a whiteboard RSO within the FlashCom application. When a user draws a shape with one of the component's tools, the parameters of a custom drawing object are sent to the shared object, and, in turn, the update is broadcast to all subscribed users. The *onSync( )* handler of the shared object either removes a shape with *MovieClip.removeMovieClip( )* or it invokes *Whiteboard.drawShape( )* to create a new text, text box, or line object on the Stage.

Creating an Application that Monitors a Connection

Now that you have a basic overview of the communication components, let's see how to use them to create an application. We'll build a Flash movie that connects to a FlashCom application using the SimpleConnect and ConnectionLight components. The SimpleConnect component will specify the URI of the FlashCom application, and the ConnectionLight instance will display the statistics of the connection.

Make sure you have installed the latest communication components for Flash MX or Flash MX 2004, as cited at the beginning of the chapter, before you begin this exercise.

Making the FlashCom Application Folder

First, set up the *basic_app* application as follows:

1. On the computer running FlashCom Server, browse to the *applications* folder. Create a new folder named *basic_app* at this location.

2. In Flash Pro or your preferred text editor, create a new ActionScript Communication document. Add the following code to the document:

   ```
   load("components.asc");
   ```

   This line of code instructs the FlashCom application to load the *components.asc* document from its *scriptlib* folder, which in turn loads the .*asc* files for each communication component.

3. Save the text document as *main.asc* in the *basic_app* folder you created in Step 1.

Your FlashCom application is now prepared to use communication components.

Building the Flash Client Movie

Now that the server-side .*asc* code is complete, we have to create the client (.*swf*) movie:

1. Create a new Flash document (File → New). Save this document as *component_ connection.fla*.

2. Rename *Layer 1* to *connect_mc*. This layer will be used to hold an instance of the SimpleConnect component.

3. Open the Components panel (Ctrl-F7 or Cmd-F7), and open the Communications Components set as shown in Figure 2-1. Drag an instance of the SimpleConnect component to the first frame of the *connect_mc* layer. Place the instance near the top-left corner of the Stage.

4. Select the new instance, and use the Properties panel to give it the instance name connect_mc. In the Parameters tab of the Properties panel, enter the path to the *basic_app* FlashCom application in the Application Directory field. For example, if you are using the Developer edition of FlashCom on the same machine as your web server, enter **rtmp:/basic_app**. Otherwise, specify the full RTMP path to your FlashCom Server and application, such as **rtmp://fcs.mydomain.com/ basic_app**.

5. Create a new layer in the Timeline panel, and name the layer *light_mc*. On frame 1 of this layer, drag an instance of the ConnectionLight component from the Components panel to the Stage. Place the instance to the right of the connect_mc instance. In the Properties panel, name this instance light_mc, and leave the default values for the component's parameters.

6. Select the connect_mc instance, and in the Properties panel, click the Communication Components field. In the Values list, click the + button and enter **light_ mc** in the field labeled 0, as shown in Figure 2-19. Click OK to close the dialog box. By specifying the light_mc instance's name, the SimpleConnect instance knows to notify it of the connection to the *basic_app* application.

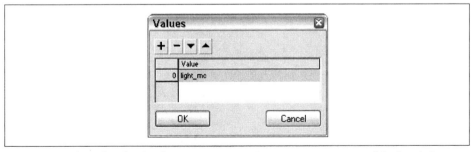

Figure 2-19. The Values list for the Communication Components parameter of the SimpleConnect component

7. Save your document, and test the movie (Control → Test Movie). As soon as the Flash movie connects to the *basic_app* application, the ConnectionLight instance turns green. If the connection fails, the light turns red. If the connection latency threshold is reached, the light turns yellow.

Building a Simple Chat Room

Now that you know how to connect to a FlashCom application using the Simple-Connect and ConnectionLight components, you can proceed to add features to the application. In the following steps, you will learn how to add the PeopleList, Chat, and UserColor components to the *basic_app* application:

1. Open the *component_connection.fla* you created in the last section. Resave this document as *component_chat.fla*.

2. Create a new layer named *list_mc*. On frame 1 of this layer, drag an instance of the PeopleList component from the Components panel to the Stage. Name the instance **list_mc** using the Properties panel. Also, place this component near the lower-left edge of the Stage, as shown in Figure 2-20.

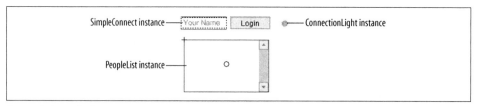

Figure 2-20. The list_mc instance

3. Create another layer named *chat_mc*. On frame 1 of this layer, drag an instance of the Chat component to the Stage. Name the instance **chat_mc** using the Properties panel. Place this component to the right of the list_mc instance, as shown in Figure 2-21.

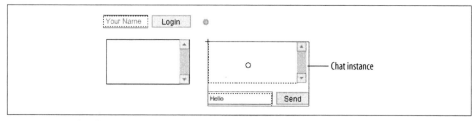

Figure 2-21. The chat_mc instance

4. Create another layer named *userColor_mc*. On frame 1 of this layer, drag an instance of the UserColor component to the Stage. Name the instance **userColor_mc** using the Properties panel. Place this instance below the Simple-Connect and ConnectionLight instances near the upper left of the Stage, as show in Figure 2-22.

5. Select the connect_mc instance on stage, and double-click its Communication Components parameter in the Parameters tab of the Properties panel. In the Values list, add the instance names of the three communication components—**list_mc**, **chat_mc**, and **userColor_mc**—as shown in Figure 2-23.

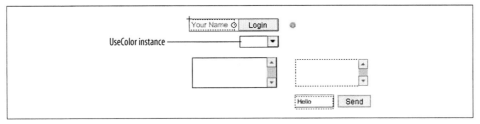

Figure 2-22. The userColor_mc instance

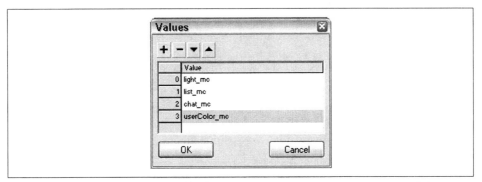

Figure 2-23. The updated Values list for the Communication Components parameter of the SimpleConnect component

6. Save your Flash document. In order to see the chat elements working properly, choose File → Publish Preview → Default - (HTML). Leave the web browser's window open, and go back to the Flash authoring environment. There, choose Control → Test Movie to open another version of the Flash movie. When the movie loads, enter your name in the username field of the SimpleConnect component and click the Login button. Your name should display in the PeopleList component, both in the Test Movie environment and the web browser window. Now, log in with another username in the Flash movie running from the browser window. Again, you should see the new name populate both movies' PeopleList instance. In each movie, choose a unique color from the UserColor component. Finally, enter a message in the chat message window, and click the Send button. You should see the message appear in the history area of both Chat instances. The color of the message text should be the same color selected in the sender's UserColor combo box.

Adding Audio and Video to the Chat Room

To add audio/video streaming capabilities to the chat room, you can add the Audio-Conference, AVPresence, or VideoConference component to the Flash document you created in the last section. In the following steps, you will add two instances of the AVPresence component and an instance of the SetBandwidth component to the movie:

1. Open the *component_chat.fla* from the last section. Resave this document as *component_avchat.fla*.

2. Create two new layers, named *av_1_mc* and *av_2_mc*.

3. On frame 1 of the *av_1_mc* layer, drag an instance of the AVPresence component from the Components panel to the Stage. Place the instance to the right of the ConnectionLight instance and above the Chat instance. In the Properties panel, name this instance **av_1_mc**.

4. Repeat the previous step for another instance of the AVPresence component. Place the new instance on frame 1 of the *av_2_mc* layer, positioned to the right of the av_1_mc instance. Name the new instance **av_2_mc**.

5. Create a new layer named *bandwidth_mc*. On frame 1 of this layer, drag an instance of the SetBandwidth component to the Stage. Place the instance below the userColor_mc instance. Name the new instance **bandwidth_mc** using the Properties panel. Your Stage should now resemble Figure 2-24.

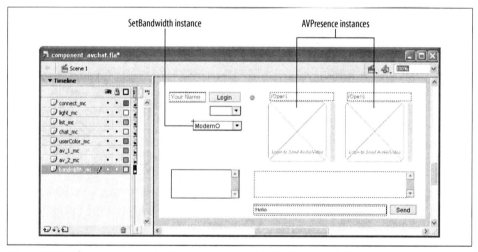

Figure 2-24. The new communication components added to the movie's Stage

6. Select the connect_mc instance on the Stage, and double-click its Communication Components parameter in the Parameters tab of the Properties panel. In the Values list, add the instance names of the three additional communication components—**av_1_mc**, **av_2_mc**, **bandwidth_mc**—as shown in Figure 2-25.

7. Save your document, and test the movie with both the Publish Preview and Test Movie commands. If you have a web cam and microphone connected to your computer, start streaming audio/video from one Flash movie's AVPresence instance. You should then see the same audio/video stream displayed in the

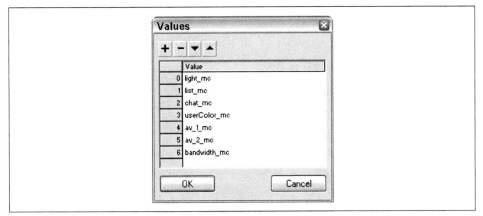

Figure 2-25. The updated Values list for the Communication Components parameter of the SimpleConnect component

other movie's AVPresence instance. (Be careful and wear headphones during these tests. If you use an open microphone and regular speakers, you'll likely experience harsh audio feedback.) Test different bit rate settings in the SetBandwidth component to see how the quality changes in both the video and audio output.

Forgoing the SimpleConnect Component

If you are building your own custom FlashCom applications and Flash client movies, you'll likely have your own login systems and user interface elements, complete with username and password fields. In such cases, you'll need to connect communication components to your FlashCom applications without the use of the Simple-Connect component. In this last section, you will learn how to enable the ConnectionLight component for an application by using your own custom client-side ActionScript code.

First, create a new server-side application. On the computer running the FlashCom Server, browse to the *applications* folder and create a new folder named *test_app* at this location. In the next section, you will create a client-side *NetConnection* object that connects to this application space.

Building the Client Movie

1. Create a new Flash document (File → New), and save the document as *no_simpleconnect.fla*.

2. Rename *Layer 1* to *light_mc*. On frame 1 of this layer, drag an instance of the ConnectionLight component from the Components panel to the Stage. Name the instance **light_mc** using the Properties panel.

3. Create a new layer, and name it *actions*. Place this layer above the *light_mc* layer.

4. Select the first frame of the *actions* layer, and open the Actions panel (F9). Add the following code:

```
app_nc = new NetConnection( );
app_nc.onStatus = function (info) {
  trace("app_nc: info.code = " + info.code);
  if (this.initLight == null) {
    light_mc.connect(this);
    this.initLight = true;
  }
};
app_nc.connect("rtmp:/test_app");
```

Here, you create a new *NetConnection* object that invokes *connect( )* on light_mc when the *onStatus( )* event handler is invoked. An internal property named initLight is used to track whether the light_mc instance's *connect( )* method has been invoked, as the *onStatus( )* handler will likely execute more than once during the session of the application. You may need to alter the RTMP URI to include the full domain name of your FlashCom Server.

5. Save your Flash document and test it. When the Flash movie loads, you should see the *trace( )* message from the *app_nc.onStatus( )* handler. If the connection was successful, the light_mc instance's status color should turn green. If the connection failed, the indicator will turn red.

You can continue to modify this example by adding more communication components. As you add component instances, you can simplify the code of the *onStatus( )* handler by creating an array to store object references to your component instances. For example, the following code creates a component_array object that connects three communication components to the app_nc connection:

```
app_nc.onStatus = function (info) {
  trace("app_nc: info.code = " + info.code);
  if (this.initComponents == null) {
    var components_array = [light_mc, bandwidth_mc, av_1_mc];
    for (var i in components_array) {
      components_array[i].connect(this);
    }
  this.initComponents = true;
  }
};
```

Conclusion

We're in only the second chapter of the book, and you've already come a long way. This chapter showed how the FlashCom communication components encapsulate commonly needed features such as chat, video recording and playback, bandwidth control, user configuration, and more. These components implement much of a FlashCom application's plumbing so you can create basic applications quickly and then enhance them with additional features as needed. We already saw how to build a simple chat room and add audio and video to it.

Now that you have a basic understanding of creating a simple FlashCom application, we'll explore the technical issues in more detail. In the next chapter, we cover creating and managing connections. In subsequent chapters, you'll master additional topics such as applications and instances, media and data streams, and the *Camera* and *Microphone* classes. You've already seen a glimpse of FlashCom's power but the journey is just beginning.

CHAPTER 3

Managing Connections

Before a Flash movie can exchange audio, video, and other data with a FlashCom Server application, it must request a network connection to the server. If an application instance on the server accepts the connection request, a TCP connection is made available to both the movie and application instance to use for ongoing communications. We saw in the preceding chapter that the SimpleConnect component can create a connection. This chapter covers connections in more depth, including how to write custom code to handle various changes in the connection status as well as different error types.

A network connection can be managed within a Flash movie using a *NetConnection* object. This object's methods are used to request, close, and monitor the status of a network connection. The *SharedObject* and *NetStream* classes, as well as Macromedia's communication components, all depend on access to a *NetConnection* object in order to communicate with the FlashCom Server.

Making a Connection

NetConnection objects are created by calling the *NetConnection( )* constructor function:

```
lobby_nc = new NetConnection();
```

In this example, the lobby_nc variable stores a *NetConnection* object, which can be used to attempt to connect to an application instance:

```
if (lobby_nc.connect("rtmp:/testLobby", userName, password)) {
  trace("Attempting connection...");
}
else {
  trace("Can't attempt connection. Is the URI correct?");
}
```

In this example, the URI *rtmp:/testLobby* is the address of an instance of an application named *testLobby* that resides on the server from which the movie was downloaded. The *connect( )* method is always passed the URI of the application instance to which to connect, followed by any number of optional parameters. In this example, a username and password are supplied after the URI. The *connect( )* method returns false if it detects a malformed URI; otherwise, it returns true, and Flash attempts to connect to the server.

 Not all malformed URIs are caught by the *connect( )* method. You must always make sure the protocol is either rtmp or rtmpt followed by a colon; otherwise, the *connect( )* method may return true and then fail.

The URI can be an absolute URI that includes a hostname or a relative URI that does not. After the *connect( )* method is called, the URI passed into it is available as the uri property of the *NetConnection* object.

Absolute URIs

An absolute URI is a string that includes protocol, host, optional port, application name, and optional instance name segments. The format of an absolute URI is:

```
rtmp[t]://host[:port]/applicationName[/instanceName]
```

The parts of the URI in square brackets are optional. An absolute URI contains all the information needed to identify an application instance to which to connect. The following sections describe all the parts of an absolute URI.

Protocol

The first part of an absolute URI is the protocol or scheme and must always be specified as rtmp, rtmpt, or rtmps, followed by :// for an absolute URI or :/ for a relative URI. RTMP is preferred because it is the native protocol for FlashCom communications. Adding the optional *t* in rtmpt indicates that HTTP tunneling is to be used. Tunneling is less efficient, because RTMP messages must be wrapped in HTTP headers, and the server must be constantly polled by the Flash movie. However, tunneling may successfully make connections through firewalls and proxy servers when RTMP access fails. Tunneling was first added to Flash Player 6.0.65.0 and Flash-Com 1.5. When run in a browser, the Flash Player uses the browser to make the HTTP connections to the server that RTMPT relies on. Since the browser normally also supports SSL, Macromedia added the ability to use the SSL by specifying the rtmps protocol instead of rtmpt. When RTMPS is used, the Flash Player attempts to establish a tunneling connection over HTTPS to FlashCom. Even though FlashCom 1.5 does not support SSL, it is possible to take advantage of RTMPS using additional server software or specialized network hardware in order to have completely encrypted real-time communications between Flash movies and FlashCom. Configuring a system to accept SSL connections is briefly discussed in Chapter 18 and at:

http://www.macromedia.com/devnet/mx/flashcom/articles/firewalls_proxy04.html

If an SSL certificate is used from an authority the browser does not recognize, anyone connecting via RTMPS will be asked to accept or install the certificate before the connection can be completed. Currently, clicking Yes to accept the connection will not work. The certificate must be installed and the connection retried.

Host and port

An absolute URI always contains a hostname after the `://` characters. Optionally, you can specify a port on the host by following the hostname with a colon and a port number. FlashCom's default port is 1935; however, it can be configured to accept connections on a different port or ports. If the `rtmp` protocol is specified and no port is given in the URI, the Flash movie attempts to connect to port 1935. If the connection attempt fails because the server cannot be reached, the Flash Player automatically attempts to connect to FlashCom on port 443. If that also fails, the Player attempts to connect to port 80. Finally, if an RTMP connection cannot be made on any of those three ports, the Player tries one last time to make a tunneling (RTMPT) connection on port 80. The sequence of ports and protocols is listed in Table 3-1.

Table 3-1. Port connection sequence

Sequence	Port	Protocol
1	1935	RTMP
2	443	RTMP
3	80	RTMP
4	80	RTMPT

The sequence in Table 3-1 is attempted only when the protocol in the URI is `rtmp` and no port is specified. If `rtmpt` is specified in the URI and no port is provided, the Flash movie attempts to connect to port 80. When `rtmps` is used, the default port is 443.

If FlashCom is configuredr to listen on a port other than 1935, 443, or 80, the port must be specified in the URI. For example, if the server is configured to use port 8080, the URI might look like this:

```
rtmp://host.domain.com:8080/conferenceRooms/room_23
```

Selecting another port is not recommended, however, because port 1935 was assigned to the Macromedia Flash Communication Server MX by the Internet Assigned Numbers Authority. A production configuration can also set up the server to listen on more than one port. Port information can be set using the *Adaptor.xml* configuration file's `<HostPort>` tag. An *Adaptor.xml* file is located inside each adaptor's directory inside the *conf* directory. On our machine with a default Windows installation, the default *Adaptor.xml* file is located here:

*C:\Program Files\Macromedia\Flash Communication Server MX\conf\\
_defaultRoot_\Adaptor.xml*

If a web server is not already running on port 443 or 80, the `<HostPort>` tag can include the port numbers 1935, 443, and 80. If no port number is supplied in the target URI and a remote firewall blocks access to the server on port 1935 but allows access via port 443, the second connection attempt will succeed. Port 443 is normally associated with encrypted communications over SSL. Neither FlashCom 1.5 nor the Flash Player provides direct SSL support.

For details on connecting to the FlashCom Admin Service application on port 1111, see Chapter 10. For an example application that uses port 1111, see Chapter 12.

Application name

The application name must be specified in the URI. On the server, the application name is the name of a subdirectory in the server's *applications* directory. Often, each application is a subdirectory in the *Macromedia Flash Communication Server MX/ applications* directory. However, a server can have multiple virtual hosts, each with its own *applications* directory. Each virtual host is associated with a domain, which is in turn mapped to an *applications* directory. To determine the location of the *applications* directory for a virtual host, check the `<AppsDir>` tag in the *Vhost.xml* file. The default *Vhost.xml* is in the *conf/defaultRoot/defaultVHost_* subdirectory of the directory in which FlashCom was installed. The *applications* directory itself is never part of the URI as the hostname maps to it.

Instance name

The instance name specifies which instance of an application to connect to. It does not have to be specified within a URI. If it is omitted, the default name _definst_ is used. These two URIs refer to the same instance:

```
rtmp://host.domain.com/conferenceRooms
rtmp://host.domain.com/conferenceRooms/_definst_
```

Application instance names can form a hierarchy. For example, a chat room application may provide many chat rooms for different courses in different university programs. To accommodate this situation, the format for instance names could follow a scheme in which the hierarchy helps to keep items organized, like this:

```
program/courseName/chatRoom
```

So some URIs might look like this:

```
rtmp://my.university.edu/chatRooms/science/phys325/room8
rtmp://my.university.edu/chatRooms/motionPicture/film001/room8
rtmp://my.university.edu/chatRooms/motionPicture/film021/room3
rtmp://my.university.edu/chatRooms/motionPicture/film021/room4
```

Each one of these URIs is an address of a separate instance of the *chatRooms* application even though two of them contain the name "room8". The instance name /chatRooms/motionPicture/film001/room8 is not the same as chatRooms/science/phys325/room8.

Relative URIs

If a *.swf* file is loaded into a browser from the same server that FlashCom is running on, you can use a relative URI in which the // characters and hostname are omitted. Here is the format for a relative URI:

```
rtmp[t]:[:port]/applicationName[/instanceName]
```

In the earlier *rtmp:/testLobby* example, the protocol is *rtmp*, the single slash indicates a relative URI, and *testLobby* is the application name. No application instance name is provided, so the _definst_ instance is assumed.

Waiting to Connect

After a successful *connect( )* method invocation (one in which the URI is properly formed), the *NetConnection* object must wait to see if the connection attempt itself is successful. This can take some time as a number of things can happen:

- The server may be down or unreachable, in which case the connection attempt will eventually fail.
- The network may be slow or the server may be busy.
- The application instance may accept the TCP network connection but place it in a pending state while it decides if it should reject or accept the connection.

Eventually, the *NetConnection* object is notified as to what happened via its *onStatus( )* method. By default, there is no *onStatus( )* method, so you should define an *onStatus( )* handler before you invoke *NetConnection.connect( )*. The *onStatus( )* method is known as an *event handler* or *callback handler* because it is invoked in response to an event occurring (in this case, the server responding to the connection attempt). The *onStatus( )* handler receives an object containing information about the event that helps interpret the response.

Here is a basic *onStatus( )* method that simply outputs the contents of the information object it receives:

```
NetConnection.prototype.onStatus = function (info) {
  trace("this.isConnected: " + this.isConnected);
  trace("      info.level: " + info.level);
  trace("       info.code: " + info.code);
  trace("info.description: " + info.description);
  if (info.application) {
    for (var prop in info.application) {
      trace("info.application." + prop + ": " + info.application[prop]);
```

```
      }
    }
    trace("\n");
  };
```

The object received by *onStaus( )*, named info in this example, has three properties:
level, code, and description. The level property indicates whether the event is an
"error" or a "status" report. The code property provides the most meaningful information and should be used in *onStatus( )* handlers to decide what action to take as
events occur. The preceding example also outputs the isConnected property of the
NetConnection object. If the connection has been established, isConnected is true;
otherwise, isConnected is false.

Example 3-1 shows a simple test movie, followed by the output messages displayed if
the connection is successful.

Example 3-1. A short test script to display connection messages

```
// Some credentials to pass to the application.
userName = "Guest";
password = "Guest";

// First, define an onStatus( ) handler.
NetConnection.prototype.onStatus = function (info) {
  trace("this.isConnected: " + this.isConnected);
  trace("      info.level: " + info.level);
  trace("       info.code: " + info.code);
  trace("info.description: " + info.description);
  if (info.application) {
    for (var prop in info.application) {
      trace("info.application." + prop + ": " + info.application[prop]);
    }
  }
  trace("\n");
};

// Next, create a NetConnection object.
lobby_nc = new NetConnection( );

// Finally, attempt to make the connection.
// The onStatus( ) handler will be invoked when the operation completes.
if (lobby_nc.connect("rtmp:/testLobby/", userName, password)) {
  trace("Attempting connection...");
}
else {
  trace("Can't attempt connection. Is the URI correct?");
}
```

If the connection is established, the code property of the information object passed to
the *onStatus( )* handler contains the string "NetConnection.Connect.Success":

```
    Attempting connection...
    this.isConnected: true
```

```
         info.level: status
         info.code: NetConnection.Connect.Success
info.description: Connection succeeded.
```

On the other hand, the connection might fail. Possible reasons for failure include that there is no *testLobby* application on the server or the server could not be found. In these cases, the handler reports an "error" status in the level property and additional status information is available in the code property of the information object (description is empty in this case):

```
Attempting connection...
this.isConnected: false
         info.level: error
         info.code: NetConnection.Connect.Failed
info.description:
```

The application instance can also refuse the connection request (for example, if the userName or password values are not acceptable). If the connection is rejected, the *onStatus( )* method is called twice—first with an error message and later with a status update. Note the values of the info object's level and code properties in each case:

```
Attempting connection...
this.isConnected: false
         info.level: error
         info.code: NetConnection.Connect.Rejected
info.description: Connection failed.
info.application.message: This application has refused your connection.

this.isConnected: false
         info.level: status
         info.code: NetConnection.Connect.Closed
info.description:
```

When an application instance rejects the connection attempt, it may return an object with additional information. If so, the object arrives as an application attribute of the info object passed into the *onStatus( )* method. To use the application object, you need to either know its properties in advance or loop through its properties with a *for-in* loop as shown in Example 3-1. If you know the properties that the designer of the application script uses, they can be accessed without a *for-in* loop. For example, a property named message can be accessed this way:

```
if (info.application) {
  trace("info.application.message: " + info.application.message);
}
```

Managing a Connection

After a successful connection is made, it can be broken by various occurrences. A well-scripted Flash movie monitors the network status and takes appropriate action as changes occur. This is easily done inside your *NetConnection.onStatus( )* handler, which is notified whenever the connection status changes. When a connection is first established, the objects and components that rely on it can begin using it. When a connection is closed, these objects may have to be disabled or disposed of. It is especially important that the user doesn't experience a sudden and unexplained loss of functionality when a network connection is dropped by the server or lost because of a network problem.

Avoiding Timing Problems

A common—and sometimes difficult to debug—problem occurs when scripts define the *onStatus( )* handler after calling the *connect( )* method:

```
nc = new NetConnection();
nc.connect(); // WRONG: do this after onStatus is defined!
nc.onStatus = function (info) {
   trace("info.code: " + info.code);
};
```

If *connect( )* is called prematurely, the network connection may be established or the connection rejected before the *onStatus( )* handler has been defined. The result is that the messages representing those events are never returned to the handler. The *onStatus( )* method must always be defined before the *connect( )* call is made. The preceding example should be rewritten as:

```
nc = new NetConnection();
nc.onStatus = function (info) {
   trace("info.code: " + info.code);
};
nc.connect();
```

For the most part, when a connection is closed, the info object passed to the *onStatus( )* method will have a level value of "status" and a code value of "NetConnection. Connect.Closed". This will happen if the network goes down, the server disconnects the client, the server stops, or the connection is closed using *NetConnection.close( )*. It is also possible that the level value will be "error" and the code value "NetConnection.Connect.AppShutdown". The following sections discuss how to deal with various connection status changes.

Dealing with Success

When Flash establishes a connection, any streams and shared objects that rely on the connection can be set up. Testing for the "NetConnection.Connect.Success" code in the *onStatus( )* handler is the easiest way to do this:

```
if (info.code = "NetConnection.Connect.Success") {
   // Initialize and connect dependent objects and components (not shown).
}
```

Dealing with Problems

When a connection cannot be established or is lost, a number of possible message sequences can be sent to an *onStatus( )* handler:

- A single error code
- An error code followed by a closed status
- A single closed status

The isConnected property of the *NetConnection* object is false when any of these events occurs. Whenever a problem occurs, you may want your script to take action, such as informing the user. The simplest way to deal with problems is to look at the isConnected property in the *onStatus( )* handler:

```
if (!this.isConnected) {
  if (info.code = "NetConnection.Connect.Rejected") {
    // Tell the user the connection was rejected by the application.
  }
  else {
    // Give the user more info based on info.code and/or info.level.
  }
  // Clean up any objects and components that need them.
  // Change state by going to another frame on the main timeline.
}
```

Displaying a message whenever isConnected is false may lead to the user seeing two messages—a reject message followed by a closed message. To avoid displaying two messages, the *onStatus( )* handler must be stopped from acting on the second message. One way to do this is to remove the *onStatus( )* handler completely by setting the onStatus property to null after the first message arrives. This can be done inside the *onStatus( )* method:

```
this.onStatus = null;
```

Removing the *onStatus( )* handler so that no further message processing can take place may seem like a drastic solution. However, the onStatus property can be reset later to a method that can handle messages. Alternatively, another *NetConnection* object, with a working *onStatus( )* handler, can be created and used to connect again. Another approach is to create an extra property of the *NetConnection* object that toggles the handling of certain messages. When messages are expected after a *connect( )* call is made or after a "success" status message, the property is set to true. When a connection has been closed, the property can be set to false. Example 3-2 shows one way to do this.

Closing the Connection from the Client

Another potential problem is that when you let the user close the connection via *NetConnection.close( )*, the *onStatus( )* handler still receives a "closed" status message. There is often little point in showing this message to the user since she was responsible for closing the connection in the first place. It may be simpler to just change the state of the application by, for example, moving the playhead of the main timeline. Again, a property can be stored in a *NetConnection* object or the *onStatus( )* method can be set to null, to avoid displaying a close message.

Example 3-2 uses a property named handleCloseEvents to indicate if error and close messages should be processed. This is just one way to write an *onStatus( )* handler using this type of flag, and it can be altered as requirements dictate. An example that assigns values dynamically to the onStatus property is included in the online version of Example 3-2 (at *http://flash-communications.net*). Figure 3-1 shows the timeline for the movie used in Example 3-2. The movie can be in one of three states, each represented by a label at the beginning of a series of frames. Init starts on the first frame and is played only when the movie first loads; the Login frame is shown when the movie is in a disconnected state and the user can try to connect; the Connected frame is shown when the movie is in the connected state.

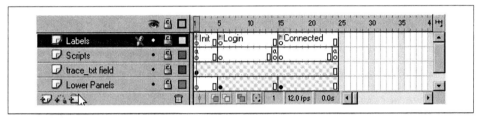

Figure 3-1. The timeline from Example 3-2

The script in Example 3-2, located on frame 1 of the *Scripts* layer of the main timeline, displays user messages in a text field. The ActionScript sends the playhead to either the Login or Connected frame depending on the state of the network connection.

Example 3-2. A script that handles connection-related events

```
// writeln( ) writes messages into a text field named trace_txt
// and is a runtime alternative to trace( ) and the Output panel.
function writeln (msg) {
  trace_txt.text += msg + "\n";
  trace_txt.scroll = trace_txt.maxscroll;
}

/* A simple onStatus( ) handler that moves the playhead to Login if a
 * connection is closed and to Connected when a connection is established.
 * User messages are written via writeln( ) into a text window.
 * The this.handleCloseEvents flag is used to make sure the user never
 * sees redundant messages.
 */
NetConnection.prototype.onStatus = function (info) {
  // Always deal with successful connections.
  if (info.code == "NetConnection.Connect.Success") {
```

Example 3-2. A script that handles connection-related events (continued)

```
    this.handleCloseEvents = true;
    writeln("Success, you are connected!");
    gotoAndPlay("Connected");
  }
  // Handle messages when the connection is closed.
  if (!this.isConnected && this.handleCloseEvents) {
    if (info.code == "NetConnection.Connect.Rejected") {
      writeln(info.application.message);
      writeln('Did you use the username "Guest" and password "Guest"?');
    }
    else {
      writeln("Error: Connection Closed.");
    }
    this.handleCloseEvents = false;
    gotoAndPlay("Login");
  }
  // Handle remote method call errors here if you need to.
};

// Create a NetConnection object.
lobby_nc = new NetConnection( );

// Called when the Connect button in the Login frames is clicked.
function doConnect ( ) {
  lobby_nc.handleCloseEvents = true;
  if (lobby_nc.connect("rtmp:/testLobby/",
                       userName_txt.text, password_txt.text)) {
    writeln("Please wait. Attempting connection...");
  }
  else {
    writeln("Can't attempt connection. Is the URI correct?");
  }
}

// Called when the Disconnect button in the Connected frames is clicked.
function doDisconnect ( ) {
  // User is requesting a close so we don't handle it in onStatus( ).
  lobby_nc.handleCloseEvents = false;
  lobby_nc.close( );
  gotoAndPlay("Login");
}

gotoAndPlay("Login");
```

The script listed in Example 3-2 needs an application to which to connect. Therefore, we need a *testLobby* subdirectory in the *applications* directory on the server from which the movie is downloaded. Once the directory is created, the *main.asc* file shown in Example 3-3 can be placed in the *testLobby* subdirectory to provide the application with its logic. This server-side script accepts connections only from users who log in using the username "Guest" and the password "Guest". Rejected clients are passed a message to display to the user.

Example 3-3. Server-side script (main.asc) to accept or reject connections based on username and password

```
/* The application.onConnect( ) method handles each client
 * connection request. In this case, users who log in
 * with userName "Guest" and password "Guest" are
 * allowed to connect. Other connection requests are rejected.
 */
application.onConnect = function (client, userName, password) {
  if (userName == "Guest" && password == "Guest") {
    client.writeAccess = "";    // Don't give write access.
    application.acceptConnection(client);
  }
  else {
    application.rejectConnection(client,
      {message: "This application has refused your connection."});
  }
};
```

Whenever a Flash movie connects to an application instance, the *onConnect( )* method of the instance's application object is called. The first parameter passed to *onConnect( )* is always a *Client* object that represents the client-side Flash movie. The remaining parameters are the parameters passed into the *connect( )* method in the movie.

Therefore, when a client attempts to connect to the *testLobby* FlashCom application, the *main.asc* file shown in Example 3-3 checks the username and password passed in. A full-fledged version could validate the username and password against a database of valid users.

Using a Connection

A *NetConnection* object represents a network connection within a Flash movie. Any object that communicates over a network connection must have access to a *NetConnection* object. For example, the *NetStream* class requires a *NetConnection* object be passed into its constructor function:

```
myStream_ns = new NetStream(myNetConnection);
```

Working with the *NetStream* class is covered in Chapter 5.

Similarly, a remote shared object's *connect( )* method must be passed a *NetConnection* object:

```
myRemote_so = SharedObject.getRemote("SOName", myNetConnection.uri, true);
myRemote_so.onStatus = onStatusFunction;
if (myRemote_so.connect(myNetConnection)) {
  trace("Connection ok so far...");
}
```

Macromedia designed both the *NetStream* and *SharedObject* classes so that, with some exceptions, they could be used as soon as a *NetConnection* object was passed to them. In both cases, the *NetConnection* object should be one that has attempted to make a connection even if the connection is not yet established. For example the process of sending data can be started via a *NetStream.send( )* or *SharedObject.send( )* method call before a connection is established. The data is held in a queue until the connection is made. Similarly, a *NetStream* object can start the process of publishing or playing audio or video before a connection is made. In this case, when the connection is made, the stream will begin to publish or play.

The important exception to this is shared object data and the shared object *onSync( )* handler described in Chapter 8. As an added convenience, if *onStatus( )* handlers are not created for *SharedObject* and *NetStream* objects, the *onStatus( )* handler of the *NetConnection* with which they are associated will be called and passed the *SharedObject* and *NetStream* information objects. In some cases, especially when data is sent, these conveniences are useful, but for the most part should be avoided. It is often easier to manage an application and provide better information to the user if objects that depend on a network connection define their own *onStatus( )* event handlers and do nothing until a connection is successfully made.

Reusing a NetConnection Object

Often a Flash movie must connect to more than one application instance. A familiar example is when Flash must first connect to a lobby so the user can select a chat room to visit. In this case, the lobby may be one application and the chat rooms may be implemented by another application. The lobby connection can be closed and then a new *NetConnection* object, with a different *onStatus( )* method, can be created to connect to the chat application. Instead of creating a new *NetConnection* object, the Flash movie can reuse an existing one. In theory, you can disconnect from one application and connect to another by calling the *connect( )* method with a new target URI. When this happens, the old connection is closed and a new one is attempted. However, two other things should normally happen. First, before a connection is closed, you should perform any required cleanup, such as closing objects and components that depend on the connection. Second, you must perform any preparatory work—at minimum you'll usually put in place a different *onStatus( )* handler—before connecting to the next application.

To follow through with the previous example, suppose an additional application, named *testChat*, is available and that once the user is in the lobby he can click a button to visit a *testChat* instance named room1. In this case, the main timeline of the movie would require separate Login, Lobby, and ChatRoom frames as illustrated in Figure 3-2.

The Chat button would be placed in the Lobby frames, and a Lobby button would be placed within the ChatRoom frames. Example 3-4 shows the *onChat( )* function that would be called when the Chat button is clicked.

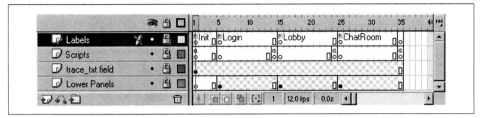

Figure 3-2. The timeline with Login, Lobby, and ChatRoom states

Example 3-4. Connecting from the lobby to a chat room

```
function doChat (btn) {
  // Don't process the next close message.
  lobbyChat_nc.handleCloseEvents = false;
  // Close the connection to the lobby.
  lobbyChat_nc.close( );

  // Set the onStatus( ) handler, defined in Example 3-5.
  lobbyChat_nc.onStatus = ChatRoom_onStatus;
  // Make sure events are handled by it.
  lobbyChat_nc.handleCloseEvents = true;

  // Try to connect to a chat room.
  if (lobbyChat_nc.connect("rtmp:/testChat/room1", userName, password)) {
    writeln("Please wait. Attempting chat room connection...");
  }
  else {
    writeln("Can't attempt connection. Is the URI correct?");
  }
}
```

In Example 3-4, event handling of close and connection error messages is turned off so that the playhead is not sent back to the Login frame when Flash calls *lobbyChat_nc.close( )*. The example assigns a new *onStatus( )* handler, named *ChatRoom_onStatus( )*, to the lobbyChat_nc object as follows:

```
lobbyChat_nc.onStatus = ChatRoom_onStatus;
```

Finally, when the connection is attempted, two global variables, userName and password, are used to retrieve the username and password to submit, because the text fields are no longer on the Stage when the user is in the lobby. Example 3-5 shows the code for the *ChatRoom_onStatus( )* function. It is used as the new *onStatus( )* handler for the lobbyChat_mc object, as indicated in the preceding code.

Example 3-5. The chat room onStatus( ) handler

```
function ChatRoom_onStatus (info) {
  // Always deal with successful connections.
  if (info.code == "NetConnection.Connect.Success") {
    this.handleCloseEvents = true;
    writeln("Success, you are connected to a chat room!");
```

Example 3-5. The chat room onStatus( ) handler (continued)

```
    gotoAndPlay("ChatRoom");
  }
  // Handle messages when the connection is closed.
  if (!this.isConnected && this.handleCloseEvents) {
    // Handle close/error messages.
    if (info.code == "NetConnection.Connect.Rejected") {
      writeln(info.application.message);
      writeln('Did you use the username "Guest" and password "Guest" ?');
    }
    else {
      writeln("Error: Connection Closed.");
    }
    this.handleCloseEvents = false;
    gotoAndPlay("Login");
  }
  // Handle remote method call errors here if you need to.
}
```

When the user is in a chat room, she can return to the lobby by clicking a Lobby button. Example 3-6 shows the code for the *doLobby( )* function called when the user
clicks the Lobby button. It is highly analogous to the *doChat( )* function in
Example 3-4. Among other things, it sets *Lobby_onStatus( )* as the new *onStatus( )*
handler for the lobbyChat_mc object. The *Lobby_onStatus( )* function declaration is
not shown here, but it is very similar to the *ChatRoom_onStatus( )* function declaration shown in Example 3-5.

Example 3-6. The doLobby( ) function

```
function doLobby (btn) {
  // Don't process the next close message.
  lobbyChat_nc.handleCloseEvents = false;
  // Close the connection to the chat room.
  lobbyChat_nc.close( );

  // Set the onStatus( ) handler (definition of Lobby_onStatus( ) is not shown).
  lobbyChat_nc.onStatus = Lobby_onStatus;
  // Make sure events are handled by it.
  lobbyChat_nc.handleCloseEvents = true;

  // Try to connect to the lobby.
  if (lobbyChat_nc.connect("rtmp:/testLobby/", userName, password)) {
    writeln("Please wait. Attempting lobby connection...");
  }
  else {
    writeln("Can't attempt connection. Is the URI correct?");
  }
}
```

Now that we've seen how to reuse a connection, let's see how we can use multiple
connections at once.

Multiple Simultaneous NetConnection Objects

Macromedia recommends against making multiple connections from a single Flash movie to a FlashCom Server or Servers at the same time. First of all, each server can handle only so many simultaneous connections and the data transfer overhead that goes with them. Furthermore, FlashCom is licensed by the number of simultaneous connections. Therefore, whenever possible, avoid designing communication applications that require multiple simultaneous connections. However, a Flash movie can connect simultaneously to different applications or different instances of the same application; it can also connect multiple times to the same application instance, if necessary. This is an especially useful feature when testing applications and in developing larger scale multi-instance applications.

The simple test script in Example 3-7 makes two connections to the same chat room instance.

Example 3-7. Using more than one NetConnection object

```
NetConnection.prototype.onStatus = function (info) {
  trace(this.name + ": " + info.code);
};
nc1 = new NetConnection( );
nc1.name = "First connection";
nc2 = new NetConnection( );
nc2.name = "Second connection";
nc1.connect("rtmp:/testChat/room1", "Guest", "Guest");
nc2.connect("rtmp:/testChat/room1", "Guest", "Guest");
```

Assuming there are no problems with the network or server, the trace output from this test will look like this:

```
First connection: NetConnection.Connect.Success
Second connection: NetConnection.Connect.Success
```

Multiple connections are useful when debugging, the topic of the next section.

Testing and Debugging Network Connections

Networked applications present some additional difficulties when testing or debugging programs, as more than one system is always involved. A connection attempt may fail for many reasons, including the following:

- The target URI may be incorrect (watch for typos).
- A username or password may be wrong.

- The maximum number of licensed clients or maximum licensed bandwidth of the server may have been exceeded.
- The network may be down or unreliable.
- A connection that worked fine in a test environment may fail because of a firewall or proxy server.

Often, the best way to understand why a network connection fails is to display all the properties of the information object returned to the *onStatus( )* method. In addition, at least until the target URI is proven to be correct, the return value of the *connect( )* method should always be checked. If it is false, the URI was malformed and should be corrected. It is a good idea to begin building a movie by always creating a default, diagnostic *onStatus( )* handler as in Example 3-1. When the connection has been tested, you can replace the *onStatus( )* handler with one more appropriate for your needs. Unfortunately, problems aren't limited to the beginning of development. As both client- and server-side scripts evolve, diagnosing the cause of a sudden loss of connectivity is difficult. To help diagnose the problem, build simple test movies that can be run outside the development environment. In fact, this is an important technique for testing much more than basic connectivity.

Test Client Movies

An excellent way to help debug connections is to write a test movie that includes a few basic components, such as:

- A large scrolling text field with scrollbar
- Connect and Close buttons
- Fields for a target URI and other *connect( )* method parameters, such as username and password

Instead of using *trace( )* statements, use a *writeln( )* function such as the one in Example 3-2 to output information to the scrolling text field. A sample test movie is supplied on the book's web site (*http://flash-communications.net*).

Using the NetConnection Debugger

Separate from the Flash MX 2004 ActionScript debugger, Macromedia supplies a NetConnection Debugger with the FlashCom Server (and with Flash Remoting). The NetConnection Debugger can display client- and server-side connection-related events such as connect requests and remote method calls and their results. To obtain the NetConnection Debugger, download and install the Macromedia Flash Remoting MX Components from:

http://www.macromedia.com/software/flashremoting/downloads/components

Once installed, to use the NetConnection Debugger, place the following `include` instruction on the first frame of the *Scripts* layer of your main timeline:

```
#include "NetDebug.as"
```

Then select Window → NetConnection Debugger from Flash's menu bar to start the debugger. To see server-side events, you must log into the administration server (Admin Service) using an administrator username and password, as described in Chapter 1. If the Filters section of the NetConnection Debugger, shown in the bottom half of Figure 3-3, is not open, click on the small triangle to open it. Enter the administrator's username and password; make sure the Flashcom_server, RTMP, and Trace checkboxes are all selected; and run your movie in the Flash development environment. Figure 3-3 shows the NetConnection Debugger after a failed attempt to connect to the server.

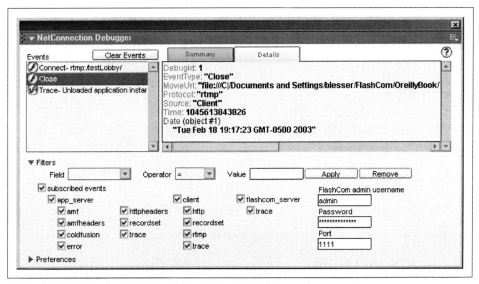

Figure 3-3. The NetConnection Debugger after a failed connection attempt

Click on an event in the Events list and select the Details tab to see the full details about each event. Client-side events are indicated by the Flash logo, and server-side events are indicated by the FlashCom logo. In Figure 3-3, the Close event details are shown. Following it in the Events list is a server-side event that reports that the application was eventually unloaded because no other clients were connected to it. Provided a *.swf* was compiled with the *NetDebug.as* file included, it can be run outside the authoring environment and its connection-related events will still be displayed in the NetConnection Debugger. As your projects evolve and you are debugging increasingly complex scripts, this is another good reason to keep around some simple test movies.

Remove the ActionScript to include *NetDebug.as* in your final movie after you no longer need the debugging features. It adds unnecessary file size to the published *.swf*.

Subclassing the NetConnection Class

You can extend the features of the *NetConnection* class by creating a subclass based on it. Creating subclasses lets you encapsulate code that operates on the *NetConnection* object within the subclass's methods such as *connect( )*, *onStatus( )*, or *close( )*. In turn, this can lead to more modular and easier to maintain applications. The key to doing this is to use the *super* operator. Example 3-8 shows a very simple example of how to extend the *NetConnection* class and then how to use it within a simple test script.

Example 3-8 uses AS 1.0 syntax so it works in both Flash MX and Flash MX 2004. This also allows you to compile using ActionScript 1.0 under File → Publish Settings → ActionScript. Example 3-10 provides an alternative implementation that uses AS 2.0 syntax and the v2 UI component's *EventDispatcher* class.

Example 3-8. A simple extension of the NetConnection class

```
// Constructor function must call super( ).
function NetConnectionSubClass ( ) {
  super( );
}

// Subclass NetConnection by assigning an instance of it
// to the prototype object of the new subclass.
NetConnectionSubClass.prototype = new NetConnection( );

// A simple demonstration onStatus( ) event handler that just
// writes out each info.code message.
NetConnectionSubClass.prototype.onStatus = function (info) {
  trace("info.code: " + info.code);
};

/* This connect( ) method may be passed any number of arguments.
 * The apply( ) method makes sure all arguments are passed into
 * the super.connect( ) method when it is called.
 */
NetConnectionSubClass.prototype.connect = function ( ) {
  return super.connect.apply(super, arguments);
};

// Create an instance of the NetConnectionSubClass subclass.
lobby_nc = new NetConnectionSubClass( );

// Attempt the connection.
if (lobby_nc.connect("rtmp:/testLobby/", "Guest", "Guest")) {
  trace("Attempting connection...");
}
else {
```

Example 3-8. A simple extension of the NetConnection class (continued)

```
  trace("Can't attempt connection. Is the URI correct?");
}
```

The *super* operator is used in two different ways in Example 3-8. First, it must be called within the constructor function as follows:

```
super();
```

Invoking *super( )* in this way calls the *NetConnection* constructor (the superclass's constructor). Second, whenever a *NetConnection* method must be called by a subclass's method, the *super* operator can be used to call the superclass's method. In this example, when the *NetConnectionSubClass.connect( )* method is called, it in turn uses *super* to call the *NetConnection.connect( )* method as follows:

```
return super.connect.apply(super, arguments);
```

Using the *apply( )* method provides a good, general purpose way to call the superclass's *connect( )* method. Passing super as a parameter ensures that *connect( )* is called as a method of the *NetConnection* superclass and passing arguments insures that all the parameters passed to the subclass's *connect( )* method are passed on to the superclass's *connect( )* method.

A simpler, but less general purpose, way to call the *NetConnection.connect( )* method is to specifically pass individual parameters this way:

```
NetConnectionSubClass.prototype.connect = function (targetURI, userName, password) {
    return super.connect(targetURI, userName, password);
};
```

In cases in which parameter values must be manipulated before being passed to the superclass's *connect( )* method or those in which not all parameters must be passed on, it is often simpler to avoid using the *apply( )* method.

On its own, Example 3-8 shows the basic mechanics of creating a subclass of the *NetConnection* class, but let's see what advantages this offers. Looking back at Example 3-4 and Example 3-6, you will see that before calling the *connect( )* or *close( )* methods, the handleCloseEvents flag had to be set each time. This is extra work that shouldn't have to be done in the *doConnect( )*, *doChat( )*, and *doLobby( )* functions.

In fact, these details can be hidden inside a *NetConnection* subclass's methods as follows:

```
// close( ) turns off the handleCloseEvents flag before closing the connection.
LobbyChatConnection.prototype.close = function ( ) {
    this.handleCloseEvents = false;
    super.close( );
};
```

If we modify the *connect( )* method to set the handleCloseEvents flag as well, the *doLobby( )* function can be greatly simplified:

```
// Called when the Lobby button in a chat room is clicked.
function doLobby(btn) {
```

```
      lobbyChat_nc.close( );
      lobbyChat_nc.connect("rtmp:/testLobby", handleLobbyConnection,
                              userName, password);
  }
```

Compare the preceding code to the *doLobby( )* function in Example 3-6. You may
notice that something else is missing. In the "Reusing a NetConnection Object" section of this chapter, two *onStatus( )* event handlers were written: one for managing
lobby connections and the other for managing chat room connections. The *doLobby( )*
and *doChat( )* functions were responsible for making sure the right *onStatus( )* handler
was in place before calling *connect( )*. In some cases, this is necessary. However, when
the *onStatus( )* handlers are almost identical, there is a more elegant solution. The main
difference between the handlers is the frame to which they move the playhead when a
connection is made. A more general purpose *onStatus( )* handler can call a function
when a connection is established. In Example 3-9, one of two simple functions is called
by the *onStatus( )* handler depending on what application it connects to:

```
// Called when a connection has been established to the testLobby app.
function handleLobbyConnection( ) {
  writeln("Success, you are connected to the lobby!");
  gotoAndPlay("Lobby");
}

// Called when a connection has been established to a chat room.
function handleChatConnection( ) {
  writeln("Success, you are connected to a chat room!");
  gotoAndPlay("ChatRoom");
}
```

How does the *onStatus( )* handler know which of these functions to call? In this
example, a reference to one of them is passed into the *connect( )* method and saved in
the connectionHandler property. Example 3-9 is a complete listing of a test script in
which the *onStatus( )* method uses the connectionHandler property to call either the
handleLobbyConnection( ) or *handleChatConnection( )* function.

Example 3-9. NetConnection subclass test script

```
// writeln( ) writes messages into a text field named trace_txt
// and is a replacement for using trace( ) and the Output panel.
function writeln (msg) {
  trace_txt.text += msg + "\n";
  trace_txt.scroll = trace_txt.maxscroll;
}

// LobbyChatConnection( ) is a constructor function for a NetConnection subclass.
// It will not work unless super( ) is called within the function.
function LobbyChatConnection ( ) {
  super( );
}

LobbyChatConnection.prototype = new NetConnection( );     // Subclass NetConnection.
```

Example 3-9. NetConnection subclass test script (continued)

```
LobbyChatConnection.prototype.handleCloseEvents = true;  // Initial value.

// connect() is always passed four parameters, updates the handleCloseEvents flag,
// and calls the superclass's connect() method.
LobbyChatConnection.prototype.connect = function (targetURI, connectionHandler,
                                                  userName, password) {
  this.connectionHandler = connectionHandler;
  this.handleCloseEvents = true;
  var result = super.connect(targetURI, userName, password);
  if (result) {
    writeln("Please wait. Attempting connection...");
  }
  else {
    writeln("Can't attempt connection to: " + this.uri);
    writeln("Is the URI correct?");
  }
  return result;
};

// close() turns off the handleCloseEvents flag before closing the connection.
LobbyChatConnection.prototype.close = function () {
  this.handleCloseEvents = false;
  super.close();
};

/* onStatus() calls the current connectionHandler when a successful connection
 * is made. It reports closed connections and errors except when closed
 * connections are expected. When a connection is closed, the playhead is
 * sent to the Login frame.
 */
LobbyChatConnection.prototype.onStatus = function (info) {
  // Always deal with successful connections.
  if (info.code == "NetConnection.Connect.Success") {
    this.handleCloseEvents = true;
    this.connectionHandler();
  }
  // Handle messages when the connection is closed.
  if (!this.isConnected && this.handleCloseEvents) {
    // Always handle rejection messages when they occur.
    if (info.code == "NetConnection.Connect.Rejected") {
      writeln(info.application.Message);
      writeln('Did you use the username "Guest" and password "Guest" ?');
    }
    else {
      writeln("Error: Connection Closed.");
    }
    this.handleCloseEvents = false;
    gotoAndPlay("Login");
  }
  // Handle remote method call errors here if you need to.
};
```

Example 3-9. NetConnection subclass test script (continued)

```
// Called when a connection has been established to the testLobby app.
function handleLobbyConnection () {
  writeln("Success, you are connected to the lobby!");
  gotoAndPlay("Lobby");
}

// Called when a connection has been established to a chat room.
function handleChatConnection () {
  writeln("Success, you are connected to a chat room!");
  gotoAndPlay("ChatRoom");
}

// Second, create a LobbyChatConnection object.
lobbyChat_nc = new LobbyChatConnection();

// When the Connect button in the Login frames is clicked, this
// function attempts to connect to the testLobby application.
function doConnect () {
  // Keep track of the username and password
  _global.userName = userName_txt.text;
  _global.password = password_txt.text;

  // Try to connect to the lobby.
  lobbyChat_nc.connect("rtmp:/testLobby", handleLobbyConnection,
                       userName, password);
}

// Called when the Lobby button in a chat room is clicked.
function doLobby (btn) {
  lobbyChat_nc.close();
  lobbyChat_nc.connect("rtmp:/testLobby", handleLobbyConnection,
                       userName, password);
}

// Called when the Chat button in the lobby is clicked.
function doChat (btn) {
  lobbyChat_nc.close();
  lobbyChat_nc.connect("rtmp:/testChat/room1", handleChatConnection,
                       userName, password);
}

// Called when the Disconnect button is clicked.
function doDisconnect () {
  lobbyChat_nc.close();
  gotoAndPlay("Login");
}

gotoAndPlay("Login");
```

The *onStatus( )* handler in Example 3-9 moves the playhead to the Login frame itself. If necessary, the more general purpose mechanism of calling a function could be used in the same way that the *connectionHandler( )* function was called.

Now let's look at how to create a *NetConnection* subclass using ActionScript 2.0. The *FCSConnector* class defined in Example 3-10 is just one way to do it. Like the previous examples, it uses an internal handleCloseEvents property to remember whether it should report a "NetConnection.Connect.Closed" code. It is also designed to take advantage of the event-passing system introduced in the UI components distributed with Flash MX 2004. Whenever *onStatus( )* is called, one of several possible events is dispatched to any objects that have added themselves as event listeners. Events are dispatched by the *dispatchEvent( )* method. You may notice in the listing that the *dispatchEvent( )* method is never defined. In fact, it is added to each *FCSConnector* object when the *EventDispatcher* class initializes the object in the *FCSConnector( )* function.

Example 3-10. An ActionScript 2.0 NetConnection subclass

```
class com.oreilly.pfcs.FCSConnector extends NetConnection {
  // EventDispatcher needs these.
  var addEventListener:Function;
  var removeEventListener:Function;
  var dispatchEvent:Function;
  var dispatchQueue:Function;

  // Internal data.
  var handleCloseEvents:Boolean = true;

  function FCSConnector () {
    super();
    mx.events.EventDispatcher.initialize(this);
  }

  function connectionClosed (type, info) {
    if (handleCloseEvents) dispatchEvent({target:this, type:type, info:info});
    handleCloseEvents = false;
  }

  function onStatus (info) {
    switch (info.code) {
      case "NetConnection.Connect.Success":
        dispatchEvent({target:this, type:"onConnect", info:info});
        break;
      case "NetConnection.Connect.Rejected":
        connectionClosed("onReject", info);
        break;
      case "NetConnection.Connect.Closed":
        connectionClosed("onClose", info);
        break;
      case "NetConnection.Connect.Failed":
        connectionClosed("onFail", info);
        break;
      case "NetConnection.Connect.AppShutdown":
        connectionClosed("onClose", info);
        break;
```

Example 3-10. An ActionScript 2.0 NetConnection subclass (continued)

```
      case "NetConnection.Connect.InvalidApp":
        connectionClosed("onReject", info);
        break;
      case "NetConnection.Call.Failed":
        dispatchEvent({target:this, type:"onCall", info:info});
        break;
    }
  }

  function connect () {
    handleCloseEvents = true;
    return super.connect.apply(super, arguments);
  }

  function close () {
    handleCloseEvents = false;
    super.close();
  }
}
```

The *FCSConnector* class does not simply create an *onStatus* event and pass on the information object as part of the event. Instead its *onStatus( )* method looks at the info.code string it receives and dispatches one of the following events: *onConnect*, *onReject*, *onFail*, *onClose*, or *onCall*. Creating separate events has advantages and disadvantages. It allows someone using the *FCSConnector* class to receive only the events he is interested in and to write separate functions to handle each type of event. However, in some applications, it may be less work to handle a single *onStatus* event. Example 3-11 lists code for a simple demonstration movie that uses the *FCSConnector* class. It imports the *FCSConnector* class, stores a single instance of it in the nc variable, and then adds the main timeline as a listener for all four connection-related events. Each event is delivered to a function or method of the same name.

Example 3-11. Importing and using the FCSConnector class in the main timeline of a movie

```
import com.oreilly.pfcs.FCSConnector;

// Create a new FCSConnector.
nc = new FCSConnector( );

// Add the _root timeline as a listener for connection-related events.
// Note: Since this code is on the main timeline this refers to _root.
nc.addEventListener("onReject", this);
nc.addEventListener("onFail", this);
nc.addEventListener("onClose", this);
nc.addEventListener("onConnect", this);

// Handle "NetConnection.Connect.Failed" messages here.
function onFail (ev) {
  var info = ev.info;
```

Example 3-11. Importing and using the FCSConnector class in the main timeline of a movie

```
    writeln("Can't reach the server.")
    writlen("Please check your network connection and try again.");
    writeln("info.code: " + info.code);
    connectButton.label = "Connect";
}

// Handle "NetConnection.Connect.Success" messages here.
function onConnect (ev) {
  var info = ev.info;
  writeln("You are now connected.");
  writeln("info.code: " + info.code);
  connectButton.label = "Disconnect";
}

// Handle "NetConnection.Connect.Rejected" messages here.
function onReject (ev) {
  var info = ev.info;
  writeln("Your connection attempt was rejected.");
  writeln("info.code: " + info.code);
  writeln("info.description: " + info.description);
  if (info.application) {
    for (var p in info.application) {
      writeln("info.application." + p + ": " + info.application[p]);
    }
  }
  connectButton.label = "Connect";
}

// Handle "NetConnection.Connect.Closed" messages here.
function onClose (ev) {
  var info = ev.info;
  writeln("Your connection was closed.");
  writeln("info.code: " + info.code);
  connectButton.label = "Connect";
}

connectButton.addEventListener("click", this);

function click (ev) {
  var button = ev.target;
  if (button.label == "Connect") {
    if (nc.connect("rtmp:/testLobby",
                   userNameTextInput.text,
                   passwordTextInput.text)) {
      button.label = "Wait...";
      writeln("Attempting to connect...");
    }
    else {
      writeln("Can't attempt connection. Check the URI.");
    }
  }
  else {
    writeln("Connection closed.");
```

Example 3-11. Importing and using the FCSConnector class in the main timeline of a movie

```
    button.label = "Connect";
    nc.close( );
  }
}

function writeln (msg) {
  msgTextArea.text += msg + "\n";
  msgTextArea.vPosition = msgTextArea.maxVPosition;
  msgTextArea.redraw( );// Fixes scrolling bug in TextArea as of Flash 7.2.
}
```

All the preceding examples are available in a Zip archive file from *http://flash-communications.net*. The archive includes the file *com/oreilly/pfcs/FCSConnector.as*. That file must be extracted from the archive with its path intact (most unZip programs have a Maintain Folders option for this purpose) and placed in a directory in the classpath of Flash MX 2004. See Chapter 9 of *Essential ActionScript 2.0* (O'Reilly) for more information on packages and the classpath.

Communication Components Without SimpleConnect

Chapter 2 showed how applications can be created using Macromedia's communication components. Macromedia supplies the SimpleConnect component to manage a network connection and connect all the other components to it. SimpleConnect allows users to log in using any name when they connect—even the same name someone else is using. If you need to develop an application that manages user identities differently but want to use Macromedia's communication components, there are two options. One is to write your own connection component. Chapters 13 through 15 describe how to build custom components. The other option is not to use a connection component at all, as illustrated in the final example in Chapter 2. The following example uses a little server-side scripting, a *NetConnection* subclass, and the communication components to demonstrate creating a basic chat room application with separate login and chat screens. The application enforces unique usernames, doesn't allow name changes while connected, and does not permit lurking. It is not designed to provide a lobby and multiple chat rooms. These and other enhancements are added in later chapters.

Creating the Application on the Server

To use the communication components without SimpleConnect, an application's *main.asc* file must load the component framework and store a username for every client that connects within the framework. A minimal *main.asc* file is shown in Example 3-12.

Example 3-12. Minimal main.asc file when SimpleConnect is not used

```
load("components.asc");

application.onConnect = function (client, userName) {
  gFrameworkFC.getClientGlobals(client).username = userName;
  application.acceptConnection(client);
};
```

Example 3-12 allows anyone to connect with any username. To reject connections in which the username is blank or already in use requires a little more work. Example 3-13 shows a listing of another *main.asc* file. The script uses an object named users to keep track of the userName associated with each Flash movie. (An object such as users, in which the item name is used to access array elements, is known as an *associative array*, *hash table*, or simply *hash*.) The *trim( )* function is used to preprocess each userName before checking whether it is null, an empty string, or already in the users object.

Example 3-13. The main.asc file for the netConnectChat application

```
load("components.asc");

// Trim any whitespace from before or after the userName.
// SSAS supports regular expressions, but client-side ActionScript does not.
function trim (str) {
  if (typeof str != "string") return "";  // Make sure str is a string.
  str = str.replace(/^\s*/, "");           // Trim leading spaces.
  str = str.replace(/\s*$/, "");           // Trim trailing spaces.
  str = str.replace(/\n/g,  "");           // Remove new lines.
  str = str.replace(/\r/g,  "");           // Remove carriage returns.
  str = str.replace(/\t/g,  "");           // Remove tabs.
  return str;
}

// Hash of client objects using the userName as a property name.
users = {};

// The onConnect( ) method rejects connection attempts
// where userName is invalid text or is already in use.
application.onConnect = function (client, userName) {
  userName = trim(userName);   // Remove leading and trailing whitespace.
  if (userName.length == 0) {  // If it is empty, reject it.
    application.rejectConnection(client, {msg: "Empty username."});
    return;
  }
  if (users[userName]) {    // If it is in use already, reject it.
    application.rejectConnection(client,
          {msg: 'The username "' + userName + '" is already in use.'});
    return;
  }
  // Store a reference to the client in the users hash.
  users[userName] = client;
  gFrameworkFC.getClientGlobals(client).username = userName;
```

```
  application.acceptConnection(client);
};

// When a client disconnects, remove the username from the
// users hash so someone can use it again.
application.onDisconnect = function (client) {
  var userName = gFrameworkFC.getClientGlobals(client).username;
  delete users[userName];
};
```

Placing the *main.asc* file from Example 3-13 into an *applications* subdirectory named *netConnectChat* allows this server-side *main.asc* script to control the *netConnectChat* application. If you were developing the *main.asc* script, you could always test it with a test client but let's push on to create the client-side part of the *netConnectChat* application in the next section.

Building the Client

Let's build a Flash movie to connect to our brand new *netConnectChat* application. For now, we'll stick with ActionScript 1.0 and the v1 UI components on which Macromedia's communication components rely. In Chapter 13, when we develop our own custom communication components, we'll switch to ActionScript 2.0 and the v2 UI components.

Using Macromedia's communication components without SimpleConnect is a two-step process: establish a network connection to the application instance and then pass the *NetConnection* object to each component's *connect( )* method. The *netConnectChat* application uses the PeopleList, Chat, and UserColor components to create a simple text chat interface. The interface can be created with everything on a single frame, as is popular when using the SimpleConnect component, or the different states of the movie can be spread over the timeline. The book's web site includes an example of a single-frame movie. In this example, we'll build the client-side movie for this application using the timeline. Figure 3-4 shows the timeline and Stage when the movie is on the Chat frame.

The Chat frame includes the following movie clips (components) and text field:

chat_mc
> A Chat component instance

peopleList_mc
> A PeopleList component instance

userColor_mc
> A UserColor component instance

userName_txt
> The text field at the bottom of the Stage

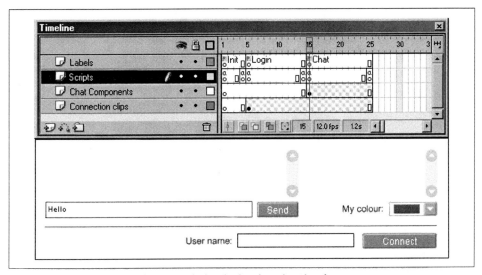

Figure 3-4. The timeline and Stage with the playhead on the Chat frame

```
connect_btn
```
   The Connect button at the bottom of the Stage

The Login frame contains only the userName_txt field and connect_btn button. If we were using the SimpleConnect component to log in the user, any other communication component would have to exist throughout the same timeline frames as Simple-Connect. In this example, the communication components do not need to be on the same frames as the username field or the Connect button. The components need only a *NetConnection* to function, so the username field and Connect button don't have to be included in the Chat frame either. However, in the Chat state, we change the Connect button label to Disconnect; the button logs out the user when clicked. The username text field is kept on the Stage to show the current user's name, but it is disabled during the chat.

The *Scripts* layer contains all but two lines of the script for the movie. The three important frames are the Init frame, which contains most of the script, and the Login and Chat frames. When the script on the Init frame has completed executing, the playhead moves to the Login frame. There is only one line of code on the Login frame of the *Scripts* layers:

```
startLoginState();
```

This statement calls the *startLoginState( )* function declared in the first frame of the timeline to initialize the elements on the Stage:

```
function startLoginState () {
  connect_btn.setLabel("Connect");
  userName_txt.selectable = true;
}
```

Similarly, there is only a single function call on the Chat frame:

```
startChatState( );
```

The *startChatState( )* function, also declared on the first frame, initializes the elements in the Chat frame:

```
function startChatState () {
  connect_btn.setLabel("Disconnect");
  userName_txt.selectable = false;
  peopleList_mc.connect(nc);
  chat_mc.connect(nc);
  userColor_mc.connect(nc);
}
```

The label on the Connect button is reset as necessary by both functions, and the selectable property of the username field is used to disable and enable the userName_txt field.

When the playhead moves to the Chat frame, the communication components are created because that is the first frame in which they exist. But they also need to be connected to a *NetConnection* object or a *NetConnection* subclass to operate. The *startChatState( )* function passes the global nc object to the *connect( )* method of each component for this purpose.

The remaining scripts on the timeline (frames 4, 14, and 24) contain only a *stop( )* function call. In addition to the components and movie clips placed directly on the Stage, the Library also contains an *AlertBox* movie clip symbol. It contains a MessageBox component named *alert_mc* from the Flash UI components set 2 and provides a way to display pop-up messages. The *AlertBox* movie clip's timeline contains code to set the title of the MessageBox and set its message text:

```
alert_mc.setTitle("Alert");
alert_mc.setMessage(message);
```

Example 3-14 shows the script from the main timeline (see *timelineComponentConnect.as* on the book's web site):.

Example 3-14. Main timeline script

```
// A simple alert function and variables to pop a message dialog box on stage.
alertLevel = 10;  // Level on which to display the alert dialog box.
upperLeft  = 10;  // _x and _y position of the alert dialog box.

// alert( ) displays msg in a pop-up alert dialog box.
function alert (msg) {
  attachMovie("AlertBox", "abox" + alertLevel, alertLevel,
              {_x: upperLeft, _y: upperLeft, message: msg} );
  // Increment the alertLevel and upperLeft position.
  alertLevel += 1;
  upperLeft += 10;
  if (upperLeft > 150) upperLeft = 10;
}
```

Example 3-14. Main timeline script (continued)

```
/* ChatConnection is a subclass of NetConnection designed to move the playhead
 * to the Chat frame when a connection is made and move it back to the Login
 * frame when it is lost.
 */
function ChatConnection () {
  super();
}

ChatConnection.prototype = new NetConnection();      // Subclass NetConnection.
ChatConnection.prototype.handleCloseEvents = true;   // Initial value.

// connect() turns on the handleCloseEvents flag before calling super.connect().
ChatConnection.prototype.connect = function () {
  this.handleCloseEvents = true;
  var result = super.connect.apply(super, arguments);
  if (!result) {
    alert("Invalid target URI: " + this.uri);
  }
  return result;
};

// close() turns off the handleCloseEvents flag before closing the connection.
ChatConnection.prototype.close = function () {
  this.handleCloseEvents = false;
  super.close();
};

/* onStatus( ) reports closed connections and errors except when closed
 * connections are expected. When a connection is closed, the playhead is
 * sent to the Login frame. When it is opened, it is sent to the Chat frame.
 */
ChatConnection.prototype.onStatus = function (info) {
  if (info.code == "NetConnection.Connect.Success") {
    gotoAndPlay("Chat");
  }
  else if (!this.isConnected) {
    if (this.handleCloseEvents) {
      var msg;
      if (info.code == "NetConnection.Connect.Rejected") {
        msg = 'Connection Rejected!';
        if (info.application) {
          msg += '\n' + info.application.msg;
        }
      }
      else {
        msg = 'Error: Connection ' + info.code.split(".").pop();
      }
      alert(msg);
      this.handleCloseEvents = false;
      gotoAndPlay("Login");
    }
```

Example 3-14. Main timeline script (continued)

```
  }
};

// Main timeline button handler functions.

/* doConnect( ) is called whenever connect_btn is clicked. If the button label
 * is Connect, the NetConnection.connect( ) method is called. If the label
 * is Disconnect, the close( ) method is called.
 */
function doConnect (btn) {
  if (btn.getLabel( ) == "Connect") {
    if (!nc.isConnected) {
      nc.connect("rtmp:/netConnectChat", userName_txt.text);
      btn.setLabel("Waiting...");
    }
  }
  else if (btn.getLabel( ) == "Disconnect") {
    if (nc.isConnected) {
      userColor_mc.close( );
      peopleList_mc.close( );
      chat_mc.close( );
      nc.close( );
      gotoAndPlay("Login");
    }
  }
}
// Main timeline state change functions.

// Called after the Chat frame is entered to connect communication components
// and change the appearance or behavior of other Flash components.
function startChatState ( ) {
  connect_btn.setLabel("Disconnect");
  userName_txt.selectable = false;
  peopleList_mc.connect(nc);
  chat_mc.connect(nc);
  userColor_mc.connect(nc);
}

// Called after the Login frame is entered to reset login components.
function startLoginState ( ) {
  connect_btn.setLabel("Connect");
  userName_txt.selectable = true;
}

// Create the chat connection object.
_global.nc = new ChatConnection( );

gotoAndPlay("Login");
```

If you test the movie in multiple browser windows, you'll see that you can log in only if the specified username is unique.

Other than that the fact the *alert( )* method has replaced *writeln( )* and that state change functions have been added, there should be little here that isn't familiar from the previous examples in this chapter. One difference is in the *onStatus( )* handler, which reports some errors a little differently:

```
msg = 'Error: Connection ' + info.code.split(".").pop();
```

The info.code property always contains a dot-delimited string. The preceding statement uses the *split( )* method to split the string into an array and then the array *pop( )* method to return the last part of the array. If info.code returns a message such as "NetConnection.Connect.Failed", the preceding statement appends the string "Failed" to "Error: Connection". When a code property is provided, the first term in the string is always the class of object with which the event is associated. The second term is usually the name of the action attempted, and the third is the result. Table 3-2 shows all the *NetConnection* information object code and level values as of FlashCom 1.5.

Table 3-2. NetConnection code and level values

Code	Level	Meaning
NetConnection.Call.Failed	Error	A remote method call was attempted on this connection and failed. The info.description property contains more details including the name of the method. Remote method calls are discussed in Chapter 9.
NetConnection.Connect.AppShutdown	Error	This message is supposed to be returned when an application instance is forced to shut down—for example when it is out of memory. However, as of FlashCom 1.5, this message is never received; "NetConnection.Connect.Closed" is received instead.
NetConnection.Connect.Closed	Status	Connection was closed by the server or the client. As of FlashCom 1.5, despite the level value of "status", it may indicate an error such as an application instance shutting down because it is using too much memory.
NetConnection.Connect.Failed	Error	The connection attempt failed. The server may not have been reachable or may be down.
NetConnection.Connect.InvalidApp	Error	This message is supposed to be returned when an application name is not registered on the server. However, as of FlashCom 1.5, this message is never received; "NetConnection.Connect.Closed" is received instead.
NetConnection.Connect.Rejected	Error	The attempt to connect was rejected by the server or by the application on the server. The reason the client was rejected depends on several factors. For example, the application may reject the connection because the user's credentials are invalid. The application may return an application object as a property of the information object. The info.description property will contain useful information if the application name was not found, if the resource limits of the application were exceeded, or if the server license does not allow more connections or the usage of more bandwidth. See Table 3-3.
NetConnection.Connect.Success	Status	A connection has been established.

The info.description property is often empty but for some messages contains important additional information. When the server returns a "NetConnection.Connect.Rejected" message, either the server or the application has rejected the connection. When an application rejects a connection, the server-side script writer has the option to return an application object to explain why. When the server rejects a connection, it returns information in the description property that explains why. A rejected description message looks like this:

```
[ Server.Reject ] : (_defaultRoot_, _defaultVHost_) : Application (appName)
    is not defined.
```

Table 3-3 lists the three types of server rejection messages included in the description property.

Table 3-3. Description values for NetConnection.Connect.Rejected messages

Message	Meaning
Server.Reject	The server rejected the connection because the application did not exist, because of a configuration error, or because of some other problem such as bad network data.
Resource.Limit.Exceeded	The resource limits for the server, virtual host, or application have been exceeded. For example, the maximum allowed number of instances or shared objects has been exceeded.
License.Limit.Exceeded	The number of simultaneous client connections or bandwidth limit has been exceeded. See the Preface for FlashCom licensing information.

Conclusion

Don't underestimate the importance of mastering the art of managing connections. The lessons learned in this chapter should serve you well in both designing and debugging your applications and their connections. In later chapters, we'll extend the *NetConnection* object in other ways as the need arises. Now that we've done some client-side scripting, it's time to move on to scripting on the server.

CHAPTER 4

Applications, Instances, and Server-Side ActionScript

FlashCom applications can be scripted on the server using Server-Side ActionScript (SSAS) and the server-side objects available to it. With SSAS, you can control who can access an application and what resources are available to each user. You can control Flash movies remotely, switch the stream source that people are watching, chain streams between FlashCom Servers, and access and update databases.

Server-Side ActionScript is a little different from the client-side ActionScript used to script Flash movies. This chapter describes how to write Server-Side ActionScript and work with the objects that control application instances and the Flash movies that connect to them. Scripting on the server is as important as scripting in Flash. This chapter is designed to get you going on the server side of things and to prepare you for the chapters that follow. Future chapters on streams, remote shared objects, and remote methods all describe how to script communication objects within Flash and their counterparts on the server.

Scripting Application Instances

A single FlashCom Server can host many different applications. Each application gets its unique server-side behavior from the scripts associated with it. You create an application by adding a subdirectory to an *applications* directory on the server. Macromedia refers to each *applications* subdirectory as a *registered application directory* because creating it registers an application with FlashCom. In turn, the server makes instances of the application available to Flash movies that try to connect to them. Every registered application directory can also be thought of as the home directory for that application. You can script an application by adding a *main.asc* file to the application's home directory. For example, adding a subdirectory named *courseLobby* to an *applications* directory creates a new application named *courseLobby*. The *main.asc* file in the *courseLobby* directory gives the application its unique server-side behavior. Server-Side ActionScript files, such as *main.asc*, are text files containing source code. They can be created with any plain text editor, such as the one included in Flash MX Professional 2004 (Flash Pro). SSAS source files almost always have the extension *.asc* (although *.js* is another option); SSAS is in fact JavaScript 1.5.

 When double-byte characters are required, such as for Kanji, you must use a text editor capable of handling UTF-8 encoding. In addition, method names containing higher-order double-byte characters must use the array operator instead of the dot operator. For example:

```
obj = {};
obj.myMethodName = function () {
  trace("myMethodName");
};
obj["myMethodName"](); // Correct
obj.myMethodName();     // Correct

obj["マイメソッド名"] = function () {
  trace("マイメソッド名");
};
obj["マイメソッド名"]();     // Correct
obj.マイメソッド名();          // Syntax Error !!
```

Instances and Resources

FlashCom can run multiple instances of an application at the same time. Each instance has its own memory, disk, stream, and shared object environment and runs its own single-threaded copy of the *main.asc* script. Instances are an important way to group users and partition the server's resources among them. Perhaps the simplest example of this is a chat application. Many instances of a chat application can be run simultaneously—each with different users connected to it—effectively creating a set of chat rooms. Users who connect to *rtmp:/courseChat/room1* can communicate with each other using the streams and shared objects associated with the room1 instance. Other users who connect to *rtmp:/courseChat/room2* can communicate among themselves using the room2 instance but will normally be unaware of the conversation occurring in the room1 instance. If instances must share streams or shared objects, one instance can make a network connection to another to gain access to its resources.

 Although you can build an application in which a single instance provides a lobby and multiple chat rooms simultaneously, it's not recommended. If a large number of users simultaneously use a single instance, performance suffers. Because an instance's ActionScript runs in a single thread, every remote method call on the server, including the delivery of chat messages, will execute sequentially.

It is difficult to give precise limits on how many clients are too many for one instance because each application makes different demands on the server. An instance that makes extensive use of Server-Side ActionScript may support fewer than 20 clients with adequate performance, while other applications may support hundreds or even a few thousand. Chapter 16 covers architectures that scale more effectively.

The streams and shared objects available to each instance are located by FlashCom using a relative URI. Most often this is just the name of the stream or shared object. For example, if a Flash movie plays a stream named intro, then "intro" is a relative URI to the instance to which the movie is connected. If the instance URI is:

rtmp://my.university.edu/courseLectures/algebra101

then the full URI to the intro video would be:

rtmp://my.university.edu/courseLectures/algebra101/intro

In practice, a full URI like that is never used, but it is useful to think of stream and shared object resources as existing in a space defined by full URIs. We'll make use of full URIs later in this chapter to show how streams are organized within an application. A Flash movie requests resources associated with an application instance using a relative URI after a connection has been attempted. For example, a movie must first request a connection to an instance before trying to publish or play a stream or get a remote shared object:

```
nc.connect("rtmp://my.university.edu/courseLectures/algebra101");
```

Once the connection has been attempted, the Flash movie can request that a recorded or live stream named intro be played:

```
ns = new NetStream(nc);      // Create a NetStream within a NetConnection.
videoArea.attachVideo(ns);   // Attach the stream to a video object on the Stage.
ns.play("intro");            // Play a stream named intro.
```

Similarly, a shared object named streamList, which contains a list of stream names, may be available for the algebra101 instance. After a connection is requested to the algebra101 instance, access to the streamList shared object could be requested as follows:

```
so = SharedObject.getRemote("streamList", nc.uri, true);
so.onSync = function (list) {
  trace("onSync> list.length: " + list.length);
};
so.connect(nc);
```

The *NetStream* and *SharedObject* classes are described in detail in Chapters 5 and 8. In both previous examples, the name of the stream and the shared object are simple relative URIs. The relative path to a stream or shared object within an instance can include directory-like names that help to separate resources into groups. For example, lectures can be grouped by subject so that a relative URI to a video stream might be *vectors/intro* while there is another video located at *matrices/intro*. A client-side *play( )* method call for one of these examples would look like this:

```
ns.play("vectors/intro");
```

Similarly, a shared object available at the relative URI *vectors/quizQuestions* would be created like this:

```
so = SharedObject.getRemote("vectors/quizQuestions", nc.uri, true);
```

Drawing a simple directory tree showing the resources within an instance is a good idea when developing an application. Figure 4-1 shows the location and relative URI of resources for the algebra101 instance of the *courseLectures* application.

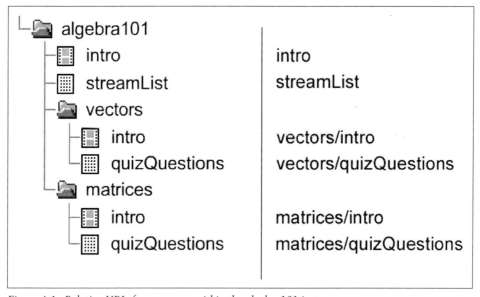

Figure 4-1. Relative URIs for resources within the algebra101 instance

All recorded streams and persistent shared object files are normally stored in the *streams* and *sharedobjects* directories in an application's home directory. The two directories are organized in a hierarchy that is consistent with the relative URI addressing of instance resources. If the streams and shared objects of this example are stored on the server, they will be found within the directory structure illustrated in Figure 4-2.

Instance names such as *algebra101* appear as top-level directories within the *stream* and *sharedobjects* directories. Within instance name directories, such as *algebra101*, are the directories and files that conform to the relative URIs used for them in Figure 4-1. For example, a stream that is recorded to the algebra101 instance's relative URI *vectors/intro*, will have a file path of:

.../applications/courseLectures/streams/algebra101/vectors/intro.flv

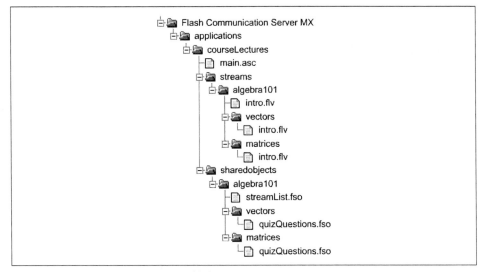

Figure 4-2. Shared object and stream file locations

Streams can be shared by all application instances by defining a special virtual directory. See "Uploading Prerecorded Streams" in Chapter 5 for more information.

Resource Name Collisions

In theory, each instance manages its own stream and shared object resources without interference from other instances. In one important case, however, stream and shared object instance names can collide (i.e., two different instances attempt to use the same resource); naturally, you want to avoid such collisions. Using the previous example of a *courseLectures* application, imagine that one client connects to this URI:

> *rtmp:/courseLectures/algebra101*

and a second client connects to a different URI:

> *rtmp:/courseLectures/algebra101/vectors*

This will start two instances of the *courseLectures* application: one instance named algebra101 and the other named algebra101/vectors. If the first instance attempts to access a shared object at the relative URI of *vectors/quizQuestions* and the second attempts to access a shared object at the relative URI of *quizQuestions*, they will both be using the same quizQuestions shared object at the full URI of:

> *rtmp:/courseLectures/algebra101/vectors/quizQuestions*

FlashCom is not designed to handle this situation.

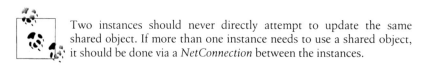
Two instances should never directly attempt to update the same shared object. If more than one instance needs to use a shared object, it should be done via a *NetConnection* between the instances.

Usually, one instance is selected as the owner of the shared object or stream and the other instances connect to it in order to access its resources. Interinstance communications is covered in detail later in this chapter and in Chapter 16.

Differences Between Flash ActionScript and Server-Side ActionScript

As alluded to earlier in this chapter and the Preface, there are two distinct types of ActionScript: client-side ActionScript—which includes both ActionScript 1.0 and ActionScript 2.0—and the server-side version, known as Server-Side ActionScript. Client-side ActionScript is used to create *.swf* movies, which run in the Flash Player on the user's machine. Server-Side ActionScript is stored in *.asc* files that run on the FlashCom Server.

Since Flash 5, client-side ActionScript has been based on the ECMA (European Computer Manufacturers Association) standards, as is JavaScript. The standard language is named ECMAScript and is defined in ECMA-262 available at: *http://www.ecma-international.org*. Client-side Flash ActionScript has never completely conformed to the ECMAScript standard because Macromedia developed the language with its unique needs and backward compatibility in mind. Client-side ActionScript has also evolved over time. The earlier implementation supported in Flash MX (and still supported in Flash MX 2004) has been retroactively dubbed ActionScript 1.0. The latest implementation—supported in Flash MX 2004 and closer to ECMA compliance than earlier implementations—is named ActionScript 2.0. For more information on the differences between Flash ActionScript 1.0 and ECMAScript, see Appendix D in *ActionScript for Flash MX: The Definitive Guide* (O'Reilly). For details on ActionScript 2.0 and how it diverges from the ECMA standards, see *Essential ActionScript 2.0*, also from O'Reilly.

Contrary to client-side ActionScript, Server-Side ActionScript conforms to the ECMAScript standard because Macromedia used the Mozilla Spidermonkey JavaScript 1.5 interpreter in FlashCom. More information on it and JavaScript 1.5 are available here:

http://www.mozilla.org/js

This section outlines the differences that you should watch out for between client-side ActionScript and Server-Side ActionScript.

Case-Sensitivity

Server-Side ActionScript is always case-sensitive, while client-side ActionScript may not be. In Flash 5 and Flash MX, most ActionScript is not case-sensitive. For example, in Flash MX, `myVariable` and `MyVariable` refer to the same variable. In server-side scripts, they do not.

Many developers continue to be confused by the case-sensitivity rules in Flash MX 2004, which depend in part on the version (SWF format) and ActionScript version (compiler version) chosen under File → Publish Settings → Flash. Realize first that we are talking about two different issues for client-side ActionScript: compile-time case-sensitivity and runtime case-sensitivity. The ActionScript 1.0 compiler is not case-sensitive, whereas the ActionScript 2.0 compiler is. However, runtime case-sensitivity is a function of the version of the SWF format to which you export, not the ActionScript version used at compile time nor the version of the Flash Player plugin in which the file is played.

Runtime case-sensitivity is summarized in Table 4-1, reproduced from Colin Moock's *Essential ActionScript 2.0*. Note that ActionScript 1.0 and 2.0 are both case-sensitive when exported in Flash Player 7–format *.swf* files and played in Flash Player 7. In other runtime cases, code is case-insensitive subject to the exceptions cited in the footnotes to the table.

Table 4-1. Runtime case-sensitivity support by language, file format, and Flash Player version

Movie compiled as either ActionScript 1.0 or 2.0 and	Played in Flash Player 6	Played in Flash Player 7
Flash Player 6–format *.swf* file	Case-insensitive[a]	Case-insensitive[a]
Flash Player 7–format *.swf* file	Not supported[b]	Case-sensitive

[a]Identifiers (i.e., variable and property names), function names, frame labels, and symbols export IDs are case-insensitive in Flash Player 6–format *.swf* files. But reserved words such as *if* are case-sensitive, even in Flash Player 6.

[b]Flash Player 6 cannot play Flash Player 7–format *.swf* files.

 Regardless of whether you are writing client-side ActionScript or SSAS, we strongly recommend maintaining consistent usage of upper- and lowercase in all your code to avoid problems.

If you are careful to always capitalize names in the same way and never use capitalization to distinguish between variable names or other identifiers, you shouldn't have any problems. However, in JavaScript it is a common practice to use capitalization to distinguish between the name of a constructor function and an instance of a class, as follows:

```
function User () {
}
```

```
// The user variable holds an instance of the User class
user = new User( );
```

In Flash 5 and Flash MX, this would essentially disable the constructor, but in SSAS, the difference in capitalization means that *User* (the class) and *user* (a variable holding an instance of the class) are different entities. A common practice to avoid confusion is to append the word "Class" onto the constructor function name:

```
function UserClass ( ) {
}
user = new UserClass( );
```

Working with Inheritance

Server-Side ActionScript does not support the formal definition of classes and interfaces supported by client-side ActionScript 2.0. SSAS supports prototype-based inheritance but is a little different from Flash ActionScript 1.0. Flash MX added the *super* operator to client-side ActionScript to make it easy to call the constructor function and methods of a superclass. Although *super* is not part of the ECMAScript version 3 language defined in ECMA-262, it is proposed for a future version of the standard. The *super* operator is not available in SSAS. However you can permit a subclass to access the constructor and methods of a superclass in a number of ways in SSAS. Example 4-1 shows one way to call the constructor and methods of a superclass in SSAS.

Example 4-1. Calling the constructor and methods of a superclass in SSAS

```
SuperClass = function (a) {
  this.a = a;
};

SuperClass.prototype.method = function ( ) {
  trace("SuperClass method called. a is: " + this.a);
};

SubClass = function (a, b) {
  SuperClass.apply(this, arguments);
  this.b = b;
};

SubClass.prototype = new SuperClass( );
SubClass.constructor = SubClass;

SubClass.prototype.method = function ( ) {
  trace("In Subclass method. a and b: " + this.a + ", " + this.b);
  SuperClass.prototype.method.apply(this, arguments);
};

subClass = new SubClass(1, 2);
subClass.method( );
```

An excellent discussion of object-oriented programming and prototype-based inheritance using JavaScript is available in *JavaScript: The Definitive Guide, Fourth Edition* (O'Reilly) by David Flanagan. Flanagan's book is especially useful for server-side scripting as it covers JavaScript 1.5—the exact same language as SSAS.

Prototype-based inheritance issues in Flash 5 and Flash MX and the various options for implementing inheritance without using *super* in Flash are discussed in detail here:

http://www.quantumwave.com/flash/inheritance.html

While the discussion centers around Flash, it is also a valuable resource for server-side scripting.

Many of the communication objects available cannot be subclassed using these sorts of techniques. For example, shared objects are not created by calling a constructor function. Instead, they are created via a static method such as *SharedObject.getRemote( )* on the client or *get( )* on the server. Often there are better ways to work with the communication classes than inheriting from them. See Chapter 15 for more details.

Single Execution Context

Client-side ActionScript provides a special _global object that provides a place to store global variables that exist outside the scope of the timeline. For example:

```
// Assume a _global object already exists.
_global.x = 3; // OK in client-side AS; however, error in SSAS.
trace (x);     // Will output: 3 in Flash MX and later.
```

In client-side ActionScript, if a variable is not found on the timeline and the _global object has a property of the same name, the _global object's property is accessed.

In SSAS there are no timelines. All server-side code executes in one global context that is associated with each application instance. So there is little point to providing a special _global object. You can create an object named _global, but it will not work as it does in client-side ActionScript. In general, you should avoid creating an object named _global in SSAS because it doesn't add anything and may create problems if you are using Flash Remoting (see Chapter 11).

When loaded into a *main.asc* file, the *netservices.asc* file creates a new _global object and assigns properties to it. The *RecordSet.asc* file also adds properties to the _global object. Furthermore, *netservices.asc* adds the *unshift( )* and *registerClass( )* methods to the *Object* class; since all classes inherit from *Object*, every object shows these methods when its properties are enumerated with a *for-in* loop. Chapter 11 contains additional information on dealing with these inconveniences. If you must use a _global object in SSAS, you should check whether it already exists before creating your own and be careful to avoid collisions with the _global properties defined in *netservices.asc*.

Accessing Undefined Variables

It is common to see tests for undefined variables in client-side ActionScript as follows:

```
if (xyz == undefined) {        // Don't do this on the server!
  trace("xyz is undefined.");
}
```

However, the preceding code will throw a reference error on the server because the variable xyz does not exist. To get around this, use the *typeof* operator, as follows:

```
if (typeof xyz == "undefined") {
  trace("xyz does not exist");
}
```

Using *typeof* is not necessary within the body of a function where the variable is local by virtue of being declared using var or passed in via the function's parameter list. The following is okay in SSAS as well as in client-side ActionScript:

```
var xyz;
if (xyz == undefined) {
  trace("xyz is undefined.");
}
```

And so is this:

```
someFunction = function (xyz) {
  if (xyz == undefined) {
    trace("xyz is undefined.");
  }
};
```

try/catch/finally Statements

If you look through the server-side communication components code in the *scriptlib/ components* folder, you will see frequent use of *try/catch* statements. For example, the server-side FCChat component is guaranteed to be defined only once by placing the definition within a *catch* block:

```
try {var dummy = FCChat;} catch (e) { // #ifndef FCChat
  // The FCChat class is defined here...
}
```

The *try/catch/finally* statement is supported in client-side ActionScript 2.0, but AS 2.0 does not support runtime type and reference checking. For details on *try/catch/finally* in ActionScript 2.0, see the chapter on exception handling in *Essential ActionScript 2. 0*. For a description of how to use *try*, *catch*, *finally*, *throw*, and *Error* objects in JavaScript (which also applies to SSAS), see *JavaScript: The Definitive Guide, Fourth Edition*.

Using *try/catch* statements has the advantage that errors, including type and reference errors, that would otherwise stop the execution of server-side scripts can be

---

caught and handled. We've already seen an example of a reference error (an error caused by trying to refer to a non-existent variable). A type error occurs if you attempt to access the property of an undefined or null object. The following short SSAS script causes execution to stop when a type error occurs. If you run it using the App Inspector (a testing utility introduced in "Admin Service, Administration Console, and App Inspector" in Chapter 1 and used later under "Testing and Debugging Server-Side Script Files"), you will see the error message "status has no properties" and the last *trace( )* statement will never be executed:

```
status = null;
trace(status.property);   // Causes a type error
trace("Unreachable trace statement.");
```

On the other hand, wrapping the same code in a *try* block makes it possible to recover from the error:

```
try {
  status = null;
  trace(status.property);
  trace("Unreachable trace statement.");
}
catch (e) {
  trace("Error name and message: " + e.name + ", " + e.message);
}
finally {
  trace("No matter what,this statement will be executed.");
}
trace("Processing can continue here...");
```

If this simple script is run in the App Inspector, the following output appears:

```
Error name and message: TypeError, status has no properties
No matter what, this statement will be executed.
Processing can continue here...
```

While ActionScript 2.0 does have a *try/catch/finally* statement, it does not support runtime type or reference checking. The same script run in Flash MX 2004 produces the following output, because trace(status.property); outputs "undefined" instead of throwing an error:

```
undefined
Unreachable trace statement.
No matter what, this statement will be executed.
```

#include and import Versus load( )

Server-Side ActionScript uses the *load( )* function in place of the #include directive (common in client-side ActionScript 1.0) to load other ActionScript source files into another script. The *load( )* method is described under "Using load( ) to Include Other Script Files" later in this chapter. The import statement is not supported in SSAS, and there is no concept of class files organized into packages as there are in

ActionScript 2.0. Again, see *Essential ActionScript 2.0* for a full discussion of client-side ActionScript classes and packages.

The Life of an Application Instance

An application instance is a process that runs in FlashCom. Each instance has:

- Its own script engine
- A namespace of streams and shared objects
- Persistent data that can be stored within its namespace

No two instances can share or update the same data directly, but they can play the same stream in a virtual stream directory (see Chapter 5).

FlashCom maintains a pool of threads for script processing, and each application uses one thread from this pool to execute server-side scripts in response to events such as loading an instance or a Flash client connecting to an instance. Server-side scripts should be designed to handle events quickly and then release the thread they are using. When an error is thrown in one instance, it will not affect the other instances.

FlashCom can run many different instances of the same application. Each instance is usually created by FlashCom in response to a connection request from a client. FlashCom receives the client's connection request and examines the RTMP address passed by the client to the server. The RTMP address forwarded by the client is the URI passed into the client-side *NetConnection.connect()* method. As described in Chapter 3, FlashCom extracts the application name and then runs an instance of the application. If no instance name is provided in the RTMP address, it creates an instance named _definst_. Otherwise, it creates the instance named in the URI. Depending on how the application is scripted and how the server is configured, some time after the last client disconnects, the instance will be destroyed. Between the time an instance is created and destroyed, a number of things can happen. To simplify how things work, they are divided here into three sections: startup, midlife, and shutdown.

Startup

An instance is normally started by FlashCom when the first client attempts to connect to it. However, it may be started manually with the App Inspector or Administration Console, or an application instance can be made to start immediately after the server is started by setting the contents of the <LoadOnStartup> tag in an *Application.xml* file (see "Using load( ) to Include Other Script Files" later in this chapter for details on where to place the *Application.xml* file).

Notice that there are two key objects related to instance and client management. The application object is a singleton object—there is only one—that represents the application instance. Each instance gets its own application object, which is an instance of the *Application* class. As shown in Example 4-2, you should add dynamic methods directly to the singleton instance, application, instead of Application. prototype. For example:

```
application.onConnect = function (client, userName, password) {};
```

A *Client* object represents a client-side Flash movie attempting to connect to an application instance. There can be more than one *Client* object (one for each user) for each application object. The methods and properties of the *Application* and *Client* classes are described in Macromedia's Server-Side Communication ActionScript Dictionary (available from *http://download.macromedia.com/pub/flashcom/ documentation/FlashCom_SS_ASD.pdf*).

Here is the startup sequence:

1. The *main.asc* file is loaded, compiled, and executed.

2. Any files that were included using the *load( )* method are loaded and executed. In turn, these files may load other files.

3. The *application.onAppStart( )* method is called. The *onAppStart( )* method is called only once and is often used to initialize the application object and the instance's shared object and stream resources.

4. If the instance has been started as a result of a client connection request using *NetConnection.connect( )*, the *application.onConnect( )* method is called and passed a *Client* object, representing the client Flash movie that tried to connect. Any optional parameters passed into *connect( )* are also forwarded to the *onConnect( )* method, where the client's connection request can be rejected, accepted, or left pending.

Midlife

Once the application instance has started, any number of clients can connect and disconnect from the instance. Whenever a Flash movie attempts to connect, the *application.onConnect( )* method is called and passed a new *Client* object representing the client-side Flash movie. *Client* objects with accepted connections are kept in the application.clients array. Whenever an accepted client disconnects, the *application.onDisconnect( )* method is called and passed a *Client* object that represents the client that has disconnected. A client can be disconnected due to network problems or problems on a remote workstation. FlashCom may not realize immediately that the client has disconnected. So, it is possible that, for a time, a *Client* object will not always represent a connected movie.

Shutdown

An instance may be unloaded by the server because it is consuming too much memory, or it may be shut down manually using the Admin Service. Barring these sorts of events, an instance is normally shut down some time after the last client disconnects. The delay between the last client disconnecting and the instance being shut down is designed to minimize the number of startups an instance must perform. This delay is controlled by three tags in three types of XML configuration files, as described in Table 4-2.

Table 4-2. Shutdown configuration tags

Tag name	Default	Location	Description
`<ApplicationGC>`	5	*Server.xml*	Interval, in minutes, when applications are asked whether they should check for instances to dispose of
`<AppInstanceGC>`	20	*Vhost.xml*	Interval, in minutes, when application instances can be checked for disposal
`<MaxAppIdleTime>`	1200	*Application.xml*	Number of seconds since the last client disconnected before the instance can be disposed of

The default values mean that every 5 minutes applications are asked whether it has been 20 minutes since they tried to dispose of their instances. If it has been 20 minutes and the last client disconnected more than 1200 seconds (20 minutes) ago, the instance will be disposed of. Unless the server is very busy, the default values will result in instances being disposed of between 20 and 25 minutes after the last client leaves. This might seem like a long delay, but it is a reasonable compromise between leaving the instance running unnecessarily and doing the extra work of shutting down and restarting an instance if another client tries to connect.

Before an instance is finally shut down, its *application.onAppStop( )* method is called. If *onAppStop( )* returns false, the instance will not be shut down. The *onAppStop( )* method is normally used to clean up any resources related to the application that may need further attention before the instance is discarded.

Running a Simple Hello World Test Script

A typical *helloWorld* test program is usually the smallest test program that produces output on the screen. While server-side programs don't normally output anything directly to the user, a simple *helloWorld* example is still useful. In SSAS, the *trace( )* function outputs text messages to the NetConnection Debugger, App Inspector, and log files on the server. During development, the App Inspector is the primary tool that allows developers to load, unload, and reload applications after a change is made in a script and needs to be tested.

Example 4-2 shows a short *main.asc* script that is the SSAS implementation of *helloWorld*. It demonstrates all the standard event handler methods of the application object.

Example 4-2. A simple server-side helloWorld test script

```
application.onAppStart = function () {
    trace("onAppStart> " + application.name + " is starting at " + new Date());
};

application.onStatus = function (info) {
    trace("onStatus> info.level: " + info.level + ", info.code: " + info.code);
    trace("onStatus> info.description: " + info.description);
    trace("onStatus> info.details: " + info.details);
};

application.onConnect = function (client, userName, password) {
    client.userName = userName;
    client.writeAccess = "/public";
    client.readAccess  = "/";
    application.acceptConnection(client);
    trace("onConnect> client.ip: " + client.ip);
    trace("onConnect> client.agent: " + client.agent);
    trace("onConnect> client.referrer: " + client.referrer);
    trace("onConnect> client.protocol: " + client.protocol);
};

application.onDisconnect = function (client) {
    trace("onDisconnect> client.userName: " + client.userName)
    trace("onDisconnect> disconnecting at: " + new Date());
};

application.onAppStop = function (info) {
    trace("onAppStop> application.name: " + application.name);
    trace("onAppStop> stopping at " + new Date());
    trace("onAppStop> info.level: " + info.level);
    trace("onAppStop> info.code: " + info.code);
    trace("onAppStop> info.description: " + info.description);
};
```

With this example code in mind, let's take a closer look at the most important event handling methods of the application object. These are invoked automatically when the application starts, when a client attempts to connect, when a client disconnects, or when the application is supposed to shut down.

application.onAppStart( )

When an application instance is accessed the first time, the script is compiled and any global code (i.e., code outside the context of an event handler) is executed. After that, the *application.onAppStart( )* method is called. In Example 4-2, the application.name property is used to output the name of the instance that has been started. The name will always be in the format *appName/instanceName*. For example, "helloWorld/_definst_" is the default instance name for the *helloWorld* application. If an instance name includes directories, the name property may contain a string such as "courseChat/chem101/room1".

application.onStatus( )

The *application.onStatus( )* method receives messages for server-side *Stream* and *Net-Connection* objects that do not have *onStatus( )* handlers, in addition to other application messages. The *onStatus( )* handler is not invoked in Example 4-2, but the handler declaration is included to show the information object properties that can be received.

application.onConnect( )

The *application.onConnect( )* method shows the interaction between the application object and the client object passed into it. The client object is an instance of the *Client* class, which provides information about the Flash movie attempting a connection, such as its IP address. An instance of the *Client* class is always passed into the *onConnect( )* method. In this example, each instance is named client. The difference in capitalization means that there is no name conflict between the *Client* class name and the individual client object passed into *onConnect( )*. If you find this confusing or want to use a naming convention that is consistent with how you write code in Flash MX, then instead of using client as an object name, use something like newClient:

```
application.onConnect = function (newClient, userName, password) {
  newClient.userName = userName;
  application.acceptConnection(newClient);
};
```

Along with the IP address (the ip property), each client has properties that contain the name of the user agent, referring page, and connection protocol. Other properties of the client object include readAccess and writeAccess, which can be used to control what relative URIs the client can access, and therefore what streams and shared objects are available to each client. In Example 4-2, the client is allowed to write to any resource in the *public* directory or its subdirectories because writeAccess is "/public". The client is allowed to read (access) any resource in any directory because readAccess has been set to "/", which is the root of any relative URI within the instance.

Properties can be added to the client object; in this example, a userName property is added dynamically. The userName variable passed into the *onConnect( )* method is the name with which the user logged in; the code stores it as a property—also named userName—of the client object so that it is available even after the *onConnect( )* handler exits.

The *onConnect( )* handler in Example 4-2 allows the client to connect to the application instance by invoking *application.acceptConnection( )*. Client connection requests can also be rejected using *application.rejectConnection( )*. Calling these methods inside *onConnect( )* is not really necessary. If *onConnect( )* returns true, the client connection is accepted; the connection is rejected if *onConnect( )* returns false. More importantly, if *onConnect( )* returns nothing or null, the client is left in a pending state and is unable to communicate with the server. Connections for pending clients can still be accepted or rejected outside of the *onConnect( )* method by calling *application.acceptConnection( )* or *application.rejectConnection( )*.

 If the *application.onConnect( )* method is not defined, all client connections are accepted and all clients are given global read and write access equivalent to setting readAccess and writeAccess to "/".

application.onDisconnect( )

The *application.onDisconnect( )* method is called when FlashCom detects that a client with an accepted or pending connection has disconnected from the instance. In the example, the client.userName property is used to identify who is leaving.

application.onAppStop( )

Finally, *application.onAppStop( )* is called just before the instance is shut down. It is passed an information object that specifies the reason for the shutdown; it can prevent the instance from shutting down by returning false.

Using the App Inspector to Run Scripts

To try out a script like the one in Example 4-2, create a text file named *main.asc* (or download it from the book's web site) and save it into a subdirectory of your *applications* folder named *helloWorld*. Find the *app_inspector.swf* movie (located in Flash-Com 1.5's *flashcom_help/html/admin* directory). This *.swf* is a testing tool known as the App Inspector.

Start the *app_inspector.swf* movie by opening it in the Flash Player, or load the *app_inspector.html* page into your browser and enter the location of the server in the Host field. If you are running FlashCom on your workstation, enter **localhost** in the Host field. If FlashCom is running on a remote server, enter the server's IP address or hostname. In the Name and Password fields, enter the administrator's username and password, which you chose during FlashCom's installation procedure.

After connecting, enter **helloWorld** in the App/Inst field and click the Load button, as shown in Figure 4-3. If the instance doesn't load, an information icon should appear near the Load button. Click on it to see what went wrong, fix and resave your script if necessary, and try again.

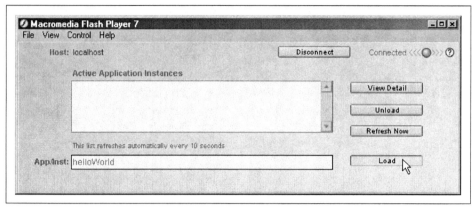

Figure 4-3. Loading an application in the App Inspector following login

If the helloWorld/_definst_ instance is not loaded successfully, click on the View Detail button, as shown in Figure 4-4.

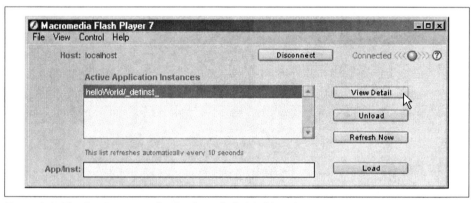

Figure 4-4. The App Inspector after loading a helloWorld application

If the helloWorld/_definst_ instance is loaded successfully, click on the Live Log tab of the App Inspector. Click the Reload App button to force the instance to restart so that you can see the output from the test script's *application.onAppStart( )* method.

Figure 4-5 shows the output in the Live Log area of the App Inspector after the *helloWorld* application was restarted.

The log shows the application instance was shut down and restarted, but the messages do not appear in the order you might expect. System messages and *trace( )* messages from the script are often intermixed. For example, the system message "Loading of app instance: helloWorld/_definst_ successful" appears in between messages generated by the *trace( )* function while the instance was unloading in the *onAppStop( )* method. The messages generated by the script in the previous output listing occur only in the *onAppStart( )* and *onAppStop( )* methods. To see messages

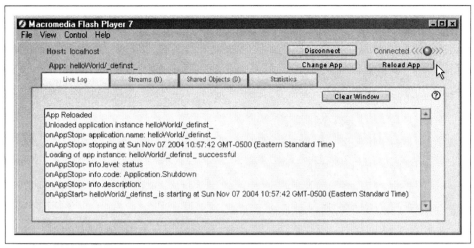

*Figure 4-5. The App Inspector after restarting helloWorld/_definst_*

related to clients connecting and disconnecting from the application instance requires a movie that connects to and disconnects from the instance. For this purpose, a test movie is supplied on the book's web site as part of the *helloWorld.zip* archive. Test movies are an important tool. A good but simple test movie should allow you to:

- Enter or select different application instance names to which to connect
- Enter a username and password or other connection parameters
- Read all the status and error messages the client receives or generates
- Easily extend it to add features as necessary

The output in Figure 4-6 shows the Live Log area when a connection is made and then dropped from a client. The IP address of 127.0.0.1 indicates that the client was running on the same system as the FlashCom Server.

Twenty-three minutes after the client disconnected, the instance shuts down and produces the output shown in Figure 4-7 in the App Inspector.

The output in the Live Log area of the App Inspector shows data such as startup and shutdown times, the client IP address and username, and when the client connects and disconnects. The App Inspector and server-side *trace( )* statements are essential for testing and debugging server-side scripts.

A More Realistic Example

Writing and testing a simple *main.asc* script for *helloWorld* is an important first step in becoming familiar with any new environment. However, while the *helloWorld* application introduces the application, *Client*, and info objects, it's not very useful.

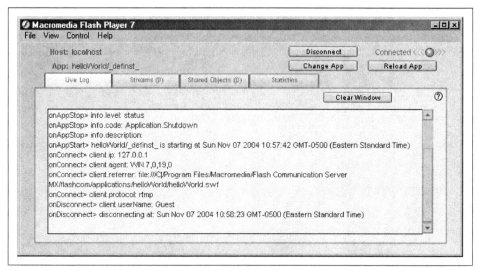

*Figure 4-6. The App Inspector after a client connects to and disconnects from helloWorld/_definst_*

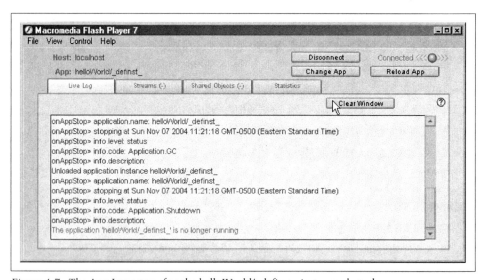

Figure 4-7. The App Inspector after the helloWorld/_definst_ instance shuts down

Although not a full-featured implementation, Example 4-3 is a bit more realistic *main.asc* script in that it shows many of the methods already discussed working in a more typical manner. The code in Example 4-3 demonstrates:

- Accepting or rejecting client connections based on a username and password
- Adding properties and methods to the *Client* object more simply, by adding an object property instead of individual properties and methods

- Limiting guest clients but not other types of clients when a maximum number of users is reached
- Using the server-side *setInterval( )* function to periodically update information about connected clients

The code listed in Example 4-3 is not commented to save space, but the version on the web site is. Take a moment to read through the code. It is described immediately after the listing.

Example 4-3. A more realistic main.asc

```
users = { Brian: {password: "secretPassword1", role: "author"},
         Robert: {password: "secretPassword2", role: "author"},
         Justin: {password: "secretPassword3", role: "author"},
           Joey: {password: "secretPassword4", role: "author"},
          Peldi: {password: "secretPassword5", role: "author"},
          Guest: {password: "Guest",           role: "guest"}
};
access = {author: {readAccess: "/", writeAccess: "/"},
          guest: {readAccess: "/public", writeAccess: ""}
};
MAXCONNECTIONS = 5;

function User (client, userName, role) {
  this.client = client;
  this.userName = userName;
  this.role = role;
  this.connectTime = new Date().getTime( );
}

User.prototype.getTimeConnected = function ( ) {
  var now = new Date().getTime( );
  return (now - this.connectTime)/1000; // seconds
};

User.prototype.getPingTime = function ( ) {
  var client = this.client;
  if (client.ping( )) {
    return client.getStats( ).ping_rtt / 2;
  }
  else{
    return "Client is not connected."
  }
};

User.prototype.getConnectionInfo = function ( ) {
  return " IP: "                 + this.client.ip +
         ", user name: "         + this.userName +
         ", connection time: " + this.getTimeConnected( ) +
         ", ping time: "         + this.getPingTime( );
};
```

Example 4-3. A more realistic main.asc (continued)

```
function listCurrentUsers ( ) {
  trace("-------------- Current Users --------------");
  var i, user;
  var total = application.clients.length;
  trace("There are " + total + " current users.");
  for (i = 0; i < total; i++) {
    user = application.clients[i].user;
    trace(user.getConnectionInfo( ));
  }
  trace("-------------------------------------------");
}

application.onAppStart = function ( ) {
  trace(application.name + " is starting at " + new Date( ));
  setInterval(listCurrentUsers, 60000);
};

application.onConnect = function (client, userName, password) {
  trace("Connection attempt from IP: " + client.ip + " userName: " + userName);
  var user = users[userName];
  if (!user || !password || user.password != password) {
    application.rejectConnection(client, {msg: "Invalid user name or password."});
    return;
  }
  if (application.clients.length >= MAXCONNECTIONS && user.role == "guest") {
    application.rejectConnection(client, {msg: "Chat is already full."});
    return;
  }
  client.user = new User(client, userName, user.role);
  client.writeAccess = access[user.role].writeAccess;
  client.readAccess  = access[user.role].readAccess;
  application.acceptConnection(client);
  trace("Connection accepted at " + new Date( ));
};

application.onDisconnect = function (client) {
  trace(client.user.userName + " is disconnecting at: " + new Date( ));
  trace(client.user.userName + " was connected for " +
  client.user.getTimeConnected( ) + " seconds.");
};

application.onAppStop = function ( ) {
  trace(application.name + " is stopping at " + new Date( ));
};
```

The following sections examine the major functionality in the code example.

Authenticating and Customizing Clients

Clients that connect to an application instance can be authenticated in a number of
ways. Chapter 11 provides an example of authenticating users using Flash Remoting

and ColdFusion; Chapter 18 describes a number of other approaches and their strengths and weaknesses.

Example 4-3 uses a simplistic approach of providing a hardcoded users object, an associative array of objects. The objects it contains can be accessed using property names like Brian, Robert, and Justin. The objects contain password and role properties for each user. For example users.Brian contains an object with Brian's password and role. Accessing Brian's password in the users object could be done using dot notation or using the square bracket operator. In Example 4-3's *onConnect( )* method, an object is retrieved from the users object this way:

```
var user = users[userName];
```

If userName contains a string that matches a property name in the users object, the user variable is assigned an object reference, and it will have a password and role property. For example, if userName is "Brian", user.password will be secretPassword1. If userName does not contain a property name that exists in users, the value of user will be undefined. All of this is taken into account in this *if* statement:

```
if (!user || !password || user.password != password) {
  application.rejectConnection(client, {msg: "Invalid user name or password."});
  return;
}
```

Each part of the condition is necessary to prevent errors and validate the user. For example, if no user were found, the user variable does not contain an object reference and will evaluate to false in the Boolean expression. In that case, the client connection will be rejected. If the user passed in an empty or undefined password string, in the Server-Side ActionScript, password will evaluate to false and again the client will be rejected. Assuming user is an object and password is a non-empty string, the user.password property can be safely accessed and compared to the password the client provided.

 Be sure that a variable contains an object before attempting to access any of its properties. Otherwise, a type error will occur on the server, and execution of the script will stop until the instance's script is allocated another thread by FlashCom when an event handler or other callback function must be called. See "try/catch/finally Statements" earlier in this chapter for another way to avoid errors halting script execution.

If the user is authenticated, the client object can be customized to store information about the user, control access to resources, and be extended with additional methods. A good way to package related information and methods together is to add an object as a new property of the client object:

```
client.user = new User(client, userName, user.role);
```

The *User* constructor can also be used to initialize the client further without cluttering the *onConnect( )* method too much. In Example 4-3, the *User* constructor also gets the connection time and stores it in the user object along with userName, role, and a copy of the client reference.

Read and write access to shared objects and streams is controlled by looking up the readAccess and writeAccess properties of objects in the access object:

```
client.writeAccess = access[user.role].writeAccess;
client.readAccess  = access[user.role].readAccess;
```

For example, if the user.role property is "guest", the previous statements will have this effect:

```
client.writeAccess = "";
client.readAccess  = "/public";
```

The empty string means that the client cannot write to or create any shared objects or publish any streams to this instance. However, the client can read data and play streams in the *public* directory or any of its subdirectories. If the user.role were "author", the statements would have this effect:

```
client.writeAccess = "/";
client.readAccess  = "/";
```

The "/" string indicates that the client has access to any resource.

Using the Client.prototype object

In Example 4-3, every client object is given a user object property before its connection is accepted. That way, every client will contain common information about each user such as his username and will contain common methods such as *user.getConnectionInfo( )*. In some application designs, where a common object is not added to each client, the most efficient way to add common methods to every object is to attach them to Client.prototype. Example 4-4 shows part of a script that uses the prototype object to make available a method for all client objects.

Example 4-4. Using the Client.prototype object to extend all clients

```
Client.prototype.getTimeConnected = function ( ) {
  var now = new Date().getTime( );
  return (now - this.connectTime)/1000; // seconds
};

application.onConnect = function (client, userName, password) {
  client.connectTime = new Date().getTime( );
  application.acceptConnection(client);
};

application.onDisconnect = function (client) {
  trace("Client connected for: " + client.getTimeConnected( ));
};
```

The *Client* class cannot be subclassed because the *Client* constructor is never called directly in a script. Whenever it is necessary to significantly extend the *Client* class, you should use composition. Adding the user object to each client and then delegating work, such as getting the client's connection information, to the user object is one example of composition. Other objects can also be added in order to take on other responsibilities on behalf of the client. For detailed discussions on attaching methods to a class's prototype, see *ActionScript for Flash MX: The Definitive Guide*. For thorough discussions of composition versus inheritance, see *Essential ActionScript 2.0*.

Limiting the Number of Client Connections

The number of currently accepted client connections is always available via the length property of the application.clients array. Restricting the number of clients that can connect at any one time is a simple matter of checking the length property and rejecting clients when it reaches a certain size. In some applications, it may be necessary to allow unlimited connections from users of one type and restrict connections of another type. In Example 4-3, guest connections are not accepted when the number of accepted clients reaches a certain point:

```
if (application.clients.length >= MAXCONNECTIONS && user.role == "guest") {
  application.rejectConnection(client, {msg: "Chat is already full."});
  return;
}
```

This example shows how to reject a connection to prevent it from being established. You can use *application.disconnect( )* at any time to disconnect a client that has already been accepted.

Performing Periodic Updates with setInterval( )

You'll often want to perform some action periodically. On the client side, this may be achieved in several ways, such as using timelines or *enterFrame* events. However, neither of these is available on the server. In server-side code, you can use *setInterval( )* to call a function or method after a certain amount of time. The function or method can be called once or many times at regular intervals. In the *onAppStart( )* method in Example 4-3, *setInterval( )*, is called and passed a reference to the *listCurrentUsers( )* function:

```
setInterval(listCurrentUsers, 60000);
```

In this example, *listCurrentUsers( )* is called once every minute (60,000 milliseconds). In turn, *listCurrentUsers( )* iterates over the application.clients array and calls each client's *user.getConnectionInfo( )* method. This method uses the properties of the client object, its user object, and *User* class methods to output text about the client. See Macromedia's Server-Side Communication ActionScript Dictionary (available in

PDF format from the URL cited earlier and also in LiveDocs format from *http://livedocs.macromedia.com/flashcom/mx2004*) for a listing of all the properties and methods of the *Client* class.

Various *Client* properties can be output to illustrate their values. The *ping( )* and *get-Stats( )* methods of the *Client* class do more than provide static information about the client. Calling *ping( )* immediately sends a test message that makes the round-trip from the server to the Flash client and back again. The message may take some time to return, so the *ping( )* method returns true if the previous ping message was returned by the client (or the server believes the client is still connected) and false if the client was not connected:

```
if (client.ping()) {
  return client.getStats().ping_rtt / 2;
}
else {
  return "Client is not connected."
}
```

If *ping( )* returns true, calling the *getStats( )* method returns an information object whose ping_rtt property contains the round-trip time in milliseconds from the last available *ping( )* call. The *ping( )* method should be used with caution because it sends each ping message at the highest available priority—potentially delaying other RTMP messages. When *ping( )* is used to determine network latency, it should not be called too frequently. As a guideline, Macromedia's ConnectionLight component's default ping interval is 2 seconds.

Instance-to-Instance Communications

The *NetConnection* class is available to server-side scripts. Analogous to the *NetConnection* class available to client-side scripts, it can be used to establish a network connection between instances on a single server or between instances on separate FlashCom Servers. When one instance attempts to connect to another, it creates and uses a *NetConnection* object in an almost identical manner to the way client-side ActionScript does. An instance that attempts to connect to another instance is treated as a client by the second instance. The instance that receives another instance's connection request will be passed a *Client* object in its *application.onConnect( )* method. In this case, the *Client* object represents the first server-side Flash-Com instance rather than a client-side Flash movie.

While an instance can request or close a connection to another instance at any time, the connection is typically made when the instance first starts and closed when the instance is about to be disposed. For example, a chat room instance may connect to a lobby instance in order to let the lobby know how many users are in the room and how active they are. This SSAS code example illustrates a chat room application connecting to a lobby on startup and disconnecting from the lobby on shutdown:

```
NetConnection.prototype.onStatus = function (info) {
  trace("NetConnection.onStatus> info.code: " + info.code);
  if (info.code == "NetConnection.Connect.Success") {
    // Initialize remote shared objects here.
  }
  else if (!this.isConnected) {
    // Handle close and other connection problems here.
  }
  if (info.code == "NetConnection.Call.Failed") {
    // Handle failed remote method calls here.
  }
};

application.onAppStart = function () {
  trace(application.name + " is starting at " + new Date());
  lobby_nc = new NetConnection();
  lobby_nc.connect("rtmp://localhost/chapter4/lobby", "Room", "secretPassword6");
};

application.onAppStop = function () {
  if (lobby_nc.isConnected) {
    lobby_nc.close();
  }
  trace(application.name + " is stopping at " + new Date());
};
```

The only difference between this server-side code and the client-side code you might find in a Flash movie is that a relative URI cannot be used (there must be a hostname) and HTTP tunneling is not available. The connecting instance is represented by the *Client* object passed into the receiving instance's *onConnect( )* method. If a username and password system is being used, the connection can be accepted or rejected based on those credentials.

On the receiving end of the connection attempt, no special code is required to handle connection requests from other instances. However, sometimes it is useful to distinguish whether the connection request originated from a FlashCom application instance or a Flash movie. One way to differentiate is to check the ip property of the incoming client object. If the IP address is 127.0.0.1, then the connection is from the same server. However, if a poorly configured proxy server is running on the same host, all clients may appear to be from 127.0.0.1. Similarly, if connections are expected from another FlashCom Server, the IP address of the remote server can be checked for. There are other ways to distinguish between client types:

* Pass different information in the optional parameters of the *connect( )* method.
* Check the client.agent property for a value such as "FlashCom/1.5.2".
* Check the client.referrer property for a value such as "rtmp://_defaultVHost_: 1935/chapter4/room".

Regardless of the approach chosen, an additional authentication step should be used. The short code snippet that follows can be placed in an *onConnect( )* method to handle instance connections before attempting to handle Flash movie connections.

The code assumes that a unique `userName` is provided by the connecting instance so that its `client` object can be kept in an object named `roomList`. The unique name could be the instance name of the room:

```
if (client.ip = "127.0.0.1" && client.agent.indexOf("FlashCom") == 0) {
  if (password == "room54780561Password") {
    roomList[userName] = client;
    return true;   // Accept the connection
  }
  else{
    trace("Invalid room connection attempt.");
    return false; // Reject the connection
  }
}
```

For variety, connections are accepted or rejected by returning `true` or `false` from within the *onConnect( )* method in the preceding example.

Now that you have a better understanding of how to manage connections, let's examine some of the mechanics of locating code and configuration files.

Script Filenames and Locations in Detail

An application comprises one or more SSAS source code files (plain text files). Let's look closer at the file organization for a server-side application.

The main Application Script File

When an application instance starts, it looks for a main script file to run. The file can have one of two names and can be stored in one of two locations. The file can be named *main* with either an *.asc* or *.js* extension (*main.asc* or *main.js*) or it can have the same name as the application's home directory with either extension. For example, if the application's home directory name is *courseChat* and if no *main.asc* file exists, the *courseChat.asc* file will be loaded. The main file can be stored in one of two places: in the application's home directory or in a subdirectory of the home directory named *scripts*. Files with the *.asc* extension take precedence over *.js* files.

Using load( ) to Include Other Script Files

Once the main file has been loaded and any global code (code defined outside event handlers such as *onConnect( )*) within it is executed, other source files can be loaded. The *load( )* method accepts the relative path of the external file to be compiled and executed. For example, a *main.asc* file in an application's home directory could load a file in the *scripts* directory this way:

```
load("scripts/myFile.asc");
```

The relative paths cannot include the "`..`" characters to indicate moving up a level in the directory tree, so there has to be another way to load source files that are common to more than one application. The FlashCom installer creates a directory named *scriptlib* where the common script files provided by Macromedia are placed. The *scriptlib* directory contains the files required for Flash Remoting and the communication components. If a file is not found in a path relative to the file that loads it, the server will attempt to find it in a relative path starting from the *scriptlib* directory. For example, when a main file loads the communication components, it calls:

```
load("components.asc");
```

Files can also be placed in subdirectories of the *scriptlib* directory. For example, the *.asc* source files for the individual communication components are found in the *scriptlib/components* directory.

The location of the *scriptlib* directory can be changed using the `<ScriptLibPath>` tag of an *Application.xml* file, and additional paths to other script library directories can be added to it. For example, an *Application.xml* file can be placed in the home directory of an application. The default tag might look something like this depending on where the server was installed:

```
<ScriptLibPath>
C:\Program Files\Macromedia\Flash Communication Server MX\scriptlib
</ScriptLibPath>
```

It could be modified to add a second path, separated from the first one with a semicolon (note that line breaks have been introduced for readability):

```
<ScriptLibPath>
C:\Program Files\Macromedia\Flash Communication Server MX\scriptlib;
C:\Program Files\Macromedia\Flash Communication Server MX\securitylib
</ScriptLibPath>
```

Appending a path in the `<ScriptLibPath>` tag has a number of advantages. You can build your own common library of scripts without placing anything in the *scriptlib* directory and possibly editing or overwriting the files supplied by Macromedia. By placing individual *Application.xml* files in the home directory of individual applications, you can make libraries available for only those applications. If you want to add a library for all applications within a virtual host, add a path in the *Application.xml* file in the virtual host directory.

Figure 4-8 shows the location of a number of source files for an application named *courseChat*. The *securitylib* directory was created to hold custom scripts that could be used by any application, and the *scripts* folder was created to hold scripts just for the *courseChat* application.

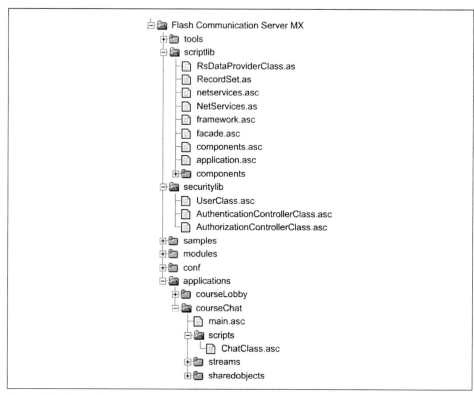

Figure 4-8. Script file locations

The first two lines of the following SSAS source code load in the files required to use Flash Remoting and the communication components. The remaining statements load in source files from the *scripts* and *securitylib* directories (the latter is configured via the <ScriptLibPath> tag in the *Application.xml* file):

```
// Load files from the scriptlib directory.
load("netservices.asc"); // Load the files required for Remoting
load("components.asc");  // Load the component framework and components

// Load a file from the scripts directory.
load("scripts/ChatClass.asc");

// Load files from the securitylib directory.
load("UserClass.asc");
load("AuthenticationControllerClass.asc");
load("AuthorizationControllerClass.asc");
```

A *scripts* directory is not required. All the source files can be kept in the home directory of the application.

Dynamically loading script files

The fact that a file is compiled and executed before other files are loaded into it leads to an interesting feature. It is possible to write global code in a file that decides what files to load based on the application's instance name or other factors. For example, suppose you want the _definst_ instance to behave as a lobby while every other instance of the application behaves as a room. The entire *main.asc* file could contain just a single *if* statement like this:

```
if (application.name == "courseChat/_definst_") {
  load("lobby.asc");
}
else {
  load("room.asc")
}
```

The *lobby.asc* and *room.asc* files would then each define a different set of application methods and therefore make the _definst_ instance behave differently from all the others.

Testing and Debugging Server-Side Script Files

Currently, no debugger that provides a way to examine data directly or step through code is available for testing and debugging server-side scripts. The primary way to get a view into the state of an executing script is to use *trace( )* statements to output information. Trace output can be examined in different ways.

The NetConnection Debugger, discussed in "Using the NetConnection Debugger" in Chapter 3, will list *trace( )* events under its Events tab and the output under its Details tab. This is most useful when you are working on a Flash movie and want to see server-side output as you make changes to the movie and have it connect and reconnect to FlashCom.

To test and fix server-side code, the primary tool for seeing trace output is the App Inspector movie (*app_inspector.swf*). Whenever a change is made in a server-side script, the instance must be reloaded so that the source files that contain the updated code are recompiled and executed. The App Inspector can be used to load, reload, and unload an application instance at any time. You can also easily select any running instance from a list and view connection and bandwidth statistics, stream and shared object status, and a live log that includes system messages and trace output.

Unlike other server development environments, trace output cannot easily be piped to a text file for later examination. However, FlashCom does provide a facility to record trace output in a recorded stream file. To enable application logging

(Macromedia's term for recording trace output), an *Application.xml* file must contain the XML tag and value as follows:

```
<RecordAppLog>true</RecordAppLog>
```

Logging can create very large files over time, so it is often best to not make this adjustment in an *Application.xml* file for an entire virtual host. An *Application.xml* file can be placed in the home directory of the application that is being developed. When logging is turned on, a stream file with an *.flv* extension and named after the instance will be saved within a folder named after the application within the *applications/admin/streams/logs/application* directory. The file can be read using the Flash Communication Server Log reader available as a separate download from Macromedia. Please see Technote 16464:

> http://www.macromedia.com/support/flashcom/ts/documents/flashcom_logging. htm

There are other alternatives for generating log output and log files. Flash Remoting can be used to send data to an application server where it can be stored in a database or written to a text file. When Remoting is used, a custom logging function must be called in place of *trace( )*. Similarly, custom Flash clients can receive data via remote method calls where they can sort and analyze data before presenting it. Remoting is described in Chapter 11, and remote method calls are covered in Chapter 9. An application-level logging system is discussed in Chapter 12.

Organizing Test Scripts

During program development and testing, *load( )* can be used to make testing of many different SSAS files a little easier to manage. If you had to create a new application home directory for every test script, you would end up with many different test folders. One trick is to use different instances to test different scripts within a single application home directory. One way to do this is to create a *main.asc* file with this one statement in it:

```
load(application.name.split('/').pop( ) + ".asc");
```

Then you can create as many test files as you like in the application's home directory. To run a test file, connect to an instance of your application with the same name. Suppose, for example, you are working on an application named *courseChat* and want to run different versions of the application's main file. You may have several main files named *mainVersion1.asc*, *mainVersion2.asc*, and so on. You can run any one of these files by using the App Inspector to load the right instance name, such as courseChat/mainVersion2, and then reload it to check the output. If client interaction is required, a test client can be set up to connect to *rtmp:/courseChat/ mainVersion2*.

Using the *main.asc* file to load other files in the application's home directory works well for testing different main file versions. When a main file is ready to go into production, it can be moved into a production directory and renamed *main.asc*.

Testing individual objects and functions is also an important part of developing applications, and you may not want to clutter the application home directory with many test script files. As an alternative, a *main.asc* file can be created that contains this short script:

```
this.tempPath = application.name.split("/");
this.tempPath.shift();
load(this.tempPath.join("/") + ".asc");
//delete this.tempPath;  // Uncomment this if you want to delete tempPath.
```

The script will load files based on the full instance name. For example, if a client connects to an instance named *rtmp:/courseChat/testBed/userClassTests*, then the *userClassTests.asc* file in the *testBed* directory will be loaded and executed.

Designing Communication Applications

Designing a communication application usually means more than designing a Flash-Com application and its instances. A communication application may involve more than one FlashCom application and many application instances. A simple example is a FlashCom lobby application and a chat room application working together to provide a chat system. Users may visit different lobby instances of the lobby application before connecting to instances of the chat room application.

Applications and application instances are the core resources FlashCom provides to partition server resources and organize communication applications. Users should be grouped into separate instances in order to maintain system performance and allocate resources such as shared objects and streams.

Designing communication applications requires planning what FlashCom applications and instances will be available, what services an application instance should provide, and what resources such as streams, shared objects, and database access are needed to provide the service. The design often includes defining how instances will be controlled and created—sometimes by other instances—and how clients will move between them.

Conclusion

This chapter introduced the application object and *Client* class and how to work with them. You'll use these important objects in all your FlashCom applications. Chapters 5 and 8 describe how to work with other SSAS classes such as *SharedObject* and *Stream* to communicate between objects and transfer data. The focus of the rest of this book shifts gradually from designing individual FlashCom applications to designing communication applications that can involve multiple applications.

Audio, Video, and Data Streams

Part II focuses on the media and data that can be transmitted to and from FlashCom applications and their clients.

- Chapter 5, *Managing Streams*
- Chapter 6, *Microphone and Camera*
- Chapter 7, *Media Preparation and Delivery*

Managing Streams

Streams are a way to organize and manage the flow of data over a network connection. Audio, video, and ActionScript data can all be carried within a stream. Data within each stream flows in only one direction, but streams can carry more than one type of data, and multiple streams can be created within a single network connection. In many applications, a stream will carry audio and video from a Flash movie to the FlashCom Server while other streams will carry audio and video from the server to the movie. Within a Flash movie the *NetStream* class is used to create and manage streams, while on the server the *Stream* class is used.

Audio and video data is transferred over a network connection by attaching it to a stream. In FlashCom 1.5.2, a stream can contain only one audio and one video channel. A movie that creates a stream within a network connection and uses the stream to send data is *publishing* data, while a movie that creates a stream to receive data is a *subscriber*. A movie must create separate streams within a connection in order to both publish and subscribe at the same time. Streams can also carry more traditional data such as strings, numbers, and objects and are FlashCom's primary method for storing very large quantities of any kind of data on the server. FlashCom streams can be recorded and saved to disk by FlashCom in Flash Video format (FLV) files.

The client-side *NetStream* class can be used to publish or subscribe to a stream. The *Stream* class is used on the server to manage or republish streams that are being published by a remote movie or that have already been stored as FLV or MP3 files on a server.

Flash movies must use both a *NetConnection* and a *NetStream* object to publish a stream to a specific application instance. Within the instance, the stream is associated with a unique relative URI that identifies the stream, which other movies can use to subscribe. In this way, the application instance acts like a hub that provides a stream namespace. A stream is published to it so that it can be subscribed to by any movie connected to the instance. Figure 5-1 shows two Flash movies connected to an instance of the *courseChat* application named algebra101. Each movie has created two separate *NetStream* objects named out_ns and in_ns. Each movie is publishing a live stream with a unique URI and has subscribed to (or is playing) another stream. A live stream is a stream that is currently being published by a movie. As the stream data arrives at the server, it is immediately sent to any movie that subscribes to it. The location of each stream's relative URI is shown within the server in Figure 5-1, and the arrows indicate the direction data is flowing within each stream.

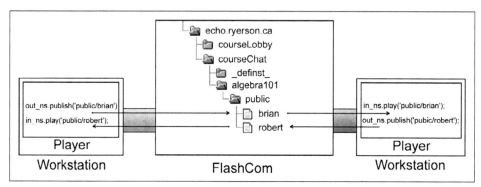

Figure 5-1. Illustration of the use of the publish( ) and play( ) methods and the stream namespace within an application instance

It is also possible to share live streams between application instances. Just as one Flash movie can connect to an application instance in order to subscribe to a stream, an application instance can also connect to another instance in order to subscribe to that instance's streams. In turn, the subscribing instances can make streams available to movies that connect to them. FlashCom instances subscribe using the server-side *Stream* class, as opposed to Flash movies, which subscribe using the client-side *NetStream* class.

Similarly, streams can be shared between FlashCom Servers by having an instance on one server connect to an instance on another and then subscribe to the other's streams, as shown in Figure 5-2. The server-side *Stream* class cannot be used to publish video or audio from sources connected to the server. Live video and audio capture must be done within a Flash movie and published to the server using the *NetStream* class. However, the server-side *Stream* class can be used to manage streams published by movies, create server-side playlists, and provide fine-grained access control to streams.

It is possible to subscribe to two types of streams: *live* and *recorded*. Both exist in the same namespace within an application instance. When movies subscribe to a live stream, each subscriber is sent its own copy of the stream data as it arrives from the publisher. When movies subscribe to a recorded stream, each movie can begin playing the stream from the beginning or randomly access different parts of the recorded stream at any time. When a movie publishes a stream, it can also be recorded on the server. As a stream is being recorded, it can be subscribed to as a live stream—in which case each movie is sent a copy of the same stream data as it arrives from the

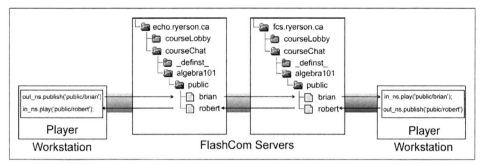

Figure 5-2. Chaining a stream between application instances running on separate FlashCom Servers

publisher at the server. A stream that is being recorded can also be played as a recorded stream—in which case movies will receive copies of what is on disk and will not be sent the live data as it arrives at the server. Streams can also be live-only—in which case they are not recorded.

A Simple Publisher/Subscriber Example

Example 5-1 is a somewhat oversimplified but complete example script that shows the essential steps in publishing one live stream and subscribing to a second live stream. The example shows how video, audio, and ActionScript data can be sent via a published stream and received by subscribing to another stream.

Example 5-1. A very basic two-way messaging client

```
// writeln() replaces trace() and writes messages into the trace_txt field.
function writeln (msg) {
  trace_txt.text += msg + "\n";
  trace_txt.scroll = trace_txt.maxscroll;
}

// onStatus() sets up the streams and buttons when a connection is
// established or lost.
NetConnection.prototype.onStatus = function (info) {
  writeln("Level: " + info.level + ", code: " + info.code);
  if (info.code == "NetConnection.Connect.Success") {
    out_ns = new NetStream(this);
    out_ns.attachAudio(Microphone.get());
    out_ns.attachVideo(Camera.get());
    in_ns = new NetStream(this);
    in_ns.showMessage = function (msg) {
      writeln(msg);
    };
    // remote_video is the instance name of an embedded video object.
    remote_video.attachVideo(in_ns);
    in_ns.play("public/" + remoteUserName);
    connect_pb.setLabel("Disconnect");
```

Example 5-1. A very basic two-way messaging client (continued)

```
      send_pb.setEnabled(true);
    }
    else if (!this.isConnected) {
      if (out_ns) out_ns.close( );
      if (in_ns) in_ns.close( );
      connect_pb.setLabel("Connect");
      send_pb.setEnabled(false);
    }
};

NetStream.prototype.onStatus = function (info) {
  for (var p in info) {
    writeln("info." + p + ": " + info[p]);
  }
};

// doSend( ) is called when the send_pb is clicked.
function doSend (msg) {
  out_ns.send("showMessage", input_txt.text);
  input_txt.text = "";
}

/* doConnect( ) is called when the connect_pb is clicked.
 * It stores the text in the userName_txt and remoteUserName_txt
 * fields in global variables for later use if a connection is
 * attempted. See the onStatus( ) method.
 */
function doConnect (pb) {
  if (pb.getLabel( ) == "Connect") {
    userName = userName_txt.text;
    remoteUserName = remoteUserName_txt.text;
    nc.connect("rtmp:/courseChat/algebra101", userName);
  }
  else {
    nc.close( );
  }
}

function doSendStream (pb) {
  if (pb.getLabel( ) == "Send Stream" && nc.isConnected) {
    pb.setLabel("Stop Stream");
    out_ns.publish("public/" + userName);
  }
  else {
    pb.setLabel("Send Stream");
    out_ns.publish(false);
  }
}

send_pb.setEnabled(false);
nc = new NetConnection( );
```

To create a *NetStream* object within a network connection, the *NetConnection* object must already exist and a connection attempt to FlashCom must have already been made by calling the *connect( )* method. In Example 5-1, a new *NetConnection* object is created and then the user must enter both his username and the name of the remote user he wants to talk to. Then he must click the Connect button. When the connection is established, the *NetConnection.onStatus( )* handler is called and two *NetStream* objects are created and initialized to send or receive data. The *NetStream* object that is designed to receive data tries to subscribe to a stream immediately, but the outgoing stream does not attempt to send anything until the user clicks the Send Stream button.

Publishing a Live Stream

In order to publish a stream, a *NetStream* object has to be created. In Example 5-1, the out_ns object is created within a connection by passing it a *NetConnection* object. The keyword this, which represents the current *NetConnection* object, is passed in this example because the *NetStream* object is created within the *NetConnection.onStatus( )* method:

```
out_ns = new NetStream(this);
```

This statement could also have been written using the nc variable defined in the last line of Example 5-1:

```
out_ns = new NetStream(nc);
```

Once the *NetStream* object out_ns exists, audio and video data sources can be attached to it:

```
out_ns.attachAudio(Microphone.get());
out_ns.attachVideo(Camera.get());
```

The *Microphone* and *Camera* classes are available only within Flash movies (not on the server) and provide a number of static methods, such as *get( )*. In the example, *Microphone.get( )* returns the *Microphone* object last selected in the movie's Player Settings dialog box. Passing the *Microphone* object to the *out_ns.attachAudio( )* method makes the sound data captured from the microphone available to the out_ns stream. The *Camera.get( )* method returns a *Camera* object and works in the same way. Attaching the *Camera* object to the stream using the *NetStream.attachVideo( )* method makes compressed video data from the camera available to the stream. Although it isn't a best practice to pass the return value from the *get( )* methods directly to the *attachAudio( )* and *attachVideo( )* methods, we use this approach for demonstration purposes. Chapter 6 considers other alternatives.

The *Camera* and *Microphone* classes provide other methods for managing video and audio sources and events, and are described in detail in Chapter 6.

Before actually publishing the stream, it is a good idea to set up an *onStatus( )* event handler that will receive notifications when stream events occur. In Example 5-1, a default *onStatus( )* handler is attached to `NetStream.prototype`, making it available to all *NetStream* instances. Any *NetStream* object that is not assigned its own handler will use the one assigned to the prototype. Defining an *onStatus( )* method on the `NetStream.prototype` is convenient for testing and exploration but is not normally used in production code. In Example 5-1, the *onStatus( )* handler simply displays the information object's properties in the `trace_txt` field.

The outbound stream is published to the server using *NetStream.publish( )* after the user clicks the Send Stream button:

```
out_ns.publish("public/" + userName);
```

The required parameter is the relative URI that identifies the stream. In this example, the stream name will depend on the username provided. If the username is "brian," the URI will be *public/brian*, which becomes the address of the published stream within the application instance to which the movie is connected. If another movie is already publishing a stream with the URI *public/brian*, the attempt to publish the stream will fail and a "NetStream.Publish.BadName" error message will be returned in the `info.code` property passed to *onStatus( )*. The directory name *public* has no special meaning in this example and was used to emphasize that stream names are relative URIs.

The *publish( )* method has a second, optional parameter (discussed later) that determines whether the stream is recorded. If the parameter is omitted, the stream is not recorded and is available as a live stream only.

Once the stream has been published, ActionScript data can also be sent on the stream at any time using the *NetStream.send( )* method. In Example 5-1, *NetStream.send( )* is used to create a simple text messaging feature. When one user enters some text in the `input_txt` field and clicks the Send button, the other user will see the text appear in her `trace_txt` field.

ActionScript data that is sent on a stream is always sent as part of a request to invoke a method. In Example 5-1, when one user enters text in the `input_txt` field and clicks the Send button, the *doSend( )* function is executed, which in turn calls *out_ns.send( )* to send the text data. The *NetStream.send( )* method is always passed the name of a remote method to call as the first parameter, as follows:

```
out_ns.send("showMessage", input_txt.text);
```

In Example 5-1, the remote method *showMessage( )* will be called on any *NetStream* objects subscribed to the stream and will receive the text the user typed into the `input_txt` field.

The *showMessage( )* method should be defined on the subscribing *NetStream*, for example:

```
in_ns.showMessage = function (msg) {
  writeln(msg);
};
```

Even if the publishing stream defines a *showMessage( )* method, it will not receive any remote method calls it sends on the stream. Only subscribed streams receive remote method calls.

In summary, the steps to publish a live stream are:

1. Create a *NetConnection* object:

   ```
   nc = new NetConnection( );
   ```

2. Use *NetConnection.connect( )* to attempt to connect to an application instance. The *connect( )* method must be called before attempting to create a *NetStream* object:

   ```
   nc.connect("rtmp:/courseChat/algebra101", userName);
   ```

3. Create a new *NetStream* object on a *NetConnection* object by passing the latter as a parameter to the *NetStream* constructor:

   ```
   out_ns = new NetStream(nc);
   ```

4. Attach any audio or video sources to the stream using *attachAudio( )* and *attach-Video( )* methods of the *NetStream* class:

   ```
   out_ns.attachAudio(Microphone.get( ));
   out_ns.attachVideo(Camera.get( ));
   ```

5. Make sure the *NetStream* object has an *onStatus( )* handler, either by defining one on NetStream.prototype or by creating a method for the individual *NetStream* object. This step is not required but is recommended.

6. Publish the stream using *NetStream.publish( )*:

   ```
   out_ns.publish("public/" + userName);
   ```

Subscribing to a Live Stream

Subscribing to a stream is a little different than publishing one. To publish audio and video in a stream, we attached a *Camera* and a *Microphone* object to the stream. However, to play a stream and display it in the Flash client, we have to attach the stream to a Video object. We also have the option of attaching the stream to a movie clip to control the stream's audio. We always start by creating a *NetStream* object within a *NetConnection* and then attach objects that display video or control audio. Methods can also be added to the stream to receive remote method calls. Here, we create a new *NetStream*, attach it to a Video object, and play the stream. Text messages received by the stream will be displayed using the *showMessage( )* method of the *NetStream* object:

```
in_ns = new NetStream(nc);
remote_video.attachVideo(in_ns);
in_ns.showMessage = function (msg) {
  writeln(msg);
};
in_ns.play("public/" + remoteUserName);
```

In Example 5-1, the in_ns stream is attached to an embedded Video object named remote_video. Embedded Video objects are similar to movie clips. They can be placed on the Stage to display video and have some of the same properties as movie clips. For example, you can manipulate the height and width of an embedded Video object by setting its _height and _width properties. To place a Video object on the Stage, use the Library panel's pop-up Options menu and choose New Video. Once an embedded Video object is available in the Library, it can be dragged to the Stage and resized, or it can be placed within a movie clip. Once on stage, a Video object must be given an instance name using the Properties panel in order to refer to it via ActionScript.

By default, audio arriving within a stream is automatically forwarded to a sound device on the local computer so that it can be heard. It is not necessary to attach a stream to anything in order to hear audio. However, to control audio volume, the stream can be attached to a movie clip and then a *Sound* object can be created on the movie clip to control the volume of the audio. For example, to set the volume to 50, an existing movie clip instance named stream_mc could be utilized this way:

```
stream_mc.attachAudio(in_ns);
soundControl = new Sound(stream_mc);
soundControl.setVolume(50);
```

 Although the *Sound* object did not work properly in the Flash Player 6 initially distributed with the Flash MX development environment, later versions properly control stream volume. The Player used in the authoring environment is not automatically upgraded when the browser Player plugin is upgraded. To upgrade the Player used in the Flash development environment, visit:

http://www.macromedia.com/support/flash/downloads.html

In summary, *NetStream* objects have *attachVideo( )* and *attachAudio( )* methods that are used to attach video and audio sources when publishing a stream. *Video* objects have an *attachVideo( )* method that is used to attach video arriving within a stream to an embedded *Video* object. Similarly, the *MovieClip* class has an *attachAudio( )* method that attaches incoming audio to a clip.

If a publishing stream calls a remote method, that method must exist on the subscribing stream or nothing will happen. In Example 5-1, the *NetStream.send( )* method is called and passed the remote method named *showMessage( )* and a text string to pass into it. Defining a *showMessage( )* method on the subscribing stream, as shown earlier, is all that is required to respond to the remote method call.

Once the in_ns stream is ready to receive audio, video, and remote method calls, you can subscribe it to a stream on the server using *NetStream.play( )*:

```
in_ns.play("public/" + remoteUserName);
```

Following through on the stream names used in Figure 5-1, if the `remoteUserName` variable contains the string "robert", then the relative URI of the stream being requested via *play( )* will be *public/robert*. If no stream of that name exists, no error will be returned. Instead, the application will simply return data from a stream of that name if and when one is published.

This short demonstration script can be used by two people to have a video, audio, and text conversation, but it does suffer from some serious limitations. For example, text messages appear only in the subscriber's text field and there is no way for either user to know the other is available and wants to chat. Also, the program should not rely on both users entering both usernames in order to chat. Some additional programming, most often using remote method calls and/or shared objects, is required to overcome these limitations. Keeping track of and managing streams using shared objects was first introduced in the *helloVideo* application in Chapter 1 and is described in detail in Chapter 8.

Stream Names

There is no stream name management system directly available in either client- or Server-Side ActionScript, though some stream management features are available through the server management application programming interface (API) as described in Chapter 10. When a movie connects to an application instance, there is no built-in way for the movie to discover what live streams may be available, what stream names it can use to publish without conflicting with another movie's stream names, and what recorded streams are available for playback. Instead, each application is responsible for managing its own streams. This may sound like a drawback, but FlashCom provides resources that give developers the flexibility to design applications with a wide variety of behaviors. When applications must provide the names of the live streams currently being published, a shared object is often used. As streams are published, the name of each stream is added to the shared object. When a published stream is closed or the publishing movie disconnects, the stream name is removed from the shared object. Collisions between stream names are often avoided by centralizing stream naming within the application instance or by allocating a unique name to each client. For example, a stream name can be based on a user's unique username or ID number. Alternately, a unique stream name, based on some other scheme such as a sequence number, can be requested from the application via a remote method call.

You can run into two related problems when stream names collide. With live streams, if two movies attempt to publish streams with the same URI, the first stream will succeed and the second will fail. Recorded streams add the possibility that streams will be unintentionally overwritten or deleted. Here are a few ways to allocate relative URIs to streams to avoid name conflicts:

- In live video conference and chat systems, use each user's unique username or ID to name the stream that each user publishes. If each user publishes more than one stream, use sequence values appended to the user's name. In some cases, the instance name of a movie clip can be appended to the user's name.

- Use directory names to group streams. For example, each user could record streams to his own directory named after his unique username. You can extend this idea even further by controlling write access to certain directories using a server-side script. For example, if a unique username is assigned to each user, then the code `client.writeAccess = "/" + userName;` will restrict the Flash movie represented by the `client` object from writing to anything unless it is within the user's own directory.

- Use remote method calls to request unique names from the server. See Chapters 8 and 9 on remote method calls and shared objects. Examples include sequence numbers generated on the server and validating user-suggested stream URIs before they are used to make sure only one user can use a URI.

- Append a timestamp or other unique sequence value to a stream name.

Publishing Streams in Detail

The *NetStream.publish( )* method can be used to publish live or recorded streams and to append data onto the end of an already recorded stream. To control how a stream is published, pass the string "live", "record", or "append" as the second parameter. For example, to append onto an already recorded stream:

```
out_ns = new NetStream(nc);
out_ns.publish("private/brian/greeting", "append");
```

When "live" or "record" is used, any previously recorded stream with the same stream URI is deleted. When "append" is used, data is appended onto the end of a preexisting stream. If a recorded stream at the same URI does not already exist, "append" creates the stream as though "record" was passed.

The stream will be saved as an *.flv* file within a subdirectory of the *streams* folder associated with the application instance. For example, assuming a Flash movie is connected to the instance albegra101 of an application named *courseChat* and that the relative URI of a published stream is:

> *private/brian/greeting*

a file named *greeting.flv* will be created within this directory:

> *.../applications/courseChat/streams/algebra101/private/brian*

The full path will vary depending on the server's operating system and on how Flash-Com was installed. See Chapter 4 for more information on resource URIs. In this example, the stream URI can be broken down into two parts. The path information:

private/brian/

and the actual stream name:

greeting

You do not have to create the application's *streams* directory or any of its subdirectories when recording a stream. They are created automatically by the server as needed when the stream is published.

onStatus( ) handlers

During development, it is a good idea to define a simple *onStatus( )* event handler that simply writes out all the properties of the information object it is passed. An easy way to do this is to define a method on the NetStream.prototype object as in Example 5-1. An *onStatus( )* handler defined this way will work for both publishing and subscribing streams. However, publishing and subscribing streams are sent different sets of messages and are generally designed to behave differently, so it is unlikely that a generic *onStatus( )* handler will apply readily to both types of streams. Another way to define an *onStatus( )* handler is to define it as the method of an individual stream:

```
out_ns = new NetStream(nc);
out_ns.onStatus = function (info) {
  if (info.code == "NetStream.Publish.BadName") {
    writeln("Invalid stream name. Please enter a different one.");
  }
};
```

Yet another approach is to create a *NetStream* subclass with an *onStatus( )* handler designed just for publishing or just for subscribing. Creating a *NetStream* subclass is described later in this chapter and is strongly recommended for applications that must always know the exact state of a stream at any given time.

 If no *onStatus( )* handler is defined for a *NetStream* object (or NetStream.prototype), the *onStatus( )* method of the *NetConnection* object to which the stream is attached will be passed any *NetStream* information objects with a level property of "error". If the *NetConnection.onStatus( )* method is not defined either, then the *System.onStatus( )* method, if any, is called.

Attaching and Detaching Audio and Video Sources

When a video or audio source is not needed, it is a good idea to detach it from a stream instead of leaving it to consume bandwidth. For example, during an online seminar, participants may need to see only the seminar leader and the person who is currently speaking. If there are 20 participants in the seminar, there is no point in sending the audio and video data for 20 people to the server. To temporarily detach audio or video data from a stream, pass null to either *NetStream.attachAudio( )* or *NetStream.attachVideo( )*. You can always call these same methods later to attach the sources again. For example:

```
out_ns = new NetStream(nc);
mic = Microphone.get( );
cam = Camera.get( )
out_ns.publish('public/' + userName);

function detachSources ( ) {
  out_ns.attachAudio(null);
  out_ns.attachVideo(null);
}

function attachSources ( ) {
  out_ns.attachAudio(mic);
  out_ns.attachVideo(cam);
}
```

Streams flow in one direction, and each point within a stream corresponds to a unique time measured in seconds. While the stream is being published, the time property of a *NetStream* object can be used to retrieve the number of seconds a stream has been publishing, provided a data source is attached to the stream. Time values are floating-point numbers that can provide values down to the millisecond. For example:

```
var millisecondTime = out_ns.time * 1000;
```

If no data is being sent in a stream, the time property will contain the last time data was sent. When a data source is attached to a publishing stream, the time value will restart at the last time value plus the time elapsed during which no data was sent. So even though the time value may pause when no data is sent, actual stream time always progresses and is reflected by the time property when data is again sent on the stream.

To stop publishing a stream without closing it, pass false to the *publish( )* method in place of the stream URI:

```
out_ns.publish(false);
```

To explicitly close a stream use *NetStream.close( )*:

```
out_ns.close( );
```

Use *publish(false)* when you plan to republish using the same *NetStream* object, and use *close( )* when you are done publishing or to reuse the same *NetStream* object to subscribe to a stream. When either method is called, any audio, video, and Action-Script data that has not been sent already will be lost.

Bandwidth and Performance Problems

Network bandwidth can vary dramatically depending on the type of connection (LAN, DSL, modem) and on the quality of all the network segments between the publishing movie and the FlashCom Server. The bandwidth may also vary significantly during the life of the connection. Each stream travels within a network connection, and multiple publishing and subscribing streams cannot send or receive more data than the connection is capable of carrying at any moment. For example, a connection via modem may allow sending a total of 56 Kbps of data while receiving 56 Kbps of data. Sending a single video stream at 16 KB/s (131 Kbps because there are 8 bits in a byte) will therefore cause a problem. Even worse, receiving three 16 KB/s streams is not possible. Most of the data will have to be dropped to reduce the total from 48 KB/s to 56 Kbps and the arrival of data will have to be delayed. Furthermore, the ideal speed of 56 Kbps is rarely achieved on a dial-up modem. Throughput of 33 Kbps is more realistic. On the other hand, someone with a good DSL connection will have no problems sending one video stream or receiving the same three video streams.

The amount of data that a movie attempts to publish within a stream largely depends on how the video and audio sources attached to the stream are configured. The resolution and frame rate of the video source and sampling rate of the audio source are just some of the adjustments that can be made to control data rates. Using the *Camera* and *Microphone* classes to control the amount of data sent in a stream is described in detail in Chapter 6. Before video data can be carried by the stream, it has to be captured from a device and compressed. The publishing system's CPU may not be able to process all the video data in real time. At high video resolutions, the system may have to drop video frames in order to avoid falling too far behind the video source. Even when the system can capture all the audio and video data, the stream may not have sufficient bandwidth available to it to carry all the data. Sending large amounts of ActionScript data can also adversely impact performance (later, we'll look at ways to minimize the bandwidth required for ActionScript data).

The RTMP protocol runs over a reliable TCP connection, which means that unlike UDP streaming protocols, any lost data packets are resent in order to guarantee they are delivered. When a stream contains more data than can be sent because of bandwidth limitations, data must be either held in a buffer until it can be sent or dropped at the source.

For live streams, when users want to communicate in real time, buffering is not a practical option. Therefore, for live streams, RTMP uses a scheme that does two things:

- Prioritizes data into three classes so that audio receives the highest priority and is therefore delivered as soon as possible. Data is given second priority, and video the lowest priority.

- Decides what data to drop if the client and network cannot keep up. Video data requires more bandwidth and is generally rated as less important than audio to most observers. Video data is therefore dropped before audio. Under extreme circumstances, if dropping video data does not reduce the amount of data to what the network can handle, audio data will also be dropped. ActionScript data is never dropped.

RTMP does not provide on-the-fly adjustments of video compression in order to dynamically adapt to bandwidth limitations. However, the `NetStream.currentFps` property returns the actual video frame rate being published, and the quality settings of the *Camera* object can be adjusted to change the level of video compression or even the video resolution.

As RTMP adapts to the difference between the amount of data it is trying to send and the capacity of the network, video may be delayed more than the audio, causing them to get out of sync. RTMP gives preference to delivering audio because it is important to hear a conversation with as little latency as possible. Audio latency and video synchronization were improved in FlashCom 1.5.

RTMP has to adapt to bandwidth twice during the publishing and playing of a stream. The Flash Player publishing the stream must adapt to the network bandwidth available between the Player and the FlashCom Server. When the server sends the stream on to each subscribing movie, it must also adapt to the bandwidth available to each subscriber. It is important to remember this when designing applications. An incoming high-bandwidth stream may arrive at the server without problems but lose most of its video frames on its way out to viewers. Stream bandwidth therefore must often be optimized for the slowest viewing connection and not for live publishing.

The amount of bandwidth any client is allocated can be capped on the server using *Client.setBandwidthLimit( )*. See "Capping client bandwidth usage" later in this chapter for more details.

Buffering When Publishing

When recording streams, buffering is a good idea to minimize dropped video frames. Instead of dropping frames that cannot be sent immediately, they can be stored in a buffer until they can be sent. If the buffer overflows, video and audio are eventually dropped, but buffering helps to improve quality, especially when video data rates fluctuate depending on changes in the scene being captured. By default, a *NetStream* object being used for publishing has a buffer time of 0 seconds (no buffering is performed). To change it, use *NetStream.setBufferTime( )*. For example, to set the buffer time to 2 seconds:

```
out_ns.setBufferTime(2);
```

During publishing, bufferLength returns the amount of data, in seconds, currently in the buffer. The bufferTime property returns the total buffer time. In practice, the buffer is always larger than the time set via *setBufferTime( )*; this allows the amount of data in the buffer to start to exceed the buffer time without any frames being immediately dropped. When the buffer time is exceeded, *NetStream.onStatus( )* is passed an information object with a code value of "NetStream.Buffer.Full". This provides an opportunity to increase the buffer time, reduce the amount of data being sent into the stream, or stop recording altogether. If the buffer length reaches one and a half times the buffer time, all video messages are dropped. If it reaches two times the buffer time, all audio and video frames are dropped. When a buffer is empty, a "NetStream.Buffer.Empty" message will be sent to the *onStatus( )* handler. See Example 5-2 and Example 5-5 for examples of responding to "NetStream.Buffer" messages.

Snapshots, Stop Motion, and Time-Lapse Video

FlashCom makes it possible to capture a single video frame or snapshot from a camera or video source, instead of capturing all the frames as they arrive from the source. The *NetStream.attachVideo( )* method has an optional second parameter named snapShotMilliseconds. When the parameter is omitted, each frame from the source is sent to the stream according to the frame rate set using *Camera.setMode( )*. If a value of 0 is passed in, a single frame of video is placed in the stream. For example:

```
out_ns.attachVideo(cam, 0);
```

To be certain the frame is not dropped and has been sent to the server before the stream is closed, two things must be done. The *NetStream.setBufferTime( )* method must be used to make sure the frame is buffered, and an *onStatus( )* handler must be used to make sure the buffer is empty before closing the stream. Example 5-2 lists the essential code that sets up a stream to publish a snapshot and then takes one when the Record button is clicked. The complete listing is available on the book's web site.

Example 5-2. Taking buffered snapshots

```
// Called after a network connection is made.
function initProgram( ) {
  if (out_ns) out_ns.close( );
  out_ns = new NetStream(nc);
  out_ns.setBufferTime(2);
  out_ns.onStatus = function (info) {
    writeln(info.code);
    if (info.code == "NetStream.Buffer.Empty") {
      this.close( );
      in_ns.play("mugshot");
    }
  };

  if (in_ns) in_ns.close( );
```

Example 5-2. Taking buffered snapshots (continued)

```
  in_ns = new NetStream(nc);
  snapshot_video.attachVideo(in_ns);
  cam = Camera.get( );
  preview_video.attachVideo(cam);
  System.showSettings(0);
  record_btn.setEnabled(true);
  connect_btn.setLabel("Disconnect");
  in_ns.play("mugshot");
}

// Called when the user clicks the Record button.
function doRecord( ) {
  if (out_ns) out_ns.close( );
  out_ns.attachVideo(cam, 0);
  out_ns.publish("mugshot", "record");
}
```

In Example 5-2, whenever a network connection is created, the code creates a *Net-Stream* object, gives it a buffer time of 2 seconds, and creates an *onStatus( )* event handler:

```
  out_ns = new NetStream(nc);
  out_ns.setBufferTime(2);
  out_ns.onStatus = function (info) {
    writeln(info.code);
    if (info.code == "NetStream.Buffer.Empty") {
      this.close( );
      in_ns.play("mugshot");
    }
  };
```

When the snapshot is taken, the buffer briefly holds some video information until it is successfully sent. When all the video data has been sent, the *onStatus( )* handler receives an info.code value of "NetStream.Buffer.Empty". At that point, it can safely close the stream without the snapshot frame being lost. To take the actual snapshot, the code calls *doRecord( )* to attach the video source to the stream and publish the stream:

```
  out_ns.attachVideo(cam, 0);
  out_ns.publish("mugshot", "record");
```

Shortly afterward, the buffer empties and the stream closes.

The snapshotMilliseconds parameter can also be used to create time-lapse videos in which snapshots are taken at regular (usually long) intervals and then played back quickly. This technique can be used to speed up an otherwise slow process, such as watching a plant grow.

To make time-lapse video work, we cannot just publish a stream, leave it open, and send snapshots at regular intervals. The stream time progresses as long as the stream is being published. When such a stream is played back, the frames change at the

---

same interval they were taken. For example, if a frame is taken every hour for 24 hours, the stream takes 24 hours to play back the 24 frames. To solve this problem, we repeatedly open the stream, capture a single frame, which is appended onto the end of the stream, and then close the stream:

```
out_ns.attachVideo(cam, 0);
out_ns.publish(streamName, "append");
```

When we play it back, the frames go by so quickly that we can't see most of them. To solve the problem, set the number of milliseconds the frame will last within the stream using the snapshotMilliseconds parameter, capture a frame, and then close the stream. For example, to play back at 10 frames per second, each frame must last 100 milliseconds:

```
out_ns.attachVideo(cam, 100);
out_ns.publish(streamName, "append");
```

The snapshotMilliseconds parameter therefore does two things. It provides a single frame from the video source and adds trailer information as to how long the frame should be played back. Example 5-3 is a simplified version of a longer working example available on the book's web site. When the user clicks the Record button, the script captures a frame every 5000 milliseconds (5 seconds). When played back, each frame plays for 100 milliseconds (one-tenth of a second).

Example 5-3. Simplified time-lapse video example

```
out_ns = new NetStream(nc);
out_ns.setBufferTime(2);
out_ns.onStatus = function (info) {
  if (info.code == "NetStream.Buffer.Empty") {
    this.close();
  }
};

function captureFrame () {
  out_ns.attachVideo(cam, 100);
  out_ns.publish(streamName, "append");
}

function doRecord (btn) {
  if (btn.getLabel() == "Record") {
    if (intervalID) clearInterval(intervalID);
    out_ns.attachVideo(cam, 100);
    out_ns.publish(streamName, "append");
    intervalID = setInterval(captureFrame, 5000);
  }
  else if (intervalID) {
    clearInterval(intervalID);
  }
}
```

Stop-motion video can be done in a similar way. Instead of using *setInterval( )* to capture a frame at regular intervals, a single frame can be captured and appended to the recorded stream whenever a button is clicked. Unlike normal video capture, every frame in a time-lapse or stop-motion video stream is a complete frame (a video keyframe, not a so-called *difference frame* that contains only the delta between two successive frames). Time-lapse and stop-motion videos will normally require much more bandwidth than regular video and should be buffered accordingly. Each application is likely to be different, but you should try experimenting with a buffer 10 times larger than you might otherwise have used.

Playing Streams in Detail

The *NetStream.play( )* method can be used to play live and recorded streams, segments of recorded streams, and a playlist of streams. The *play( )* method has a number of optional parameters that make this possible:

```
in_ns.play(streamURI | false, [, start [,length [, flushPlaylists]]]);
```

The first parameter is required and must be either a relative URI that identifies the stream to play or the value `false`, which stops the current stream from playing. The remaining parameters, shown inside square brackets, are optional. The nesting of the square brackets indicates that if one optional parameter is included, then so must all previous ones. For example, to use the `length` parameter, the `start` parameter must also be provided.

Playing Live or Recorded Streams

The `start` parameter can be used to indicate more than its name implies. The possible values for `start` are:

-2

> Plays the live stream at the specified URI or plays the recorded stream at that location if the live stream is not found. If a recorded stream is also not found, the *NetStream* object waits for the stream to be published.

-1

> Plays only a live stream at the specified URI. If a live stream is not found, the *NetStream* object waits for one to be published. A recorded stream at the same URI will not be played.

0

> Plays only a recorded stream at the specified URI from its beginning. If a recorded stream is not found, an information object is returned to *NetStream. onStatus( )*.

Greater than 0

> Same as passing 0, but indicates how many seconds into the recorded stream to begin playing.

If a start value is not passed into the *play( )* method, the default is -2 (plays a live or recorded stream).

The `length` parameter defines how many seconds the live or recorded stream should play. For example, to play a stream beginning 1 minute into the stream for 30 seconds, call *play( )* as follows:

```
in_ns = new NetStream(nc);
in_ns.play("announcements", 60, 30);
```

If the `length` parameter is -1 or omitted, the stream plays until it ends. Note that, by definition, live streams always start playing at the current time; only recorded streams can be started at some offset. But the length of time to play a stream can be limited even for live streams by specifying a time limit with the `length` parameter.

Creating playlists

By default, invoking *play( )* overrides any previous *play( )* command for that *Net-Stream* object, closing the previous stream immediately and playing the new stream. However, you can create a playlist in which the server treats a sequence of recorded streams as a continuous stream; the server provides seamless buffering so that there are no interruptions when the source stream changes.

To add a stream to a playlist, pass `false` as the fourth, optional parameter (flushPlaylists) when invoking *play( )*. This tells FlashCom not to close the previous stream. Instead, the stream is queued and buffered to play after the streams already in the playlist. Here is a short example. Note that if `flushPlaylists` is specified as true or omitted, as shown in the first *play( )* invocation, FlashCom reinitializes the playlist:

```
in_ns = new NetStream(nc);
in_ns.play("announcements", 60, 30);
in_ns.play("live_Camera_1", -1, 15, false);
in_ns.play("live_Camera_2", -1, 15, false);
in_ns.play("prod_trailer",   0, -1, false);
```

The preceding code creates a playlist that plays the following sequence:

1. 30 seconds of the recorded stream named *announcements*, starting 60 seconds into the stream

2. 15 seconds of the *live_Camera_1* stream

3. 15 seconds of the *live_Camera_2* stream

4. The entire recorded *prod_trailer* stream

The `flushPlaylists` parameter can also be used to control how ActionScript data is streamed. See the "Stream logs" section later in this chapter.

Stream Time

As a live or recorded stream plays, stream time increases. If the stream pauses, stream time stops until the stream begins to play again. Stream time is 0 at the beginning of a recorded stream or when a live stream is first published. The stream time in seconds is available from the `NetStream.time` property. However, if no data is being received while a stream is playing, the `time` property reflects the last moment that data was received on the stream. When data arrives within the stream, the `time` property jumps to the correct value. For example, if a stream containing video plays for 30 seconds, at which point the video stops, the stream time will remain at 30 until more data of some type arrives. If more data arrives after another 20 seconds, the time value will suddenly change to 50 and continue increasing as long as data continues to arrive. Playlists are treated as though they are a single stream. When each stream in the playlist begins, stream time is not reset to 0. Therefore, the stream time is relative to when the stream started, not when the current content started playing. For example, if each playlist video clip is 30 seconds, the beginning of the second clip will have a stream time of 30, not 0.

Internally, whenever data is attached to a stream by a publisher, a timestamp is generated and embedded within the stream at the start of the audio, video, or Action-Script message. The timestamp is used to establish correct stream time when the stream is played. After a period of time while a stream is playing but no audio, video, or ActionScript data messages have arrived, the timestamp at the beginning of the next message to arrive is used to update the stream time.

Playback Events

The *NetStream.onStatus( )* handler, if defined, is called when errors or significant events occur. It receives an information object containing five fields that describe the event: `level`, `code`, `details`, `description`, and `clientid`. For example, when the chat movie described at the beginning of this chapter first attempts to subscribe to a stream named *public/robert*, the information object passed to *onStatus( )* contains the following property values:

```
info.level: status
info.code: NetStream.Play.Reset
info.description: Playing and resetting public/robert.
info.details: public/robert
info.clientid: 58996536
```

The `level` property will contain either "error" or "status", depending on the type of event. The `code` property contains the most useful message for determining what has happened. In this case, the stream has been reset, which indicates that any other pending *play( )* commands have been dropped. The `details` property contains the stream URI to which the message relates.

When a *NetStream* object attempts to subscribe to a live stream, its *onStatus( )* handler will normally be called twice and receive the `info.code` values "NetStream.Play. Reset" and "NetStream.Play.Start".

If the live stream is available, it will begin to play without *onStatus( )* being called again. However, the stream may not have started publishing yet, in which case no data will be received from FlashCom. The subscribing stream will therefore wait without generating any further calls to *onStatus( )*. When the stream is finally published, the *onStatus( )* handler will be called a third time and passed an information object with a `code` property of "NetStream.Play.PublishNotify".

There is no notification if a live stream is not available the moment an attempt is made to subscribe to it.

When a *NetStream* object attempts to connect to a recorded stream without a `start` parameter or with a `start` parameter of -2, it is not clear to FlashCom whether the NetStream is attempting to play a live or recorded stream. Consequently, even if the recorded stream does not exist, the NetStream will behave as though it is attempting to play a live stream. However, if a `start` parameter of 0 or greater is passed into *play( )*, the NetStream looks for a recorded stream only. In such a case, if the recorded file is found, the *onStatus( )* handler is called twice with the `code` values "NetStream.Play.Reset" followed by "NetStream.Play.Start".

If the file is not found and `start` is 0 or greater, FlashCom passes an information object with a `code` value of "NetStream.Play.StreamNotFound" to the *onStatus( )* handler.

The next few sections describe typical operational sequences and the status events they generate. Later, under "Putting the User in Control," we'll explain how to use these events to modify the user interface dynamically to help the user monitor and control various operations.

Playing MP3 Files

FlashCom 1.5 introduced the ability to stream recorded MPEG layer 3 (MP3) compressed audio files. MP3 files can be saved into a subdirectory of an application's *streams* subdirectory in order to make them available for streaming. Once available, they can be played using a stream URI that begins with the `mp3:` prefix. For example, if an MP3 file is stored in the following file path:

.../applications/radio/streams/_definst_/jazz/track1.mp3

and a *NetConnection* is established from a Flash movie to the `_definst_` instance of the *radio* application, then the following statement subscribes to a stream that plays the MP3 file:

```
in_ns.play("mp3:jazz/track1", 0, -1);
```

MP3 files can contain tagged information in the ID3 format that may contain information such as the song title, artist, album, year, genre, and a comment. To read the ID3 information, use a separate *play( )* statement in which the relative URI of the stream begins with the id3: prefix. For example:

```
in_ns.play("id3:jazz/track1");
```

To actually read the ID3 data, you must define a *NetStream.onId3( )* handler. Example 5-4 shows a short demonstration script that reads the ID3 information, writes it into the Flash development environment's Output panel, and then starts to play the audio stream. The ID3 tag names and values are returned as the property names and values of the information object passed into the *onId3( )* handler.

Example 5-4. Reading the ID3 tags and playing MP3 audio using one stream

```
NetStream.prototype.onId3 = function (info) {
  trace("NetStream.onId3>");
  for (var p in info) {
    trace("    " + p + ": " + info[p]);
  }
};

nc = new NetConnection( );
nc.connect("rtmp:/radio");

ns = new NetStream(nc);
ns.setBufferTime(10);
ns.play("id3:jazz/track1");
ns.play("mp3:jazz/track1", 0, -1, false);
```

In order to make sure that all the ID3 information is received before the audio is played, the code sets the flushPlaylists parameter to false when *play( )* is called a second time. Two separate streams can also be used—one to retrieve the ID3 information and another to play the audio.

FlashCom 1.5 returns the code value of "NetStream.Play.Failed", not "NetStream.Play.StreamNotFound", when an MP3 file is not found.

Uploading Prerecorded Streams

Prerecorded media files in both FLV and MP3 format can be uploaded to a Flash-Com Server where they can be played. FLV files that are not recorded by the Flash-Com Server can be created using Sorenson Squeeze for Flash MX 2004 or other utilities, such as Squeeze Lite, which is included with the Macromedia Video Kit for Dreamweaver. There are two options as to where FLV and MP3 files can be stored on the server for playback. (FLV files recorded by FlashCom can also be copied to other locations on the server where they can be played by other instances.) One option is to place FLV or MP3 files in the *streams/instanceName* subdirectory of an application's home directory where *instanceName* is an instance name such as _definst_. However, the files are available only for that instance of the application. The second option is to specify a virtual directory so that every instance of every application can access the same files. A virtual directory is a pathname that is mapped to an actual directory path. The mapping is defined within the <Streams> tag of a *Vhost.xml* configuration file. For example, to map the common name music to the path *C:\CommonFiles\music*, use the following <Streams> tag:

```
<Streams>music;C:\CommonFiles\music</Streams>
```

A semicolon must separate the virtual pathname and the actual directory path. If multiple mappings are required, use multiple <Streams> tags.

Buffering When Subscribing

Live streams that support real-time chats and video conferences should not be buffered. Any delay due to buffering of a stream will only make conversation more difficult. The amount of lag, or delay, in seconds of a live stream can be determined by checking the NetStream.liveDelay property. For recorded streams, or even live streams that are not part of a real-time conversation, buffering can be used to provide a more seamless and higher-quality playback than live bufferless streaming provides.

When recorded streams are played, a small default buffer time of 10 milliseconds (0.01 second) is used even if the buffer time is set to 0. If stream data arrives more slowly than it is being played, eventually the buffer will empty and playing will stop until the buffer refills. With a fast connection and low data rates, this may never happen. However, if data arrives too slowly to be continuously played, the stream may start and stop repeatedly. Setting the buffer time to a higher value will guarantee that longer sections of a stream play continuously.

If a recorded stream is played and then the same *NetStream* object is used to play a live stream, a buffer time will still be set on the stream. Clear it by setting the buffer time to 0.

To set the buffer time for a stream, use *NetStream.setBufferTime( )*:

```
in_ns.setBufferTime(10);
```

To determine the number of seconds of data currently in the buffer, use the NetStream.bufferLength property. During testing, you can watch the buffer length change with a simple test script that displays the length in a text field:

```
in_ns.play(streamName);
in_ns.setBufferTime(10);
function onEnterFrame( ) {
  bufferLength_txt.text = in_ns.bufferLength;
}
```

The bufferLength property is often used to set the size of a progress bar after buffering begins. In fact, it is often a good idea to display a movie clip that shows a progress bar whenever the buffer is empty until the buffer refills and then hide the progress bar. When a stream stops, the user will see the progress bar gradually increase until it reaches 100%, and then it will disappear when the stream starts to play again. An exception occurs if the stream is buffering very near the end. It may not need to completely fill the buffer in order to play to the end. One way to determine when to show or hide a buffering progress indicator movie clip is to watch for three buffer-related code values in the information objects passed to *onStatus( )*, namely "NetStream.Buffer.Empty", "NetStream.Buffer.Full", and "NetStream.Play. Stop". "NetStream.Play.Stop" indicates that buffering is complete when the stream is near the end and does not need to fill the buffer completely before starting to play.

Detecting the End of the Stream

When the publisher of a live stream stops publishing a stream, the *onStatus( )* method of any subscribing *NetStream* objects are called and passed an information object with a code value of "NetStream.Play.UnpublishNotify". So there is no ambiguity about when a live stream ends. However, when a recorded stream is being played, two things happen. First, the server stops sending data to the Flash movie. Second, any data still in the stream buffer continues playing within the Flash movie until the buffer is empty. When the server stops sending data to the movie, *onStatus( )* is passed a code value of "NetStream.Play.Stop". Then, when the buffer empties shortly afterward, *onStatus( )* is called again with a code value of "NetStream.Buffer. Empty". The following output shows the information objects' code values during playback of a stream from start to finish:

```
NetStream.Play.Reset
NetStream.Play.Start
NetStream.Buffer.Full
NetStream.Buffer.Empty
NetStream.Buffer.Full
NetStream.Play.Stop
NetStream.Buffer.Empty
```

Someone viewing this stream does not see or hear it start to play until the first "NetStream.Buffer.Full" value occurs. The stream stops playing when the first "NetStream.Buffer.Empty" value is returned and does not start again until the second "NetStream.Buffer.Full" value is returned. Finally, the stream stops playing completely after the last "NetStream.Buffer.Empty" value occurs.

Seeking Within a Stream

When a recorded stream is being played, *NetStream.seek( )* can be used to jump to any time within the recorded stream and begin playing the stream from that point. The *seek( )* method takes one required parameter—the number of seconds from the beginning of the stream to seek to. For example, this statement stops the playing stream and restarts it 20 seconds from the beginning of the recorded stream:

```
in_ns.seek(20);
```

Calling *seek( )* empties the buffer and restarts buffering of the stream. Consequently, the following code values will be passed in three successive *onStatus( )* handler calls:

```
NetStream.Seek.Notify
NetStream.Play.Start
NetStream.Buffer.Full
```

The stream will not visibly or audibly begin to play again until the "NetStream.Buffer.Full" code value is received. If the seek cannot be carried out, a code value of "NetStream.Seek.Failed" will be returned.

To seek to another time in the stream relative to the current stream time, convert it to absolute time by adding the `NetStream.time` property as an offset. For example, to seek to 5 seconds before the current time, subtract 5 from the current time to get the absolute time:

```
relativeSeekTime = -5;
in_ns.seek(in_ns.time + relativeSeekTime);
```

Compressed video data is almost always made up of keyframes separated by difference frames. Most recorded video frames are therefore not full video frames but rather updates from the last keyframe. When seeking within a stream, the requested time usually does not fall on a keyframe. When this happens, FlashCom's default behavior is to start playing the stream from the closest preceding keyframe. The alternative is to have FlashCom seek to the previous keyframe, read the difference frames up until the seek time, and construct a new video frame dynamically. This process is called *enhanced seeking* and can be enabled using an *Application.xml* file's <EnhancedSeek> flag. By default, enhanced seeking is disabled because it is a more computationally expensive operation. To turn on enhanced seek for one application, place an *Application.xml* file in the home directory of an application with the following tag:

```
<EnhancedSeek>true</EnhancedSeek>
```

Using enhanced seeking for all applications is not recommended because it requires the server to perform the extra work of reading the preceding frames to create the current frame. For a complete description of the *Application.xml* and other XML configuration files, consult *Managing Flash Communication Server*, available at:

http://www.macromedia.com/support/flashcom/documentation.html

Pausing and Unpausing a Stream

The *NetStream.pause( )* method can be used to pause and unpause playback of a recorded stream. When called without any parameters, it toggles between pausing and playing the stream. Calling *pause(true)* pauses the stream; calling *pause(false)* resumes playback. Unfortunately, when a stream is paused, the stream's buffer empties, so that when the stream is unpaused, the stream must refill the buffer before it can begin playing again. When a stream is paused and unpaused, *NetStream.onStatus( )* is called four times. The information objects' code values will be:

```
NetStream.Pause.Notify
NetStream.Unpause.Notify
NetStream.Play.Start
NetStream.Buffer.Full
```

After the "NetStream.Buffer.Full" code value is received, the stream will appear to play to the user. If *seek( )* is called while a stream is paused, the current stream time changes to reflect the *seek( )* request and the video frame at the seek time is displayed. When the stream is unpaused, the stream plays starting from the new time. In such a case, the information objects' code values received in succession by *onStatus( )* are:

```
NetStream.Pause.Notify
NetStream.Seek.Notify
NetStream.Play.Start
NetStream.Unpause.Notify
NetStream.Play.Start
NetStream.Buffer.Full
```

In between "NetStream.Pause.Notify" and "NetStream.Unpause.Notify", the "NetStream.Seek.Notify" code indicates the seek operation succeeded and "NetStream.Play.Start" indicates that the server sent data to the subscriber. No buffer-related message occurs between the pause codes.

Putting the User in Control

A common task in developing Flash communication applications is creating an audio/video stream player with volume, mute, pause, stop, start, and seek/progress controls and a pop-up buffering indicator. It is also desirable to visibly disable and enable controls or otherwise change their text or appearance depending on the state of an application. To make everything work properly, an application has to know the current state of the stream, be informed when it changes, and be able to track requests made of a *NetStream* object. Most of the work of interpreting what a stream is doing begins in the *onStatus( )* handler. The information objects that are passed into *onStatus( )* provide most of the low-level information about a stream; however, they do not describe the state of the stream at the level an application may need. For example, in order to know when to pop up a movie clip that shows the buffering status of the stream, we need to know when the stream has paused in order to refill its buffer. No single information object delivered to the *onStatus( )* handler indicates when the stream has paused to refill its buffer. So, before looking at writing a complete *onStatus( )* handler, let's look at some common problems in writing one designed to help a stream playback application determine what a stream is doing.

NetStream.Buffer.Empty

When the code property of an information object indicates the buffer is empty, either the stream has played through to the end, or the stream has simply run out of data and must pause to refill the buffer. How do you tell the difference? A first good answer starts with the recognition that, when the stream has played to the end, the "NetStream.Play.Stop" message precedes the "NetStream.Buffer.Empty" one. We might try to differentiate between the two states by introducing a stopped property to act as a flag as follows:

```
in_ns.onStatus = function (info) {
  writeln(info.code);
  switch (info.code) {
    case "NetStream.Play.Stop":
      this.stopped = true;
      break;
    case "NetStream.Buffer.Empty":
      if (this.stopped) {
        this.reportChange("playingAtEnd");
      }
      else {
        this.reportChange("buffering");
      }
      break;
    case "NetStream.Buffer.Full":
      this.reportChange("playing");
      break;
  }
};
```

In this code snippet, a function named *reportChange( )* is passed a string that indicates the current state of the stream. In turn, *reportChange( )* will pass on the message to another object that is responsible for controlling the stream—something I'll discuss later. For now, we just want to properly inform some other object of what the stream is doing. Now imagine that the user watches the stream through to the end so that "NetStream.Play.Stop" and "NetStream.Buffer.Empty" code values are passed to *onStatus( )*. The *onStatus( )* handler will correctly report that the stream has played through to the end. Now, what happens if the user restarts the stream? Whenever the buffer empties from now on, *onStatus( )* remembers that it has seen a "NetStream.Play.Stop" code and incorrectly reports that the stream has played to the end. The solution is to add another *case* clause to reset the stopped flag when the stream plays:

```
case "NetStream.Play.Start":
  this.stopped = false;
  break;
```

NetStream.Seek.Notify

When a seek occurs while a stream is playing, the buffer is emptied and the stream stops until the seek is complete and the buffer is refilled. However, there is no "Net-Stream.Buffer.Empty" message to indicate the buffer is empty in this situation. So, the "NetStream.Seek.Notify" message must serve the same purpose. But there is a complication! If the stream is paused when the user seeks to a new location, the stream does not start to fill the buffer (the buffer fills only when the stream is playing). So just as an empty buffer message may mean more than one thing, the notify message alone does not indicate the state of the stream. What to do? Again we can resort to tracking whether the stream is paused by setting a paused property, which we add to the *NetStream* object. We can therefore add *case* clauses as follows:

```
case "NetStream.Seek.Notify":
  if (!this.paused) {
     this.reportChange("buffering");
  }
  break;
case "NetStream.Pause.Notify":
  this.paused = true;
  this.reportChange("paused");
  break;
case "NetStream.Unpause.Notify":
  this.paused = false;
  break;
```

With six *case* clauses in our *switch* statement so far, you may wonder how far we have to go to write an *onStatus( )* handler that will reliably describe what a *NetStream* is really doing while subscribed to a recorded stream. The answer is that it depends on what your application needs to do. But rather than writing numerous *onStatus( )* handlers for different applications and run the risk of mishandling some events, you should write one *onStatus( )* handler that handles all the events related to playing a recorded stream. In fact, for convenience, a good way to do this is to create a *NetStream* subclass that can be used in many different applications. Example 5-5 shows one way to create a *NetStream* subclass using ActionScript 1.0–style syntax.

Example 5-5. A NetStream subclass for use in subscribing to recorded streams

```
function NetStreamPlaybackClass (nc) {
  this.stopped  = false;
  this.paused   = false;
  super(nc);
}

NetStreamPlaybackClass.prototype = new NetStream( );

NetStreamPlaybackClass.prototype.play = function (streamURI, start,
                                            length, flushPlaylists) {
  // Preprocess parameters if necessary.
  super.play.apply(this, arguments);
};
```

```
NetStreamPlaybackClass.prototype.pause = function (flag) {
  // Preprocess parameters if necessary.
  if (flag != undefined) {
    this.paused = flag;
  }
  else {
    this.paused = !this.paused;
  }
  super.pause.apply(this, arguments);
  // Notify immediately.
  if (this.paused) {
    this.onStatus({code: "NetStream.Pause.Notify", level: "status"});
  }
};

NetStreamPlaybackClass.prototype.reportChange = function (state) {
  this.state = state;
  this.obj[this.method](state, this);
};

NetStreamPlaybackClass.prototype.onStatus = function (info) {
  this.lastInfo = info;
  if (info.level != "status") {
    this.reportChange(info.level);
    return;
  }
  switch (info.code) {
    case "NetStream.Play.Start":
      if (!this.paused)
        this.reportChange("buffering");
        this.stopped = false;
      break;
    case "NetStream.Play.Stop":
      if (this.bufferLength == 0) {
        this.reportChange("playingAtEnd");
      }
      else {
        this.reportChange("playing");
      }
      this.stopped = true;
      break;
    case "NetStream.Buffer.Empty":
      if (this.stopped) {
        this.reportChange("playingAtEnd");
      }
      else {
        this.reportChange("buffering");
      }
      break;
    case "NetStream.Buffer.Full":
      this.reportChange("playing");
      break;
```

Example 5-5. A NetStream subclass for use in subscribing to recorded streams (continued)

```
      case "NetStream.Seek.Notify":
        if (!this.paused) {
          this.reportChange("buffering");
        }
        else {
          this.reportChange("seeking");
        }
        break;
      case "NetStream.Pause.Notify":
        this.paused = true;
        this.reportChange("paused");
        break;
      case "NetStream.Unpause.Notify":
        this.paused = false;
        break;
   }
};

// setChangeHandler() must be passed a method and an object.
NetStreamPlaybackClass.prototype.setChangeHandler = function (method, obj) {
  this.method = method;
  this.obj = obj;
};

NetStreamPlaybackClass.prototype.getLastInfo = function () {
  return this.lastInfo;
};
```

The *NetStreamPlaybackClass* subclass defined in Example 5-5 operates behind the scenes but does not directly affect an application's UI. On its own, it does not enable or disable buttons or move sliders; instead, it tells an object that registers itself as a change handler what the stream is doing. To tie together button components, a custom slider, or other interface elements with *NetStreamPlaybackClass*, a good design choice is to create an object that acts as a mediator (sometimes called a director) between the interface controls and a *NetStream* object or *NetStream* subclass. To be effective, a mediator object must register itself as the change handler for all the interface elements and for the *NetStreamPlaybackClass* instance. When a change notification arrives from another object, the mediator must determine how to respond by manipulating the stream or interface elements. This design has the advantage that all state management code is centralized in one place. Example 5-6 shows how a mediator object works with two movie clips—buffer_mc, a clip that shows a progress bar, and seek_mc, a clip that contains a slider. The example shows a partial listing for a mediator class named *PlayBackDirector* and some of the code used to connect it to other objects. The complete code for this example is available on the book's web site.

Example 5-6. Partial listing of the PlayBackDirector class

```
function PlayBackDirector () {
  this.soundOn = true;
```

Example 5-6. Partial listing of the PlayBackDirector class (continued)

```
  this.lastStateName = "";
}

PlayBackDirector.prototype.playing = function (obj) {
  // Hide the buffer status movie clip.
  delete buffer_mc.onEnterFrame;
  buffer_mc._visible = false;

  // Start tracking the stream time.
  seek_mc.onEnterFrame = function () {
    this.setPosition(stream.time);
  }

  // Set the buttons to the right state.
  play_pb.setEnabled(true);
  play_pb.setLabel("Stop");

  pause_pb.setEnabled(true);
  pause_pb.setLabel("Pause");
};

PlayBackDirector.prototype.buffering = function (obj) {
  // Show the buffer status movie clip.
  buffer_mc.setMaxValue(stream.bufferTime)
  buffer_mc.onEnterFrame = function () {
    this.setPosition(stream.bufferLength);
  }
  buffer_mc._visible = true;

  // Stop tracking the stream time.
  delete seek_mc.onEnterFrame;

  // Set the buttons to the right state.
  play_pb.setEnabled(true);
  play_pb.setLabel("Stop");

  pause_pb.setEnabled(true);
  pause_pb.setLabel("Pause");
};

PlayBackDirector.prototype.onStreamChange = function (stateName, obj) {
  if (stateName == this.lastStateName) return;
  this.lastStateName = stateName;
  this[stateName](obj);
};

// This handler calls seek( ) on the stream and disables the slider until
// the stream starts to play again.
PlayBackDirector.prototype.onSliderChange = function (pos, obj) {
  delete seek_mc.onEnterFrame;
  stream.seek(pos);
};
```

Example 5-6. Partial listing of the PlayBackDirector class (continued)

```
PlayBackDirector.prototype.onPlayRequest = function (btn) {
  if (btn.getLabel() == "Play") {
    this.playing(stream);
    stream.play("public/Ryerson_High_Speed");
  }
  else {
    stream.close();
    btn.setLabel("Play");
    delete seek_mc.onEnterFrame;
    delete buffer_mc.onEnterFrame;
    buffer_mc._visible = false;
    pause_pb.setEnabled(false);
  }
};
```

The *onStreamChange( )* method is called whenever the state of the stream object changes. For example, if *onStreamChange( )* is passed a stateName value of "buffering", *PlayBackDirector.buffering( )* is called. The *buffering( )* method is responsible for setting everything controlled by *PlayBackDirector* to the correct state when the stream is buffering. The buffer_mc clip's range is adjusted to reflect the stream buffer's time, an *onEnterFrame( )* method is created for the clip so that on each frame it will show the current buffer length, and finally, the buffer_mc clip is made visible. On the other hand, if a "playing" message arrives, the buffer_mc clip is hidden and its *onEnterFrame( )* method is deleted. Ideally, there should be one method for each stream state, which guarantees that all the objects and movie clips controlled by *PlayBackDirector* always respond appropriately to changes in stream state.

As of Flash Player 6.0.79.0, "NetStream.Buffer.Empty" events are not always generated when a stream pauses to buffer before continuing to play. A version of *NetStreamPlaybackClass* is provided on the book's web site that fixes the problem by regularly checking whether the stream is playing and calling the *onStatus( )* method with a "NetStream.Buffer.Empty" message if it has paused to buffer. Macromedia expects to fix this for Flash Player 8, due to be released in the second half of 2005.

Managing Bandwidth

Matching the size of the data stream to the client's available bandwidth is the most important factor in determining how well a stream plays for any user. FlashCom cannot further compress a stream to suit the bandwidth available for each client or interpolate video frames to lower resolutions to cope with lower-bandwidth connections. As will be discussed in Chapter 7, the best way to tailor a stream to different bandwidths is to create separate streams for typical connection speeds. Often this means creating one stream for modem users, another for DSL users, and possibly one for users on a LAN. However, once a stream is selected for playing by a client, there

---

are still some things beyond buffering that can be done to improve playback performance when bandwidth is less than optimal.

Shutting off audio or video

The *receiveAudio( )* and *receiveVideo( )* methods of a *NetStream* object can be used to stop and start the server sending audio or video in a stream. Both methods are passed a Boolean value that determines whether audio or video data should be sent by the server. Example 5-7 shows a method that is called when an audio Mute button is clicked.

Example 5-7. A method for toggling sound on and off

```
PlayBackDirector.prototype.onMuteAudioRequest = function (obj) {
  this.soundOn = !this.soundOn;
  stream.receiveAudio(this.soundOn);
  if (this.soundOn) {
    muteAudio_pb.setLabel("Mute Audio");
  }
  else {
    muteAudio_pb.setLabel("Restore Audio");
  }
};
```

When a stream is already playing and the audio is muted by instructing the server to stop sending audio, the audio will not stop playing in the client immediately if there is still audio data in the stream's buffer. Similarly, if video data is in a buffer when a request to restart sending audio data is received, it may be some time before audio is heard on the client system. Stopping the server from sending video using *receiveVideo(false)* may improve stream playback performance. Without the need to download and buffer video data, audio and ActionScript data can fill the buffer faster, leading to fewer pauses for buffering.

Capping client bandwidth usage

The maximum bandwidth a client can use to send or receive data is capped by the server according to the <Bandwith>, <ServerToClient>, and <ClientToServer> tags in the *Application.xml* file that controls an application. The default settings allow a client to send 250,000 bytes/sec (244 KB/s) to the server as well as to receive 250,000 bytes/sec. A client connected via modem is likely to be able to send and receive much less data—often less than 4000 bytes/second. When a client is subscribed to a stream, FlashCom attempts to monitor network traffic and drops video frames as necessary. To help the server determine the bandwidth available, each client's bandwidth limit can be set using *Client.setBandwidthLimit( )*, as shown in Example 5-8.

Example 5-8. Server-side script that relies on a connection type string being passed to the server from the client when it connects

```
connectionSettings = {
  modem: {up: 4000, down: 4000},
  dsl:   {up: 16000, down: 62000},
  lan:   {up: 1250000, down: 10000000}
}

application.onConnect = function (client, connectionType) {
  var setting = connectionSettings[connectionType];
  if (setting) {
    client.setBandwidthLimit(setting.up, setting.down);
  }
  return true;
};
```

Conferences and bandwidth

Live conferences in which users see and hear one another simultaneously can create a heavy processing load on each Flash movie and the FlashCom Server hosting the conference, and tax the bandwidth available to the client and server. The processing and bandwidth load for each client scales linearly with the number of participants. The load and bandwidth demands on the server increase as the square of the number of clients. Figure 5-3 shows the outgoing stream from each client and the incoming streams for small conferences of two or three participants.

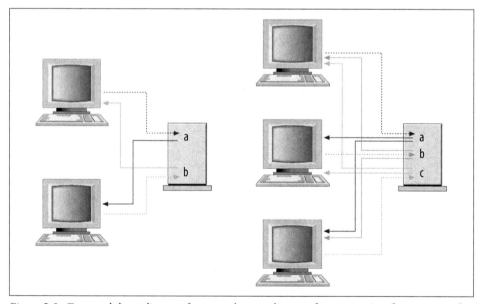

Figure 5-3. Two- and three-client conferences: the two-client conference requires four streams; the three-client conference, nine streams

Each client must send one stream to the conference instance and receive as many streams as there are other participants. In other words, if there are n participants, each will have to send one and receive $n - 1$ streams:

```
Total client streams = 1 + n - 1 = n
```

The server will receive a stream from each client and send out to each client one stream from all the other clients. Therefore, the total number of streams handled by the server will be:

```
Total server streams = n * (1 + n - 1) = n²
```

Conferences with too many participants—all sending and receiving audio and video—can quickly swamp some clients with data and may contribute to bandwidth and load problems on the server. There is no magic solution to this problem—it is the nature of live conferences. When designing and hosting conference systems, consider making sure that clients do not attempt to send more audio and video data than absolutely necessary, that there is a limit on the number of participants, or that a token passing system is used to restrict the number of clients actually sending audio and video at one time. Assuming each video stream requires 8 KB/s, Table 5-1 shows how bandwidth demand increases per client connection.

Table 5-1. Bandwidth demands for number of client connections

Number of clients	Client upstream demand	Client downstream demand	Server demand
2	8 KB/s	8 KB/s	32 KB/s
3	8 KB/s	16 KB/s	72 KB/s
4	8 KB/s	24 KB/s	128 KB/s
5	8 KB/s	32 KB/s	200 KB/s
10	8 KB/s	72 KB/s	800 KB/s
20	8 KB/s	152 KB/s	3.2 MB/s
50	8 KB/s	392 KB/s	20 MB/s

The Stream Class

The server-side *Stream* class is designed to provide a proxy and control mechanism for live and recorded streams. It is unlike the client-side *NetStream* class in that it cannot create a new and original audio/video stream because it cannot be used to attach video or audio data sources to a stream. Instead, the server-side *Stream* object can be used to create new streams that incorporate already existing live and recorded streams, manage existing streams, or create new data-only streams. It can be used to:

- Create a single stream on the server that sequentially plays a list of other streams. Flash movies have to subscribe to only the one server-side–generated stream to receive the contents of a sequence of streams played from the server.

- Create a single stream that acts as a switcher between other streams. Flash movies subscribe to the one stream while the source of the stream is switched on the server. The effect is similar to a video switcher used in a television studio to control which camera signal is broadcast to the world. The stream can also be recorded, creating a new edited stream.
- Chain streams between application instances on one server or between many servers. Chaining streams between servers is one way to provide the capacity to serve a very large number of subscribers to a single live stream.
- Control access to individual streams. The *Stream* class can be used to provide very fine-grained access control for each user.
- Record ActionScript data streams that can contain very large amounts of data, for example, a log file.

Getting a Recorded Stream's Length

The *Stream* class has one static method, *length( )*, which, before the release of FLV 1.1 files, was the only way to directly determine the length of a recorded stream from the stream file itself. See Chapter 7 for more information on determining the stream length from FLV 1.1 files. To determine the length of a recorded stream, call *length( )* as follows:

```
len = Stream.length("lectures/vectors03");
trace("The stream is " + len + " seconds long");
```

If the stream is not found, *length( )* returns 0. It is often useful to provide a function that will calculate the length of a number of streams, as shown in Example 5-9.

Example 5-9. Getting the length of a list of streams (server-side script)

```
function sumStreamLengths ( ) {
  var sum = 0;
  var i = arguments.length;
  while (i--) {
    sum += Stream.length(arguments[i]);
  }
  return sum;
}
```

The *sumStreamLengths( )* function in Example 5-9 can be used to retrieve the length of more than one stream (as in a playlist) this way:

```
len = sumStreamLengths("lectures/vector01", "lectures/vector02");
```

The *sumStreamLengths( )* function can also be called to get the length of only one stream:

```
len = sumStreamLengths("public/recordedStream");
```

The simplest way to access the *Stream.length( )* method from a Flash movie requires calling a method on the server, which in turn calls *Stream.length( )* and returns the result to the client. Example 5-10 shows a segment of a client-side script that requests the length of a single recorded stream using a remote method call. Note the use of *NetConnection.call( )* to invoke a server-side script from the client.

Example 5-10. Retrieving the length of a stream from the server using a client-side script

```
function doGetStreamLength ( ) {
  nc.call("getStreamLength", new ResultObject( ), streamName_txt.text);
}

function ResultObject ( ) {
}

ResultObject.prototype.onResult = function (len) {
  trace( "The stream length is: " + len);
};
```

The *doGetStreamLength( )* function is called after the user types a stream URI into the streamName_txt field and clicks a button. Within the *doGetStreamLength( )* function, *NetConnection.call( )* calls a remote method named *getStreamLength( )* on the server. Example 5-11 shows the server-side script and how the *Client.getStreamLength( )* method is defined on the server that responds to the request.

Example 5-11. Defining the client.getStreamLength( ) method on the server

```
application.onConnect = function (client) {
  // Define client.getStreamLength( ) on the server to be invoked from the client.
  client.getStreamLength = function (streamName) {
    return Stream.length(streamName);
  }
  return true; // Accept the client connection.
};
```

Remote method calls and how they work are described in detail in Chapter 9. If the total length of all the streams in a playlist is required, a *Client* object can be given a method that calls *sumStreamLengths( )*, as shown in this server-side code:

```
client.getPlaylistLength = function ( ) {
  return sumStreamLengths.apply(null, arguments);
};
```

The server-side *client.getPlaylistLength( )* method can be called using this client-side code:

```
nc.call("getPlaylistLength", new ResultObject( ),
        "lectures/vector01", "lectures/vector02");
```

Don't get confused by the remote method invocation. The *Client* instance is a server-side entity that represents the client connected to the server. The client-side *NetConnection.call( )* method is used to invoke a method (in this case, *getPlaylistLength( )*) attached to the server-side *Client* instance.

Republishing with Stream Objects

Often, the server-side *Stream* class is used to create a new *Stream* object. A newly created stream can be used to republish another stream under the new stream's name. For example, the following server-side script creates a new stream at the URI *public/TVChannel_1* and republishes the prerecorded stream *hidden/promo_97*:

```
channel1Stream = Stream.get("public/TVChannel_1");
channel1Stream.play("hidden/promo_97", 0, -1);
```

Assuming that a stream at the URI *public/TVChannel_1* does not already exist, the *Stream.get( )* method creates a new stream. Every Flash movie that subscribes to *public/TVChannel_1* will see the *hidden/promo_97* stream being played. Even though the server-side *Stream.play( )* method has similar parameters to the client-side *NetConnection.play( )* method, the former provides a different service. It plays a live or recorded stream within the *Stream* object. When a recorded stream is played into another stream, subscribers will see the recorded stream as it is being played. In effect, the recorded stream is "streamed live" so that subscribers will not be able to seek within it.

The name of the stream specified in the *Stream.get( )* method is the name of the stream clients must subscribe to in order to play it.

Server-side playlists

A mixture of live and recorded streams can be treated as a playlist and streamed in a preprogrammed sequence as one live stream, as shown in Example 5-12.

Example 5-12. Creating a server-side playlist

```
channel_1Stream = Stream.get("public/TVChannel_1");
channel_1Stream.onStatus = function (info) {
  trace("code: " + info.code);
  trace("details: " + info.details);
};
channel_1Stream.play("hidden/promo_97", 0, -1);
channel_1Stream.play("hidden/camera_1", -1, 300, false);
channel_1Stream.play("hidden/camera_2", -1, 300, false);
channel_1Stream.play("hidden/promo_98", 0, -1, false);
```

In Example 5-12, subscribers to the *public/TVChannel_1* stream will see the *hidden/promo_97* stream play from the beginning (start set to 0) through to the end (length set to -1), watch 300 seconds (5 minutes) of each of two live streams, and then see the final recorded stream play from the beginning to the end. The fourth parameter of the *Stream.play( )* method, reset, plays the same role as the `flushPlaylists` parameter of *NetStream.play( )* (namely, whether to begin a new playlist or append to the existing playlist).

Like client-side *NetStream* objects, server-side *Stream* objects may also have an *onStatus( )* handler defined and will receive information objects that are very similar to *NetStream* information objects. Example 5-12 produces the following output in the *app_inspector.swf* movie:

```
code: NetStream.Publish.Start
details:
code: NetStream.Play.Reset
details: hidden/promo_97
code: NetStream.Play.Start
details: hidden/promo_97
code: NetStream.Play.Start
details: hidden/camera_1
code: NetStream.Play.Start
details: hidden/camera_2
code: NetStream.Play.Start
details: hidden/promo_98
```

In some circumstances, it may be necessary to prevent access to recorded streams except when they are played live by a server-side stream. In Example 5-12, two paths—*public* and *hidden*—are used. If read access is provided to the *public* path only, the recorded stream in the *hidden* path cannot be accessed directly:

```
application.onConnect = function (client) {
  client.readAccess = "/public";  // Allow access to the public directory only.
  client.writeAccess = "";        // Stop all write access.
  return true;
};
```

Switching streams

When the reset parameter is either omitted or set to true when calling *Stream.play( )*, the currently playing stream is closed and the *Stream* object immediately plays the new stream. This feature can be used to dynamically switch the source of a *Stream* object at any time. The server-side code segment in Example 5-13 shows how a simple remote method can be defined for clients that need to be able to switch streams. The *getUserRole( )* function was omitted to reduce the size of the listing but is included on the book's web site.

Example 5-13. Defining a switchStream() method for a client object (server-side code)

```
channel_1Stream = Stream.get("public/TVChannel_1");
channel_1Stream.play("hidden/camera_1");

application.onConnect = function (client, userName, password) {
  var userRole = getUserRole(client, userName, password);
```

```
  if (userRole == "CONTROLLER") {        // User has the control panel.
    client.switchStream = function (streamName) {
      channel_1Stream.play(streamName);
    };
  }
  else {                                 // Assume user is an anonymous viewer.
    client.readAccess = "/public";       // Provide read access to the public
    client.writeAccess = "";             // directory and no write access.
  }
  return true;                           // Accept all connections.
};
```

A client movie designed to act as a video switcher will call *Client.switchStream( )* on the server side using the client-side *NetConnection.call( )* method:

```
function doShowCamera2 () {
  nc.call("switchStream", null, "hidden/camera_2");
}
```

Chaining streams

The server-side *Stream.play( )* method differs from the client-side *NetStream.play( )* method in that it takes a fifth parameter, remoteConnection. A remoteConnection parameter must be a *NetConnection* object that has connected to another application instance. Example 5-14 shows a simple server-side script that connects to another application instance on another FlashCom Server and plays a stream from it.

Example 5-14. Chaining a stream from one server to another

```
nc = new NetConnection( );
nc.onStatus = function (info) {
  trace("NetConnection> code: " + info.code);
  if (info.code == "NetConnection.Connect.Success") {
    rebroadcast_s = new Stream.get("rebroadcast");
    rebroadcast_s.onStatus = function (info) {
      trace("Stream> code: " + info.code);
      trace("Stream> details: " + info.details);
    };
    rebroadcast_s.play("public/Ryerson_56K", 0, -1, true, nc)
  }
};
nc.connect("rtmp://echo.ryerson.ca/campusCameras/connector");
```

Recording streams

A *Stream* object can also record the streams it plays. The *Stream.record( )* method takes a single parameter, as follows, that determines how recording proceeds:

"record"

Deletes any existing recorded stream and begins recording

"append"
> Appends onto an existing recorded stream or begins a new one if none exists

false
> Stops recording

When a stream is recorded, the string URI that was passed into the *Stream.get( )* method is used to determine the stream filename and path to which to record. The following example records a playlist as well as makes it available as a live stream. The filename of the recorded stream in this example will be *TVChannel_1.flv*:

```
channel_1Stream = Stream.get("public/TVChannel_1");
channel_1Stream.play("hidden/promo_97", 0, -1);
channel_1Stream.play("hidden/camera_1", -1, 300, false);
channel_1Stream.play("hidden/camera_2", -1, 300, false);
channel_1Stream.play("hidden/promo_98", 0, -1, false);
channel_1Stream.record("record");
```

Recording can be stopped at any time by calling:

```
channel_1Stream.record(false);
```

Deleting Streams

A Flash Video format (FLV) file can be deleted using a *NetStream* or *Stream* object. Batches of files—including MP3 files—can be deleted using the server-side application object.

Deleting an FLV file with a NetStream object

To delete a recorded FLV stream using a Flash movie, publish a live stream with the same relative URI as the recorded stream. For example, to delete the file *junk.flv* at the URI *public/junk*, you can use this client-side code:

```
ns = new NetStream(nc);
ns.onStatus = function (info) {
  for (var p in info) {
    trace(p + ": " + info[p]);
  }
};
ns.publish("public/junk", "live");
ns.close( );
```

The *onStatus( )* information object will not indicate that a stream has been deleted. It will show only that the stream has been successfully published:

```
clientid: 64144408
description: Publishing public/junk.
code: NetStream.Publish.Start
level: status

clientid: 64144408
description: public/junk is now unpublished.
```

```
code: NetStream.Unpublish.Success
level: status
```

The second message with a code of "NetStream.Unpublish.Success" results from closing the stream. MP3 files cannot be deleted this way, as a client cannot publish MP3 files.

Deleting an FLV file with a Stream object

You can also delete a recorded FLV stream using the server-side *Stream* class. A *Stream* instance can *get( )* a stream and then delete it by calling its *clear( )* method. Here is another way to delete the same *junk.flv* file from the preceding example, this time using server-side code:

```
junkStream = Stream.get("public/junk");
junkStream.onStatus = function (info) {
  for (var p in info) {
    trace(p + ": " + info[p]);
  }
};
junkStream.clear();
```

When a server-side *Stream* object clears a stream this way, FlashCom invokes *onStatus( )* with an information object whose code value is "NetStream.Clear.Success", which indicates the stream file has been deleted:

```
code: NetStream.Clear.Success
level: status
```

MP3 files cannot be deleted this way, because a server-side *Stream* object cannot publish, and therefore cannot *get( )*, an MP3 URI.

Deleting MP3 and FLV files with the application object

The only way to programmatically delete MP3 files (which also works for FLV files) and to delete more than one file at a time using a URI pattern as with *application. clearStreams( )*. Using *clearStreams( )*, you can delete either a single MP3 or FLV file, a batch of either MP3 or FLV files using a wildcard pattern, or all the MP3 or FLV files belonging to an application instance. To delete an individual file, pass the relative URI of the file to the *clearStreams( )* method:

```
if (application.clearStreams("flv:/public/junk")) {
  trace("Stream was successfully deleted or did not exist.");
}
else {
  trace("Stream was not deleted.");
}
```

The URI does not require the first forward slash—*flv:public/junk*—will also work. The *application.onStatus( )* method is not invoked when *clearStreams( )* is called. Instead, *clearStreams( )* returns true if the file was deleted or no file was found. If a file is found but could not be deleted, it returns false. The flv: prefix at the

---

beginning of the URI makes it clear that an FLV file is to be deleted. However, if the flv: prefix is not included, it is assumed. To delete an MP3 file, mp3: must be prefixed to the URI. For example:

```
application.clearStreams("mp3:/music/boringTrack");
```

will delete *boringTrack.mp3* from the *music* directory. If mp3: is not prefixed, the *clearStreams( )* method will attempt to delete an FLV file named *boringTrack.flv*. If it doesn't find one, it will still return true.

Two wildcard characters, * and ?, can be used to delete files matching a wildcard pattern within a directory and all its subdirectories. For example, the following statement will delete all the files beginning with the string "junk" in the *public* directory and all its subdirectories:

```
application.clearStreams("/public/junk*");
```

An asterisk (*) can be used on its own to indicate that either all FLV or all MP3 files in a directory and its subdirectories should be deleted. For example, to delete all FLV files in the *public* directory and all its subdirectories use:

```
application.clearStreams("/public/*");
```

The asterisk is not really necessary. For example, you can delete all the files in the *public* directory and all its subdirectories this way:

```
application.clearStreams("/public/");
```

If all files in a directory, such as *public*, and its subdirectories are deleted as a result of a *clearStreams( )* call, the directory (in this case, *public*) and all its subdirectories will also be deleted.

The ? character can also be used to match a single character. For example, to delete all the files that start with "log_" followed by exactly four characters, use the following:

```
application.clearStreams("/private/log_????");
```

The preceding examples delete FLV files because the file type was not specified. To delete MP3 files, prefix the stream URI with the string mp3: as in this statement:

```
application.clearStreams("mp3:/music/*");
```

 Unfortunately, wildcard patterns do not work in FlashCom versions 1.5 through 1.5.2 but do work in version 1.0. You can still clear all the files in a directory this way:

```
application.clearStreams("/public/");
```

To delete all the FLV stream files of an instance, use a single forward slash as the stream URI. For example:

```
application.clearStreams("/");
```

Or you can prefix the slash with flv:

```
application.clearStreams("flv:/");
```

To delete all the MP3 stream files of an instance, use:

```
application.clearStreams("mp3:/");
```

Publishing and Playing ActionScript Data

ActionScript data can be added to a published stream at any time. The data is always added as part of a method invocation request. For example, we can't just add the text string "Hi Robert, how are you?" to a stream. Instead, we have to name a method that will receive our text. In Example 5-1, we chose to have each client publishing an out_ns stream specify the method name "showMessage" and the text to pass to it:

```
out_ns.send("showMessage", input_txt.text);
```

The *NetStream.send( )* method sends a method name, parameters, and timestamp to the server along with the published stream.

The *out_ns.send( )* method invocation adds the name of the method ("showMessage"), the data to be passed into the method (the text from the input_txt.text field), and a stream timestamp to the published stream.

In the case of a live stream, the method name, parameters, and timestamp will be sent to the server along with any audio and video. The server forwards the ActionScript data on to any clients subscribed to the stream. When each client receives the ActionScript data from the server, nothing will happen unless the *NetStream* object playing the stream has a *showMessage( )* method defined on it. From Example 5-1:

```
in_ns.showMessage = function (msg) {
  writeln(msg);
};
```

Since the *showMessage( )* method is usually invoked on a client other than the sender, it is referred to as a *remote method*.

Not only does the server send on ActionScript data to live subscribers of a stream, but it also stores the ActionScript data in the stream's FLV file if the stream is being recorded. Clients that subscribe to a recorded stream will also receive the recorded ActionScript data in sync with stream time and any audio or video that was recorded.

 Sending ActionScript data in a stream can be tremendously useful. The data can be used to record all sorts of events, such as someone adding text to a chat, showing a slide during a presentation, or starting to publish a different stream.

Chapter 15 includes an entire session recording and playback framework based on recording and playing back ActionScript data in a stream. However, there are other ways to send a remote method request to other clients that are often more practical than sending data in a stream. Chapter 9 covers all the options for invoking remote methods in detail.

The client-side *NetStream.send( )* method and the server-side *Stream.send( )* method both allow you to send ActionScript data in a stream. There are two essential steps to making remote method invocation work: defining a method on the subscribing *NetStream* object and sending the request to the method within a published stream.

Defining a Remote Method

Defining a remote method to be executed on a *NetStream* object is no different than defining a method on any ActionScript object. The method can be defined on NetStream.prototype, which makes it available to every *NetStream* object, or as an individual method of a particular *NetStream* instance. The following code snippet shows two simple method definitions. Both methods rely on a function or object (not shown) to do the real work:

```
// Defining a method on the prototype object for all instances.
NetStream.prototype.showMessage = function (msg) {
  writeln(msg);
};

ns = new NetStream(nc);

// Defining a method for a single instance.
ns.doCommand = function (command) {
  commandHandler.doCommand(command);
};
```

Both methods can be invoked only if the *NetStream* object ns is playing a stream. Publishing streams cannot invoke their own methods using *send( )*. When a *NetStream* method such as *showMessage( )* or *doCommand( )* is invoked, it cannot return a value the way a normal ActionScript function can. If a remote method does attempt to use a return statement to return a value, the value is discarded.

Sending a Request

A request to invoke a remote method can be sent by a publishing *NetStream* object or by a subscribed server-side *Stream* object. Both objects use the *send( )* method to make a request. The first parameter of the *send( )* method is always the name of the remote method (handler name) to invoke. Any optional parameters passed after the method name are passed as parameters into the remote method when it is invoked:

```
// Passing a single string parameter.
out_ns.send("showMessage", input_txt.text);
```

```
// Passing a complex object.
cObj = {command: "rewriteField", text: "Sample Text.", scroll: 1};
out_ns.send("doCommand", cObj);
```

On the server, method invocation requests can also be made by a *Stream* object:

```
s = Stream.get("monitorStream");
s.send("showMessage", "New client logged in from " + client.ip);
```

Stream logs

The *send( )* method can be used to write log data into a recorded stream file. In fact, this is the way FlashCom stores all its log files.

 The advantage to using streams to store log data is that streams, unlike shared objects, can store very large amounts of data with little impact on client or server memory.

The data can be read back by defining a method on a *NetStream* object and then playing the stream.

In the simple homegrown Example 5-15, a server-side *Stream* object is used to record events as they occur.

Example 5-15. Simple application logging

```
log_s = Stream.get("log");
log_s.record("append");

application.onAppStart = function ( ) {
  log_s.send("onLog", {event: "onAppStart",
                      time: new Date( ),
                      appInstance: application.name});
};

application.onConnect = function (client, userName, password) {
  log_s.send("onLog", {event: "onConnect",
                      time:  new Date( ),
                      ip:    client.ip,
                      userName: userName});
  return true;
};

application.onDisconnect = function (client) {
  log_s.send("onLog", {event: "onDisconnect",
                      time:  new Date( ),
                      ip:    client.ip,
                      userName: userName});
  return true;
};
```

Playing the log file back from a remote client is done by connecting to the instance and then playing the log stream. However, since this is a log file that may have taken many hours to record, we don't want to wait for hours to get back all the Action-Script data. To play all the ActionScript data immediately, we can set the flushPlaylists parameter to a value of 2 or 3:

```
ns = new NetStream(nc);
ns.onLog = function (info) {
  for (var p in info) {
    trace(p + ": " + info[p]);
  }
};
ns.play("log", 0, -1, 3);
```

In this example, the value 3 is specified as the *NetStream.play( )* method's flushPlaylists parameter. If a value of 2 or 3 is passed in, all remote method call requests are retrieved immediately before any stream audio or video begins to play. A value of 3 resets the playlist while a value of 2 maintains the current playlist.

Here is some sample output:

```
time: Sat May 24 22:42:51 GMT-0400 2003
event: onAppStart
appInstance: customLog/_definst_
userName: Guest
time: Sat May 24 22:42:51 GMT-0400 2003
ip: 127.0.0.1
event: onConnect
userName: blesser
time: Sat May 24 22:43:04 GMT-0400 2003
ip: 127.0.0.1
event: onDisconnect
```

In fact, you don't have to go to all this work to log events. FlashCom can write out *trace( )* messages to an application log for you if you ask it to. The messages are saved in a stream file as *onLogMsg( )* requests and can be read back with a utility such as the one cited shortly. To turn on application logging, use the <RecordAppLog> tag in any *Application.xml* file. Replace the default false value with true:

```
<RecordAppLog>true</RecordAppLog>
```

Logging can use a great deal of disk space, so you may want to place individual *Application.xml* files with the <RecordAppLog> tag set to true in the home directory of the applications you want to log. The log file will be saved to the *.../admin/streams/ logs/application/appName* directory and will be named after the application instance name, for example, *_definst_.flv*. FlashCom can also create a server access log that records information about when users logged in and out of the system.

A utility to read log files and more information on FlashCom logs are available at:

http://www.macromedia.com/support/flashcom/ts/documents/ flashcom_logging.htm

See Chapter 12 for another approach to application-level logging and Chapter 18 for a discussion of logging options.

Sending and recording events

The *send( )* method can be used to send and record information to be acted on in sync with audio and video. For example, during an online lecture, a professor may wish to bold a section of text in a text field in order to focus attention on it. When the professor clicks a Send button, each student will see the section of text bolded in the Flash movie she is watching. Later, when the recorded version of the stream is played back, the bolding of text will again occur, synchronized to the audio stream of the professor's voice.

Making a system like this work requires building a Flash movie or movies that capture audio and events from the professor, translate the events into some form of data, such as an object, and send them in the stream. When the data in the stream arrives at the subscribing movie, it must be acted on to produce the required effect.

When an object is used to send an instruction—for example to tell another movie to bold text in a text field—it is often called a *command object*. See the *Command* design pattern in the book *Design Patterns* by Erich Gamma et al. (Addison Wesley).

Example 5-16 shows a partial listing of code that creates an object containing information about the formatting of text in a text field. (The complete example is available on the book's web site.) The formatTextCommand object is an instance of the *FormatTextCommandClass* class and contains the starting and ending positions of the text to select and bold. It is created after the user highlights some text and clicks a Send button.

Example 5-16. Sending a command to set selected text in bold

```
function FormatTextCommandClass (start, end) {
  this.startIndex = start;      // Beginning of selection
  this.endIndex = end;         // End of selection
}

FormatTextCommandClass.prototype.destination = "code_mc";
FormatTextCommandClass.prototype.command = "formatText";
FormatTextCommandClass.prototype.repaint = false;

// Called when the Send button is clicked.
function doSend () {
  if (lastTextobj.focusedField == code_txt) {
    // Show the professor the text set in bold.
    code_txt.setTextFormat(normalFormat);
    code_txt.setTextFormat(lastTextObj.startIndex,
                           lastTextObj.endIndex,
                           highlightFormat);
    // Create a command object and queue it up.
    var formatTextCommand = new FormatTextCommandClass(lastTextObj.startIndex,
```

Example 5-16. Sending a command to set selected text in bold (continued)

```
                                                  lastTextObj.endIndex);
    sender.queueCommand(formatTextCommand);
  }
  sender.send();
}
```

The `lastTextObj` and `sender` objects are not shown. The `sender` object contains a queue of events and sends them in a stream using the following statement (where `obj` is a command already in the sender's queue):

```
    ns.send("doCommand", obj);
```

When the stream is playing (live or recorded), command objects are passed into the *doCommand( )* method of subscribing streams:

```
    ns.doCommand = function (command) {
      command.time = this.time;
      commandHandler.doCommand(command);
    };
```

In this case, the `commandHandler` object passes the command on to an object that finds the destination movie clip (in this case named code_mc) and calls its *formatText( )* method. The *formatText( )* method, shown in Example 5-17, sets the formatting of the code_txt field and then uses the information in the command to bold a section of the text.

Example 5-17. Processing the command to bold a text selection

```
highlightFormat = new TextFormat();
highlightFormat.bold = true;
highlightFormat.color = 0x004433;

normalFormat = new TextFormat();
normalFormat.bold = false;
normalFormat.color = 0x006655;

function formatText (command) {
  code_txt.setTextFormat(normalFormat);
  code_txt.setTextFormat(command.startIndex, command.endIndex, highlightFormat);
}
```

Creating Synchronized Presentations

One of the most compelling features of FlashCom-enabled applications is the way Flash content and streaming audio and video can be merged into a seamless and full-featured presentation. With some careful scripting, you can create a presentation that includes optional viewing of closed captions, animated slides, dynamic repositioning of video, and other effects all synchronized to video playback. There are two approaches to synchronizing events, such as displaying closed captions, to stream time.

The first approach is to embed information about events directly in a stream using the *NetStream.send( )* method. The advantages of *send( )* are that synchronization is as precise as it can be and that it often requires less scripting. The disadvantages are that *send( )* must be called on the publishing stream while it is being recorded and, if the user is allowed to seek to different parts of a stream, additional scripting is required to replay or reestablish the events up to the time the user seeks to. In the future, FLV editors may become available that allow postproduction embedding and editing of remote method calls.

The second approach is to synchronize a list of instructions to a stream by regularly checking (polling) the stream time to see if an instruction should be executed. An instruction can be used to display a caption, resize or hide a video object, or display an animation. For presentations, especially when prerecorded video and audio from multiple sources must be assembled, synchronizing lists of instructions to a stream by regularly checking stream time is the most practical approach.

Adding Closed Captions

Closed captions are a good place to experiment with synchronizing presentation events to a stream. When someone is speaking, the caption containing the correct words must be displayed. A simple and flexible way to provide closed captioning data is to provide a list of caption start times along with the text of each caption in an XML file:

```
<closedCaptions>
  <caption seconds="0.0"><![CDATA[]]></caption>
  <caption seconds="3.0"><![CDATA[Welcome to my presentation.]]></caption>
  <caption seconds="7.0"><![CDATA[I hope you enjoy it.]]></caption>
</closedCaptions>
```

Each <caption> tag contains a seconds attribute, which is the stream time at which the caption should first be displayed. Within each <caption> tag, a <![CDATA[]]> tag is used to contain unencoded text. Any unencoded text, including the & and < characters, can safely be placed in a CDATA section. When Flash parses the XML, the contents of the CDATA section will be converted to a text node. The first <caption> tag contains no text so that when the stream starts, no caption text will be visible. Other empty captions can be added to a list of captions to pad the list for intervals when no one is speaking.

When the XML data is loaded into a Flash movie, it can be used to create an array of objects. Each object can have a time property and a text property.

During playback of the stream, the stream time must be checked at regular intervals against the caption that is currently displayed. If the wrong caption is displayed, the correct one must be found and displayed. Either *setInterval( )* or *onEnterFrame( )* can be used to regularly call a function to check the stream time against the current caption. Unless a very low frame rate is used, checking with *onEnterFrame( )* is a good practice as it will be called just before the next frame is redrawn. There is often little point in choosing an interval that checks several times in between frames or more often than the movie's frame rate.

Since the stream time will be checked repeatedly, the process of finding the correct caption should be as efficient as possible. A simple and efficient way to check the caption is to store caption objects in an array sorted by time, as depicted in Figure 5-4. An index into the array can be used to keep track of the current caption and easily get the time of the next caption.

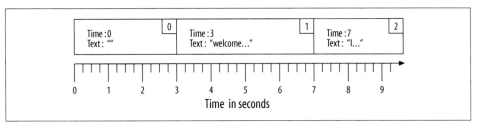

Figure 5-4. An array of caption objects laid out against time

Assuming the stream begins to play at 0 seconds and proceeds forward linearly, the first caption can be displayed, and the time of the next caption—in the illustration, 3 seconds—kept in a variable. As long as the current stream time is less than the next caption time, nothing has to be done. When the time finally progresses to being equal to or greater than the time of the next caption, the next caption can be displayed and the time of the one following it retrieved. Later, when time becomes equal to or greater than 7, the next caption is shown. Assuming that an array named captionList containing caption objects with time properties is available, a simple *onEnterFrame( )* function might look something like this:

```
// Start with caption number 0.
currentIndex = 0;
// Get the time of the next caption.
nextCaptionTime = captionList[1].time;
// Deal with the case where there is no next caption.
if (!nextCaptionTime) nextCaptionTime = Number.POSITIVE_INFINITY;
// Show the current caption.
showCaption(currentIndex);

// As the stream plays, keep checking the stream time.
function onEnterFrame () {
  // If the stream time has progressed far enough, show the next caption.
  if (ns.time >= nextCaptionTime) {
    currentIndex++;
    nextCaptionTime = captionList[currentIndex + 1].time;
    if (!nextCaptionTime) nextCaptionTime = Number.POSITIVE_INFINITY;
    showCaption(currentIndex);
  }
}
```

The *showCaption( )* function is not shown but is responsible for displaying the text of a caption. A strategy like this works well if the stream only plays through from the beginning to the end. If the user is allowed to navigate to any part of the stream at any time, another approach must be used to find the current caption in the array. Since the captions are stored in time order, a binary search can be performed on the array to quickly find the current caption when necessary. When the stream begins to play again, the script can go back to checking the time of the next caption.

Captions are much like other events that have to be synchronized to stream time, so it makes sense to create a general purpose container to hold events and keep them synchronized to a stream.

The book's web site includes a complete tech note that describes the design and development of a *SynchronizedEventsList* class, which can store, find, and return events given a stream time. The tech note contains a complete sample presentation and source code. The sample combines closed captioning with repositioning, hiding, and showing of video as the presentation progresses and synchronized animations. For the sake of brevity, the entire application, which includes a *NetStream* subclass; the *ClosedCaptionsManager*, *CaptionEvent*, and *PlaybackDirector* classes; and methods to read and parse an XML file, is not listed here.

Adding Synchronized Slides

The presentation on the book's site uses the *SynchronizedEventsList* class from within other objects to synchronize events to a stream. A *SynchronizedEventsList* instance can be used by another object to store events and then to find an event for a specific time. For example, another object that has the responsibility of responding to stream events by always displaying the correct caption can create its own *SynchronizedEventsList* instance and then use it to store captions and find the right one at any time. In fact, it is a good idea to use a separate events list because it makes searching for the correct event much simpler than trying to mix caption and other types of events within a single array.

The presentation implements custom *SlideManager* and *SlideEvent* classes. As the slideshow stream plays, the playhead of the client movie's timeline must be moved to a labeled frame representing each slide at the appropriate time. The example uses an XML file to define the start times in seconds when each frame label should be played.

The NetStream and Stream Information Objects

The *onStatus( )* method of a client-side *NetStream* or server-side *Stream* object is called and passed information objects as significant stream events occur. We've already made use of many of them throughout this chapter. The properties within the information object are more formally described in Table 5-2.

Table 5-2. Information object property names

Property name	Description
clientid	A unique server-side ID for the client
code	A dot-separated string code for the event such as "NetStream.Buffer.Empty"
description	A longer description of the event than provided by the code property
details	The name of the stream
level	The type of message—either "status" or "error"

The code property values are described in detail in Table 5-3 (all codes start with "NetStream.", which is omitted from the code column). Each entry shows the level value and whether the code applies to the *NetStream* and/or *Stream* class.

Table 5-3. Code strings

Code	Level	NetStream	Stream	Comments
Buffer.Empty	status	X		The stream buffer is empty. An empty buffer can mean two things on a subscribing stream. If data is not arriving as quickly as it is being played, the buffer will empty and the stream will stop audibly or visually playing until the buffer refills. If the stream has come to the end of the server so that no more data is being sent, the buffer will eventually be emptied, indicating that the stream has finished playing. For a publishing stream, an empty buffer indicates that all the stream data that was waiting in the buffer to be sent to the server has been sent.
Buffer.Full	status	X		The stream buffer has reached or exceeded the stream buffer time value in seconds of data. On subscribing streams, a full buffer indicates that a stream has enough stream data in it to begin audibly or visually playing. On a publishing stream, a full buffer indicates that so much data is waiting in the buffer to be sent to the server that the buffer has reached or exceeded the stream's buffer time value.
Clear.Failed	error		X	At least one of the stream files to be deleted by *application.clearStreams( )* could not be deleted.
Clear.Success	status		X	A recorded stream or streams were successfully cleared by the *application.clearStreams( )* method.
Failed	error	X	X	An attempt to use a *Stream* or *NetStream* method failed for a reason not described by another code value.
Pause.Notify	status	X		A subscribing stream has paused playback. See also Unpause.Notify.

Table 5-3. Code strings (continued)

Code	Level	NetStream	Stream	Comments
Play.Failed	error	X		A *play( )* request failed for a reason not described by another code value.
Play.PublishNotify	status	X		If a live stream is not immediately available when *NetStream* objects attempt to subscribe to it, they will wait until it is. When the stream is published, all waiting subscribers receive this message.
Play.Reset	status	X		All pending *play( )* requests have been dropped and the playlist has been reset.
Play.Start	status	X		Stream data has started to arrive from the server. This message is received whenever the server starts sending data to a subscribing stream. Examples include when the stream first starts to play and when it begins to play after a seek or pause.
Play.Stop	status	X		Stream data has stopped arriving from the server. When subscribed to a recorded stream, this code indicates the server has come to the end of the stream and does not need to send more data.
Play.StreamNot-Found	error	X		An attempt to subscribe to a recorded stream has failed because the stream file could not be found. This code value will not be returned if the subscribing stream attempts to play a live or recorded stream using a start parameter value of -2 or omits a start parameter value entirely.
Play.UnpublishNotify	status	X		When a live stream stops publishing, all subscribers receive this message.
Publish.BadName	error	X	X	The stream could not be published because a live stream with the same name is currently being published.
Publish.Idle	status	X		The message is received by a publisher that has not sent any data on the stream for a long time.
Publish.Start	status	X		Informs the publisher that the stream is being successfully published to the server.
Record.Failed	error	X	X	The stream could not be recorded for a reason not described by another code value.
Record.NoAccess	error	X	X	The publisher attempted to record a stream without write access.
Record.Start	status	X	X	Recording has started.
Record.Stop	status	X	X	Recording has stopped.
Seek.Failed	error	X		A subscriber's attempt to seek to a time in a stream failed.
Seek.Notify	status	X		A subscriber's attempt to seek to a time in a stream has succeeded.
Unpause.Notify	status	X		The subscriber has resumed playing a paused stream.
Unpublish.Success	status	X	X	Notice to the publisher that the stream has stopped publishing.

Stream Enhancements and Limitations

Macromedia has been improving the streaming capability of FlashCom and the ability of the Flash Player to play streams. FlashCom 1.5 introduced the ability to stream MP3 files, and Flash Player 7 introduced the ability to progressively download and play streams from a web server, a feature not covered here as it does not rely on FlashCom (refer to the Preface). Some of the many other small improvements are covered in this section.

Server-Side send( ) Enhancements

FlashCom 1.5.2 fixed a problem with adding *send( )* methods to a stream on the server. Whenever a server-side *Stream* object was used to send a method request within a stream, any subscribers to the live stream received the request just after it was sent. However, when a recorded stream was played back, any messages generated on the server all played back either at the beginning of the stream or in blocks during playback. The reason for the requests being received out of sync was that the stream time was determined by the publishing client and not by the server-side *Stream* object. The publishing client's *NetStream* sent a timestamp when audio or video was attached to the stream and whenever *send( )* was called. The server-side *Stream* object could not determine the precise stream time when it inserted a method request, so the time of the request was set to the timestamp of the last message in the stream. The problem was resolved in FlashCom 1.5.2 by having the server keep track of stream time and adjusting the time difference for each *send( )* method added to the stream. While the change may seem like a small one, it makes possible developing server-side recordings of chats and other applications. See Chapter 15 for more information.

Prior to FlashCom 1.5.2, remote methods defined on a server-side *Stream* object were never called. As of FlashCom 1.5.2, methods can be defined on a server-side *Stream* just as they can be defined on a client-side *NetStream* instance. When Action-Script data is played, the server-side *Stream* object's method will be called.

Sound Performance

FlashCom 1.5.2 also reduced the load on the server caused by sending audio to multiple subscribers. CPU load is often a determining factor in how many streams a server can manage. During live streams, the server does not immediately send each packet of sound information on to each subscriber as it arrives. Instead, the server waits until it has collected a small batch of sound samples and sends them at once. The result is a significant decrease in CPU usage when there are a large number of subscribers.

ActionScript 2.0

ActionScript 2.0 introduced strong typing to client-side ActionScript. In Flash MX 2004 and Flash Pro, the *NetStream* class is not defined as being a dynamic class. As a result, predefined methods such as *onStatus( )* can be dynamically redefined without the compiler complaining, but new methods—such as those required to receive remote method calls—cannot be added using the dot operator. The following short snippet will produce the compiler error "There is no property with the name 'show-Message'":

```
var nc = new NetConnection( );
var ns:NetStream = new NetStream(nc);
ns.onStatus = function (info) {
  trace(info.code);
};
ns.showMessage = function (msg) { // Compiler error!
  trace(msg);
};
```

One way around the problem is to simply not use strong typing—do not declare the ns variable as being a *NetStream*. Instead, simply use:

```
var ns = new NetStream(nc);
```

If you want to use strong typing, an alternative solution is to use the [ ] operator:

```
nc = new NetConnection( );
var ns:NetStream = new NetStream(nc);
ns.onStatus = function (info) {
  trace(info.code);
};
ns["showMessage"] = function (msg) {
  trace(msg);
};
```

Synchronization Limitations

In FlashCom 1.5.2 and earlier, each stream can carry only one audio and one video channel. Consequently, to play multiple video and audio channels at the same time requires more than one stream. However, there is no way to prebuffer and queue multiple streams to begin playing at the same time or to keep them synchronized while they play. Consequently, accurate synchronization of multiple streams is not currently possible.

Conclusion

The *NetStream* and *Stream* classes are the core classes for organizing and moving large amounts of data back and forth between Flash and FlashCom. In conjunction with the *SharedObject* class, the *NetStream* and *Stream* classes provide an amazing

---

wealth of options for delivering real-time or recorded audio, video, and ActionScript data. In the remaining chapters, streams will be used for video conferencing, to play chat histories, and to record and play back application events—you'll find them everywhere. After a while, using them whenever you need to move data will become second nature.

CHAPTER 6

Microphone and Camera

Flash movies can capture live audio and video from a microphone and camera attached to the user's computer using the *Camera* and *Microphone* classes. However, to share live audio and video content with other users, you need to publish the audio and video streams to a FlashCom application. You can use this feature to conduct live audio/video conferences with several online users or to monitor remote locations. You can also script your Flash movie to record live audio and video directly to the FlashCom application.

Generally, the Flash *.swf* file must be Flash Player 6 format or later (and played in Flash Player 6 or higher) to publish camera and microphone content. However, not all devices have built-in support for all features. For example, publishing audio from the Pocket PC requires an external microphone attached to the unit. As you'll learn later in this chapter, you can check the Camera.names property to determine if the user has a recognized video capture (or camera) driver.

Working with Microphone/Audio Input

Flash Player 6 and higher support the intrinsic *Microphone* class, enabling Flash to accept audio input from the client. The *Microphone* class does not interface directly with FlashCom, but it does provide the means by which you can capture the input and send it over a stream to the FlashCom application on the server. In the simplest scenario, working with microphone input requires very minimal code. Of course, many other scenarios will require more sophistication. In the following sections, you'll get the chance to learn how to use the *Microphone* class to create applications of varying complexity.

Getting the Microphone/Audio Input

Before you can do anything with microphone input, you need to open a *Microphone* instance that references the device. The static *Microphone.get( )* method returns a reference to a *Microphone* instance, which creates a connection to a specific device attached to the computer:

```
// Create a Microphone instance, which creates a
// connection to the default audio device.
user_mic = Microphone.get( );
```

A computer may not have an audio input device, in which case *get( )* returns null. If an audio device is present but currently locked exclusively by another application, the Flash Player won't be able to use it, though it won't report null either. Most devices on Windows do not enable exclusive locks. Macintosh audio devices aren't exclusively locked either. Furthermore, it's very unlikely that two applications would try to gain exclusive use of an audio device at the same time. Therefore, it's not likely to be an issue.

A computer may have more than one audio device connected. In most scenarios, you will want to use the default device. The user can and should select the default device from the Macromedia Flash Player Settings panel's Microphone tab. (This panel is accessible by choosing Settings from the Flash Player context menu.) This not only puts the user in control, it ensures that the same device is active for all applications that use a microphone. When you call *get( )* with no parameters, Flash creates an object (a *Microphone* instance) that connects to the default device.

However, in other, less common scenarios, you may want to programmatically select a different device. Each audio device connected to the computer has an integer index. You can pass the corresponding index to *get( )* in order to instruct the Flash Player to create a *Microphone* instance that references the specified device:

```
// Create a Microphone instance that creates a
// connection to the audio device with index 1.
user_mic = Microphone.get(1);
```

The indexes you can use with *get( )* represent elements of the Microphone.names array, which contains a list of audio devices detected by Flash. For example, if your computer has two sound cards recognized by Flash, then the following code would display 2 in the Output panel:

```
trace(Microphone.names.length);
```

Once you've created a *Microphone* instance, you can also retrieve the index and name of the device to which it connects, using the index and name properties:

```
trace(user_mic.index);
trace(user_mic.name);
```

Note that the first device is index 0, not 1.

Understanding Microphone Permissions

The Flash Player allows the user to make decisions about what happens with regard to his computer, including the Player's access to audio devices. When you invoke

Microphone.get( ), Flash creates an object that contains information about an audio device connected to the computer. However, before you can do anything useful with the device, the user has to grant permission.

Users grant (or deny) permission via the Macromedia Flash Player Settings panel, as shown in Figure 6-1. The Settings panel opens automatically when the Flash application attempts to obtain data from a *Microphone* object, such as getting Microphone. activityLevel or attaching a microphone to a published stream. However, attaching a *Microphone* object to a stream that is not being published will not open the Settings panel. If the stream is published afterward, the panel will open.

Figure 6-1. Asking permission to access the local microphone

The Settings panel appears only if the dimensions of the Flash Player exceed 215 x 138. Otherwise, the panel will not display, and there will be no further notification to the user.

When the user is presented with the Settings panel, she has the option to either allow or deny access to the audio device. If she allows access, Flash will have access to the microphone input. However, your program must also deal gracefully with the user denying access to the audio devices. Therefore, you need a way to detect what option the user selected. Fortunately, the *Microphone.onStatus( )* method is called automatically when the user changes the permission for the device via the Settings panel. Flash passes a single parameter to the method—an information object with a code property of "Microphone.Muted" or "Microphone.Unmuted". The following is an example of an *onStatus( )* event handler as you might define it for testing purposes on a *Microphone* object named user_mic:

```
user_mic.onStatus = function (info) {
  if (info.code == "Microphone.Muted") {
    trace("You have denied access to the following audio device: " + this.name);
  }
  else if (info.code == "Microphone.Unmuted") {
    trace("You have allowed access to the following audio device: " + this.name);
  }
};
```

The Settings panel opens automatically when you attempt to use microphone audio in the Flash application. However, the panel can be opened in two other ways. The user can manually open the Settings panel by choosing Settings from the Flash Player context menu (available by right-clicking atop the Flash Player window on Windows or Ctrl-clicking on Macintosh). Alternatively, Flash can programmatically open the Settings panel using the *System.showSettings( )* method:

```
System.showSettings();
```

When the Settings panel opens automatically, it merely enables the user to grant or deny permission, as shown in Figure 6-1. When opened either programmatically or by way of the context menu, the panel offers more options, as shown in Figure 6-2.

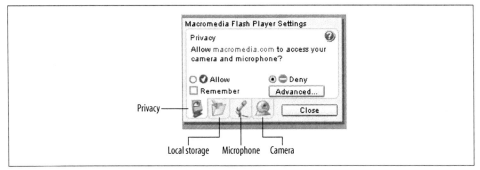

Figure 6-2. The full-fledged Macromedia Flash Player Settings panel

By default, *showSettings( )* opens the Settings panel to the tab that was last open. You can also specify an integer from 0 to 3 as a parameter to *showSettings( )*, which tells Flash which tab to display:

0

Opens the Privacy tab where the user can allow or deny access to the camera and microphone devices. The Advanced button opens the Settings Manager URL on Macromedia's site where the user can configure privacy and storage settings on a per–web site basis, plus set global preferences for privacy, storage, security, and automatic notifications.

1

Opens the Local Storage tab, allowing the user to control the amount of local storage allocated to the domain.

2

Opens the Microphone tab, allowing the user to select an audio input device, set recording volume, and control echo suppression.

3

Opens the Camera tab, allowing the user to select a video input device.

Many users find it invasive for a program to open the Settings panel without the user initiating it. Instead, provide a button that allows the user to open the panel. The following code assigns an *onRelease( )* event handler method to a button instance so that it opens the Settings panel when clicked. The button is initially made invisible, but if the user denies access to the audio device, the button is made visible:

```
settings_btn.onRelease = function () {
  System.showSettings(0);
};
settings_btn._visible = false;
user_mic.onStatus = function (info) {
  if (info.code == "Microphone.Muted") {
    settings_btn._visible = true;
  }
  else if (info.code == "Microphone.Unmuted") {
    settings_btn._visible = false;
  }
};
```

Detecting the Microphone Privacy Setting

If your Flash application requires access to the microphone, you'll need a way to detect whether the user has allowed such access.

Your application can check the read-only, Boolean Microphone.muted property to determine whether the user has granted access to the microphone. The property is false if access is allowed. However, the default is true (indicating access denied) until the user grants permission or if the user has remembered a deny status.

So let's imagine that your application attempts to publish audio input from the microphone.

If the user has not yet been asked for permission to access the microphone:

1. The initial value of the muted property is true.
2. The Settings panel shown in Figure 6-1 opens automatically, prompting the user to either allow or deny access.
3. After the user makes a selection, Flash invokes the *Microphone.onStatus( )* method.
4. You can check the muted property from within *onStatus( )* to determine whether the user has allowed access and act accordingly.

But as discussed earlier, if the Settings panel is opened programmatically or via the context menu, the user can also choose whether to remember the Allow or Deny setting, as shown in Figure 6-2. If a user selects the Remember option, Flash remembers that privacy setting for other movies run from the same domain.

If the user previously remembered an "Allow" setting (allow state), the muted property is false and access to the audio device is allowed, so your Flash movie can access the microphone.

But if the user previously remembered a "deny" setting (deny state), the muted property is true and the Settings panel will not open automatically. Because Flash invokes *onStatus( )* only when there is a change in the privacy status, *onStatus( )* won't be invoked. However, you shouldn't assume from the muted property alone whether the user has yet to be prompted for permission or whether he has remembered a deny state!

If the user has chosen to remember a deny state, it may be rude to display the Settings panel programmatically and ask him to reconsider. We need a more graceful way to determine what to do next.

One possible solution is as follows:

1. Before attaching or publishing the audio, check the value of the muted property. If muted is false, the user has granted access to the microphone, so your application can skip the remaining steps and proceed as normal.

2. Otherwise, the muted property is true, so continue with Steps 3 through 6.

3. Use *setInterval( )* to create a timeout after a specified interval. If the timeout is reached, assume the user had previously selected that the Player should remember a deny state. Therefore, the timeout handler should decide whether to abort the application, prompt the user to change his mind, or continue running the application without microphone input.

4. Add an *onStatus( )* event handler method that clears the interval created in Step 3. The handler should also check the muted property to determine whether the user chose to allow or deny access to the audio device and proceed accordingly.

5. Attach or publish the audio.

6. If the timeout is reached, assume the user had previously selected that the Player should remember a deny state, and proceed as described in Step 3. If *onStatus( )* is called, it can check the muted property as described in Step 4.

The following code illustrates the basic idea:

```
// Get a microphone object.
var user_mic = Microphone.get( );

// Declare a variable to hold the interval identifier.
var mutedInterval;

// If muted is false, the user has remembered an allow state,
// so proceed as normal. Otherwise, set an interval for the timeout.
if (!user_mic.muted) {
  okay( );
}
else {
  // Set an interval for the timeout. This example uses a 5-second
  // timeout after which the muted( ) function is called.
  mutedInterval = setInterval(muted, 5000);
}
```

```
// Define an onStatus() method.
user_mic.onStatus = function (info) {
  // Clear the interval to prevent the timeout handler from executing.
  clearInterval(mutedInterval);

  // Call the appropriate function based on the user's selection.
  if (info.code == "Microphone.Muted") {
    muted();
  }
  else {
    okay();
  }
};

// Attach the audio (may trigger the Settings panel, depending on remember status).
this.attachAudio(user_mic);

/* The following functions simply display messages in the Output panel so that you
 * can see the way in which the code works. In an actual application you would
 * likely want to have the functions route the user's experience appropriately
 * depending on whether the user has allowed access to the audio device.
 */
function okay () {
  trace("okay");
}
function muted () {
  trace("muted");
}
```

The preceding solution is not without possible flaws. The key is determining the
optimal length for the timeout interval. If the timeout is too long, the user will have
to wait for a long time before she is notified of the status. But if the timeout is too
short, the application could make a decision while the user is still choosing to either
allow or deny access.

Attaching and Publishing Audio

Once you've created a *Microphone* instance, you can attach it to a movie clip so that
the audio plays back locally or attach it to a *NetStream* object and publish it to a
FlashCom server.

To play the audio locally, pass the *Microphone* instance to the *MovieClip.attachAu-
dio()* method:

```
controller_mc.attachAudio(user_mic);
```

To publish the input from a *Microphone* instance, first attach it to a stream using the
NetStream.attachAudio() method, as follows:

```
publisher_ns.attachAudio(user_mc);
```

You can then publish the stream using *NetStream.publish()*. The overhead of a net
stream without any data is negligible, so you can start publishing the stream without

having to check whether the user has granted permission to the audio device. See the previous section for details on determining whether the user has granted permission.

Adjusting Microphone Settings

Once you've created a *Microphone* instance and the user has granted permission to use the device, you can make some programmatic adjustments to the settings, including gain, rate, minimum activity level, and echo suppression. The gain and echo suppression properties correspond to options within the Settings panel. The rate and minimum activity–level properties are settable via ActionScript but do not have any corresponding options in the Settings panel.

Working with gain

The gain determines the audio recording level. The default value is 50, midway between the minimum value of 0 and a maximum value of 100. The higher the value, the louder the audio will sound. Keep in mind that the gain is not exactly the same thing as the volume level. Increasing the gain boosts the incoming signal, but it has the potential to increase feedback and distortion. If the user has the volume at the device level too low, he should adjust those settings. For example, if the user has the volume for the "mic in" channel of the sound card set to the minimum value, increasing the gain in the Flash Player is more likely to result in distortion and feedback than if the sound card level is set at higher values instead. Ideally, the user should set the volume of the microphone in the microphone driver's setting dialog box, because the appropriate volume usually applies to all applications. Unfortunately, some users will not set the microphone volume level properly, so setting the gain programmatically may be the only option to improve their audio input.

You can set the gain using the *setGain( )* method, passing a value from 0 to 100:

```
user_mic.setGain(50);
```

You can also retrieve the current gain with the read-only gain property:

```
trace(user_mic.gain);
```

The following code uses a NumericStepper component named cnsGain to allow the user to control the gain for a *Microphone* instance named user_mic (a NumericStepper is simply a numeric entry box with arrows to increase or decrease the values):

```
var gainListener = new Object();
gainListener.change = function (event) {
  user_mic.setGain(event.target.value);
};
cnsGain.addEventListener("change", gainListener);
cnsGain.minimum = 0;
cnsGain.maximum = 100;
cnsGain.value = user_mic.gain;
```

Working with rate

You can also programmatically control the sampling rate (in kHz) at which the audio is retrieved. Use the *setRate( )* method to set the rate to a value of 5, 8, 11, 22, or 44. Any other value is rounded to the nearest supported value:

```
user_mic.setRate(44);
```

Use the read-only rate property to retrieve the current rate:

```
trace(user_mic.rate);
```

The following code uses a combo box named ccbRate to allow the user to select a rate and apply it to the audio from a *Microphone* instance named user_mic:

```
// Populate the combo box with the possible rates.
ccbRate.dataProvider = [5, 8, 11, 22, 44];
// Set the initial value of the combo box, by selecting
// the item that matches the current rate.
for (var i:Number = 0; i < ccbRate.length; i++) {
  if (ccbRate.getItemAt(i) == user_mic.rate) {
    ccbRate.selectedIndex = i;
    break;
  }
}
// Set up a listener to update the rate when the combo box selection changes.
var rateListener = new Object();
rateListener.change = function (event) {
  user_mic.setRate(event.target.value);
};
ccbRate.addEventListener("change", rateListener);
```

Working with activity level

The activity level of a *Microphone* instance ranges from 0 (no activity) to 100 (maximum activity). Low-level ambient noise can register little to no activity (levels of 0 to 2) if the gain is low to normal. At high gain settings (or when there is loud computer equipment or nearby air conditioners), ambient noise can cause readings of 20 or more. You can retrieve the current activity level for a *Microphone* instance using the read-only activityLevel property. The following code uses *setInterval( )* to poll the activity level every 100 milliseconds and display the value in a text input component named ctiLevel:

```
setInterval(showLevel, 100);
function showLevel () {
  ctiLevel.text = user_mic.activityLevel;
}
```

Different applications may require different specifications with regard to how microphones function. In some scenarios, you may want to record every sound over a duration of time. In other applications, you may want to publish audio only when the activity level is above a certain threshold (voice-activated recording).

Also keep in mind that, when publishing audio, bandwidth can be a major issue. Publishing audio, even when the audio consists of just ambient noise, requires a lot of bandwidth. Consider the audio in a conferencing application—only one or two people are likely to be speaking at a time, yet tens or even hundreds of users may be participating. Flash provides you with the *setSilenceLevel( )* method in order to adjust the minimum activity level required for the microphone to set itself to active.

The default minimum activity level to activate a microphone is 10.

With a two-person conference, each user can adjust the listening volume on the receiving end, but with three or more participants, the volumes must be set correctly on the sending end, since they are mixed together on the receiving end.

 Ideally, each user should set her microphone gain in the Microphone tab of the Settings panel so that the default silence level of 10 is appropriate. If all users in a multiuser conference normalize their settings this way, their audio should all be at about the same volume (enabling everyone to hear everyone else).

However, you can adjust the minimum activity level programmatically to any value from 0 to 100. The following code sets the minimum activity level to 0, effectively making the microphone active regardless of activity level:

```
user_mic.setSilenceLevel(0);
```

A microphone remains active as long as the activity level remains above the minimum. After the activity level drops below the minimum, Flash does not deactivate the microphone until a timeout is reached. The default timeout is 2000 milliseconds (2 seconds). You can adjust the timeout as well as the minimum activity level using *setSilenceLevel( )*. Simply pass a second parameter to the method indicating the number of milliseconds you want Flash to wait before deactivating the microphone:

```
user_mic.setSilenceLevel(50, 1000);
```

When the microphone is deactivated, no audio is published over a *NetStream*. Instead, a single message is sent to the server to indicate that the audio stream is silent (a "silent" user consumes no bandwidth). Once the minimum activity level is surpassed again, the microphone starts sending audio data again.

Each time the microphone is activated or deactivated, the *Microphone.onActivity( )* event handler method is called. Flash passes the method a Boolean parameter indicating whether the microphone is active (true) or inactive (false). The following code writes a value to a text area component instance named ctaActivity each time the microphone is activated or deactivated:

```
user_mic.onActivity = function(active) {
  ctaActivity.text += active + newline;
};
```

You can use the read-only silenceLevel and silenceTimeout properties to retrieve the current values for the minimum activity level required to activate a microphone and the timeout before the microphone is deactivated.

Working with echo management

Microphones and speakers often cause unwanted echo, resulting in feedback. Feedback is normally a symptom of the microphone being placed so that it picks up audio from speakers. The best way to avoid speaker audio feeding back into the microphone is to advise users to use a closed headset instead of speakers. Most users have headsets from portable audio devices if not headsets purchased specifically for use with their computers. Some headsets have a built-in microphone and often provide the best echo protection, but even a standard headset will usually work well.

If a user must use speakers rather than headphones, no amount of programmatic attempts will take the place of good microphone placement. The microphone should be placed facing the user and away from the audio speakers. Assuming the speakers and the microphone are in front of the user, the microphone should be nearer to the user and the speakers should be further away. Furthermore, the microphone should be directional. If the microphone is omnidirectional, it will pick up speaker output no matter how it is placed relative to the speakers.

Though the effect is fairly minimal, you can manage echo and feedback slightly using the *Microphone.setUseEchoSuppression( )* method. You can call the method with a value of true to turn on echo suppression (the default value is false):

```
user_mic.setUseEchoSuppression(true);
```

The read-only useEchoSuppression property reports the current value.

> The echo suppression feature works by temporarily halving the gain when audio is playing through the speakers/headphones.

Working with Camera Input

Just as the *Microphone* class supports audio input, the *Camera* class allows your Flash application to display and publish video from a camera or other video input device. The following sections show how to use the *Camera* class to get video input and apply various settings to it.

Getting Camera Input

Getting camera input is practically identical to getting microphone input. Use the static *Camera.get( )* method in order to create a new *Camera* object that connects to a specific video device on the computer:

```
var user_cam = Camera.get();
```

As with *Microphone.get( )*, the *Camera.get( )* method uses the default video device if no parameter is specified. However, you can also pass the method an integer value representing a different device. The indexes you can use with *get( )* represent elements of the Camera.names array, which contains a list of the video input devices detected by Flash. Ideally, however, the user will select the default video input device using the Camera tab of the Macromedia Flash Player Settings panel from Figure 6-2.

Regardless, once you've created a *Camera* instance, you can retrieve the index and name of the device to which it connects using the index and name properties.

A video device may already be locked exclusively for use with another application. In that case, the Flash Player will not be able to make a connection to the device. When that occurs, Flash does not provide you with any explicit notification that the connection was unsuccessful. It will still return a new *Camera* object when you call the *get( )* method. Programmatically it will appear as though everything worked just fine. If you want to be able to detect that a connection was made successfully, you can use the currentFps property. While it is not foolproof, a currentFps property of 0 usually indicates that Flash was unable to connect to the device. In that case, you may want to ask the user to check the device and close any other application monopolizing it.

Understanding Camera Permissions

Camera permissions work just like microphone permissions. When you attempt to use the video input via a *Camera* object, Flash checks whether the user has granted permission. If the user didn't previously check the Remember box in the Settings panel, the panel will open, prompting the user to allow or deny access. When the user selects an option, the *Camera.onStatus( )* method is called. Otherwise, if the user has selected the Remember checkbox previously, you'll need to use the Camera. muted property to determine whether the user has granted permission. See "Detecting the Microphone Privacy Setting" for more details. The API and procedure for camera and microphone permissions are identical. Whenever the privacy setting changes, *onStatus( )* is invoked on all *Camera* and *Microphone* objects that define such a handler, and the muted property is updated for each object as well.

Attaching and Publishing Video

Once you've created a *Camera* object, you can attach the input to a local Video object (so the user can monitor it) and/or publish the input to a FlashCom application via a *NetStream* object (so that other users can receive it).

If you want to attach the input to a Video object:

1. Create a Video symbol by opening the Library panel and selecting New Video from the Library panel's Options menu.
2. Drag an instance of the Video symbol to the Stage.

3. Name the instance using the Properties panel.

4. Attach the video input to the object using *Video.attachVideo( )*.

The following code attaches the input from a *Camera* object named user_cam to a Video object named content_vid:

```
content_vid.attachVideo(user_cam);
```

If you want to publish the camera input to a FlashCom application, attach the input to a stream using *NetStream.attachVideo( )* and publish the stream using *NetStream. publish( )*:

```
publisher_ns.attachVideo(user_cam);
publisher_ns.publish("cameraStream", "record");
```

Unlike audio, video is not "silent" even if the motion level falls below a certain threshold. So publishing video to a stream will necessarily use some bandwidth, even if there's no motion. However, the bandwidth requirement is low enough to be considered negligible in most cases.

Adjusting Camera Settings

Even more so than audio input, video input often requires that you optimize some settings. The following sections explain how to programmatically adjust a *Camera* object to affect video quality, dimension, frame rate, keyframe interval, and camera responsiveness.

Working with modes

Most cameras are capable of varying *modes* distinguished by different widths, heights, and frame rates. By default, Flash uses dimensions of 160 x 120 pixels and 15 frames per second (fps) when connecting to a camera. However, *Camera.set-Mode( )* specifies the camera mode programmatically.

The *setMode( )* method requires at least three parameters to specify the requested camera mode: the width, height, and frame rate. For example, the following code instructs Flash to attempt to set the mode of the camera associated with user_cam to 320 x 240 at 30 fps:

```
user_cam.setMode(320, 240, 30);
```

While *setMode( )* may seem fairly unassuming, each camera is preconfigured with a set of modes at which it can operate, and different cameras may support different modes. Therefore, when you set a camera's mode to 320 x 240 at 30 fps, the actual result may differ slightly (or drastically). In order to predict what kinds of behaviors *setMode( )* can produce, it can be helpful to understand the logic that it uses. That said, *setMode( )* attempts to make sensible choices so that ActionScript programmers don't have to worry about the details.

The *setMode( )* method follows some general rules. It won't set the camera to a mode that exceeds the parameters passed to it. However, it will, if necessary, use a mode with smaller dimensions and/or a lower frame rate. The algorithms that the method uses are fairly complex. In brief, Flash compares the area of the requested dimensions with the area of each of the native modes, selecting the best match available. If the selected mode does not match the aspect ratio, the video is cropped. If the selected mode does not match the frame rate, frames are dropped.

The important point is that you won't get exactly the mode you ask for if the camera doesn't support it.

By default, the frame rate is given priority in finding an appropriate mode. You can give priority to the area calculation by passing true as the fourth, optional parameter to *setMode( )*. Let's look at a few example scenarios in order to see how *setMode( )* works.

In some cases, selecting whether the area or frame rate gets priority simply doesn't matter. Consider the following *setMode( )* call, which attempts to set the camera to 320 x 240 at 30 fps:

```
user_cam.setMode(320, 240, 30, true);
```

Now consider a camera that supports the following native modes (sorted by fps, then by area in descending order):

> 176 x 144 @ 30 fps
> 160 x 120 @ 30 fps
> 128 x 96 @ 30 fps
> 80 x 60 @ 30 fps
> 320 x 288 @ 25 fps
> 320 x 240 @ 25 fps
> 352 x 288 @ 15 fps
> 640 x 480 @ 13 fps
> 512 x 288 @ 13 fps

The preceding *setMode( )* command selects the 320 x 240 at 25 fps mode because it is an identical area match and also a close match for the frame rate.

In this example scenario, even if frame rate is given priority (as indicated by omitting the fourth parameter or passing false):

```
user_cam.setMode(320, 240, 30, false);
```

the same final native mode is selected, because the available 30 fps native modes support only areas that are less than the requested dimensions.

However, sometimes the area/frame rate priority setting can have an effect, even a drastic one. The following example assumes the camera has the same native modes as in the preceding example. However, in this case, *setMode( )* is called to specify dimensions of 640 x 480 at 30 fps. If area is given priority:

```
user_cam.setMode(640, 480, 30, true);
```

the chosen mode is 640 x 480 at 13 fps because it is the best match for the area. When area is given priority, if the *Camera* class is unable to match the dimensions exactly, it will retrieve the next largest settings and then crop the image (unless the requested dimensions exceed those supported by the camera).

However, if frame rate is given priority:

```
user_cam.setMode(640, 480, 30, true);
```

the selection is 320 x 288 at 25 fps—very different indeed! Because the available 30 fps native modes were too small an area compared to the requested 640 x 480, *setMode( )* chose the mode with the biggest area that supported a high frame rate (in this case 25 fps is reasonably close to 30 fps).

The preceding scenarios are only two of many possible ones. For complete details on the algorithm used to select the native mode that best matches the requested parameters, see:

http://flash-communications.net/technotes/setMode/index.html

You can retrieve the current mode's settings using the read-only width, height, and fps properties of a *Camera* object. The fps property determines the maximum frame rate at which Flash will capture video using the current device settings. However, it does not necessarily mean that it will always capture at that rate. If necessary, Flash will drop the frame rate in order to be able to continue to publish a stream given other settings and the amount of bandwidth available. You can retrieve the actual frame rate at any given point by reading the value from the read-only currentFps property.

One logical approach might be to query the camera to obtain a list of native modes, display them in a listbox, and prompt the user to select a supported mode. Unfortunately, the ActionScript API does not provide a method to obtain a list of native modes supported by a camera (whatever method Flash uses internally to determine the available modes is not exposed to ActionScript).

Professionals responsible for buying cameras and setting up high-quality conferencing and live event broadcasts should select cameras based, in part, on the available modes. If you have a camera with known modes, script your application to select—or allow an operator to select—from a list of modes appropriate for the event. If you don't have control over the equipment, in which case the camera's native modes are unknown, consult the URL cited earlier to help determine how to select available modes with reasonable bandwidth requirements.

You can publish only one size stream from a web cam at a time. If you create two separate instances with *Camera.get( )* that refer to the same video source, changes made via *setMode( )* to either instance are applied to both instances. To publish two different bit rates of the "same" footage, you need two capture sources. (Likewise, to capture audio input at different sampling rates simultaneously, you need two separate microphones.)

There are hardware and software solutions that make a single camera appear like multiple devices to the Flash Player, such as ViewCast's SimulStream for Osprey Video cards:

> *http://www.viewcast.com/simulstream_main.html*

Working with quality

Video data can require a lot of bandwidth, which depends on the video's dimensions, frame rate, and quality (amount of compression). If your FlashCom application is running on a high-speed intranet in which bandwidth is not an issue, you can use higher-quality settings. But even in such cases, there are limits to what a PC can reasonably capture; for example, you shouldn't exceed 80% of CPU capacity on Windows.

However, most applications are deployed over the Internet, an environment in which the bandwidth requirements profoundly affect the application's functioning and the user experience. Therefore, you must optimize the video quality given the bandwidth of the user's connection. Using *setMode( )* to select the smallest appropriate dimensions and lowest acceptable frame rate will assist you in managing bandwidth considerations. Additionally, the quality setting of the video plays a major role, so you can further tune the bandwidth requirements of the video using the *Camera.setQuality( )* method.

The *setQuality( )* method accepts two parameters that indicate the trade-off between data rate and appearance quality: an integer indicating the number of bytes per second to which the video data should be compressed and an integer from 0 to 100 indicating the quality of the video. The three basic scenarios when using *setQuality( )* are:

Bandwidth is the priority
> Specify the bytes per second value and set the second parameter to 0. Flash will reduce the quality (increase compression) to keep the video within the specified bandwidth.

Quality of the video image is the priority
> Specify 0 for the first parameter; the higher the second parameter (from 0 to 100), the higher the image quality. If necessary, Flash will drop motion quality and the frame rate in order to maintain the image quality of the video.

Quality and bandwidth are equally important

Specify non-zero values for both parameters. Flash will try to compress the video within the quality and bandwidth settings. If necessary, Flash will drop the frame rate in order to maintain the bandwidth and quality.

Table 6-1 gives you some general starting points when using *setQuality( )*. Macromedia uses 16,000 bytes/sec (about 16 KB/s) for the default video bandwidth over a modem. Although a dial-up modem cannot handle 16 KB/s, Flash dynamically adjusts the frame rate as necessary.

Table 6-1. Suggested bandwidth and image quality settings for video over various connection types

Connection	Prioritize bandwidth	Prioritize image quality
56K modem	setQuality(4000, 0)	setQuality(0, 65)
DSL/cable	setQuality(120000, 0)	setQuality(0, 90)
LAN	setQuality(400000, 0)	setQuality(0, 100)

The effects of *setQuality( )* are visible only in the compressed version of the video. The video that is published over a *NetStream* object is compressed, so any subscriber to that stream will see the effect of the *setQuality( )* settings. However, if you attach video input directly to a local Video object, the compression will not be visible by default. Regardless of how much compression you apply, the video will still appear as crisp and smooth as the device can capture. To view the compressed video within the same client movie that is capturing the video, use *setLoopback(true)* to emulate the compression (passing false indicates no compression locally):

```
user_cam.setLoopback(true);
```

Using loopback is processor-intensive because it requires the Player to compress the video and then decompress it for display. Therefore, the loopback mode is typically used only during the development and testing phases.

The following code allows you to see the effects of *setQuality( )*. You can include it on the main timeline of a Flash file in which you have placed a Video object named content_vid and NumericStepper components named cnsQuality and cnsBandwidth on stage:

```
var user_cam = Camera.get( );
// Display the video in the Video object.
content_vid.attachVideo(user_cam);
// Set the loopback so that you can view the compressed video.
user_cam.setLoopback(true);
var qualityListener = new Object( );
qualityListener.change = function (event) {
  user_cam.setQuality(user_cam.bandwidth, event.target.value);
};
cnsQuality.addEventListener("change", qualityListener);
cnsQuality.minimum = 0;
cnsQuality.maximum = 100;
```

```
cnsQuality.value = user_cam.quality;
var bandwidthListener = new Object( );
bandwidthListener.change = function (event) {
  user_cam.setQuality(event.target.value, user_cam.quality);
};
cnsBandwidth.addEventListener("change", bandwidthListener);
cnsBandwidth.minimum = 0;
cnsBandwidth.maximum = 400000;
cnsBandwidth.stepSize = 1000;
cnsBandwidth.value = user_cam.quality;
```

Test the movie and adjust the quality and bandwidth sliders to see their effect on the video.

Working with keyframes

Video in Flash uses keyframes in a way that is different from the way the Flash time-line uses keyframes. Depending on the bandwidth available and *setMode( )* and *set-Quality( )* settings, Flash compresses video data within each 8 x 8 pixel block of each video frame. High levels of compression produce images with noticeable "blocki-ness" as a result. However, to reduce bandwidth consumption further, Flash does not always send complete frames. Frames for which complete image information is sent are called keyframes. The frames in between keyframes contain image data for only regions in which changes have occurred. The keyframes (called delta or differ-ence frames) contain information about every pixel of the image regardless of whether or not anything has changed since the previous keyframe. Keep in mind, however, that a keyframe's quality may still be low, even though it contains com-plete image information. The amount of compression applied to the video still affects the quality of keyframes.

By default, Flash video is published with a keyframe every 15 frames. However, you can adjust the keyframe interval (from 1 to 48) to better suit your application and audience. Setting the value to 1 means that each frame is a keyframe—in other words, the data for each frame is complete. This dramatically increases the band-width and workstation processor requirements. A higher value for the keyframe interval generally means that the bandwidth requirements are decreased. There is no loss of video quality introduced by reducing the number of keyframes. However, if the video frame's contents are changing rapidly, more frequent keyframes can actu-ally reduce the overall bandwidth requirements by reducing the size of each delta frame. That is, increasing the keyframe interval saves bandwidth most effectively when the contents of the frame aren't changing very much. Fortunately, this applies to most FlashCom applications, in which the video is often a talking head (however, it works best if the subject doesn't move around a lot).

You can set the keyframe interval using the *setKeyFrameInterval( )* method. Simply call the method and pass it an integer value from 1 to 48:

```
user_cam.setKeyFrameInterval(10);
```

You can retrieve the current keyframe interval using the read-only `keyFrameInterval` property.

Understanding Video Objects

When you want to display Flash video via a *Camera* object or a *NetStream* object, you need to use a *Video object*. There is no programmatic way to directly create a Video object. Instead, you have to create a Video symbol in the Library and add an instance of that symbol to the Stage. Furthermore, even after you have created a Video symbol in the Library, there is no way to directly attach an instance to the Stage programmatically. However, you can work around the issue by creating a movie clip symbol that contains a Video object.

Movie clip symbols can be attached to the Stage programmatically if you set them to export for ActionScript in the symbol's Linkage Settings dialog box in the Library. Therefore, if you create a movie clip symbol containing a Video object, you can programmatically use it to add a Video object to the Stage at runtime. Although a Video object has properties such as `_width` and `_height`, you should place it inside a movie clip for greater programmatic control, because the *MovieClip* class supports additional properties and methods.

Working with activityLevel

Just as you can programmatically work with the sound activity level for a *Microphone* object, you can perform analogous operations with the motion activity level of a *Camera* object. The main difference is the slight variations in the names of properties and methods used.

To read the current activity level of a *Camera* object, use the read-only `activityLevel` property, just as you would with a *Microphone* object. The range of values for `activityLevel` is from 0 to 100.

The *Camera.setMotionLevel( )* method sets the threshold at which to notify your application of motion. The *setMotionLevel( )* method requires at least one parameter—an integer from 0 to 100—indicating the minimum motion level required for the *Camera* object to be activated. The default value is 50. You can optionally specify a second parameter that indicates the number of milliseconds before the object times out after the activity level falls below the minimum. The default value is 2000 milliseconds (2 seconds). This sets the motion level threshold to 35 and sets the timeout period to 1 second of inactivity:

```
user_cam.setMotionLevel(35, 1000);
```

You can retrieve the current minimum motion level and timeout setting with the read-only `motionLevel` and `motionTimeOut` properties.

Although *Camera.setMotionLevel( )* is analogous to *Microphone.setSilenceLevel( )*, there is at least one major distinction due to the differences in how video and audio are treated. When audio and video are being published, the microphone or camera has to capture data to determine if the activity threshold is reached. If the threshold specified by *Microphone.setSilenceLevel( )* is not reached, the application does not transmit the audio to FlashCom. (That is, the data is discarded if the input is deemed "silent.") However, even if the video capture is not changing very much (low motion), the video is still transmitted to keep the picture up-to-date.

Therefore, *Camera.setMotionLevel( )* specifies the value at which the *Camera.onActivity( )* event handler should be called, not whether the video data should be transmitted. The *onActivity( )* method of a *Camera* object works just like the corresponding method of a *Microphone* object. The method is passed a Boolean parameter indicating whether the object has been activated (true) or deactivated (false):

```
user_cam.onActivity = function (activated) {
  trace("Is the camera activated? " + activated);
};
```

If you want to literally stop transmitting data when activity is low, you can unpublish the stream in the *onActivity( )* handler. However, low-motion video (in which the picture is not changing much and the video has very small delta frames) with a long keyframe interval uses very little bandwidth (though clearly not zero, like audio silence).

 One prudent use of an *onActivity( )* handler is to determine if no one is standing in front of a camera-enabled kiosk. If the program detects no motion activity, you might cycle back to an attract loop. In this case, you should use *setMotionLevel( )* to set the motion threshold and time-out period as appropriate for your kiosk environment.

Building a Message-Taking Application

You've had a chance to learn about the intricacies of the *Microphone* and *Camera* classes in theory. Next you can put what you've learned into practice by building a simple message-taking (and retrieval) application.

In order to create the application, complete the following steps:

1. Create a new FlashCom application on the server. In the *applications* directory of the FlashCom Server, create a new subdirectory named *message_taker*.
2. Create a new Flash document and save it as *MessageTaker.fla*.
3. Within the Flash document, create a new Video symbol in the Library.

4. On the Stage add the following, as shown in Figure 6-3:

   a. Two instances of the Video symbol. Give them instance names of record_vid and playback_vid. Place record_vid to the left and playback_vid to the right. The Video objects will display the video while recording and playing back a message.

   b. Two Button component instances below record_vid. Give them instance names of cbtPreview and cbtRecord. The Button instances allow the user to preview the settings without recording or to record a new message.

   c. One ComboBox component instance below the Button instances. Give it an instance name of ccbRate. The component allows the user to adjust the rate at which the microphone is capturing data.

   d. Three NumericStepper component instances below ccbRate. Give them instance names of cnsGain, cnsQuality, and cnsBandwidth. The components allow the user to adjust the microphone gain, video quality, and video bandwidth.

   e. One List component instance below playback_vid. Give it an instance name of clMessages. The List component displays the dates and times—in a form similar to "Thu Dec 9 22:32:32 GMT-0500 2004"—of messages that have been previously recorded.

   f. One Button component instance below clMessages. Give it an instance name of cbtPlayback. The Button instance allows the user to play back the selected message.

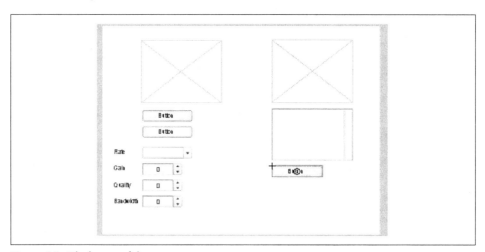

Figure 6-3. The layout of the components

5. Rename the default layer to *Components*, and create a new layer named *Actions* above it.

6. Select the first keyframe of the *Actions* layer, and open the Actions panel.

7. Add the following code to the Actions panel:

```
// Create the Microphone and Camera objects.
var user_mic = Microphone.get();
var user_cam = Camera.get();

// Create the NetConnection object.
var fcs_nc = new NetConnection();

// Create listener objects to be used with the components.
var recordListener     = new Object();
var playbackListener   = new Object();
var previewListener    = new Object();
var rateListener       = new Object();
var gainListener       = new Object();
var bandwidthListener  = new Object();
var qualityListener    = new Object();

var rsoMessages;       // Variable to store the RSO.
var mcMain = this;     // Store a reference to the main timeline.
var record_ns;         // NetStream for recording.
var playback_ns;       // NetStream for playback.
var sMessageTitle;     // Store title of message being recorded.

// Initialize the microphone threshold and camera mode and quality.
user_mic.setSilenceLevel(10, 2000);
user_cam.setMode(320, 240, 15);
user_cam.setQuality(0, 100);

// Set the loopback to true so user can see what the output stream looks like.
user_cam.setLoopback(true);

// Connect to the FlashCom application.
fcs_nc.connect("rtmp:/message_taker");

// Get the RSO that keeps track of the messages.
rsoMessages = SharedObject.getRemote("messages", fcs_nc.uri, true);
rsoMessages.connect(fcs_nc);

// When the RSO synchronizes, assign the data to the data provider for the List.
rsoMessages.onSync = function (info) {
  clMessages.dataProvider = this.data.messages;
};

// Set up the ComboBox instance.
ccbRate.dataProvider = [5, 8, 11, 22, 44];
for (var i:Number = 0; i < ccbRate.length; i++) {
  if (ccbRate.getItemAt(i) == user_mic.rate) {
    ccbRate.selectedIndex = i;
    break;
  }
}

// Define the listener for the Rate combo box.
```

```
rateListener.change = function (event) {
  user_mic.setRate(event.target.value);
};
ccbRate.addEventListener("change", rateListener);

// Define the listener for the gain stepper.
gainListener.change = function (event) {
  user_mic.setGain(event.target.value);
};
cnsGain.addEventListener("change", gainListener);
cnsGain.minimum = 0;
cnsGain.maximum = 100;
cnsGain.value = user_mic.gain;

// Define the listener for the quality stepper.
qualityListener.change = function (event) {
  user_cam.setQuality(user_cam.bandwidth, event.target.value);
};
cnsQuality.addEventListener("change", qualityListener);
cnsQuality.minimum = 0;
cnsQuality.maximum = 100;
cnsQuality.value = user_cam.quality;

// Define the listener for the bandwidth stepper.
bandwidthListener.change = function (event) {
  user_cam.setQuality(event.target.value, user_cam.quality);
};

cnsBandwidth.addEventListener("change", bandwidthListener);
cnsBandwidth.minimum = 0;
cnsBandwidth.maximum = 400000;
cnsBandwidth.stepSize = 1000;
cnsBandwidth.value = user_cam.quality;

// Define the listener for the Record button.
recordListener.click = function (event) {
  // The Record toggle button has a selected value of true or false.
  // If true, start recording the video.
  if (event.target.selected) {
    // Set the label of the button to Stop while in Record mode.
    event.target.label = "Stop";

    // Display the video in the Video object.
    record_vid.attachVideo(user_cam);

    // Create the NetStream object, and add the audio and video.
    record_ns = new NetStream(fcs_nc);
    record_ns.attachAudio(user_mic);
    record_ns.attachVideo(user_cam);

    // Create a unique message title with the Epoch milliseconds prefixed by
    // "message". It becomes the stream filename, such as message1102647695650.flv
    sMessageTitle = "message" + (new Date()).getTime();
```

```
    // Publish the stream.
    record_ns.publish(sMessageTitle, "record");
  }
  else {
    /* Otherwise, the Record button is toggled to the deselected state, so
     * stop recording the video.
     * Set the button label back to Record while in stopped mode.
     */
    event.target.label = "Record";

    // Clear the video and audio from the Video and NetStream objects.
    record_vid.attachVideo(null);
    record_vid.clear();
    record_ns.attachAudio(null);
    record_ns.attachVideo(null);

    // Stop publishing and close the stream.
    record_ns.publish(false);
    record_ns.close();

    // If the RSO doesn't have a messages property, define one as an array.
    if (rsoMessages.data.messages == undefined) {
      rsoMessages.data.messages = new Array();
    }
    /* Add the message to the array. This creates a label property string from the
     * current date and time similar to "Thu Dec 9 22:32:32 GMT-0500 2004".
     * The data property is the stream name (used to retrieve the .flv file).
     */
    rsoMessages.data.messages.push({label: new Date(), data: sMessageTitle});
  }
};

// When the user clicks the Play Message button, play the selected stream.
playbackListener.click = function (event) {
  if (clMessages.value != undefined) {
    playback_ns = new NetStream(fcs_nc);
    playback_ns.play(clMessages.value);
    playback_vid.attachVideo(playback_ns);
  }
};

// When the user clicks the Preview button, display the video and preview
// the audio.
previewListener.click = function (event) {
  if (event.target.selected) {
    event.target.label = "Stop";
    mcMain.attachAudio(user_mic);
    record_vid.attachVideo(user_cam);
  }
  else {
    event.target.label = "Preview";
    mcMain.attachAudio(null);
    record_vid.attachVideo(null);
    record_vid.clear();
```

```
    }
};
// Set the properties for the Button instances (Preview, Record, Play Message).
cbtPreview.toggle = true;
cbtPreview.addEventListener("click", previewListener);
cbtPreview.label = "Preview";

cbtRecord.toggle = true;
cbtRecord.addEventListener("click", recordListener);
cbtRecord.label = "Record";

cbtPlayback.addEventListener("click", playbackListener);
cbtPlayback.label = "Play Message";
```

8. Test the movie. Try the different features, including previewing, adjusting settings, recording messages, and playing back messages.

The preceding steps used quite a lot of code, so it may benefit from some further explanation.

Obviously, one of the first steps is to create *Microphone* and *Camera* objects:

```
var user_mic = Microphone.get();
var user_cam = Camera.get();
```

Following that, the code sets up a *NetConnection* object because you'll be connecting the Flash interface to a server-side FlashCom application:

```
var fcs_nc = new NetConnection();
```

The code then creates a series of listener objects used to handle events dispatched by the components. That way you can have Flash take the appropriate actions when buttons are clicked, combo boxes are changed, or new values are selected from numeric steppers:

```
var recordListener    = new Object();
var playbackListener  = new Object();
var previewListener   = new Object();
var rateListener      = new Object();
var gainListener      = new Object();
var bandwidthListener = new Object();
var qualityListener   = new Object();
```

Set values for the microphone activity threshold and camera mode and quality (the audio gain, video quality, and video bandwidth can be changed via the UI but you have to change this code if you prefer a different activity threshold or camera mode):

```
user_mic.setSilenceLevel(10, 2000);
user_cam.setMode(320, 240, 30);
user_cam.setQuality(0, 100);
```

We want the user to be able to preview the video as it would appear when the stream is playing back. Therefore, we set the loopback to true:

```
user_cam.setLoopback(true);
```

The listeners for the numeric steppers and the combo box simply update the internal values based on the user input.

The *recordListener.click( )* method handles click events dispatched by cbtRecord. The Record button is a toggle button, which means that it has two possible states—selected and deselected. You can use the Boolean selected property, which indicates the current state of the button, to determine which action to take:

```
recordListener.click = function (event) {
    if (event.target.selected) {
```

If the button is selected, the code instructs Flash to start recording the video and audio to a stream. It attaches the audio and video to a *NetStream* object and then calls *publish( )* to record it to the server. Additionally, the code attaches the video to the Video object so the user can see it while the stream is recording:

```
event.target.label = "Stop";
record_vid.attachVideo(user_cam);
record_ns = new NetStream(fcs_nc);
record_ns.attachAudio(user_mic);
record_ns.attachVideo(user_cam);
sMessageTitle = "message" + (new Date()).getTime( );
record_ns.publish(sMessageTitle, "record");
```

Notice that the title of the message stream is generated using *Date.getTime( )*, which returns the current time in Epoch milliseconds (a long integer, such as 1102647695650, representing the number of milliseconds since January 1, 1970). Using the current timestamp is a simple way to make sure the stream names, such as message1102647695650, will be unique. It is unlikely that two users will start recording at exactly the same time (down to the millisecond) even for high-traffic applications. The stream name becomes the name of the *.flv* file that will be stored, such as *message1102647695650.flv*.

If the Record button is in the deselected state, the code tells Flash to stop recording the stream. It invokes *attachAudio( )* and *attachVideo( )* with a parameter value of null to remove the camera and microphone data. Calling *publish( )* with a value of false stops publishing the stream. And calling *NetStream.close( )* closes the stream:

```
event.target.label = "Record";
record_vid.attachVideo(null);
record_vid.clear( );
record_ns.attachAudio(null);
record_ns.attachVideo(null);
record_ns.publish(false);
record_ns.close( );
```

The application uses a remote shared object (RSO) to store information about the messages that have been recorded. That way, it can retrieve that information each time the application is run and use it to populate the List component. Therefore, use the *SharedObject.getRemote( )* method to get the connection to the shared object and then connect to it:

```
rsoMessages = SharedObject.getRemote("messages", fcs_nc.uri, true);
rsoMessages.connect(fcs_nc);
```

Once the user finishes recording the stream, the code updates the RSO to include information about the stream that was just recorded. Each element of the messages array contains an object with two properties: label and data. The label property contains the date and time at which the message was recorded. The data property contains the stream name:

```
if (rsoMessages.data.messages == undefined) {
    rsoMessages.data.messages = new Array();
}
rsoMessages.data.messages.push({label: new Date(), data: sMessageTitle});
```

We create the messages array in this manner because the List component expects to be populated with precisely such an array of objects; we can use messages as a data provider for the List component without any modification. Each time the shared object data updates, the *onSync( )* event handler updates the List component (which displays the label of each element in the messages array):

```
rsoMessages.onSync = function(info) {
  clMessages.dataProvider = this.data.messages;
};
```

Playing back the selected stream is quite simple. Just check to make sure a value has been selected from the List component. Then, create a *NetStream* object and play the corresponding stream:

```
playbackListener.click = function (event) {
  if (clMessages.value != undefined) {
    playback_ns = new NetStream(fcs_nc);
    playback_ns.play(clMessages.value);
    playback_vid.attachVideo(playback_ns);
  }
};
```

Like the Record button, the Preview button is a toggle button. Therefore, in the *previewListener.click( )* method, you can check for the current selected state. If the button is selected, attach the *Microphone* object to the main timeline to preview the audio and attach the *Camera* object to the record_vid Video object to preview the video. Otherwise, if the selected state is false, remove the attached audio and video using the *attachAudio( )* and *attachVideo( )* methods with values of null:

```
previewListener.click = function (event) {
  if (event.target.selected) {
    event.target.label = "Stop";
    mcMain.attachAudio(user_mic);
    record_vid.attachVideo(user_cam);
  }
  else {
```

```
    event.target.label = "Preview";
    mcMain.attachAudio(null);
    record_vid.attachVideo(null);
    record_vid.clear( );
  }
};
```

Building a Surveillance Application

In the previous example, you had the chance to build an application that uses the *Camera* and *Microphone* classes. Next, we'll build a simple surveillance application that records to a stream only when the activity levels are high enough to warrant it.

To build the application, complete the following steps:

1. Create a new FlashCom application on the server. Within the FlashCom *applications* directory, create a new subdirectory named *surveillance*.

2. Create a new Flash document, and save it as *Surveillance.fla*.

3. Within the Flash document, create a new Video symbol in the Library.

4. Create an instance of the Video symbol on the main timeline, and give it the instance name content_vid. Place the instance approximately in the center of the Stage.

5. Create a TextArea component instance on the Stage just below the Video object. Use the Properties panel to give it an instance name of ctaLog and change its dimensions to 160 x 200.

6. Rename the default layer to *Contents*, and create a new layer above it named *Actions*.

7. Select the first keyframe of the *Actions* layer, and open the Actions panel.

8. Add the following code to the Actions panel:

```
// Create the Camera and Microphone objects.
var user_mic = Microphone.get( );
var user_cam = Camera.get( );

// Create the NetConnection object to connect to the server.
var fcs_nc = new NetConnection( );

// Create a NetStream variable.
var record_ns;

// Initialize two Boolean variables to false. They indicate whether the
// activity level is high enough and whether the stream is currently recording.
var activity = false;
var recording = false;

// Set the minimum activity level for the microphone and camera.
user_mic.setSilenceLevel(10, 2000);
user_cam.setMotionLevel(50, 2000);
```

```
// Set the camera mode and quality.
user_cam.setMode(320, 240, 30);
user_cam.setQuality(0, 100);

// Attach the video to the Video object.
content_vid.attachVideo(user_cam);

// Connect to the FlashCom application, and open a stream.
fcs_nc.connect("rtmp:/ surveillance");
record_ns = new NetStream(fcs_nc);

// Determine when the microphone and camera are activated and deactivated.
// In all cases, call the calculate() function.
user_mic.onActivity = function (activated) {
  calculate(activated);
};

user_cam.onActivity = function (activated) {
  calculate(activated);
};

// calculate() determines what action should take place when
// the microphone and/or camera is activated or deactivated.
function calculate (activated) {
  activity = activated;
  if (activity && !recording) {
    startRecording();
  }
  else if (!activity && recording) {
    pauseRecording();
  }
};

// Start recording the stream.
function startRecording () {
  recording = true;
  record_ns.attachAudio(user_mic);
  record_ns.attachVideo(user_cam);
  record_ns.publish("security", "append");
  // Display date/time recording begins, such as "Thu Dec 9 22:32:32 GMT-0500 2004"
  ctaLog.text += "Started recording" + new Date() + newline;
}

// Stop recording the stream.
function pauseRecording () {
  recording = false;
  record_ns.publish(false);
  ctaLog.text += "Paused recording" + new Date() + newline;
}

// Initialize application by starting to record.
startRecording();
```

9. Test the movie. You should see the TextArea report when the video is recording and pausing.

10. Create a new Flash document, and save it as *SurveillanceView.fla*.

11. Create a new Video symbol in the Library of *SurveillanceView.fla*.

12. Create an instance of the Video object on the Stage, and give it an instance name of content_vid.

13. Rename the default layer to *Content*, and create a new layer named *Actions*.

14. Select the first keyframe of the *Actions* layer, and open the Actions panel.

15. Add the following code to the Actions panel:

```
// Create the NetConnection object, and connect to the FlashComm
// application on the server.
var fcs_nc = new NetConnection( );
fcs_nc.connect("rtmp:/surveillance");

// Create the NetStream object, and play back the stream.
var playback_ns = new NetStream(fcs_nc);
playback_ns.play("security");
content_vid.attachVideo(playback_ns);
```

16. Test the movie. You should see the surveillance stream play. Only the portions in which the activity level was high enough were recorded.

The code from *SurveillanceView.fla* is fairly straightforward. However, the code from *Surveillance.fla* is complex enough that it could benefit from some further explanation.

As with any application that uses audio and video input, the first step is to create *Camera* and *Microphone* objects:

```
var user_mic = Microphone.get( );
var user_cam = Camera.get( );
```

After creating the *NetConnection* object and a variable to store the *NetStream* object, you next want to declare and initialize two Boolean variables. The activity variable indicates whether the activity level of the microphone and/or camera is currently high enough. The recording variable simply indicates whether the stream is currently recording.

```
var activity = false;
var recording = false;
```

The application records audio and video only when the activity levels exceed the thresholds set via *Microphone.setSilenceLevel( )* and *Camera.setMotionLevel( )*. In the example code, the minimum activity levels are set to 10 and 50, with a 2-second timeout. You may want to adjust those levels in your own application if you find that they are not optimal.

```
user_mic.setSilenceLevel(10, 2000);
user_cam.setMotionLevel(50, 2000);
```

Even when the stream is not recording, the code still displays the video. Cameras usually take a short while to initialize, and so the delay could cause difficulties if you had to reinitialize the camera connection each time you resumed recording. By continuously displaying the camera input in the Video object, we initialize the camera only once:

```
content_vid.attachVideo(user_cam);
```

The *onActivity( )* event handlers are called automatically when the microphone or camera is activated or deactivated. This surveillance application handles both in the same way, so each of the event handler methods simply proxies the call to a custom function called *calculate( )*.

The *calculate( )* function determines what action should take place when a camera and/or microphone is activated and/or deactivated. It's not as simple as starting to publish the stream when one of the devices is activated and stopping it when one of the devices is deactivated. Remember that, since either device can cause the stream to start publishing, you need to check to see whether the stream is already being published. The *calculate( )* function does that. It starts to publish the stream (by calling *startRecording( )*) only if the activity level is high enough and if the recording variable is false. Otherwise, it stops publishing the stream only if the activity level is not high enough and the stream is currently publishing.

Publishing the stream is fairly basic. Of course, you'll want to set the recording variable to true so that Flash will be able to make the appropriate calculations subsequently. Then, as usual, attach the audio and video to the *NetStream* object and publish it. Additionally, add a line of text to the text area to indicate when the stream started recording:

```
function startRecording () {
  recording = true;
  record_ns.attachAudio(user_mic);
  record_ns.attachVideo(user_cam);
  record_ns.publish("security", "append");
  // Display date/time recording begins, such as "Thu Dec 9 22:32:32 GMT-0500 2004"
  ctaLog.text += "Started recording" + new Date() + newline;
}
```

Pausing the stream is also very basic. Of course, you'll want to set recording to false so adjustments can be made correctly when a microphone or camera is activated or deactivated. Then, as usual, call *publish( )* with a value of false to stop publishing the stream. And add a line of text to the text area to indicate when the stream paused:

```
function pauseRecording () {
  recording = false;
  record_ns.publish(false);
  ctaLog.text += "Paused recording" + new Date() + newline;
}
```

Conclusion

This chapter explained how to use both the *Microphone* and *Camera* classes to record live streams. These classes are at the heart of most communication applications, including the sample applications demonstrated here. There are hundreds of possible FlashCom applications that make use of audio and video, from conferencing to surveillance to technical support. Armed with what you've learned so far about managing connections and streams, you're ready to create some really interesting applications with the *Camera* and *Microphone* classes. The next chapter covers video preparation of recorded streams in detail.

CHAPTER 7

Media Preparation and Delivery

FlashCom Server can deliver high-quality audio and video experiences to just about any audience connected to the Internet. Whether you're streaming your own image and voice live with a web cam and microphone or publishing a prerecorded movie trailer, news clip, or training video, all your audience needs is Flash Player 6 or higher to view and hear the content. This chapter shows how to take more control over audio/visual material (or sources) employed by a FlashCom application.

Audio and Video Compression

Most digital audio and video content is compressed for efficient storage and transmission. Uncompressed content requires large file sizes; for example, 1 second of uncompressed broadcast television–quality video consumes at least 26 MB of storage. Such bandwidth requirements are unrealistic for real-time viewing over even the fastest networks. As a result, media formats—such as Windows AVI (Video for Windows) and Apple QuickTime—use various codecs to compress and decompress audio and video information. One of the more popular consumer video formats, DVD-Video, uses the MPEG-2 codec. Some codecs are specific to the file format or platform. However, the Sorenson Spark codec used for the Flash Video (FLV) files is built into the Flash Player and therefore supported on all platforms. Sorenson Spark is the primary video codec used by Flash Player 6 (or higher), as well as FlashCom Server.

When not using FlashCom, Flash Player 6 requires the video to be embedded in a FLA file (it is included within the published SWF file), but Flash Player 7 supports progressive download video. This allows external FLV files to be played from a standard web server over HTTP and delivered to a browser equipped with Flash Player 7. FlashCom uses the same file format (FLV) but offers streaming capabilities and other features not supported by a web server alone, as described in the Preface.

With the release of the Flash Video Exporter version 1.1 (and now version 1.2) included with Flash Pro, Macromedia added a metadata field named totalTime to

FLV files. FLV files that contain this extra piece of information are dubbed FLV 1.1 files, while earlier FLV files are considered version 1.0. If you install the latest Updater 2 to your FlashCom Server installation, the server will also record this extra metadata to your FLV files. You can use either FLV 1.0 or 1.1 files with any version of FlashCom Server. Both versions can also be loaded progressively with Flash Player 7. See the related notes under "Exporting Video from QuickTime Player Pro with the FLV Exporter" and "MediaPlayback Component" later in this chapter.

The Sorenson Spark Codec

The Sorenson Spark codec allows the Flash Player to play video content. The Spark codec is built right into Flash Player 6 and later, so no extra system files or installation is required. (Other video players, such as Apple QuickTime, support external codecs that are installed by default or downloaded separately.) Sorenson Spark can be used to play back streams from a FlashCom application. It can also be used to encode real-time, live video from a web cam or other video source and send it to a FlashCom application.

The fact that the Spark codec is built into Flash Player 6 and later saves Flash developers a lot of grief—other multimedia authoring engines, such as Macromedia Shockwave, rely on external video players such as QuickTime, which may require additional downloads to install more components or the necessary codec.

The Sorenson Spark codec can encode (compress) video material in one of two ways: *constant bit rate* (CBR) compression or *variable bit rate* (VBR) compression. The following sections discuss the difference between these two encoding options.

Constant bit rate (CBR) compression

Constant bit rate (CBR) compression is most common for live streaming video. When you publish or subscribe to a live stream delivered from a FlashCom Server, the video is using CBR compression. The term *basic* or *standard* Spark codec refers to the CBR encoding mechanism.

In CBR compression, each video frame is encoded with uniform data size constraints, regardless of content changes. A stream using CBR will "dice up" the available bandwidth over the number of frames delivered over a given amount of time. For this reason, the amount of change occurring within the video frame should be kept to a minimum. Talking heads or any other slow-moving content work reasonably well with CBR compression applied. However, fast-moving content, such as hockey players skating over ice following a puck, will not fare well with CBR compression—the content within the video frame changes at a rapid rate; as a result, more compression must be applied to each frame to keep it within the bit rate constraints. More compression means lower quality, appearing as "blocky" or chunky video.

Refer to Chapter 6 for more information about controlling the quality and bandwidth limits for live video streams using the *Camera* class.

Variable bit rate (VBR) compression

While CBR compression is the only option for live streaming video, you can use variable bit rate (VBR) compression for video content that you have already recorded or created with another software application, such as a 3D modeling program or a recording device like a professional video camcorder.

 VBR compression is one of the features available in the Sorenson Spark Pro edition codec. Sorenson Squeeze, discussed later in this chapter, utilizes the Pro edition of the codec and offers several encoding options unavailable in other Flash Video utilities.

A variable bit rate allows the encoding mechanism of Sorenson Spark to change the amount of data stored in each frame, enabling it to utilize any leftover bandwidth for more intensive frames (i.e., a frame that has substantially more content changes). During the VBR encoding process, the entire video clip is analyzed, frame by frame. The encoder makes a log of the analysis and decides which frames it can group together because there is little or no difference among them. With these similar frames, the encoded video file stores only the changes from one frame to the next. In truth, CBR-encoded video can also do similar *interframe* detection, but not nearly as efficiently. The additional analysis performed during VBR encoding, however, makes it impossible to use for real-time (live) encoding. Within a group of similar frames, a VBR encoder can minimize the bandwidth required and "borrow" the bandwidth it saved for use on more intensive frames (actually exceeding the bandwidth cap).

The qualitative differences between CBR and VBR compression cannot be overemphasized. VBR compression will always yield better looking video content and usually results in substantially smaller file sizes as well. Figure 7-1 shows a black-and-white (grayscale) video frame encoded with CBR and VBR compression.

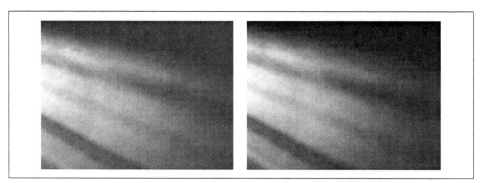

Figure 7-1. Comparison of CBR encoding (left) and VBR encoding (right)

If you can't see the difference in print, you can find a demo comparing encoding types at:

   http://www.flash-communications.net/examples/ch07/encoding.html

In order to compress video with Sorenson Spark's VBR codec, you need to use a dedicated software utility. Macromedia Flash MX Professional 2004 (Flash Pro) includes the Flash Video Exporter Tool, an add-on to Apple QuickTime, enabling you to create VBR-encoded FLV files. (The Flash Video Exporter is also known as simply the FLV Exporter.) Third-party applications such as Sorenson Squeeze and Wildform Flix can also be used to create high-quality FLV files with VBR compression. We cover all of these utilities later in this chapter.

The Speech Codec

Flash Player 6 and later also includes a built-in Speech codec, specifically added for streaming live audio. The Speech codec is the only audio codec available for live streaming audio from the Flash Player. The Speech codec uses a constant bit rate to encode audio information. You can control the quality (and bandwidth intensity) of the audio stream using the *Microphone.setRate( )* method. The Speech codec can use the following sampling rates: 5, 8, 11, 22, or 44 kHz. The higher rates yield higher-quality (better sounding) audio at the expense of higher bandwidth.

When you publish an audio source to FlashCom, the audio encoded by the Speech codec can support only monaural sound. Stereo sound cannot be published to a FlashCom application. Refer to Chapter 6 for more information regarding the control of audio quality with the *Microphone* class.

Prerecorded Versus FlashCom-Recorded Media

Chapter 6 taught you how to record content to a FlashCom application with the *Camera* and *Microphone* classes. When you record live content to FlashCom from a video source captured by the Flash Player, you have the following limitations:

- The video source is encoded with the Sorenson Spark codec using CBR compression, limiting the quality of the video image.
- The audio source is encoded with the Speech codec using CBR compression.
- The audio source is converted to mono sound.

However, if you record or capture your content with an external application, your media options expand greatly. You can control the following options with one or more of the applications discussed later in this chapter:

Video codec type
   With the FLV Exporter tool included with Flash Pro, you can choose between the Sorenson Spark codec or the Screen Recording codec. See the later section "The Screen Recording Codec" for more information.

Audio compression

With any of the Flash Video encoding utilities, you can encode the audio channel of your source file with MP3 compression, which supports stereo sound and higher bit rates than the Speech codec.

Regardless of how you create the FLV files used by your FlashCom application, you can view any FLV files over HTTP with the progressive download option for *NetStream* instances in Flash Player 7. Refer to the Preface for details on how this option differs from streaming support provided by FlashCom.

The Screen Recording Codec

One of the benefits of the Flash Video Exporter over other third-party FLV encoders is the capability to encode FLV files with the Screen Recording codec. As its name implies, this lossless codec is designed to work with desktop screen captures. If you have recorded an AVI or MOV file of a task performed with a desktop application (e.g., a tutorial video demonstrating how to use a program such as Flash MX 2004), you can create a compressed FLV file with the Screen Recording codec for optimal clarity of screen details. Make sure you use a low frame rate (6 to 10 fps) and a high keyframe interval (60 or higher) to keep your FLV bit rate from being too demanding for your target audience's bandwidth availability.

Converting Prerecorded Material to FLV Format

It's not very likely that all of the audio/video material you want to stream to your users was recorded by your FlashCom Server. Chances are, you'll have content that you've recorded with other higher-quality capture sources, such as a mini-DV camcorder or video output from 3D modeling applications. Your business clients may even provide you with high-quality video footage for movie trailers, sports or news clips, or product demonstrations. Most of these files are not going to be in a digital video format directly supported by FlashCom. For that reason, you'll need a way to convert disparate video formats to the FLV file format, the only one that FlashCom supports.

 If you need some sample video content to convert to FLV files, you can download sample Windows AVI and QuickTime MOV files from the book's web site.

Recompressing Video Files

A sure sign of a less than ideal digital video workflow is the act of recompressing digital video files that have already been significantly compressed with some other encoder. For example, a business client of yours may provide you with Windows Media (WMV) files. Since FlashCom supports only the FLV file format, you'll need to convert the WMV files with one of the utilities discussed in this section. However, WMV files already have been compressed from some other source footage. It's likely that the WMV files already show signs of compression, such as artifacts (digital noise around the edges of video images). Applying yet another compressor such as Sorenson Spark to this footage will only introduce more artifacts. So you should always attempt to get the original source videotape (or transfer) and capture the video yourself in your preferred video editing application. Alternatively, ask your client to provide you with broadcast-quality digital video files.

Using Flash MX 2004 to Create FLV Files

You may already know that Flash MX and Flash MX 2004 enable you to import and embed digital video files into Flash movies (SWF files). But did you know that you can also reexport those embedded video files as FLV files that you can use with FlashCom Server? Admittedly, the Flash MX or Flash MX 2004 authoring environment can encode video only with the Sorenson Spark Basic edition codec (a.k.a. CBR encoding). Thus, the quality of video is significantly lower than that of the other tools we discuss in this section. The quality is good enough, though, if you just need a quick conversion of video formats to use in a FlashCom Server application.

 If you have Flash Pro, you can use the included FLV Exporter tool with most QuickTime-enabled applications, including Apple Quick-Time Player Pro. This utility is discussed in the next section.

The following tutorial provides an overview of the Video Import Wizard in Flash MX 2004. For more specific information on the options available in the Video Import Wizard, refer to the Help panel in Flash MX 2004.

To import a digital video file into a Flash MX 2004 document:

1. Before you begin, make sure your Flash document is using the frame rate you want to use with the video clip from FlashCom. With a new Flash document (FLA file) open, choose Modify → Document (Ctrl-J or Cmd-J). In the Frame Rate field, enter your desired frame rate. Most video delivered over the Internet uses a frame rate of 12, 15, or 24. Click OK to close the dialog box.

2. Choose File → Import → Import to Library. In the Import to Library dialog box, browse to a digital video file that you want to encode in FLV format. Flash MX 2004 supports most popular video file formats, including QuickTime (MOV), Video for Windows (AVI), Windows Media (ASF, WMV), and MPEG files.

3. After you have selected a digital file to import, the Video Import Wizard appears. The first screen of the wizard will vary according to the file format you chose. Figure 7-2 shows the first screen when a QuickTime file has been selected

for import. If you want Flash MX 2004 to convert the file to the FLV format, choose the Embed Video in Macromedia Flash Document option and click the Next button.

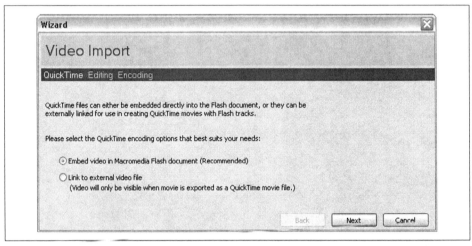

Figure 7-2. The QuickTime import screen of the Video Import Wizard

4. After you have selected the QuickTime embed option (or if you have selected a non-QuickTime file format in Step 2), the Video Import Wizard proceeds to the Editing phase. As shown in Figure 7-3, you can decide whether you want to import the entire video or choose various clips within the source footage to import. For the purposes of this exercise, choose the Import the Entire Video option, and click the Next button.

5. Now you have reached the Encoding phase of the import process. On this screen, shown in Figure 7-4, you can choose the compression and filter options for the clip. You can choose a predefined compression profile for your desired bit rate, or you can create a custom profile by choosing Create New Profile from the Compression Profile drop-down menu. For the purposes of this exercise, choose the DSL/Cable 256 Kbps profile. If you click the adjacent Edit button, you can see the options for profiles and the specific settings for this preset on the Compression Settings screen, as shown in Figure 7-5. After you review these settings, click the Back button to return to the main Encoding screen. Select Create New Profile from the Advanced Settings drop-down menu. This brings up the Advanced Settings screen, as shown in Figure 7-6, where you can change color characteristics of the video image, scale and crop the video area, control how the clip is imported into the current timeline, and enable/disable the audio track of the video clip. Click the Back button to return to the main Encoding screen.

6. Once you have determined the compression and filter settings for the clip, you're ready to let Flash MX 2004 encode the digital video file. In the Video Import Wizard, click the Finish button. As Flash encodes the video, a dialog box indicates the progress of the import as shown in Figure 7-7.

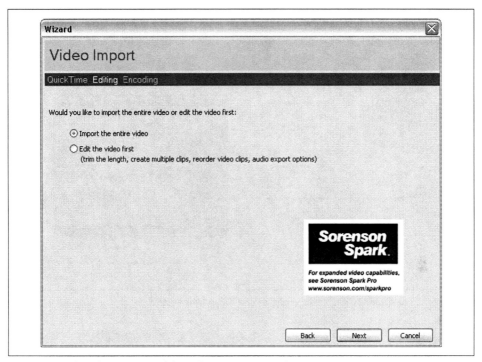

Figure 7-3. The Editing screen of the Video Import Wizard

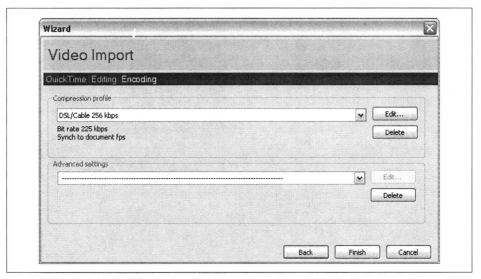

Figure 7-4. The Encoding screen of the Video Import Wizard

Figure 7-5. The Compression Settings used by the Video Import Wizard

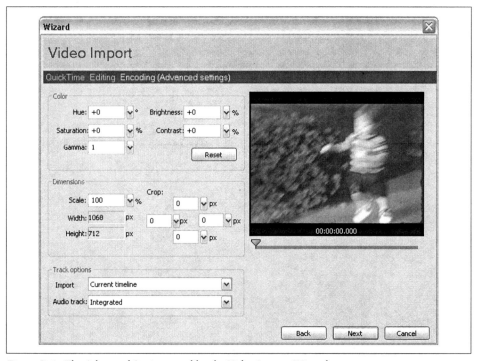

Figure 7-6. The Advanced Settings used by the Video Import Wizard

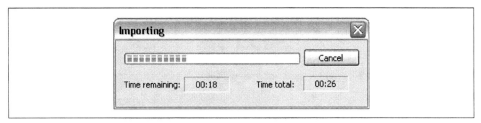

Figure 7-7. The Importing progress dialog box

To export the embedded video clip to an external FLV file:

1. After the video clip has been imported into the Flash document, open the Library panel (Ctrl-L or Cmd-L). Right-click (or Ctrl-click on Mac) the Embedded Video symbol that represents the video file you imported and choose Properties as shown in Figure 7-8.

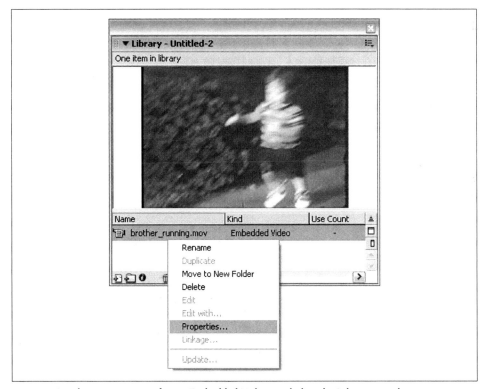

Figure 7-8. The context menu for an Embedded Video symbol in the Library panel

2. In the Embedded Video Properties dialog box, shown in Figure 7-9, click the Export button. In the Export FLV dialog box, specify the name of a new FLV file and click the Save button.

3. Move the FLV file to the *streams/_definst_* folder of your FlashCom application.

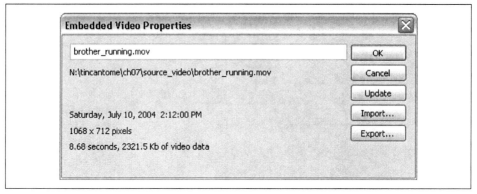

Figure 7-9. *The Embedded Video Properties dialog box*

If your FlashCom *applications* folder doesn't have a *streams* subfolder, refer to "Configuring the FCS Application" later in this chapter. There, you will learn how to create the appropriate folders in which to store your FLV files.

Exporting Video from QuickTime Player Pro with the FLV Exporter

If you are using Flash Pro, your installation CD or downloaded installer files include a *Flash_Video_Exporter.exe* file (or *Flash_Video_Exporter.dmg* on Mac). Make sure that you have run this installer file before continuing with this section. This installer does not create a standalone application with which you can encode digital video files. Rather, it installs a QuickTime plugin that enables FLV export from most QuickTime-enabled applications.

 In January 2004, Macromedia released Video Update 1.2 for Flash Pro. This updater improves the capabilities of the Flash Video Exporter. Among other features, the updater adds two-pass VBR encoding to the exporter's options and embeds the length of the video clip into the FLV file for use by the media components, discussed later in this chapter. You can obtain the updater from *http://www.macromedia.com/support/flash/downloads.html*.

A good indication that your preferred video editing application supports QuickTime is to check for a File → Export Movie option. Usually, the Export Movie option of a video application enables you to output QuickTime files. Some video applications such as Adobe Premiere Pro 7 support QuickTime files but do not have a feature to export movies in various encoders like the FLV format.

In order to export FLV files from Apple QuickTime Player, you need to buy a registration key for the Pro version. You can find more details about QuickTime Pro at *http://www.apple.com/quicktime/upgrade.*

The primary difference between Flash Pro's Flash Video Exporter and the built-in Video Import Wizard of Flash MX 2004 is VBR encoding. The Video Import Wizard can compress video only with CBR encoding, while all of the other tools discussed in this chapter support VBR encoding. As you learned earlier, you can achieve better visual images and smaller file sizes if you use VBR encoding.

To export the video in FLV format from QuickTime Pro:

1. Open the digital video file in QuickTime Pro.

2. Optionally, drag the in and out markers (the small triangles below the progress bar, shown in Figure 7-10) to trim the clip. Be sure to choose Edit → Trim after you have changed the markers' positions.

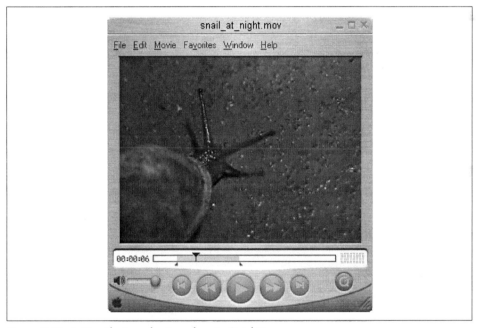

Figure 7-10. Setting the in and out markers in QuickTime

3. Choose QuickTime's File → Export Movie command. In the Save Exported File As dialog box (Figure 7-11), choose Movie to Macromedia Flash Video (FLV) in the Export drop-down menu. Specify a location and filename for the new FLV file. Click the Options button in the dialog box to view and edit the compression settings to be applied by the Flash Video (FLV) Exporter, as shown in Figure 7-12.

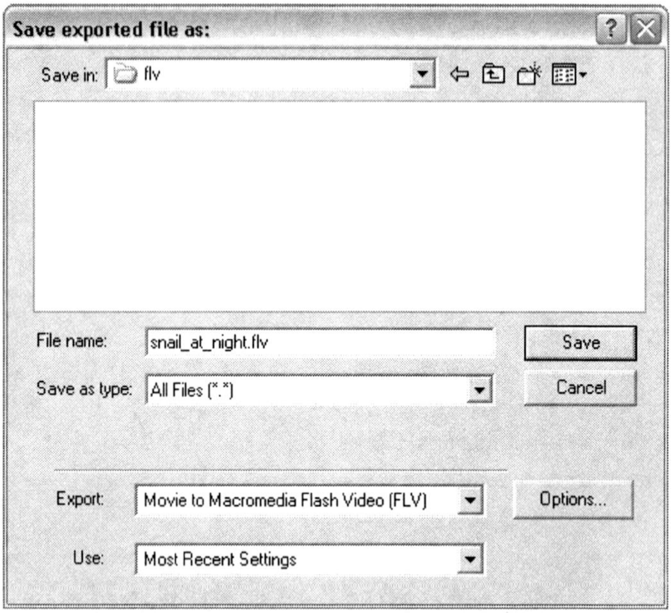

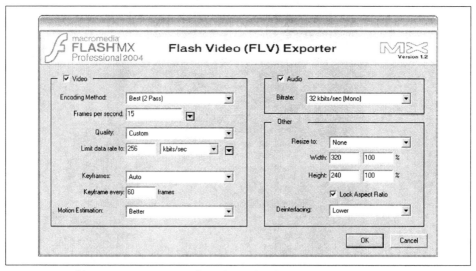

Figure 7-11. QuickTime's Save Exported File As dialog box

Figure 7-12. The FLV Exporter settings for video and audio compression

Unless you've got to be somewhere in a hurry, always use the Best (2 Pass) option for compressing your FLV files. The visual quality and file size are always better, compared to other compression options.

4. After you have determined which compression settings you'd like to use, click the Save button to begin the export process. QuickTime shows the export progress in a dialog box. (We discuss appropriate settings throughout the remainder of the chapter.)

5. When the FLV file has finished exporting, copy the file to the appropriate *streams* folder of your FlashCom application, as described under "Configuring the FCS Application" later in this chapter.

Optimizing Media with Sorenson Squeeze

One of the first products on the market to create FLV files was Sorenson Squeeze. Naturally, Sorenson would have an edge on the competition, given that they created the Spark codec. By far, Sorenson Squeeze gives you the most control over the subtleties of compression with the Spark Pro codec. You can also batch process several files with the same settings or even choose multiple output settings for the same file. For example, if you want to create FLV files for specific bit rates, you can add a new output setting for each bit rate you wish to create. You can also capture DV (Digital Video) footage directly from your Firewire-connected camcorder with Sorenson Squeeze. In this section, we provide you with an overview on the media creation process in Squeeze. To learn more about Sorenson Squeeze, visit *http://www.sorenson.com*.

Sorenson Squeeze is offered in two editions for Flash users: Sorenson Squeeze 4.0 for Flash MX (which, despite the name, is also appropriate for Flash MX 2004) and Sorenson Squeeze Compression 4.0 Suite. The Compression Suite enables you to compress video in several output formats, including MPEG-2 DVD video to Flash Video (FLV). The Macromedia Video Kit includes Sorenson Squeeze 4.0 Lite for Flash MX, which has a reduced feature set from Squeeze 4.0 for Flash MX. You can find a comparison of features at *http://www.macromedia.com/ software/studio/flashvideokit/sorenson_comparison.html*.

The figures in this section depict the Compression Suite version, but the features discussed are available in both editions. While you can also use Squeeze to output Flash movies (SWF files), this section discusses only FLV output.

To export FLV files from Sorenson Squeeze 4.0:

1. Open the Sorenson Squeeze application.

2. Choose File → Import Source (or click the Import File button in the Input panel), and browse to a location containing a digital video file.

3. When the video clip opens in Squeeze (see Figure 7-13), you can preview the video clip and choose in and out points for the clips if you need to trim footage from the original clip. Squeeze 4.0 offers a new cropping tool, available directly in the preview window.

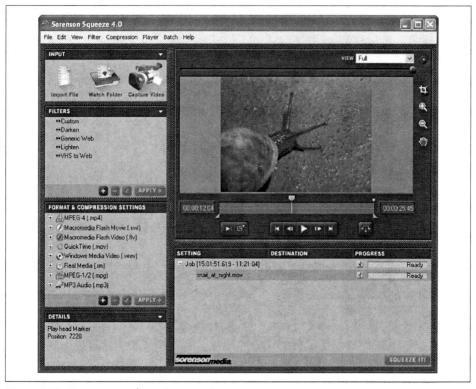

Figure 7-13. Previewing a clip in Sorenson Squeeze

4. If you want to adjust the image contrast or brightness or make other audio/video tweaks, you can use one of the presets available in the Filters panel (shown on the left in Figure 7-13) or create your own by choosing Filter → New or clicking the plus (+) button in the toolbar of the Filters panel. As shown in Figure 7-14, the Filter dialog box provides image adjustment controls. Any changes to the Contrast, Brightness, Gamma, White Restore, Black Restore, or Cropping values update the video clip image in the preview window of the main application interface. You can control the video clip's current position while you edit the image adjustment values. While most of these filters' effects can be previewed immediately, the benefits of some filter settings cannot be appreciated until you have actually compressed the clip:

   a. Video Noise Reduction

      This setting can be used to eliminate grainy looking video. Video noise is usually found in footage shot in low light, with an inexpensive mini-DV camcorder or footage transferred from VHS tape. As a rule of thumb, use the Light setting for footage captured from a low-end mini-DV camcorder (i.e., a single-chip or CCD camcorder) and use the Heavy setting for VHS transferred footage.

b. Normalize Audio

When selected, option analyzes the audio track of the video clip and looks for the highest audio level. If that audio level is very low, Squeeze will amplify it to a "normal" level and adjust the rest of the audio track accordingly. For example, if your DV camcorder's microphone was pointing at a person lecturing from a podium and that person's voice wasn't very loud (relative to the microphone's position), normalizing the audio can increase the volume so that it's more audible. However, normalization usually increases background noise and silence in audio gaps as well.

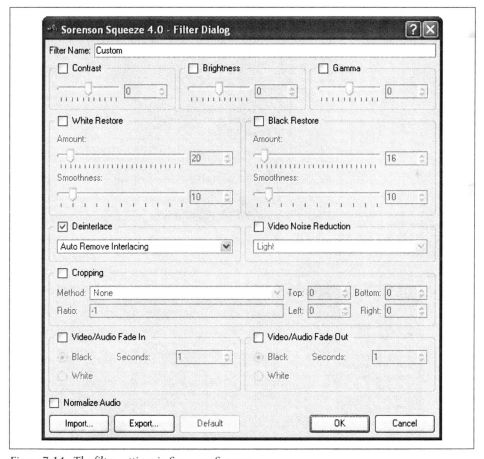

Figure 7-14. The filter settings in Sorenson Squeeze

5. If you created a custom filter, select Custom in the Filters panel and click the Apply button. The selected filter is now added to the current clip in the Job list below the video preview area, as shown in Figure 7-13.

6. Now you're ready to select the output format. Expand the Macromedia Flash Video (.flv) listing in the Format & Compression Settings panel, as shown in Figure 7-15. Choose the bit rate settings for your target audience; you can Shift- or Ctrl-click as many bit rate settings as you require. For footage that you want to use with FlashCom Server, start with one of the bit rates ending with the _Stream suffix. For this example, we selected the 256K_Stream option. After you have selected a bit rate, click the Apply button. The output setting appears below the clip name in the Job list, as shown in Figure 7-16.

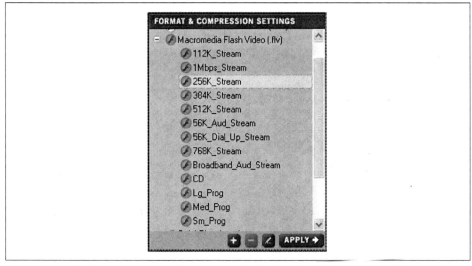

Figure 7-15. The bit rate options in the Macromedia Flash Video (.flv) category in the Format & Compression Settings panel

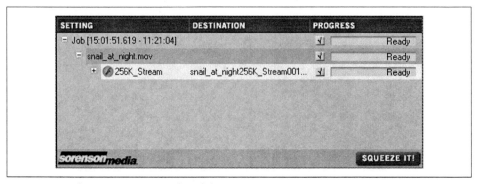

Figure 7-16. The output settings in the Job list

7. You can use the default compression settings that Squeeze has predefined in the output profile, or you can adjust the settings to suit your tastes. Click the + button next to 256K_Stream in the Job list, and you will see the expanded output setting shown in Figure 7-17. Double-click either the MP3 or Spark Pro list item. Double-clicking either opens the Audio/Video Compression Settings dialog box shown in Figure 7-18. Again, while the VBR compression process takes longer than CBR, you'll get better visual quality in your video clip if you choose Sorenson 2-Pass VBR in the Method combo box, located in the Video section of this dialog box. Among other compression options, you can also provide Squeeze with a file size limit (in the Constrain File Size field). If your desired compression settings exceed this limit, Squeeze will reduce the quality to meet your file size expectations.

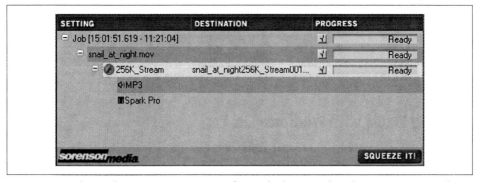

Figure 7-17. Change the compression settings of your clip by expanding the output setting and double-clicking the MP3 or Spark Pro entry

8. Once you have finessed the output settings, you're ready to let Squeeze do its job. Click the Squeeze It! button, as seen in Figure 7-17, and Squeeze starts to analyze the video clip and compress it in FLV format. The resulting FLV file is located in the same directory as your original video clip, unless you specified a different output location. You can change the output location by selecting the output setting in the Job list and choosing Batch → Change Destination. You can also right-click (or Ctrl-click on Mac) the output setting and choose Change Destination.

9. After Squeeze has finished creating the FLV file, copy the FLV file to the appropriate *streams* folder of your FlashCom application.

If you want to compress two or more source video clips in a batch, you can continue to import more source files using File → Import Source or clicking the Import File button. Select the new clip in the Job list, and choose your filter and compression options. Repeat the process for each additional source clip. You can also select multiple output settings for each individual clip. When you have all of your source clips and output settings configured, click Squeeze It! to begin processing the batch.

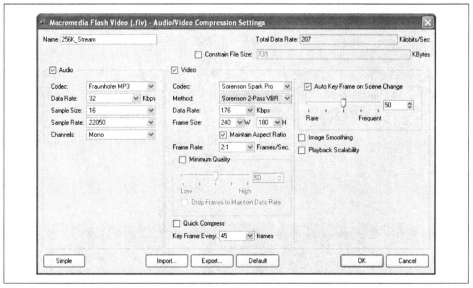

Figure 7-18. Squeeze's Audio/Video Compression Settings dialog box

Creating Media with Wildform Flix Pro

You can also encode FLV files with Wildform Flix Pro. Nearly all of the features in Sorenson Squeeze 4.0 are available in Flix Pro 4.0. Flix Pro does not have a watch folder as Squeeze does (see the sidebar), but Flix can batch process files with a few extra filenaming options. Flix Pro version 4.0 is currently available only for Windows; the latest Macintosh version is 3.0.

 Flix can also create vector versions of your digital video source clips, as Flash movies (SWF files). These movies cannot be streamed from a FlashCom application, but they can be used to create frame-by-frame masks for Flash video. To see a sample of vector output from Flix, go to *http://www.wildform.com/resources/gallery_vv.php*.

To export an FLV file from Flix Pro 4.0:

1. When you start Flix Pro 4.0, the File tab, as shown in Figure 7-19, is visible. Click the Browse button to the right of the Input setting to select a source clip. Flix will automatically assign an output file in the same location, with the file extension of the output format you are using. such as *.flv* or *.swf*. By default, Flix assumes you are outputting to a *.swf* file, so change it to *.flv*.

2. Choose a compression profile in the Preset drop-down menu. For this example, choose the 300K Broadband Video (MX FLV) profile, as shown in Figure 7-20.

Using Watch Folders in Sorenson Squeeze to Create Streams

One of the great features of Sorenson Squeeze is its capability to batch compress several video clips in the same location. Moreover, Squeeze will continue to monitor that folder for new video clips and compress them automatically. The process to batch compress and/or set up a watch folder is nearly the same as the steps outlined in the previous section:

1. Move all of your video clips to the same folder location (such as *C:\video_compress*).

2. In Sorenson Squeeze, choose File → Watch Folder (or click the Watch Folder button), and select the location you used in Step 1. The video preview area will not display any video footage, but the Job list will list the folder's name.

3. Proceed to choose output file format(s), filter settings, and compression options.

4. After you choose a compression option, the Job list displays the option's information. Note that the output filename includes the compression setting name as a suffix that will be added to each source video clip's filename. For example, if you choose the 256K_Stream preset, a source clip named *snail.mov* will have a counterpart output filename of *snail256K_Stream001.flv*.

5. Click the Squeeze It! button, and Squeeze will begin compressing the files in the folder location. At this point, Squeeze creates two subfolders in the watch folder location: *CompletedSource* and *CompressedOutput*. After Squeeze has finished compressing a source clip in the watch folder location, it moves the source clip to the *CompletedSource* folder. The compressed FLV file for each source clip is created in the *CompressedOutput* folder.

6. After Squeeze has finished compressing the original source clips in the watch folder location, it continues to monitor the folder for new source clips as long as the Squeeze application runs. As new clips are added, Squeeze creates new output files with the compression options you specified earlier.

You can create a virtual directory in your FlashCom virtual host settings that is mapped to the *CompressedOutput* folder of the watch folder, or you can create a script that moves the compressed files to another location. For example, you could move the compressed files using the `<cfschedule>` tag in a ColdFusion page. In this way, you can stream new files from FlashCom applications without additional intervention.

3. If necessary, click and drag the in and out pointers below the video preview area. The selected range is shaded blue (which appears gray in Figure 7-21).

4. Click the Video Filters button in the lower right corner of the File tab. The Editor dialog box (shown in Figure 7-22) offers similar options to the filter settings of Sorenson Squeeze. Unlike Squeeze, though, you can finesse the video noise reduction with a precise numeric slider. You can also boost saturation values; NTSC video (the video signal recorded to DV camcorder tape) often appears less saturated when viewed on a computer monitor compared to a standard TV

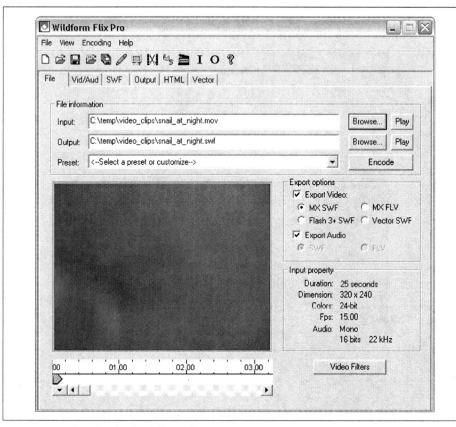

Figure 7-19. The File tab of Wildform Flix Pro 4.0

screen. You can use the Saturation slider to revive footage that looks washed out. Or you can remove all saturation to create black-and-white (grayscale) video. You can also check the Deinterlace option to remove the flicker from NTSC video footage shot with North American camcorders. While Sorenson Squeeze will automatically detect that your footage is interlaced, you need to let Flix know if you want your footage deinterlaced.

5. If you'd like to finesse the video and audio compression settings for your chosen preset, click the Vid/Aud tab (shown in Figure 7-23). One of the nice features of Flix is that the original source (or input) clip's information is juxtaposed next to your output clip settings. You can easily determine whether you're specifying an output dimension or audio sampling rate that exceeds the original—generally, you do not want to upsample video or audio quality in your output file.

6. Now you're ready to output the FLV file. Select the File tab and click the Encode button to the right of the Preset option, as seen in Figure 7-21. Flix opens an Encoding dialog box (as seen in Figure 7-24) enabling you to monitor the bit rate settings during analysis and compression.

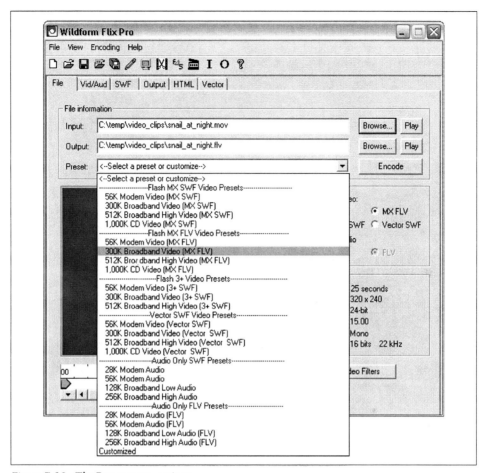

Figure 7-20. The Preset menu options

7. When Flix has finished the encoding process, a preview window appears and plays the FLV file. If you missed the playback of the preview, you can replay the FLV file by clicking the Play button to the right of the Output setting of the File tab.

8. Copy the FLV file to the appropriate *streams* folder of your FlashCom application.

If you want to encode several source clips with the same preset, choose Edit → Batch Process to select the clips.

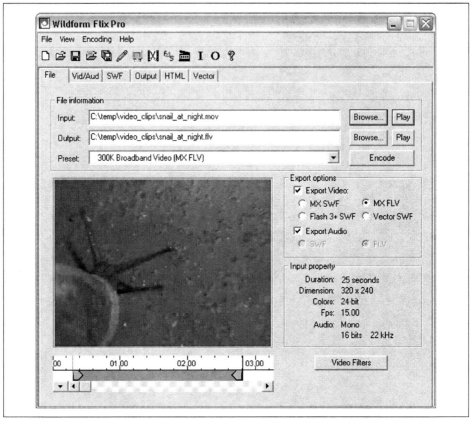

Figure 7-21. The markers below the video preview area control the in and out points

 For an open source solution to FLV compression, try *ffmpeg*, which uses libraries of audio and video codecs to transcode digital audio and video formats. FLV is among the many formats that the tool recognizes. The *ffmpeg* utility can also capture and create live streams. For more information on this handy utility, visit *http://ffmpeg.sourceforge. net*. For more information on open source programming in general, go to *http://opensource.org*.

Using Flash Pro's Media Components

Once you've created FLV files with any of the tools described earlier in this chapter, you're ready to put them to use in your own FlashCom applications. In this section, you learn how to use components designed to stream FLV files from a FlashCom application. If you don't know your *NetStream* basics, be sure to read Chapter 5 before proceeding with the examples shown in this section.

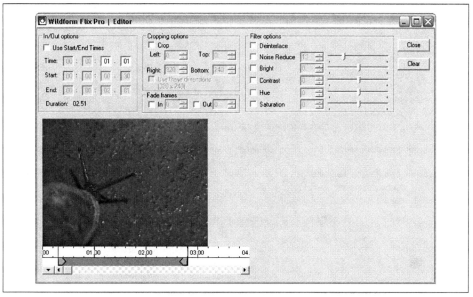

Figure 7-22. The Flix Pro Editor dialog box

Among the several add-ons Macromedia includes in Flash Pro, beyond the standard edition of Flash MX 2004, the media components enable you to quickly add audio or video stream playback to your applications. The media components take care of everything from stream initialization to stream playback control.

MediaPlayback Component

The all-in-one MediaPlayback component enables you to play FLV files from a Flash-Com Server application over RTMP or from a web server over HTTP. The component features a display area for the video portion of your stream, a playback controller, and a Halo-themed background. For our purposes, we review only the FlashCom-specific features of this component. For a review of the component's API, search for "MediaPlayback" in Flash MX 2004's Help panel.

As with other Flash components, you can add and control a MediaPlayback instance with ActionScript alone, or you can drag an instance to the Stage of your Flash document and specify its settings in the Parameters tab of the Component Inspector panel, as shown in Figure 7-25.

The following parameters are configurable. Most apply only to FLV files:

FLV or MP3
> Specify the type of media you want to load with the component instance, either from a web server or from a FlashCom Server application. When you select

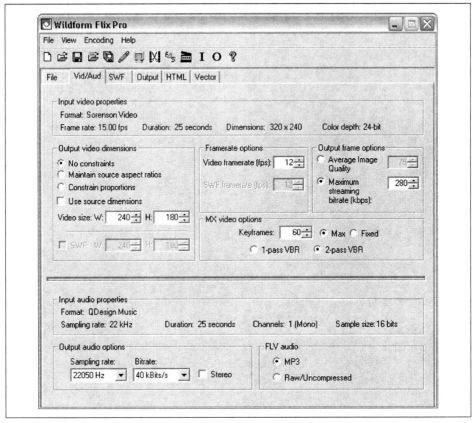

Figure 7-23. The Flix Pro Vid/Aud tab

MP3, the display area of the component shrinks, accommodating only the progress bar (and hidden controls).

Video Length

Use these text fields to enter the duration of your FLV video clip in hours, minutes, seconds, and milliseconds. If the Milliseconds checkbox is cleared, the last field is measured in frames instead of milliseconds, and the frame rate (FPS) option becomes active.

 Unless the FLV file is created with Flash Communication Server 1.5.2 or with Flash Video Exporter 1.2 (or higher), you need to specify the video length values for your media file. FCS 1.5.2 and Flash Video Exporter 1.2 automatically embed the duration value into FLV files. This data is retrieved using the new *NetStream.onMetaData( )* callback. If you are using another utility to create your FLV files, consider using the FLV MetaData Injector, available at *http://www.buraks.com/flvmdi*, to insert the necessary metadata in FLV files to be compatible with the media components.

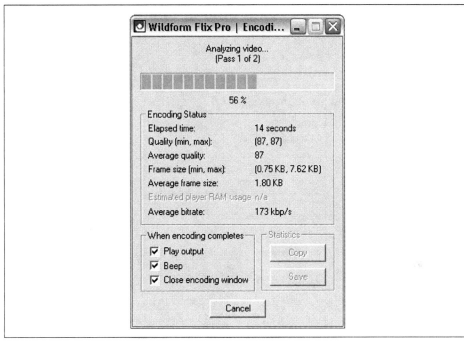

Figure 7-24. The Flix Pro Encoding dialog box

URL

> Enter the RTMP path to your FlashCom application, including the stream name, or the HTTP path (relative or absolute) for the media file. If you are loading an FLV file from a FlashCom application, you can omit the *.flv* extension from the file path. For example, if you have a file named *test.flv* in the *streams/_definst_* folder of an application folder named *broadcast*, you would use the following RTMP path (the path need not include the instance name when connecting to the default instance):
>
> > *rtmp://fcs-server.com/broadcast/test*
>
> or
>
> > *rtmp://fcs-server.com/broadcast/test.flv*
>
> The MediaPlayback component can also load FLV or MP3 files from an instance-specific folder within the *streams* folder of your FlashCom application. The following URL streams the MP3 file named *song.mp3* from the *streams/music* folder of the application named *jukebox*:
>
> > *rtmp://fcs-server.com/jukebox/music/song.mp3*

Automatically Play

> If you want your media file to play back as soon as the MediaPlayback instance loads onto the Stage, select this checkbox. Otherwise, the user must click the control bar's Play button to begin playback.

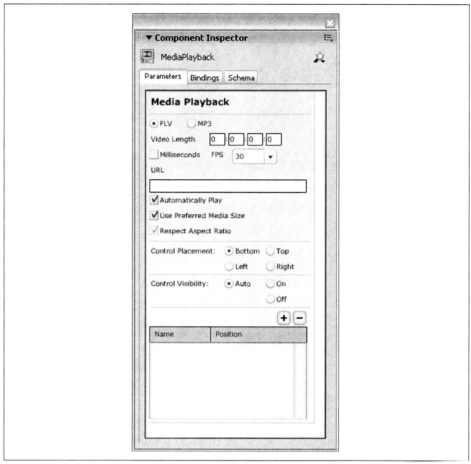

Figure 7-25. The parameters for the MediaPlayback component

Use Preferred Media Size

This checkbox determines whether the video stream is displayed at its original width and height, as you encoded it. The only exception is if your video stream is larger than the width and height of the component instance. In that case, the video is scaled to fit within the boundaries of the component. However, if the component's video display area exceeds the width and height of the original video stream, the video stream does not scale up to fit within the component.

Respect Aspect Ratio

This option determines whether the video image is stretched to accommodate the width and height of the display area of the component instance. If this option is selected, the aspect ratio of the original video file is honored. If the option is cleared, the video image is stretched close to the edges of the component instance's display area.

Control Placement

Use this parameter to place the progress bar and control bar relative to the video display area. You can choose from Bottom, Top, Left, and Right.

Control Visibility

This option determines the behavior of the sliding control bar that displays next to the progress/playback bar. By default, the Auto option hides the control bar until the user mouses over the progress bar area. You can force the display of the control bar by choosing On, or you can disable the control bar by choosing Off.

Cue Points

Using the Add (+) or Remove (-) buttons, you can add or remove cue points to or from your media file. If you add a cue point to a media component, the instance fires an event whenever the cue point is reached. For example, you can click the Add button, enter test into the Name column, and enter 0:0:10.0 into the Position column. Thereafter, you can use a listener in your ActionScript code to detect when the media file has reached the 10 second position. The media components broadcast a *cuePoint* event when a cue point value is reached. Using cue points, you can add information overlays to your video for medical diagrams, instructional videos, and so forth.

For more information on adding event listeners for cue points, search for "Media. addCuePoint" in Flash MX 2004's Help panel.

To practice using the MediaPlayback component, follow these steps:

1. In Flash Pro, create a new Flash document. Save the document as *mediaPlayback.fla*.

2. Open the Components panel (Ctrl-F7 or Cmd-F7). In the panel, open the Media Components folder, and drag an instance of the MediaPlayback component to the Stage.

3. Select the instance on the Stage, and use the Properties panel to name the instance cmpStream.

4. In the Properties panel, click the Launch Component Inspector button. If the Component Inspector panel is docked, undock and expand the panel to see all of the options (as shown in Figure 7-25).

5. In the Component Inspector panel, make sure the FLV radio button is selected. In the URL field, enter the following RTMP path:

   rtmp://209.29.151.23/ch07/brother_running.flv

   This FLV file is publicly accessible on the book's official FlashCom Server. For the purposes of this example, the other options in the panel should be kept at their default values. You do not need to enter a Video Length value, as the FLV file's metadata contains the duration information.

6. Save the Flash document, and test it (Control → Test Movie, or Ctrl-Enter or Cmd-Enter). Once the stream has been buffered from the book's server,

playback will begin. Familiarize yourself with the component's UI, as shown in Figure 7-26. If you roll over the progress bar, the control bar expands below the display area. You can pause and resume playback with the Play button to the left, and you can rewind with the left arrow button. The right arrow button, which enables you to advance to the end of a media file, is disabled for FLV file playback. You can also control the volume of the audio track in the FLV file with the slider at the right of the control bar. When you roll off the control bar area, it hides itself again. Finally, click the top-right corner of the MediaPlayback instance and the window expands to fill the entire Flash movie Stage, scaling the video. Clicking the right corner again scales the component back to its original size.

Figure 7-26. The UI of the MediaPlayback component

MediaController and MediaDisplay Components

The MediaController and MediaDisplay media components can work either together or on their own. These components are essentially the main elements of the Media-Playback component without the background chrome skin. MediaDisplay loads an FLV or MP3 file (and displays the video feed of an FLV file), while MediaController manages the playback of the media resource. You can build your own display clip or component to be used with the MediaController, build your own controller to be used with MediaDisplay, or use both together.

To use the MediaDisplay and MediaController components in concert with each other:

1. Open a new Flash document, then open the Components panel (Ctrl-F7 or Cmd-F7).

2. Drag an instance of the MediaDisplay component to the Stage. In the Properties panel, name the instance cmdStream.

3. Click the Launch Component Inspector button in the Properties panel. In the Component Inspector panel, make sure the FLV media type is selected, and specify the following RTMP path:

```
rtmp://209.29.151.23/ch07/brother_running.flv
```

 Unlike the MediaPlayback component, the MediaDisplay component requires a path that ends with an *.flv* extension. Feel free to substitute the RTMP path with one of your own.

4. Save your document as *mediaDisplay_mediaController.fla,* and test it (Ctrl-Enter or Cmd-Enter). You should see the FLV file play in the component. Because the component is using the Automatically Play option, the stream plays back on its own. Also, the video picture is larger than the component instance width and height because the Use Preferred Media Size option is enabled by default.

5. Now, drag an instance of the MediaController component onto the Stage. Place the instance below the MediaDisplay instance from Step 2. Name this instance cmcControl. Use the default values for the component parameters.

6. In order for the MediaController instance to work with the MediaDisplay instance, you need to add some ActionScript. Create a new layer in the timeline named *Actions*. Select frame 1 of the *Actions* layer, and open the Actions panel (F9). Add the following lines of code:

```
import mx.controls.MediaDisplay;
var cmdStream:MediaDisplay;
cmdStream.associateController(cmcControl);
```

7. Save your Flash document, and test it. The stream automatically plays, and if you roll the mouse over the progress bar, you can control the stream.

Enabling Multiple Bit Rate FLVs Within an Application

As you build audio/video streaming–enabled applications with FlashCom, you'll want to know how to serve streams designed to meet the bandwidth restrictions of each client connecting to the application. For example, if you have an FLV file that was encoded for 256 Kbps, chances are that stream won't play very well to someone using a 56 Kbps dial-up connection. One of the drawbacks to FlashCom's audio/video streaming is that it cannot recompress an FLV file on the fly. Other AV streaming servers, such as the Apple QuickTime Streaming Server, can take a high-resolution QuickTime movie (MOV file) and compress it further for low-bandwidth clients. With FlashCom, you have two options when faced with this problem.

- Change the frame rate of the stream for the receiving client. With client-side ActionScript, you can use the *NetStream.receiveFps( )* method to lower the frame rate of a streaming FLV published from a FlashCom application.

- Encode multiple FLV files, with each file targeted at a specific bit rate. For example, if you know that you'll have dial-up and broadband users subscribing to streams on your FlashCom Server, you could encode your source video clips at 39 Kbps and 384 Kbps, respectively. The higher bit rate stream could be viewed by the broadband users, while the lower bit rate stream would be available for the dial-up users.

In this section, you learn how to efficiently handle the latter option by building a Flash movie that can dynamically switch between two FLV files of the same content. To see an example of the system you're about to dissect, check out the following URL:

http://www.flash-communications.net/examples/ch07/MultiBitrateStreamer

Because FlashCom can seek anywhere within a stream and serve specific portions of that stream, the MultiBitrateStreamer component used in this exercise does not have to download either stream in its entirety.

Preparing the FLV Files

The first step to enabling multiple bit rate streams for your FlashCom application is to create an FLV file for each bit rate. With the MultiBitrateStreamer component used in this section, you can switch between two qualities of the same content. Thus, two FLV files can be created with your preferred FLV encoding application. In the following example, download the MPEG-2 file from the Open Video Project web site:

http://www.open-video.org/details.php?videoid=4425

Once you have downloaded this video clip (or have located a source clip of your own), you're ready to compress two versions of the clip in FLV format. We recommend using an encoder that can batch process files, such as Sorenson Squeeze or Wildform Flix. Otherwise, you can use the Flash Video Exporter tool that ships with Flash Pro.

To create two bit rate–specific FLV files using Sorenson Squeeze 4.0:

1. In Squeeze's Input panel, click the Import File button. Browse to the location of your source clip.

2. In Squeeze's Format & Compression Settings panel (see Figure 7-13), expand the Macromedia Flash Video (.flv) group, and select the 384K_Stream preset. Ctrl-click (Cmd-click on Mac) the 56K_Dial_Up_Stream preset. Click the Apply button. The presets are now applied to the source clip in the Job list (located at the lower right of the Squeeze UI).

3. In the Job list, expand the 384K_Stream node and double-click the Spark Pro setting. In the Video settings of the dialog box, change the Method setting to Sorenson 2-Pass VBR. Clear the Maintain Aspect Ratio checkbox, and set the Frame Rate to 24, as shown in Figure 7-27. The 2-Pass VBR option produces higher-quality video output. Since the source footage for our example is already MPEG, the source aspect ratio is 1:1, instead of 4:3.

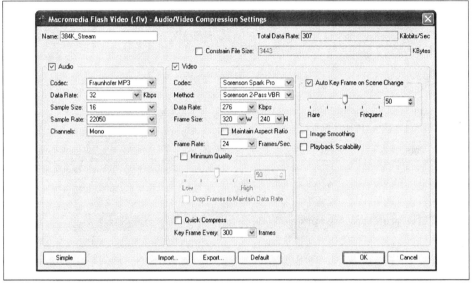

Figure 7-27. Optimal settings for the source clip at 384 Kbps

4. Repeat Step 3 for the 56K_Dial_Up_Stream preset. Instead of using a frame rate of 24, choose 10, as shown in Figure 7-28.

5. Click the Squeeze It! button located at the lower-right corner of the Squeeze UI. Squeeze starts to compress the source clip with the selected presets.

6. When Squeeze has finished creating the FLV files, rename the 384 Kbps file to *sample_high.flv*. Rename the 56 Kbps file to *sample_low.flv*. Read the next section for information on relocating these files to their final destination.

Configuring the FCS Application

The process for using multiple bit rate FLV files is the same as utilizing any FLV file for a FlashCom application. The FLV files are copied to an instance folder of the *streams* folder within your application folder. For example, if you want your FLV files accessible to the default instance, _definst_, of an application named *broadcast*, you would create the folder structure shown in Figure 7-29.

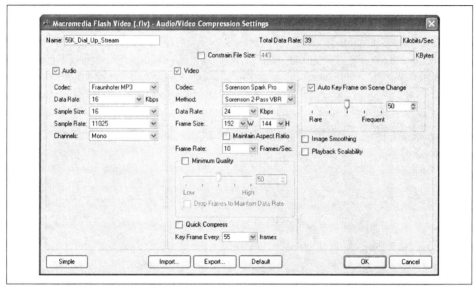

Figure 7-28. Optimal settings for the source clip at 56 Kbps

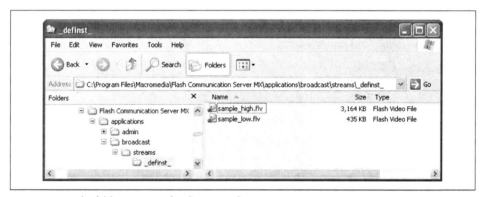

Figure 7-29. The folder structure for the stream locations

You can also set up your FlashCom Server to point to a location outside of your application instance folder by using a virtual directory. Virtual directories are visited later in this chapter and discussed in "Uploading Prerecorded Streams" in Chapter 5.

Once you have copied your FLV files to the *streams/_definst_* folder (or your preferred application instance folder), you need to add the Server-Side ActionScript code necessary for the custom StreamController component used for this exercise. At the root of your application folder (e.g., *applications/broadcast*), create a text file named *main.asc* with the following code:

```
Client.prototype.getLength = function (streamName) {
  return Stream.length(streamName);
};
```

The *getLength( )* method enables the StreamController component to retrieve the duration (in seconds) of a stream or FLV file, accessible from the application instance.

Providing an Interface to Select and Switch the Streams

To understand how a multi-bitrate controller works, download the following file from the book's web site:

> *http://www.flash-communications.net/examples/ch07/MultiBitrateStreamer/*
> *MultiBitrateStreamer_100.zip*

After you have downloaded the file, uncompress the archive to access the *.fla* and *.as* files associated with this sample. Open *MultiBitrateStream_100.fla* in Flash MX 2004, and open the Library panel. Double-click the MultiBitrateStreamer component. As shown in Figure 7-30, this component has three primary elements:

Display area

> The mcVideo instance at the top of the component's Stage is a movie clip instance containing a nested Video object named vWindow. The mcVideo instance can scale based on the dimensions of the source video clip it is displaying.

Control bar

> Below the mcVideo instance is the cscControl instance, which is an instance of the StreamController component, located in the *MultiBitrateStreamer assets* folder of the Library. This component works much like the MediaController component, yet it adds less weight to the overall file size of the Flash movie. The StreamController can pause, play, and scrub the video stream. The current time and duration of the stream are also displayed below the control interface.

Radio buttons

> Two RadioButton instances are located below the cscControl instance. The crbLow instance, labeled Low, is the default option. When this button is selected, the stream playing in the mcVideo instance will be the low-quality FLV stream. The crbHigh instance, labeled High, enables the high-quality FLV stream to play.

The StreamController and RadioButton instances use a Miniml font face called *hooge 05_53*. While you may not be able to see this font display within the Flash MX 2004 IDE, the published file loads the font from the *MultiBitrateStreamer_library.swf* file. This file must be uploaded to the web server along with the Flash movie containing the MultiBitrateStreamer component. You can purchase several pixel-based fonts designed for Flash movies at *http://www.miniml.com*.

Now, open the *MultiBitrateStreamer.as* file. This is the class file used by the MultiBitrateStreamer component. For the purposes of this example, the publicly inspectable variables of the component are discussed, in addition to the *switchQuality( )* method. At the top of the .as file, the following public variables are exposed.

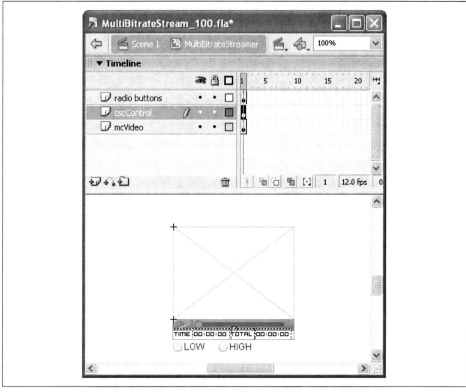

Figure 7-30. The timeline of the MultiBitrateStreamer component

You can set these values in the Parameters tab of the Properties panel for each instance of the MultiBitrateStreamer component:

```
[Inspectable(defaultValue=false)]
public var initHigh:Boolean;
[Inspectable(defaultValue=160)]
public var lowWidth:Number;
[Inspectable(defaultValue=120)]
public var lowHeight:Number;
[Inspectable(defaultValue="stream_low")]
public var lowStreamName:String;
[Inspectable(defaultValue=320)]
public var highWidth:Number;
[Inspectable(defaultValue=240)]
public var highHeight:Number;
[Inspectable(defaultValue="stream_high")]
public var highStreamName:String;
[Inspectable(defaultValue="rtmp://localhost/broadcast")]
public var fcsURL:String;
```

The first variable, initHigh, determines whether the high-quality stream is the first stream displayed in the mcVideo instance. By default, the value is set to false.

The lowWidth and lowHeight values establish the dimensions of the low-quality stream, as displayed by the mcVideo instance. The lowStreamName value sets the low-quality stream's name, which is the name of the low-quality FLV file you compressed earlier in this section—without the *.flv* extension.

The highWidth, highHeight, and highStreamName values work the same as their low counterparts, except that they are used with the high-quality stream.

The fcsURL is the RTMP path to your FlashCom application instance.

The *switchQuality( )* method is the listener method used by the crbLow and crbHigh instances, as initialized by the *init( )* method. The *switchQuality( )* method stops the currently playing stream by invoking *play(false)* and begins playback of the alternative stream. The playedTime variable retrieves the current time of the stream from the *StreamController* instance, cscControl. Note that this time value is not equivalent to the NetStream.time of the currently playing stream—NetStream.time is a relative time value; it will reset to 0 each time you initialize a new *NetStream.play( )*:

```
public function switchQuality (oEvent:Object):Void {
  var newQuality:String = oEvent.target.data;
  var owner = oEvent.target._parent;
  var playedTime:Number = owner.cscControl.time;
  var streamToPlay:String =
      newQuality == "low" ? owner.lowStreamName : owner.highStreamName;
  owner.activeStream.play(false);
  owner.vWindow.attachVideo(null);
  owner.activeStream.play(streamToPlay, playedTime,
                    (owner.cscControl.isPaused ? 0 : -1) );
  owner.vWindow.attachVideo(owner.activeStream);
  owner.cscControl.streamName = streamToPlay;
  if (!owner.cscControl.isPaused) owner.cscControl.streamTime =  playedTime;
  owner.streamQuality = newQuality;
  owner.size( );
}
```

If you go back to the main timeline of the *MultiBitrateStream_100.fla* document and select the instance of the component on the Stage, you'll notice that the Properties panel contains working values for the sample stream compressed earlier in this section. If you test the movie and have a connection to the Internet, the low-quality FLV stream will load into the mcVideo instance. Clicking the high-quality radio button resizes the mcVideo instance and loads the high-quality stream. If you have configured your FlashCom Server with an application instance containing your multiple bit rate FLV files, go back to the Flash MX 2004 IDE and change the fcsURL path in the Properties panel to reflect the location of your application.

Streaming MP3 Audio

One of the additions to FlashCom 1.5 from the original 1.0 release is the capability to stream MP3 audio files from a FlashCom application. Now, you may be scratching your head, thinking, "Can't I already load MP3 files into the Flash Player with *Sound.loadSound( )*?" And you're right. However, *loadSound( )* operates with HTTP, and so requires that the MP3 files (or source) are accessible from a web server. Also, it's possible for someone to discover this source and access the MP3 files directly, without the use of Flash Player. With FlashCom, you can protect your MP3 sources and be fairly confident that the right to access those files is managed. Just like FLV files, MP3 files streamed with FlashCom over RTMP (or HTTP tunneling) are never cached as whole files on the end user's computer. The MP3 data is stored only temporarily as chunks within the Flash Player's buffer. After the sound has played, there's nothing left over on the user's machine. Because of this security feature, you may decide to use FlashCom Server as your MP3 streaming server as well as your video streaming server.

For a review of stream basics and an introduction to MP3 streaming, including use of the *NetStream* and *Stream* classes, refer to Chapter 5.

Considerations for MP3 Playback

Unlike the FLV format, the MP3 audio format is very popular and widely accessible. There are more MP3 audio converters than you can shake a stick at, and many of them are freely available on *http://www.download.com*. Apple iTunes includes a free MP3 encoder, with several customizable compression options.

Like the Sorenson Spark codec, the MP3 audio codec has two primary encoding methods: CBR (constant bit rate) or VBR (variable bit rate). While VBR encoding takes a bit longer to complete, the better audio quality is worth the wait. In our experience, FlashCom can stream just about any MP3 file you want to stream. If you are going to encode a batch of files in the MP3 format with the hope of streaming them on FlashCom, you should create a few test files with your preferred encoder and compression options to use with a sample FlashCom application. Once you know your flavor of MP3 files works with FlashCom, proceed to encode the rest of the files in the same manner.

Using the MediaPlayback Component to Play MP3 Files

In this section, you learn how to create a list of MP3 sound effects and play them with the MediaPlayback component that ships with Flash Pro. Download the following Zip file containing four MP3 files:

> *http://www.flash-communications.net/examples/ch07/mp3.zip*

Once you have downloaded the Zip file, uncompress the MP3 files (*dog.mp3, cat.mp3, bird.mp3, duck.mp3*) and move them to the following application path on your Flash-Com Server:

> *applications/broadcast/streams/_definst_*

If you haven't created the *main.asc* for the *broadcast* application as discussed in the previous section, review the "Configuring the FCS Application" section for more details.

Now that you have the MP3 files ready to stream from your FlashCom Server, you're ready to build the user interface in Flash Pro:

1. Open a new document in Flash Pro. Save this document as *MediaComponent_ mp3.fla*.

2. Rename *Layer 1* to *clbSounds*. On frame 1 of this layer, drag an instance of the List component from the UI Components folder of the Components panel to the Stage. Place the instance near the top-left corner of the Stage. In the Properties panel, name this instance clbSounds.

3. Create a new layer, and name it *cmpPlayer*. On frame 1 of this layer, drag an instance of the MediaPlayback component to the Stage, to the right of the clbSounds instance. In the Properties panel, name this instance cmpPlayer and set its height to 80. Click the Launch Component Inspector button, and in the Parameters tab of the Component Inspector panel, select the MP3 option and the On value for the Control Visibility setting, as shown in Figure 7-31.

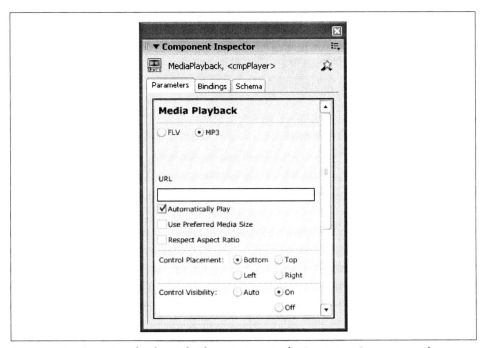

Figure 7-31. The settings for the MediaPlayer instance in the Component Inspector panel

4. Now you're ready to add the ActionScript code to populate the list and trigger the MediaPlayback component when an item in the list is selected. Create a new

layer named *Actions*, and drag this layer to the top of the layer stack. Select frame 1 of this layer, and open the Actions panel (F9). Add the following code:

```
import mx.controls.List;
import mx.controls.MediaPlayback;

var clbSounds:mx.controls.List;
var cmpPlayer:mx.controls.MediaPlayback;

var dp:Array - [ {label: "Dog", data: "dog.mp3"},
                 {label: "Cat", data: "cat.mp3"},
                 {label: "Duck", data: "duck.mp3"},
                 {label: "Bird", data: "bird.mp3"}];

clbSounds.dataProvider = dp;

var oSounds:Object = new Object();
oSounds.change = function (oEvent:Object) {
  var sVal:String = oEvent.target.selectedItem.data;
  cmpPlayer.contentPath = "rtmp://209.29.151.23/ch07/" + sVal;
  cmpPlayer.play();
};
clbSounds.addEventListener("change", oSounds);
```

This block of code creates a data provider for the clbSounds instance. The dp array contains four objects, each with a label and data property. The oSounds object is a listener whose *change( )* method is invoked whenever an item in the list is clicked. For this example, the contentPath of the cmpPlayer instance uses the public URL on the book's server, but you can change this path to reflect the location of your own broadcast application.

5. Save the document, and test the movie (Ctrl-Enter or Cmd-Enter). When you click the Dog item in the list, you will hear the sound of a dog barking. The *dog. mp3* file is streaming from the FlashCom Server. If you select another item in the list, you will hear that sound play.

Conclusion

It doesn't do much good to design a communication application that can't deliver the media to the end users in an efficient manner. The best-designed application will fail miserably if the media isn't properly prepared. Even if you aren't responsible for creating the video and audio files, in order to master FlashCom application development, you must also understand media preparation and delivery. This understanding allows you to determine whether the programming or the media, or a combination of the two, is at fault when an application does not perform as it should.

This chapter has covered many details for compressing and streaming audio and video. It should put you in good stead creating efficient, media-centric communications applications. In Chapter 17, we revisit bandwidth considerations to make sure your client's connection is not overtaxed. In the next chapter, we shift gears to talk about shared objects, which offer a way to transmit data to and from the server.

Remote Connectivity and Communication

Part III covers communication between FlashCom applications and their clients or communicating with other application servers using Flash Remoting.

- Chapter 8, *Shared Objects*
- Chapter 9, *Remote Methods*
- Chapter 10, *Server Management API*
- Chapter 11, *Flash Remoting*
- Chapter 12, *ColdFusion MX and FlashCom*

Shared Objects

Remote shared objects are used in FlashCom applications to do everything from sharing the position of spaceships in a game to broadcasting chat text messages. They are a good way to keep track of what users are doing in a conference, let movies know what streams are available, and allow users to disconnect and reconnect to an application without losing track of the application's state.

Shared objects are an extension of ActionScript objects that allow objects to be shared by more than one movie and to be stored for later use. Local shared objects (LSOs) can be stored and retrieved locally by Flash movies between sessions and, under some circumstances, by more than one movie. Remote shared objects (RSOs) can be shared in real time by Flash movies connected to the FlashCom Server. When one movie changes a property of its copy of an RSO, updates are sent automatically to all the other movies sharing the same object. RSOs can be stored locally and on the FlashCom Server. RSOs have a *send( )* method similar to *NetStream* objects that can be used to broadcast messages to every movie connected to a shared object.

Objects and Shared Objects

ActionScript objects are implemented as associative arrays. Each object property associates a value with a property name. The property name is a string that is used to store and retrieve a value in a slot, or location, within the object. Objects are similar to arrays—they have slots that hold values. Arrays are designed to provide access to the value in each slot via an index number, while objects provide access to values via a string property name. Example 8-1 reviews how to add properties to a generic ActionScript object.

Example 8-1. Creating and adding properties to an ActionScript object

```
// Create a simple object named user.
user = new Object( );
// Use dot notation to add a userName property.
user.userName = "blesser";
```

```
// Use the [] operator to add a password property.
user["password"] = "bigSecret";
// Add a function as a property of this generic object.
user.showProperties = function () {
  for (var prop in this) {
    trace(prop + ": " + this[prop]);
  }
};
// Call the function.
user.showProperties();

// Output to the Output panel for this script:
showProperties: [type Function]
password: bigSecret
userName: blesser
```

In ActionScript, objects are the foundation on which custom classes are built. However the *SharedObject* class cannot be extended the same way as other classes. Shared objects always store data in a simple associative array. Shared objects can contain instances of other classes in their *slots* (i.e., properties); however, there are some restrictions on the type of data that can be stored in a shared object's slots. With one exception, a shared object slot can contain any native ActionScript type such as a *Number, String, Date, Boolean, Object,* or *Array.* However, an LSO cannot be used to store and retrieve a function in a later session, and RSOs cannot make a function available to remote movies by assigning one to a slot. However, with an added step of registering a class in a movie, a shared object slot can contain custom classes, provided they are also defined in each Flash movie or in the server-side application where they are accessed.

Getting a Shared Object in Flash

One reason shared objects cannot be extended, or subclassed, to create custom classes is that they are created by static methods of the *SharedObject* class rather than constructed using the *new* operator. In client-side Flash ActionScript, the two static methods to create shared objects are *SharedObject.getLocal( )* and *SharedObject. getRemote( ).*

Getting and Using a Local Shared Object

SharedObject.getLocal( ) returns a local shared object (LSO):

```
local_so = SharedObject.getLocal("ConfigData");
```

Once returned, a local shared object can be used immediately. Properties and values can be created, stored in, and retrieved from the shared object's data property (data is a generic *Object* instance):

```
// Set up an onStatus( ) handler for this LSO.
local_so.onStatus = function (info) {
  if (info.code == "SharedObject.Flush.Failed") {
    trace("Unable to save user information - space request not granted.");
  }
};
// Set two properties of the shared object.
local_so.data.userName = "blesser";
local_so.data.password = "bigSecret";
// Try to write the data to disk.
var result = local_so.flush( );
if (result == false) {
  trace("Can't save user information because local storage is set to Never.");
}
```

The Flash editor provides code hints for shared objects when variable names end in "_so".

Local shared objects are not covered in detail in this book. See *ActionScript for Flash MX: The Definitive Guide* (O'Reilly) for a complete description of how to work with LSOs. A comparison of local path options for local and remote shared objects is included in "Locally and Remotely Persistent Shared Objects" later in this chapter. However, you may also want to consult the previously referenced book for a description of how to share local objects between movies from the same domain and how to use the local path parameter in *getLocal( )*.

Getting and Using a Remote Shared Object

Remote shared objects are created using *SharedObject.getRemote( )* but do not dynamically share information until they are connected to the server using a *NetConnection* object and have been synchronized with a copy of the shared object on the server. Setting up an RSO is a multistep process that begins with creating an unconnected RSO. The RSO must be associated with a relative URI (the shared object's name) and an RTMP address (the URI of the application instance), both of which must be passed into the *getRemote( )* method:

```
nc = new NetConnection( );
nc.connect("rtmp:/courseChat");
remote_so = SharedObject.getRemote("UsersData", nc.uri);
```

Normally, a *NetConnection* object's uri property is passed into the *getRemote( )* method as the RTMP address, but a string can be used as well:

```
remote_so = SharedObject.getRemote("UsersData", "rtmp:/courseChat");
```

RSOs work across the network, so the next step is to connect the RSO instance in the Flash movie with the server by calling the shared object's *connect( )* method and passing it a *NetConnection* object:

```
if (remote_so.connect(nc)) {
  trace("Connection object and URIs are OK. Wait for first onSync.");
```

```
  }
  else {
    trace("Can't connect - check URIs and the NetConnection object.");
  }
```

If the connection succeeds, the *SharedObject.connect( )* method returns true, but the shared object is still not ready for use. The server may have to create its own copy of the shared object or copy the contents of an already existing shared object to the local copy that has just connected. When the server has completely synchronized its own copy of the shared object with the movie's copy, the *onSync( )* method of the movie's shared object is called. The *onSync( )* method should be defined before *connect( )* is called to ensure that *onSync( )* calls are not missed. The *onSync( )* method is passed an array of information objects when it is called. After the initial call to *onSync( )* indicates that synchronization has taken place, each information object will normally contain a message about a slot in the shared object. Example 8-2 shows a simple default *onSync( )* handler that outputs all the information it receives, which is often useful during testing. This code belongs in the client-side Flash movie. The *writeln( )* function is shown in Example 5-1.

Example 8-2. A default onSync( ) handler

```
SharedObject.prototype.onSync = function (list) {
  writeln("=====SharedObject.prototype.onSync=====");
  if (!this.synchronized) {
    writeln("This shared object has been synchronized.");
    this.synchronized = true;
  }
  for (var i in list) {             // Loop through all the objects in the array.
    writeln("------------------");
    var info = list[i];           // Get the object at position i in the array.
    for (var p in info) {         // Loop through all the properties of the object.
      writeln("i: " + i + ", " + p + ": " + info[p]);
      if (p == "oldValue") {      // If a value changed, show the new one too.
        writeln("newValue: " + this.data[info.name]);
      }
    }
  }
};
```

Once *onSync( )* has been called at least once, the shared object is ready for use.

> In client-side ActionScript, all data exchange is performed through the data property of a shared object. (Properties assigned directly to the shared object are ignored.) To write data to a slot, assign a value to a property of the shared object's data object. To read data from a slot, read a property of the shared object's data object.

This example shows how to write properties to the data property of the shared object:

```
// Assign numbers or other primitive types using the dot operator.
remote_so.data.ball_1_x = 0; // Assign a number.
remote_so.data.ball_1_y = 0; // Assign a number.

// Create an array.
var shapeList = new Array();
shapeList[0] = "lineStyle";
shapeList[1] = 2;
shapelist[2] = "moveTo";
shapeList[3] = 0;
shapeList[4] = 0;
shapeList[5] = "lineTo";
shapeList[6] = 125;
shapeList[7] = 0;
shapeList[8] = "Z"; // Sentinel value to force drawing of the last command

// Assign an array to a slot, in this example using the [] operator.
var shapeName = "line_20";
remote_so.data[shapeName] = shapeList;

// Assign an object, in this example using an object literal and the [] operator.
var userName = "blesser";
remote_so.data[userName] = {fullName: "Brian Lesser", status: "Offline"};
```

Similarly, reading data from a shared object requires accessing the properties of the data object:

```
// Move a movie clip to the coordinates stored in a shared object.
ball_1_mc._x = remote_so.data.ball_1_x;
ball_1_mc._y = remote_so.data.ball_1_y;

// Create a new movie clip and draw within it using an array in a shared object.
var sList = remote_so.data["line_20"];
var mc = this.createEmptyMovieClip("line_20_mc", 100);
startData = -1;
endData = -1;
for (var i = 0; i < sList.length; i++) {
  var token = sList[i];
  if (typeof token == "string") {
    if (lastCommand != undefined) {
      mc[lastCommand].apply(mc, sList.slice(startData, endData));
    }
    lastCommand = token;
    startData = i + 1;
  } else {
    endData = i + 1;
  }
}

// Fill in the fields of a form using an object in a shared object.
fullName_txt.text = remote_so.data[userName].fullName;
status_txt.text = remote_so.data[userName].status;
```

Movie clips should not be stored in a shared object slot; their properties, such as _x and _alpha, will not be sent to the server and other clients:

```
remote_so.data.ball_1 = ball_1_mc; // Error: mc properties cannot be shared!
```

A shared object cannot send movie clip properties to the server because the properties cannot be accessed by a *for-in* loop. Similarly, an object's properties that have been hidden using *ASSetPropFlags( )* will not be sent to the server and other clients. Individual properties, such as MovieClip._x, can be assigned to a shared object slot.

Deleting a slot in a shared object is done using the *delete* operator:

```
// Delete properties of the shared object.
delete remote_so.data.ball_1_x;
delete remote_so.data.ball_1_y;

var shapeName = "line_20";
delete remote_so.data[shapeName];

var userName = "blesser";
delete remote_so.data[userName];
```

To delete all the properties of a shared object, you can loop through all the properties of the data object using a *for-in* loop and delete each one:

```
for (var p in so.data) {
   delete so.data[p];
}
```

However, depending on how your application is designed, another client can add a new property at the same time you are trying to clear the shared object of all its properties. A shared object can be reliably cleared using Server-Side ActionScript (SSAS).

You cannot replace the data object with your own object by assigning it to the data property of a shared object. If you try to assign something to the data object itself, nothing happens:

```
remote_so.data = new Object( ); // Illegal (does nothing)
```

Instead, assign the value to a property of the data object, as follows:

```
remote_so.data.someObj = new Object( );  // This works
```

Private versus shared data

Whenever a slot in the data object is created, updated, or deleted, the corresponding slot on every other instance of the RSO is updated accordingly. However, properties that are added directly to the shared object itself remain private to the instance and do not cause a remote update:

```
// Add a new property to the shared object that will not be copied
// to remote instances.
remote_so.synchronized = false;
```

If you intended to create a shared property, use this instead:

```
remote_so.data.synchronized = false;
```

> When you call *SharedObject.getRemote( )* to get a reference to a shared
> object, it always returns the same object (if it is successful), regardless
> of how many times you call it. Consider the following short script:
>
> ```
> r1_so = SharedObject.getRemote("UsersData", nc.uri);
> r2_so = SharedObject.getRemote("UsersData", nc.uri);
> r1_so.synchronized = false;
> trace(r2_so.synchronized); // false
> ```
>
> Both r1_so and r2_so refer to the same remote shared object instance
> and have identical properties.

Updating Objects and Arrays in Shared Object Slots

When a shared object's slot contains an object or array, modifying an element in the object or array causes the entire contents of the shared object's slot to be sent to FlashCom and copied to all the remote instances of the shared object. For example, if a property of a shared object named line_20 contains an array, the following statement causes the entire array to be copied to every remote copy of the shared object:

```
remote_so.data.line_20[4] = 3;
```

This may sound very inefficient, and at times it is.

> It is often necessary to design shared objects differently than you
> might design local objects in order to avoid large updates caused by
> small changes in data.

However, shared objects are not updated as soon as a change occurs. They are updated once within a set time interval and only if a change has occurred. Often this reduces the amount of redundant data being sent when many changes are made on an object or array in a slot. Update intervals are described in "Updates and Frame Rates" later in this chapter.

Reassigning the same value to an existing shared object slot will not cause an update. However, assigning new arrays or objects containing identical values will cause an update:

```
// Changing the value in a shared object slot causes an update.
remote_so.data.ball_1_x = 2;
// Assigning the same value again will not cause an update.
remote_so.data.ball_1_x = 2;

// Changing the array in a slot causes an update.
remote_so.data.line_20[4] = 4;
// Assigning the same value that is already there does not.
```

```
remote_so.data.line_20[4] = 4;

var userName = "peldi";
var user1 = {fullName: "Giacomo Guilizzoni", status: "Online"};
var user2 = {fullName: "Giacomo Guilizzoni", status: "Online"};

// When adding a new property, the slot will be created on all copies.
remote_so.data[userName] = user1;
// Assigning a different object with identical contents will force an update.
remote_so.data[userName] = user2;
```

When an object or array in a slot is updated, a new copy of that object or array is created in all the remote shared objects (except in the movie where the slot was updated). The old object or array is replaced with a new one. This can produce surprising results if you are using a reference to an object or array in a shared object slot. For example, if one movie creates a reference to an object in a shared object slot this way:

```
// Movie #1 gets a reference to an object in a slot.
var peldi = this.data.peldi;
```

then another movies updates the same slot in its copy this way:

```
// Movie #2 changes the status property of the object in the same slot.
this.data.peldi.status = "Offline";
```

When the update is complete, the `peldi` object will not refer to the same object as the one stored in `remote_so.data["peldi"]`. After the update, the following test will produce the results listed after each statement:

```
// Movie #1 now has two separate objects with a different peldi property.
trace(peldi == this.data.peldi);   // false
trace(peldi.status);               // Online
trace(this.data.peldi.status);     // Offline
```

To fix this problem, the old reference should be overwritten with a reference to the new object once the change has occurred (see the next section for how to detect a slot change):

```
// Movie #1 retrieves the most recent object in the slot.
peldi = this.data.peldi;
```

The ActionScript garbage collection process will dispose of the old object.

onSync( ) and Managing Change

Whenever the content of a shared object slot is created, updated, or deleted in one movie, the changes are sent to the server. If the update is successful, every movie connected to the same shared object will eventually have its copy of the slot updated. Updates occur at set intervals (and only if changes were made), so several slots may be updated in one batch. When the updates for one interval are complete, the *onSync( )* method of the shared object is called and passed an array of information objects. Each information object contains a code property that indicates what happened (usually either a slot has changed or all slots have been deleted). Information objects may also have a name property, which contains the slot name, and an oldValue property, which contains the slot's value just before the slot was updated. When a movie attempts to add a new slot to a shared object or update an existing slot, the change will be either accepted or rejected by the server. The supported code values are described in Table 8-1.

Table 8-1. Properties of information objects passed to onSync( )

Code	Description	Name	oldValue
"success"	Indicates a slot change by the current movie was accepted. Other movies receive a "change" event for this slot.	Name of the new or updated slot	None
"change"	A slot was changed or added by another movie or by a server-side script. The first time *onSync( )* is called after connecting to the shared object, existing values on the server are copied to the connecting movie's shared object.	Name of the new or updated slot	Indicates previous value (or none if a new slot)
"delete"	The local movie or a remote movie deleted a slot (sent to all movies connected to the shared object).	Name of the deleted slot	None
"reject"	Server rejected a movie's attempt to change a shared object slot. This can happen when there is contention between movies to update a shared object or when a locally and remotely persistent shared object connects.	Name of the rejected slot	Indicates previous value
"clear"	Indicates the shared object has been cleared—that is, it had no slots before the current set of updates. Occurs when *onSync( )* is called for the first time after synchronizing with a temporary shared object or when a persistent shared object has gotten so out of sync with the server's copy of the shared object that it has to be cleared—all its slots were deleted.	None	None

Even though the array passed into *onSync( )* contains information objects that may contain any of the codes in Table 8-1, some or even all of them can often be ignored. Example 8-3 contains the definition of a short *onSync( )* method that simply deletes the contents of a ListBox component and then repopulates it using shared object data.

Example 8-3. Tying together a shared object and a listbox

```
Chat.prototype.init = function (nc) {
  this.userList_so = SharedObject.getRemote("UserList", nc.uri);
  this.userList_so.owner = this;
  this.userList_so.onSync = function (list) {
    this.owner.peopleList_lb.removeAll();
    for (var p in this.data) {
      this.owner.peopleList_lb.addItem(p, this.data[p]);
    }
  };
```

Example 8-3. Tying together a shared object and a listbox (continued)

```
  this.userList_so.connect(nc)
};
```

One reason for this simple approach is that the ListBox component does not provide a way to efficiently search for, update, and delete elements in the data provider array in which it stores list items. So, we call its *removeAll( )* method to delete all the items and then use a *for-in* loop to repopulate the listbox using the *addItem( )* method. In Example 8-3, the name and value of each shared object property are passed into *addItem( )* as the label string and data parameters. See Example 13-1 and Chapter 15 for more efficient ways to update ListBox and DataGrid components with shared object data. Creating and managing shared objects within another object, such as the *Chat* object, is a common practice. In Example 8-3, this statement adds a reference in the shared object to the *Chat* object for later use:

```
    this.userList_so.owner = this;
```

Since the owner property is not assigned to the data property of the shared object, it is simply a private property of the shared object and will not cause a shared object update. Within the shared object's *onSync( )* method, it is used to get the *Chat* object and its properties:

```
    this.userList_so.onSync = function (list) {
      this.owner.peopleList_lb.removeAll( );
      for (var p in this.data) {
        this.owner.peopleList_lb.addItem(p, this.data[p]);
      }
    };
```

Within *onSync( )*, the keyword this refers to the shared object and not the *Chat* object. So this.owner refers to the *Chat* object and this.data refers to the shared object's data object. Example 8-3 shows only how to repopulate a listbox after a shared object's data has been updated. You may be wondering how the user-list data gets populated in the first place. The code that adds and deletes the properties of the user list is shown in Example 8-5. In that example, the user list shared object's properties are set using Server-Side ActionScript as clients connect and disconnect from an application instance. Server-side scripting of shared objects is described under "Scripting Shared Objects on the Server" a little later in this chapter.

Yet Another Shared Ball Example

A shared ball sample application in which users drag around a movie clip so that other users see it move, has become the FlashCom equivalent of "hello world" for introducing shared objects. Macromedia's version of this application can be found in the server's *samples/tutorial_sharedball* directory. It displays real-time shared object updates as the ball is dragged around on the Stage, including responding to those updates when someone else drags the ball around.

Example 8-4 is a slightly more involved version of the same basic idea. A shared object, named BallPosition, contains the x and y coordinates of a shared ball movie clip. The slot names are named after the movie clip. If the shared ball movie clip is named ball_1_mc, the x and y coordinate slots are named ball_1_mc_x and ball_1_mc_y. When a copy of the shared ball movie first starts, the ball is colored red to indicate that its shared object is not synchronized. It can still be moved around on stage without any effect on other movies. After the movie connects and the shared object is synchronized for the first time, the ball turns green. If one or more movies are already connected and their movie clips of the shared ball are already synchronized, the most recently connected ball jumps to the latest position defined in the shared object. If no other movies are connected, the ball's current position is saved in the shared object. From then on, when the movie clip is dragged around the Stage, the following events occur:

1. The global x and y coordinates of the mouse are retrieved and clipped to the rectangular area the ball is allowed to move within.

2. The shared ball movie clip is moved to the x and y coordinates.

3. The BallPosition shared object's slots are updated with the new x and y coordinates of the movie clip, and the changes are sent to other connected movies.

4. The data objects of all movies are updated, after which the *onSync( )* method of every copy of each movie's shared object is called. The *onSync( )* method in the movie that changed the ball position is passed a list of slots with information objects (normally one for the x position and one for the y position) with a code value of "success." The other movies receive a code value of "change".

5. The movies that receive a "change" notification move the ball movie clip to the coordinates in the shared object.

In summary, if one movie changes the x and y coordinates in the shared object, all the movies are notified of the change. The movie that made the change is notified that the change was successful, and the movies that did not make the change are notified that the data in their copy of the BallPosition shared object has changed. In response to the notification, the movie that made the change does not have to do anything. It has already placed the movie clip of the ball in the correct place. Every movie that receives a "change" notification must move the ball movie clip to its new location on stage.

What happens if two or more movies try to move the ball at the same time? One movie will be successful, and all the other's changes to the shared object will be rejected. Instead of a "success" code, a value of "reject" is received in the information objects in the list; the movie receiving the rejection must update the clip position to match the location stored in the shared object from the last movie that moved the ball.

Like Example 8-3, Example 8-4 places the code that gets and manipulates the shared object within another object. In this case, the *SharedBall* class defines the behavior of a shared ball movie clip and contains all the shared object code. The code in Example 8-4 is the complete listing for the *SharedBall* class, but the listing does not show the complete working example, which is available on the book's web site. When a ball is created in the movie, it is passed a reference to the *NetConnection* object that has just connected to the server. The *SharedBall* class takes it from there. Note that Example 8-4 uses some AS 2.0 syntax. The book's web site also contains an AS 1.0 version of this example.

Example 8-4. A SharedBall class containing a shared object

```
class SharedBall extends MovieClip {

  var xSlot:String; // Slot holding _x location of the shared ball
  var ySlot:String; // Slot holding _y location of the shared ball
  var bounding_mc;  // Initially, the name of the parent clip's bounding area
  var left:Number, right:Number, top:Number, bottom:Number; // Travel limits
  var so;  // SharedObject, but not typed, so we can add the synchronized property
  var color:Color;
  var ballColor_mc:MovieClip;

  /* SharedBall constructor function. The bounding_mc property may be set
   * in the property dialog box or within the init object passed to attachMovie( )
   * when this clip is created.
   */
  function SharedBall () {
    // Save the name of the slots this shared ball will use in the shared object,
    // such as ball_1_mc_x and ball_1_mc_y
    xSlot = _name + "_x";
    ySlot = _name + "_y";

    // Set the left, top, right, and bottom properties that act as movement limits.
    setTravelLimits();

    // Get a color object for the movie clip that gives the overall clip its color.
    color = new Color(ballColor_mc);
    color.setRGB(0xff0000);
  }

  /* The registration point for this clip is the center of the ball.
   * The radius is, therefore, half the width or half the height.
   * Keeping the center one radius length from the bounding box's edge
   * keeps the ball entirely within the bounding box.
   * If the bounding_mc property is the name of a clip in the parent,
   * use it as the bounding box; otherwise use the Stage as the bounding box.
   */
  function setTravelLimits () {
    bounding_mc = _parent[bounding_mc];
    if (!bounding_mc) {
      bounding_mc = {_width: Stage.width, _height: Stage.height};
    }
```

Example 8-4. A SharedBall class containing a shared object (continued)

```
  var radius  = _width / 2;
  left    = bounding_mc._x + radius;
  right   = bounding_mc._x + bounding_mc._width - radius;
  top     = bounding_mc._y + radius;
  bottom  = bounding_mc._y + bounding_mc._height - radius;
}

/* onConnect( ) is called after the movie has connected to the application
 * instance. It is passed a reference to the connected NetConnection object.
 * It sets up the BallPosition shared object.
 */
function onConnect (nc) {
  // Get the RSO named BallPosition
  so = SharedObject.getRemote("BallPosition", nc.uri);
  // Create a private flag property named synchronized
  so.synchronized = false;
  // Create a private reference, named owner, to the Ball object.
  so.owner = this;
  // Define the onSync( ) handler.
  so.onSync = function(list) {
    // If synchronized is not set, this is the first call.
    if (!this.synchronized) {
      this.synchronized = true;
      // Tell the ball clip we have just synchronized.
      this.owner.onSynchronized( );
    }
    /* If any movies have changed the ball's position, tell the
     * ball clip that a change has occured. We do not need to watch
     * for "success" codes here, as the ball has already been moved
     * by this movie when a "success" code is received. If an update
     * is rejected, move back.
     */
    for (var i in list) {
      if (list[i].code == "change" || list[i].code == "reject") {
        this.owner.onChange( );
        break;
      }
    }
  }
  // Don't forget to connect to the shared object!
  so.connect(nc);
}

// Color the ball green when the ball is synchronized.
function onSynchronized( ) {
  // Turn green to show the ball is synchronized to the shared object.
  color.setRGB(0x00ff00);
  // If there are no _x and _y values in the shared object
  // for this ball, set them.
  if (typeof so.data[xSlot] == "undefined") {
    so.data[xSlot] = _x;
    so.data[ySlot] = _y;
```

Example 8-4. A SharedBall class containing a shared object (continued)

```
    }
  }

  // Change the ball position—see so.onSync( ).
  function onChange( ) {
    _x = so.data[xSlot];
    _y = so.data[ySlot];
  }

  // Color the ball red when the network connection is closed.
  function onDisconnect ( ) {
    color.setRGB(0xff0000);
  }

  /* When the user clicks on the ball movie clip, define an onMouseMove() method
   * to move the ball within the travel limits defined by the left, top, right,
   * and bottom properties. Then update the shared object with the new position.
   */
  function onPress ( ) {
    onMouseMove = function( ) {
      // Get the mouse position.
      var x = _root._xmouse;
      var y = _root._ymouse;

      // Make sure x and y are within their travel limits.
      if (x < left) {
        x = left;
      } else if (x > right) {
        x = right;
      }
      if (y < top) {
        y = top;
      } else if (y > bottom) {
        y = bottom;
      }

      // Move the clip to (x, y), and store the coordinates in the shared object.
      so.data[xSlot] = _x = x;
      so.data[ySlot] = _y = y;
    }
  }

  // Stop dragging when the mouse is released over the clip.
  function onRelease ( ) {
    delete onMouseMove;
  }

  // Stop dragging when the mouse is released outside the clip.
  function onReleaseOutside ( ) {
    delete onMouseMove;
  }
}
```

Inside the *SharedBall.onMouseMove( )* method are two statements that attempt to both set both the position of the shared ball movie clip and update the shared object:

```
so.data[xSlot] = _x = x;
so.data[ySlot] = _y = y;
```

In the code snippet, the x and y variables contain the coordinates to which to move the ball. Sometime after these statements are executed, the *onSync( )* method of the *SharedBall* clip is called and this short *for-in* loop checks each information object in the list:

```
for (var i in list) {
  if (list[i].code == "change" || list[i].code == "reject") {
    this.owner.onChange( );
    break;
  }
}
```

Inside the *onSync( )* method, this refers to the shared object. The code property of each information object in the list is checked for the value "change" or "reject". If either value occurs, the *SharedBall* clip is told to change its position to the coordinates currently in the shared object. The *onSync( )* method notifies the *SharedBall* clip that a change has occurred by calling a method of its owner object, which is in fact the *SharedBall* clip—see the *SharedBall.onConnect( )* method, which sets the shared object's owner property to refer to the *SharedBall* clip. Here is the *SharedBall. onChange( )* method that sets the position of the ball:

```
function onChange ( ) {
  _x = so.data[xSlot];
  _y = so.data[ySlot];
}
```

In this example, the *SharedBall* class contains the shared object and is completely responsible for creating, updating, and responding to it.

Example 8-4 also fixes a small bug in the shared ball sample that ships with Flash-Com versions 1.0 and 1.5. The *onMouseMove( )* method in the Macromedia example sets the location of the movie clip in the shared object before checking to see if the mouse cursor has moved off stage. You can therefore drag and release the ball off stage and it will sometimes stay completely out of view where you can no longer click on it to drag it around. If you quickly drag the ball off stage and release it, the shared object position is set to the offstage position, but the movie clip's position is set back to being on stage. However, when *onSync( )* is called, it moves the clip to whatever coordinates are in the shared object. To correct the bug, make the shared object update the last statements in the *onMouseMove( )* method as shown in Example 8-4.

Updates and Frame Rates

If you were to add a *trace( )* statement in the *onMouseMove( )* and *onSync( )* methods from Example 8-4, connect the movie, and start quickly dragging the ball around, you might get output that looks something like this:

```
onMouseMove> ball_1_mc_y: 239.95
onMouseMove> ball_1_mc_x: 138
onMouseMove> ball_1_mc_y: 245.95
onMouseMove> ball_1_mc_x: 144
onMouseMove> ball_1_mc_y: 246.95
onMouseMove> ball_1_mc_x: 147
onSync> ball_1_mc_y: 246.95
onSync> ball_1_mc_x: 147
onMouseMove> ball_1_mc_y: 243.95
onMouseMove> ball_1_mc_x: 149
onMouseMove> ball_1_mc_y: 229.95
onMouseMove> ball_1_mc_x: 149
onMouseMove> ball_1_mc_y: 216
onMouseMove> ball_1_mc_x: 148
onMouseMove> ball_1_mc_y: 211
onMouseMove> ball_1_mc_x: 143
onSync> ball_1_mc_y: 211
onSync> ball_1_mc_x: 143
```

There are more *mouseMove* events than synchronization events. So, although the shared object's data is updated each time *onMouseMove( )* is called, not every update is sent to the server and synchronized.

Shared objects post updates at regular intervals. At the end of each time interval, if any changes have occurred in the properties of the data object, the changed properties and their values are sent in one batch to the server. If no changes have occurred since the last batch of updates were sent, no update occurs.

With rapidly changing data, sending all the updates to the server could generate more network traffic than is really needed. The shared ball is a simple example. Other examples are shared cursors, avatar positions, game element positioning, and scrolling or highlighting text in a shared text field.

Of course, some situations require that a sequence of messages be sent to FlashCom without loss of any in-between values. In those cases, remote method invocation can be used. You can use the *send( )* method of a *SharedObject* or *NetStream* object or the *call( )* method of a *NetConnection* or *Client* object. Remote method invocations are reliably sent to and queued on the server; they are covered in more detail in Chapter 9.

By default, shared objects post updates to the server at a regular interval equal to the movie's frame rate, which may be slower or faster than desirable. The *SharedObject. setFps( )* method changes the update rate for shared object data. For example, inserting the following statement in the *onConnect( )* method of Example 8-4 sets the number of updates to three per second, regardless of the movie's frame rate:

```
so.setFps(3);
```

Just as Flash frame rendering can slow down during demanding operations, under heavy network load or over a slow connection, the rate of shared object updates may also slow down. When the shared object update rate slows down, only the most recent data values are sent. Any in-between values from a dropped frame are discarded. Before a new update is sent, the shared object always waits for the results of any outstanding updates. In other words, before the shared object sends an update request to the server, it waits until the server responds to the previous update request. The server may accept the changes or reject them. Until the shared object receives notification of what has happened, it does not send any new (pending) updates.

Why not just set a high frame rate, such as 24 fps, and let the movie and server handle it as described? In some applications, such as games, you may want to. But you may also be creating more network traffic than necessary and therefore consuming bandwidth better spent on sound or video.

Also, consider what happens if a movie is running at 24 fps but it takes 100 milliseconds (one-tenth of a second) for a message to get from the movie to FlashCom and return: FlashCom cannot achieve more than a 10 fps shared object update interval for a client with a 100 ms round-trip time. It also takes time for the server to process update requests. By attempting to send messages 2.5 times faster than they can be processed over the connection, you waste bandwidth; the server will discard updates for clients with higher network latency, resulting in different update rates for different clients. A more realistic approach is to set the update rate 30 to 50 percent slower than the average latency. For example, if you have an average 100 ms latency (10 fps), use an update rate of 5 to 7 fps.

If you set the shared object update rate to 0, the shared object will stop sending updates to the server entirely. Stopping updates temporarily is a good idea when you have a large number of updates that you would like to send in one batch. For example:

```
// Stop all updates.
so.setFps(0);
// Change all the properties in one batch.
for (var p in streamInfo) {
    so.data[p] = streamInfo[p];
}
// Restart updates.
so.setFps(7);
```

A modified version of Example 8-4 on the book's web site allows you to adjust the update rate while moving the shared ball to see how it affects the appearance of motion.

Scripting Shared Objects on the Server

Working with remote shared objects in Server-Side ActionScript is a little different than working with them in the Flash client. Example 8-5 shows a short *main.asc* file that forces users to sign into an application with a unique username and keeps track of each user in a remote shared object.

Example 8-5. main.asc file for a simple video chat application

```
// trim( ) removes whitespace from the beginning and end of a string.
function trim (str) {
  if (typeof str != "string") return "";  // Make sure str is a string.
  str = str.replace(/^\s*/, "");          // Trim leading spaces.
  str = str.replace(/\s*$/, "");          // Trim trailing spaces.
  str = str.replace(/\n/g,  "");          // Remove new lines.
  str = str.replace(/\r/g,  "");          // Remove carriage returns.
  str = str.replace(/\t/g,  "");          // Remove tabs.
  return str;
}


// Get a temporary (non-persistent) RSO for a read-only list of usernames.
application.onAppStart = function ( ) {
   userList_so = SharedObject.get("public/userList");
};

/* Accept a client whose username is a unique, non-empty string
 * and update the userList shared object.
 * Each slot value in userList is the path to which each client
 * has write access and where other clients should look for
 * a stream to which to subscribe.
 */
application.onConnect = function (client, userName) {
  userName = trim(userName);
  if (userName.length == 0) {
    application.rejectConnection(client, {msg: "Blank or missing user name."});
    return;
  }

  var userPath = userList_so.getProperty(userName);
  if (userPath) {
    application.rejectConnection(client,
        {msg: "The user name '" + userName + "' is already in use."});
    return;
  }
  client.readAccess  = "public";
  client.writeAccess = "public/chat";
  client.writeAccess = "public/textchat";
  client.userName = userName;
  userList_so.setProperty(userName, "public/chat/" + userName);

  return true;
};
```

Example 8-5. main.asc file for a simple video chat application (continued)

```
// Delete records of clients when they disconnect.
application.onDisconnect = function (client) {
   userList_so.setProperty(client.userName, null);
};
```

The server-side *SharedObject.get( )* method is used in place of the client-side *SharedObject.getRemote( )* method in Flash and does not require a URI to the application instance (because it is executed from within the FlashCom application):

```
userList_so = SharedObject.get("public/userList");
```

Like streams, shared objects are identified by partial URIs that are relative to the application instance. In Example 8-5, the userList shared object is created within the *public* path. In the *application.onConnect( )* method, all clients are given read-only access to the *public* path so that they can read but not update the userList shared object.

Since the server controls the shared object, there is no need in server-side scripts to call a server-side *connect( )* method (there isn't one) or wait for an *onSync( )* event.

Another difference from client-side ActionScript is that server-side shared objects don't have a data property. Assigning and retrieving values of server-side shared objects is done via the *getProperty( )* and *setProperty( )* methods. The following statement sets a property of the shared object. The first parameter in *setProperty( )* is always a string property name, while the second parameter can be data of any built-in ActionScript datatype—with the same exceptions and caveats mentioned earlier:

```
userList_so.setProperty(userName, "public/chat/" + userName);
```

If an object, array, or other non-primitive data is placed in a shared object's slot and an element in the object or array is updated later, *setProperty( )* must be called again to update the shared object. For example:

```
// Create an object.
var loc = {x: 10, y: 30};
// Copy it into the shared object property named location.
userList_so.setProperty("location", loc);
// Update the object.
loc.x = 89;
// You must copy the object back into the shared object to update it.
userList_so.setProperty("location", loc);
```

To delete a slot of a shared object in Server-Side ActionScript, call *setProperty( )* and pass null as the second parameter. In Example 8-5, this deletes the entry for a user when her client disconnects:

```
userList_so.setProperty(client.userName, null);
```

To retrieve the value of a shared object's property in SSAS, use *getProperty( )*:

```
var userPath = userList_so.getProperty(userName);
```

If a property does not exist, *getProperty( )* returns null.

Working with server-side shared objects is not as convenient as working with them in client-side Flash ActionScript. The data object of client-side shared objects is not available on the server, and you have to call *setProperty( )* every time you want to update any part of an object or array within a slot. The data object and automatic updates available in Flash were left out of the server implementation for performance reasons. Detecting and managing changes to elements of the data object is both a CPU- and memory-intensive process. However, you should not shy away from scripting shared objects on the server. It is often the right place to control updates, as described in Chapters 15 and 18. Let's look at a quick example. In Example 8-5, clients are given read-only access to a shared object. The shared object is created before any client connections are accepted, and all the updates are done on the server side. It is not uncommon for applications to simply deny write access to every client, as follows:

```
application.onConnect = function (client) {
    client.writeAccess = ""; // No write access
    client.readAccess = "/"; // Read anything
};
```

Now consider what happens if the server doesn't create the shared object before the first client is allowed to connect. If a shared object does not exist when a client with read-only access attempts to connect to it, the connection attempt will fail. To avoid the problem, shared objects are often created and initialized in the *application. onAppStart( )* method as in Example 8-5.

Server-Side onSync( )

In Flash, a shared object's *onSync( )* handler can be defined either on SharedObject. prototype or on an individual shared object instance. On the server, you cannot use the prototype to define an *onSync( )* handler for all shared objects; for performance reasons, *onSync( )* handlers must be defined for an individual instance. One way to define an *onSync( )* handler for a *SharedObject* instance is by using a function expression, also called a function literal:

```
ball_so = SharedObject.get("BallPosition");
ball_so.onSync = function (list) {
  trace("ball_so.onSync> list.length: " + list.length);
  for (var i in list) {
    trace("---------- list item number: " + i + " ------------");
    var info = list[i];
    for (var p in info) {
      trace(p + ": " + info[p]);
    }
  }
};
```

Another option is to use a function declaration (also called a function statement) to define the function and then assign it to an individual instance as necessary:

```
function genericOnSyncHandler (list) {
  trace("ball_so.onSync> list.length: " + list.length);
  for (var i in list) {
    trace("---------- list item number: " + i + " ------------");
    var info = list[i];
    for (var p in info) {
      trace(p + ": " + info[p]);
    }
  }
}
ball_so = SharedObject.get("BallPosition");
ball_so.onSync = genericOnSyncHandler;
```

The shared ball example does not require a *main.asc* script. However, if we wrote one and added the code from either of the previous examples to it, when you drag the ball around, the output in the App Inspector movie would be similar to:

```
Loading of app instance: chapter8/sharedBall/version_1 successful
ball_so.onSync> list.length: 2
---------- list item number: 0 ------------
code: change
name: ball_1_mc_x
oldValue: undefined
---------- list item number: 1 ------------
code: change
name: ball_1_mc_y
oldValue: undefined
ball_so.onSync> list.length: 1
---------- list item number: 0 ------------
code: change
name: ball_1_mc_y
oldValue: 82
```

Whenever a change occurs as a result of an update from a Flash movie, the list array passed into the server-side *onSync( )* method includes information objects with a code value of "change" or "delete" and will always contain an oldValue property—even if its value is undefined. When a change is made using the server-side *setProperty( )* method, *onSync( )* is not called on the server; however, the client-side *onSync( )* method is called for each copy of the shared object in connected Flash movies, subject to the constraints described in the next section.

Locking a Shared Object

Client-generated updates of shared objects do not run in the same thread on the server as SSAS, so shared object updates can occur in between server-side *setProperty( )* method calls. To guarantee that a shared object cannot be updated by a client until a unit of work is complete on the server, use the shared object's *lock( )* and *unlock( )* methods. A locked shared object will not notify clients of updates until it is unlocked, so locking a shared object on the server is also a good way to group updates together so they are all sent in one batch to clients. The client-side shared object's *onSync( )* method will be called only after all the data has been incorporated into the local copy of the shared object. The following server-side code demonstrates using *lock( )* and *unlock( )* properly:

```
// initPuzzlePieces() creates a shared object for each puzzle piece
// containing the initial coordinates, x and y velocity, and state.
function initPuzzlePieces (nClips, xMin, xMax, yMin, yMax) {
    var so;
    puzzlePieces = [];
    for (var i = 0; i < nClips; i++) {
        so = SharedObject.get("PuzzlePiece_" + i, true);

        // Stop client update requests and stop sending updates to clients.
        so.lock();

        // Select a random position within the travel limits.
        so.setProperty("x", Math.floor(Math.random()*(xMax-xMin) + xMin));
        so.setProperty("y", Math.floor(Math.random()*(yMax-yMin) + yMin));

        // Select a random direction in which to start moving this clip.
        so.setProperty("xVel", Math.floor(Math.random()*12) - 5);
        so.setProperty("yVel", Math.floor(Math.random()*12) - 5);

        // Mark the puzzle piece as being available.
        so.setProperty("state", "free");

        // Send the new properties for this shared object now.
        so.unlock();

        // Keep a reference to each shared object.
        puzzlePieces.push(so);
    }
}
```

Locks can be nested, so be sure you have a matching *unlock( )* call for every *lock( )* you issue. FlashCom maintains a version number for the shared object as a whole and for each shared object slot. When *lock( )* is called on a shared object, the version number is not incremented until the shared object is unlocked. The version number for the shared object is available in its version property and is normally incremented after every *setProperty( )* call. The version number of each individual slot is not available to ActionScript.

Clearing a Shared Object

Three server-side approaches can be used to reliably clear all the properties of a shared object, so that none are left. One approach is to lock the shared object, get all its properties' names using *getPropertyNames( )*, and then delete each property using *setProperty( )*, as follows:

```
so = SharedObject.get("SOName");
so.lock();
```

```
var names = so.getPropertyNames( );
for (i in names) {
  so.setProperty(names[i], null);
}
so.unlock( );
```

Executing a loop like this will also result in the client shared object's *onSync( )* method being passed a list of information objects. Each item's code property will have a value of "delete." However, it is much simpler to use the server-side *clear( )* method:

```
so = SharedObject.get("SOName");
so.clear( );
```

In this case, each client's shared object *onSync( )* handler will receive an array containing one information object with a code value of "clear."

The *application.clearSharedObjects( )* method can also be used to clear shared objects as discussed in "Clearing and Deleting Persistent Shared Objects" later in this chapter.

Checking the Size of a Shared Object

The *size( )* method, available only on the server, returns the number of properties in a shared object and is a convenient way to check whether a shared object is already in use:

```
if (so.size( ) == 0) {
  // Initialize some shared object properties.
}
```

Temporary and Persistent Shared Objects

The preceding examples in this chapter all used temporary shared objects. Each temporary shared object is created either by a server-side script or when the first client with write access tries to connect to the shared object. The shared object is disposed of as soon as it is no longer in use by the server-side script and by its clients. At the very latest, it will be disposed of when the application instance shuts down. If you tried out the shared ball example, you may have noticed that if every client disconnected, the application did not remember the last position of the ball. The ball position was simply reset by the first client to connect. The shared ball example does not use a server-side script, so the shared object is created when the first client connects and then disposed of when the last client disconnects.

If you need to retain shared object data even after the application instance quits, you can create a persistent shared object, which is stored on the server and available the next time an instance starts up. Use persistent shared objects whenever you need to maintain application state between instance sessions.

When creating shared objects, you can make them temporary or persistent (persistent ones can be made to persist only on the server or on both the client and server). Shared objects that are persistent only on the client are called local shared objects and are not covered here (they are created with *SharedObject.getLocal( )* as discussed in *ActionScript for Flash MX: The Definitive Guide*). If you need to share data between clients only while an application is running, use temporary shared objects.

Persistent shared objects are stored as *.fso* files in each application's *sharedobjects* directory. A shared object that persists on the server can also be saved locally on the client. When remote shared objects are stored locally, they have an *.sor* extension, which is different from the *.sol* extension given to local shared objects. Locally persistent remote shared objects enable your application to update the shared object offline and resynchronize with the server when the connection is reestablished.

When using the *getRemote( )* method on the client, the optional third parameter, persistence, is a Boolean or string that determines whether and where the object should persist:

```
SharedObject.getRemote(SharedObjectURI, AppInstanceURI [, persistence]);
```

To request a temporary shared object (one not persisted on the server), pass false or null or omit the persistence parameter altogether. Passing true requests a persistent shared object that is stored on the server only. To store a remote shared object both on the server and locally, pass in a string that defines the path for local persistence, as described later under "Locally and Remotely Persistent Shared Objects." The *getRemote( )* method will return null if it detects that any of the parameters passed to it are invalid.

On the server, the second parameter of the *SharedObject.get( )* method specifies persistence:

```
SharedObject.get (SharedObjectURI [, persistence [, netConnection]]);
```

Passing true makes the shared object persistent while passing false or omitting the parameter means a temporary shared object will be returned. The optional netConnection parameter is described later under "Proxied Shared Objects."

Persistent and temporary shared objects occupy different namespaces. For example, the following two client-side statements return different shared objects even though the shared object's relative URI ("Test") and the application URI ("rtmp:/testSO") are the same:

```
x1_so = SharedObject.getRemote("Test", "rtmp:/testSO", true);
x2_so = SharedObject.getRemote("Test", "rtmp:/testSO", false);
```

If you specify persistence on the client and non-persistence on the server (or vice versa), only client-side updates are visible on the client and only server-side updates are visible on the server. The problem is that the two shared objects are different—they exist in different namespaces even though they appear to have the same name. Make sure that you are consistent with the type of persistence you specify on the client and on the server.

For example, to create a temporary shared object on the server, you can use:

```
userList_so = SharedObject.get("public/userList");
```

To connect to the same temporary shared object in Flash, use:

```
userList_so = SharedObject.getRemote ("public/userList", nc.uri);
```

To persist the shared object on the server between sessions, pass true as the second parameter:

```
userList_so = SharedObject.get("public/userList", true);
```

and in Flash, pass true as the third parameter:

```
userList_so = SharedObject.getRemote("public/userList", nc.uri, true);
```

Temporary shared objects exist within an application instance only while a client or the application instance has a reference to it. For example, if a single client creates a temporary shared object and then disconnects, the shared object is disposed of. If several clients connect to the same temporary shared object, when the last one disconnects or closes the shared object, the shared object is disposed of.

If a temporary shared object must last through an application instance session, the application instance should use *SharedObject.get( )* to get a reference to the shared object and keep it from being disposed of until the instance itself is disposed of. The *application.onAppStart( )* method is a good place to *get( )* a temporary shared object. Provided the application does not close the shared object, the shared object and the data it contains will be available until the application instance is disposed of.

When the last connection to a persistent shared object is closed, the server writes the latest state to the shared object's *.fso* file and disposes the shared object from memory. Later, if a client connects to the shared object, the contents of the *.fso* file are read into memory again by the server and copied to the client's version of the shared object.

Synchronizing Temporary and Persistent Shared Objects

Temporary and persistent shared objects are not synchronized in the same way. When you write an *onSync( )* method for a shared object, you must match your event handling approach to the persistence option you select. Whenever a client connects to a temporary shared object, any data already in the client's copy of the shared object is cleared (deleted). As a result, the client must wait until it gets the first *onSync( )* call before it updates the shared object. Persistent shared objects are not synchronized in the same way. Their data properties might not be deleted before the first *onSync( )* is called. Since handling synchronization is perhaps one of the most complex aspects of FlashCom development, let's walk through the differences between synchronizing temporary and persistent shared objects in detail.

After a Flash movie connects to a shared object with *SharedObject.connect( )*, the local copy of the shared object is synchronized with the remote shared object on the server. When a temporary shared object is synchronized, any properties in the local copy are cleared and any data in the remote shared object is downloaded to the movie's shared object. As a result, the *onSync( )* method of the movie's shared object will always be passed a list containing one information object with a code value of "clear" followed by information objects with code values of "change" for each property in the remote shared object.

For example, if a movie connects to a temporary shared object that already has three properties named a, b, and c, then the list passed into the *onSync( )* method will contain four information objects:

```
{code: "clear"}
{code: "change", name: "a"}
{code: "change", name: "b"}
{code: "change", name: "c"}
```

Since temporary shared objects are always cleared whenever they are synchronized, they cannot be used to read or write data until they are synchronized. That is why it is essential to wait until the *onSync( )* method of a temporary shared object is called the first time before using a temporary shared object in a movie. A common way to make sure the shared object has been synchronized before using it is to use a private flag in the shared object to trigger an initialization function. The shared ball in Example 8-4 uses the same technique to show when the ball has been synchronized:

```
so = SharedObject.getRemote("myTemporarySharedObject", nc.uri);
// Create a private flag property named synchronized.
so.synchronized = false;
// Define the onSync( ) handler.
so.onSync = function (list) {
  // If synchronized is not set, this is the first call.
  if (!this.synchronized) {
    this.synchronized = true;
    // Call a function or object method, which can now use this shared object.
  }
  // Do other synchronization work here.
};
// Don't forget to actually connect to the shared object!
so.connect(nc);
```

Persistent shared objects are not automatically cleared when they are synchronized. For example, if a movie creates a persistent shared object and connects for the first time to a shared object on the server that already has properties a, b, and c, the list passed into the *onSync( )* method will contain only three information objects:

```
{code: "change", name: "a"}
{code: "change", name: "b"}
{code: "change", name: "c"}
```

If there are no properties on the server's copy of the shared object, the *onSync( )* method will be passed an empty list.

When using persistent shared objects, the movie may set properties of the shared object before calling its *connect( )* method. In this short code snippet, two properties named a and b are created before connecting the shared object. When *connect( )* is called, the local copy of the shared object will send any data it already has to the server:

```
// Get a reference to the shared object.
// nc.connect() must have been called already (to create the net connection).
so = SharedObject.getRemote("myPersistentSharedObject", nc.uri, true);

// Define a simple onSync() method for testing.
so.onSync = function (list) {
  writeln("----onSync list.length: " + list.length + "----");
  for (var i = 0; i < list.length; i++) {
    var info = list[i];
    for (var p in info) {
      writeln(i + ": " + p + ": " + info[p]);
    }
  }
};

// Set some initial values for the shared object.
so.data.a = "A is for alienation.";
so.data.b = "B is for the boss...";

// Now, connect the shared object.
so.connect(nc);
```

If the shared object on the server doesn't have any properties already, the code produces this output. Note the *onSync( )* method is called twice. The first time it is called with an empty list. The second time, you can see that the server has accepted the new a and b slot data from the local copy of the shared object and added them to the server's copy:

```
----onSync list.length: 0----
----onSync list.length: 2----
0: code: success
0: name: a
1: code: success
1: name: b
```

If the properties a and b already exist in the shared object on the server, *onSync( )* is called only once:

```
----onSync list.length: 2----
0: oldValue: A is for alienation.
0: code: reject
0: name: a
1: oldValue: B is for the boss...
1: code: reject
1: name: b
```

If the shared object on the server already has just two properties, x and y, then this output occurs:

```
----onSync list.length: 2----
0: code: change
0: name: x
1: code: change
1: name: y
----onSync list.length: 2----
0: code: success
0: name: a
1: code: success
1: name: b
```

In this case, *onSync( )* was called twice—once to notify us about what properties had been added to the local copy by the server and the second time to tell us what happened to the properties of the shared object that existed before we tried to connect.

You can close the connection to a persistent shared object by calling the shared object's *close( )* method. Later, the shared object can be reconnected by calling the shared object's *connect( )* method again without necessarily deleting data in the local copy of the shared object. This feature makes it possible to build applications in which the client does not have to be connected to keep working with shared object data.

Every time the client connects to a persistent shared object and synchronization takes place, the server compares each shared object slot's version number in the client to the version number for each slot on the server. The server sends slot data to the client only for slots that are not current in the movie's shared object. For example, if the only property of the shared object that has changed since the movie's shared object was closed is a property named c, then *onSync( )*, containing only one information object, is called:

```
{code: "change", name: "c"}
```

If there have been no changes, *onSync( )* is passed an empty list.

The persistent shared object synchronization process also manages the deletion of slots. If a local copy contains a slot that has since been deleted in the remote version of the shared object, when the local copy connects again, the local slot will be deleted. For example, if slot c was deleted on the server and still exists in the local copy, an information object will be returned in the *onSync( )* list:

```
{code: "delete", name: "c"}
```

Similarly, if a property of the local shared object is deleted while the local copy of a shared object is not connected and no changes to that property are made in the remote copy, when the shared object reconnects, the property will be deleted on the server. If the property was updated on the server while the client was disconnected, the request to delete the property will be rejected.

Clearing and Deleting Persistent Shared Objects

Even if all the properties of the shared object have been cleared, the *.fso* file on the server, if it exists, will not be deleted.

If you want to delete the *.fso* file of a persistent shared object you must call *application.clearSharedObjects( )*. It is similar to the *application.clearStreams( )* method in that it will clear and delete many shared objects at once and is passed a path string that can contain the * and ? wildcard characters. The ? character matches a single character, while the * matches any number of characters. The *clearSharedObjects( )* method returns true if the shared objects within the path were deleted and false if they were not. If the following list of shared object URIs are used to create persistent shared objects, several directories will be created within the application instance's *sharedobjects* directory:

```
userList
chat/index
chat/history_01
chat/history_02
private/blesser/streamList
private/blesser/accessLog
```

The actual file paths will be:

```
.../applications/appName/sharedobjects/instanceName/userList.fso
.../applications/appName/sharedobjects/instanceName/chat/index.fso
.../applications/appName/sharedobjects/instanceName/chat/history_01.fso
.../applications/appName/sharedobjects/instanceName/chat/history_02.fso
.../applications/appName/sharedobjects/instanceName/private/blesser/streamList.fso
.../applications/appName/sharedobjects/instanceName/private/blesser/accessLog.fso
```

where the path to the *applications* directory depends on where FlashCom is installed, and *appName* and *instanceName* are placeholders for actual application and instance names.

To delete an individual file, pass the URI for the shared object to *clearSharedObjects( )*. For example, to clear and delete only the userList shared object, use:

```
application.clearSharedObjects("/userList");
```

To clear and delete only the chat/index shared object, use:

```
application.clearSharedObjects("/chat/index");
```

To delete shared objects beginning with "history", use either the * or ? wildcard character. Deleting the entire contents of the *chat* path also deletes the index shared object. See the comments for each statement:

```
// Delete by matching any last two characters after "history_".
application.clearSharedObjects("/chat/history_??");
// Delete by matching any characters after "history".
application.clearSharedObjects("/chat/history*");
// Delete everything in the chat directory and its subdirectories using a "*".
application.clearSharedObjects("/chat/*");
// Delete everything in the chat directory and its subdirectories
// using a trailing forward slash after "/chat".
application.clearSharedObjects("/chat/");
```

To clear and delete all the shared objects in the *private* directory and all its subdirectories, use either of the following two statements:

```
application.clearSharedObjects("/private/");
application.clearSharedObjects("/private/*");
```

Either statement will delete both the *private* and *blesser* directories as well as the shared object files in them.

To clear all the properties and delete all the *.fso* files of all the shared objects owned by an application instance, use a path string of "/":

```
application.clearSharedObjects("/")
```

Any shared object subdirectories that no longer have any files in them will also be deleted.

Locally and Remotely Persistent Shared Objects

Persistent RSOs can also be stored locally much like local shared objects. Local persistence makes it possible to extend how long a user can work offline before having to connect to the server. A user can work with a local copy of a persistent shared object without connecting to the server, save his work locally, and quit the application. Later, he can retrieve the locally persistent copy and keep working. Finally, when he needs to connect to FlashCom, his data will be synchronized with the data on the server. Locally persistent RSOs can also reduce the bandwidth required to synchronize to the server, as described a bit later under "Resynchronization Depth."

When connected to the FlashCom Server, both the local and remote copies of the shared object are updated. While disconnected from FlashCom, only the local copy can be updated.

To request that a remotely persistent object also persist locally, the persistence parameter of the *SharedObject.getRemote( )* method must contain a local path string similar to the `localPath` string required to create a local shared object:

```
SharedObject.getRemote(SharedObjectURI, AppInstanceURI [, persistence]);
```

The local path string must be part of the path information from the URL to the movie's *.swf* file. For example, if a *.swf* is downloaded from:

```
rtmp://host.domain.com/so/sample1.swf
```

then the local path string can be any one of the following:

```
/
/so
/so/sample1.swf
```

To avoid the possibility that two different Flash movies might inadvertently over-write each other's local copy of a shared object, use the full path to the movie. In the preceding example:

```
/so/sample1.swf
```

note that *sample1.swf* is the name of a subdirectory, not the name of a *.swf* file. The shared object is stored in a subdirectory based on the local path string, plus the application instance's URI.

For example, if a shared object named Test were acquired via a call to *getRemote( )* this way:

```
SharedObject.getRemote("Test", "rtmp:/myApp/myInstance", "/so/sample1.swf");
```

it would show up on my Windows 2000 computer under the file path:

```
C:\Documents and Settings\blesser\Application Data\Macromedia\Flash Player\
host.domain.com\so\sample1.swf\myApp\myInstance\Test.sor
```

The first part of the path, down to the *Flash Player* subdirectory, is where all local shared object data is stored for my account on my computer. The last part of the path:

```
\host.domain.com\so\sample1.swf\myApp\myInstance\Test.sor
```

has four parts:

`host.domain.com`
> The hostname of the system from which the movie was downloaded. There will be a directory for each host accessed.

`so\sample1.swf`
> The path to the *.swf* file available at the named host. In this example, the subdi-rectory is named *sample1.swf* after the movie that stored the shared object in the */so/sample1.swf* local path.

`myApp\myInstance`

The FlashCom application name and instance name where the remote shared object exists. It is always added after the local path in order to separate locally persistent shared objects that belong to different applications and instances.

`Test.sor`

The file containing the local copy of the remote shared object. The *.sor* extension is used for locally persistent remote shared objects. The *.sol* extension is used for purely local shared objects.

Under some circumstances, it may be desirable that more than one movie on a given client have access to the same remote shared object as well as its local copy. Any movie available from the same hostname and within the path defined by the local path string can access the local copy of the remote shared object of a different movie.

When a Flash movie disconnects from a remote shared object or disconnects completely from the server, it can continue to update the local copy of the shared object. When the movie reconnects to the server, the local and remote copies are synchronized. The server uses slot version numbers to determine if each slot in the local copy of the shared object should overwrite the corresponding slots in the remote version or if the remote data should overwrite some or all of the local data. If a slot in the local copy of the shared object has a higher version number, it will overwrite the slot in the remote version. In practice, this means that if a local slot in a shared object has been updated and the remote slot has not been updated, the local value will overwrite the remote value. However, if the remote version has changed at all since the client disconnected, the remote version will overwrite the local version—the server version takes precedence.

The client-side *onSync( )* method of the remote shared object will be called when the movie reconnects to the shared object. Whenever a local value is used to update the remote shared object, an info object will contain a code value of "success." If a local change is rejected, an info object will contain a code value of "reject". When a local change is rejected, the old local value is included in the info object's `oldValue` property.

Prior to Version 7.2 of Flash MX 2004, ActionScript 2.0's strict type checking caused an error when using a local path string as the persistence parameter passed to *SharedObject.getRemote( )*. To solve the problem, you should upgrade to the latest release. If for some reason you can't upgrade, change the *SharedObject* definition file at *.../First Run/Classes/SharedObject.as* from:

```
static function getRemote(name:String,
    remotePath:String, persistence:Boolean):SharedObject;
```

to:

```
static function getRemote(name:String,
    remotePath:String, persistence:Object):SharedObject;
```

to fix the problem.

Using flush( ) to Write to a Persistent Shared Object

Normally, when a persistent shared object is created and data added to it, an *.fso* file is not immediately written to the server's disk by the application instance. The file may be written to disk some time later or when the instance shuts down. In fact, if no file exists and a persistent shared object has no properties when the instance shuts down, no *.fso* file is created. You can force the instance to write out the current state of a shared object by calling the Server-Side ActionScript *SharedObject.flush( )* method. On the client side, you can also use *SharedObject.flush( )* to write the shared object to local storage if the remote shared object is locally persistent (it also works for purely local shared objects). In each case, the *flush( )* method affects only the system on which it is called. On the server, calling *flush( )* forces a write to the server's disk, while on the client, *flush( )* forces a write to local disk.

In two cases, calling *flush( )* on the server does not write the RSO to the disk. Updating any slot in a shared object increments the version property of the shared object. If the version number has not changed since the last time the file was written to disk, calling *flush( )* has no effect (there is no point in writing to disk if the data has not changed since the last write). The second case is when you *lock( )* a shared object. All updates to a locked shared object are considered part of one batch, so the version number does not increment until *unlock( )* is called. Therefore, if you call *flush( )* on a locked shared object, there is no guarantee anything will be written to disk. A short code snippet illustrates:

```
so.setProperty("balance", 0);
so.flush( );  // The shared object has changed, so it will be written to disk

so.lock( );   // The lock freezes the version number
so.setProperty("balance", 100);  // Property change does not increment version
so.flush( );  // flush( ) does nothing because the version number has not changed
so.unlock( );
```

To guarantee that the latest version of the shared object is written to disk, unlock the shared object before calling *flush( )*:

```
so.lock( );   // The lock freezes the version number
so.setProperty("balance", 100); // Make a property change
so.unlock( ); // Unlocking allows FlashCom to increment the version number
so.flush( );  // Updated data is written to disk
```

Resynchronization Depth

By default, persistent shared objects are never cleared of data when they connect or reconnect to the remote shared object managed by the server. Version numbers are used to determine what local properties must be updated on the remote shared object and what slot changes in the local copy must be rejected. This scheme can be very efficient for large shared objects because reconnections may require fewer updates. For example, if a remote shared object has 1000 properties, the first time a client connects to it, all 1000 properties must be sent by the server to the movie. However, if the client movie also saves a local copy of the shared object, when it reconnects later, only the slots on the remote shared object that have changed must be downloaded to the local copy. If only 10 slots have changed, synchronization is much faster than if all 1000 slots must be downloaded. However, for applications in which an object is locally and remotely persistent and many deletions must be performed, it may be more efficient to simply clear all the local slots and download all the data from the remote shared object.

Server-side shared objects have a property named `resyncDepth` that can be used to control how many remote version changes must occur before reconnecting shared objects are cleared and repopulated with data from the remote shared object. For example, the resynchronization depth can be set this way:

```
my_so.resyncDepth = 5;
```

As a consequence, when a persistent shared object connects, its local version number is added to the `resyncDepth` value. If the total is less than the current version number of the remote shared object on the server, all its properties will be cleared and all the properties of the remote shared object will be downloaded.

When the data in a slot is deleted on the server, the actual slot and its associated version number are not deleted. The `resyncDepth` property also controls when properties of a shared object are completely deleted. If the version number of a slot plus `resyncDepth` is less than the shared object's current overall version number, the slot is completely deleted. The default value for `resyncDepth` is -1, which effectively sets the resynchronization depth to infinity so that the actual slot is never deleted.

Setting the resynchronization depth of a shared object is not always the best way to control the complete deletion of shared object slots. An alternative is to purge stale slots as necessary by calling the *purge( )* method, which accepts a version threshold for the purge. For example:

```
my_so.lock( );
my_so.purge(my_so.version - 5);
my_so.unlock( );
```

In this example, if the version number of the shared object is 100, any slots with a version number less than 95 will be completely deleted.

Using the *purge( )* method may lead to some surprising synchronization behaviors when locally and remotely persistent shared objects are reconnected. For example, a property may be saved both locally and remotely before disconnecting from an application. Later, while disconnected, the remote property may be deleted by another client and eventually purged. When the local copy reconnects, there will be no record on the server that the property was deleted, so the local version of the property will successfully update the remote shared object.

When either the resyncDepth property or *purge( )* method is used, the complete deletion of slots frees memory for the application. Applications that are long lived—that is, not frequently garbage collected—and those that create and delete large numbers of shared object slots should completely delete them to reduce memory usage.

Proxied Shared Objects

Every shared object belongs to one application instance. The *master instance*, also called the *home instance*, is the only one that can use Server-Side ActionScript to lock a shared object. However, other application instances can access a shared object belonging to a master instance using a network connection. The process of connecting to another instance in order to access its shared object is very much like the process used by a Flash movie to connect to an instance's shared objects.

One instance uses a *NetConnection* object to connect to the master instance. Then it creates a *SharedObject* and connects it to a shared object in the master instance. Once synchronization takes place, it can get and set data in the shared object belonging to the master instance. Many instances can connect to the master instance and update the master's shared objects. Figure 8-1 shows two instances—named chatApp/room2 and chatApp/room1—connected to a master instance named chatApp/_definst_. The master instance contains one shared object with a relative URI of *private/roomList*. The other two instances have connected to the master instance and to its private/roomList shared object.

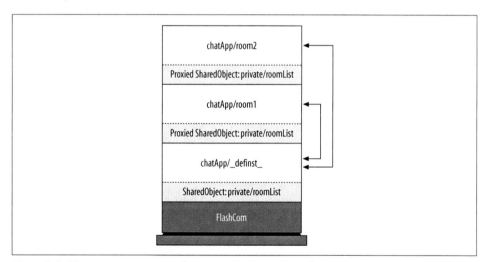

Figure 8-1. Two instances connected to a master instance in order to access its private/roomList shared object

The following short SSAS code snippet shows how an instance can connect to the _definst_ instance of an application named *chatApp* and then connect to the master instance's roomList shared object. We'll learn more about this application in the next section:

```
// Create a new NetConnection object.
nc = new NetConnection();
/* Connect to the _definst_ instance of the chatApp application.
*/ The _definst_ instance is the master instance.
/* See Example 8-6 and Example 8-7.
*/
nc.connect("rtmp://localhost/chatApp", "room");
// Create a proxy of the master's private/roomList shared object
// using the net connection, nc.
roomList_so = SharedObject.get("private/roomList", false, nc);
```

In SSAS, there is no *SharedObject.connect( )* method to call, so, instead, the *NetConnection* object is passed directly into the *SharedObject.get( )* method where it is used to connect the local and remote copies of the shared object. Another difference from client-side ActionScript is that regardless of whether the shared object is temporary or persistent, the instance must wait until the shared object's *onSync( )* method is called before trying to read or update the shared object, as shown in Example 8-8. When a room instance updates the shared object, the update is passed to the master instance, where the remote shared object is updated. Updates are then sent by the master instance to every client copy of the shared object.

When an instance connects to a master instance's shared object, it automatically makes the master's shared object available to its own movies. In Figure 8-2, the Flash clients connected to the room instances can access the master instance's shared object via the room instances. Each movie connects to a shared object using the relative URI of *private/roomList* as though the shared object belongs to the room instance. The shared object to which the Flash movies are connected is, in fact, a stand-in for the master's shared object. (That is, each room provides a proxy of the master's shared object for its client movies to connect to.)

The proxy process—in which one instance makes available a shared object, stream, or method belonging to another instance—is important for building large-scale applications and for applications that require collaboration between instances.

One example in which instances must cooperate is when one application instance acts as a lobby and the others as chat rooms. The lobby must inform its clients what chat rooms are active and how many people are in them. The information about how many visitors are in each room originates in each chat room instance and must somehow be shared with the lobby. In some applications, visitors in chat rooms may also want to know how many people are in each of the other rooms—information the lobby instance collects from all the rooms.

One way to share room information across the lobby and room instances is for the lobby to create and manage a room list shared object. Each slot in the room list can be named after a room instance and contain the number of visitors in that room. To

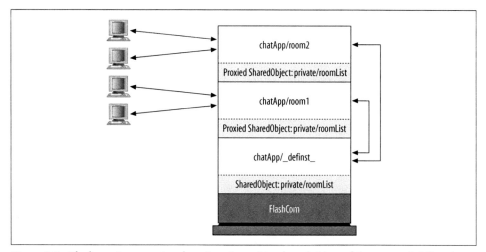

Figure 8-2. Flash movies accessing the private/roomList shared object of the master (_definst_) movie via the other instances

get information into the lobby's room list, every chat room instance opens a *NetConnection* to the lobby and connects to the lobby's room list shared object. Whenever a client enters or leaves a chat room, each room updates its copy of the room list shared object.

Any Flash clients that connect to the lobby can also connect to the room list shared object and will be notified of any room list updates. Similarly, clients that connect to a room can also connect to the room's copy of the room list and will also receive notices of updates via the *onSync( )* method. Each room's copy of the shared object acts as a proxy, or stand-in, for the master instance's shared object. A Flash movie connecting to a room instance connects to the room list shared object as though it is owned by the room instance. However, the movie is really connecting to a proxied shared object, and its messages to and from the shared object are passed by the room to the master instance (the lobby).

Lobby and Chat Room Example

Example 8-6 lists the code for the *main.asc* file for the *chatApp* application. The file has one purpose: when a request for the _definst_ instance of the application is received, it loads the *lobby.asc* file. When a request for any other instance occurs, it loads the *chatRoom.asc* file. In this simple scheme, there is, therefore, only one lobby, which is the default instance of the application. See Chapter 16 for alternatives.

Example 8-6. The main.asc file for chatApp, which delegates to the lobby.asc or chatRoom.asc file

```
// Use regular expressions to separate the instance and application name
// from the application.name property.
application.instanceName   = application.name.replace(/.*?\//, "");
application.applicationName = application.name.replace(/\/.*/, "");

if (application.instanceName == "_definst_") {
   load("lobby.asc");
}
else {
   load("chatRoom.asc");
}
```

The script guarantees that when any movie or instance attempts to connect to the default instance of the application, the *lobby.asc* script is run; all other instances are run with the *chatRoom.asc* file loaded.

The *lobby.asc* file, shown in Example 8-7, provides the server-side lobby behavior for the application. It sets up the room list and accepts connections from Flash movies and from other application instances (typically rooms).

Example 8 7. The lobby.asc file

```
application.onAppStart = function () {
   // Since rooms will also connect, keep track of the
   // number of Flash clients in a separate variable.
   this.clientCount = 0;
   // Get a temporary shared object for the room list.
   roomList_so = SharedObject.get("private/roomList");
   // Update the number of users in the lobby.
   roomList_so.setProperty(this.instanceName, this.clientCount);
};

application.onConnect = function (client, userName, instanceName) {
   // Test to see if a room or regular Flash client is trying to connect.
   if (client.ip == "127.0.0.1" &&
       client.agent.indexOf("FlashCom") == 0 &&
       userName == "room") {
      // It's a room connecting.
      client.type = "room";
      client.instanceName = instanceName;
      client.readAccess  = "private";
      client.writeAccess = "private";
      return true;
   }
   else {
      // It's not a valid room connecting,
      // so assume client is a Flash client.
      this.clientCount++;
      client.type = "client";
      client.readAccess  = "/";
      client.writeAccess = "public";
      roomList_so.setProperty(this.instanceName, this.clientCount);
      return true;
```

Example 8-7. The lobby.asc file (continued)

```
   }
};

application.onDisconnect = function (client) {
  if (client.type == "client") {
    this.clientCount--;
    roomList_so.setProperty(this.instanceName, this.clientCount);
  }
  else {
    roomList_so.setProperty(client.instanceName, null);
  }
};
```

For good measure, the lobby keeps track of each Flash client that connects to it and updates a slot named _definst_ in the room list shared object with the number of Flash clients in the lobby. Inside the *onAppStart( )* method, in this statement:

```
      roomList_so.setProperty(this.instanceName, this.clientCount);
```

the this.instanceName property is used to name the lobby's slot _definst_, and the clientCount property is used to track the number of Flash clients. Why not use the application.clients.length property that automatically keeps track of the number of client connections to the lobby instance? The problem is that both room instances and Flash movies can connect to the lobby; the lobby's *onConnect( )* method must determine whether a new client object is a Flash movie or a room instance. Since application.clients.length includes room instances attached as clients, the lobby keeps track of how many Flash movies have connected in the clientCount property.

The room instances don't have the same problem. They can use the application. clients.length property to count the number of clients, because only Flash clients (not other instances) connect to rooms. Example 8-8 shows the code that implements a chat room instance for the application.

Example 8-8. The chatRoom.asc file

```
function roomListOnSync (list) {
  if (!this.ready) {
    this.ready = true;
    this.setProperty(application.instanceName, application.clients.length);
  }
}

application.onAppStart = function () {
  nc = new NetConnection();
  nc.connect("rtmp://localhost/" + this.applicationName, "room",
             this.instanceName);
  roomList_so = SharedObject.get("private/roomList", false, nc);
  roomList_so.ready = false;
  roomList_so.onSync = roomListOnSync;
};
```

Example 8-8. The chatRoom.asc file (continued)

```
application.onConnect = function (client, userName) {
  roomList_so.setProperty(application.instanceName, application.clients.length + 1);
  return true;
};

application.onDisconnect = function (client) {
  roomList_so.setProperty(application.instanceName, application.clients.length);
};
```

In *chatRoom.asc*'s *application.onAppStart( )* method, the room connects to the lobby, requests a shared object named private/roomList, and assigns an *onSync( )* method for the shared object. After the *NetConnection.connect( )* to the lobby succeeds, the shared object is automatically connected, synchronization takes place, and the *onSync( )* handler of the proxied shared object is called for the first time. If the *onSync( )* method is being run for the first time, it updates the shared object with the current number of clients in the room. The *onConnect( )* and *onDisconnect( )* methods also update the shared object as each client connects to or leaves the room.

Although both the *onConnect( )* and *onDisconnect( )* methods update the shared object, having *onSync( )* also update the shared object is necessary to report the correct number of connected clients when the first user arrives. The reason for this is that a room instance is created when the first client connects. The room instance starts the process of connecting to the lobby and its private/roomList shared object. However, while waiting for the connection process to complete, the room's *onConnect( )* method is called and passed a *Client* object representing the first client. Since the shared object may not be synchronized yet, updating it may have no effect.

Let's look at the problem in detail. When a client connection request starts up a room instance, the following sequence occurs:

1. The *main.asc* file is loaded.
2. The *main.asc* file loads *chatRoom.asc*.
3. The *application.onAppStart( )* method in *chatRoom.asc* is invoked automatically.
4. The *chatRoom* instance starts the process of connecting to the lobby instance and proxying its roomList shared object. The connection process is asynchronous. *NetConnection.connect( )* returns immediately even though the connection is not established immediately.
5. The *application.onConnect( )* method in *chatRoom.asc* is invoked automatically (based on the original client request to connect to this application).
6. The *application.onConnect( )* method attempts to update the roomList_so shared object before the shared object is synchronized.
7. The network connection is established to the lobby instance.
8. The *roomList_so.onSync( )* method is called, and the roomList_so is now ready for updates.

The problem is that the shared object is not ready when the first client connects to a new chat room. So the shared object must be updated with the number of clients after it finally connects.

With every chat room instance creating a proxy to the lobby's private/roomList shared object, a Flash movie does not have to distinguish between connecting to the lobby or chat room to connect to the private/roomList shared object and display the number of users in each room in a listbox. Here is a short function that could be called within a Flash movie to connect to either the lobby instance or a chat room instance depending on the URI in the instanceURI variable:

```
function doConnect () {
  nc.close();
  nc.connect(instanceURI);

  roomList_so = SharedObject.getRemote("private/roomList", nc.uri);
  roomList_so.onSync = function (list) {
    roomList_lb.removeAll();
    for (var p in this.data) {
      roomList_lb.addItem(this.data[p] + ": " + p);
    }
  };
  roomList_so.connect(nc);
}
```

In the lobby/chat room example, only the lobby or chat room instances update the shared object. In fact, each movie is given only read access to the shared object. However, an application can allow write access to a proxied shared object—for example, to allow text chat across more than one instance.

With some alteration to the previous sample code, the lobby could be a separate application on one server, and the chat rooms could exist on more than one server in order to distribute the processing load across multiple servers. That is, instances can connect to other instances and their shared objects, on the same server or across servers.

Each network connection from one instance to another is counted by the communication server's license manager as one client network connection. Consequently, an application that uses interinstance connections will consume client licenses faster than one that does not.

Shared Objects and Custom Classes

With a little extra work, you can store instances of a custom class in the slot of a shared object. For example, if you are developing a shared whiteboard, a shared object could contain all the shapes that define each graphic in the whiteboard. The client-side *Rectangle* class in Example 8-9 can be used to create a simple Action-Script *Rectangle* instance using the *new* operator that will draw itself into a movie clip. The *Rectangle* object can also be stored in a shared object slot so that other movies can use it to draw the same rectangle.

Registering the class using the *Object.registerClass( )* method is the essential step that makes storing and calling methods on an instance of a class possible in a shared object slot.

Example 8-9. A client-side Rectangle class

```
// Rectangle constructor called when instantiated using new Rectangle( )
// and when a rectangle object is copied into a remote shared object.
function Rectangle (xMin, yMin, xMax, yMax) {
  if (typeof xMin == "undefined") return;  // Return if being deserialized
  this.xMin = xMin;
  this.yMin = yMin;
  this.xMax = xMax;
  this.yMax = yMax;
}

// Register the Rectangle class.
Object.registerClass("Rectangle", Rectangle);

/* Default prototype properites.
 * Note: methods are not saved in the shared object;
 * they must be defined in each movie.
 */
Rectangle.prototype.bThickness = 2;
Rectangle.prototype.bRGB = 0x0000AA;
Rectangle.prototype.bAlpha = 100;

// A simple draw( ) method that expects to be passed a movie clip reference.
Rectangle.prototype.draw = function (mc) {
  mc.lineStyle (this.bThickness, this.bRGB, this.bAlpha);
  mc.moveTo (this.xMin, this.yMin);
  mc.lineTo (this.xMin, this.yMax);
  mc.lineTo (this.xMax, this.yMax);
  mc.lineTo (this.xMax, this.yMin);
  mc.lineTo (this.xMin, this.yMin);
};
Rectangle.prototype.setBThickness = function (thickness) {
  this.bThickness = thickness;
};
Rectangle.prototype.setBRGB = function (rgb) {
  this.bRGB = rgb;
};
Rectangle.prototype.setBAlpha = function (alpha) {
  this.bAlpha = alpha;
};
```

For example, a movie that includes the definition for the *Rectangle* class from Example 8-9 can create a *Rectangle* object using the *new* operator, draw with it, and save it into a shared object:

```
var r = new Rectangle(10, 10, 32, 30);
r.setBRGB(0xFF0000);
r.draw(canvas_mc);
shapes_so.data.myRectangle = r;
```

Later, another movie—provided it also includes the definition for the *Rectangle* class from Example 8-9—can use the *Rectangle* object in the shared object to draw:

```
shapes_so.data.myRectangle.draw(canvas_mc);
```

You must do three important things to make this work:

- The class must be defined wherever it is used. In this example, the *Rectangle* class definition must be present in any movie that wants to create and store a *Rectangle* object in a shared object and must be defined in any movie that wants to draw a *Rectangle* object stored by another movie.

- The class must be registered using *Object.registerClass( )*. A more common use for *registerClass( )* is to associate a movie clip symbol with a class. In this example, the arbitrary string "Rectangle" is used since the *Rectangle* class is not associated with a movie clip. When a custom class is a subclass of *MovieClip*, movie clip properties such as _x and _y will not be copied to remote shared objects.

- The constructor is called when a movie creates an object before placing it in a shared object slot. When movies receive a copy of the object, the properties of the object are loaded into the object and then the object's constructor is called without any parameters. To make sure the constructor does not overwrite the data already copied into the object, the constructor must test whether it is safe to overwrite any properties. In Example 8-9, the constructor checks to see whether any parameters are being passed in before updating the object.

Custom classes can also be used in shared objects in SSAS. However, the constructor of a server-side object is called before an object's properties are copied into it. The *onInitialize( )* method, if any, is called just after the property data is copied into the object. Example 8-10 is an SSAS implementation of the *Rectangle* class and is designed as a complement to the client-side *Rectangle* class in Example 8-9.

Example 8-10. Server-side Rectangle class definition

```
function Rectangle () {
  // Serialized properties are not available yet.
}

Rectangle.prototype.onInitialize = function () {
  // Serialized properties are available.
};

Rectangle.prototype.getXML = function () {
  var buffer = '<Rectangle ';
  buffer += 'xMin="' + this.xMin + '" ';
  buffer += 'yMin="' + this.yMin + '" ';
  buffer += 'xMax="' + this.xMax + '" ';
```

Example 8-10. Server-side Rectangle class definition (continued)

```
  buffer += 'yMax="' + this.yMax + '" ';
  buffer += 'bRGB="' + this.bRGB + '" ';
  buffer += 'bThickness="' + this.bThickness + '" ';
  buffer += 'bAlpha="' + this.bAlpha + '" ';
  buffer += '/>';
  return buffer;
};

application.registerClass("Rectangle", Rectangle);
```

Example 8-10 does not include a *draw( )* method, as there is no point in having one on the server (the server application has no Stage on which to display graphics) but includes a *getXML( )* method, which generates an XML tag representing the shape for storing in an XML text file.

In a whiteboard component, the client-side part of the component could respond to a user request to draw a rectangle by placing a rectangle instance in a shared object slot. Other clients would detect the new slot and add the rectangle instance to the whiteboard. If the whiteboard must be saved, the server-side part of the whiteboard could generate XML to represent each part of the drawing.

Avoiding Collisions

When a movie attempts to update slots in a shared object, the server locks the properties of the server-side copy of the shared object the movie is attempting to update. Any other movies that attempt to update a slot while it is locked will receive an information object with a `code` value of "reject" for each locked slot in the list passed into the shared object's *onSync( )* method. So, if multiple movies attempt to update the same property of a shared object at nearly identical times, only one movie will succeed. The other movies will receive notice that their change requests were rejected. In some applications, rejected updates are an inevitable and necessary feature of the application. In others, steps should be taken to avoid slot update collisions. For example, it is interesting to see several people try to control the shared ball at the same time. The ball may move erratically around the Stage, but no harm is done. However, multiple users sharing a whiteboard application will prefer that each person has complete control of a drawing tool and can complete part of a drawing without interference from other users.

Here are a number of ways to avoid shared object slot update collisions:

Use separate shared objects.
> For example, if each user is represented by an avatar that follows the movement of his mouse, separate shared objects can maintain the coordinates and color of each user's cursor. Each shared object should have a unique name based on the username or an ID number.

Use a naming convention for slots to keep them separate.

For example, if each user has a unique user ID (a name or number will do), the ID can be used as a prefix for every property name. An avatar system could use three properties in the same shared object for each avatar, separated from the ID with a common character such as an underscore. For example:

blesser_x: 23

blesser_y: 76

blesser_color: #ff0000

peldi_x: 301

peldi_y: 216

peldi_color: #00ffff

Use a cooperative system mediated by the server.

When a slot must be updated by more than one movie, control of the slot can be cooperatively assigned to one movie at a time. Often remote method calls (see Chapter 9) are used to request access to a shared object or shared object slot because they are reliably queued by the server. The server can pass control to each movie in turn or use some other method to allocate control.

Do not update shared objects in the client.

A common approach when updates may conflict or where no updates can be dropped is to send data to the server using *NetConnection.call( )*, which is described in Chapter 9. The server processes the updates it receives from each client and writes whatever data is necessary into the shared object.

Optimizing Shared Object Performance

While it is possible to store complex data structures such as objects or arrays in a shared object slot, doing so is often not a good idea. The reason goes back to the fact that when one property in the object or array changes, the entire data structure is copied to the remote shared object and distributed to every client. To avoid the unnecessary copying of data, shared objects should be designed to reduce redundant updates. For example, a natural and seemingly logical way to design a list of users would be to create a shared object with each property value containing an object with information about each user. In SSAS we might create a structure like this:

```
userList_so = SharedObject.get("public/userList");
userList_so.lock();
userList_so.setProperty("blesser", {cn: "Brian Lesser", status: "Offline"});
userList_so.setProperty("peldi", {cn: "Giacomo Guilizzoni", status: "Offline"});
userList_so.setProperty("reinhardt", {cn: "Robert Reinhardt", status: "Offline"});
userList_so.unlock();
```

Although this approach seems logical (in that it keeps information about each user in one object), it will waste network bandwidth. In this case, imagine that the status property of the object in each slot is regularly updated to show when a user is online, away from her computer, busy, offline, and so on. Each time the status property changes, the cn (common name) property and its data will be sent to every client as well. One common solution to this problem is to use separate shared objects—one for personal information and another for status information. When separate objects are used, each movie must know what shared objects it should connect to. The most common way to work this out is to have separate objects or components look for their own shared objects based on some prearranged naming convention. A user list movie clip or component will attempt to connect to a shared object named userList, and a status movie clip or component will attempt to connect to a shared object named status. An alternative scheme is to use separate slots in the same shared object as described earlier in the second item in the list under "Avoiding Collisions."

Broadcasting Remote Method Calls with send( )

When data changes in one copy of a shared object, that data is copied to every other copy of the shared object, after which every shared object's *onSync( )* method is called. Shared objects provide another way to broadcast information to every copy of a shared object without storing data or calling the *onSync( )* method. Custom methods of the shared object can be defined so that they can be executed and passed data. For example, a custom *showMessage( )* method can be defined that will show text passed to it within a text field. One copy of a shared object can then send some text to every copy of the shared object and ask that the text be processed by the method named *showMessage( )*. Asking remote shared objects to execute a method is one mechanism of remote method invocation (RMI); see Chapter 9 for more information on RMI.

A request to invoke a method will succeed only on the shared objects that define a method with that name. Requests to invoke a method are made using *SharedObject. send( )*. A common use for *send( )* is to broadcast the text messages that show up in a chat component. As an oversimplified example, if this statement is executed:

```
messages_so.send("showMessage", "Hi Everyone");
```

then the *showMessage( )* method of every copy of the messages_so shared object is called and passed the text "Hi Everyone". Here is one implementation of *showMessage( )* that just displays the text in a text field and scrolls the text field down as far as possible:

```
messages_so.showMessage = function (msg) {
  chat_txt.text += msg + "\n";
  chat_txt.scroll = chat_txt.maxscroll;
};
```

Note that *showMessage( )* is defined as a property of the shared object, not attached to the shared object's data property.

Text Chat Example

The previous two snippets of code do not show how the shared object is created and managed in a real application. A common way to create a text chat is to create a *Chat* object or component that contains a shared object. When a message needs to be sent to the other movies participating in the chat, the user will click a button or press the Enter key so that a method of the *Chat* object is called. It will retrieve text from an input field and then send it using the shared object's *send( )* method by invoking a custom method named *showMessage( )*:

```
Chat.prototype.sendMessage = function () {
  var msg = trim(this.send_txt.text);
  if (msg == "") {  // Don't send empty messages
    return;
  }
  this.send_txt.text = ""; // Clear the text field
  this.messages_so.send("showMessage", this.userName + ": " + msg);
};
```

The *Chat* object is also responsible for getting the shared object and defining its *showMessage( )* method:

```
Chat.prototype.init = function (nc, userName) {
  this.messages_so = SharedObject.getRemote("public/textchat/messages", nc.uri);
  this.messages_so.owner = this;
  this.messages_so.ready = false;
  this.messages_so.onSync = function (list) {
    if (!this.ready) {
      this.ready = true;
      this.owner.onMessagesReady(this);
    }
  };
  this.messages_so.showMessage = function (msg) {
    this.owner.showMessage(msg);
  };
  this.messages_so.connect(nc);
};
Chat.prototype.showMessage = function (msg) {
  this.chat_txt.text += msg + "\n";
  this.chat_txt.scroll = this.chat_txt.maxscroll;
};
Chat.prototype.onMessagesReady = function (so) {
  this.setEnabled(true);
};
```

This example should look a little like the previous shared ball example. The *Chat* object contains a shared object that no other class uses, just as the *SharedBall* class contained a shared object. The shared object is stored as a property of the *Chat* object:

```
this.messages_so = SharedObject.getRemote("public/textchat/messages", nc.uri);
```

Also, as in the shared ball example, the shared object is given a private property named owner that holds a reference back to the *Chat* object:

```
this.messages_so.owner = this;
```

When a *showMessage* broadcast arrives, the shared object's *showMessage( )* method uses its owner property to pass the text message on to the *Chat* object:

```
this.owner.showMessage(msg);
```

In the *Chat* class example, the shared object acts as a conduit for broadcasting text messages between chat objects. It does not store any data.

 The accumulated text of the chat session is not stored in the shared object. Doing so might require very large messages to be sent, consuming too much bandwidth. Instead, the newly entered text is passed as a parameter to the *showMessage( )* handler. Each client is responsible for maintaining and updating its own copy of the text; latecomers do not receive text that was sent before they joined the chat.

Differences Between Shared Objects and NetStream.send( )

NetStream and *Stream* objects can publish *send( )* method requests very much like shared objects can broadcast method requests. (See "Sending a Request" in Chapter 5.) However, there are some important differences between how shared objects and streams handle *send( )* requests. When a shared object sends a remote method invocation request, the request is sent to the server and then to every copy of the shared object, including the shared object that originated the request. In the example of the text chat, that means the request to invoke a method is also sent back to the originator of the message. In the previous example of the text chat object, the text sent by a user will not show up on the screen until it is received back from the server. The *NetStream.send( )* method works differently. There is only one publisher of each stream, and when the publisher sends a message, only the subscribers to the stream receive the method request. *NetStream* subscribers cannot invoke *send( )* to send remote method requests, and the publisher does not receive back its own send requests. The other important difference is that recorded streams will store any method requests made on them in the *.flv* file of the stream so that the recorded methods will be executed when the stream is played later. Shared objects have no internal mechanism to record method calls (that is, remote method calls invoked via a shared object are not automatically stored or retrievable).

A Simple Video and Text Chat Application

Chapter 5 described a very simple two-way chat that required each user to know that the other user was online and to manually subscribe to the other user's stream by name. Shared objects provide the facilities required to make movies aware of all the users connected to a chat or conferencing application instance and to notify the movies about all the streams that are available.

We've already seen in Example 8-5 a server-side script that forces users to log in with a unique username. As each user logs in, his username is used as the name of a shared object property that contains a unique path assigned to him by the script. For example, if three users named "rreinhardt", "blesser", and "peldi" are logged in, the public/userList shared object contains the following properties:

```
blesser: public/chat/blesser
peldi: public/chat/peldi
rreinhardt: public/chat/rreinhardt
```

Movies that connect to the application instance can read the shared object and present to each user a list of usernames. Each movie can also use the unique path associated with its user's name to publish an audio and video stream and can subscribe to the stream of all the other users by retrieving the unique path for each user from the shared object.

The complete version of Example 8-11 on the book's web site contains all the files necessary to implement a chat/conference room with the following features:

- Each user is forced to log in with a unique username.
- A list of users is displayed in each movie and updated as users leave or log in to the chat room.
- Every movie automatically publishes one live stream to a relative path based on the user's username: *public/chat/username*. A pop-up movie clip shows the video stream being published and allows the user to stop or start sending audio or video.
- Every movie uses the public/userList shared object to get the path to subscribe to every other movie's stream and displays a pop-up movie clip that displays the video and allows the user to mute or unmute the incoming audio and video.
- A text chat is provided using the *send( )* method of the public/textchat/messages shared object.

Example 8-5 already lists the server-side script that forces each user to log in with a unique username and updates the public/userList shared object, and earlier code snippets showed excerpts from the *Chat* class that implements the text chat feature. The remainder of this chapter describes how the user list is implemented and how shared objects and streams work together to provide an audio/video chat facility. The entire application, though not complex, is too large to describe in detail here.

The application has three states: Init, Login, and Chat. Each state is represented by a separate labeled sequence of frames on the timeline, as shown in Figure 8-3.

The Init frame contains a global *trim( )* function, a *NetConnection* subclass, and an application object that controls changing state between the Login and Chat frames.

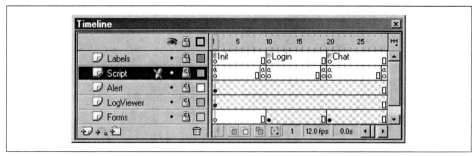

Figure 8-3. Timeline state labels for the chat application

When the movie starts, these objects are created and initialized, and the playhead is sent to the Login frame. When the user submits a username, the application object attempts to connect to an application instance. If successful, the playhead is sent to the Chat frame where the real work of the movie is done. The Chat frame contains an onstage instance of the *Chat* movie clip symbol with the following elements:

welcome_txt
   A text field that displays the current user's name

peopleList_lb
   A listbox that displays the usernames of everyone in the chat room

chat_txt
   A text field that displays text chat

send_txt
   An input text field for writing text chat messages

send_pb
   A push button for sending text chat messages

More importantly, there are two movie clip symbols in the Library that are attached to the *Chat* movie clip as needed:

StreamController
   A movie clip symbol that displays the video being published by the *Chat* object and allows muting of video and audio

StreamViewer
   A movie clip symbol that plays a stream and allows its audio or video to be muted

Both movie clip symbols are designed to be attached to another movie clip and expect to be passed a streamName variable containing the relative URI of a stream to either publish or subscribe to. Example 8-11 is the complete listing of the *Chat* class including comments that describe each method. See the book's web site for the complete *.fla* including the code for the *StreamController* and *StreamViewer* symbols.

Example 8-11. Chat class for the video chat application

```
#initclip
// Chat constructor function. Most of the setup work for this class
// is done in the init() method.
function Chat() {
  this.enabled = false;     // Current enabled state—see setEnabled() method
  this.streamLevel = 100;   // Level to place stream viewer and controller clips
  this.streamClipCount = 0; // Number of clips—for pop-up clip positioning
}
Chat.prototype = new MovieClip();
Object.registerClass("Chat", Chat);

// onLoad() sets component properties that must wait for an onLoad event.
Chat.prototype.onLoad = function () {
  this.send_pb.setEnabled(this.enabled);
  this.send_txt.selectable = this.enabled;
};

// setEnabled() locks or unlocks the text chat's input text field.
Chat.prototype.setEnabled = function (flag) {
  if (this.enabled == flag) {
    return;
  }
  else {
    this.enabled = !this.enabled;
  }
  this.send_pb.setEnabled(this.enabled);
  this.send_txt.selectable = this.enabled;
  if (!this.enabled) {
    this.send_txt.text = "";
  }
};

/* init() is called when the playhead reaches a frame containing the Chat
 * movie clip to set up the chat. It must be passed the user's current
 * username and a reference to a NetConnection object that has already
 * established a connection to the application instance.
 */
Chat.prototype.init = function (nc, userName) {
  this.nc = nc;
  this.userName = userName;
  this.setEnabled(false);
  this.welcome_txt.html = true;
  this.welcome_txt.htmlText = "Welcome <B>" + userName + "</B> to the chat area.";
  // Set up the userList_so shared object so that it notifies the Chat clip when
  // it needs to redraw the people list and show/delete stream clips.
  this.userList_so = SharedObject.getRemote("public/userList", nc.uri);
  this.userList_so.owner = this;
  this.userList_so.onSync = function (list) {
    this.owner.redrawPeopleList(this, list);
    this.owner.displayStreams(this, list);
  };
  // Set up the messages_so shared object to receive text messages.
```

Example 8-11. Chat class for the video chat application (continued)

```
  this.messages_so = SharedObject.getRemote("public/textchat/messages", nc.uri);
  this.messages_so.owner = this;
  this.messages_so.ready = false;
  this.messages_so.onSync = function (list) {
    if (!this.ready) {
      this.ready = true;
      this.owner.onMessagesReady(this);
    }
  };
  this.messages_so.showMessage = function (msg) {
    this.owner.showMessage(msg);
  };
  // Connect the shared objects.
  this.userList_so.connect(nc);
  this.messages_so.connect(nc);
  // Publish a stream for this user with video and audio.
  this.ns = new NetStream(nc);
  this.cam = Camera.get( );
  this.ns.attachVideo(this.cam);
  this.mic = Microphone.get( );
  this.ns.attachAudio(this.mic);
  // Use the username to set the URI for the stream to publish.
  this.ns.publish("public/chat/" + userName);
};

// redrawPeopleList( ) is called by userList_so.onSync( ).
Chat.prototype.redrawPeopleList = function (so, list) {
  this.peopleList_lb.removeAll( );
  for (var p in so.data) {
    this.peopleList_lb.addItem(p, so.data[p]);
  }
};

/* displayStreamController( ) attaches a StreamController clip to the Chat clip
 * and passes it the name of the stream and screen position to appear in.
 * See the displayStreams( ) method.
 */
Chat.prototype.displayStreamController = function (name, streamName, x, y) {
  this.attachMovie("StreamController", name, this.streamLevel++,
           {_x:x, _y:y, name:name, streamName:streamName, ns:this.ns,
            cam:this.cam, mic:this.mic});
};

// displayStreamView( ) attaches a StreamViewer clip to the chat.
Chat.prototype.displayStreamViewer = function (name, streamName, x, y) {
  this.attachMovie("StreamViewer", name, this.streamLevel++,
           {_x:x, _y:y, name:name, streamName:streamName});
};

/* displayStreams( ) is called by userList_so.onSync( ) whenever a user
 * is added or removed from the user list. It is passed both a
 * reference to the userList_so shared object and the information
```

Example 8-11. Chat class for the video chat application (continued)

```
 * object list passed to onSync( ).
 */
Chat.prototype.displayStreams = function (so, list) {
  for (var p in list) {
    // Get the information object.
    var obj = list[p];
    // If the code value is "delete" and there is a stream clip attached
    // to the chat clip, delete the stream clip.
    if (obj.code == "delete" && this[obj.name]) {
      this[obj.name].removeMovieClip( );
      this.streamClipCount--;
    }
    // Otherwise, if a "change" code is received, add a stream clip for new user.
    else if (obj.code == "change") {
      var name = obj.name;
      if (!this[name]) {
        var x = (this.streamClipCount % 4) * 180;
        var y = (((this.streamClipCount % 8) < 4) ? 0 : 1) * 185;
        this.streamClipCount++;
        // Add a StreamController clip if the name is this user's username.
        if (name == this.userName) {
          this.displayStreamController(name, so.data[name], x, y);
        }
        else {
          this.displayStreamViewer(name, so.data[name], x, y);
        }
      }
    } // End else-if.
  }
};

// onMessagesReady( ) is called when the messages shared object is first
// synchronized and is used to visibly enable the text chat fields.
Chat.prototype.onMessagesReady = function (so) {
  this.setEnabled(true);
};

// showMessage( ) is called from messages_so.showMessage( ) when text chat arrives.
Chat.prototype.showMessage = function (msg) {
  this.chat_txt.text += msg + "\n";
  this.chat_txt.scroll = this.chat_txt.maxscroll;
};

// sendMessage( ) uses the messages_so shared object to send( ) a message.
Chat.prototype.sendMessage = function ( ) {
  var msg = trim(this.send_txt.text);
  if (msg == "") {
    return;
  }
  this.send_txt.text = "";
  this.messages_so.send("showMessage", this.userName + ": " + msg);
};
```

Example 8-11. Chat class for the video chat application (continued)

```
#endinitclip
send_pb.setClickHandler("sendMessage", this);
send_txt.enterChar = String.fromCharCode(Key.ENTER);
send_txt.onChanged = function () {
  var lastChar = this.text.charAt(Selection.getEndIndex() - 1);
  if (lastChar == this.enterChar) {
    sendMessage();
  }
};
```

If you read through the code, you'll see that the *Chat* class's *init( )* method sets up both the messages_so and the userList_so shared objects. The earlier "Broadcasting Remote Method Calls with send( )" section describes how the messages_so shared object is used to implement a text chat. The userList_so shared object's *onSync( )* method is very simple:

```
this.userList_so.onSync = function (list) {
  this.owner.redrawPeopleList(this, list);
  this.owner.displayStreams(this, list);
};
```

It calls the *Chat* object's *redrawPeopleList( )* and *displayStreams( )* methods and passes a reference to the shared object and the information list to them. The *displayStreams( )* method examines each information object in the list array looking for code values of "change" or "delete". When a user connects to the chat, her username is added to the user list by the server-side script and deleted when her client disconnects. After each of these events, the *userList_so.onSync( )* method is called.

If the code value of an information object is "delete", then a user has left the chat application. If a *StreamViewer* movie clip for that user already exists, it must be deleted:

```
var obj = list[p];
if (obj.code == "delete" && this[obj.name]) {
  this[obj.name].removeMovieClip();
  this.streamClipCount--;
}
```

Each *StreamViewer* movie clip is named after the unique username that each person logged in with and is attached to the *Chat* movie clip. Since, in this case, obj.name contains the username, this[obj.name] returns a reference to a *StreamViewer* movie clip if it exists.

When the information object's code value is "change", a user has logged in. However the code checks whether the user is someone connecting from another Flash movie or is the person logged in using this Flash movie:

```
var name = obj.name;
if (name == this.userName) {
  this.displayStreamController(name, so.data[name], x, y);
}
else {
```

```
    this.displayStreamViewer(name, so.data[name], x, y);
}
```

If the user connected via another Flash movie, a *StreamViewer* movie clip is attached to the *Chat* movie clip by the *displayStreamViewer( )* method. Otherwise, we're dealing with the user who logged in with this Flash movie, so a *StreamController* movie clip is attached to the *Chat* clip. In either case, the relative URI to the stream will be retrieved from the user list shared object and used by the *StreamViewer* to subscribe to the stream or by the *StreamController* to control the stream:

```
    so.data[name]
```

Designing with Shared Objects

In this chapter, you've seen two related ways to design applications using shared objects in some detail. In the shared ball example, the *SharedBall* class uses a shared object to share its x and y coordinates with other instances of itself in other movies. In that case, shared objects simply extend the idea of containing data within an object to containing data within the same object running in several clients. Internal data in an object determines the current state of an object. The shared ball position is an example of object state, and shared objects provide a mechanism for manipulating the state of every ball object in every movie.

The user list shared object does more than extend data within an object into instances of the object in several Flash movies. When the user list is updated in one place (on the server), the information in it is used by more than one object. When data in the user list changes, the people list in every client is updated and stream viewers are created or deleted.

Conclusion

Shared objects are an excellent way to share information within a single class of objects or across objects or components in an application. Whenever you need to create an object or component with shared behavior, you should consider creating a shared object or accessing one provided by another object. For example, if you create a video conference component, consider storing information about each user's stream and video window in a shared object or objects. Information such as the video resolution, video and audio quality, x and y location of each video window, and the audio or video mute state can all be written into a shared object. As long as one instance of an object is responsible for updating its part of the video conference data, the others can reliably react to changes in shared objects.

Chapters 13 and 14 cover creating communication components, and Chapter 15 describes how to build components and real applications using shared objects. The next chapter, Chapter 9, covers another way to communicate between movies and the server, using remote method invocation.

Remote Methods

Remote procedure calls—one of the building blocks of any client/server architecture—were first defined in 1976 ("A high-level framework for network-based resource sharing" by J. E. White, in *Proc. National Computer Conference*, June 1976) and made popular by "Implementing Remote Procedure Calls" by A. Birrel and B. Nelson in 1984 (*ACM Transactions in Computer Systems*, vol. 2, no. 1, February 1984).

A *remote procedure call* (RPC) occurs when code on one computer invokes a function (procedure) on another computer. Object-oriented systems provide a similar feature referred to as *remote method invocation* (RMI) because the methods of remote objects are invoked instead of functions.

FlashCom provides developers with an elegant and powerful set of mechanisms to invoke methods remotely. A movie can invoke methods on the server and the server can invoke methods in movies. Method calls can be broadcast to every movie and application instance connected to a shared object or stream, or they can be sent to and from individual movies. An application instance can even create proxies of methods belonging to another application instance.

This chapter shows several examples of how to use the RMI methods and why you might choose one over others. Each section contains a sample application or code snippet to help understand the concepts. Toward the end of the chapter, we also cover optimizations because RMI calls can be significantly slower than local code execution.

Why Use Calls?

Chapters 5 and 8 already showed you examples of using the *send( )* method to call remote methods:

- *NetStream.send( )* and *Stream.send( )* invoke a method on all the clients that are playing that net stream. Furthermore, the method call can be buffered and saved as part of the stream itself, allowing the creation of powerful recording and play-back interfaces (see Chapter 15). Chapter 5 provides details on how to use this particular type of RMI.

- Conversely, the *SharedObject.send( )* command invokes a method on all the clients connected to that shared object. This can be used to invoke a method on a subset of your clients (the ones connected to a particular shared object). Chapter 8 includes an example of how to use this type of RPC.

The send( ) and call( ) Methods

The stream and shared object *send( )* methods both provide a mechanism to send method invocation requests to multiple movies at the same time. Both *send( )* methods are one-way—once the method is invoked on the *Stream*, *NetStream*, or *SharedObject*, no result can be collected. We can only hope that the method existed and that it ran successfully.

This chapter introduces the *call( )* method of the *NetConnection* and *Client* classes. The *call( )* methods provide a way to invoke a method on one recipient at a time. Unlike *send( )*, *call( )* makes it possible to receive the return value of a remote method. The *call( )* method can invoke methods on numerous objects attached to the *Client* or *NetConnection* objects (we'll see how). The *call( )* method provides fine-grained messaging control from client to server to clients, if necessary, and has advantages and disadvantages in securing an application (as elaborated upon in Chapter 18). Using *send( )* has been described in detail in Chapters 5 and 8, so this chapter focuses almost entirely on the *call( )* method. However, the methods are complementary and, as you will see, may be used together.

Client-to-Server Calls

Clients can ask the server to perform some operation using the *NetConnection.call( )* method, supported in Flash Player 6 and higher.

The syntax for *NetConnection.call( )* is:

```
my_nc.call(serverMethodName, resultObject | null, [, p1, ...pn]);
```

where my_nc is the instance name of a *NetConnection* object.

The first parameter of *call( )* is serverMethodName, a string (such as "test" or "getServerTime") that specifies the name of the method to invoke on the server.

Almost any valid identifier name can be used as a method name; however, the name cannot include spaces and you shouldn't use reserved words and methods such as agent, call, getBandwidthLimit, getStats, ip, onAppStart, onAppStop, onConnect, onDisconnect, onStatus, protocol, ping, readAccess, referrer, setBandwidthLimit, or writeAccess.

The second parameter passed to *call( )* can be either null or a result object (as explained shortly).

The optional parameters p1, ...pn are passed as parameters to the method on the server.

For the call to work, you must define a method on the server with the exact same name of your first parameter (serverMethodName) and attach it to the server-side *Client* object.

Let's see some examples.

Simple call( ) Example: "Server, Limit My Bandwidth"

As described in Chapter 5, FlashCom can limit how much data is sent to or received from each client using *Client.setBandwidthLimit( )*. These limits allow users to have a great multiuser experience even at different connection speeds (modem, ADSL, T1, or LAN). The *setBandwidthLimit( )* method is available only on the server-side *Client* object, which makes for a great example of a simple client-to-server call.

Place a ComboBox component on the main timeline, give it the instance name speed_cb, and attach the following client-side ActionScript to frame 1 of the *Actions* layer (a scripts-only layer you've created for that purpose):

```
_root.speed_cb.addItem("Modem", {up: 33, down:33});
_root.speed_cb.addItem("DSL", {up: 100, down: 400});
_root.speed_cb.addItem("LAN", {up: 1000, down: 1000});
```

Now define a change handler for it, like this:

```
_root.speed_cb.addEventListener("change", _root);
_root.change = function (evt:Object):Void {
  var selected = _root.speed_cb.value;
  trace("Asking server to set my limits to: up:" + selected.up +
       ", down:" + selected.down);
  nc.call("setMyBandwidth", null, selected.up, selected.down);
};
```

where nc is the *NetConnection* object used to connect this client to the FlashCom Server.

Here's how you can define the *setMyBandwidth( )* method on the *Client* object in the server-side *main.asc* file:

```
application.onConnect = function (clientObj) {
  // ...some regular onConnect( ) code.

  // Called by the client
  clientObj.setMyBandwidth = function (clientToServer, serverToClient) {
    this.setBandwidthLimit(1000*serverToClient/8, 1000*clientToServer/8);
  };

  application.acceptConnection(clientObj);
};
```

When each client (.swf movie) makes a connection to the server, FlashCom invokes *main.asc*'s *application.onConnect( )* method, with a reference to the client connection (clientObj) as a first parameter. On this *Client* instance, the code defines the *setMyBandwidth( )* method, which just calls *setBandwidthLimit( )* on the *Client* instance itself (as represented by the keyword this), using the parameters passed in to the call. Finally the code accepts the connection to the client movie (which receives a "NetConnection.Connect.Success" status in the *NetConnection.onStatus( )* handler, if defined). When the user selects a value using the speed_cb combo box, *change( )* is invoked, which uses the *NetConnection.call( )* method to invoke *setMyBandwidth( )* on the server, passing the two parameters provided. Since we defined *setMyBandwidth( )* on clientObj, the method is found and invoked, and the *Client.setBandwidthLimit( )* method is used to throttle this client's bandwidth. No return value or result is needed from the execution of *setMyBandwidth( )*, so the second parameter of the *NetConnection.call( )* method is set to null.

 The Server-Side ActionScript (SSAS) language is strictly case-sensitive. Always copy and paste the method name from your *call( )* parameter to the function definition (or vice versa) to avoid typos.

This sample showed how to execute a simple remote method from a client to the server and how to pass parameters to it. As we will see, the *setMyBandwidth( )* method could also be defined on Client.prototype instead of on the instance (clientObj).

Other Parameter Types

In the previous example, we passed two integers to a server-side method. You can also pass arrays, like this:

```
var myArray = [0,1,2];
nc.call("myMethod", null, myArray);
```

or, more commonly, simple records (which in ActionScript are implemented as objects with properties containing data but not methods):

```
nc.call("myMethod", null, {name:"Peldi", presenter:true, age:29});
```

As discussed later, you can also pass full-blown objects (with methods) as parameters to *call( )*.

Result Object Example: "Server, What Time Is It?"

As mentioned earlier, remotely invoked methods can return a value to the invoking client. Let's see how to handle a return value. Imagine an application that displays the time on the server, so that users connected around the world can synchronize their watches (maybe they're planning a jewel heist).

Place a Button component on the main timeline and give it the instance name getServerTime_pb. Also create a dynamic text field on the main timeline and name it serverTime_txt. Now you can assign it a click handler by attaching this client-side ActionScript to frame 1 of the *Actions* layer:

```
_root.getServerTime_pb.addEventListener("click", _root);
_root.click = function (evt:Object):Void {
  var resObj = new Object();
  resObj.onResult = function (val):Void {
    trace("The time on the server is:" + val);
    _root.serverTime_txt.text = val;
  };
  nc.call("getServerTime", resObj);
};
```

As you can see, we are passing a *result object* reference, resObj, as the second parameter of the *call( )* invocation; it is used to obtain the result of the call. In order to be a valid result object, resObj must define an *onResult( )* method. This method will be triggered by the Flash Player as soon as the result arrives back from the server (don't forget that, just like the call itself, this is an asynchronous operation; you should make no assumption as to how long it will take for the result to arrive). Note that the *onResult( )* method accepts a val parameter, which will contain the result returned from the remote method invocation.

Now let's define the *getServerTime( )* method on the server:

```
application.onConnect = function (clientObj) {
  // ...some regular onConnect() code.

  // Called by the client
  clientObj.getServerTime = function () {
    var now = new Date();
    return now.toUTCString();
  };
  application.acceptConnection(clientObj);
};
```

This example is very similar to the previous one. When each client (*.swf* movie) makes a connection to the server application (*main.asc*), FlashCom invokes *application.onConnect( )* and passes it a reference to the client connection (clientObj). On this object, we define the *getServerTime( )* method, which returns the date as a string, using *Date.toUTCString( )*. In this example, *getServerTime( )* doesn't require any parameters, so none were passed to *call( )* on the client side. When the user clicks the getServerTime_pb button, Flash invokes the *click( )* handler. A new result object (resObj) is created, and the call is made to *getServerTime( )*. The server executes the call and returns the string to the Flash Player, which invokes the *onResult( )* handler for the registered result object. All that's left to do is *trace( )* the value and set the text of the dynamic text field (serverTime_txt) to it.

The datatype of the val parameter received by *resObj.onResult( )* is wholly dependent on the return value of *clientObj.getServerTime( )*. In this example, it is a string, but it could be any native datatype.

Another Example: "Server, How Long Is This Stream?"

Here's a similar example that retrieves the length (in seconds) of a recorded *.flv* file from the server. As you have seen in Chapter 5, the Stream.length property is available only on the server. So if a Flash client wants to know how long a stream is in seconds, it has to ask the server. Here are some code snippets that do the trick. On the client movie, we'll do things a little differently this time, to show a different approach that might be useful sometimes. The outcome is the same: a call is made to the server and the result is displayed to the client through a text field. This code belongs on the client side:

```
// Define a StreamLengthResultHandler object.
StreamLengthResultHandler = function (owner, streamName:String):Void {
  this.owner = owner;
  this.streamName = streamName;
};
StreamLengthResultHandler.prototype.onResult = function (val:Number):Void {
  trace("The length in seconds of " + this.streamName + " is " + val);
  this.owner.streamLength_txt.text = "Length of " + this.streamName +
      ": " + val + "sec";
};

_root.getLength_pb.addEventListener("click", _root);
_root.click = function (evt:Object):Void {
  var name = _root.streamName_txt.text;
  nc.call("getStreamLength", new StreamLengthResultHandler(_root, name), name);
};
```

The difference in this client-side code is that we define a full-blown result handler object, with a constructor and an *onResult( )* method. This technique is commonly used when doing asynchronous calls (when using Flash Remoting, for example). It's a way to have the result object "remember" some values that might come in handy when the result actually arrives. In this example, we store the owner and streamName properties passed into the constructor, and use them in the *onResult( )* handler to display the stream name and to find the streamLength_txt text field in the correct scope (_root, in this case).

The server-side code for this example is nothing new at this point:

```
application.onConnect = function (clientObj) {
  // ...some regular onConnect() code.

  // Called by the client
  clientObj.getStreamLength = function (name) {
    return Stream.length(name);
  };
```

```
    application.acceptConnection(clientObj);
};
```

Client.method Versus Client.prototype.method

As we have seen in the previous examples, in order for a server-side method to be invoked by a *.swf* movie, it needs to be attached to a *Client* object. In the previous examples, we attached the method to the clientObj instance passed to *application. onConnect( )*.

Alternatively, Server-Side ActionScript allows you to attach the method to Client. prototype, saving memory and processor time on the server. In ActionScript (and JavaScript and Server-Side ActionScript), if you attach a method to the prototype of the object (in this case, the *Client* class), every instance of that class (in our case, every client that connects) will contain that method automatically. Here's how you could rewrite the server-side methods used in the previous examples:

```
Client.prototype.setMyBandwidth = function (clientToServer, serverToClient) {
    this.setBandwidthLimit(1000*serverToClient/8, 1000*clientToServer/8);
};

Client.prototype.getServerTime = function ( ) {
    var now = new Date( );
    return now.toUTCString( );
};

Client.prototype.getStreamLength = function (name) {
    return Stream.length(name);
};
```

You'll find that there are times when using one syntax is better than the other, and sometimes you'll want to use a combination of the two. Look at the following code, for example:

```
application.onConnect = function (clientObj, username) {
    // ...some regular onConnect( ) code.

    if (username == "admin") {
        // Define a method to be called by the admin user only.
        clientObj.kickUser = function (id) {
            application.disconnect(application.clientsByID[id]);
        };
    }

    application.acceptConnection(clientObj);
};

// This can be called by any client.
Client.prototype.setMyBandwidth = function (clientToServer, serverToClient) {
    this.setBandwidthLimit(1000*serverToClient/8, 1000*clientToServer/8);
};
```

```
// This can be called by any client.
Client.prototype.getServerTime = function () {
  var now = new Date();
  return now.toUTCString();
};
```

As you can see in this example, we define *setMyBandwidth( )* and *getServerTime( )* on Client.prototype, making them available to be called by any client movie. Conversely, the *onConnect( )* method defines another method, *kickUser( )*, only for clients who connected with a username equal to "admin". If a non-admin client tries to make the following call:

```
nc.call("kickuser", null, 3);
```

it will fail, because the *kickuser( )* method is not defined on that *Client* instance.

> As a rule of thumb, attach methods needed by every *Client* object to Client.prototype. Define methods on client instances if you want a subset of your users to be able to invoke those methods.

Server-to-Client Calls

We've seen how to invoke a server-side function from a client. Let's look at the reverse scenario in which server-side scripts ask a particular client movie to perform some operation using *Client.call( )*.

The server-side syntax is very similar to the client-side *NetConnection.call( )* method discussed earlier. Here is the server-side code:

```
my_client.call(clientMethodName, resultObject | null, [, p1, ...pn]);
```

where my_client is the instance name of the *Client* object you want to invoke the method on.

The first parameter of *call( )* is clientMethodName, a string (such as "test", or "setUserID") that specifies the name of the method to invoke on the client side.

Almost any valid identifier name can be used as a method name. Avoid strings with spaces and don't use reserved words and methods such as call, close, connect, isConnected, onStatus, and uri.

The second parameter can be either null or a result object.

The optional parameters p1, ...pn are passed as parameters to the method on the client. All the parameter types discussed earlier under "Other Parameter Types" can be passed to this call as well.

The server-side *Client.call( )* method returns a Boolean (true if the call was sent, false if it failed immediately). In order for the call to work, you will need to define a method on the client side that matches the name of your first parameter (clientMethodName) and attach it to the client-side *NetConnection* object.

Let's see some examples.

Simple call( ) Example: "Client, Here's Your ID"

Since server-side code executes in a single thread, a typical task performed on the server is assigning a unique ID to each connecting client. Here's some code, which can be placed in a *main.asc* file, that does the trick:

```
application.onAppStart = function () {
  this.nextID = 0;
};
application.onConnect = function (clientObj) {
  clientObj.userID = this.nextID++;
  trace("client " + clientObj.userID + " is connecting");
  this.acceptConnection(clientObj);
  clientObj.call("setUserID", null, clientObj.userID);
};
application.onDisconnect = function (clientObj) {
  trace("client " + clientObj.userID + " is leaving");
};
```

The code resets the counter (nextID) every time the application starts and increments it every time a user connects. Right after accepting the client connection, we can start making calls to the client safely, as we do in this line:

```
clientObj.call("setUserID", null, clientObj.userID);
```

We need to define a method in the client and attach it to the *NetConnection* object, in order for the method to be invoked by the server. Here is the client-side code:

```
my_nc.setUserID = function (id) {
  _root.myID = id;
  // ...other code to set up the UI.
};
```

where my_nc is the name of the *NetConnection* object instance on the client side. In this example, we store the unique ID as a property of _root.

Contacting Clients

In a common scenario, the server wants to tell something to all (or a subset of) the clients connected to the application. You can do this in several ways:

- Use *NetStream.send( )* as described in Chapter 5.
- Use *SharedObject.send( )* as described in Chapter 8.
- Have all the clients you want to notify connect to a shared object and set a property on that shared object using the *SharedObject.setProperty( )* method. This will trigger an *onSync( )* on all clients, as also discussed in Chapter 8.

- Loop through the `application.clients` array and make a server-to-client call to all the clients you want to notify, as discussed next.

Looping through the clients array

Here's a little server-side code snippet that loops through the `application.clients` array:

```
for (var i = 0; i < application.clients.length; i++) {
  var c = application.clients[i];
  if (c.role == "viewer") {
    c.call("showViewerUI", null);
  }
}
```

The code loops through all the clients connected to the application and saves a reference to each client in the c variable. The code checks whether the role property of the client (attached to the client instance somewhere else in your script; not shown) is equal to "viewer"; if so, the code invokes *showViewerUI( )* on the selected client.

Using a Result Object: "Client, Are You OK?"

Just as a client-to-server *NetConnection.call( )* method can return a value to the client, the server-to-client *Client.call( )* method can return a value to the server. The syntax is identical, so let's dive down into an example.

Sometimes you want to make a round-trip call to a client to make sure it's still alive. Here's the server-side code to check whether a client is alive:

```
// Define a class that just stores the client ID.
AreYouOkResultHandler = function (clientID) {
  this.clientID = clientID;
};
// Handle the result of calling areYouOk( ).
AreYouOkResultHandler.onResult = function (val) {
  trace("Client " + this.clientID + " returned " + val);
};

application.pingClient = function (clientObj, clientID) {
  // Invoke a message on the client.
  clientObj.call("areYouOk", new AreYouOkResultHandler(clientID));
};
```

On the client side, we can define the simple *areYouOk( )* method and attach it to the *NetConnection* object, like this:

```
my_nc.areYouOk = function () {
  return true;
};
```

Using a return object in a server-to-client call is very rare, as one would usually make use of shared objects to maintain information about clients. It's more common in server-to-server calls, which we will discuss in the next section.

How to Remember the Syntax

Most developers get confused at first by the asymmetry of making calls and attaching methods on the *NetConnection* and the *Client* objects when using remote methods in FlashCom. Here's a little reminder.

For client-to-server calls, the *NetConnection* is the only way out of the client, so the call should start there. Invoke *NetConnection.call( )* from the client-side Flash movie, specifying the name of the handler to be invoked on the server:

```
my_nc.call("serverHandlerName");
```

and from the server's point of view, every connection to the outside world is a different client movie, so define the SSAS handler as a method of the server-side *Client* object:

```
clientObj.serverHandlerName = function () {/* Code goes here */};
```

Conversely, for server-to-client calls, the server connects to many client movies, so calling a method on a particular client is done by invoking *Client.call( )* from SSAS:

```
clientObj.call("clientHandlerName");
```

and from the client point of view, the only way in from the server is the *NetConnection* object, so it's logical to define the client-side method on *NetConnection*:

```
my_nc.clientHandlerName = function () { /* Code goes here */ };
```

If you think about it, it's logical. Just remember that the *Client* object is used exclusively on the server—it represents the client making the connection.

Server-to-Server Calls

A powerful but often overlooked feature of FlashCom is the ability for a server-side script to create a *NetConnection* to another application instance on the same server or on any other machine running the FlashCom Server. This is a very important feature, which can be used to create lobby/rooms-style applications or to make applications scalable across multiple servers, as discussed in Chapter 16.

The server-to-server model closely mimics the client-to-server calls discussed in previous sections. In a server-side script, you can create a *NetConnection* object and connect it to a regular RTMP address, and the other application instance will treat the connecting instance just like any other client. One instance can connect to another one by creating a *NetConnection* object and then calling *connect( )*:

```
nc = new NetConnection();
nc.connect("rtmp://localhost/appName/instanceName");
```

The only way the server-side call differs from a client-side *NetConnection.connect( )* call is that a full URI must be supplied, including the hostname. On many systems, "localhost" can be used to refer to the same server on which FlashCom is running. On others, "localhost" cannot be used, so the full hostname or IP address must be specified.

The instance being connected to receives a connection request from another instance, just like requests from Flash movies. The *application.onConnect( )* method is called in the receiving application and passed a *Client* object that represents the connection request from the other application instance. Handling requests from both clients and instances can complicate the code within *onConnect( )* methods. To differentiate between requests from Flash *.swf* files and those from other FlashCom instances, examine the ip, referrer, and agent properties of the *Client* object passed to *onConnect( )*. For example:

```
application.onConnect = function (client) {
  if (client.ip == "127.0.0.1" && client.agent.substr(0,8) == "FlashCom"
      && client.referrer.split("/")[3] == "lobby_rooms") {
    // It is a lobby_rooms application instance
    // running on the same server (127.0.0.1) trying to connect.
    application.acceptConnection(client);
  }
  else {
    // Otherwise, we assume the client represents a .swf.
     client.writeAccess = "public";
     client.readAccess = "public";
    application.acceptConnection(client);
  }
};
```

The following section describes a full-blown example that uses client-to-server, server-to-client, and server-to-server calls to create a powerful lobby/rooms communication system. If you understand every line of code in the example, you have mastered the fundamentals of RMI in FlashCom.

A Simple Lobby/Rooms Application

This example brings together all the topics we have covered so far in this chapter. You'll see how to use each kind of RMI in FlashCom to create much of the core code required to build real-world lobby/rooms applications.

In this scenario, we want users to connect to a lobby application, see a list of all the rooms on the site, create a room (with a password, for privacy), see how many people are in each room, and be able to join a room or delete one. The example does not include user authentication nor does it include user controls on who can create or delete particular rooms. However, it does provide the essential structure to which those features could be added. See Chapter 18 for more information on user authentication and authorization.

Using the Same Application Folder for the Lobby and Rooms

Since there is only one lobby and multiple rooms, one way to implement this on the server side is to use the default instance (_definst_) for the lobby and all other instances for rooms. As should be familiar from the preceding chapter, here's our *main.asc* file, which checks the instance name to decide whether to load *lobby.asc* or *room.asc*:

```
var slashPos = application.name.indexOf("/");
gAppName = application.name.slice(0, slashPos);
gRoomName = application.name.slice(slashPos + 1);

// _definst_ is used for the lobby; any other instance is a room.
if (gRoomName == "_definst_")
  load("lobby.asc");
else
  load("room.asc");
```

This approach allows us to keep all the server-side code for this application (lobby and rooms included) in the same application folder (in this sample, we'll call it *lobby_rooms*), which makes it easier to deploy.

This example requires two separate Flash movies: one to connect to the lobby instance, which lets the user view, create, and delete rooms, and another to connect to an individual room instance. Let's look at the lobby part of the application first, followed by the room client and server code.

The Lobby

Here are some of the functions performed by the lobby:

- Keep a list of rooms (each room's unique ID, name, password, and number of occupants)
- Allow users to create new rooms
- Allow users to delete rooms
- Allow users to join rooms through client-side code
- Interact with other application instances (the rooms) through server-side code

The client-side lobby.as code

Figure 9-1 shows the user interface of the lobby movie. A user can connect to a room by highlighting its name in the list and clicking the Join button. Selecting a room and clicking the Delete button results in a *call( )* to the *deleteRoom( )* method in the lobby instance, which deletes the room. Entering a room name and password and clicking the Create button results in a *call( )* to the *createNewRoom( )* method in the lobby, which creates a new room.

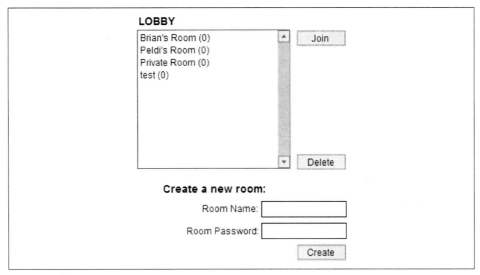

Figure 9-1. The lobby client interface

In the Flash authoring tool, place the following assets on the first frame of your Stage:

A List component
Give it the instance name roomList_lb.

Three Button components
Give them the instance names join_pb, create_pb, and delete_pb.

Two input TextFields
Give them the instance names roomName_txt and roomPwd_txt.

We stick with this example in AS 1.0 format for simplicity purposes, but the book's web site has a full-blown AS 2.0 code example.

Add the following code to the first frame of your movie (it's good practice to keep ActionScript in external *.as* files):

```
#include "lobby.as"
```

Save your movie as *lobby.fla*, and create an empty *lobby.as* text file in the same folder.

Let's go through the *lobby.as* code, one section at the time.

First, we define some constants and set up some UI handlers:

```
// Location of your room's .swf movie, used in getURL() in joinRoom().
this.roomSwfURL = "http://myserver.com/lobby_rooms/room.swf";

// Set up UI handlers.
this.create_pb.addEventListener("click", this);
this.join_pb.addEventListener("click", this);
```

```
this.delete_pb.addEventListener("click", this);
this.click = function (evt) {
  switch (evt.target) {
    case this.create_pb:
      createNewRoom( );
      break;
    case this.join_pb:
      joinRoom( );
      break;
    case this.delete_pb:
      deleteRoom( );
      break;
  }
}
```

We'll define the UI handlers (*createNewRoom( )*, *joinRoom( )*, and *deleteRoom( )*) shortly.

Next, we create a *NetConnection* for this client:

```
// Set up the room's NetConnection.
this.nc = new NetConnection( );
this.nc.mc = this;
this.nc.onStatus = function (info) {
  trace(info.code);
  if (info.code == "NetConnection.Connect.Success") {
    // Connected; now connect assets.
    this.mc.onConnect( );
  }
};
// Connect to the lobby.
this.nc.connect("rtmp:/lobby_rooms/_definst_"); // The lobby is _definst_
```

Nothing special here. We call the *onConnect( )* method once the connection to the lobby instance (_definst_) is established. The *rtmp:/lobby_rooms* URI notation assumes that the two applications are running on the same server. Refer to Chapter 3 for more information about the *NetConnection.connect( )* method.

Next comes the definition for *onConnect( )*:

```
// Called by onStatus( ) on success.
this.onConnect = function () {
  // Get the shared object with the room names and user counts.
  this.rooms_so = SharedObject.getRemote("public/roomNamesAndUsers",
                                         this.nc.uri, true);
  this.rooms_so.mc = this;
  this.rooms_so.onSync = function (list) {
    this.mc.updateRoomList( );
  };
  this.rooms_so.connect(this.nc);
};
```

We get the remote shared object containing the room names and number of users and set up a simple *onSync( )* method, which calls *updateRoomList( )*, defined next:

```
// Called by rooms_so.onSync().
this.updateRoomList = function () {
  // Not very scalable, but does the trick.
  this.roomList_lb.removeAll();
  // Loop through the data array and add rooms to the list.
  for (var roomID in this.rooms_so.data) {
    this.roomList_lb.addItem(this.rooms_so.data[roomID].name + " (" +
                             this.rooms_so.data[roomID].users + ")", roomID);
  }
  this.roomList_lb.sortItemsBy("label","ASC");
};
```

So every time we get an *onSync()* message on the shared object, we completely re-create the List component's contents; for each line, we add the name of the room and how many users are in it. For more efficient ways to update a list from the contents of a shared object, see Chapters 8 and 15.

All we have left to do is define the three *click()* button handlers. First, the one for the Create button:

```
// Button handler for create_pb.
this.createNewRoom = function () {
  // We could check for duplicate names here, but in this example
  // we're going to allow them.
  this.nc.call("createNewRoom", null,
               this.roomName_txt.text, this.roomPwd_txt.text);
  this.roomName_txt.text = this.roomPwd_txt.text = "";
};
```

The preceding method makes a client-to-server call to *createNewRoom()* (defined in *lobby.asc*, shown later), passing it the new room's name and password from the input text fields.

Now let's create the handler for the Delete button:

```
// Button handler for delete_pb.
this.deleteRoom = function () {
  var selectedRoomID = this.roomList_lb.selectedItem.data;
  if (selectedRoomID!= undefined)
    this.nc.call("deleteRoom", null, selectedRoomID);
};
```

The preceding method simply gets the roomID of the selected room from the listbox and makes a client-to-server call to *deleteRoom()* (defined in *lobby.asc*) to ask the server to delete the room.

Finally, here is the handler for the Join button:

```
// Button handler for join_pb.
this.joinRoom = function () {
  var selectedRoomID = this.roomList_lb.selectedItem.data;
  if (selectedRoomID!= undefined) {
    // Open the room swf in a new browser window, passing the roomID as a parameter
    getURL(this.roomSwfURL + "?room=" + selectedRoomID, "_blank");
  }
};
```

The preceding code is the last method of *lobby.as* and is also very simple; it takes the selected roomID from the listbox and passes it to the room *.swf*, which we open in a new browser window with a *getURL( )* call.

That's all the code necessary for the client side of the lobby application. Now let's look at the server side.

The server-side lobby.asc code

Let's step through the server-side *lobby.asc* file, which is loaded by the *main.asc* file if the application instance name is _definst_.

First, we set up all the shared objects and data structures we need to function:

```
trace("IN LOBBY");

application.onAppStart = function () {
  // Retrieve the last used roomID from a persistent private shared object.
  this.lastRoomID_so = SharedObject.get("private/lastID", true);
  if (this.lastRoomID_so.size() == 0) {
    this.lastRoomID = 0;
    this.lastRoomID_so.setProperty("id", this.lastRoomID);
  }
  this.lastRoomID = this.lastRoomID_so.getProperty("id");

  // Get the shared object that contains the password for each room.
  this.roomPasswords_so = SharedObject.get("private/roomPasswords", true);

  // This shared object saves the name of the room and how many users are in it.
  this.roomNamesAndUsers_so = SharedObject.get("public/roomNamesAndUsers", true);

  // This is a hash table in which we save the server-to-server connections
  // to each room, used in swf_deleteRoom( ).
  this.serverSideConnectionsByRoomID = new Object();
};
```

The code is pretty self-explanatory. It gets a private shared object named lastID, containing a counter used to create unique room IDs.

Then the code gets another two shared objects:

- A private shared object containing an array of room passwords (roomID is used to index into the array)
- A public shared object (to which the client movies subscribe, as we've seen before) containing room names and user counts

We split the shared objects this way for security (so that clients never get room passwords sent to them via *onSync( )* or in any other way).

We also create a hash table for saving references to server-to-server connections, which we will use in *swf_deleteRoom( )* (described later).

Here comes the most interesting part of this example. Since the room names and passwords are kept only in shared objects used by the lobby, other server-side application instances (the rooms) will have to connect to the lobby (server-to-server connection) to ask for their own name and password. As we will see, all a room knows when it starts is its roomID. Also, we want the lobby to notify a room once it is deleted, so that it can in turn notify the *.swf* movies connected to it and stop accepting client connections.

The lobby's *onConnect( )* method, therefore, needs to be smart enough to understand what type of client it is dealing with—a *.swf* movie or a server-side room application instance. As seen earlier, we use the *Client*'s agent and referrer properties to identify a connection from another FlashCom instance:

```
// Two types of clients connect to this app: .swf movies and room app instances.
application.onConnect = function (client) {
  // Clients cannot write to any shared object (or stream) directly.
  client.writeAccess = "";

  // Check the client.agent property and the app name.
  if ( (client.agent.substr(0,8) == "FlashCom") &&
       (client.referrer.split("/")[3] == "lobby_rooms") ) {
    trace("This is a connection from room.asc!");

    // This type of client can only interact with us using calls.
    client.readAccess = "";
    client.writeAccess = "";

    // Get its room ID from the client.referrer property. This is done for
    // added security; each room can make calls only about itself.
    client.roomID = client.referrer.split("/")[4];

    trace("roomID: " + client.roomID);

    // Attach only the methods we want this client to be able to call.
    client.getRoomInfo = asc_getRoomInfo;
    client.personJoined = asc_personJoined;
    client.personLeft = asc_personLeft;

    // Save a reference to this client in the serverSideConnectionsByRoomID
    // table, used in swf_deleteRoom( ).
    this.serverSideConnectionsByRoomID[client.roomID] = client;
  } else {
    trace("This is a connection from a .swf movie!");

    // .swf movies can read the public shared objects and streams.
    client.readAccess = "public";
    client.writeAccess = "";

    // Attach only the methods we want this client to be able to call.
    client.createNewRoom = swf_createNewRoom;
    client.deleteRoom = swf_deleteRoom;
  }
  application.acceptConnection(client);
};
```

Notice how we don't allow server-to-server connections to subscribe to any shared object (by setting readAccess and writeAccess to an empty string), because we want them to interact with us only via calls (once again for security reasons). Client-side *.swf* movies, on the other hand, need to subscribe to the public/roomNamesAndUsers shared object, so they need to have read access set to "public".

Also notice how we attach only the appropriate methods to each type of client. Room instances will be able to invoke the *getRoomInfo( )*, *personJoined( )*, and *personLeft( )* methods, while *.swf* movies will be able to invoke only the *createNewRoom( )* and *deleteRoom( )* methods. We don't attach any method to Client. prototype in this case, because we don't have any method that we want both types of clients to be able to call.

A last thing to notice is how we infer the roomID of the server-to-server connection from the client.referrer property. This trick, combined with the fact that *getRoomInfo( )* doesn't take a roomID as input (as we will see shortly), makes the server-side application more secure.

Next, we have to define the three methods accessible by the rooms' application instances. We'll define the two methods accessible by the *.swf* movies later. Here's the code for the first method, to get the room information:

```
// Methods for room.asc to call. None of these calls take a roomID parameter
// because it is inferred from the client.referrer property in onConnect( ).

// Called by room.asc in onAppStart( )
function asc_getRoomInfo( ) {
  trace("getRoomInfo called by " + this.roomID); // this is the client

  var roomSlot = application.roomNamesAndUsers_so.getProperty(this.roomID);
  if (roomSlot == undefined) {
    trace("The room doesn't exist.");
    return {name: null, pwd:null};
  } else {
    roomName = roomSlot.name;
    var roomPwd = application.roomPasswords_so.getProperty(this.roomID);
    return {name:roomName, pwd:roomPwd};
  }
}
```

This method is called by *room.asc* as part of the application startup code. This is how the room finds out its name and password. If the room doesn't exist (it's possible that someone tried to guess a roomID and attached it to the URL of the *room.swf* or simply is going to an old room that has since been deleted), we return a {name: null, pwd:null} object; otherwise, we get the values from the roomNamesAndUsers_so and roomPasswords_so shared objects and return them to *room.asc*.

The two methods that handle users joining and leaving a room are very similar to each other:

```
// Called by room.asc in verifyPassword( )
function asc_personJoined ( ) {
```

```
      var roomSlot = application.roomNamesAndUsers_so.getProperty(this.roomID);
      if (roomSlot == undefined)
        return;
      roomSlot.users++;
      // This will trigger an onSync() on the clients connected to the lobby.
      application.roomNamesAndUsers_so.setProperty(this.roomID, roomSlot);
    }

    // Called by room.asc in onDisconnect()
    function asc_personLeft () {
      var roomSlot = application.roomNamesAndUsers_so.getProperty(this.roomID);
      if (roomSlot == undefined)
        return;
      roomSlot.users--;
      // This will trigger an onSync() on the clients connected to the lobby.
      application.roomNamesAndUsers_so.setProperty(this.roomID, roomSlot);
    }
```

This code is how a room instance tells the lobby that a user has successfully authenticated or that a user has left, and the lobby should update the users counter for the room. Notice how these methods don't return any value to the room and how *setProperty( )* is used to trigger *onSync( )* events on all *.swf* clients subscribed to the public/roomNamesAndUsers shared object (as we have seen, the *onSync( )* method updates the roomList on the client side).

Figure 9-2 shows the code execution flow when a user enters a room. As you can see, *room.asc* connects to *lobby.asc* to notify it that someone has entered the room. The *asc_personJoined( )* method updates the roomNamesAndUsers_so shared object, triggering a UI update in all the *.swf* clients connected to the lobby application.

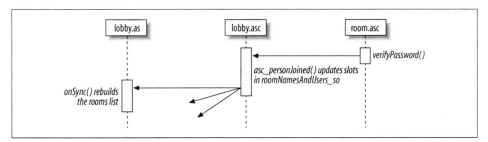

Figure 9-2. Sequence diagram for a user entering a room

All that's left is to define the two methods that we saw the client-side lobby invoke in the previous section: *createNewRoom( )* and *deleteRoom( )*. Here is the server-side code for *createNewRoom( )*:

```
    // Methods for the .swf movies to call.
    // Called by the lobby clients to create a new room
    function swf_createNewRoom (roomName, roomPwd) {
      trace("createNewRoom: " + roomName + "," + roomPwd);

      // Increment the lastRoomID counter and save it in the shared object.
```

```
    application.lastRoomID++;
    application.lastRoomID_so.setProperty("id", application.lastRoomID);

    // Create a unique roomID that's hard to guess.
    var roomID = "c" + application.lastRoomID + "r" + Math.round(Math.random( )*1000);

    // Save an entry for the new room in the public roomNamesAndUsers_so
    // RSO (this will trigger an onSync( ) on the clients).
    application.roomNamesAndUsers_so.setProperty(roomID, {name:roomName, users:0});

    // Save the password for the new room in the private roomPasswords_so  RSO.
    application.roomPasswords_so.setProperty(roomID, roomPwd);
    trace("New Room Created:" + roomID);
  }
```

First, the code increments the `lastRoomID` counter and saves it in the `lastRoomID_so` shared object (this guarantees us a unique ID). Then it manufactures a new `roomID` by using the counter and a random number, which makes it harder to guess.

We add the new entry to the `roomNamesAndUsers_so` shared object, which will trigger an *onSync( )* on the clients (so that they can update their `roomList_lb`), and save the password provided in the `roomPasswords_so` shared object. Figure 9-3 shows the process for creating a new room.

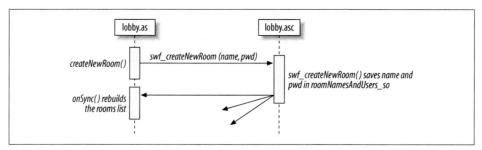

Figure 9-3. Sequence diagram for the creation of a new room

The last method of *lobby.asc* is *deleteRoom( )*:

```
    // Called by the lobby clients to delete a room
    // (we could add a password check here).
    function swf_deleteRoom (roomID) {
      trace("deleteRoom: " + roomID);

      // Delete the slot from the shared objects.
      // This will trigger an onSync( ) on the clients.
      application.roomNamesAndUsers_so.setProperty(roomID, null);
      application.roomPasswords_so.setProperty(roomID, null);

      // Server-to-server call to the room instance, which will notify
      // the .swfs connected to it that their room has been deleted.
      if (application.serverSideConnectionsByRoomID[roomID] != null)
        application.serverSideConnectionsByRoomID[roomID].call("roomDeleted", null);
    }
```

This code deletes the appropriate slots from the two shared objects, then makes a server-to-server call, this time from the lobby to the room instance, to notify that the room has been deleted. We use the client reference saved in the application. serverSideConnectionsByRoomID table (we saved it during *onConnect( )*) to find the appropriate application instance to call.

The Room Application

The room can perform a number of functions: it can be a video chat room, a multiuser game, or any other application you can imagine. Of interest for this chapter is how you connect to and get into the room with a password, and how you react to a room when it is deleted; the rest of the room application is left up to the reader.

The client-side room.as code

Figure 9-4 is a screenshot of the sample room we are going to build.

```
ROOM: Peldi's Room

Room Password: [****        ]   [ Enter ]
```

Figure 9-4. The login screen for a room

To create the room, in the Flash authoring tool, place the following assets on the first frame of your main timeline:

Two dynamic TextFields
    Give them the instance names roomName_txt and feedback_txt.

An input TextField
    Give it the instance name pwd_txt.

A Button component
    Give it the instance name enter_pb.

Add the following code to the first frame of your movie:

```
#include "room.as"
```

Save your movie as *room.fla* and create an empty *room.as* text file in the same folder.

Let's go through the client-side *room.as* code, one section at the time:

```
trace("Room = " + _root.room);

if (_root.room == undefined) {
  this.feedback_txt.text = "Invalid Room ID";
}
else {
  this.roomID = _root.room;
```

```
      // The movie's NetConnection
      this.nc = new NetConnection( );
      this.nc.mc = this;
      this.nc.onStatus = function (info) {
        trace(info.code);
        if (info.code == "NetConnection.Connect.Success")
          trace("Connection successful, waiting until user enters correct password");
        else if (info.code == "NetConnection.Connect.Rejected")
          this.mc.feedback_txt.text = info.application.message;
      };

      // Called by the server, sending us the name for this room
      this.nc.setRoomName = function (val) {
        this.mc.roomName_txt.text = val;
      };

      // Called by the server if this room gets deleted
      this.nc.roomDeleted = function ( ) {
        this.mc.feedback_txt.text = "This room has been deleted";
        this.close( ); // Closing the connection
      };

      // Connecting to the server
      this.nc.connect("rtmp:/lobby_rooms/" + this.roomID);
    }
```

As we saw in the *joinRoom( )* method of *lobby.as*, the *room.swf* is passed a _root.
room parameter. If the parameter was deleted by the user, we show an error. Otherwise, we define the movie's *NetConnection*, attach a regular *onStatus( )* handler to it,
and attach two methods—*setRoomName( )* and *roomDeleted( )*—that are going to be
invoked by the server side. The *setRoomName( )* method simply updates the
roomName_txt text field to display the name of this room. The *roomDeleted( )* method
displays some feedback to the user and closes the *NetConnection*. Finally, we connect to the application instance (which has the same name as the roomID).

The second half of the client-side code for *room.as* follows:

```
    this.onPasswordAccepted = function ( ) {
      // The code for the actual room (chat, AVPresence, etc.) can now be initialized.
      this.feedback_txt.text = "You would go inside the room now";
    };

    this.enter_pb.addEventListener("click", this);
    this.click= function (evt) {
      var res = new Object( );
      res.mc = this;
      // verifyPassword( ) returns true (password correct) or false (wrong password).
      res.onResult = function (val) {
        trace("verifyPassword returned " + val);
        if (val == true)
          this.mc.onPasswordAccepted( );
        else
          this.mc.feedback_txt.text = "Wrong Password, try again.";
```

```
};
    this.nc.call("verifyPassword", res, this.pwd_txt.text);
};
```

We define a method, *onPasswordAccepted( )*, which is the gateway to the actual application. This method gets invoked only after the user has entered the correct password in the pwd_txt text field. Typically, one would show a different UI and connect any other asset (or communication components) to the main *NetConnection* at this point.

In order to get past the login screen, the user needs to send the correct password to the server. This is done through a client-to-server call to *verifyPassword( )*, which returns true or false to the result object.

The server-side room.asc code

Let's step through *room.asc*; as we saw earlier, it is loaded by the *main.asc* file if the application instance name is not _definst_.

The *onAppStart( )* logic for *room.asc* is more complex than usual:

```
trace("IN ROOM");

// This is in a global function because we want to call it both upon
// application startup and if the connection to the lobby is closed (reconnect).
function connectToLobby( ) {
  trace("Connecting to lobby...");
  application.toLobby_nc.connect("rtmp://localhost/" + gAppName + "/_definst_");
  // Note that _definst_ is the lobby.
}

application.onAppStart = function () {
  application.roomDeleted = false;

  // Server-to-server NetConnection to the lobby.
  application.toLobby_nc = new NetConnection();

  application.toLobby_nc.onStatus = function (info) {
    trace("Connection to Lobby onStatus:" + info.code);

    if (info.code == "NetConnection.Connect.Success") {
      // The lobby accepted our connection,
      // now get this room's name and password.
      var res = new Object();
      res.mc = this;
      // getRoomInfo( ) returns an object of the form {name: "xxx", pwd:"xxx"}.
      res.onResult = function (val) {
        trace("getRoomInfo returned: " + val.name + ", " + val.pwd);

        // If name and pwd are null, the room no longer exists; notify all clients.
        if ((val.name == null) && (val.pwd == null)) {
          trace("This room doesn't exist any more");
          this.mc.roomDeleted();
```

```
      return;
    }
    // Save the name and pwd in global variables.
    application.roomName = val.name;
    application.roomPwd = val.pwd;

    // Notify all clients of the room name now that we know it.
    for (var i = 0; i < application.clients.length; i++)
      application.clients[i].call("setRoomName", null, application.roomName);
  };
  this.call("getRoomInfo", res);
}
else if (info.code == "NetConnection.Connect.Closed") {
  // Connection lost, reconnect.
  connectToLobby( );
}
};

// Called by lobby.asc when somebody deletes this room
// or by the preceding result object if getRoomInfo() returns {null, null}
application.toLobby_nc.roomDeleted = function ( ) {
  application.roomDeleted = true;
  trace("This room has been deleted");

  // Notify all clients (they will disconnect themselves).
  for (var i = 0; i < application.clients.length; i++)
    application.clients[i].call("roomDeleted", null);
};

// Create a permanent RTMP connection with the lobby.
connectToLobby( );
};
```

First, we define a global function that just connects the room's application instance to the lobby.

In *onAppStart( )*, the code first sets the roomDeleted flag to false. Then it creates a server-to-server *NetConnection* to the lobby application (application.toLobby_nc). Just as we would if the room instance were a Flash client, we define an *onStatus( )* handler on the *NetConnection* object. If the *onStatus( )* handler notices that the *NetConnection* has been lost, it calls *connectToLobby( )* to reconnect immediately. If the connection is successful, the room application instance immediately issues a server-to-server call, which invokes *getRoomInfo( )* on the lobby, to find out its name and password. The *getRoomInfo( )* function is defined in *lobby.asc*, as shown in the previous section. The code saves the results from *getRoomInfo( )* in the global application.roomName and application.roomPwd variables. Because remote procedure calls are asynchronous, once we get the room name, we notify all the clients we might have accepted in the meantime, with the server-to-client call *setRoomName( )*. If the result is {null, null}, it means that the room has been deleted in the meantime, so we tell each client to disconnect itself by calling the *roomDeleted( )* method described later.

Next, we need to define a *roomDeleted( )* method on this *NetConnection*, so that *lobby.asc* can notify us if this room gets deleted. In *roomDeleted( )*, we set the roomDeleted flag to true, then we loop through all the connected clients and make a server-to-client call to the *roomDeleted( )* method defined in *room.as*. That method will make the clients disconnect themselves after displaying a message.

Next we need to define an *onConnect( )* method for *room.asc*:

```
application.onConnect = function (client) {
  if (application.roomDeleted) {
    application.rejectConnection(client, {message: "This room no longer exists"});
    return;
  }

  application.acceptConnection(client);

  // If getRoomInfo() already returned, pass the room name to this client.
  if (this.roomName != undefined)
    client.call("setRoomName", null, this.roomName);

  // A client is not considered to be in the room until the user
  // enters the correct password.
  client.inRoom = false;
};
```

This code first checks whether the room has been deleted. If so, we reject the connection with a feedback message and return. Otherwise, we accept the connection, and if the *getRoomInfo( )* call already returned (i.e., if application.roomName is already defined), we call *setRoomName( )* on this client. If this is not the case, *setRoomName( )* will be called on the client when *getRoomInfo( )* returns, as we saw in the *onAppStart( )* function. Last, we set the inRoom flag to false; although the connection has been accepted, the user is not considered in the room until she submits a valid password.

The asynchronous nature of the room-to-lobby (server-to-server) connection is a tricky point, which is best explained with the sequence diagrams in Figure 9-5 and Figure 9-6. Figure 9-5 shows the execution flow when a user connects to a room instance that's not already running. As the user connects, *application.onAppStart( )* is triggered right before *application.onConnect( )*. The room's *onAppStart( )* method performs an asynchronous *NetConnection.connect( )* to connect to the lobby instance, and the *onConnect( )* method accepts the client's connection before the server-to-server connection is established (*onStatus( )* isn't invoked yet). When the *onStatus* event finally arrives, the room calls *getRoomInfo( )* on the lobby, which is also an asynchronous call. Only when the call returns do we decide what to do. We either notify the connected client that the room was deleted (through server-to-client calls to *roomDeleted( )*), or we tell the client the room name (through server-to-client calls to *setRoomName( )*).

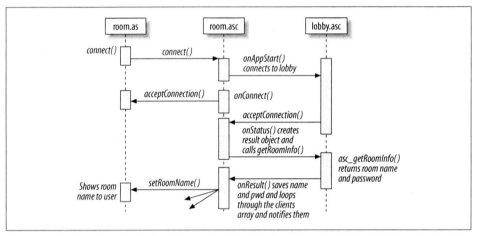

Figure 9-5. Sequence diagram for connecting to a room that's not already running

The execution flow for a second client that connects to the already running application instance is much simpler as shown in Figure 9-6. Because the room already knows its name and password (from the previous execution of *getRoomInfo( )*), the *onConnect( )* handler can simply decide what to call on the client that's trying to connect (either reject the connection if the room has been deleted or call *setRoomName( )* right after accepting the new client's connection).

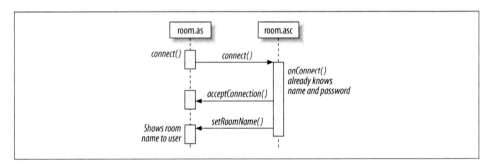

Figure 9-6. Sequence diagram for connecting to a room that's already running

Next, we define an *onDisconnect( )* function for *room.asc*:

```
application.onDisconnect = function (client) {
  trace("onDisconnect");
  if (application.roomDeleted)
    return;

  // If the client was counted within the room, tell the lobby to decrease
  // the occupant count when he leaves.
```

```
    if (client.inRoom)
      this.toLobby_nc.call("personLeft");
};
```

If the room has been deleted since a client connected, the code simply returns. Otherwise, if this client is already included in the occupant count for this room, we make a server-to-server call to the lobby to tell it that a person has left this room.

To finish our server-side *room.asc* code, we attach a function to `Client.prototype`, so that clients can call it to submit a password:

```
// Called by the client
Client.prototype.verifyPassword = function (pwd) {
  if (pwd == application.roomPwd) {
    // Password is correct; this client is now in the room.
    this.inRoom = true;
    // Tell the lobby to increase the occupant count for this room.
    application.toLobby_nc.call("personJoined");
    return true;
  } else
    return false;
};
```

The *verifyPassword( )* handler checks the submitted password against the one returned by *getRoomInfo( )*. If the password is valid, the code sets the inRoom flag to true, and we tell the lobby (through another server-to-server call) that another person has joined this room.

That concludes our example. As is often the case when developing multiuser client/server applications, it feels as if all the different methods are like pieces in a puzzle, and one cannot see the full picture until all the pieces are in place.

This, and the asynchronous nature of remote calls, are perhaps the biggest challenges of developing client/server applications. We encourage you to ponder the previous example until you understand it fully, as it encompasses most of the concepts you will ever face when making use of remote procedures calls in client-side and Server-Side ActionScript.

Debugging Calls

Debugging in Flash is relatively difficult, and trying to debug client/server interactions is even harder. Luckily, some helpful tools and methods are built into the communication objects' classes.

The Communication App Inspector Is Your Best Friend

For any FlashCom developer, the Communication App Inspector—as described in Chapter 4 under "Testing and Debugging Server-Side Script Files"—is an irreplaceable tool for debugging every aspect of your client/server applications. When dealing with remote calls, it is important to know if your client-to-server or server-to-server calls are getting triggered at the right time, with the right number of arguments, or if your server-to-client calls are failing for any reason. The App Inspector's Live Log tab displays the output from any *trace( )* statements in SSAS, which helps monitor and debug all these interactions.

A handy trick is to create a shortcut to *app_inspector.swf* (usually found in the *flashcom_help\html\admin* folder under your server's directory). This will give you one-click access to the App Inspector, even when the Flash authoring tool is not running, and will let you open more than one instance of it easily.

Let's look at some common errors and ways to fix them.

Error: msg sent before connection established

If you see the error message "Error: msg sent before connection established" in your application's live log in the App Inspector, you have a flaw in your server-side code logic. Most often, this means that you tried to invoke a method on a client before accepting the connection from that client.

This code, for instance, will trigger that warning:

```
application.onConnect = function (client) {
  // This is wrong.
  client.call("test", null, 123);
  application.acceptConnection(client);
};
```

The correct code would have the order of the *Client.call( )* and *application.acceptConnection( )* calls reversed; you need to accept a client's connection before making server-to-client calls on that client. The error might look pretty obvious in the preceding example, but the connection logic could be much more complex (as we will see in Chapter 18), so having the server warn us when we accidentally call a method on a client before we accept its connection is very useful.

The same error message is also triggered if you try to make a server-to-client call to a client that no longer exists (i.e., after it disconnects).

Debugging Server-to-Server Calls

When debugging server-to-server calls, it's very useful to open two instances of the App Inspector and put them side by side, one looking at the calling instance's logs, the other at the responding instance's logs. It's a small trick, but invaluable when debugging server-to-server calls.

Trapping onStatus Whenever Possible

ActionScript, on both the client and server sides, provides methods to debug your application and deal with runtime failures. The main debugging tool for remote method invocations is trapping the *onStatus* event in an *onStatus( )* handler.

Look at this example of a client-to-server call:

```
var resObj = new Object( );
resObj.onResult = function (val) {
  trace("The time on the server is:" + val);
  _root.serverTime_txt.text = val;
};
resObj.onStatus = function (info) {
  trace("getServerTime.onStatus: " + info.code);
  for (var i in info)
    trace("  " + i + ": " + info[i]);
};
nc.call("getServerTime", resObj);
```

It's the same example we saw at the beginning of this chapter, but with an *onStatus( )* method added to the result object. This method will get called by the Flash Player whenever there's a problem with the call.

The same technique (defining an *onStatus( )* method on the result object) applies to Server-Side ActionScript, but with a twist. On the server side, in fact, *Client.call( )* returns a Boolean value, which tells us whether the call was sent or failed immediately. Look at this example:

```
AreYouOkResultHandler = function (clientID) {
  this.clientID = clientID;
};
AreYouOkResultHandler.onResult = function (val) {
  trace("Client " + this.clientID + " returned " + val);
};
AreYouOkResultHandler.onStatus = function (info) {
  trace("Call to areYouOk to " + this.clientID
        + " failed asynchronously: " + info.code);
};

application.someFunction = function (client, clientID) {
  var callSent = client.call("areYouOk",
                 new AreYouOkResultHandler(clientID));
  if (!callSent)
    trace("Call to areYouOk to " + clientID + " failed synchronously!");
};
```

Notice how we deal with potential failures in two different ways: we create an *onStatus( )* method on the result object, which will get called if there is a problem with the execution of the call; furthermore, we use the callSent variable to check the return value of the call, which tells us whether the call executed at all. The return value may be false if the server has already disconnected the client we are trying to invoke, for example.

The info object returned as a parameter to the *onStatus( )* call (on both the client and server sides) contains the following properties:

code
> Will have the value "NetConnection.Call.Failed" if an error occurred

description
> Will have the value "Method not found (methodname)" if the method was not defined; will have the value "Failed to execute method (methodname)" if the execution of the remote method generated a runtime error

level
> Will be "error"

If you don't need the fine granularity of having a different *onStatus( )* handler for each result call, you can define a global *onStatus( )* handler and attach it to your *Net-Connection* object on the client side and to the application object on the server side. This will trap all errors that aren't caught by per-call *onStatus( )* handlers. Look at this server-side code, for example:

```
application.onStatus = function (info) {
  for (var i in info)
    trace("-" + i + ": " + info[i]);
};
```

Because this is a more generic *onStatus( )* handler, which catches all sorts of application-wide errors, the info object on the server side will have slightly different values:

code
> Will have the value "Application.Script.Error" if an error occurred

description
> Will have the value "Method not found (_error:69882672)" if the method was not found or the method generated a runtime error

level
> Will be "error" in case of an error; "status" otherwise

Hopefully you will find these debugging techniques helpful in diagnosing application problems, resulting in more error-resilient code.

Advanced Topics

Now that you know how remote methods in FlashCom work, you're ready for the fun stuff! This section covers some advanced topics and offers tips on how to really use RMI in FlashCom to its fullest potential.

Passing Variable Numbers of Arguments

One common trick to achieve polymorphism (calling the same function with a variable number of arguments) in ActionScript is the use of the arguments object to create methods that can have a variable number of arguments passed in.

For example, you can invoke the following *addNumbers( )* function with differing numbers of parameters:

```
function addNumbers( ) {
  var res = 0;
  for (var i = 0; i < arguments.length; i++)
    res += arguments[i];
  return res;
}
```

For example:

```
var sum = addNumbers(1, 2);
var sum = addNumbers(10, 9, 8, 7, 123, 42, 456, 76, 3453, 56, 0, 345);
```

In client-side ActionScript (including methods attached to *NetConnection*), the arguments property can be treated like an array. It contains the parameters passed into the function.

In SSAS, arguments is a hash table with a special .length property, not an array, so it must be looped through manually if you want to create an array out of it.

A different kind of polymorphism can be reached in client-to-server calls by writing a simple "proxy" method to other methods. The following server-side code example shows how to create a method on the *Client* object that calls any method on the application instance, using the *apply( )* method:

```
Client.prototype.makeCall = function (methodName /* , p1, p2, ...pn*/) {
  var params = new Array( );
  params.push(this);
  for (var i = 1; i < arguments.length; i++)
    params.push(arguments[i]);

  return application[methodName].apply(application, params);
};
```

Notice how the arguments are transformed in a proper array by looping through them and how a reference to the calling client (this) is inserted as a first parameter to the call.

So, for example, if your application has the following two methods:

```
application.getClientStats = function (clientObj) {
  return clientObj.getStats( );
};

application.setUserInfo = function (clientObj, name, age, height) {
  clientObj.name   = name;
```

```
    clientObj.age    = age;
    clientObj.height = height;
};
```

you can call them like this:

```
nc.call("makeCall", res, "getClientStats");
nc.call("makeCall", null, "setUsername", "MyName", 29, "185 cm");
```

Notice the client-to-server polymorphism—you are executing the same call (*make-Call( )*), but with a variable number of arguments; *makeCall( )*, in turn, passes the arguments to the method you want to call.

Inserting a reference to the calling client as a first parameter allows the called method to read client-specific variables or make a server-to-client call on the reference.

For a more elaborate example of how to use the arguments object on the server side, search for "arguments" in some of the communication component framework's server-side files: *framework.asc*, *facade.asc*, and *application.asc*. Of particular interest is the *__toArray__( )* method, which converts the arguments object into a real array, so that other array functions such as *concat( )* can be used with it.

Making Calls Without Waiting for connect( )

There is a little-known feature in the Flash Player that allows you to make client-to-server calls on the *NetConnection* even before the *NetConnection* is established. For example, the following code will work:

```
nc = new NetConnection( );
nc.connect("rtmp:/test");
nc.call("myCall", null);
```

This code makes the asynchronous operation of connecting to the server look synchronous. It creates the *NetConnection*, connects, and makes a call, all without waiting. The Flash Player does the queuing up for us, delivering the call on the server side only after the connection handshake has completed.

While this feature makes programming for FlashCom more approachable to beginning client/server coders, it is not a best practice. What if the server decides to reject our connection? Our calls will have failed by the time we find out about it (in the *onStatus( )* handler, if we took the trouble to define one). To work around it, we would have to define a queue of calls invoked before the connection was established, which takes us back to square one.

 The best practice is to wait to make additional calls from *onStatus( )* after checking whether the *connect( )* call succeeded.

The following code shows how to implement the operation consistent with best practices:

```
nc = new NetConnection();
nc.onStatus = function (info) {
  if (info.code == "NetConnection.Connect.Success") {
    setUp();
  }
  // ...other code to handle failure modes.
};
nc.connect("rtmp:/test");

function setUp () {
  nc.call("myCall",null);
  // ...any other code that should run only if the connection is successful.
}
```

The code first creates a *NetConnection* object, then defines an *onStatus( )* handler on it. The *onStatus( )* handler calls a global *setUp( )* function only once and only if the connection is established. Calling *connect( )* on the *NetConnection* triggers *onStatus( )* when the call completes. Therefore, *setUp( )* isn't called until after the *connect( )* call succeeds.

As Chapters 5 and 8 discussed, you can make calls on streams and shared objects before the connection is established as well, though we wouldn't recommend it as a best practice.

This feature is most commonly used on shared objects with occasionally connected applications such as Macromedia Central.

Reusing Result Objects

A good way to save memory is to reuse the same result object for more than one call. After defining it once, you can use it multiple times. Consider the following example in which the result object is defined only once:

```
var res = new Object();
res.onResult = function (val) {
  trace("Returned:" + val);
};
function doCall () {
  nc.call("doCall", res, _global.index++);
}
doCall();
doCall();
doCall();
```

Contrast the preceding code with the following. They do the same thing, but this code creates a new result object inside *doCall( )*:

```
function doCall () {
  var res = new Object();
```

```
      res.onResult = function (val) {
        trace("Returned:" + val);
      };
      nc.call("doCall", res, _global.index++);
    }
    doCall( );
    doCall( );
    doCall( );
```

The first bit of code is more efficient because it defines the result object only once, while the second example creates a new result object for every call we make to *doCall( )*.

Calling obj1/obj2/method and obj1.obj2.method

A very handy feature of FlashCom is the automatic resolution of complex method names.

As we have seen before, calling *nc.call("someMethod")* on the client side will invoke *someMethod( )* on the instance of the *Client* object in the server-side script. Consider this server-side code in which we define a *UserPreferences* object; the code creates an instance (userPrefs) and attaches it to the instance of the *Client* object for the client connecting to the application:

```
    function UserPreferences (client) {
      this.client = client;
    }
    UserPreferences.prototype.setName = function (name) {
      this.name = name;
    };
    UserPreferences.prototype.getName = function () {
      return this.name;
    };

    application.onConnect = function (client) {
      client.userPrefs = new UserPreferences(client);
      application.acceptConnection(client);
    };
```

Thanks to the automatic resolution of method names, we can invoke this code from the client side as follows:

```
    nc.call("userPrefs.setName", null, "Dave");
    nc.call("userPrefs/getName", res);
```

and everything will magically work! There is no need to build wrapper methods to relay the invocation; the server automatically finds the userPrefs object attached to the calling client and invokes *setName( )* and *getName( )* on it. Using the dot (.) or the slash (/) is equivalent in client-to-server calls.

This also works for server-to-client calls, but the dot (.) syntax is not allowed. You have to use the slash (/) to delimit objects when making a server-to-client call.

Nesting works too, so you can call "userPrefs/memberObj1/memberObj2/function-Name". There is no set limit to how many levels of nesting you can have, but your machine's RAM will eventually run out! Also, if you need that many levels of nesting, you may want to consider restructuring your code.

Consider again the server-side code for the earlier lobby/rooms example. This code:

```
// Attach only the methods we want to this client.
client.getRoomInfo = asc_getRoomInfo;
client.personJoined = asc_personJoined;
client.personLeft = asc_personLeft;
```

would be a lot cleaner if we encapsulated those three methods in a *RoomHandlers* object, saved in a separate *.asc* file, like this:

```
RoomHandlers = function () { };
RoomHandlers.prototype.getRoomInfo   = function () { /* same code as before */ };
RoomHandlers.prototype.personJoined  = function () { /* same code as before */ };
RoomHandlers.prototype.personLeft    = function () { /* same code as before */ };
```

This would make the *lobby.asc* file a lot cleaner to read. Then all we'd have to do to attach the three methods to the client object is:

```
client.roomHandlers = new RoomHandlers();
```

Then whenever *room.asc* wants to call any of these methods, it would just have to prepend the roomHandlers name to the call, like this:

```
application.toLobby_nc.call("roomHandlers/personJoined");
```

Routing Remote Calls Through a Common Function

Sometimes it's useful to define one big method that operates as a "bottleneck" for function calls that have something in common. Imagine wanting to localize your application and have all the strings accessed through the same function or wanting to have all your *trace( )* statements pass through one function, so that they can all be turned off by commenting out one line of code. You can put the common code in the "router" function and write smaller, cleaner subfunctions. Here's an example of a client-side router function, which gets invoked every time something goes wrong on the server side:

```
nc.serverSideError = function (code, title, msg) {
  hideRegularUI();
  showErrorUI();

  switch (code) {
    case 100: // Remoting error
      showErrorMessage(title, msg, "Retry");
      break;
    case 200: // Script error
      showErrorMessage(title, msg, "Quit");
      nc.close();
      break;
```

```
            case 300: // Disconnect yourself
               showErrorMessage("You have been ejected",
                     "User " + msg + " has removed you from the room", "");
               break;
            default:
               trace("Unknown server-side error code:" + code);
         }
      };
```

This function could be called by the server in any of the following ways:

```
      client.call("serverSideError", null, 100, "Remoting Error 103",
               "There was an error executing xyz call");

      System.onStatus = function () {
         for (var i = 0; i < application.clients.length; i++)
            application.clients[i].call("serverSideError", null, 200,
                  "Script Error!", info.code);
      };

      client.call("serverSideError", null, 300, "", "Peldi");
```

Here's a similar example of a server-side router method, called by clients to perform some operation on another user:

```
      Client.prototype.updateUser = function (command, userID, param2) {
         switch (command) {
            case "delete":
               application.users_so.setProperty(userID, null);
               break;
            case "change-name":
               var userObj = application.users_so.getProperty(userID);
               userObj.name = param2;
               application.users_so.setProperty(userID, userObj);
               break;
            case "promote":
               application.updateRole(userID, param2);
               break;
            default:
               trace("Unknown command " + command);
         }
         application.clientsByID[userID].isDirty = true;
      };
```

which could be invoked by clients in a number of ways:

```
      nc.call("updateUser", null, "delete", 3);
      nc.call("updateUser", null, "change-name", 1, "Sam");
      nc.call("updateUser", null, "promote", 2, "admin");
```

You get the idea. For more information about design patterns in FlashCom applications, refer to Chapter 15.

Using a Façade Method on the Server-Side

A façade pattern allows you to group method calls within one or more simpler method calls so that you do not have to make repeated RMI calls to do a complex transaction. In other words, you call one function across the network that calls several functions on the server one at a time, processing intermediate results if necessary.

A façade method on the server side can be very helpful. Imagine the following examples:

- In a complex, componentized application, such as Breeze Live, a user promotes another user to "presenter" status. Here a single client-to-server call to an *updateRole(id, role)* façade method could do the trick. The *updateRole( )* method would then notify the server side of each component that the role of user ID has changed, without having each client-side portion of each component make a *set-Role( )* client-to-server call itself.

- A connection component is charged with setting up all other components in an application. A simple approach would be to have each component set up its server-side portion with a *connect( )* call. A façade approach would call a *setUp(componentsArray)* function on the server side only once, which would then call *connect( )* on the server-side portion of each component in the array.

> Because RMI calls are so slow compared to code execution, you should strive to minimize their number. Façade methods on the server side are often the solution.

___resolve( ) and apply( )

Perhaps the most powerful feature of Server-Side ActionScript is the *__resolve( )* method, which is invoked every time a non-defined method is called or an undefined property is accessed on the server side (by a server-side script or a client call). It's a "last chance" that the server gives us before failing, either with a script error or with a "Method not found" error. Here's an example that will make it clear. On the client side, we have this code, which attempts to invoke *myCall( )* on the server:

```
nc = new NetConnection();
nc.connect("rtmp:/test");
nc.call("myCall", null, "test", true);
nc.call("myCall", null, "two", false);
```

Assume that on the server side we don't have a *myCall( )* method defined. If we run this code, we would get a "Method not found (myCall)" error on the server side and a "NetConnection.Call.Failed" error on the client side.

Now let's add the following __resolve( ) handler to the server-side code *Client* proto-type:

```
Client.prototype.__resolve = function (name) {
  trace("__resolve " + name);
  Client.prototype[name] = function (a, b) {
    trace(name + "! " + a + "," + b);
  };
  return Client.prototype[name];
};
```

Reload the application, restart the client-side movie, and you will see the following server-side traces:

```
__resolve myCall
myCall! test,true
myCall! two,false
```

What's happening? The first time we call *myCall( )* from the client, the method is not found on the server, so __resolve( ) is invoked on the *Client* object. The parameter automatically passed to the __resolve( ) function is the name of the undefined method. We trace it, then we define a function with that name on the fly, attaching it to the Client.prototype object. In the __resolve( ) method, you should always return something that has the same type of what you were looking for. In this case, __resolve( ) was invoked because of a missing method, so we return the method we just created.

The next time we call *myCall( )*, the __resolve( ) method doesn't even get triggered, because now Client.prototype already has a method called *myCall( )*—it's the one we created in the __resolve( ) method!—so it just gets invoked.

This feature, combined with the arguments object, can be used to create very powerful automatic call routing based on naming schemes. Perhaps the best-known example of code that does just this is the *facade.asc* file that is part of the communication components server-side framework, which you can find in the *scriptlib* folder of your FlashCom installation.

Using call( ) and send( ) together

Sometimes server-to-client calls are more easily achieved using *SharedObject.send( )*. Look at the *sendMessage( )* method in *chat.asc* in your *scriptlib/components* folder, for example. This method is used to broadcast a new chat message from a client to all the other clients:

```
// Send a message to all others participating in the chat session.
FCChat.prototype.sendMessage = function (client, mesg) {
  mesg = this.hiliteURLs(mesg);
  // ...some other code.
  this.message_so.send("message", mesg);
};Whenever a client hits
```

Whenever a client hits the Send button in the chat session, *sendMessage( )* is invoked through a client-to-server call. The message is checked for URLs, appended to the chat history, and broadcast to all the clients connected to the application, using:

```
this.message_so.send("message", mesg);
```

If you wanted to use server-to-client calls instead, you would have to loop through the application.clients array, like this:

```
for (var i = 0; i < application.clients.length; i++)
  application.clients[i].call("message", null, mesg);
```

which would require each client to have a *message( )* method attached to its *NetConnection* object. Using *SharedObject.send( )* is simpler. Because we know that all the clients looking at the chat are subscribed to the message_so shared object, we can just invoke *send( )* on it and define a *message( )* method on it on the client side.

This saves us a loop, but doesn't give us the same fine granularity. We might, for example, want to send a message to a subset of clients (private messages or messages to presenters). In that case, looping through the application.clients array is the way to go (so that you can perform checks on each client object):

```
for (var i = 0; i < application.clients.length; i++) {
  if (application.clients[i].role == "presenter") {
    application.clients[i].call("message", null, mesg);
  }
}
```

Using application.registerProxy( )

Here's a problem. Let's suppose you are designing a large application distributed across multiple servers and the client isn't connected directly to a given application instance on another server. How do you make a client-to-server call to your server-side script, have it make a server-to-server call to another application instance, and return the result to the client?

Well, with the knowledge you have gained in this chapter, this shouldn't be too hard to solve. Here's the client-side code:

```
nc = new NetConnection( );
nc.owner = this;
nc.onStatus = function (info:Object):Void {
  if (info.code == "NetConnection.Connect.Success")
    this.owner.setUp( );
};
nc.connect("rtmp://127.0.0.1/myApp");

this.setUp = function ( ) {
  nc.regularAddResult = function (val) {
    trace("regularAddResult:" + val);
  };
  nc.call("regularAdd", null, 4, 5);
};
```

Here's the server-side script for the first application, *myApp*:

```
application.onAppStart = function () {
  this.nc = new NetConnection();
  this.nc.connect("rtmp://127.0.0.1/otherApp/");
};
Client.prototype.regularAdd = function (a, b) {
  res = new Object();
  res.client = this;
  res.onResult = function (val) {
    this.client.call("regularAddResult", null, val);
  };
  application.nc.call("regularAdd", res, a, b);
};
```

And here's the server-side script for *otherApp*:

```
Client.prototype.regularAdd = function (a, b) {
  return (a + b);
};
```

The client calls *regularAdd( )* on *myApp*, which in turn calls *regularAdd( )* on *otherApp*, grabbing the result. Then, in order to pass the result to the client, *myApp* needs to make a server-to-client call to *regularAddResult( )*.

One very little known feature of FlashCom named *application.registerProxy( )* allows you to solve the problem with a lot less code.

Here's the revised client-side code:

```
nc = new NetConnection();
nc.owner = this;
nc.onStatus = function (info:Object):Void {
  if (info.code == "NetConnection.Connect.Success")
    this.owner.setUp();
};
nc.connect("rtmp://127.0.0.1/myApp");

this.setUp = function () {
  res = new Object();
  res.onResult = function (val) {
    trace("onResult:" + val);
  };
  nc.call("doAdd", res, 2, 3);
};
```

Here's the *myApp* server-side code:

```
application.onAppStart = function () {
  this.nc = new NetConnection();
  this.nc.onStatus = function (info) {
    if (info.code == "NetConnection.Connect.Success")
      application.registerProxy("doAdd", this);
  };
  this.nc.connect("rtmp://127.0.0.1/otherApp/");
};
```

And here's the *otherApp* server-side code:

```
Client.prototype.doAdd = function (a, b) {
  return a + b;
};
```

In this revised version, when the client calls *doAdd( )*, it can specify a result object, and the result of *doAdd( )* on *otherApp* will be automatically proxied from *otherApp* to *myApp*, all thanks to *application.registerProxy( )*.

The *registerProxy( )* method also takes a third parameter, so that your methods can have different names in different application instances. For example, we could change the call to *registerProxy( )* as follows:

```
application.registerProxy("doAdd", this, "addTwoNumbers");
```

and have the code of *otherApp* be:

```
Client.prototype.addTwoNumbers = function (a, b) {
  return a + b;
};
```

The second parameter passed to *registerProxy( )* can be either a reference to a *Net-Connection* connected to another application instance or a reference to a client connected to the application. This way you could have one client execute some methods, having other clients thinking that they are executing methods on the server side.

This technique is useful to offload call processing to another client or instance. For example, you could choose to do the script processing of all database-related methods in an instance specifically set up to handle that task. You could do the same thing in Server-Side ActionScript, but using *registerProxy( )* on a client is convenient and sometimes faster to develop (you might already have a standalone client-side application that talks to a database). Simply modify the code to connect to Flash-Com and use *registerProxy( )* to register the database-related functions for other clients to use.

Passing Objects as Parameters

An extremely rarely used feature of FlashCom allows you to pass full-fledged typed objects as parameters to a client-to-server or server-to-client call.

To understand this feature, let's build an example of the *command design pattern*, in which commands are sent to a dispatcher that executes them blindly. Usually in the command pattern, there is a Command interface like this:

```
interface Command {
  public function execute(Void):Void;
}
```

and command classes that implement it. Here's an example:

```
class SetUpGlobalsCommand implements Command {
  private var m_name:String;
  private var m_id:Number;

  // Constructor
  function SetUpGlobalsCommand (name:String, id:Number) {
    m_name = name;
    m_id = id;
  }

  public function execute (Void):Void {
    // Do something
  }
}
```

Another example command could be the following:

```
class ResetAllColorsCommand implements Command {
  // Constructor
  function ResetAllColorsCommand (Void) {
  }

  public function execute (Void):Void {
    // Do something
  }
}
```

Now imagine wanting to implement the command pattern with the preceding commands coming from the server side and going to a client. First, let's build it using the methods already described in this chapter.

This could be your server-to-client call to trigger *SetUpGlobalsCommand( )*:

```
aClient.call("commandDispatcher", null, {type:"setUpGlobals", name:"Brian", id:0});
```

The *ResetAllColorsCommand( )* method could be invoked like this:

```
aClient.call("commandDispatcher", null, {type:"resetAllColors"});
```

The client-side handler for both calls would look like something like this:

```
nc.commandDispatcher = function (cmdRecord) {
  switch (cmdRecord.type) {
    case "setUpGlobals":
    var newCommand = SetUpGlobalsCommand(cmdRecord.name, cmdRecord.id);
    newCommand.execute();
    break;
    case "resetAllColors":
    var newCommand = ResetAllColorsCommand();
    newCommand.execute();
    break;
  }
}
```

As you can see, the type property of the record passed as a parameter is used to determine which command to instantiate and execute.

Passing typed objects as parameters offers another way to solve the same problem.

Look at this server-side script:

```
function SetUpGlobalsCommand (name, id) {
  this.m_name = name;
  this.m_id = id;
}
application.registerClass("SetUpGlobalsCommand", SetUpGlobalsCommand);

function ResetAllColorsCommand () {
}
application.registerClass("ResetAllColorsCommand", ResetAllColorsCommand);
```

Basically, the code creates two objects and uses *application.registerClass( )* to tell FlashCom to serialize the constructor of these classes when passing instances of them as parameters to remote calls.

 Only the constructor gets serialized, so there is no point in defining an *execute( )* method on these classes here (unless of course you want to use the commands on the server side as well). Remember that no methods get passed through, only the constructor and the class members that are assigned in it.

Here's what the server-to-client calls would look like now:

```
aClient.call("commandDispatcher", new SetUpGlobalsCommand("Brian", 0));
aClient.call("commandDispatcher", new ResetAllColorsCommand( ));
```

Notice how we pass class instances instead of simple objects. This is what the client-side code would look like now:

```
nc.commandDispatcher = function (cmdInstance) {
  cmdInstance.execute( );
}
```

The Flash Player will automatically create an instance of the appropriate class when deserializing the parameter, so all that's left to do is call *execute( )* on it.

See how much simpler the handler gets? Okay, admittedly, not that much simpler. We told you this feature was used extremely rarely.

You can pass typed objects in a similar fashion in client-to-server calls. For an example, refer to the *Server-Side Communication ActionScript Dictionary* documentation that comes with FlashCom.

Conclusion

We've covered a tremendous amount in the short span of this chapter. We've seen ways that FlashCom can invoke methods remotely (from client to server or server to client). Furthermore, we've seen how to broadcast method calls to every movie and application instance connected to a shared object or stream, or send them to and from individual movies. We've even seen how an application instance can create proxies of methods belonging to another application instance.

After reading this chapter, you should understand the different RMI methods. With practice or the advice of colleagues, you'll get better at deciding which approach to use for your given situation. We covered a lot of practical examples such as requesting specific information from the server or a client. We also studied the framework of a Lobby/Rooms application to give you both theoretical understanding and a working knowledge of this complex topic. Toward the end of the chapter, we covered monitoring, debugging, and optimization techniques, because RMI calls can be significantly slower than local code execution.

In the next three chapters, we'll use remote method invocation extensively. Chapter 11 covers the powerful Server Management API, which allows a Flash client to perform administrative functions remotely. Chapters 12 and 13 use Flash Remoting and ColdFusion to extend the power of FlashCom with access to remote scripts and databases.

CHAPTER 10

Server Management API

The FlashCom Server installation includes an additional application that is used to administer the server and the installed applications. If you use the Communication App Inspector (*app_inspector.swf*) or the Administration Console (*admin.swf*), you are already familiar with some of the tasks that can be performed by the FlashCom Admin Service, which was introduced in Chapter 1. With the Admin Service, you can inspect all running applications, get vital statistics on the resources that the server and applications are consuming, and perform most of the server configurations. The Admin Service also gives access to the NetConnection Debugger as shown in Figure 3-3. The debugger can be used to see the messages sent across the wire to diagnose any problems.

 Impressively, Macromedia provides a complete ActionScript API to the features of the Admin Service. This allows you to create administrative applications that run as Flash movies on the client. These applications are typically for testing and administration, but you can also access features that give powerful control over the FlashCom Server, applications, instances, and users. See "Server Management API Uses" at the end of the chapter for more ideas.

Let's first see how to establish a connection. We'll explore more about what you can do with the Admin Service later under "Using the Server Management API."

Connecting to the Admin Service

Connecting to the Admin Service is nearly as simple as connecting to a FlashCom Server application. The connection to the Admin Service is protected with a username and password. These credentials are set in the *Server.xml* configuration file. This file is located in the *conf* directory in the Macromedia Flash Communication Server MX installation folder.

By default, the encrypt attribute in the Password node is true. This controls whether the password is encrypted in the configuration file. Since the password is encrypted by default, you cannot open the file to recover a lost password. To create a new password, you can set the encrypt attribute to "false" and enter a new password for the value of the node:

```
<Server>
  <UserList>
    <User name="admin">
      <Password encrypt="false">adminPassword</Password>
    </User>
  </UserList>
</Server>
```

After resetting the password, you can log on with the new password using the Administration Console (*admin.swf*). Then use the Administration Console to change your password, which will automatically rewrite the *Server.xml* configuration file with the new password encrypted. The password is always encrypted when set via the Server Management API with *changePswd( )*.

The *NetConnection* class is used to create the connection to the Admin Service, and the username and password must be passed to the *NetConnection.connect( )* method. The Admin Service listens on a different port than the FlashCom Server. The Admin Service listens on port 1111 and you must specify the port in the connection string passed to the *connect( )* method. The options to change the Admin Service port are discussed later. The following example illustrates how to connect to the Admin Service on a FlashCom Server.

Example 10-1 shows how to connect to the Admin Service. You need to specify the port (1111) in the call to *NetConnection.connect( )* so that Flash connects to the Admin Service and not a different FlashCom application. You do not need to specify any application name or instance path at the end of the RTMP string (in fact, if you do, it will be ignored), because there is only once instance of the Admin Service.

Example 10-1. Establishing the Admin Service connection

```
adminConnection = new NetConnection( );
adminConnection.onStatus = function (info) {
  if (info.code == "NetConnection.Connect.Success") {
    trace("The connection was successful");
  } else {
    trace(info.code + newline + info.description);
  }
};
adminConnection.connect("rtmp://host.com:1111", "username", "password");
```

The success code returned from the Admin Service in the information object passed to the *onStatus( )* handler is "NetConnection.Connect.Success", the same string returned when establishing a FlashCom connection.

As stated earlier, the default port of the Admin Service is 1111, which there is no compelling reason to change. Nonetheless, this port can be changed in the *Server. xml* configuration file. The <HostPort> tag allows you to set the IP address and port to bind the Admin Service to:

```
<HostPort>192.168.1.10:1111</HostPort>
```

If your server has multiple IP addresses and you want the Admin Service to respond to all of them, omit the IP address, and just specify the port preceded by a colon:

```
<HostPort>:1111</HostPort>
```

Changing the port will not add any security to the Admin Service; it will only increase the amount of time an attacker needs to find the port. You definitely should restrict access to the Admin Service by either network configuration or system configuration so only the approved list of IP addresses can connect to the admin port. If you are hosting a public FlashCom Server, you can use a firewall to deny access to the Admin Service to either a single IP address or a range of IP addresses, depending on the capabilities of the firewall. Additional configuration settings for each admin user can be set to control access in the *Server.xml*. For example:

```
<Server>
  <UserList>
    <User name="admin">
      <Password encrypt="false">adminPassword</Password>
    <Allow>192.168.1</Allow>
    <Deny>192.168.1.100</Deny>
    <Order>Allow,Deny</Order>
    </User>
  </UserList>
</Server>
```

The <Allow> tag lets you specify a domain name, a subnet, or IP addresses that can access the Admin Service with that username. You can specify multiple entries, separated by commas, in the <Allow> tag. The <Deny> tag has the opposite effect of the <Allow> tag; <Deny> lets you specify addresses that cannot access the Admin Service.

The <Order> tag controls how the <Allow> and <Deny> tags are applied. If the <Order> tag is set to Allow,Deny, all IP addresses listed in the <Allow> tag will have access except for those specified in the <Deny> tag. This lets you specify a broad subnet in the <Allow> tag and further restrict specific IP addresses in the <Deny> tag. If the <Order> tag is set to Deny,Allow, all connections will be allowed access unless they are specifically listed in the <Deny> tag. In this case, the <Allow> tag lets you specify IP addresses to which to grant access even if they are in a denied subnet.

Clearly, setting the <Order> tag to Allow,Deny provides greater security, as you have to then specify which IP addresses or ranges can access the Admin Service.

Note that <Allow>, <Deny>, and <Order> tags also appear in the *Adaptor.xml* file, which has no direct relationship to the *Server.xml* file discussed here. Within the <UserList> tag of the *Server.xml* file, these tags determine the IP address(es) from which users can log into the Admin Service. In the *Adaptor.xml* file, these tags determine the IP address(es) from which users can log into other FlashCom applications.

You will also notice that no path to an application or instance is present in the connection string passed to the *connect( )* method. Since there is only one instance of the Admin Service running on each FlashCom Server, you do not need to specify any additional application or instance information.

Example 10-2 shows the code for the *FCSAdminConnector* class, which is a convenient subclass of the *NetConnection* class, tailored to initialize an admin connection. This class and all related classes can be downloaded from the book's web site.

Example 10-2. The FCSAdminConnector class

```
import com.oreilly.pfcs.FCSConstants;

class com.oreilly.pfcs.admin.FCSAdminConnector extends NetConnection {
  public  var dispatchEvent:Function;
  public  var addEventListener:Function;
  public  var removeEventListener:Function;
  private var __username:String;
  private var __password:String;
  private var __host:String;
  private var __port:Number = 1111;

  function FCSAdminConnector (ahost, aport, auser, apass, aeventObj) {
    super();   // Call the superclass constructor.
    mx.events.EventDispatcher.initialize(this);
    host = ahost;
    port = aport;
    username = auser;
    password = apass;
    addEventListener("connect", aeventObj);
    addEventListener("fault", aeventObj);
  }

  public function setCredentials (uname:String, pass:String):Void {
    username = uname;   // Set the username.
    password = pass;    // Set the password.
  }

  public function get username ():String {
    return __username;
  }

  public function set username (uname:String):Void {
    __username = uname;
  }

  public function get password ():String {
    return __password;
  }
```

Example 10-2. The FCSAdminConnector class (continued)

```
public function set password (pass:String):Void {
  __password = pass;
}

public function get host ():String {
  return __host;
}

public function set host (ahost:String):Void {
  __host = "rtmp://" + ahost;
}

public function get port ():Number {
  return __port;
}

public function set port (aport:Number):Void {
  __port = aport;
}

// See com.oreilly.pfcs.FCSConstants.as on the book's web site for the mapping of
// FCSConstants to the actual string codes returned from the server.
// For example, FCSConstants.SUCCESS  maps to "NetConnection.Connect.Success".
private function onStatus (info:Object):Void {
  switch (info.code) {              // Key on the code.
    case FCSConstants.SUCCESS:      // If the code is connection success.
      info.type = "connect";        // Set the event type.
      dispatchEvent(info);          // Send the event out to the listeners.
      break;
    default:
      info.type = "fault";          // Default event type is "fault".
      dispatchEvent(info);          // Send the event.
      break;
  }
}

public function connect (ahost, auser, apass):Void {
  if (arguments.length == 3) {
    super.connect.apply(super, arguments);
  } else if (arguments.length == 1) {
    super.connect(ahost, username, password);
  } else {
    var uri = host + ":" + port;
    super.connect(uri, username, password);
  }
}
}
```

The *FCSAdminConnector* class provides getter and setter methods for the host, port, username, and password properties so they can easily be set via ActionScript or data binding. The class also uses the methods defined in the *EventDispatcher* class to be consistent with the v2 UI components. The class will send two different events: *connect* and *fault*.

The *onStatus( )* handler in Example 10-1 checks the info.code property against the raw response string typically returned by the FlashCom Server to indicate success ("NetConnection.Connect.Success"). In contrast, the *onStatus( )* handler in Example 10-2 checks the info.code against the constant FCSConstants.SUCCESS. Why the difference? *FCSConstants* is a custom class included in the com.oreilly.pfcs package on the book's web site. As a convenience, it provides a property definition equivalent for each string status code that the FlashCom Server may return. This makes the code easier to read and is useful within intelligent development environments (IDEs) that provide syntax tips and code completion, so you don't have to memorize all the codes (as you do with their string equivalents, because code completion doesn't work with strings in most IDEs).

Example 10-3 demonstrates how to create an admin connection with this class.

Example 10-3. Implementing the FCSAdminConnector Class

```
import com.oreilly.pfcs.admin.FCSAdminConnector;

listener = new Object( );
listener.connect = function (eo) {
  // Handle the connection.
};

listener.fault = function (eo) {
  // Handle the connection failure.
};

var adminConn = new FCSAdminConnector ("www.yourhost.com",
                "1111", "username", "password", listener);
adminConn.connect( );
```

Now that you understand how to connect to the Admin Service, let's see how to use it to your benefit.

Using the Server Management API

Once a connection to the Admin Service has been established, you can use the Server Management API to query the Admin Service to monitor the running and installed applications, manage the server and administrators, and edit the server's configuration settings. The API provides the necessary remote methods to perform these actions. Accessing the remote methods on the Admin Service is done the same way as accessing remote methods in a FlashCom application as illustrated in Chapter 9. The *NetConnection.call( )* method is used to access every admin method:

```
adminConn.call("remoteMethod" [, responder [, arg1, ...argn]]);
```

The first parameter to the *call( )* method is the method name to run on the Admin Service. The second parameter is the responder object to handle the information returned from the Admin Service. Additional parameters can be passed as arguments that the remote method expects, which vary by method.

If the connection to the remote method succeeds, an information object containing the data generated by the remote method is returned. Whether the method succeeds or fails, the *onResult( )* callback method of the responder object is always triggered. Unlike calls to typical FlashCom application methods, Server Management API calls made to the Admin Service do not call an *onStatus( )* handler to report errors. Instead, the level and code properties of the response object passed to the *onResult( )* method indicate whether the method was successful or there was some error during execution. Table 10-1 lists the properties of the response object returned by the Admin Service to the *onResult( )* handler.

Table 10-1. Response object properties returned by the Admin Service

Property	Description
code	If the remote method failed, the code is "NetConnection.Call.Failed" (FCSContstants.CALL_FAILED), "NetConnection.Admin.CommandFailed" (FCSConstants.ADMIN_COMMAND_FAILED), or "NetConnection.Call.BadValue" (FCSConstants.ADMIN_BAD_VALUE). If the remote method succeeds, the code is "NetConnection.Call.Success" (FCSConstants.CALL_SUCCESS).
data	Optional property. Most methods will return a data object with additional return parameters.
description	Optional property. If the method fails, some remote methods will also return a description property with additional information on why the method failed.
level	The type of response returned. Either "status" or "error".
timestamp	The server time at which the method was executed.

The response object passed back from the Admin Service has properties similar to the object returned to the *NetConnection.onStatus( )* method. The Admin Service response object also has a timestamp property, which can be used to track how old the current data set is, and an optional data property, which may contain many additional pieces of information relative to the API operation that was performed.

The Server Management API methods can be grouped into four main categories: application, instance, server, and configuration methods. The entire list of API methods is long and well documented by Macromedia. A comprehensive Help panel entry for the Server Management API is installed with the communication components in Flash MX 2004. The Server Management ActionScript Dictionary, which documents the Server Management API, can also be downloaded in PDF format or accessed as LiveDocs in HTML format from the Macromedia web site:

http://www.macromedia.com/support/documentation/en/flashcom

The *FCSAdminAdaptor* class shown in Example 10-4 is a client-level wrapper to the Server Management API. Along with hiding the actual *NetConnection* implementation, this ActionScript 2.0 class provides an equivalent method for each Server Management API method, but in a format that is more familiar to most developers. The methods are also strictly typed so the compiler will catch any errors to speed up the overall development and debugging process of an application. The rest of this chapter will rely upon this class. The class file can be downloaded from the book's web site and is included here so you can browse it to get an understanding of all of the methods that the Server Management API exposes.

Example 10-4. The FCSAdminAdaptor Class

```
import com.oreilly.pfcs.admin.FCSAdminConnector;
import com.oreilly.pfcs.admin.PendingAdminCall;

class com.oreilly.pfcs.admin.FCSAdminAdaptor extends Object {

  private var __adminConn:FCSAdminConnector;

  function FCSAdminAdaptor (aconn:FCSAdminConnector) {
    __adminConn = aconn; // store the connection locally
  }

  function addAdmin (aname:String, apassword:String,
                     ascope:String):PendingAdminCall {
    return doRMI("addAdmin", arguments);
  }

  function addApp (aname:String):PendingAdminCall {
    return doRMI("addApp", arguments);
  }

  function broadcastMsg (scope:String, methodName:String):PendingAdminCall {
    return doRMI("broadcastMsg", arguments);
  }

  function changePswd (adminName:String, password:String,
                       scope:String):PendingAdminCall {
    return doRMI("changePswd", arguments);
  }

  public function gc (Void):PendingAdminCall {
    return doRMI("gc");
  }

  public function getActiveInstances (Void):PendingAdminCall {
    return doRMI("getActiveInstances");
  }

  public function getAdaptors (Void):PendingAdminCall {
    return doRMI("getAdaptors");
  }

  public function getAdminContext (Void):PendingAdminCall {
```

Example 10-4. The FCSAdminAdaptor Class (continued)

```
    return doRMI("getAdminContext");
  }

  public function getApps (Void):PendingAdminCall {
    return doRMI("getApps");
  }

  public function getAppStats (applicationName:String):PendingAdminCall {
    return doRMI("getAppStats", arguments);
  }

  public function getConfig (key:String, scope:String):PendingAdminCall {
    return doRMI("getConfig", arguments);
  }

  public function getInstanceStats (instanceName:String):PendingAdminCall {
    return doRMI("getInstanceStats", arguments);
  }

  public function getIOStats (Void):PendingAdminCall {
    return doRMI("getIOStats");
  }

  public function getLicenseInfo (Void):PendingAdminCall {
    return doRMI("getLicenseInfo");
  }

  public function getLiveStreams (instanceName:String):PendingAdminCall {
    return doRMI("getLiveStreams", arguments);
  }

  public function getLiveStreamStats (instanceName:String,
                             streamName:String):PendingAdminCall {
    return doRMI("getLiveStreamStats", arguments);
  }

  public function getMsgCacheStats ():PendingAdminCall {
    return doRMI("getMsgCacheStats");
  }

  public function getNetStreams (instanceName:String):PendingAdminCall {
    return doRMI("getNetStreams", arguments);
  }

  public function getNetStreamStats (instanceName:String,
                             streamName:String):PendingAdminCall {
    return doRMI("getNetStreamStats", arguments);
  }

  public function getScriptStats (instanceName:String):PendingAdminCall {
    return doRMI("getScriptStats", arguments);
  }
```

Example 10-4. The FCSAdminAdaptor Class (continued)

```
public function getServerStats ( ):PendingAdminCall {
  return doRMI("getServerStats");
}

public function getSharedObjects (instanceName:String):PendingAdminCall {
  return doRMI("getSharedObjects", arguments);
}

public function getSharedObjectStats (instanceName:String,
                                   sharedObjectName:String):PendingAdminCall {
  return doRMI("getSharedObjectStats", arguments);
}

public function getUsers (instanceName:String):PendingAdminCall {
  return doRMI("getUsers", arguments);
}
public function getUserStats (instanceName:String,
                           userID:String):PendingAdminCall {
  return doRMI("getUserStats", arguments);
}

public function getVHosts (adaptorName):PendingAdminCall {
  return doRMI("getVHosts", arguments);
}

public function ping ( ):PendingAdminCall {
  return doRMI("ping");
}

public function getVHostStats (adaptorName:String,
                             vHostName:String):PendingAdminCall {
  return doRMI("getVHostStats", arguments);
}

public function reloadApp (instanceName:String):PendingAdminCall {
  return doRMI("reloadApp", arguments);
}

public function removeAdmin (adminName:String, scope:String):PendingAdminCall {
  return doRMI("removeAdmin", arguments);
}

public function removeApp (applicationName:String):PendingAdminCall {
  return doRMI("removeApp", arguments);
}

public function restartVHost (scope:String):PendingAdminCall {
  return doRMI("restartVHost", arguments);
}

public function setConfig (key:String, value:String,
                         scope:String):PendingAdminCall {
```

Example 10-4. The FCSAdminAdaptor Class (continued)

```
    return doRMI("setConfig", arguments);
  }

  public function startServer (type:String):PendingAdminCall {
    return doRMI("startServer", arguments);
  }

  public function startVHost (vHostName:String):PendingAdminCall {
    return doRMI("startVHost", arguments);
  }

  public function stopServer (type:String):PendingAdminCall {
    return doRMI("stopServer", arguments);
  }

  public function stopVHost (vHostName:String):PendingAdminCall {
    return doRMI("stopVHost", arguments);
  }

  public function unloadApp (instanceName:String):PendingAdminCall {
    return doRMI("unloadApp", arguments);
  }

  private function doRMI (aname, argsCol):PendingAdminCall {
    if (argsCol == undefined) argsCol = new Array();
    var pc:PendingAdminCall = new PendingAdminCall(aname);
    argsCol.unshift(pc);
    argsCol.unshift(aname);
    __adminConn.call.apply(__adminConn, argsCol);
    return pc;
  }
}
```

To gain access to the simplified API, you must first construct an *FCSAdminConnector* instance and pass that connection to the *FCSAdminAdaptor* constructor as shown in Example 10-5; this creates a new instance of the *FCSAdminAdaptor* class on which you can invoke methods of the Server Management API.

Example 10-5. Constructing the FCSAdminAdaptor Instance

```
import com.oreilly.pfcs.admin.FCSAdminAdaptor;
import com.oreilly.pfcs.admin.FCSAdminConnector;

listener = new Object();
listener.connect = function (eo) {
  // this is the FCSAdminConnector instance stored in adminConn
  _global.adminAPI = new FCSAdminAdaptor(this); // Create the API adaptor.
};

listener.fault = function (eo) {
  trace("The connection attempt was unsuccessful");
};
```

Example 10-5. Constructing the FCSAdminAdaptor Instance (continued)

```
adminConn = new FCSAdminConnector ("www.yourhost.com",
                "1111",  "username", "password", listener);
adminConn.connect( );
```

To execute a method of the API, you call the method directly on the instance of the *FCSAdminAdaptor*. The method will then return a *PendingAdminCall* object as the result. Here, we call the *getApps( )* method on the _global.adminAPI, which is an *FCSAdminAdaptor* instance we created in Example 10-5.

```
var pendingCall:PendingAdminCall = _global.adminAPI.getApps( );
```

The *PendingAdminCall* object is your way of receiving the results from the Admin Service. The *PendingAdminCall* class internally defines the *onResult( )* method for you and tests whether the method invocation was successful. If the method call was a success, the instance will dispatch a *result* event and pass on the returned data from the Admin Service. If the method call failed, the instance will dispatch a *fault* event and pass along the status code from the Admin Service. This saves time writing error handling tests for each method invocation so your *onResult( )* handlers do not end up looking like this:

```
response.onResult = function (result) {
  if (result.code == "NetConnection.Call.Failed" ||
      result.code == "NetConnection.Admin.CommandFailed" ||
      result.code == "NetConnection.Call.BadValue") {
    // Body to handle failure
  } else {
    // Body to handle success
  }
};
```

You can register a listener for the *result* and *fault* events with the *addEventListener( )* method:

```
listener = new Object( );
listener.result = function (resObj) {
  // Handle the results passed in resObj
}
listener.fault = function (errObj) {
  // Handle the error passed in errObj
}

pendingCall.addEventListener("result", listener);
pendingCall.addEventListener("fault", listener);
```

However, the *PendingAdminCall* object already has a listener attached as the responder property. The listener is already registered to receive both the *result* and *fault* events. It is up to you to define the method that handles those events by overriding the *result( )* and *fault( )* methods of that responder object as follows:

```
pendingCall.responder.result = function (resObj) {
  // Handle the results
};
pendingCall.responder.fault = function (errObj) {
  // Handle the error
};
```

Example 10-6 illustrates how to execute a Server Management API method with the *FCSAdminAdaptor* class and handle the expected results using the *PendingAdmin-Call* object and the default listener in the responder property.

Example 10-6. Executing an API method

```
// Using the same connection and initialization code from Example 10-5...
import com.oreilly.pfcs.admin.PendingAdminCall;

// Make a call on the _global.adminAPI instance created in Example 10-5.
var pendingCall:PendingAdminCall = _global.adminAPI.getApps();

// Handler for successful attempt.
pendingCall.responder.result = function (result) {
  // Handle the results here
}

// Handler for failed attempt.
pendingCall.responder.fault = function (result) {
  // Handle the error here.
}
```

The *FCSAdminAdaptor* and the *PendingAdminCall* classes provide a framework to execute methods of the Server Management API and handle the resulting data and errors. Using these classes will result in writing less code while making the code more readable.

Now that we have discussed how to use these tools, let's discuss the different Server Management API methods that we can call.

Application Methods

The application-related methods of the Server Management API allow you to obtain a list of and statistics on installed applications, add an application directory, and delete an application. The application-related methods are:

getApps( )
getAppStats(applicationName)
addApp(applicationName)
removeApp(applicationName)

Example 10-7 illustrates how to execute the *getApps( )* method and map the results to a List component.

Example 10-7. Using the getApps( ) method

```
import com.oreilly.pfcs.admin.PendingAdminCall;

// Using the same adminAPI object from Example 10-5...
var appsCall:PendingAdminCall = adminAPI.getApps( );
appsCall.responder.result = function (res) {
  // This is the list of installed applications.
  _root.appsList.dataProvider = res.data;
};
```

Once you have the list of installed applications, you can use that information to
gather the statistics for each one or delete one of the applications. If you are using a
List component to display the applications, you can set the component's
dataProvider property to the data property of the result because the List component
will accept an array of strings as the dataProvider, which is exactly what the Admin
Service returns as the data property. You can access the selected application name
with the List instance's selectedItem property. (A similar operation is performed in
Example 10-9.) Example 10-8 creates a listener for the *change* event broadcast by the
List component and retrieves the statistics for the selected application.

Example 10-8. Using the getAppStats( ) method

```
function change (event) {
  var target = event.target;
  var appName = target.selectedItem;
  var appStatsCall:PendingAdminCall = adminAPI.getAppStats(appName);
  appStatsCall.responder.result = function (res) {
    for (var i in res.data) {
      trace(i + " : " + res.data[i]);
    }
  };
}
_root.appsList.addEventListener("change", this);
```

The statistics returned by the *getAppStats( )* method are cumulative for all of the
instances of that application and are located in the data property of the result object.
Sample output from the *getAppStats( )* method follows. These are the many properties of the data object returned in the response:

```
up_time : 804046
launch_time : Thu Nov 25 13:35:39 GMT-0600 2004
total_instances_unloaded : 5466
total_instances_loaded : 5495
rejected : 0
accepted : 44276
connected : 41
total_disconnects : 44235
total_connects : 44276
msg_dropped : 1812162
msg_out : 210880117
msg_in : 40181444
```

```
bytes_out : 16123434107
bytes_in : 2718399445
bw_out : 38080
bw_in : 3601
```

The *addApp( )* and *removeApp( )* methods allow you to add and remove an application. The *addApp( )* method will create a directory for an application. Since no application files are required for a FlashCom application, the application will run even without a *main.asc* file. In the absence of a *main.asc* file to manage connection requests, the default behavior is to accept all connections and grant users unlimited read and write access to streams and shared object data. That would allow arbitrary users to upload any data or stream any audio or video from a client they've constructed that accesses your server. So use caution when using the Server Management API to add an application. If you do not write a *main.asc* file to the application directory (which isn't supported via the API), you may unwittingly expose the server to unwanted users. The *removeApp( )* method deletes the specified application folder and all associated stream and shared object files contained within.

 The *addApp( )* method can create an empty application that effectively exposes your server. The *removeApp( )* method does not offer any additional prompts, warnings, or chances to abort the operation, so consider it extremely dangerous. If the integrity of the Admin Service is ever compromised, this method would allow any attacker to destroy all of the application files. If a person knows the administrative username and password, he can execute any method of the Server Management API on the server or virtual hosts for which he has privileges. Superusers can do whatever they want to the entire server and any virtual host. Virtual host administrators can do whatever they want within the context of a virtual host. For these reasons, limit administrative access to only the most trusted and knowledgeable developers.

Instance Methods

The instance-related methods of the Server Management API provide the ability to monitor running instances and their users, shared objects, and streams. The list of instance methods is:

getActiveInstances( )
getInstanceStats(instanceName)
getLiveStreams(instanceName)
getLiveStreamStats(instanceName, streamName)
getNetStreams(instanceName)
getNetStreamStats(instanceName, streamId)
getScriptStats(instanceName)
getSharedObjects(instanceName)
getSharedObjectStats(instanceName, soName, persistence)
getUsers(instanceName)

getUserStats(instanceName, userId)
reloadApp(instanceName)
unloadApp(instanceName)

To start inspecting an instance of an application, you first need to get the list of all of the active instances. This can easily be done by calling the *getActiveInstances( )* method:

```
function listInstances () {
  var appsCall:PendingAdminCall = adminAPI.getActiveInstances();
  appsCall.responder.result = function (res) {
    _root.appsList.dataProvider = res.data;
  };
}
```

The results of the *getActiveInstances( )* method contain a data property that is an array of all the instance names of the running applications. This array can then be bound to the `dataProvider` property of any list-based component.

Once you have a list of all of the available instances, you can use the List component to control the currently selected application. In that case, the `selectedItem` property of the List component can be used as the argument for the other instance methods to create a list of the shared objects, streams, and users for an item selected in the list. The instance name can also be used to unload and reload the application with the appropriate methods.

Other methods to drill down into specific statistics on shared objects, streams, and users are available. Like the other instance methods, these methods require that you either know the unique name representing the resource or you use one of the available methods to gather the available names of the resource to choose from and use in the API call. For example, if we wanted to further inspect the available information about a particular user, we would call *getUsers( )* first and then use the list of connected users to call the *getUserStats( )* method, as Example 10-9 illustrates.

Example 10-9. Using getUserStats( ) to display statistics for a user

```
function listUsers () {
  var rCall:PendingAdminCall = adminAPI.getUsers(_root.appsList.selectedItem);
  rCall.responder.result = function (res) {
    _root.userList.dataProvider = res.data;
  };
}

function change (e) {
  var rCall:PendingAdminCall = adminAPI.getUserStats(_root.appsList.selectedItem,
                                    _root.userList.selectedItem);
  rCall.responder.result = function (res) {
    // Display the resulting data to the user somehow (not shown).
  };
}
```

```
_root.userList.addEventListener("change", this);

/* Example results from the getUserStats() method.
stream_ids {
    0 : 1
}
msg_queue {
    other : 0
    video : 0
    audio : 0
    total_queues : 3
}
protocol : rtmp
connect_time : Fri Dec 3 10:37:08 GMT-0600 2004
msg_dropped : 0
msg_out : 921
msg_in : 14
bytes_out : 279434
bytes_in : 660
*/
```

Server Methods

The set of methods supported by the Server Management API related to monitoring and controlling the server is thorough enough to be able to monitor the vital statistics of the server and bandwidth consumption. FlashCom Servers can also be configured to serve multiple-host environments, and the Server Management API has a collection of methods capable of handling a virtual host configuration. The list of server-related methods is as follows (items in square brackets are optional arguments):

> *broadcastMsg(scope, methodName [, arg1, ... argn]);*
> *gc( )*
> *getAdaptors( )*
> *getAdminContext( )*
> *getIOStats( )*
> *getLicenseInfo( )*
> *getMsgCacheStats( )*
> *getServerStats( )*
> *getVHosts( )*
> *getVHostStats([adaptorName, vhostName])*
> *ping( )*
> *restartVHost([scope])*
> *startServer(type)*
> *startVHost(vhostName)*
> *stopServer(type)*
> *stopVHost(vhostName)*

The server-related methods of the Server Management API are bound to a more strict security policy than the application- and instance-related methods. There are two levels of administrative access for the FlashCom Admin Service: server administrators and virtual host administrators. Server administrators have superuser access and are not restricted in any way. Virtual host administrators have the capability to manage only a single virtual host and cannot access any server-wide methods or execute methods on another virtual host.

broadcastMsg( )

The *broadcastMsg( )* method is not documented in the official API documentation but is a powerful method that provides the mechanism to distribute a message to any user connected to the server. This method requires two arguments and can accept additional optional arguments to be supplied to the corresponding handler on the client side. The scope argument specifies the reach of the message. You can send a message to all connections to the server, to an adaptor, to a virtual host, to all instances of an application, or to a single instance of an application, depending on the scope parameter. The various possibilities for scope are:

"Server"
Send a message to the entire server.

"VHost"
Send a message to the virtual host that you are connected to.

"App:name"
Send a message to all instances of an application.

"App:name/instance"
Send a message to a single instance of an application.

"Adaptor"
Send a message to the adaptor to which you are connected.

"Adaptor:name"
Send a message to another adaptor.

"Adaptor:name/VHost:name"
Send a message to a virtual host on a different adaptor.

"Adaptor:name:VHost:name/App:name"
Send a message to an application on another virtual host.

"Adaptor:name:VHost:name/App:name/instanceName"
Send a message to an application instance on another virtual host.

The methodName argument, the second parameter sent to *broadcastMsg( )*, specifies the method name to be executed on the client. The optional additional arguments represent the parameters that you want to pass to that method. The method definition in the connecting clients must be assigned to the *NetConnection* object used to connect to the FlashCom Server. Example 10-10 shows how to use *broadcastMsg( )* from a client to send a message to all connected clients.

Example 10-10. broadcastMsg( ) example

```
// Broadcasting code, invoked from the client to control the Admin Service.
adminAPI.broadcastMsg("Server", "onAdminMessage", "message from admin");

// Reception code on the client.
my_conn = new NetConnection( );
mY_conn.connect("rtmp://flashcomserver.yourdomain.com/app/instance");
my_conn.onAdminMessage = function (msg) {
  trace("A message came from the Server Management API : " + msg);
};
```

Other server-related methods

Most of the other server-related methods of the Server Management API provide a means to gather the statistics of the server. For example, the *getServerStats( )* method returns a collection of data including the CPU and memory consumption of the FlashCom Server as well as the current and historical bandwidth use.

Like the instance-related methods, the server-related methods provide a way to inspect each adaptor and virtual host and provide methods to list the adaptors and virtual hosts configured on the server. The configuration options of the server allow you to have multiple adaptors and have multiple virtual hosts linked to each adaptor, forming a possibly complex tree of virtual hosts. In order to inspect a virtual host, you will first have to list the adaptors and choose the virtual host that is linked to that specific adaptor before you can survey the statistics for a single virtual host.

The server-related methods also provide the means to start and stop the entire FlashCom Server (*stopServer( )*) or a virtual host (*stopVHost( )*). These methods do not provide any opportunities to back out, so use them cautiously.

Configuration API Methods

The last group of methods in the Server Management API is used to configure the server. These methods provide a developer-level API to access the various *.xml* configuration files that control how the server operates.

Allowing a friendly GUI to these files is a convenient way to handle the server's configuration but is also very dangerous if the proper controls are not established to restrict intruders from accessing the interface. There are no safeguards or checks built into the API methods, so an unwanted change to a configuration file could be disastrous.

The configuration-related methods of the Server Management API are:

addAdmin(userName, password [, scope])
changePswd(userName, newPassword [, scope])
getConfig(key [, scope])
setConfig(key, value [, scope])

The *addAdmin( )* method allows you to create additional username/password combinations to allow users to log into the Admin Service. The scope argument allows the ability to give a new administrator access to either the entire server by specifying "Server" or to a virtual host by specifying the path to the virtual host as "*adaptorName/vhostName*". Administrators have access to all the API calls available for the server or virtual host to which they are granted access.

The *changePswd( )* method changes the password of an existing administrative account without specifying the old password. The second parameter is the new password. Virtual host administrators can change only their own password.

The *getConfig( )* and *setConfig( )* methods are more complex; they provide direct access to the *.xml* configuration files. These methods should be considered very dangerous and probably should be left alone. The configuration files are easy to edit with a simple text editor. Keeping client access to remote configuration options to an absolute minimum will keep the FlashCom Server secure.

Server Management API Uses

Now that we have covered the Server Management API basics, we can discuss some possible uses for the Admin Service and the ActionScript API that grants access to it. The obvious example is to create a Flash movie that monitors a FlashCom Server. The Communication Application Inspector is an example of such a Flash movie. Also available on the book's web site is a sample application that extends the features of the App Inspector, some features of which are discussed shortly.

Monitoring a FlashCom Server

The vital statistics that you need to know about any FlashCom Server are the memory, processor, and bandwidth consumption. These statistics are the key pieces of information that indicate how well an application is performing and if it is under significant load and possibly near a critical state. To access this information, use the *getServerStats( )* method. Example 10-11 illustrates how to poll the server and display these statistics in a TextArea component.

Example 10-11. Monitoring a FlashCom Server

```
import com.oreilly.pfcs.admin.FCSAdminConnector;
import com.oreilly.pfcs.admin.FCSAdminAdaptor;
import com.oreilly.pfcs.admin.PendingAdminCall;

adminConn = new FCSAdminConnector( );
adminConn.host = "www.yourhost.com";
adminConn.username = "admin";
adminConn.password = "flash";
adminConn.addEventListener("connect", this);
adminConn.connect( );

adminAPI = new FCSAdminAdaptor(adminConn);

function connect (e:Object) {
  monitorServer( );
  monitorInterval = setInterval(this, "monitorServer", 1000);
}

var lastBandwidthIn = 0;
var lastBandwidthOut = 0;

function monitorServer ( ) {
  var pcall:PendingAdminCall = adminAPI.getServerStats( );

  pcall.responder.result = function (result) {
    var data = result.data;
    var io = data.io;
    var out = "";

    out += "Current Users : " + io.connected + newline;
    out += "CPU : " + data.cpu_Usage + newline;
    out += "RAM : " + data.memory_Usage + newline;
    if (lastBandwidthIn > 0) {
      out += "Bandwidth Out : " + calcBW(io.bytes_out, lastBandwidthOut) + newline;
      out += "Bandwidth In : " + calcBW(io.bytes_in, lastBandwidthIn) + newline;
    }
    _root.output.text = out;

    lastBandwidthOut = io.bytes_out;
    lastBandwidthIn = io.bytes_in;
  };
}

function calcBW (currentBW, lastBW) {
  return (Math.round(((currentBW - lastBW) * (8 / 1024))*100)/100) + " Kbps";
}
```

This example first establishes a connection to the server with the *FCSAdminConnector* class and then creates an interval that polls the server every second for server statistics. Once per second, the data is returned and displayed to the user. Only a few elements of the data are actually displayed in this example and the rest of the properties are ignored, but you can experiment with it and add other useful properties to display.

 All of the values returned by the Server Management API regarding bandwidth are in bytes. The license for the FlashCom Server, as well as most network ratings, are measured in bits.

Multiply the number of bytes by 8 to determine the number of bits. To convert bits to kilobits, divide by 1000. To convert bits into megabits divide by 1,000,000. This will be the actual number to use to determine how close you are to the license limits.

Monitoring these statistics can be taken further as well. The data returned from the Server Management API doesn't have to be destroyed every second. You could collect that data in various storage formats. For example, you could use a local shared object, remote shared object, or data stream to collect a sample of the data to later run an analysis. You could also ship the data off to a database for more robust and flexible storage. This data can be invaluable in determining peak usage times and general capacity for making hardware and software purchasing decisions.

A sample application that exposes most of the features of the Server Management API can be downloaded from the book's web site. This application provides an example of how to view the detailed data that can be gathered from the Admin Service and can be used as the basis to build more sophisticated monitoring applications that can further collect data for analysis.

Polling Room Statistics

If you are creating a multiroom application, such as a chat room system, or other similar scenarios, you could also use the Server Management API to gather statistics about each instance of the application to display to the users. For example, if you had multiple chat rooms, you could use the Server Management API to list the total number of users in each room. You could obviously implement this in other ways, including using proxy shared objects, but each of those methods requires additional interinstance connections, which consume part of your server license. Connections to the Admin Service do not count against the FlashCom license, so this can be a useful way to conserve license slots and add the global room data necessary to make a rich multiroom application.

Imagine that we have an application named *ChatRooms*. This application has multiple rooms, and we want to display the current number of participants in each room. The previous examples in this chapter used client-side ActionScript 2.0. Server-Side ActionScript is still based on ActionScript 1.0, but the basic ideas of using the *NetConnection* object and its methods still apply to any server-side examples; only the syntax will look slightly different. The Server-Side ActionScript in Example 10-12 periodically polls the Server Management API for all of the instances of the application and gathers how many users are connected to each instance.

Example 10-12. Polling room statistics

```
application.onAppStart = function () {
  this.adminConn = new NetConnection();
  this.applicationName = this.name.split("/")[0];
  this.adminConn.onStatus = function (info) {
    if (info.code == "NetConnection.Connect.Success") {
      this.loopInterval = setInterval(application, "loopRoomStats", 10000);
      application.loopRoomStats();
    }
  };
  this.adminConn.connect("rtmp://localhost:1111",
                         "username", "password");
  this.roomTotals = SharedObject.get("roomTotals", false);
};

application.loopRoomStats = function () {
  var instanceResponder = new Object();
  instanceResponder.onResult = function (result) {
    var data = result.data;
    for (var i in data) {
      var name = data[i];
      if (name.indexOf(application.applicationName) == 0) {
        application.getRoomStats(name);
      }
    }
  };
  this.adminConn.call("getActiveInstances", instanceResponder);
};

application.getRoomStats = function (roomName) {
  var resp = new Object();
  resp.roomName = roomName;
  resp.onResult = function (result) {
    var data = result.data;
    application.roomTotals.setProperty(this.roomName, data.connected);
  };
  this.adminConn.call("getInstanceStats", resp, roomName);
};

application.onAppStop = function () {
  this.adminConn.close();
  this.roomTotals.close();
  clearInterval(this.loopInterval);
};
```

In the *application.onAppStart( )* method, we first create the *NetConnection* object and connect it to the Admin Service. At the same time, we create a shared object that is used to cache the room statistics gathered from the API and deliver the data to the connected clients. When the *onStatus( )* callback method executes, we initialize an interval to run every 10 seconds and gather the room statistics. The *application.loop-RoomStats( )* method calls *getActiveInstances( )* to list the available rooms and call *application.getRoomStats( )* on each room. Once the room statistics have been gathered, the `connected` property is mapped as the value for the room name in the shared object.

To display this data on the client side, all we would have to do is subscribe to the `roomTotals` remote shared object and map the room count properties to a visual display. Each room instance will have a corresponding entry in the `roomTotals` shared object that holds the total number of users connected to each instance. This approach is a proven strategy to gather data from a multiple-instance application and will work for many situations.

The connection to the Admin Service should never be inserted into a publicly available FlashCom client application. This would expose the authentication credentials to the world. This would also require that the Admin Service is configured to be accessible from any IP address—and not a private one on a local LAN—or just the IP address(es) of the FlashCom administrators.

Let's be clear that we are talking about two different things. First, by its very nature, a client application used to monitor a FlashCom Server should never be publicly available (i.e., don't post it to an unsecured web server). Second, a FlashCom application that could benefit from using the Server Management API should never expose the login information on the client. It might be tempting or more convenient to put the connection to the Admin Service in the client application and poll the data directly, rather than have the FlashCom Server connect to the Admin Service and write the data to a shared object. However, exposing the Admin Service login credentials would be a severe security risk. Leave the connection code and all related interaction with the Admin Service in your *.asc* files and not in your *.swf* files!

Subscribing to the Log Streams

Along with the ActionScript API discussed throughout this chapter, several log streams are available from the Admin Service. Fundamentally, the log streams are the same as any other FlashCom stream, except these streams contain only data and are available only if you are logged in to the Admin Service. The two types of log streams available are access logs and application logs. Like other FlashCom streams, these streams can also be recorded and used for later playback. Turning on the recording feature of the streams is handled in the configuration files. The access log stream is handled at the virtual host level, and that configuration setting is found in the *Vhost.xml* file for each adaptor. Set the following flag to `true` to record (store) the access log:

```
<RecordAccessLog>true</RecordAccessLog>
```

The configuration for the application logs is found in each *Application.xml* file. Set the following flag to true to record (store) the application log:

```
<RecordAppLog>true</RecordAppLog>
```

 If either of these values is set to false, the server will not record the streams. The log streams illustrated in this chapter can still be accessed as live streams.

Either of the logs can be played as live streams or recorded streams. Playing the stream as a live stream will listen in real time for new events to be posted to the stream. If you play the log stream as a recorded stream, all of the historical data will be either played back in real time or immediately flushed to the client, depending on the parameters passed to the *NetStream.play( )* method.

The access log is simply a record of all of the connection attempts to the server. This stream will contain a lot of connect and disconnect messages including basic information about what clients connected to and where they connected from.

The application logs are a bit more complicated and display all of the compile and runtime errors generated by an application. The application logs are also the stream to which server-side *trace( )* methods are sent. Regardless of the stream type or the source of the message, the method triggered on the listening *NetStream* object is always *onLog( )*. The *onLog( )* method should accept a single argument, an information object. This object is formatted similarly to other FlashCom response arguments and is a collection of properties including, but not limited to, description, code, and level.

Example 10-13 demonstrates how to play an access log stream.

Example 10-13. Playing the access log stream

```
accessLog = new NetStream(adminConn);
accessLog.onLog = function (msg) {
  for (var i in msg) trace(i + " : " + msg[i]);
};
// Play it as a live stream.
accessLog.play("logs/access", -1);
// Or play it as a recorded stream.
accssLog.play("logs/access", 0, -1, 3);
```

This code should look really familiar, as it is akin to playing any other FlashCom stream. The two versions of the *accessLog.play( )* call illustrate listening to the stream as a live stream or a recorded stream. In the latter example, the value 3 is used as the fourth parameter to indicate that we want all of the data events to be flushed immediately and we want to reset any playlists that might be stored on the server.

Application log streams work exactly the same as access log streams—the only difference is the stream name. The stream name for an application log stream consists of the same "logs/" prefix but with an additional "application" prefix followed by the full application instance name. The full format is as follows:

```
logs/application/applicationName/instanceName
```

Example 10-14 demonstrates how to play an application log stream.

Example 10-14. Playing an application log stream

```
myAppLog = new NetStream(adminConn);
myAppLog.onLog = function (msg) {
  for (var i in msg) trace(i + " : " + msg[i]);
};
myAppLog.play("logs/application/pfcschat/adminchapter", -1);
```

There are a couple of additional special log streams that do not seem to have corresponding configuration file entries and are not listed in any available documentation. A special stream named *logs/application/?* is used as a catchall log. If a log is not attached to a particular application, the warning and trace messages are sent to this special log. For example, an application that has a compile error and was not recently running would send its compile error messages to the catchall log. Another special stream, named *logs/system*, appears to be rarely used.

Conclusion

The Admin Service and the ActionScript API available to access it are oft-neglected resources. The Communication Application Inspector is useful for introductory purposes and simple debugging, but it does not present many of the useful features and data that you can access via the Server Management API. You should make use of the API to monitor your applications and the performance of your server. You can also use it for more advanced purposes by integrating the Admin Service into your multi-instance applications to perform instance-reporting tasks that otherwise would consume licenses.

In the second half of the chapter, we saw some important sample applications built using the Server Management API, including monitoring a FlashCom Server, gathering statistics on application instances, and managing the log streams. These operations are important for monitoring both the performance and security of your FlashCom Server, topics we'll cover in depth in the last few chapters of the book.

CHAPTER 11

Flash Remoting

Server-Side ActionScript (SSAS) supported by FlashCom 1.5.2 does not offer all the same features as client-side ActionScript. SSAS does not support the *LoadVars* or *XML* classes used by client-side ActionScript to load external data. With FlashCom applications, you cannot directly access server-side scripts, CGI applications, XML files, or the local filesystem. The good news is you can use Flash Remoting to communicate with an application server to accomplish these necessary tasks.

Flash Remoting has two parts: the client-side API used to create a connection to an application server and a server gateway that acts as the bridge between the client logic and the application server. The client-side APIs are built into the FlashCom Server as well as the Flash Player. This chapter discusses the entire Flash Remoting process but will focus on the client-side API used to connect to the application server. Throughout this chapter, the term *client* refers to either a SWF running in the Flash Player or a FlashCom application. That is, when using Flash Remoting with FlashCom, the FlashCom Server acts as the client. The techniques provided are valid for either situation.

The Remoting Gateway

The rest of this chapter focuses on the client code and techniques used in Flash Remoting, but let's take a moment to discuss the entire process. Flash Remoting enables you to make a request to the application server, have the server process the data using business logic, and return the results back to the client. The request/response system of Remoting works similarly to the technique of calling a remote FlashCom method, as discussed in Chapter 9. The process is asynchronous as well, so the results are not immediately returned but trigger an event in the client. However, unlike FlashCom remote methods, Flash Remoting calls use a non-persistent connection and use the HTTP protocol to communicate. Instead of sending RTMP data over the network, Remoting uses Action Message Format (AMF).

AMF is a binary message format modeled after SOAP, a protocol designed to exchange structured data in a distributed environment. SOAP uses XML tags to describe and package data and was designed to be abstract and versatile, which unfortunately resulted in the schema being complex and verbose. AMF was designed to be an efficient, compact format to pass ActionScript datatypes over the network. AMF uses binary flags to describe and package data. An AMF packet will always be smaller than an equivalent SOAP packet, which translates to faster response times and faster processing times when creating and processing AMF packets instead of SOAP.

Figure 11-1 depicts the process performed during a remoting call.

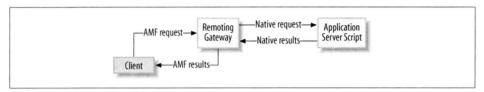

Figure 11-1. The process performed in response to a remoting call

When a request is made to an application server:

1. The client serializes data—including the parameters that the remote process expects—into AMF data. That binary data is wrapped in an HTTP packet and sent over the network to the destination server.

2. The application server receives the request and passes it on to the Flash Remoting gateway, which converts the AMF data into native datatypes of the application server (something that the server can understand).

3. The application server performs the necessary processing and generates a response. The response is serialized back into AMF by the remoting gateway and wrapped in an HTTP packet and sent back to the client.

4. The client receives the results and deserializes the response AMF data into ActionScript objects.

There are several server-side implementations of the Flash Remoting gateway. Although Flash Remoting is not included with FlashCom, Macromedia bundles it with ColdFusion and JRun. Macromedia also offers Flash Remoting for separate purchase for J2EE and .NET. There are several open source implementations of Flash Remoting for PHP, Java, and Perl such as AMFPHP (*http://www.amfphp.org*), OpenAMF (*http://www.openamf.org*), and AMF::Perl (the remoting gateway formerly known as FLAP at *http://simonf.com/amfpython*). FlashORB (*http://www.flashorb.com*) is a third-party alternative. For extensive details on Flash Remoting, including its use with ColdFusion, Java, PHP, .NET, and Server-Side ActionScript—a version that differs slightly from the SSAS supported by FlashCom—see *Flash Remoting: The Definitive Guide* (O'Reilly).

Remoting Basics

All of the processing and conversion of AMF is handled internally by the FlashCom Server (or Flash Player) and the Flash Remoting gateway, so you never have to deal with it. The *NetConnection* class, the base class for RTMP communications, also serves as the foundation for Remoting. A *NetConnection* instance on the client provides the developer interface to create the binary data and transmit it to the destination server.

Let's start with a simple example in which the Flash Player is the client. You could also run this example script inside a FlashCom application if the path to the imaginary service were correct. Example 11-1 shows how to use a *NetConnection* object to call a remote method on an application server with the remoting gateway installed.

Example 11-1. Flash Remoting with NetConnection

```
my_conn = new NetConnection( );
my_conn.connect("http://localhost/flashservices/gateway");

response = new Object( );
response.onResult = function (result) {
  trace(result);
};

my_conn.call("services.TestService.dataEcho", response, "test message");
```

The first two lines should look familiar to anyone building a FlashCom connection. In this case, the URI passed to the *connect( )* method refers to the remoting gateway that comes bundled with ColdFusion residing on the local host. Unlike an RTMP connection, the call to *connect( )* does not actually make a connection to the server, so the call will always return true. Internally, the client (in this case, the Flash Player) checks the protocol used for the connection. If the protocol is rtmp://, rtmpt://, or rtmps://, the Flash Player immediately tries to establish a socket connection with the remote host, and the *connect( )* method returns a Boolean value indicating whether the URI is valid. If the protocol is unspecified or is anything other than rtmp, rtmpt, or rtmps, the Flash Player doesn't try to make a connection to the remote host and always returns true.

The next segment of code creates a *response object* (also known as a responder), named response, with an *onResult( )* method to handle the response to the remote method call. When the server sends back a response, the Player automatically calls the *onResult( )* method of the specified object and passes the results as a single argument. Within this body of this method is where you would either process the result or forward the result to another object for processing.

The final line uses *NetConnection.call( )* to invoke the remote procedure, using the following format:

```
NetConnection.call(remoteMethod, resultObject | null [, p1, ...pn])
```

The *remoteMethod* parameter is a dot-delimited path to the file, in which the method name is the last part of the string. Depending on the server configuration, the full path from the server root will have to be specified. The remote method format is:

```
topfolder.subfolder.file_no_extension.method
```

In Example 11-1, *remoteMethod* is "services.TestService.dataEcho". This means that the remote method named *dataEcho( )* exists in a file named *TestService.cfc* (for ColdFusion) within a directory named *services*, which resides in the server root directory.

The *resultObject* parameter is the object that receives the results from the remote call. If the object has an *onResult( )* method defined, it receives a single argument containing results returned by the remote method. If the remote method fails for any reason, the *onStatus( )* method, if any, is called instead of *onResult( )*. The *onStatus( )* method receives a single argument, an information object, which has a minimum of three properties: level, code, and description. These properties describe the nature of the error as well as a description of the problem. If the remote procedure does not return any results or you do not need to receive the results, you can pass null as *resultObject*.

In Example 11-1, *resultObject* was the response object previously created. The response object's *onResult( )* handler simply traces the results returned from the remote method. The response object did not define an *onStatus( )* method and therefore will ignore any errors returned by the method call.

The last group of arguments, (p1,...pn), are the optional parameters to supply to the remote method. In Example 11-1, the only argument was a string with the value "test message".

Remoting Classes

Flash Remoting offers features beyond the ability to perform remote method calls. Remoting supports pageable recordsets, session management, adding and responding to special headers, and more. The Flash Remoting components bring even these advanced features, such as navigating through a pageable recordset, to all Flash developers. The components hide the underlying implementation and make implementing a remoting connection easier.

Although the Flash Remoting components include many classes, the *NetServices* and *RecordSet* classes are used for almost every remoting application. *NetServices* is the main interface for creating remoting connections. The *RecordSet* class represents the results from a database query and provides the implementation to manipulate and negotiate pageable recordsets. The components were originally developed for Flash MX and ported over for FlashCom, so the code to communicate with a remote service can be used in both environments with little or no modifications (client-side

ActionScript 1.0 and Server-Side ActionScript—equivalent to JavaScript 1.5—are very similar).

Google web service

Let's see how to use the Remoting classes to accomplish some common goals. Example 11-2 shows how to consume the Google web service with the *NetServices* package, allowing you to add a Google search capability to your application. This example assumes that you have Flash Remoting installed and configured to accept web services. The client-side ActionScript in the example should be entered in the first frame of the *Actions* layer of a Flash movie. Look over the code, and we'll discuss it momentarily.

Example 11-2. Implementing the Google search web service

```
// To run this example from a FlashCom appication,
// use load("netservices.asc") instead of #include "NetServices.as".
#include "NetServices.as"
// To run this example from a FlashCom appication, wrap the rest of this
// example in an application.onAppStart() function.
NetServices.setDefaultGatewayUrl("http://localhost/flashservices/gateway");
my_conn = NetServices.createGatewayConnection();

GoogleService = my_conn.getService("http://api.google.com/GoogleSearch.wsdl", this);

this.doGoogleSearch_Result = function (data) {
  trace("we have data");
  searchdata = data;
};

this.doGoogleSearch_Status = function (error) {
  for (var i in error) {
    trace(i + " : " + error[i]);
  }
};

// You need to insert your Google developer key as a string for the key property.
params = {
  key:"Your developer key goes here",
  q:"amfphp",
  start:0,
  maxResults:10,
  filter:true,
  restrict:"",
  safeSearch:false,
  lr:"",
  ie:"UTF-8",
  oe:"UTF-8"
}

GoogleService.doGoogleSearch(params);
```

As in the first line of the example, you must include *NetServices.as* to use the Flash Remoting components. This loads the *NetServices* class and several other classes. In a FlashCom application, the SSAS syntax to load the *NetServices* class is:

```
load ("netservices.asc");
```

The *setDefaultGatewayUrl( )* method provides a means to set a URL to use for all calls to *createGatewayConnection( )*. The *createGatewayConnection( )* method also accepts a URL that overrides the default gateway URL.

You can use either of the following to create the gateway connection:

```
NetServices.setDefaultGatewayUrl("http://localhost/flashservices/gateway");
my_conn = NetServices.createGatewayConnection( );
```

or:

```
my_conn = NetServices.createGatewayConnection(
            "http://localhost/flashservices/gateway");
```

Using *setDefaultGatewayUrl( )* to set the default gateway avoids having to specify the connection path every time you create a gateway connection with *createGateway-Connection( )*.

The *createGatewayConnection( )* method returns a *NetConnection* object that is used to communicate with the remote server. (The *NetServices.as* file adds several remoting-specific methods to the *NetConnection* class.) You must assign the results of *createGatewayConnection( )* to a variable, or the connection object will be destroyed; it is not cached locally within the *NetServices* class.

The *getService( )* method, one of the methods of *NetConnection* added by *NetServices.as*, builds and returns an object that acts as a proxy to the remote service definition:

```
myService = NetConnection.getService(serviceName[, responseObject]);
```

The *serviceName* parameter is the path to the service definition for the remote server. Its format is the same as the first parameter for the *NetConnection.call( )* method without the method name included in the string. In Example 11-2, its value is "http://api.google.com/GoogleSearch.wsdl".

The *responseObject* is the object that should respond to all methods called through this service object. This parameter is optional, and in most applications not practical. Typically, unless there is a specific reason to do so, using a single object to respond to all remote calls will end in an unnecessarily complicated result definition. Instead, you'll usually implement separate responders for each method called through the service.

Example 11-2 shows one way to handle the results of a remote method invocation. The *doGoogleSearch_Result( )* method handles the results returned by the call to *doGoogleSearch( )* (The Flash Remoting components automatically look for a handler of the same name with "_Result" appended for this purpose.) The example simply traces a message stating that results were returned by the call and stores the result data in a variable named searchdata. You can use the Debug → List Variables command in the Flash authoring tool's Test Player to inspect the format of the returned results. The NetConnection Debugger, discussed in Chapter 3, is also useful for analyzing data transmitted via Flash Remoting.

The *doGoogleSearch_Status( )* method is triggered if the service returns any errors (again, Flash automatically looks for a handler of the same name with "_Status" appended for this purpose). We will come back to handling errors later; the method here simply traces the error message if something goes wrong.

Finally, the remote method is executed. The Google web service requires many parameters, which are passed in a single parameters object. The two important properties of the parameters object are key and q. The key property is a required string assigned to each developer. A developer obtains a key by registering to use the Google search web service at *http://www.google.com/apis*. The q property is the string for which you want to search. The other parameters manipulate how the search is processed and returned. Consult Google's documentation at the preceding URL for details of each parameter. Finally, *doGoogleSearch( )* is invoked on the GoogleService service to execute the remote procedure.

Services

The syntax to access remote services varies slightly depending on the Flash Remoting gateway version (ColdFusion, Java, .NET, etc.). Furthermore, the types of services available via Remoting vary slightly as well. For example, accessing a remote web service via Java or JRun requires a wrapper, which is not necessary with ColdFusion or .NET. Once connected to a service, however, the service's methods are accessed from the client code in a uniform way that is independent of the Flash Remoting gateway or the server-side technology implementing the remote services.

To provide access to its services, the remote application server supports a *service class*, which provides access to one or more remote methods. The techniques required to define a service class vary, so check the documentation of your server (ColdFusion, .NET, Java, etc.) or consult *Flash Remoting: The Definitive Guide*. For our purposes, we assume you have created a remote application and properly configured your application server to allow remote access to it.

Connecting to a remote service class (or simply a service) is accomplished by supplying the service's dot-delimited path to the *getService( )* method. This path is typically the full path from the web root of the server. Some server implementations such as ColdFusion, JRun, and AMFPHP provide a mechanism to specify a classpath or a service directory, in which case the service path supplied can be relative to that location.

The syntax for most of the remote services requires that you omit the file extension of the service class file. For example, here, we omit the *.cfml* or *.cfc* extension of a ColdFusion service:

```
UtilityService = my_conn.getService("cfcs.jwatkins.CommonUtils");
```

Web services are supported by many of the remoting implementations. Example 11-2 illustrated how to connect to the Google search web service. Connecting to a web service is as simple as specifying the *.wsdl* file as the service name passed to *getService( )*:

```
TempService = my_conn.getService(
        "http://www.xmethods.net/sd/2001/TemperatureService.wsdl");
```

A single connection object can be shared for all services located at a gateway URL.

 Flash Remoting calls are batched together when the Flash client makes multiple remote calls on the same frame or when FlashCom makes multiple remote calls from within the same function. When calls are batched, you do not receive a response from any method calls until all of the remote methods have finished.

The following two remote calls are batched together even though one is mapped to a local service class and the other is a web service. The results are not returned from the remoting server until both of the methods have completed processing:

```
someFunction = function ( ) {
  NetServices.setDefaultGatewayUrl("http://localhost/flashservices/gateway");
  my_conn = NetServices.createGatewayConnection( );
  UtilityService = my_conn.getService("cfcs.jwatkins.CommonUtils");
  TempService = my_conn.getService(
          "http://www.xmethods.net/sd/2001/TemperatureService.wsdl");
  UtilityService.searchString(needle, haystack);
  TempService.getTemp("61310");
};
```

This automated batching of remote calls is an important issue that may impact your implementation of performing remote calls. If a remote method takes a long time to execute or returns a large amount of data, it will slow other processes down. So you should ensure that such methods execute separately from other methods. This can be accomplished by chaining the remote calls (i.e., waiting for the results of one before executing another) or by using separate connection objects for each method call. Here is an example using separate connections:

```
someFunction = function ( ) {
  NetServices.setDefaultGatewayUrl("http://localhost/flashservices/gateway");
  my_conn1 = NetServices.createGatewayConnection( );
  my_conn2 = NetServices.createGatewayConnection( );

  UtilityService = my_conn1.getService("cfcs.jwatkins.CommonUtils");
  TempService = my_conn2.getService(
```

```
        "http://www.xmethods.net/sd/2001/TemperatureService.wsdl");

    UtilityService.searchString(needle, haystack);
    TempService.getTemp("61310");
};
```

Methods

Once you've established a connection and created a service object, you can make calls on that object to access methods of the service. The *getService( )* method returns a proxy object to the service. The proxy object uses the *NetConnection.call( )* syntax internally but provides a familiar way to invoke a remote method. The syntax to call a remote method is similar to any other method invocation:

```
    serviceProxy.methodname([responseObject] [, arg1, ...argn])
```

The first parameter, *responseObject*, is an optional response object, which overrides the default response object passed to the *getService( )* method. This approach allows you to use different responders for each method call instead of using the same handler for all methods invoked on the service. In most situations, this is the preferred approach. It lets you handle the results differently for each type of method invoked, or even for each invocation of a given method.

If the first argument is an object defining an *onResult( )* method, Flash strips it from the argument list passed to the remote service and uses it as a response object instead (the response object parameter is not passed to the remote method).

 However, if you set a response object via *getService( )* and attempt to specify another response object when invoking a remote function, it won't work. The response object will be passed as a parameter to the remote function instead of being stripped out of the argument list. See "Creating Responder Functions" in Chapter 4 of *Flash Remoting: The Definitive Guide* for many more details.

The remaining parameters in the remote method invocation are the arguments that the remote method expects. You can pass the arguments in two ways. The first approach is to pass the parameters as individual arguments separated by commas. Here is an example in which the optional response object is included as the first parameter:

```
    serviceProxy.someMethod(someResponseObj, "one", "two", "three");
```

Here is the same method invocation without the optional response object:

```
    serviceProxy.someMethod("one", "two", "three");
```

Passing unnamed parameters is similar to how parameters are passed when invoking any ActionScript method, and the names of the parameters do not need to be known to the client. However, the order that the remote server expects the arguments must be known to and observed by the client code. Normally with remote methods that require a single or only a few parameters, this is not an issue. But with remote methods that require many parameters, such as the Google search service, this can be a major source of problems.

The second approach is to wrap all of the parameters into a single object as name/value pairs and pass the object as the only parameter (besides the optional response object, not used in this example):

```
params = {one:"one", two:"two", three:"three"};
serviceProxy.someMethod(params);
```

The major advantage to this approach is that the order and number of the arguments becomes irrelevant because they are named values. The disadvantage is that the client must know the names that the server expects for each parameter.

 Not all implementations of the Flash Remoting gateway support passing the arguments as properties of a single object. Check your remoting implementation's documentation.

Handling results

You have already been introduced to two ways to handle a response to a remoting call: using a *methodname_Result( )* method or using an *onResult( )* method attached to a response object. Both approaches handle the results in the same manner.

To handle the results with *methodname_Result( )*, simply define a function using the same name as the remote method call and append "_Result" to the end:

```
doGoogleSearch_Result = function (data) {
  trace(data);
};
```

This approach is the easiest to implement. If you do not pass a default responder to the *getService( )* method, the response methods must be defined in the same scope as the service proxy object. However, if you specify a default responder to *getService( )*, the response methods must be defined as methods of that object.

To handle the results with an *onResult( )* method, you must define an object with an *onResult( )* method and register that object as the responder. You can either pass the object to the *getService( )* method:

```
responder = new Object( );
responder.onResult = function (data) {
  trace(data);
};
myService = my_conn.getService("AuthenticationService", responder);
```

or you can pass the object as the first parameter of the remote method call:

```
myService.authenticateUser(responder, "jwatkins", "abcd");
```

If you aren't very comfortable using objects, the *methodname_Result( )* approach allows you to handle results by simply defining functions with the appropriate names. If you are comfortable with object-oriented programming, you can also implement the *methodname_Result( )* approach by designing a class to handle the results from the remoting calls. You can create all of the response methods in the class and pass an instance of the class as the default response object to the *getService( )* method:

```
function ResultsClass () {...}
ResultsClass.prototype.method1_Result = function ...
ResultsClass.prototype.method2_Result = function ...

myService = my_conn.getService("TestService", new ResultClass());
```

There are several drawbacks to using *methodname_Result( )*, however. Because the response handler's name depends on the remote function's name, you must define separate *_Result* handlers for each method. Furthermore, if the name of a remote function changes, you must change the name of its corresponding *_Result* handler.

Using an *onResult( )* method instead of a *_Result* handler is cleaner from an object-oriented standpoint. Simply pass an object that defines an *onResult( )* method. The object can be either an anonymous object or an instance of a class. This approach makes it easier to share response-handling logic across different remote calls; you can pass the same response object to several remote methods or set up one object as the default responder and override it when necessary.

The *NetServices* package dispatches the *onResult* event from a remote call in the following order, stopping when it finds an appropriate handler:

1. First, it looks for a function named *methodname_Result( )* defined on the response object or the current timeline.

2. Otherwise, if a response object with an *onResult( )* method was specified in the call to *getService( )*, results are sent to that *onResult( )* method.

3. Otherwise, if the first argument passed to the remote method invocation is an object that defines an *onResult( )* method, results are sent to that *onResult( )* method.

4. Otherwise, if the movie is playing in the authoring environment, results are sent to the Output window.

5. Otherwise, the results are lost.

Using the *onResult( )* approach is also slightly faster. When you do not specify an object with an *onResult( )* method, the *NetServices* classes have to create an additional object to handle the results from the server and forward the request to the *methodname_Result( )* method.

A bug in the *NetServices* class prevents responder objects with an *onResult( )* method from working as expected. This bug existed in prior versions but is fixed in the Updater 2 for FlashCom 1.5.

If you prefer to name your response handler something other than *onResult( )*, Example 11-3 defines a custom class that forwards the results to an object and method name of your choosing. The class defines an *onResult( )* method that calls the object and method name originally passed to the *RelayResponder* class constructor.

Example 11-3. Using a RelayResponder

```
#include "NetServices.as"

NetService.setDefaultGatewayUrl("http://localhost/flashservices/gateway");

function RelayResponder (targetObject, targetMethod) {
  this.targetObject = targetObject;
  this.targetMethod = targetMethod;
}
RelayResponder.prototype.onResult = function (data) {
  this.targetObject[this.targetMethod](data);
};

function FictionalDataClass ( ) {
}

var o = FictionalDataClass.prototype;
o.getData = function ( ) {
  this.conn = NetServices.createGatewayConnection( );
  this.service = this.conn.getService("DataService");
  this.service.getData(new RelayResponder(this, "receiveData"));
};
o.receiveData = function (data) {
  trace("The request was forwarded here");
};

myData = new FictionalDataClass( );
myData.getData( );
```

Handling errors

Up to this point, we have assumed that everything will always work, which is unfortunately not the case during either development or production. When relying on an external resource to perform processing, the external resource may change or be unavailable, or parameters that were once valid may no longer be valid. Remoting has the capability to alert the client that something has gone wrong and provide additional details that may help determine what has happened.

If a remote server fails to process a call, it returns an error object and invokes a *status method* (in this case, "status" is a euphemism for "error"). Regardless of how you handle the error message, which depends on how you defined your response object, Flash Remoting always passes a single error object to the status method. The error object returned by the remote server includes level and description properties specifying the error severity and an explanation of why the server couldn't perform the request. The values of these properties, while not always completely accurate, are invaluable in debugging the error.

If you use the *methodname_Result( )* approach for your responder, you should specify a *methodname_Status( )* function to catch any errors. There are still yet other options, however. The *NetServices* package dispatches the *onStatus* error from a remote call in the following order, stopping when it finds an appropriate handler:

1. First, it looks for a function named *methodname_Status( )* defined on the response object or the current timeline.

2. Otherwise, if a response object with an *onStatus( )* method was specified in the call to *getService( )*, status errors are sent to that *onStatus( )* method. (If you pass a response object with an *onResult( )* method as the first parameter to the remote method call, an *onStatus( )* method is called only if it is attached directly to the response object. If you pass such a response object to each remote method call, the handlers cited in Steps 3 and 4 are never called.)

3. Otherwise, the *_root.onStatus( )* method, if any, is used.

4. Otherwise, the *_global.System.onStatus( )* method, if any, is used.

5. Otherwise, if the movie is playing in the authoring environment, results are sent to the Output window.

6. Otherwise, the results are lost.

In many situations, there is not any meaningful action that the client can take to correct the problem at runtime. Depending on the application, you may simply report the error to the user, stating that the remote service is unavailable. In other cases, the error can be corrected by adjusting the parameters that are sent to the remote server. At other times, intermittent connection errors, such as with HTTP calls, can be solved by simply trying again. When an HTTP call fails in Breeze Live, the application typically retries it five times at 1-second intervals. (You should avoid being so aggressive in retrying as to create an inadvertent denial-of-service attack.)

Passing Datatypes

All the basic ActionScript datatypes can be passed through AMF with remoting. A remote server can interact with the passed datatype using its native syntax. The actual translation of datatypes varies by remoting implementation; consult *Flash Remoting: The Definitive Guide* or your remoting gateway documentation to see how each datatype is deserialized on the server. Passing most ActionScript datatypes requires no configuration or additional code; all you need to do is pass the variable as a parameter to the remote method.

Custom classes

You can also send and retrieve an instance of a custom class with Flash Remoting. Some remoting implementations allow you to have a definition for the class available on the server side and have the class restored as an instance of the server-side class. Likewise, you can receive an instance of a custom class and have it constructed back to an instance of the class available in the client code.

Passing an instance of a custom class is a useful tool. Using methods instead of accessing properties directly is an excellent way to hide the internal implementation of the data and is the most flexible approach in case the data structure changes in the future. Any code that accesses the data will not need to be modified if it uses the methods to access the data (assuming the method definitions are updated correctly). You could also define methods that create unique displays of the data. For example, you could have a firstName and lastName property in the data and have a method that returns the full name as follows:

```
DataClass.prototype.getName = function () {
    return this.firstName + " " + this.lastName;
};
```

The *getName( )* method simply returns the firstName and lastName properties joined together with a space. Using such a method is easier than joining the two properties together every time the name needs to be displayed or used in this format.

Having the custom class defined does not automatically deserialize the passed object as an instance of the class. In a FlashCom application, you also need to register the class using *application.registerClass( )*:

```
application.registerClass(className, constructor);
```

The *className* parameter is the name of the class as a string. The *constructor* property is the physical function that should be used to reconstruct the instance of the class object.

```
function myClass () {}
application.registerClass("myClass", myClass);
```

This example will register the class myClass as a class that can be deserialized.

 Setting properties in the constructor will break any deserialized data!

Recordsets

Databases are common tools for storing and organizing data. Databases are also very scalable in terms of performance and the amount of data that can be stored. Often an application will require the use of a database, and FlashCom cannot access a database without Flash Remoting.

RecordSet is a special custom class available in the *NetServices* package. The *RecordSet* class represents the query results from a database. Using *RecordSet* provides many methods to access query results and control how the results (known as a recordset or result set) are returned from the server. The remote server can interface directly with a database by executing either SQL code or stored procedures. The server returns the query results back to the client (in this case, FlashCom). In the FlashCom application, the results can be constructed into an instance of the *RecordSet* class as shown in Example 11-4.

Example 11-4. RecordSet example

```
load("netservices.asc");

application.onAppStart = function () {
  NetServices.setDefaultGatewayUrl("http://www.myhost.com/flashservices/gateway");
  var conn = NetServices.createGatewayConnection();
  var dataService = conn.getService(
                  "com.oreilly.pfcs.chapter11.PlayListService");

  var response = new Object();
  response.onResult = function (result) {
    application.playList = result; // Save the playlist to a persistent scope
    application.outStream = Stream.get("radiochannel"); // Get a live stream

    var l = result.getLength();                  // Get the recordset length
    for (var i = 0; i < l; i++) {
      var record = result.getItemAt(i);
      // Use the filename from the recordset.
      application.outStream.play(record.filename,
        record.starttime,              // Get the start time from the recordset
        record.length,                 // Get the length from the recordset
        false);                        // Add each record to the playlist
    }
  };
  response.onStatus = function (info) {
    trace("The PlayListService is unavailable right now");
    for (var i in info) trace(i + " : " + info[i]);
  };
  // Invoke the method to retrieve the recordset.
  dataService.GetPlayList();
};
```

Example 11-4 assumes that a database table stores the following columns: name, filename, starttime, and length. It uses remoting to retrieve the list of tracks to play and builds a server-side playlist with the *Stream* object. This example also shows one simple way to interact with recordset data in your application. The most commonly used methods of the *RecordSet* class are *getLength( )* and *getItemAt( )*. The *getLength( )* method counts the number of records returned by the remoting service, which you can use to loop through the results. The *getItemAt( )* method returns the record at the specified index (zero-relative). The returned record is an object with the database columns as the properties. You can retrieve a list of the column names returned by the query with the *getColumnNames( )* method. This method returns an array of strings that correspond to the column names.

The results from the server can be broken up into smaller batches and distributed to the client in several ways, as controlled by the *RecordSet.setDeliveryMode( )* method. The three modes are "ondemand", "fetchall", and "page". By default, recordsets operate in fetchall mode, in which all of the results are returned in a single batch. Pageable recordsets can be sent entirely in one batch, sent in multiple smaller batches, or stored on the server until the desired record is requested. For many scenarios, using pageable recordsets is not necessary. Often there are other solutions to limit the amount of data that needs to be displayed. However, there are times when the amount of data is just too large to transfer and display at once.

You can enable recordset paging in ondemand mode by passing a `pagesize` property in the parameters object when you call the remote method:

```
params = new Object( );
params.pagesize = 5;
my_service.getData(params);
```

In ondemand mode, only the specified number of records is returned to the client. The remaining records are returned on an as-needed basis when you call *getItemAt( )*. If the results contained 50 records and you set the initial page size to 5, if you try to access a record between 6 and 50, the record will need to be fetched from the server. In ondemand mode, the client fetches only a single record when it is requested. You cannot immediately access a record that is still residing on the server after calling *getItemAt( )*. You must wait for the server to return the results, which causes it to issue a *modelChanged* event. If the record still needs to be loaded, the *getItemAt( )* method will return the string "in progress". If the record has already been downloaded, you can access the record immediately.

```
listener = new Object( );
listener.modelChanged = function (eventObj) {
  // This event is triggered when the data changes.
};
my_rs.addView(listener);
```

At any time during the ondemand mode, you can change the delivery mode to either fetchall or page using *setDeliveryMode( )*. Changing the mode to fetchall requests the server to return the remainder of the recordset in a single batch or optionally in smaller batches. You can set fetchall mode as follows:

```
my_rs.setDeliveryMode("fetchall"[, pagesize]);
```

Using the same scenario of a 50-record result set, the request mechanism will request only pagesize records at a time until all of the records have been downloaded. If the resultset is large, breaking it up into smaller batches allows the client to display the records that have been downloaded without waiting for the entire resultset.

The page delivery mode is somewhere between ondemand and fetchall. It delivers records when they are requested but optionally returns more than a single record. You can set page mode as follows:

```
my_rs.setDeliveryMode("page", pagesize[, prefetch]);
```

Setting the mode to "page" sets a delivery mechanism similar to how most search engines work. When you perform a search, the engine returns a limited number of results with the ability to navigate through the additional results. Each set of results returned by the search engine is a page. The pagesize parameter determines how many records should be listed in each collection, and the prefetch parameter determines how many total pages should be downloaded additionally, so they are cached and ready to access.

If you set the mode to "page" after receiving the first five records, the client requests additional records only when you use *getItemAt( )* to try to access a record that still resides on the server. If you request a record that has not been loaded locally, the server returns a full page of records starting at the index passed to *getItemAt( )* plus the additional number of complete page collections specified by prefetch. To calculate the total number of records that could be downloaded, multiply pagesize by prefetch + 1. This example downloads 15 records every time a record that has not been previously fetched is requested:

```
my_rs.setDeliveryMode("page", 5, 2);
```

Using page mode is an effective way to manage extremely large results. If the number of returned records is in the thousands, using a paged view of the data will make navigating and interacting with the data an easier task.

Each delivery mode has benefits and drawbacks.

Using fetchall mode to send the data in a single batch is the easiest for the server to perform because it doesn't have to allocate additional memory to store the server-cached records. The fetchall mode uses the least overall bandwidth if you are going to need the entire result set, because only two communications—the client request and the server results—take place. Being able to break the fetchall process into smaller pages makes displaying records to the client faster as well. However, fetchall mode does not work well for very large result sets because it is difficult for the client application and end user to process large amounts of data. It is also wasteful if all the records in the result set are not needed.

The ondemand mode works great for applications in which only one record is viewed at a time. For example, if you have an application that displays contact information, the ondemand mode will minimize the amount of bandwidth necessary to display a single record from a result set. However, if you need to retrieve all the records in a result set, ondemand mode uses the most bandwidth because there is one request and one response for each record. The ondemand mode also consumes additional server memory and processing to store the cached results.

The page mode is effective for displaying smaller groups of results. This usually applies when you are performing a search function and need to show the end user multiple records simultaneously for faster browsing but need to limit the number of records displayed for simplicity and performance reasons. Like ondemand mode, page mode requires additional server memory to store the cached results.

Action Message Format

While AMF is a compact format, it is still important to understand the size implications of each datatype. AMF is used both in remoting and when you embed data into a *NetStream*. It also is the basis for the format of data stored in shared objects. Since data embedded in a stream has the highest priority and is never dropped, it is important to understand how the size of the data can force a client on a slower connection to drop video and even audio frames.

All AMF packets sent with remoting contain five parts:

- Packet version header
- Header count
- Array of header messages
- Body message count
- Array of body messages

The version, header count, and body count add 6 bytes to the packet. The header and body messages vary by the count and the data contained in each. Each type of object passed over AMF carries its own overhead in bytes. The byte counts in Table 11-1 include a 1-byte flag (indicating the datatype) that precedes the data for each type.

Table 11-1. AMF datatypes and byte count

Datatype	Byte count
null	1
undefined	1
Boolean	2
Number	9
Date	10
String	2 + string length
XML	5 + *XML.toString( ).length*
Array	5 + (*n* for each array index value)
Object	4 + (2 + string length for each property name) + (*n* for each property value)

Table 11-1. AMF datatypes and byte count (continued)

Datatype	Byte count
Associative array	8 + (2 + string length for each property name) + (n for each property value)
Custom class	6 + class name length + (2 + string length for each property name) + (n for each property value)

The table is sorted by byte count to help you manage bandwidth usage, but of course the exact bandwidth varies by the contents of complex datatypes, such as arrays.

> As illustrated in Table 11-1, passing the number 1 adds 7 more bytes to the packet than passing the Boolean true; they are not equivalent! If both the client and server implementations can handle sending and receiving Boolean values, using a Boolean instead of a number can save precious bytes. Of course, multiple Boolean values can be coded as bits in a single number and decoded using bitwise operators.

It is not usually necessary to pay such granular attention the number of bytes in an AMF packet when dealing with remoting from a FlashCom application, since the connection from server to server is usually very fast. It becomes more important to consider the impact of the data packets when you are embedding data into an audio and video stream or when managing *SharedObject* data.

Role of Remoting in FlashCom Applications

FlashCom is not the most effective environment for storing and manipulating data. Managing large and complicated data structures is better handled by a filesystem or a relational database management system (RDBMS). FlashCom is designed for sharing real-time multimedia information and data across multiple users. Using data, however, is a common need for most applications, and it is important to understand when and how to implement remoting to solve a given problem. As a general rule, if the data should be shared by multiple users, then the remoting implementation should be built in FlashCom. The FlashCom Server has the ability to cache the results from a remoting request into a shared object, which can then be easily distributed to all the listening clients. Using the FlashCom Server to gather the remote data and cache the results will dramatically reduce the load required by the remote server. On the other hand, there are important cases in which remoting should be implemented by the Flash client, such as when personal or private information is involved.

The following sample application demonstrates various examples of when and how to implement remoting. The application is a messaging system that provides users with the ability to maintain a profile and a friend list, have private conversations with another user, and have group conversations with multiple users. The application code and files are too numerous to include here, so only the remoting-specific sections are highlighted and explained. However, the entire application can be downloaded from the book's web site.

The first screen the user sees is the login screen with the option to create a profile. Since the user is not part of the system, she needs to create a profile. The creation of a user profile is a private action and should be handled strictly between the Flash client and the remote server. Once the user data is collected, the application sends it to the remote server to add the user to the system. Example 11-5 shows the client-side Flash ActionScript that handles the user registration event when adding a user's profile to the database.

Example 11-5. Adding a user's profile

```
#include "NetServices.as"
NetService.setDefaultGatewayUrl("http://www.yourhost.com/flashservices/gateway");

function register (userObj) {
  var remote_conn = NetServices.createGatewayConnection( );
  var messengerService =
         remote_conn.getService("com.oreilly.pfcs.chapter11.fcsmessenger");
  var response = new Object( );
  // Handle the results.
  response.onResult = function (result) {
    // The server could return -1 if the action failed.
    if (result > -1) {
      _root.gotoAndStop("Login");              // Send the user to the login screen
    }
  };
  // Catch any errors
  response.onStatus = function (error) {
    Alert.show(error.description, error.type); // Create a modal alert window
  };
  messengerService.addUser(response, userObj);
}
```

The *register( )* method accepts an object as its argument. The userObj parameter would store all the local user properties that need to be collected by basic form elements (username, address, telephone number, etc.). The remote *addUser( )* method would take the user properties and insert them into the database, successfully registering the user into the system. The *onResult( )* handler could then proceed to the login screen by moving the playhead to the Login frame label.

Once the user has established her profile, she needs to log into the application. There are several different techniques to implement the login system. In Example 11-6, the user object is passed off to the FlashCom server; it builds the authentication mechanism in SSAS. This is a convenient approach if your application doesn't require any trusted security measures, because the client can simply establish a connection with the FlashCom Server and let the server manage validation of the user credentials needed to log on.

Example 11-6. Logging the user into the application

```
load("netservices.asc");

// trim( ) removes whitespace from the beginning and end of a string.
function trim (str) {
  if (typeof str != "string") return "";   // Make sure str is a string
  str = str.replace(/^\s*/, "");            // Trim leading spaces
  str = str.replace(/\s*$/, "");            // Trim trailing spaces
  str = str.replace(/\n/g,  "");            // Remove new lines
  str = str.replace(/\r/g,  "");            // Remove carriage returns
  str = str.replace(/\t/g,  "");            // Remove tabs
  return str;
}

application.onAppStart = function ( ) {
  userList_so = SharedObject.get("private/userList");
  application.gatewayURI = "http://www.yourhost.com/flashservices/gateway";
  application.service = "com.oreilly.pfcs.chapter11.fcsmessenger";
  NetServices.setDefaultGatewayUrl(application.gatewayURI);
};

application.onConnect = function (client, user) {
  if (typeof user == "undefined" || ! user.userName) { // Validate the user obj
    application.rejectConnection(client, {msg: "Invalid user object."});
    return false;
  }

  user.userName = trim(user.userName);
  if (user.userName.length == 0) {
    application.rejectConnection(client, {msg: "Invalid or empty user name."});
    return false;
  }

  var conn = NetServices.createGatewayConnection( );
  var messengerService = conn.getService(application.service);

  var loginResponse = new Object( );
  loginResponse.onResult = function (userProfile) {
    if (userProfile == -1) {
      application.rejectConnection(client,
        {msg: "The username and password could not be verified"});
      return false;
    }

    var item = userProfile.getItemAt(0);

    var tempUser = userList_so.getProperty(item.userid);
    if (tempUser) {
      application.rejectConnection(client,
        {msg: "Only one simultaneous login is allowed"});
    }

    user.password = "";      // Make sure the password is cleared
```

Example 11-6. Logging the user into the application (continued)

```
    delete user.password;    // Delete the password
    user.web = item.web;
    if (!item.hide_email) {
      user.email = item.email;
    }
    user.firstname = item.firstname;
    user.lastname = item.lastname;
    user.arrival  = new Date( );
    user.__ID__  = item.userid;
    client.user = user;
    userList_so.setProperty(item.userid, user);
    application.acceptConnection(client);
  };

  messengerService.login(loginResponse, user.userName, user.password);
};
```

The login process is slightly more complicated than registering a new user. In *application.onAppStart( )*, we initialize the necessary objects and properties for later. The userList_so shared object is used to ensure that only one login is allowed per user at a time. Once the user has established a connection and we have verified that she has provided the proper login credentials, the script writes an item to the shared object indicating that the user is present. When the user disconnects, the script removes the user record from the shared object so she will be able to log in again.

The first part of the *application.onConnect( )* method validates the user object and verifies that a username was passed. Once we know that at least something was passed for the user object and username, we need to verify the user's credentials with the database:

```
    var conn = NetServices.createGatewayConnection( );
    var messengerService = conn.getService(application.service);
    messengerService.login(loginResponse, user.userName, user.password);
```

Finally, the *onResult( )* method checks the results from the *login( )* action, adds the additional information to the user object, and accepts the user's connection. The remote procedure verifies the user's credentials and returns either the entire user record or -1 if the process failed. In the handler if the result is -1, we reject the connection:

```
    if (userProfile == -1) {
      application.rejectConnection(client,
        {msg: "The username and password could not be verified"});
      return false;
    }
```

The rest of the handler grabs the actual *RecordSet* item, checks to see if the user is already logged in, and adds the missing profile information to the user object.

Using this process to validate a user's credentials and log the user into a FlashCom application is a convenient approach because it creates a logical, linear flow of information. The user information is packaged and shipped to the FlashCom Server. The FlashCom server validates the information with the application server and accepts or denies the connection accordingly.

Because FlashCom doesn't natively support Secure Sockets Layer (SSL) connections and the credentials are sent in clear text over the network, this method doesn't offer any security, only a convenient means to establish a verified connection with a user. Other methods of authentication typically require the Flash client to validate credentials directly with an authenticating server first, then contact the FlashCom Server separately to connect to an application. Using this approach allows you to use SSL encryption for the information over the network. See Chapter 18 for more information.

Now that the user has been authenticated and logged in to the FlashCom Server, we need to request the friend list. The friend list will be similar to a buddy list used in an instant messaging client. The user can request to add and remove friends from his own list. The user can also see whether each friend is online and be notified if the friend's online status changes. To accomplish this, we use an approach similar to the login process. The Flash client requests the friend list from the FlashCom Server. The FlashCom Server grabs the actual list from the database and loops through all the friends to check whether they are currently online.

From the client scripts, we initiate the sequence by using the *NetConnection.call( )* method:

```
conn.call("getFriendList", null);
```

The server-side script defines the *getFriendList( )* method to request the list from the server and checks to see which friends are online:

```
Client.prototype.getFriendList = function () {
  var conn = NetServices.createGatewayConnection();
  var messengerService = conn.getService(application.service);

  var response = new Object();
  var theClient = this;
  response.onResult = function (friendList) {
    var len = friendList.length;
    for (var i = 0; i < len; i++) {
      var item = friendList.getItemAt(i);
      item.online = userList_so.getProperty(item.userid) == null;
    }
    theClient.call("receiveFriendList", null, friendList);
  };
  messengerService.getFriendList(response, this.user.userid);
};
```

The *getFriendList( )* method makes the request to the server for the list of friends for the passed userid. Once the results have been returned from the method, the handler loops through all of the results and finds the friends who are online by looking for them in the userList_so shared object. If the friend's userid is present in the shared object, then she is currently online.

Notice that the *getFriendList( )* method does not simply return the friendList, but it uses the *Client.call( )* method to call the *receiveFriendList( )* method on the client. Remoting calls are asynchronous, so the *return* statement would execute long before the results were actually returned from the server.

The last two remote methods, *addFriend( )* and *removeFriend( )*, are implemented in a similar way. The *addFriend( )* method should be sent through FlashCom, because the user who added the friend would like to see if the friend is currently online. The *removeFriend( )* method doesn't need to involve the FlashCom Server at all because it simply removes the friend from the list.

Of course, the possible applications are many and varied, but this gives you the basis for understanding how and when to use remoting in a typical scenario. Remember to see the book's web site for the full example files.

Securing Access

Protecting the server resources and the content that is shipped over the network is important to keeping unwanted intruders out of your application. When implementing a remoting method that requires the data to be secure, the best way to encrypt the data is to implement the remoting from the client to the server over an SSL connection. Since remote data that needs to be secure is typically personal information, this should be handled between a client application and an authenticating server, as described in Chapter 18. This can easily be done with a SWF running in the browser and connecting to the gateway with:

```
https://www.yourserver.com/flashservices/gateway
```

Protecting the remote methods on the server is also important. If you enable a remote method for public access, it is likely that those methods can be accessed from outside of your application. Fortunately, most remoting implementations provide a way to protect the methods with roles-based security. In ColdFusion, you can add the roles attribute to the method declaration (the <cffunction> tag) to restrict the access of the method to users who have been authenticated on the server and have been declared with the specific role:

```
<cffunction name="remoteMethod" access="remote" roles="authenticatedUser">
<!--- method body -->
</cffunction>
```

By declaring the role on the method, you force the user to log into the server before he can access the method. This can be done in two ways. The first way is to implement the *setCredentials( )* method on the client:

```
#include "NetServices.as"
NetServices.setDefaultGatewayUrl("http://www.yourhost.com/flashservices/gateway");
my_conn = NetServices.createGatewayConnection( );
my_conn.setCredentials("username", "password");
```

The *setCredentials( )* method adds a Credentials header to the outbound AMF packet and forces the server to initialize the login routine. In ColdFusion, this is usually defined in the *Application.cfm* file within a <cflogin> tag. Inside the <cflogin> tag, you define the authentication mechanism to verify the username and password passed in the Credentials header. Alternatively, you can also create your own custom login routine by declaring a public method that is not restricted with a roles attribute that will log in the user with the <cfloginuser> tag.

If your FlashCom application relies heavily upon remoting and you absolutely need the FlashCom application server data to be secure, you can create your network so only the FlashCom Server can access the resources defined on the server. This will guarantee that only the FlashCom Server has access to the remote resources and they cannot be abused by an outside party. See Chapter 18 for more information on security.

Conclusion

This chapter has demonstrated how Flash Remoting can be used to add data connectivity to FlashCom applications. Flash Remoting can access web services, server-side scripts, CGI applications, XML files, or the local filesystem with the help of an application server such as ColdFusion. Just your luck, the next chapter covers ColdFusion to perform numerous utility functions and database queries not possible with FlashCom alone.

We're almost done with our tour of FlashCom internals and associated technologies. By now, you should have a solid theoretical foundation but you may be having trouble seeing the forest for the trees. Don't fret; subsequent chapters deal with component frameworks, application development, performance tuning, security, and more.

CHAPTER 12

ColdFusion MX and FlashCom

In the previous chapter, you had the opportunity to learn about using Flash Remoting in conjunction with Flash Communication Server. In this chapter, you can learn some specifics involved in using Flash Remoting with ColdFusion MX and Flash-Com. You'll get a chance to see some practical, working examples so you can better understand some of the many ways in which you can leverage the benefits of Flash Remoting in conjunction with FlashCom.

Understanding ColdFusion MX and Flash Remoting

ColdFusion is a rapid application deployment service with a simple but powerful scripting language offering a remarkably easy learning curve. A free trial version of ColdFusion and information on installing and using it can be found at:

http://macromedia.com/software/coldfusion/

To perform the exercise in this chapter, which relies on ColdFusion, download and install the trial version from the preceding URL. The sample files are all available on the book's web site. Even if you don't install ColdFusion and test the example, it is informative to read through the code. For ColdFusion hosting services, refer to the resources cited in the Preface.

ColdFusion is often described as an application server, but it is technically a service of the application server. ColdFusion Markup Language (often referred to as CFML or ColdFusion) is a tag-based programming language, so you can use any text editor, such as the one included in Dreamweaver, HomeSite, or Flash Pro to write your CFML code. Many third-party editors, such as PrimalScript (*http://www.sapien.com/primalscript.aspx*), are also available. ColdFusion Server interprets the CFML logic and effectively converts it to an HTML page that can be served to any web browser.

ColdFusion offers a powerful underlying platform to develop applications that perform database queries, HTTP requests, FTP operations, file and directory system operations, email services, and much more. ColdFusion encourages good programming practices, such as separating business logic from page content and storing reusable chunks of CFML in ColdFusion components, which make it easy to create *n*-tiered applications. That, in turn, provides a great foundation for using ColdFusion in conjunction with Flash Remoting. In addition, ColdFusion has Flash Remoting technology built in, so no additional elements need be installed in order to use ColdFusion, Flash Remoting, and FlashCom Server together.

Using CFML and ColdFusion Components

CFML is an XML/HTML-like language you can use to create the two basic types of ColdFusion elements: ColdFusion pages (stored in *.cfm* or *.cfml* files) and ColdFusion components (stored in *.cfc* files). ColdFusion pages are part of the presentation tier and therefore don't really fit into the Flash Remoting model. ColdFusion components (CFCs), however, can form the business logic of a ColdFusion application and are, therefore, an appropriate choice when using ColdFusion in conjunction with Flash Remoting.

Let's take a few minutes to discuss the basics of building a CFC using CFML. If you're not already familiar with CFML or CFCs, consider getting a good ColdFusion reference such as *Programming ColdFusion MX, 2nd Edition* (O'Reilly). If you have a good programming background, you may find that this simple introduction and the online CFML documentation included with ColdFusion provide ample resources.

Like all ColdFusion code, CFCs can be created in any text editor. A CFC must always have a <cfcomponent> tag as the root element and should be stored in a text file with the extension *.cfc*. Enclosed within that are one or more methods defined using <cffunction> tags. The following code defines a CFC with a single method named *getProducts( )*, albeit one that doesn't do anything:

```
<cfcomponent>
  <cffunction name="getProducts">
  </cffunction>
</cfcomponent>
```

Typically, a method includes one or more lines of CFML between the opening and closing <cffunction> tags. A method can return a value using a <cfreturn> tag. The following code defines a CFC with a *getProducts( )* method in which ColdFusion queries a database and returns a recordset (additions shown in bold):

```
<cfcomponent>
  <cffunction name="getProducts">
    <cfquery datasource="fcs_products" name="qProducts">
      SELECT *
      FROM products
    </cfquery>
```

```
    <cfreturn qProducts />
  </cffunction>
</cfcomponent>
```

The query has been named qProducts using the name attribute in the <cfquery> tag. The results of the query are returned in the query object named qProducts. You can also define method parameters using <cfargument> tags. The following rewrite of the CFC adds a single parameter that allows the caller to specify the product category (additions shown in bold):

```
<cfcomponent>
  <cffunction name="getProducts">
    <cfargument name="category" type="string" />
    <cfquery datasource="fcs_products" name="qProducts">
      SELECT *
      FROM products
      WHERE category = '#category#'
    </cfquery>
    <cfreturn qProducts />
  </cffunction>
</cfcomponent>
```

By default, any parameter you define is required. However, you can make a parameter optional by specifying "false" for the required attribute of the <cfargument> tag. You can also set a default value with an optional parameter. The following rewrite of the CFC makes the category parameter optional. If no value is specified, ColdFusion uses a default value of "software" (changes shown in bold):

```
<cfcomponent>
  <cffunction name="getProducts">
    <cfargument name="category" type="string" required="false" default="software" />
    <cfquery datasource="fcs_products" name="qProducts">
      SELECT *
      FROM products
      WHERE category = '#category#'
    </cfquery>
    <cfreturn qProducts />
  </cffunction>
</cfcomponent>
```

When using CFCs with a standard ColdFusion presentation tier (ColdFusion pages), the preceding examples work just fine. However, if you want to make a CFC method accessible to Flash Remoting, you need to set the correct access for the method. You can make the *getProducts( )* method accessible to Flash Remoting by specifying a value of "remote" for the access attribute of the <cffunction> tag. The final version is as follows (changes shown in bold):

```
<cfcomponent>
  <cffunction name="getProducts" access="remote">
    <cfargument name="category" type="string" required="false" default="software" />
    <cfquery datasource="fcs_products" name="qProducts">
      SELECT *
      FROM products
```

```
        WHERE category = '#category#'
      </cfquery>
      <cfreturn qProducts />
   </cffunction>
</cfcomponent>
```

ColdFusion components should be saved into a directory accessible to the web server just as you'd save a ColdFusion template (*.cfm*). CFCs are standard text documents, so you can create them using any text editor. A CFC can define multiple functions (with separate <cffunction> tags), and you can give the component any name, such as *FCSUtilities.cfc*. The *.cfc* filename becomes the name of the service, and the functions defined within it become methods of the service as described in subsequent sections.

Using Flash Remoting with ColdFusion

You need to know five basic pieces of information in order to use Flash Remoting with ColdFusion from FlashCom:

- What is the Flash Remoting gateway URL?
- What is the service address?
- What is the name of the service method?
- What parameters does the method require/accept, and how can you pass those parameters to the method?
- What kind of data does the method return, and how should you handle the return data?

In truth, these issues are identical regardless of whether you are using Flash Remoting with ColdFusion or some other server-side technology such as Java, .NET, or PHP. Consult the online documentation for your server, or see *Flash Remoting: The Definitive Guide* for details on the slight differences in, say, the URL of the Flash Remoting gateway.

Determining the Flash Remoting gateway URL

Every Flash Remoting request and response is routed through a gateway. In the case of ColdFusion MX, the gateway is a servlet running in the */flashservices/gateway* context. For example, if you want to connect your FlashCom application to a ColdFusion Server on the same domain, use the following gateway URL:

> *http://localhost/flashservices/gateway*

The following code illustrates how to create a *NetConnection* object that connects to a Flash Remoting gateway in which ColdFusion is running on the same domain as FlashCom:

```
load("NetServices.asc");
application.onAppStart = function () (
```

```
NetServices.setDefaultGatewayUrl("http://localhost/flashservices/gateway");
var nc = NetServices.createGatewayConnection();
};
```

Determining the service address

Once you've created a connection to the Flash Remoting gateway, you next need to specify the address of the service. The service, in the case of ColdFusion, is a CFC. CFCs should be referenced using the fully qualified name. That means you include any package names delimited by dots, but you should not include the *.cfc* file extension. For example, if you have a CFC named *FCSUtilities.cfc* accessible within the root context of the web server on the ColdFusion machine, you can create a service object as follows:

```
var frservice = nc.getService("FCSUtilities", this);
```

The preceding code assumes that nc is a valid *NetConnection* object created using *NetServices.createGatewayConnection( )*.

If *FCSUtilities.cfc* is within the */fcs/cfcs* context, then the corresponding ActionScript code would be:

```
var frservice = nc.getService("fcs.cfcs.FCSUtilities", this);
```

Calling the service method

Calling the service method is simple. Just invoke the method on the service object using dot notation. The following code calls a CFC method named *getProducts( )* from a service object named frservice:

```
frservice.getProducts();
```

Passing parameters to a service method

You can pass parameters to a service method in one of two ways: positional or named. To use positional parameters, pass a comma-delimited list of values between the parentheses following the function name, such as:

```
frservice.addProfile(param1, param2, param3, param4);
```

Consider the following CFC method code:

```
<cffunction name="addProfile" access="remote">
  <cfargument name="name_first" type="string" />
  <cfargument name="name_last" type="string" />
  <cfargument name="city" type="string" />
  <cfargument name="category" type="string" />
  <cfquery datasource="fcs_profiles">
    INSERT INTO profiles(name_first, name_last, city, category)
    VALUES('#name_first#', '#name_last#', '#city#', '#category#')
  </cfquery>
  <cfreturn true />
</cffunction>
```

The *addProfile( )* method defined in the preceding code requires four parameters: name_first, name_last, city, and category. If you use standard, positional parameters when you call it from FlashCom, you need to specify the parameters in exactly the order in which the <cfargument> tags appear within the method definition. For example:

```
frservice.addProfile("Kevin", "Singh", "New York", "student");
```

Optionally, you can use named parameters. When you use named parameters, you pass the method a single object in which the names of the properties match the names of the parameters defined in the CFC method. The following is an example using the *addProfile( )* method:

```
frservice.addProfile({name_first: "Kevin", name_last: "Singh",
                      city: "New York", category: "student"});
```

If you use named parameters, then the order in which the properties appear within the object does not matter. The following code works just like the previous example, even though the order of the properties is different:

```
frservice.addProfile({name_last: "Singh", name_first: "Kevin",
                      category: "student", city: "New York"});
```

The named parameters option poses a potential quirk if you want to pass a single associative array (*Object* instance) as the parameter to a CFC method. For example, you may have a CFC defined as follows:

```
<cffunction name="addData" access="remote">
  <cfargument name="data_structure" type="struct" />
  <cfquery datasource="fcs_example">
    INSERT INTO sample(a, b, c, d)
    VALUES('#data_structure.a#', '#data_structure.b#',
           '#data_structure.c#', '#data_structure.d#')
  </cfquery>
</cffunction>
```

However, if you attempt to call that method from FlashCom in the following way, you'll get an error:

```
frservice.addData({a: "a", b: "b", c: "c", d: "d"});
```

ColdFusion reports an error saying that the method expects a parameter named data_structure and not parameters named a, b, c, and d. Because just one parameter is being passed and because that parameter is an associative array, Flash Remoting and ColdFusion will treat it as a series of named parameters. To solve the problem, simply wrap the associative array in another object as follows:

```
frservice.addData({data_structure: {a: "a", b: "b", c: "c", d: "d"}});
```

Handling return values

As you've already learned, Flash Remoting works asynchronously. Therefore, if a service method returns a value, you cannot use a simple assignment statement when calling the method via Flash Remoting. For example, the following will not work to assign to products_rs the value returned by *getProducts( )*:

```
var products_rs = frservice.getProducts( );
```

Instead, you need to handle the results with a response object as discussed in Chapter 11. The response object can be any ActionScript object to which you add appropriately named methods to handle the response. You can tell FlashCom how to handle the response by passing the response object when you call *getService( )*, as in the following:

```
var frservice = nc.getService("fcs.cfcs.FCSUtilities", this);
```

Here, the keyword this indicates that the current object will handle the response. If the preceding code appears within a method attached to the application object, it means the application object will handle any responses from any calls made to the service's methods.

The response object should have a method whose name takes the form: *serviceMethodName_Result*. For example, if the service method is named *getProducts( )*, the response object should have a method named *getProducts_Result( )*. The following is an example of such a method defined for the application object:

```
application.getProducts_Result = function (products_rs) {
  trace(products_rs.getLength( ) + " products were returned.");
};
```

For other ways to specify response objects, see Chapter 11.

Using Flash Remoting to Log Events

The following example shows how to use Flash Remoting to create a FlashCom logging system in conjunction with ColdFusion. A logging system can be very useful with your FlashCom applications. The Admin Service application included with FlashCom uses a logging system. However, that logging system writes to a stream, so the log is accessible only to applications that read the stream's binary FLV format, most notably FlashCom. In the following example, the logging system uses Flash Remoting to write the log data to a database so that the data can later be read from a variety of clients. You can then use SQL and ColdFusion features such as charting to create various reports, for example.

The FlashCom logging application has six basic parts:

- The database into which the log events are saved
- The Server-Side ActionScript (SSAS) class that takes care of caching and then sending the events to the database via ColdFusion and Flash Remoting
- The ColdFusion component that takes the event data sent from FlashCom and records it to the database

- The FlashCom application that utilizes the aforementioned ActionScript class
- The Flash client that connects to the FlashCom application
- The ColdFusion page that allows a user to view and filter events

Setting Up the Database

Before writing any ColdFusion or ActionScript code, you need to determine what data should be logged and create the database tables to store that data. You can approach recording log events in various ways. For the purposes of this example application, we'll record the following information:

Event type
> A FlashCom developer should be able to create arbitrary event types and record those in the database. For example, one application developer may want to differentiate between the application starting and stopping. Another developer may also want to log an event each time a user connects to the application.

Event description
> Allowing for a description of the event means developers can record more detailed information about the event.

Event time
> We record the time at which the event occurred.

Information object
> The information object allows developers to store any additional information they want. For example, when a client connects to the application, a developer may want to record the client's IP address.

Application name
> We record the name of the application.

Logger object name
> An application might have more than one logger object. Therefore, users may later want to be able to filter events based on the logger that recorded the event data.

You can use any database management system you want in order to create the database tables. The scripts provided in this chapter have been tested with MySQL, but generally should work with other standard database management systems.

The database we'll use in the example has a single table with seven fields. Table 12-1 describes the database table.

Table 12-1. The fields in table fcs_event

Field	Datatype
event_id	varchar(50)
event_type	varchar(50)

Table 12-1. The fields in table fcs_event (continued)

Field	Datatype
event_description	text
event_timestamp	datetime
info_object	text
application_name	varchar(50)
logger_name	varchar(50)

The following SQL script creates the database and table if run from many database management systems:

```
CREATE DATABASE 'fcs_log';
USE 'fcs_log';
CREATE TABLE 'fcs_event' (
  'event_id' varchar(50) NOT NULL default '',
  'event_type` varchar(50) default NULL,
  'event_description' text,
  'event_timestamp' datetime default '0000-00-00 00:00:00',
  'info_object' text,
  'application_name' varchar(50) default NULL,
  'logger_name' varchar(50) default NULL,
  PRIMARY KEY ('event_id')
) TYPE=MyISAM;
```

No indexes are created for this table, but depending on how the table will be used, indexes could be created for a number of the attributes.

Once you've created the database and table, you should make sure to register the database as a datasource within the ColdFusion Administrator.

You can register a datasource in ColdFusion by selecting the Data Sources link from the navigation menu on the left of the screen. Once at the next screen, enter **fcs_log** as the datasource name, select MySQL as the datasource, and click the Next button. From there, you'll be prompted to specify the server information so that ColdFusion can connect to the database.

In the example code, we'll use the datasource name of fcs_log.

Creating the Logger Class

Logging is managed on the server side by a Server-Side ActionScript class that we'll call *PFCSLogger*. The *PFCSLogger* class has the following specifications:

- Each instance should have a name it can use to distinguish itself from other instances.
- Instances of the class should write events to a stream and store the events until a maximum number of events is cached. Once the cache maximum is reached, it

should send the event data to the CFC in a single batch. That way, fewer Flash Remoting calls are made.

- The class should have an API that allows the developer to specify the event type, description, and info object when calling the *log( )* method. The event timestamp, application name, and logger name should be inserted automatically by the *PFCSLogger* class.

In order to define the *PFCSLogger* class, create a new SSAS file named *PFCSLogger.asc* and place it in a directory named *fcs_log* under the FlashCom *applications* directory.

Add the following code to *PFCSLogger.asc*:

```
// Load the NetServices classes.
load("NetServices.asc");

// Define the constructor. A single parameter specifies a unique instance name.
function PFCSLogger (name) {
  // If the name parameter is undefined, use a default value and issue a warning.
  if (name == undefined) {
    this.name = "defaultLogger";
    trace("PFCSLogger WARNING: Default logger name used. " +
        "Pass a parameter to the constructor to use a different logger name.");
  }
  this.name = name;

  // Create a new stream within a directory with the same name as the logger.
  this.cache = Stream.get(this.name + "/log_cache");

  // Start appending data to the stream.
  this.cache.record("append");

  // Create a new stream for playing back the data recorded in the cache stream.
  this.cache_playback = Stream.get("log_cache_playback");

  // Add a reference to the stream within which the data is recorded.
  this.cache_playback.log_cache = this.cache;

  // Specify a default maximum number of cached events.
  this.cache_playback.max_cached = 10;

  // Every event is recorded using send(), specifying log() as the method passed to
  // the send() call. Therefore, each event that is read from the stream calls the
  // log() method. So define log() such that it appends events to an array.
  this.cache_playback.log = function (info) {
    this.events.push(info);
  };

  // Use onStatus() to determine when the stream has stopped playing, so you'll
  // know when the events have been read from the stream.
  this.cache_playback.onStatus = function (info) {
    if (info.code == "NetStream.Play.Stop") {
      // Check whether the number of events in the stream exceeds the maximum
      // number of cached events. Also, if flush is true, call the service method
```

```
    // to record the events to the database. Call the stream's record( ) method
    // with parameter "record" to overwrite previous events that had been cached.
    if (this.events.length >= this.max_cached || this.flush) {
      this.fr_service[this.method](this.events);
      this.log_cache.record("record");
      this.flush = false;
    }
  }
};

  // Set an interval to check the cached events (default interval is 10 seconds).
  this.interval = setInterval(this, "checkCache", 10000);
}

// log( ) adds an event to the stream using send( ). The method has three parameters:
// the event type, the event description, and an optional info object.
PFCSLogger.prototype.log = function (event_type, description, info_object) {
  // Specify the log( ) method when calling send( ), so log( ) is called
  // when the events are read from the stream. Pass to the stream an object
  // containing the event type, event description, and info object, plus the
  // application name, the event timestamp, and the logger name.
  //
  this.cache.send("log", {event_timestamp: (new Date( )), event_type: event_type,
              description: description, info_object: info_object,
              application_name: application.name, logger_name: this.name});
};

// Define a method so that the default maximum cache value can be overwritten.
PFCSLogger.prototype.setMaxCached = function (max_cached) {
  this.cache_playback.max_cached = max_cached;
};

// Define a method so that the default poll interval can be overwritten.
PFCSLogger.prototype.setPollInterval = function (poll_interval) {
  clearInterval(this.interval);
  this.interval = setInterval(this, "checkCache", poll_interval);
};

// Define a method that allows the Flash Remoting information to be set.
PFCSLogger.prototype.setFlashRemoting = function (url, service_name, method) {
  NetServices.setDefaultGatewayUrl(url);
  var nc = NetServices.createGatewayConnection( );
  this.cache_playback.fr_service = nc.getService(service_name, this);
  this.cache_playback.method = method;
};

// flush( ) allows the data to get sent immediately to the CFC regardless of
// whether the maximum number of cached events has been stored.
PFCSLogger.prototype.flush = function ( ) (
  this.cache_playback.flush = true;
  this.checkCache( );
};

// checkCache( ) gets called at an interval to read the event data from the stream.
```

```
PFCSLogger.prototype.checkCache = function () {
  this.cache_playback.events = new Array();
  this.cache_playback.play(this.name + "/log_cache", -2, -1, 3);
};
```

Much of the preceding code is fairly self-explanatory. However, some portions warrant a more detailed explanation.

Each instance should have a name property that is set in the constructor. The name property allows the logger instance to create a stream that is unique to it. As you can see in the code, the stream that the logger creates is named log_cache, and it is placed within a directory with the same name as the name property:

```
function PFCSLogger(name) {
  if (name == undefined) {
    this.name = "defaultLogger";
    trace("PFCSLogger WARNING: Default logger name used. " +
         "Pass a parameter to the constructor to use a different logger name.");
  }
  this.name = name;
  this.cache = Stream.get(this.name + "/log_cache");
```

The stream should initially be set to record in append mode because the application could have restarted while previous events were still in cache. Using the append mode makes sure those previous events are not overwritten:

```
this.cache.record("append");
```

In order to play back the events recorded in the stream, you'll need a second stream. The cache_playback property creates a second stream in order to handle that task:

```
this.cache_playback = Stream.get("log_cache_playback");
```

Since streams are recorded in real time, you cannot read the events in the way you might read the contents of a shared object or an array. Instead, you need to play the stream, then use an *onStatus( )* event handler to determine when the end of the stream has been reached. When the end of the stream has been reached, the method will get called with an information object whose code property is "NetStream.Play. Stop". At that point, you can check how many events are recorded in the stream. If the maximum number of cache events has been reached, send the events to ColdFusion via Flash Remoting. Then, call the *record( )* method in record mode to overwrite the previously cached events:

```
this.cache_playback.onStatus = function (info) {
  if (info.code == "NetStream.Play.Stop") {
    if (this.events.length >= this.max_cached) {
      this.fr_service[this.method](this.events);
      this.log_cache.record("record");
    }
  }
};
}
```

The logger calls the *checkCache( )* method at a polling interval to read the contents of the stream. Each time the method is called, it should create a new, empty array into which to store the events and call the *play( )* method to play back the stream. The empty array is used to count the number of events. Each time the *log( )* method of the playback stream is called, you can add the event to the array. The *play( )* method plays back the stream to which the events are getting recorded. Notice that it uses a value of 3 for the fourth parameter passed to *play()*; this tells FlashCom to return the data in the stream immediately rather than in real time:

```
PFCSLogger.prototype.checkCache = function () (
  this.cache_playback.events = new Array();
  this.cache_playback.play(this.name + "/log_cache", -2, -1, 3);
};
```

Creating the CFC

The next step is to create the CFC that records the data in the database. The CFC has one method: *record( )*. The method accepts a single parameter, which should be an array of events. Each event is an associative array (in ColdFusion, they are called structures or structs) with the following properties: event_type, description, event_timestamp, logger_name, and application_name. It may also have an info_object property. The CFC method is fairly simple; it loops through each of the elements of the array and inserts the event data as database records. For the purposes of this example, create a subdirectory named *fcs_log* in the web root, and create a new file named *Logger.cfc* with the following CFC code in the *fcs_log* folder:

```
<cfcomponent>
  <!---
  # Define the record() method, and allow remote access from Flash Remoting.
  # Define one parameter named events, which should be an array.
  --->
  <cffunction name="record" access="remote">
    <cfargument name="events" type="array" />

    <!--- Loop through each of the elements in the events array. --->
    <cfloop from="1" to="#ArrayLen(events)#" index="i">

      <!--- Use CreateUUID() to create a primary key. --->
      <cfset event_id = CreateUUID() />
      <cfset event = events[i] />

      <!--- If info_object is defined, use WDDX to serialize the data into
            a string that can get inserted into the database.
            Otherwise, use an empty string.
      --->
      <cfif IsDefined("event.info_object")>
        <cfwddx action="cfml2wddx" input="#event.info_object#"
                output="info_object_wddx" />
```

```
      <cfelse>
        <cfset info_object_wddx = "" />
      </cfif>

      <!--- Insert the data into the database. --->
      <cfquery datasource="fcs_log">
      INSERT INTO fcs_event(event_id, event_type, event_description,
                      event_timestamp, info_object, application_name, logger_name)
      VALUES('#event_id#', '#event.event_type#', '#event.description#',
            #CreateODBCDateTime(event.event_timestamp)#, '#info_object_wddx#',
            '#event.application_name#', '#event.logger_name#')
      </cfquery>
    </cfloop>
  </cffunction>
</cfcomponent>
```

The CFC method is very basic—it takes the array of events and inserts the data into the database. A few details, however, could use some additional explanation.

Auto-incrementing integer fields can be used as primary keys in most database management systems. However, most database systems have a different way of defining auto-incrementing fields or sequences. While often less efficient than product-specific options such as Oracle Sequences, you can use a varchar field as the primary key and use a universally unique identifier value. ColdFusion has a function called *CreateUUID( )* that generates such a value. So the following code simply creates the ID and assigns it to a variable:

```
<cfset event_id = CreateUUID( ) />
```

Besides working with any database, *CreateUUID( )* has other advantages. For example, if you want to insert a new record and then retrieve the primary key, you can use *CreateUUID( )* to create the primary key in the code before the INSERT statement. That provides the key without having to do an INSERT and then a SELECT, as you would need to do if relying on the database system to generate a unique ID.

The event.info_object property is a ColdFusion structure. That means it is a complex datatype, and it would be rather difficult to parse the data, determine the datatypes of each of the values in the structure, and insert those values into the database in an efficient manner. Instead, it is much more convenient to serialize the structure as a WDDX packet. WDDX is an XML-based language specifically designed to represent complex data (arrays, associative arrays, recordsets, etc.) as strings so the data can be sent via protocols such as HTTP or, in this case, inserted into a text field in a database. ColdFusion has built-in WDDX support using the <cfwddx> tag, allowing you to quickly serialize (and deserialize) data. The following code converts the event.info_object structure to a WDDX packet and stores it in a variable named info_object_wddx:

```
<cfwddx action="cfml2wddx" input="#event.info_object#" output="info_object_wddx" />
```

Building the FlashCom Application

The next step is to create the FlashCom application, which simply creates instances of the *PFCSLogger* class and writes log events. Place the following code in your application's *main.asc* file. Assuming you named the FlashCom application's directory *fcs_log*, you can alternatively name the main file *fcs_log.asc*:

```
// Load the file that defines the PFCSLogger class.
load("PFCSLogger.asc");

application.onAppStart = function () (
  // When the application starts, create a new logger instance named "application."
  this.logger = new PFCSLogger("application");

  // Set the Flash Remoting information.
  this.logger.setFlashRemoting("http://localhost/flashservices/gateway",
                               "fcs_log.Logger", "record");

  // Write an event that indicates the application started.
  this.logger.log("app_start", "The application started");

  // Set an interval that calls log() every minute, just to generate test data.
  setInterval(this.logger, "log", 60000, "poll", "A poll interval ellapsed");
};

application.onConnect = function (newClient, username) {
  this.acceptConnection(newClient);
  newClient.username = username;

  // Create a new logger instance as a property of the client.
  newClient.logger = new PFCSLogger("client_" + username);
  newClient.logger.setFlashRemoting("http://localhost/flashservices/gateway",
                                    "fcs_log.Logger", "record");

  // Write a log event that says the user has connected.
  newClient.logger.log("client_connect", "A client connected to the application",
                   {username: username, ip: newClient.ip});
};

application.onDisconnect = function (disconnectingClient) {
  // Write a log event that indicates the user disconnected. Then call flush() to
  // send the data to the CFC.
  disconnectingClient.logger.log("client_disconnect", "A client disconnected",
             {username: disconnectingClient.username, ip: disconnectingClient.ip});
  disconnectingClient.logger.flush();
};

// When the application stops, send a log event and flush the cache.
application.onAppStop = function () (
  this.logger.log("app_stop", "The application stopped");
  this.logger.flush();
};
```

```
// Define a client method that simply returns an array of connected users.
// Write a log event each time the method is called.
Client.prototype.getUserList = function () {
  this.logger.log("get_user_list", "Client requested user list.",
                  {client: this.username, ip: this.ip});
  return application.clients;
};
```

The application code is fairly straightforward and doesn't require much additional explanation. It creates *PFCSLogger* instances—one as a property of the application object and one as a property of each connected client. The application logger logs events when the application starts and stops. Additionally, and simply for testing purposes, the application uses *setInterval( )* to log poll events once per minute. The client logger logs events when clients connect, disconnect, or call the *getUserList( )* method.

Creating the Flash Client

In order to test the application and the loggers, you next need to create a Flash movie to serve as the client. The client is very simple. It should contain two component instances—a Button component named cbt and a List component named user_list. Create a file named *loggerClient.fla*, add the two components using the Components panel, and give them instance names using the Properties panel. Then, rename the first layer to *Actions* and add the following ActionScript code to the first frame of the layer on the main timeline:

```
// Define a response object to handle responses from FlashCom client method calls.
var response = new Object();
response.onResult = function (data) {
  // When an array of users is returned, assign it to the data provider of the list.
  user_list.dataProvider = data;
};

// Define a listener object to handle click events dispatched by the button.
var listener = new Object();

// When a user clicks the button, call FlashCom application's getUserList() method.
listener.click = function () {
  nc.call("getUserList", response);
};

// Register the listener object with the button.
cbt.addEventListener("click", listener);

// Create the NetConnection.
var nc = new NetConnection();

// Connect to the application with a username of "some_user".
nc.connect("rtmp:/fcs_log", "some_user");
```

Once you've created and saved the Flash client movie, run it a few times. Running the client starts the FlashCom application and logs the corresponding events. Click the button to retrieve the user list, which also logs an event.

Now that we have some events, we need a way to view the event log.

Viewing the Events

The final step in the logger example is to create a simple ColdFusion page to view the events. You can define a ColdFusion page within the *fcs_log* directory in the web root. Name the page *log_view.cfm*, and add the following code to it:

```
<!--- Add three queries to retrieve the distinct event types, application names,
      and logger names.
--->
<cfquery datasource="fcs_log" name="qEventTypes">
SELECT DISTINCT event_type
FROM fcs_event
</cfquery>

<cfquery datasource="fcs_log" name="qApplications">
SELECT DISTINCT application_name
FROM fcs_event
</cfquery>

<cfquery datasource="fcs_log" name="qLoggers">
SELECT DISTINCT logger_name
FROM fcs_event
</cfquery>

<html>
  <head>
    <title>FCS Log</title>
  </head>
  <body>
    <!--- Define a form that posts back to itself. --->
    <form action="<cfoutput>#CGI.SCRIPT_NAME#</cfoutput>" method="post">
      <table>
        <!--- Define three select controls that allow the user to select event
              types, application names, and logger names to filter the records.
        --->
        <tr>
          <td>Event Type:</td>
          <td>
            <select name="event_type">
              <option value="*">any event type</option>
              <cfoutput query="qEventTypes">
                <option
                value="#qEventTypes.event_type#"> #qEventTypes.event_type#</option>
              </cfoutput>
            </select>
          </td>
```

```
      </tr>

      <tr>
        <td>Application:</td>
        <td>
          <select name="application_name">
            <option value="*">any application</option>
            <cfoutput query="qApplications">
              <option value="#qApplications.application_name#">
                            #qApplications.application_name#
              </option>
            </cfoutput>
          </select>
        </td>
      </tr>

      <tr>
        <td>Logger:</td>
        <td>
          <select name="logger_name">
            <option value="*">any logger</option>
            <cfoutput query="qLoggers">
              <option
                    value="#qLoggers.logger_name#">#qLoggers.logger_name#</option>
            </cfoutput>
          </select>
        </td>
      </tr>

      <tr>
        <td colspan="2">
          <input type="submit" name="submit_button" value="View Events" />
        </td>
      </tr>
    </table>
</form>

<!--- If the form has been submitted, display the records. --->
<cfif IsDefined("FORM.submit_button")>
  <!--- Add a query that retrieves the matching event records. --->
  <cfquery datasource="fcs_log" name="qEvents">
    SELECT *
    FROM fcs_event
    WHERE 1 = 1
    <cfif FORM.event_type NEQ "*">
      AND event_type = '#FORM.event_type#'
    </cfif>
    <cfif FORM.application_name NEQ "*">
      AND application_name = '#FORM.application_name#'
    </cfif>
    <cfif FORM.logger_name NEQ "*">
      AND logger_name = '#FORM.logger_name#'
    </cfif>
  </cfquery>
```

```
       <table cellpadding="5">
         <tr>
           <td></td>
           <td>event type</td>
           <td>description</td>
           <td>timestamp</td>
           <td>application</td>
           <td>logger</td>
           <td>info object</td>
         </tr>
         <cfoutput query="qEvents">
           <tr bgcolor="##FFF5DF">
             <td>#qEvents.CurrentRow#</td>
             <td>#qEvents.event_type#</td>
             <td>#qEvents.event_description#</td>
             <td>#DateFormat(qEvents.event_timestamp, "medium")#
                 #TimeFormat(qEvents.event_timestamp, "medium")#</td>
             <td>#qEvents.application_name#</td>
             <td>#qEvents.logger_name#</td>
             <td>
               <cfif qEvents.info_object NEQ "">
                 <cfwddx action="wddx2cfml" input="#qEvents.info_object#"
                         output="info_object_deserialized" />
                 <cfloop collection="#info_object_deserialized#" item="item">
                   #item#: #info_object_deserialized[item]#<br />
                 </cfloop>
               </cfif>
             </td>
           </tr>
         </cfoutput>
       </table>
     </cfif>
   </body>
 </html>
```

Once you've created the ColdFusion page or copied the version from the book's web site to your server, you can browse to it and view the events that have been logged.

This event-logging application is but one example of the kinds of applications you can build using Flash Remoting to communicate between FlashCom and ColdFusion.

Getting a List of Streams

ColdFusion can be used to do more than just create log files. One particularly useful feature that FlashCom does not have is the ability to return the contents of a directory—such as the name of the streams contained within an application. If ColdFusion is running on the same computer as FlashCom, it is quite simple to use the <cfdirectory> tag to retrieve a list of .flv files within a directory. Being able to search through the *streams* folder of an application is an important feature of administrative applications that must monitor disk utilization, clear out older streams, or provide alerts. It is a simpler alternative to maintaining stream names in a database.

You could design your application so that each client Flash movie makes separate Flash Remoting calls to request a list of stream names. However, this approach could generate many Flash Remoting calls, especially if the Flash clients continually poll ColdFusion for updated lists. If each of 100 clients each polls once per minute, 100 Flash Remoting requests are sent to the server per minute. A much more efficient approach is to make the Flash Remoting calls from the server. Then, even if 100 clients are polling once per minute, only one Flash Remoting call is made per minute. Using a remote shared object (RSO), the server can update the clients as needed. And, if done appropriately, the only data that the RSO will need to send to the clients is the data that has changed. Therefore, if the directory listing doesn't change during 10 minutes, no directory data is sent to the clients during that time. For each new stream added, one piece of data, rather than the entire directory listing, is sent to each of the clients. The following example builds an application that uses Flash Remoting calls from FlashCom to retrieve a listing of streams within the application. It then uses an RSO to update any connected clients. The example has four parts:

- The streams
- The CFC
- The FlashCom application
- The Flash client

Setting Up the Streams

The first step in the example is to set up the streams. You should create a new FlashCom directory for the application named *fcs_streams*. Then, within that directory, create a subdirectory named *streams*, and within the *streams* directory, create a subdirectory named *_definst_*. The *streams/_definst_* directory is the default location for streams within a FlashCom application. You can also add subdirectories within that directory. In the example, we'll add subdirectories to illustrate how ColdFusion can recurse through the subdirectories to retrieve the streams. So within the *streams/_definst_* directory, create another subdirectory named *archived*.

Once you've set up the directory structure, the next step is to add the streams. If you don't already have some *.flv* files you can move to the directory, you can download an archive of sample streams from the book's web site (*http://www.flash-communications.net*). Copy two streams (*.flv* files) to the *streams/_definst_* directory and two streams to the *streams/_definst_/archived* directory.

Creating the CFC

Once you've set up the application and placed the *.flv* files in the appropriate directories, the next step is to create the CFC that can read the contents of those directories. You should create a new directory in the web root and name it *fcs_streams*.
Then, within that directory, create a new file named *DirectoryUtilities.cfc*, and add
the following code to it:

```
<cfcomponent>
 <!---
 # Define getFiles() with remote access. Declare two parameters specifying
 # the subdirectory and main path. For example, the subdirectory may be \ and the
 # main path may be C:\Program Files\Macromedia\Flash Communication Server
 # MX\applications\fcs_streams\streams\_definst_.
 --->
 <cffunction name="getFiles" access="remote">
   <cfargument name="sub_path" />
   <cfargument name="main_path" />

   <!--- Define two local variables; they must be local variables because the
         method calls itself recursively and, otherwise, incorrect values result.
   --->
   <cfset var aFiles = "" />
   <cfset var stData = "" />

   <!--- Retrieve the directory listing for the specified directory. --->
   <cfdirectory action="list" directory="#main_path##sub_path#" name="qFiles" />

   <!--- Create a new array. --->
   <cfset aFiles = ArrayNew(1) />

   <!--- Loop through each of the items in the directory listing. --->
   <cfloop query="qFiles">

     <!--- If the type of element is a directory, call getFiles() recursively.
           Otherwise, just add the file to the array.
     --->
     <cfif qFiles.type EQ "Dir">

       <!--- Determine the correct path to send to the getFiles() method. --->
       <cfif sub_path EQ "\">
         <cfset new_path = "\" & qFiles.name />
       <cfelse>
         <cfset new_path = sub_path & "\" & qFiles.name />
       </cfif>
       <cfset directory_files = getFiles(new_path, main_path) />

       <!--- Add each of the files from the return array to the aFiles array. --->
       <cfloop from="1" to="#ArrayLen(directory_files)#" index="i">
         <cfset ArrayAppend(aFiles, directory_files[i]) />
       </cfloop>
     <cfelse>
       <!--- If the element is a file, create a new structure, populate it
```

```
                 with some information about the file, and add it to the array.
            --->
            <cfset stData = StructNew( ) />
            <cfset stData.name = qFiles.name />
            <cfset stData.path = sub_path />
            <cfset stData.main_path = main_path />
            <cfset ArrayAppend(aFiles, stData) />
          </cfif>
       </cfloop>
       <!--- Return the array. --->
       <cfreturn aFiles />
     </cffunction>
  </cfcomponent>
```

The CFC code isn't very big, but it does use recursion, which can appear somewhat confusing at first. So some further explanation will help clarify the code.

Recursive methods are methods that call themselves. The *getFiles( )* method is recursive so that it can retrieve the files from subdirectories as well. Therefore, the method takes two parameters: the main directory path and the subdirectory path:

```
<cffunction name="getFiles" access="remote">
  <cfargument name="sub_path" />
  <cfargument name="main_path" />
```

The main directory path remains the same with each recursive call to the method, but the subdirectory path changes to indicate from which subdirectory the method should retrieve a listing of contents.

Next, you want to make sure you define two variables as local variables. Using the var keyword in CFML, as in ActionScript, scopes the variable to the method or function:

```
<cfset var aFiles = "" />
<cfset var stData = "" />
```

In the case of aFiles and stData, the variables must be local; otherwise, each time the method is called recursively, the previous values would be overwritten and the return value would be incorrect. Making the variables local ensures they are not overwritten by recursive calls.

The <cfdirectory> tag allows ColdFusion to work with directories on the server running ColdFusion. When the action attribute is set to "list", the tag retrieves a list of the contents of the specified directory as a query object and assigns it to the variable specified by the name attribute. Therefore, the following code creates a new query object named qFiles with the contents of the directory:

```
<cfdirectory action="list" directory="#main_path##sub_path#" name="qFiles" />
```

In order to store and return information about each stream, create an array and assign it to the aFiles local variable:

```
<cfset aFiles = ArrayNew(1) />
```

The next step is to loop through each of the records in the qFiles object:

```
<cfloop query="qFiles">
```

Every record in a query object returned by `<cfdirectory>` contains several fields, including type and name. The type can be either "Dir" or "File". If the type is "Dir", the element is a directory. In that case, the code calls *getFiles( )* recursively using the new subdirectory in order to retrieve that subdirectory's listing:

```
<cfif qFiles.type EQ "Dir">
  <cfif sub_path EQ "\">
    <cfset new_path = "\" & qFiles.name />
  <cfelse>
    <cfset new_path = sub_path & "\" & qFiles.name />
  </cfif>
  <cfset directory_files = getFiles(new_path, main_path) />
```

Once you've retrieved the subdirectory's listing of files, you can add each element to the aFiles array:

```
<cfloop from="1" to="#ArrayLen(directory_files)#" index="i">
  <cfset ArrayAppend(aFiles, directory_files[i]) />
</cfloop>
```

If the element is a file, the code creates a new structure and stores the name of the file, the subdirectory path, and the main path to the file. It then appends that structure to the aFiles array:

```
<cfelse>
  <cfset stData = StructNew( ) />
  <cfset stData.name = qFiles.name />
  <cfset stData.path = sub_path />
  <cfset stData.main_path = main_path />
  <cfset ArrayAppend(aFiles, stData) />
</cfif>
```

Writing the FlashCom Application

The next step is to create the FlashCom application, which is responsible for polling ColdFusion to get updated listings of streams and then updating connected clients using a remote shared object. To create the FlashCom application, create a new file named *main.asc* or *fcs_streams.asc* in the *fcs_streams* FlashCom directory. Then add the following code to the file. Look over the code briefly, and we'll discuss it momentarily. Note that each slot in the RSO uses a unique key composed of the subdirectory path and the name of the stream file:

```
load("NetServices.asc");

application.onAppStart = function ( ) {
  NetServices.setDefaultGatewayUrl("http://localhost/flashservices/gateway");
  var ncFlashRemoting = NetServices.createGatewayConnection( );
  this.frservice = ncFlashRemoting.getService("fcs_streams.DirectoryUtilities",
                                              this);
```

```
// Create a NetConnection to connect to the Admin Service application.
this.ncAdmin = new NetConnection();

// Once the Admin Service connection has been established, call getConfig()
// within that app to retrieve the physical path to the current application.
this.ncAdmin.onStatus = function (info) {
  if (info.code == "NetConnection.Connect.Success") {
    var key = "Adaptor:_defaultRoot_/VirtualHost:_defaultVhost_/AppsDir";
    this.call("getConfig", application, key, "/");
  }
};
// Connect to the admin application using the correct username and password.
// Replace the username and password with those you've set in your Admin Service.
this.ncAdmin.connect("rtmp://localhost:1111/admin",
                     "adminuser", "adminpassword");

// Create a remote shared object to store the streams information.
this.files_so = SharedObject.get("files");
};

// The onResult() method is called once the Admin Service returns a response
// from the getConfig() call.
application.onResult = function (value) {
  // Call the getFiles() CFC method to get the streams within the current
  // application. Use an interval to poll every 10 seconds.
  var application_path = application.name.split("/");
  var path = value.data + "\\" + application_path[0] + "\\streams\\" +
             application_path[1];
  this.file_interval = setInterval(this.frservice, "getFiles", 10000, "\\", path);
  this.frservice.getFiles("\\", path);
};

application.getFiles_Status = function (info) {
  for (var item in info) {
    trace(item + " " + info[item]);
  }
};

// The getFiles_Result() method is called when the CFC method returns a response.
application.getFiles_Result = function (files) {

  // Lock the RSO so it doesn't send updates until every file has been checked.
  this.files_so.lock();

  var key;
  var previous_data;
  var update;

  // Loop through every one of the files returned by the CFC method.
  for (var i = 0; i < files.length; i++) {

    // Create a key to use with the RSO. Use the subdirectory path and the
    // filename to ensure a key that is unique to the stream.
```

```
  key = "file" + files[i].PATH.split("\\").join("_") + "_" +
                 files[i].NAME.split(".")[0];

  // Retrieve the data stored in the RSO currently for the key.
  previous_data = this.files_so.getProperty(key);

  // Assume the file didn't change and the clients don't need to be updated.
  update = false;

  // If the previous data was null, it is a new stream, so set update to true.
  // Otherwise, loop through the elements of the previous data; if any values
  // differ from the data returned by the CFC method, set update to true.
  if (previous_data == null) {
    update = true;
  }
  else {
    for (var item in previous_data) {
      if (previous_data[item] != files[i][item]) {
        update = true;
      }
    }
  }

  // Change the RSO element only if its value differs from the previous version.
  if (update) {
    this.files_so.setProperty(key, files[i]);
  }
}

// You also need to check whether a stream was removed. So get
// the keys of the RSO in order to loop through it.
var keys = this.files_so.getPropertyNames();

// If there are no keys in the RSO, unlock the shared object and exit the method.
if (keys == undefined) {
  this.files_so.unlock();
  return;
}

var remove;

// Loop through each of the keys of the shared object.
for (var i = 0; i < keys.length; i++) {
  remove = true;

  // Loop through each of the files to make sure the element in the
  // shared object still exists on the server.
  for (var j = 0; j < files.length; j++) {
    key = "file" + files[j].PATH.split("\\").join("_") + "_" +
                   files[j].NAME.split(".")[0];
    if (key == keys[i]) {
      remove = false;
      break;
    }
```

```
      }
      // If no matching element was found, remove the element from the shared object.
      if (remove) {
        this.files_so.setProperty(keys[i], null);
      }
    }
    this.files_so.unlock( );
  };
```

The preceding code is complex enough that it deserves some further explanation.

When the application starts, you want to programmatically determine the physical path to the application on the server. You can retrieve that information using the Admin Service application that comes with FlashCom. So you should connect to the Admin Service using a *NetConnection* object (just as the Admin Console client, *admin.swf*, that comes with FlashCom does). Make sure you use the correct username and password in order to connect to the application (these are set in the Admin Service application). Once a "NetConection.Connect.Success" message is returned, you can call the *getConfig( )* method to retrieve the physical path to the *applications* directory:

```
this.ncAdmin = new NetConnection( );
this.ncAdmin.onStatus = function (info) {
  if (info.code == "NetConnection.Connect.Success") {
    var key = "Adaptor:_defaultRoot_/VirtualHost:_defaultVhost_/AppsDir";
    this.call("getConfig", application, key, "/");
  }
};
this.ncAdmin.connect("rtmp://localhost:1111/admin",
                     "adminuser", "adminpassword");
```

The response from the *getConfig( )* method is handled by the application object. Once the response is returned, you next want to calculate the path to the streams in the application and then call the *getFiles( )* CFC method. The following code assumes you are using FlashCom on a Windows machine and, therefore, need to convert forward slashes to backslashes. Additionally, it sets up a polling interval to call *getFiles( )* every 10 seconds:

```
application.onResult = function (value) {
  var application_path = application.name.split("/");
  var path = value.data + "\\" + application_path[0] + "\\streams\\" +
             application_path[1];
  this.file_interval = setInterval(this.frservice, "getFiles", 10000, "\\", path);
  this.frservice.getFiles("\\", path);
};
```

Once the response is returned from the *getFiles( )* call, the first step is to lock the shared object. Locking the shared object makes sure that the connected clients aren't updated as soon as a property within the RSO is changed. Instead, it will wait until *unlock( )* is called:

```
application.getFiles_Result = function (files) {
  this.files_so.lock( );
```

Checking the returned files against the existing RSO data takes two steps. The first is to loop through each of the elements of the returned array to check whether any elements have been added. Each element in the RSO uses a unique key composed of the subdirectory path and the name of the stream file:

```
for (var i = 0; i < files.length; i++) {
  key = "file" + files[i].PATH.split("\\").join("_") + "_" +
             files[i].NAME.split(".")[0];
  previous_data = this.files_so.getProperty(key);
  update = false;
  if (previous_data == null) {
    update = true;
  }
  else {
    for (var item in previous_data) {
      if (previous_data[item] != files[i][item]) {
        update = true;
      }
    }
  }
  if (update) {
    this.files_so.setProperty(key, files[i]);
  }
}
```

The second step is to loop through each of the elements of the RSO to see whether any elements have been removed from the server. Each element of the RSO needs to be compared to each element of the files array. If the RSO key is not found in the files array, then it means the stream was removed from the server. Therefore, it should be removed from the RSO as well:

```
for (var i = 0; i < keys.length; i++) {
  remove = true;
  for (var j = 0; j < files.length; j++) {
    key = "file" + files[j].PATH.split("\\").join("_") + "_" +
               files[j].NAME.split(".")[0];
    if (key == keys[i]) {
      remove = false;
      break;
    }
  }
  if (remove) {
    this.files_so.setProperty(keys[i], null);
  }
}
```

Once the comparisons and updates have taken place, next call the *unlock( )* method to send updates to the clients if necessary:

```
this.files_so.unlock( );
```

Making the Streams Client

The remaining step in the example is to create the client that retrieves the stream listing from the FlashCom application. In order to create the client, make a new Flash document, name it *streamList.fla,* and add two items to the Stage: a List component instance named files_list and a Video object named playback_vid. Then, add the following code to the first frame of the *Actions* layer on the main timeline. The client displays a list of streams in a listbox and plays back the stream selected by the user:

```
// Create the connection to the FlashCom application.
var nc = new NetConnection( );
nc.connect("rtmp:/fcs_streams");

// Create the RSO.
var rso = SharedObject.getRemote("files", nc.uri);

// When the RSO synchronizes, remove the elements from the list, and
// repopulate it with the contents in the RSO.
rso.onSync = function (list) {
  files_list.removeAll( );
  for (var item in this.data) {
    files_list.addItem(this.data[item].NAME, this.data[item]);
  }
};

// Connect the RSO.
rso.connect(nc);

// Define a listener object to listen to change events dispatched by the list.
var oListener = new Object( );

// A change event means the user selected a stream from the list,
// so play back the selected stream.
oListener.change = function (oEvent) {
  // Use split( ) to split the path of the stream data using a backslash as the
  // delimiter. Then, remove the first element from the array to get rid of the
  // empty string element.
  var path_array = oEvent.target.value.PATH.split("\\");
  path_array.shift( );

  // Next, if the first element is still an emtpy string, remove it as well.
  if (path_array[0] == "") {
    path_array.shift( );
  }

  // Join the elements of the path array again using a forward slash since that is
  // the format FlashCom uses to play streams.
  var path = path_array.join("/");

  // If the path is not an empty string, append a trailing forward slash.
  if (path.length > 0) {
    path += "/";
  }
```

```
// Add the stream name to the path. Use split( ) to remove the file extension.
path += oEvent.target.value.NAME.split(".")[0];

// Play the stream.
ns.play(path);

// Attach the stream to the Video object.
playback_vid.attachVideo(ns);
};

// Register the listener object with the List instance.
files_list.addEventListener("change", oListener);

// Define the NetStream object to play back the streams.
var ns = new NetStream(nc);
```

Once you've added the preceding code, you can test the movie. You should get a list-ing of the streams in the *streams/_definst_* directory as well as the *streams/_definst_/ archived* directory. If you select one of the streams from the list, it will play back. Additionally, with the client still running, notice what happens when you move streams in and out of the *streams/_definst_* and *streams/_definst_/archived* directo-ries. Because of the polling interval on the server, it may take up to 10 seconds to see the newly updated stream list.

This example demonstrates one of many FlashCom applications that use ColdFu-sion's powerful features to make the application more capable or efficient.

Using ColdFusion and FTP to Mirror Streams

If your FlashCom application gets enough traffic, you may need to have more than one FlashCom Server running. Depending on what your application does, you may need to make sure that the lists of streams on each of the servers are synchronized. For example, users may have the option of recording videos that are viewable by any-one else using the application. However, if the user who records the video is con-nected to FlashCom Server A and another user is connected to FlashCom Server B, the user connected to Server B won't be able to view the video from Server A. The following example shows one way to use ColdFusion, Flash Remoting, and FTP to keep the streams on multiple servers in sync. The application consists of five basic parts:

- A Server-Side ActionScript class to manage streams
- A simple Server-Side ActionScript class to represent an FTP server
- A CFC to manage the FTP operations
- The FlashCom application file
- A simple Flash client movie to record new streams

Additionally, in order to successfully run the application, you'll need access to at least one FTP server. Even though the general idea of the example is to mirror streams on a cluster of FlashCom Servers, you don't need to have more than one FlashCom Server to run the basic example and see how it works. In fact, its usefulness isn't limited to synchronizing files on other FlashCom Servers. The same system can be used to back up streams to another server; you also can use it to copy streams from a dedicated recording server to individual distribution servers or to a storage area network.

Creating a Stream Manager

The example assumes that users can record new streams and, as soon as the stream has finished publishing, you want to make copies to one or more other servers. Therefore, you'll need a stream manager class on the server that can generate unique stream names and listen to get notified when the stream has finished publishing.

The *PFCSStreamManager* class does three basic things:

- Generates a new, unique stream name for each stream
- Connects to the stream
- Once the client finishes publishing to the stream, the manager dispatches an event to listeners, notifying them that the stream is ready to copy

You can create the *PFCSStreamManager* class within a new FlashCom application named *fcs_ftp*. In the *fcs_ftp* directory, create a new file named *PFCSStreamManager.asc*, and add the following code to the file:

```
function PFCSStreamManager( ) {
  // Create a new associative array to store the streams that are publishing.
  this.streams_publishing = new Object( );
}

PFCSStreamManager.prototype.getNewStreamID = function ( ) {
  // Create two numbers—one based on epoch milliseconds and one based on a
  // random number from 0 to 100,000. Then, concatenate those to form a unique
  // stream identifier (the chance that the ID isn't unique is very low).
  var number_1 = (new Date()).getTime( );
  var number_2 = Math.round(Math.random( ) * 100000);
  var id = "stream_" + number_1 + "_" + number_2;

  // Create a new Stream object.
  this.streams_publishing[id] = Stream.get("playback_" + id);

  // Tell the stream its ID.
  this.streams_publishing[id].id = id;

  this.streams_publishing[id].parent = this;
  this.streams_publishing[id].onStatus = function (info) {
    // The "NetStream.Play.UnpublishNotify" code is recevied when the client stops
    // recording the stream. Dispatch a publish_done event to notify listeners.
```

```
    if (info.code == "NetStream.Play.UnpublishNotify") {
      // Dispatch a publish_done event, and pass the stream ID in the event object.
      this.parent.dispatchEvent({type: "publish_done", id: this.id});
      // Delete the stream.
      delete this.parent.streams_publishing[id];
    }
  };

  // Start playing the stream.
  this.streams_publishing[id].play(id);

  // Return the new stream's ID.
  return id;
};

// Define a dispatchEvent() method to notify listeners.
PFCSStreamManager.prototype.dispatchEvent = function (event) {
  // Loop through each of the listeners for the specific event type. Call the
  // method of the listener that matches the event name. Pass it the event object.
  for (var i = 0; i < this["listeners_" + event.type].length; i++) {
    this["listeners_" + event.type][i][event.type](event);
  }
};

// Add new listeners.
PFCSStreamManager.prototype.addEventListener = function (type, listener) {
  if (this["listeners_" + type] == undefined) {
    this["listeners_" + type] = new Array();
  }
  this["listeners_" + type].push(listener);
};
```

The preceding code is quite straightforward and doesn't require much further explanation. However, a few items are worth discussing in more detail.

The *getNewStreamID( )* method generates a new, unique stream ID. Since potentially many FlashCom Servers will allow users to record streams and copy them to other servers, it's important to generate IDs that are likely to be unique across servers. Although it doesn't absolutely guarantee that the same ID won't be generated twice, concatenating the epoch milliseconds with a random number makes duplicate stream IDs exceedingly unlikely:

```
var number_1 = (new Date()).getTime();
var number_2 = Math.round(Math.random() * 100000);
var id = "stream_" + number_1 + "_" + number_2;
```

You can next create a new stream to which to subscribe and listen for events of the stream to which the client will publish. The *onStatus( )* method is called with a "Net-Stream.Play.UnpublishNotify" code when the user finishes publishing to the stream. It simply dispatches a *publish_done* event to listeners:

```
this.streams_publishing[id] = Stream.get("playback_" + id);
this.streams_publishing[id].id = id;
this.streams_publishing[id].parent = this;
```

```
this.streams_publishing[id].onStatus = function (info) {
  if (info.code == "NetStream.Play.UnpublishNotify") {
    this.parent.dispatchEvent({type: "publish_done", id: this.id});
    delete this.parent.streams_publishing[id];
  }
};
this.streams_publishing[id].play(id);
```

Now that the stream manager class is complete, let's tackle the FTP server class.

Creating an FTP Server Class

The next step is very simple. You want to create a basic class that represents the data for an FTP server, including:

url

The URL of the FTP server, such as "publicstreams.flashcommunications-net", excluding the ftp: protocol.

username

A username that has write access to the FTP server.

password

The password corresponding to the username for access to the FTP server.

directory

The initial (root) directory to which to copy files.

passive_mode

Whether to use passive mode for the FTP transfer. Passive FTP (a.k.a. PASV FTP) allows a connection to be initiated from the client rather than from the server. Passive mode may be required for users behind some gateways or router-based firewalls. However, some FTP servers support active transfers only. Cold-Fusion supports both, which is why we leave it as a configurable option that is specified for each FTP server individually.

You can create a new file named *FTPServer.asc* in the *fcs_ftp* directory, and add the following SSAS code to it:

```
function FTPServer (url, username, password, directory, passive_mode) {
  this.url = url;
  this.username = username;
  this.password = password;
  this.directory = directory;

  // Make passive_mode an optional parameter. It can have values of
  // either "yes" or "no" (defaults to "no" if no value is passed in).
  if (passive_mode == undefined) {
    this.passive = "no";
  }
  else {
    this.passive = passive_mode;
  }
}
```

We'll use *FTPServer* instances to describe each FTP server to which to copy the stream. The CFC that we'll write next uses this data to perform the FTP transfers.

Using ColdFusion with FTP

You next want to create a CFC that will use FTP to copy a file from one server to one or more other servers. The method should accept four parameters:

ftp_servers
> An array of *FTPServer* objects

file
> The name of the file to copy, such as an *.flv* stream

path
> The path to the file on the local machine

transfermode
> An optional parameter indicating the transfer mode (ASCII or binary); defaults to binary, as should be used for *.flv* files

Create a new CFC document named *FTPUtilities.cfc*, and save it to a directory named *fcs_ftp* in the web root. Add the following code to the file:

```
<cfcomponent>
  <cffunction name="copyFile" access="remote">
    <cfargument name="ftp_servers" type="array" />
    <cfargument name="file" type="string" />
    <cfargument name="path" type="string" />
    <cfargument name="transfermode" type="string"
                required="false" default="binary" />

    //Loop through FTPServer objects, and use <cfftp> to copy the file.
    <cfloop from="1" to="#ArrayLen(ftp_servers)#" index="i">

      //Create the connection to the server.
      <cfftp action="open" server="#ftp_servers[i].url#"
             username="#ftp_servers[i].username#"
             password="#ftp_servers[i].password#" connection="ftp_connection" />

      //Copy the file.
      <cfftp action="putfile" transfermode="#transfermode#"
             localfile="#path##file#" remotefile="#ftp_servers[i].directory##file#"
             passive="#ftp_servers[i].passive#" connection="ftp_connection" />

      //Close the connection to the server.
      <cfftp action="close" connection="ftp_connection" />
    </cfloop>
  </cffunction>
</cfcomponent>
```

Our ColdFusion component implements a *copyFile( )* method that copies the specified file to all the FTP servers specified by ftp_servers, an array of *FTPServer* objects (one describing each FTP server).

Making the FlashCom Application

The next step is to assemble the FlashCom application. The application should allow a client to connect, request a stream ID, and publish to the stream. Once the client stops publishing, the FlashCom application should automatically copy the file to one or more servers.

Create a new file named *fcs_ftp.asc* (or *main.asc*) and save it to the *fcs_ftp* subdirectory in the FlashCom *applications* directory. Add the following code to the file:

```
load("PFCSStreamManager.asc");
load("FTPServer.asc");
load("NetServices.asc");

application.onAppStart = function () (
  // Create a Flash Remoting connection.
  NetServices.setDefaultGatewayUrl("http://localhost/flashservices/gateway");
  var ncFlashRemoting = NetServices.createGatewayConnection();
  this.frservice = ncFlashRemoting.getService("fcs_ftp.FTPUtilities", this);

  // Create a connection to the Admin Service to get the current
  // application's physical path.
  this.ncAdmin = new NetConnection();
  this.ncAdmin.onStatus = function (info) {
    if (info.code == "NetConnection.Connect.Success") {
      var key = "Adaptor:_defaultRoot_/VirtualHost:_defaultVhost_/AppsDir";
      this.call("getConfig", application, key, "/");
    }
  };
  // Replace the username and password with those you've set in your Admin Service.
  this.ncAdmin.connect("rtmp://localhost:1111/admin",
                       "adminusername", "adminpassword");

  // Create a new stream manager.
  this.stream_manager = new PFCSStreamManager();

  // Create a listener to listen for publish_done events.
  this.stream_manager_listener = new Object();

  // When the stream is done publishing, the stream manager dispatches a
  // publish_done event. The event handler calls the copyFile() method.
  this.stream_manager_listener.publish_done = function (event) {
    application.copyFile(event.id);
  };
  this.stream_manager.addEventListener("publish_done",
                                       this.stream_manager_listener);

  // Create an array of FTP servers to which the files should be copied.
```

```
    this.servers = new Array( );

    // Add one or more FTPServer instances to the array. You need to add trailing
    // slashes after the streams directory but exclude the ftp protocol. For example:
    //    "fcs/some_application/streams/_definst_/".
    this.servers.push(new FTPServer("ftp.somefcsserver1.com", "username", "password",
                        "streams_directory", "yes"));
    this.servers.push(new FTPServer("ftp.somefcsserver2.com", "username", "password",
                        "streams_directory", "no"));
};

    // onResult( ) is called when the response is returned from the Admin Service.
    // Calculate the physical path to the streams.
    application.onResult = function (value) {
      var application_path = application.name.split("/");
      this.streams_path = value.data + "\\" + application_path[0] + "\\streams\\" +
                                      application_path[1] + "\\";
};

    // Create an empty method to handle the response from the copyFile( ) method.
    // Otherwise, the onResult( ) method would get called.
    application.copyFile_Result = function ( ) {};

    // When the copyFile( ) method is called, invoke the copyFile( ) method of the CFC.
    // This always copies .flv files.
    application.copyFile = function (id) {
      this.frservice.copyFile(this.servers, id + ".flv", this.streams_path, "binary");
};

    // Add a getNewStreamID( ) method to the client objects that simply proxies
    // a call to the stream manager's getNewStreamID( ).
    Client.prototype.getNewStreamID = function ( ) (
      return application.stream_manager.getNewStreamID( );
};
```

Much of the FlashCom application code is either straightforward or very similar to code used in the previous example application. Note the ftp:// protocol need not be included in the *FTPServer* instance's url parameter (although FTP servers often have names that begin with "ftp" such as "ftp.somedomain.com"). This example shows two FTP servers, one for which we used passive transfers and one for which we did not.

Also note that the *application.copyFile( )* method automatically appends the *.flv* extension to the filename, so you should not include it when specifying a stream's filename. It always uses the binary transfer mode, as is appropriate for *.flv* streams. To transfer other types of files, you could modify *application.copyFile( )* to accept the transfer mode as a second optional parameter and to not automatically append *.flv* to the filename.

Creating the Publishing Client

In order to test the FlashCom stream-copying application, you'll need a simple client that publishes a stream. The client should connect to the FlashCom application. When the user clicks a button to start publishing, the client should send a request to the FlashCom application for a stream ID. Once it gets the new stream ID, it can start publishing. Then, when the user clicks the button to stop publishing, the stream manager on the server will get notified automatically, and the FTP operations will occur.

Create a new Flash document named *streamCopy.fla*. Add a Button component instance to the Stage, and give it an instance name of cbt_publish. Then, add the following code to the first frame of the *Actions* layer on the main timeline:

```
// Define a response object to handle response from the getNewStreamID( ) call.
var response = new Object( );

// Once the FlashCom application returns a response with the stream ID,
// attach the camera and start publishing.
response.onResult = function (id) {
  ns.attachVideo(Camera.get( ));
  ns.publish(id, "record");
};

// Create a NetConnection to connect to the FlashCom application.
var nc = new NetConnection( );
nc.connect("rtmp:/fcs_ftp");

// Create a NetStream over which to publish the stream.
var ns = new NetStream(nc);

// Define a listener to handle the click events from the button.
var listener = new Object( );
listener.click = function (event) {
  // If the button is selected, get a new stream ID. Otherwise, stop
  // publishing the stream.
  if (event.target.selected) {
    nc.call("getNewStreamID", response, null);
  }
  else {
    ns.publish(false);
  }
};

// Register the listener to handle click events.
cbt_publish.addEventListener("click", listener);

// Add a label and set the button to toggle.
cbt_publish.label = "Publish";
cbt_publish.toggle = true;
```

The client code is basic enough that it doesn't require any further explanation. Simply run the client movie; to test it, publish a stream and then stop publishing. Then, check on the FTP server in the correct directory, and you should see the copy of the stream. Other applications running on secondary servers should then be able to access the streams.

Conclusion

In this chapter, you had a chance to see how to use ColdFusion, Flash Remoting, and FlashCom in conjunction with one another in a variety of practical examples including event logging, accessing local files, and copying files via FTP. You may be able to use some of the example code and ideas in your own FlashCom applications. However, don't feel limited to the specific examples in this chapter. The possibilities when combining the technologies are quite large. So use this chapter as a reference and a springboard.

This concludes the section of the book focusing on core classes and the technical foundation of FlashCom application development. The final section focuses on higher-level concepts such as the communication components and the component framework, design patterns and best practices, building scalable applications, performance tuning, and security. Your mastery of the fundamentals will serve you well as you learn more about architecting FlashCom applications.

Design and Deployment

Part IV covers building and extending components, application design, scalability, managing latency and bandwidth limitations, and creating secure applications.

- Chapter 13, *Building Communication Components*
- Chapter 14, *Understanding the Macromedia Component Framework*
- Chapter 15, *Application Design Patterns and Best Practices*
- Chapter 16, *Building Scalable Applications*
- Chapter 17, *Network Performance, Latency, and Concurrency*
- Chapter 18, *Securing Applications*

Building Communication Components

The preceding chapters have introduced the classes that form the foundation of every communication application. The core communication classes in client-side Flash ActionScript are *Video*, *Camera*, *Microphone*, *NetStream*, *NetConnection*, and *SharedObject*. In FlashCom Server-Side ActionScript, the core classes are *Application*, *Client*, *SharedObject*, *Stream*, and *NetConnection*. Describing and demonstrating how to work with each class has taken up more than half of this book for good reason: facility with the core communication objects is a necessity for building applications. The preceding chapters included many small test and demonstration programs and, if you have been reading through them sequentially, you may be wondering how to turn the many examples you've seen into full-featured applications. The remainder of this book is devoted to providing you with the information and examples you need to build useful, robust, secure, and scalable applications.

This chapter describes the first and arguably most important step in building full-fledged applications. It introduces how to design and build custom communication components. Building communication components makes it possible to partition applications into well-defined building blocks that can be built and tested separately and then assembled to make a variety of applications. One advantage of composing an application out of communication components is that many components can manage their own stream and shared object resources without the rest of the application having to manipulate them. Similarly, the code and logic for communication functions such as text chat, video conferencing, shared text areas, and people lists can be encapsulated within each component. In this respect, communication components often resemble miniature applications—each may make use of multiple user interface components, employ client- and server-side code, and manage its own data. Since each communication component is relatively self-contained, adding a component to an application is relatively simple.

If you've looked in Flash's Library panel, in the server's *scriptlib* folder of Macromedia's communication components and component framework, or at Macromedia's v1 or v2 user interface component sets, you may feel that components are complex and time-consuming to understand and build. In fact, they are not so difficult to make. The communication components in this chapter do not rely on Macromedia's communication component framework or any of Macromedia's communication components. Using, modifying, and creating your own components within Macromedia's framework is described in the next chapter.

This chapter begins by building a simple people list component that shows who is connected to an application instance. It isn't much more than a visible list of users generated from the contents of a shared object. Then, we'll extend the simple people list to manage its own shared object, work with a separate user status component, and display connection status icons beside each user's name. Other components, including a text chat, shared text, video conference, video window, and people grid are also described. Some of the components are designed to work together or be used independently.

The word "component" has many different meanings, so it is important to explain its use in this chapter. In general, a component is software that has been built according to a well-defined standard or *component model*. The component model may include a set of interfaces, an event model, and a set of base classes from which you can derive your own components. If the component conforms to the component model, it can be incorporated into applications without being modified.

Flash provides a component model (a.k.a. a *component framework*) and comes with a number of ready-made components. The most often used are the UI components such as the Button, TextInput, and List components. At the most fundamental level, a Flash component is a movie clip that can be imported into a Flash movie's Library and used with little or no configuration. A component movie clip often contains assets such as imported image, video, and sound files; other Flash symbols; and ActionScript code. The Flash component model has evolved from support for so-called Smart Clips in Flash 5, through the v1 component architecture of Flash MX, to the v2 component architecture introduced in Flash MX 2004. Flash components that are imported into a Library can be dragged to the Stage, resized, and customized using the Properties panel, Component Inspector, or ActionScript without having to alter the internal elements of the component itself.

Flash components can be used to build larger and more complex Flash components. For example, a text chat component will often contain TextArea, TextLabel, and Button components. However, a text chat component is also a communication component. It requires a connection to a FlashCom Server and may include server-side scripts as an essential part. This chapter is about building communication components, but for brevity we often refer to *communication components* simply as *components*.

Unlike the v1 and v2 component architectures created by Macromedia, there is no special way to package the server-side script (and server-side media files) of a communication component. Installing scripts on the server requires copying ActionScript files to the server and, often, editing the *main.asc* file. The Macromedia communication components' architecture, described in the next chapter, does provide important elements of a server-side component model.

So, for the purposes of this chapter, communication components are Flash components coupled with server-side scripts that work together. The components presented in this chapter all use the v2 component set and message handling system introduced in Flash MX 2004.

 Most of the code examples in the remainder of the book use Action-Script 2.0. In order to compile these examples, set the ActionScript version to ActionScript 2.0 under File → Publish Settings → Flash. Many examples require the components that are included only in Flash Pro and will therefore not compile in the standard edition of Flash MX 2004.

The documentation included with Flash update 7.2 has improved coverage of the v2 component architecture, but it is still incomplete in some respects. This chapter contains some helpful information on building v2 components; however, building components is a large topic so you may wish to refer to some of the following references:

Macromedia's LiveDocs often includes additional comments, notes, and examples; see the section on using components:

> *http://livedocs.macromedia.com/flash/mx2004/index.html*

The Macromedia Developer Center section on Flash Components page provides articles and sample source code for most components:

> *http://www.macromedia.com/devnet/mx/flash/components.html*

The source code for the Flash MX 2004 components can be found at a path similar to:

> *C:\Program Files\Macromedia\Flash MX 2004\en\First Run\Classes\mx*

At UltraShock's site, see the Tutorials/Flash MX 2004 section:

> *http://ultrashock.com*

Nigel Pegg wrote many of the components and has posted useful information about using and customizing them in his blog at:

> *http://www.markme.com/nigel*

See Joey Lott's article on creating components here:

> *http://www.person13.com/articles/components/creatingcomponents.html*

Source Files

The components that are described in this chapter are available in one of three sample applications named after the type of component used to show who is online. Each application is contained in one Zip file on the book's web site:

SimplePeopleList.zip
> A very simple application that does little more than display who is connected

PeopleList.zip
> An application that includes the PeopleList, Status, TextChat, and SharedText components

PeopleGrid.zip
> An application that includes the PeopleGrid, Status, TextChat, SharedText, and Questions components

Each file contains all the source and *.swf* files required to install the application as well as rebuild it. Recompiling the source files requires Flash MX Professional 2004.

People Lists

People list components can be very basic—a simple one can show the username of everyone connected to an application instance and nothing more. As each user connects, his name appears in the list, and as each leaves, it disappears. You can add features from there. People lists normally show the connection status of each person, such as online or away from the keyboard. You may want to show other information, such as whether each person has audio or video resources. In an online course system, you may want to know if someone is waiting to ask a question. People lists often aggregate and display information from other components or from multiple shared objects to present a summary of information about each user. Of all the component types, people lists are ones you may find yourself building and rebuilding. Throughout this chapter, we'll build three people lists. After reading it, you may not have to build so many!

A Simple People List

To begin with, let's build a simple people list component that displays the username of each person connected to an application instance and provides additional information such as a user's full name, email address, and connection time whenever a user clicks on someone's name in the list. To keep things manageable, this simple people list does not even manage its own shared object—it uses one managed by the server-side *main.asc* file.

Before we start, let's consider some questions you should ask before you build any component:

- Are any database, stream, or shared object resources already available to the component?
- What resources must the component create and manage by itself?
- What user interface components should the component contain?
- What information must the component make available to other components or objects?

In the case of a simple people list, here are some answers:

- Components often create and manage their own streams and shared objects. In the case of a people list, a shared object containing information about users may already be provided by a server-side script. In other cases, a server-side people list component may be responsible for providing user information. For the simple people list, we can assume the information is already available in a shared object and that each slot name is a user's username and each slot value is an object containing the user's full name, email address, and connection time.
- Since the people list component will use a preexisting shared object, it doesn't have to create any other resources.
- There are a few contenders for UI components the people list might use. The most common is a List component, which performs much faster than a DataGrid when used properly. However, a DataGrid has the advantage that columns in the grid can contain different icons so that different information about each user can be shown graphically. Finally, a Tree component can be used. Opening and closing person nodes in the tree can show additional information. For the simple people list, a List component is sufficient.
- When the user clicks on a username in the people list, any object that needs to know about the user will receive an object containing the username, full name, email address, and connection time for that user. We'll use the v2 component architecture available in Flash MX 2004 to provide this feature with a minimum of fuss.

Building the Component

Our custom SimplePeopleList component is a subclass of the *UIComponent* class provided as part of the v2 component framework; it contains only two movie clips. One is the BoundingBox movie clip that is normally used to provide an initial size for many components and a List component to display the username of each person. The SimplePeopleList component was created by inserting a new movie clip symbol in a Flash movie and giving it a linkage identifier of *SimplePeopleList* and an AS 2.0 class name of *SimplePeopleList* using the Linkage Properties dialog box. (In this chapter, we do not use packages. They are used in Chapter 15 when introducing a simple alternative communication component framework.)

 Whenever building a component based on the v2 component set, you should not drag components from the Components panel into your own component. Instead, select File → Import → Open External Library, then open the *StandardComponents.fla* file from the *.../First Run/ComponentFLA* directory. When you need assets from the v2 component set, drag them from the external Library into your movie's Library or onto the Stage.

The SimplePeopleList needs the following assets from the *StandardComponents.fla* file's Library:

BoundingBox movie clip
    A simple movie clip that is often used to provide an initial size for a component when it is first instantiated. Obtain it from the Library's Flash UI Components 2 → Component Assets folder.

List component
    A component used to create the visible list of users. Obtain it from the Library's Flash UI Components 2 folder.

UIComponent class
    The base class on which every component in this chapter is based, located in the Library's Flash UI Components 2 → Base Classes → FUIObject Subclasses → FUIComponent Subclasses folder. You don't need to include it manually because each component manages its own dependencies, so the List component will include it automatically. However, if you build a component that doesn't include an existing subcomponent, you'll need to include the UIComponent class manually.

The SimplePeopleList component is really just a movie clip symbol in the Library that is associated with the *SimplePeopleList.as* class file, has been exported for ActionScript, and has the linkage identifier *SimplePeopleList*. Figure 13-1 shows the two frames that make up the *SimplePeopleList* movie clip symbol.

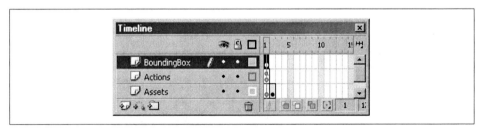

Figure 13-1. The timeline of the SimplePeopleList movie clip symbol

The BoundingBox clip has been placed at the origin (0, 0) of the SimplePeopleList component in frame 1 and has been named boundingBox_mc. The action in the *Actions* layer is a simple *stop( )* statement to keep the playhead from moving to the second frame. Finally, the second frame of the *Assets* layer is where the List component has been placed. The *stop( )* statement on the first frame guarantees that the second frame will never be reached. Therefore, assets—such as the List component—that must be in a movie's Library are placed in the second frame. When the component is imported into a movie, the assets will also be imported and appear in the movie's Library. Since the playhead will never reach the second frame, the List clip in the second frame will never be instantiated and is never directly used. With these elements in place, the real work of creating the SimplePeopleList component, including attaching a List component, is done in the *SimplePeopleList.as* class file. Example 13-1 shows the complete listing of the *SimplePeopleList* class definition; this client-side ActionScript 2.0 code must be placed in an external *SimplePeopleList.as* file. However, this listing does not show all the code necessary to create a working example; see the *SimplePeopleList.zip* file on the book's web site for the complete code.

Many of the examples throughout this chapter use *getter* and *setter* methods. These are just methods that are called automatically when a corresponding property is set or retrieved. They provide a way to have assignment and retrieval operations for a property managed by a function, while allowing the developer to read or assign the property in the typical way (without having to invoke a function manually). For more information on these methods, see the section "Getter and Setter Methods" in Chapter 4 of *ActionScript for Flash MX: The Definitive Guide* (O'Reilly).

Example 13-1. A SimplePeopleList component

```
class SimplePeopleList extends mx.core.UIComponent {
  // Connect component class and symbol.
  var className:String = "SimplePeopleList";
  static var symbolName:String = "SimplePeopleList";
  static var symbolOwner:Object = SimplePeopleList;

  // Subcomponents and movie clips.
  var list:mx.controls.List;
  var boundingBox_mc:MovieClip;

  // Externally supplied NetConnection.
  var __nc: NetConnection;
  // Shared object obtained via the NetConnection.
  var userList:SharedObject;
  // Default path to resources for this component.
  var __resourcePath:String = "pfcs/SimplePeopleList/main/";

  // Constructor function calls UIComponent's constructor.
  function SimplePeopleList () {
  }

  // init() is called after createChildren() and before onLoad().
```

Example 13-1. A SimplePeopleList component (continued)

```
function init () {
  super.init();
  boundingBox_mc._visible = false;
  boundingBox_mc._width = boundingBox_mc._height = 0;
}

// No drawing is required as the List subcomponent is the entire GUI.
function draw () {
  size();
}

// Resize the List to take up the entire area of the compoent.
function size () {
  super.size();
  list.setSize(width, height);
}

// Attach the List to this component.
function createChildren () {
  var depth = 1;
  createObject("List", "list", depth++, {_x:0, _y:0});
  list.vScrollPolicy = "auto";
}

// The simplePeopleList.resourcePath = "mypath" setter method.
public function set resourcePath(resourcePath:String) {
  if (!resourcePath) {
    trace("SimplePeopleList Error: Empty or undefined resourcePath.");
    return;
  }
  __resourcePath = resourcePath;
}

// The simplePeopleList.nc = myNC setter method. Assumes resourcePath is correct.
public function set nc (nc:NetConnection) {
  if (!nc) {
    trace("SimplePeopleList Error: nc was null or undefined.");
    return;
  }
  __nc = nc;
  if(!nc.isConnected) {
    trace("SimplePeopleList Error: nc must be connected before use.");
    return;
  }
  // Get the temporary shared object.
  // SharedObjectFactory is explained shortly.
  userList = SharedObjectFactory.getRemote(__resourcePath + "userList", nc.uri);
  userList.addEventListener("onSync", this);
  // Assume this component "owns" the userList and is responsible for
  // connecting to it.
  userList.connect(nc);
}
```

Example 13-1. A SimplePeopleList component (continued)

```
  // Passes through add listener requests to the List subcomponent.
  function addEventListener(type, dest) {
    list.addEventListener(type, dest);
  }

  // Passes through remove listener requests to the List subcomponent.
  function removeEventListener(type, dest) {
    list.removeEventListener(type, dest);
  }

  // A simple event handler for the userList shared object that
  // manipulates the List's dataProvider directly.
  function onSync (ev) {
    var dp = list.dataProvider;
    dp.splice(0);
    for (var p in userList.data) {
      dp.push({label:p, data:userList.data[p]});
    }
    dp.dispatchEvent({target: dp, type:"modelChanged"});
  }

  // When this component is disposed of, release resources.
  function onUnload ( ) {
    close( );
  }

  // close( ) releases resources.
  function close ( ) {
    userList.removeEventListener("onSync", this);
  }
}
```

The SimplePeopleList component's code can be broken down into two broad categories: the code required to produce the graphical user interface and the part that ties
together the userList shared object and the List component. Let's look at each separately.

Building the graphical interface

By extending the *UIComponent* class and setting the className, symbolName, and
symbolOwner variables, the *SimplePeopleList* class inherits all the properties and methods of the *UIComponent* class and connects the *SimplePeopleList* symbol in the
Library with the *SimplePeopleList* class for the v2 component framework. Of particular interest here are the following methods that will be called in order when a *Simple-
PeopleList* object is instantiated:

SimplePeopleList( )
     The *SimplePeopleList* constructor function is called first and simply returns.

init( )

> The *init( )* method is called and in turn calls *UIComponent.init( )* and then hides the boundingBox_mc clip. The clip already exists because it was placed on the SimplePeopleList component's Stage in frame 1.

createChildren( )

> The *createChildren( )* method is called before the clip is shown in a movie frame and is used to attach clips to the component and initialize them. In Example 13-1, a List component instance is attached to the SimplePeopleList component, given the name list, positioned at (0, 0), and set to autohide the vertical scrollbar.

draw( )

> The *draw( )* method is called after the clip is loaded. If an *onLoad( )* method had been defined, it would have been called before *draw( )*. The *draw( )* method is responsible for updating the visual appearance of the component. Since the entire user interface of the SimplePeopleList component is a List component that can draw itself, the *draw( )* method simply calls the *size( )* method.

size( )

> The *size( )* method just passes the width and height of the clip to the List subcomponent so that it resizes itself to fill the area allocated to the SimplePeopleList.

Both the list instance of the List component and the boundingBox_mc instance of the BoundingBox movie clip must be declared as variables within the class definition to avoid compiler errors.

Tying the list to the shared object

The *SimplePeopleList* class has a property named __nc reserved to hold a *NetConnection* object. For the purposes of designing a simple people list component, we assume that the Flash movie that it is being used connects to a FlashCom application instance and can provide a connected *NetConnection* object for the SimplePeopleList to use. Rather than providing a method that can be used to pass in a reference to the *NetConnection* object, the SimplePeopleList component defines a setter method. The setter method will be called when the component's nc property is set this way:

```
peopleList.nc = nc;
```

The setter method—with comments and error checking removed—is as follows:

```
public function set nc (nc:NetConnection) {
    __nc = nc;
    userList = SharedObjectFactory.getRemote(__resourcePath + "userList", nc.uri);
    userList.addEventListener("onSync", this);
    userList.connect(nc);
}
```

The public nc property is saved in the private __nc property for later use. Then the *NetConnection* object and the *SharedObjectFactory* class are used to get a reference to the userList shared object. The path to the shared object is composed from two strings:

```
__resourcePath + "userList"
```

If the __resourcePath property has not been changed from its default, the path to the userList shared object is:

```
pfcs/SimplePeopleList/main/userList
```

In previous chapters, shorter paths have been used. However, in this chapter, a regular naming scheme is used to identify and keep separate the shared object and stream resources each component manages. The userList path has three parts preceding the name of the shared object itself:

pfcs

> The first term in the path is a directory that contains resources that are available to most Flash clients. Chapter 18 describes in detail using directories to secure resources. Creating a *pfcs* folder makes it possible to deny access to other folders.

SimplePeopleList

> The second term in the path is a directory that is reserved for resources needed by any instance of one type of component—in this case, the SimplePeopleList component.

main

> The third term in the path is the folder that is reserved for an instance of the component. In this case, *main* is the default folder name that is normally used by the "main" people list of an application. In a scenario in which more than one people list is used, the third term in the path can be used to distinguish between component resources.

The *SharedObjectFactory* class is a custom class written to return shared objects that can broadcast events. This class makes it possible to call *addEventListener( )* on the userList shared object. The *SharedObjectFactory* class is discussed in detail in the next section.

The *nc( )* setter method adds the SimplePeopleList component instance as a listener of the userList for *onSync( )* events. Once again, here is the code that gets the shared object and sets up the SimplePeopleList as a listener for *onSync* events:

```
userList = SharedObjectFactory.getRemote(__resourcePath + "userList", nc.uri);
userList.addEventListener("onSync", this);
```

The component's *onSync( )* handler is called whenever the shared object's *onSync( )* method is called. The *addEventListener( )* and *removeEventListener( )* methods are the standard methods v2 components provide to add and remove event listeners.

Finally, the *nc( )* setter method connects the shared object using the *NetConnection* object:

```
userList.connect(nc);
```

When the connection to the userList shared object occurs, the *SimplePeopleList.onSync( )* method is called:

```
function onSync (ev) {
  var dp = list.dataProvider;
  dp.splice(0);
  for (var p in userList.data) {
    dp.push({label:p, data:userList.data[p]});
  }
  dp.dispatchEvent({target: dp, type:"modelChanged"});
}
```

When *onSync( )* is called, the contents of the List component instance are simply removed and re-created using the shared object's data property. Each list item's label is set to the slot name (username) of each slot in the user list, and the item's data is set to the data in the slot. In this case, the data will be an object containing the full name, email address, and connection time of the user. Since the *onSync( )* method must delete the entire contents of the list and rewrite it each time the shared object changes, it manipulates the list's dataProvider property directly to improve performance. The contents of the list are deleted by calling *splice( )*, and new items are added using *push( )*. Unlike the List component's *removeAll( )* and *addItem( )* methods, *splice( )* and *push( )* do not tell the list to redraw itself. Directly updating the dataProvider avoids redundant update requests to the list as each item is added. Instead, the data provider's *dispatchEvent( )* method is called once to ask the list to redraw itself after all the items have been added.

While it is not used in the *SimplePeopleList.onSync( )* method, the *onSync( )* method is passed an event object. The list of information objects that was passed to the shared object's *onSync( )* method is contained within the event object and is available in its ev.list property.

If the *nc( )* setter and *onSync( )* methods connect to and display the contents of the userList shared object, you may be wondering how the user information gets into the shared object in the first place. In the case of the SimplePeopleList component, the work of adding and removing user information is done by the *main.asc* script on the server. The complete file is available in the *SimplePeopleList.zip* file on the book's web site. Here is an excerpt from the *main.asc* file that shows how user information is added and removed from the userList shared object:

```
application.onAppStart = function () {
  userList_so = SharedObject.get("pfcs/SimplePeopleList/main/userList");
};

application.onConnect = function (client, user) {
  client.user = user;
```

```
  client.user.arrival = new Date( );
  userList_so.setProperty(client.user.userName, client.user);
  return true;
};

application.onDisconnect = function (client) {
  userList_so.setProperty(client.user.userName, null);
};
```

The *main.asc* script is coded on the assumption that the client will pass a second parameter in the *NetConnection connect( )* method when it connects. The parameter should contain an object with userName, fullName, and email properties that will be stored in the userList shared object. The user object is also stored as a property of each *Client* object in this and later examples, so that the server-side part of any component can easily retrieve user information associated with a client.

The *SimplePeopleList* class is responsible for managing the userList shared object within the client. (Later, we'll create a people list component that also adds users to the shared object.) So it needs to provide a way to retrieve the user object for any user that appears in its list. Like all Flash MX 2004 v2 components that must broadcast events, the List component has *addEventListener( )* and *removeEventListener( )* methods.

When a user clicks on the List subcomponent within the SimplePeopleList component, a *change* event is generated. Other components or objects can add themselves as event listeners in order to know when an item has been selected in the list. When they receive a *change* event, they can use the event's target property to get a reference to the list and use the list's selectedItem property to get the data object from the selected item.

The SimplePeopleList component provides two methods that allow other objects and components to subscribe to list selection events:

```
function addEventListener (type, dest) {
  list.addEventListener(type, dest);
}

function removeEventListener (type, dest) {
  list.removeEventListener(type, dest);
}
```

The methods simply pass through an event listener request to the list component instance. When the user selects an item in the people list, the list component instance broadcasts an event to any listeners that have used the people list's *addEventListener( )* method to listen for the event. For example, the following statement adds an application object as a listener for change events:

```
peopleList.addEventListener("change", application);
```

Other components will require more complex *addEventListener( )* methods and may need to be able to broadcast their own custom events.

In Example 13-1, the `target` property of each *change* event will be the
List component and not the SimplePeopleList. Instead of passing event
listener requests through to the List, SimplePeopleList could add itself
as a listener to the List, then redispatch List events to its own listeners. Unfortunately, redispatching events is not enough to emulate the
List's functionality. The SimplePeopleList must also provide the standard List methods and properties such as `selectedItem` and
`selectedIndex` that listeners expect to be able to use on the event target. The effort and increase in code size needed to make the `target`
property point to the List instead of the SimplePeopleList may not be
justified.

Now that we've described how the SimplePeopleList component works, how do you
use it in a Flash movie? Briefly, you must add it to the Library of a movie and attach
it to the Stage manually at authoring time or using ActionScript. Once on the Stage
or attached with ActionScript, it must be passed a reference to an already connected
NetConnection object. In the example *.fla* found in the *SimplePeopleList.zip* file, an
application object creates a *NetConnection* object, and the *SimplePeopleList* instance
(named `peopleList`) is connected this way:

```
// First tell the people list about events we want to listen for.
peopleList.addEventListener("change", application);
// If necessary, replace the default resource path (not necessary here).
peopleList.resourcePath = "pfcs/SimplePeopleList/main/";
// Provide an already connected NetConnection to the component.
peopleList.nc = application.nc;
```

See *SimplePeopleList.zip* on the book's web site for a complete example including
both the server-side *main.asc* script and all the client-side files.

You'll find the *SimplePeopleList* movie clip symbol in the Library of *SimplePeopleList.fla*
in the Zip archive. The SimplePeopleList could also have been compiled into a SWC
file. A SWC file is an archive that contains a *catalog.xml* file that describes the other
contents of the archive, ActionScript files that define component classes, and the SWF
files that implement each component. A SWC file may also contain other assets. See
Understanding SWC Files in the Flash MX 2004 Help. Converting a movie clip symbol
into a compiled SWC is relatively easy. Select the symbol in the Library, right-click
(Windows) or Ctrl-click (Macintosh) to open the contextual menu, and select Export
SWC File. Then save the SWC file. SWC files are not used in this book—partly
because of problems using them as subcomponents within other components. However, they are a good way to package component sets. For more information on creating and compiling components see:

   http://www.person13.com/articles/components/creatingcomponents.html

The SimplePeopleList component was developed to show how a component can
manage and coordinate the work of both v2 user interface components and communication resources such as the `userList` shared object. It is a subclass of the

---

UIComponent class, implements many of the core *UIComponent* methods, and uses the v2-style setter methods. The SimplePeopleList component has two shortcomings that will be addressed later in this chapter: it doesn't provide a way to show the connection status of users, and it relies on code in the *main.asc* file to populate a shared object. The PeopleList and Status components developed later provide these features.

Listenable Shared Objects

The SimplePeopleList component provides a view of the data in a userList shared object by listing the shared object's data properties. Other components may also need to use the userList shared object and be notified when the *onSync( )* method is called. In one respect, the SimplePeopleList treats the userList shared object as it treats its List component; it simply adds itself as an event listener for *onSync* events. Remote shared objects must be modified in order to dispatch events or add and remove event listeners. When an object or component in this chapter needs to connect to a shared object, it uses the *SharedObjectFactory* class listed in Example 13-2 instead of the *SharedObject* class. The *SharedObjectFactory* class retrieves a remote shared object and then adds methods and properties to it so that one or more objects or components can add themselves to the shared object as event listeners. It uses the *EventDispatcher* class provided as part of the v2 UI component framework to perform part of the customization of each shared object. The code in Example 13-2 must be placed in a file named *SharedObjectFactory.as*. Read through the heavily commented example if you are interested in how the *SharedObjectFactory* converts a remote shared object into a v2-style event dispatcher.

Example 13-2. The SharedObjectFactory class

```
class SharedObjectFactory extends Object {
  /* getRemote( ) calls SharedObject.getRemote( ) to get a shared object reference
   * and then uses the mx.events.EventDispatcher object to make the shared
   * object into a v2 component-style event broadcaster. Also, an isConnected
   * flag is maintained to implement an onFirstSync event and to keep track of
   * the shared object's connection state. Finally, two methods have been added
   * to dynamically add and remove remote methods to and from the shared object.
   */
  static function getRemote (name, uri, persistence) {
    // Get the remote shared object.
    var so = SharedObject.getRemote.apply(SharedObject, arguments);
    // If it exists and has not been modified to be a broadcaster...
    if (so && !so._onFirstSync) {
      // Make it an event broadcaster.
      mx.events.EventDispatcher.initialize(so);
      // Define an _onFirstSync( ) method that can be assigned to onSync
      // whenever an attempt is made to connect the shared object.
      so._onFirstSync = function (list:Array) {
        this.isConnected = true;
```

Example 13-2. The SharedObjectFactory class (continued)

```
      this.dispatchEvent({type:"onFirstSync", target: this, list:list});
      this.onSync = this._onSync;
      this.onSync(list);
    };
    /* Define an _onSync( ) method to assign to onSync after the first
     * onSync( ) has been called. Note the event.list property contains
     * the list normally passed to onSync( ).
     */
    so._onSync = function (list:Array) {
      this.dispatchEvent({type:"onSync", target: this, list:list});
    };
    // Keep a reference to the SharedObject.connect( ) method.
    so._connect = so.connect;
    // Replace connect( ) with a method that modifies onSync and isConnected
    // before calling the original connect( ) method.
    so.connect = function (nc:NetConnection) {
      this.onSync = this._onFirstSync;
      this.isConnected = false;
      this._connect(nc);
    };
    // Keep a reference to the original SharedObject.close( ) method.
    so._close = so.close;
    // Modify the close( ) method to set the isConnected flag before
    // actually closing the shared object.
    so.close = function ( ) {
      this.isConnected = false;
      this._close( );
    };
    /* Dynamically attach a remote method to the shared object. Note
     * the method simply dispatches an event to any interested listeners
     * and includes the arguments object so listeners can deal with the
     * remote call themselves. Listeners must use addEventListener( ) on the
     * shared object to receive remote method call notifications.
     * addRemoteMethod( ) and removeRemoteMethod( ) are discussed later.
     */
    so.addRemoteMethod = function (methodName) {
      so[methodName] = function ( ) {
        this.dispatchEvent({type:methodName, target: this, args:arguments});
      };
    };
    // Delete the remote method if it is no longer needed.
    so.removeRemoteMethod = function (methodName) {
      delete so[methodName];
    };
  }
  return so;
}
}
```

If you use the *SharedObjectFactory* class in place of the *SharedObject* class to get a remote shared object, you should never have to customize another shared object again. All you have to do is get the shared object with *SharedObjectFactory*.

getRemote( ) and decide what events a listener needs to receive. You can add remote methods to the shared object using *addRemoteMethod( )* and receive remote method events by having a listener listen for remote calls by name.

Example 13-3 is a short demonstration of how the *SharedObjectFactory* class can be used. It demonstrates adding event listeners for both *onFirstSync* and *onSync* events and defining and listening for a remote method (arbitrarily named *rmiCheck( )* in this example). The *TestSOListener* class can be used to create a simple soListener object for test purposes. The *onFirstSync* event was created as an extra event beyond *onSync* to provide notice only when the shared object first connects. The *TestSOListener* class listing is extensively commented and is provided in Example 13-3 so you can see how to listen for each type of event and extract information from each event object.

Example 13-3. The TestSOListener class is designed to show how to use the SharedObjectFactory class

```
class TestSOListener {
/* TestSOListener is a test/demonstration class that shows
 * how a class can work with a shared object returned by
 * the SharedObjectFactory.getRemote( ) method.
 */
function TestSOListener ( ) {}

  /* onFirstSync( ) is called once after the shared object first connects.
   * ev.target is a reference to the shared object.
   * ev.list is the list of information objects passed into the
   * shared object's onSync( ) method the first time it was called.
   */
  function onFirstSync (ev) {
    var list = ev.list;
    var so = ev.target;
    // Write out some information about the list.
    trace("onFirstSync> list length: " + list.length);
    // Write out the properties of the shared object.
    for (var p in so.data) {
      trace(p + ": " + so.data[p]);
    }
    // Test remote method invocation (RMI) by sending
    // an rmiCheck message with two parameters.
    so.send("rmiCheck", "First Parameter", "Second Parameter");
    // Test the onSync( ) method by adding data to the shared object.
    so.data.hello = "Greetings!";
  }

  /* onSync( ) is called immediately after the onFirstSync event and
   * is passed the same list onFirstSync( ) was passed. Afterward, it is
   * called whenever onSync( ) is called on the shared object.
   * ev.target is a reference to the shared object.
   * ev.list is the list of information objects passed into the
   * shared object's onSync( ) method.
```

Example 13-3. The TestSOListener class is designed to show how to use the SharedObjectFactory class (continued)

```
     */
  function onSync (ev) {
    var list = ev.list;
    var so = ev.target;
    trace("onSync> list length: " + list.length);
    for (var i in list) {
      var info = list[i];
      for (var p in info) {
        trace(p + ": " + info[p]);
      }
    }
  }


  /* rmiCheck() is called whenever the rmiCheck() method is invoked
   * on the shared object.
   * ev.target holds a reference to the shared object and
   * ev.args holds a reference to the arguments passed by the
   * remote method call.
   */
  function rmiCheck (ev) {
    var args = ev.args;
    var so   = ev.target;
    // Show that we have been called.
    trace("rmiCheck> args.length: " + ev.args.length);
    // Trace out the arguments passed to this method.
    for (var i in args) {
      trace("arg " + i + ": " + args[i]);
    }
    // If you don't want to look through the arguments, call
    // another method this way.
    this.rmiCheckHandler.apply(this, ev.args);
  }


  // rmiCheckHandler() is called from rmiCheck() using apply()
  // and shows that normal parameter passing can be used.
  function rmiCheckHandler (first, second) {
    trace("rmiCheckHandler>");
    trace("   first: " + first);
    trace("   second: " + second);
  }
}
```

The simplest way to try out the class is to create an instance of it on the main timeline, connect to the server, get a test shared object, and set up soListener as a listener for *onFirstSync* and *onSync* events. We also set up a remote method named *rmiCheck()* on the shared object and set up the soListener to receive an event whenever *rmiCheck()* is called:

```
    soListener = new TestSOListener();

    nc = new NetConnection();
```

```
nc.onStatus = function (info) {
  trace("nc.status> " + info.code);
  if (info.code == "NetConnection.Connect.Success") {
    so = SharedObjectFactory.getRemote("Test", nc.uri);
    so.addEventListener("onSync", soListener);
    so.addEventListener("onFirstSync", soListener);
    so.addRemoteMethod("rmiCheck");
    so.addEventListener("rmiCheck", soListener);
    so.connect(nc);
  }
};
nc.connect("rtmp:/empty");
```

Output from this test script shows that *onSync( )* is always called immediately after *onFirstSync( )* is called and is passed the same information list. This is a convenience that provides flexibility in how the two events are handled. For example, one listener may listen for only the *onSync* event and not the *onFirstSync* event while another may listen for only the *onFirstSync* event or for both.

```
nc.status> NetConnection.Connect.Success
onFirstSync> list length: 1
onSync> list length: 1
code: clear
rmiCheck> args.length: 2
arg 1: Second Parameter
arg 0: First Parameter
rmiCheckHandler>
    first: First Parameter
  second: Second Parameter
onSync> list length: 1
code: success
name: hello
```

The remainder of this chapter and Chapter 15 make extensive use of the *SharedObjectFactory* class to create remote shared objects that don't require any further customization.

Status and People List

Most instant messaging and conferencing systems provide a way for the user to indicate that he is too busy to respond, has gone out briefly, or is offline although still connected. The Status component described here is designed to give the user a way to indicate his status. In this example, every user's status appears in a PeopleList component.

There are two basic approaches to adding user status input and display. One is to build a PeopleList component that includes a combo box, to let each user select a status. The other is to build two separate components: a Status component that is visually little more than a combo box and a PeopleList that knows how to display each user's status along with his username.

Regardless of the internal implementation, the user interface might be similar. Figure 13-2 shows such a setup with a PeopleList component on the left and a separate Status component on the right. When a user selects a different status, the icon beside his username in the PeopleList changes.

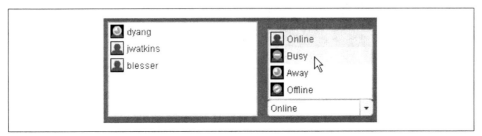

Figure 13-2. A PeopleList component (left) and a separate Status component (right)

In some respects, the first design option (using a PeopleList without a separate Status component) is simpler. A status property can be added to each person's entry in a userList shared object that indicates the user's status. When a user changes his status, the status property of the user's entry is changed to some value such as "Offline", "Busy", or "Away". The change in the user's entry in the shared object results in an *onSync( )* call on the shared object. When the PeopleList component detects that a user's entry has changed, it changes the icon beside the user's username to show his new status.

In this first design option, a single shared object includes user and status information. Each slot contains a single object with firstName, lastName, and status properties. Although this design option works and is simple to implement, it has two disadvantages. First, whenever the status property of a shared object slot is updated, the entire object in the slot—instead of just the updated status property—must be sent to every client. Resending redundant information wastes a small amount of bandwidth (and user information such as the full name and email address are unlikely to change during a session). Second, the status combo box and people list are tied together in a single design. There may be cases in which a status combo box is not needed or a design calls for it to be located away from the people list.

The second design option requires more work and involves both the creation of separate Status and PeopleList components and the maintenance of two separate shared objects: one containing an object for each user and one holding the status of each user. In the second design, the Status component updates the status shared object with the current status of a user. The PeopleList component must be set up to listen for changes in the status shared object as well as for changes in the people shared object (we'll call it the people shared object to distinguish it from the userList shared object used in the SimplePeopleList). When the status of a user changes, the PeopleList component must update the status icon for the user.

There are, of course, still other approaches, such as using *SharedObject.send( )* to update clients, as described in Chapter 8. For clarity and simplicity, this chapter demonstrates the second design approach using two shared objects.

Each slot in the `people` shared object contains an object with `firstName` and `lastName` properties. A simple object illustrates how the data is organized:

```
people = {blesser: {firstName:"Brian",   lastName:"Lesser"},
          peldi:   {firstName:"Giacomo", lastName:"Guilizzoni"},
          jwatkins:{firstName:"Justin",  lastName:"Watkins"}};
```

Each slot in the `status` shared object contains a string indicating a user's status:

```
status = {blesser: "Online",
          peldi:   "Busy",
          jwatkins:"Away"};
```

The Status component is relatively simple to build. It contains only one user interface component, a combo box.

Designing and Building the Status Component

Let's return to the some of the questions we asked when designing the SimplePeopleList:

- What resources must the component create and manage by itself?
- What user interface components should the component contain?
- What information must the component make available to other components or objects?

The Status component described here must manage a status shared object that contains the current status of each user. Each slot in the shared object is named after a user's username and contains a string value describing the user's status. The user interface for the Status component will be a v2 ComboBox that allows each user to select a status and shows the icon that will appear in the PeopleList for each selection. The Status component, therefore, must make the icons available for the PeopleList to use as well, as shown in Figure 13-2. Since the Status component is responsible for connecting to and managing the status shared object, it must also provide a reference to the status shared object for any other component that needs it. Status changes are broadcast as changes in the shared object to any interested component.

In the design implemented here, the Status component has two parts: a client-side component and a server-side class that works in partnership with it. When a user changes the selection in the Status component's ComboBox, the component makes a remote method call to its server-side counterpart, asking it to change the appropriate entry in the status shared object. The server-side *Status* object makes sure the correct user's entry is set with a valid status string in the shared object. An alternative to this approach is to update the shared object in the client. However, there are advantages to performing updates on the server, such as being able to serialize and securely validate updates. Chapters 15 and 18 discuss these in detail. Any components listening for changes on the shared object will receive updates when a user's status changes. However, the Status component doesn't need to receive any updates since it is set by the user.

Building the client-side Status component

With our design in mind, it is time to start coding. Example 13-4 lists the complete AS 2.0 client-side code for the Status component, while Example 13-6 lists the server-side *Status* class. Example 13-4 is quite long. You may want to skip over the *get column( )* method for now and return to it when you reach the section on the PeopleGrid component.

Example 13-4. The client-side Status component

```
import mx.controls.gridclasses.DataGridColumn;

class Status extends mx.core.UIComponent {
  // Connect component class and symbol.
  var className:String = "Status";
  static var symbolName:String = "Status";
  static var symbolOwner:Object = Status;

  // Default path and name.
  var __name:String = "main";
  var path:String = "pfcs/Status/main/";

  // Subcomponents and movie clips.
  var combo:mx.controls.ComboBox;
  var boundingBox_mc:MovieClip;

  // Externally supplied NetConnection—should already be connected.
  var __nc:NetConnection;
  // Internally aquired remote SharedObject, if needed by another component.
  var __status_so:SharedObject = null;

  // Constructor function calls UIComponent's constructor.
  function Status( ) {
  }

  // init( ) is called before createChildren( ) and before onLoad( ).
  function init( ) {
    super.init( );
    boundingBox_mc._visible = false;
    boundingBox_mc._width = boundingBox_mc._height=0;
  }
  // No drawing is required as the combo box is the entire GUI.
```

Example 13-4. The client-side Status component (continued)

```
function draw( ) {
  size( );
}

// Resize the list to take up the entire area of the component.
function size( ) {
  super.size( );
  combo.setSize(width, height);
}

// Attach the combo box to this component.
function createChildren( ) {
  var depth = 1;
  createObject("ComboBox", "combo", depth++, {_x:0, _y:0});
  combo.addItem({label:"Online", icon:"Status_Person_Online"});
  combo.addItem({label:"Busy", icon:"Status_Person_Busy"});
  combo.addItem({label:"Away", icon:"Status_Person_Away"});
  combo.addItem({label:"Offline", icon:"Status_Person_Offline"});
  combo.dropdown.iconField = "icon";
  combo.addEventListener("change", this);
}

/* change( ) is a callback invoked when the combo box selection changes.
 * It calls the remote method setStatus( ) to notify the server-side
 * Status object that the status for this user has changed.
 */
function change (ev) {
  var status = combo.selectedItem.label;
  __nc.call(path + "setStatus", null, status);
}

// set name changes the path and name for the component.
// The default name is "main".
function set name(name:String) {
  if (!name) name = "main";
  __name = name;
  path = "pfcs/" + className + "/" + __name + "/";
}

// getter method for the name. Could use a get path method too.
function get name( ) {
  return __name;
}

// The Status.nc setter method.
public function set nc (nc:NetConnection) {
  __nc = nc;
}

/* get column creates what might be called a column transfer object.
 * It is designed to work with the PeopleGrid component.
 * It returns an object that contains the following properties:
```

Example 13-4. The client-side Status component (continued)

```
 *    name:
 *       The name of the column.
 *    so:
 *       The SO that contains the data that must be displayed in the column.
 *    dgColumn:
 *       A DataGridColumn for insertion into a DataGrid.
 *    propertyName:
 *       The property name to add into each item in the DataGrid's data provider.
 *    getPropertyValue:
 *       A method to extract, from an SO slot, the data that must be added
 *       into an item in the DataGrid's dataProvider. (i.e., if the slot contains
 *       a record, the getPropertyValue( ) method will extract the right
 *       information to put into each item in the DataGrid).
 */
public function get column( ) {
  if (!__status_so && __nc) {
    __status_so = SharedObjectFactory.getRemote(path + "status",__nc.uri);
    __status_so.connect(__nc);
  }

  var col = {
    name: path,
    so: __status_so,
    propertyName: "status",
    dgColumn: new DataGridColumn("status"),
    target: this
  }
  col.dgColumn.cellRenderer = "StatusCellRenderer",
  col.dgColumn.headerRenderer = "StatusHeaderRenderer";
  col.dgColumn.width = 24;
  col.getPropertyValue = function (slot) {
    return slot;
  };
  return col;
}

/* get status_so uses __nc to get a reference to a status
 * temporary remote shared object. The shared object's relative URI
 * depends on the path of this component. By default, it is found
 * at pfcs/Status/main/status but could be elsewhere. For example:
 * pfcs/Status/breakoutRoom_3/status.
 */
public function get status_so ( ) {
  if (!__nc) {
    return null;
  }
  if (!__status_so) {
    __status_so = SharedObjectFactory.getRemote(path + "status",__nc.uri);
    __status_so.connect(__nc);
  }
  return __status_so;
}
```

Example 13-4. The client-side Status component (continued)

```
  // Pass through listener requests to the ComboBox.
  function addEventListener(type, dest) {
    combo.addEventListener(type, dest);
  }

  function removeEventListener(type, dest) {
    combo.removeEventListener(type, dest);
  }

  // Call close( ) to make sure the component is cleaned up.
  function onUnload( ) {
    close( );
  }
  // Clean up.
  function close( ) {
    combo.removeEventListener("change", this);
  }
}
```

Much of the code for the Status component is similar to the SimplePeopleList component. The *UIComponent* class is used as a base class, the ComboBox is attached to the component in the *createChildren( )* method, the path is set as the resourcePath was earlier, and the __nc *NetConnection* object is set in much the same way. One difference is that the options for the combo box are set by adding item objects to the combo instance:

```
    combo.addItem({label:"Online", icon:"Status_Person_Online"});
```

The string "Status_Person_Online" is the linkage identifier of a movie clip in the *Assets* layer of the Status component. The timeline and Stage for the Status movie clip symbol are shown in Figure 13-3. Every icon needed by the Status component has been placed on the second frame of the *Assets* layer in order to guarantee that they will travel with the Status component into the Library of the Flash movie in which they are used. The icon property identifies which icon to display for each item.

The drop-down list of the ComboBox is a List component, so the following statement is all that is needed to make the icons show up in the drop-down list:

```
    combo.dropdown.iconField = "icon";
```

See the help entry for the dropdown property of the ComboBox component and the iconField entry of the List component in the Flash MX 2004 Help system for more information.

The Status component also sets itself up as a listener on the combo subcomponent so that it knows when the combo instance has been changed:

```
    combo.addEventListener("change", this);
```

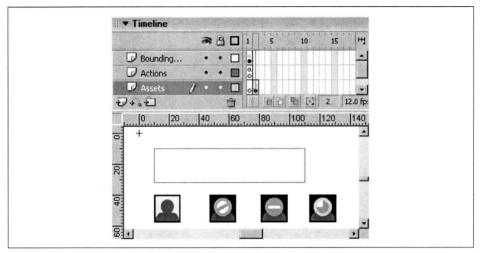

Figure 13-3. The timeline and Stage of the Status movie clip symbol; the Stage contains a ComboBox and four icons

When the *change( )* method is called, it notifies the server-side *Status* object that it should make a change using a remote method call:

```
function change (ev) {
  var status = combo.selectedItem.label;
  __nc.call(path + "setStatus", null, status);
}
```

The *change( )* method gets the label string from the combo box such as "Offline" or "Away" and calls a remote method using the __nc *NetConnection* object. The remote method name is a concatenation of the path and the method name, *setStatus( )*. If the path is "pfcs/Status/main/", the remote method being called will be named *pfcs/Status/main/setStatus*. When the remote call arrives at the server, the *Client* object that represents the Flash movie will have the *pfcs/Status/main/setStatus( )* method invoked on it—if it has one. For example, if the status string passed to it is "Away", it will be as though the following method call was made:

```
client.pfcs.Status.main.setStatus("Away");
```

Before moving on to describe how the server-side *Status* object is set up to receive and handle a *setStatus( )* call, let's cover one other detail about the client-side Status component.

The Status component is responsible for managing the status shared object. If another component needs access to the status shared object, the Status component must supply it. The getter method *get status_so( )* uses the *NetConnection* object to connect to the shared object and return a reference to it:

```
public function get status_so ( ) {
  if (!__nc) {
    return null;
```

```
    }
    if (!_status_so) {
        _status_so = SharedObjectFactory.getRemote(path + "status",_nc.uri);
        _status_so.connect(_nc);
    }
    return _status_so;
}
```

We're done building the client-side *Status* class, so let's move on to the server-side *Status* class and the main server-side application that loads it.

Building the server-side Status object

Whenever a client connects to the server, any methods that will be called remotely must be attached to the *Client* object. Potentially every component may have to attach remote methods to the *Client* object. To avoid writing long and complicated *application.onConnect( )* methods, a good practice is to call a method of a server-side component whenever a client connects. That way, the component can set up the client to receive any remote method calls and can add information into a shared object about the client if it needs to. When the client disconnects, the component should also get a chance to recover resources or remove an entry from a shared object. The *main.asc* file in Example 13-5 loads a separate *.asc* file for a Status and PeopleList component. Each file contains a class definition for the server-side part of a component. Within the *onAppStart( )* method, instances of the *Status* and *PeopleList* classes are created. Whenever a client connects, the *Client* object is passed to the *addClient( )* method of both components, and when a client disconnects, each component's *removeClient( )* method is called.

Knowing how to divide your code between the client side and server side, or even following an example of how it's done, can all be a bit confusing. When an event occurs on the server, such as a client connecting or disconnecting, any shared object updates should be handled primarily on the server side. Reacting to client-side events, such as button clicks or text messages, are more complicated—shared objects can be updated on the client or on the server. We'll see several variations throughout this chapter and describe best practices in Chapter 15. Figure 13-4 shows an interaction diagram that illustrates how the client- and server-side parts of the Status component work together to update the status shared object. When *addClient( )* or *removeClient( )* is called on the server, the status is updated. When the client-side Status component calls its server-side counterpart, the server-side *Status* object updates the shared object. In the next section, we'll build a PeopleList component that will receive *onSync( )* calls whenever the status changes.

Example 13-5 shows the code for the *main.asc* file that that loads the *Status.asc* and *PeopleList.asc* files, initiates the server-side application, and hands off most of the work to the status and peopleList objects. Some functions and error checking have been omitted.

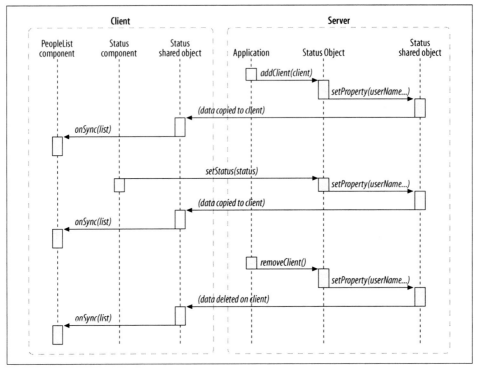

Figure 13-4. An overview of how the Status component updates the PeopleList component

Example 13-5. A main.asc file that loads the Status.asc and PeopleList.asc files

```
load("Status.asc");
load("PeopleList.asc");

application.onAppStart = function () {
  userList_so = SharedObject.get("private/userList");
  status     = new Status();
  peopleList = new PeopleList();
};

application.onConnect = function (client, user) {
  var tempUser = userList_so.getProperty(user.userName);
  if (tempUser) {
    application.rejectConnection(client, {msg: "The user name " +
                                user.userName + " is already in use."});
    return false;
  }
  client.user = user;
  client.user.arrival  = new Date();
  peopleList.addClient(client);
  status.addClient(client);
  userList_so.setProperty(client.user.userName, client);
  return true;
};
```

Example 13-5. A main.asc file that loads the Status.asc and PeopleList.asc files (continued)

```
application.onDisconnect = function (client) {
  status.removeClient(client);
  peopleList.removeClient(client);
  userList_so.setProperty(client.user.userName, null);
};
```

A good deal of error checking and other code has been removed from Example 13-5. The complete source is available in the *PeopleList.zip* file on the book's web site.

Example 13-6 is the complete listing of the server-side *Status* class contained in the *Status.asc* file. The class uses a scheme similar to the client-side *Status* class to allow it to address different resource paths in order to keep resources for different components separate.

Example 13-6. The server-side Status class definition from the Status.asc file

```
function Status(name) {
  if (!name) name = "main";
  this.name = name;
  this.path = "pfcs/" + this.className + "/" + name;
  this.so = SharedObject.get(this.path + "/status");
}

Status.validStates = {
  Online: true,
  Offline: true,
  Away: true,
  Busy: true
}

Status.prototype.className = "Status";

/* Adds an object path to a client object.
 * This effectively parses the path, such as "client/pfcs/Status/main"
 * to create a hiearchy of properties that match the namespace,
 * such as client.pfcs.Status.main.
 * Each time through the for loop, a new object, such as
 * client, client.pfcs, client.pfcs.Status, and client.pfcs.Status.main
 * is created, if it does not exist already.
 */
Status.prototype.addObjectPath = function (client) {
  var pathArray = this.path.split("/");
  var obj = client;
  var name;
  for (var i = 0; i < pathArray.length; i++) {
    name = pathArray[i];
    if (!obj[name]) {
      obj[name] = {};
    }
    obj = obj[name];
  }
};
```

```
Status.prototype.addClient = function (client) {
  this.addObjectPath(client);
  var thisComponent = this;
  client.pfcs[this.className][this.name].setStatus = function (status) {
    // Pass the client object and status to the Status
    // component's setStatus() method.
    thisComponent.setStatus(client, status);
  };
  this.so.setProperty(client.pfcs.user.userName, "Online");
};

Status.prototype.removeClient = function (client) {
  this.so.setProperty(client.pfcs.user.userName, null);
  if (client.pfcs &&
      client.pfcs[this.className] &&
      client.pfcs[this.className][this.name])
    delete client.pfcs[this.className][this.name];
};

Status.prototype.setStatus = function (client, status) {
  if (typeof status != "string") return;
  if (!Status.validStates[status]) return;
  this.so.setProperty(client.pfcs.user.userName, status);
  //trace("setStatus> " + client.pfcs.user.userName + ", " + status);
};

Status.prototype.close = function () {
};
```

Whenever a client connects, its *Client* object is passed to the component's server-side *addClient( )* method. The *addClient( )* method has to attach a *setStatus( )* method to the server-side client object so the client-side Status component can invoke *setStatus( )* on the server. The *setStatus( )* method could be attached directly to Client. prototype, so as to be available to all clients as discussed under "Using the Client prototype object" in Chapter 4. But we chose the more flexible approach of customizing each client, to allow us to differentiate between them. Chapter 18 makes good use of this to give users different privileges based on their roles.

To distinguish the remote methods belonging to each component, the *addClient( )* method has to do more than add a *setStatus( )* method directly to the client object. Just as each client's streams and shared objects are named in a way to avoid one component overwriting the streams or shared objects belonging to another component, remote methods are named using the same convention:

```
pfcs/ComponentClassName/componentInstanceName/remoteMethodName
```

When a remote method is called, the same format is used. So a client-side Status component instance named main will call the server-side *setStatus( )* method this way:

```
_nc.call(path + "setStatus", null, status);
```

If we evaluate the path variable, we can see this is the same as calling:

```
_nc.call("pfcs/Status/main/setStatus", null, status);
```

This will call a method on the server-side `client` object just as though we executed a server-side statement that looks like this:

```
client.pfcs.Status.main.setStatus(status);
```

Let's look at this method call in detail. The *setStatus( )* method is being called on the main object. The `main` object is a property of the `Status` object, which is a property of the `pfcs` object, which is a property of the `client` object. Despite their names, all of these objects, except the `client`, are just generic objects that are created simply to have a place to put methods like *setStatus( )*. The name of each object conforms to the naming convention used throughout the remainder of this book. Later we'll see other examples of calling remote methods using the same naming convention—for example, when a TextChat component calls its *sendMessage( )* method on the server:

```
client.pfcs.TextChat.main.sendMessage(...)
```

and when the SharedText component calls a server-side method:

```
client.pfcs.SharedText.main.edit(...)
```

For each of these remote method calls to work, nested generic objects following the *pfcs/ComponentClassName/ComponentInstanceName* naming convention must be added to the `client` object.

Returning to the Status component: in order to call the *setStatus( )* method, a number of generic objects must already exist in the `client` instance. A `pfcs` object must already be a property of the `client` object. In turn, a `Status` object must be a property of the `pfcs` object, and a `main` object must be a property of the `Status` object. When all these object properties are in place, a *setStatus( )* method must be attached as a property of the `main` object. The work of creating the `pfcs`, `Status`, and `main` object properties within the `client` object is done by the *addObjectPath( )* method. Note that the Status component's path property already contains the string "pfcs/Status/main" when *addClient( )* calls *addObjectPath( )*:

```
this.addObjectPath(client);
```

When *addObjectPath( )* returns, the `client.pfcs.Status.main` object exists, and the *setStatus( )* method can be added to it. The following short snippet of code adds the *setStatus( )* method:

```
var thisComponent = this;
client.pfcs[this.className][this.name].setStatus = function (status) {
  thisComponent.setStatus(client, status);
};
```

When *client.pfcs.Status.main.setStatus( )* is called, it does little more than call the Status component's own *setStatus( )* method. In other words, the `client.pfcs.Status.main` object is really just a stand-in (proxy) for the actual Status component and merely passes on requests to the Status component itself.

In order to call the Status component's *setStatus( )* method, some way is needed to refer to the actual Status component from within the main object's *setStatus( )* method. At first glance, you might think you could just use this to refer to the Status component. However, when *client.pfcs.Status.main.setStatus( )* is called, this refers to the main object. The solution is to use another variable. In this case, the thisComponent variable is passed a reference to this inside the *addClient( )* method. When the *client.pfcs.Status.main.setStatus( )* method is called, thisComponent still refers to the Status component and can be used to call the component's *setStatus( )* method.

This is a nice feature of JavaScript (and Server-Side ActionScript which is JavaScript 1.5). When the *client.pfcs.Status.main.setStatus( )* method is defined inside the *Status* class's *addClient( )* method, any variable defined inside *addClient( )* and its current value, can be used inside the *client.pfcs.Status.main.setStatus( )* method. Behind the scenes, JavaScript creates a special closure object in order to store the variable thisComponent and the value it contained when the *client.pfcs.Status.main.setStatus( )* was defined. The same thing happens with the client variable. When the *client.pfcs. Status.main.setStatus( )* is defined, the client variable refers to the client on which it is being defined on. So, the client variable will always refer to the *Client* it is called on. If that seems a little esoteric, don't worry; it is. The main thing is that you can use variables defined inside the *addClient( )* method inside the *client.pfcs.Status.main. setStatus( )* method, and they will retain the values they had when *addClient( )* was called.

When *client.pfcs.Status.main.setStatus( )* is called, this method is called by it:

```
Status.prototype.setStatus = function (client, status) {
  if (typeof status != "string") return;
  if (!Status.validStates[status]) return;
  this.so.setProperty(client.user.userName, status);
};
```

The method is passed a reference to the client object it was called from and so can get the userName associated with the client variable and set the new status in the status shared object:

```
this.so.setProperty(client.user.userName, status);
```

The Flash movie doesn't need to pass the username to the server. Note that the user object, which contains the userName property, was attached to the client property in the *main.asc* script when the client connected, as a simple way to associate user information with each client object. Other more complex designs are possible that do not require adding user data directly to the client object and are usually part of a more complex server-side component framework.

Finally, the Status component's *addClient( )* method sets the initial connection status for the client in the status shared object:

```
this.so.setProperty(client.user.userName, "Online");
```

When the client disconnects, the server-side *Status.removeClient( )* method is called. It removes the entry for the client from the status shared object:

```
this.so.setProperty(client.user.userName, null);
```

That was a fair bit to follow, and it's easy to lose track of the big picture. In summary, the Status component's *addClient( )* method sets up each server-side client object so it can receive *setStatus( )* calls from the client-side part of the Status component. The *addClient( )* method also updates the status shared object so that the user's initial status is "Online". From then on, whenever the user changes his status, the series of events in Figure 13-4 will occur. Have a look at Figure 13-4 from top to bottom to see how one event leads to another.

That's it—you've seen all the pieces that make the Status component work. It's time to turn to designing and building the PeopleList component that will listen to the status shared object and display the right icon for each user.

Designing and Building a PeopleList Component

The SimplePeopleList component introduced earlier was designed to be as simple as possible in order to introduce the basic requirements of building a v2 Flash component. It was not responsible for adding data to the userList shared object and was not capable of showing a user's status. The PeopleList component addresses both shortcomings. A server-side *PeopleList* object is used to maintain a people shared object to which the client-side *PeopleList* object connects (this replaces the userList used in the SimplePeopleList component). Furthermore, if a Status component passes a reference to the status shared object to the PeopleList component, the latter also displays status icons; otherwise, PeopleList works correctly without displaying any icons.

Fortunately, the code for the *PeopleList.asc* file, which implements the server-side *PeopleList* class is short and relatively simple, as shown in Example 13-7.

Example 13-7. The server-side PeopleList class definition from the PeopleList.asc file

```
function PeopleList(name) {
  if (!name) name = "main";
  this.name = name;
  this.path = "pfcs/" + this.className + "/" + name;
  this.so = SharedObject.get(this.path + "/people");
}

PeopleList.prototype.className = "PeopleList";

PeopleList.prototype.addClient = function (client) {
  this.so.setProperty(client.pfcs.user.userName, client.pfcs.user);
};
```

```
PeopleList.prototype.removeClient = function (client) {
  this.so.setProperty(client.pfcs.user.userName, null);
};

PeopleList.prototype.close = function () {
};
```

The server-side *PeopleList* class does two things. It adds an entry for each user into the people shared object when the client connects, and it removes the entry when the client disconnects. The entry it adds is an object that was passed into the *application. onConnect( )* method. (See the *main.asc* file listing in Example 13-5.) Creating a separate shared object for the PeopleList component makes it possible to separate the public from the private information passed in by the client and reduce shared object updates to those needed by just the PeopleList component. In this example, the user object is just added to the PeopleList's people shared object. In later chapters, only public information is added.

The PeopleList component does not receive remote method calls from its client-side counterpart the way the Status component does. The shared object path is in the now-familiar path of *pfcs/PeopleList/main/people*.

The client-side PeopleList component contains the same asset as the SimplePeopleList component—a List component. Much of the code in the client-side PeopleList component is the same as the code in the SimplePeopleList component, so the entire class definition is not reproduced here. See the *PeopleList.as* file in the *PeopleList.zip* archive on the book's web site for the complete listing. The setter method that is passed a *NetConnection* object is almost identical. The only difference is that it gets a shared object at the path path + "people" instead of the path resourcePath + "userList" used by the SimplePeopleList component. In either case, the client-side PeopleList component uses the *NetConnection* object to get a reference to the remote shared object, sets itself as listener on it, and connects it. The *PeopleList* class has an additional setter method that can be used to pass a reference to a status_so shared object to it, as shown in the client-side code in Example 13-8.

Example 13-8. Passing in a status shared object to the PeopleList component

```
public function set status_so (so:SharedObject) {
  if (so instanceof SharedObject) {
    __status_so = so;
    __status_so.addEventListener("onSync", this);
    list.iconFunction = function (item) {
      var status = item.data.status;
      if (status) {
        return "Status_Person_" + status;
      }
    };
    if (__status_so.isConnected) {
```

```
      onSync({target:__status_so, type:"onSync", list:[]});
   }
 }
}
```

The method makes the PeopleList component instance a listener of the status shared object so that the *PeopleList.onSync( )* method will receive updates from both the people and status shared objects. It also adds an *iconFunction( )* method to the List object.

The method is called whenever a list item needs to be redrawn inside the List. It finds the value of the list item's data.status property and returns the linkage identifier of a status icon to display beside the item's text label. Finally, if the status shared object has already been connected by the Status component, its isConnected property will be true. In that case, the *set status_so( )* method calls *onSync( )* once itself to make sure the list is redrawn based on any status information that is already available.

Before moving on to describe the *onSync( )* method, where most of the interesting work of the client-side PeopleList component takes place, one more setter method—the one to hide offline users—needs to be described:

```
    public function set hideOfflineUsers(hideOfflineUsers:Boolean) {
      __hideOfflineUsers = hideOfflineUsers;
    }
```

When a user wants to appear offline, he can select the offline option in the status combo box. In some applications, his name will be completely removed from everyone's PeopleList. In others, it may be more appropriate to show an offline icon. Setting hideOfflineUsers to true ensures that an offline user's icon and username will disappear from the PeopleList display.

Finally, Example 13-9 shows the source code for the *PeopleList.onSync( )* method from the *PeopleList.as* class file.

Example 13-9. The PeopleList onSync( ) method that handles both PeopleList and Status onSync( ) calls

```
function onSync (ev) {
  // Get the list's dataProvider property and truncate it.
  var dp = list.dataProvider;
  dp.length = 0;
  // Fill the dataProvider property using the Array.push( ) method.
  for (var p in __people_so.data) {
    var obj = clone(__people_so.data[p]);
    var status = __status_so.data[p];
    if (status) {
      obj.status = status;
      // To make a person disappear from the PeopleList when
      // he or she is offline, skip this record if necessary:
```

```
        if (__hideOfflineUsers && obj.status == "Offline") continue;
    }
    dp.push({label:p, data:obj});
  }
  dp.dispatchEvent({target:dp, type:"modelChanged"});
}
```

The username of each person connected to an application is used to name each slot in the people and status shared objects.

The *onSync( )* method may be called when either the people or status shared object is updated. In either case, it does the same thing. It replaces all the items in the list with new ones based on the contents of the people and status shared objects. If no status list exists, no status information is included in the list. As shown in Example 13-9, the *onSync( )* method gets the object stored in each slot of the people shared object, makes a copy of it using the *clone( )* method, and adds a status property to it if there is one.

This is necessary because a property cannot be added to a people shared object slot without forcing another shared object update. So instead, a copy is made and updated.

If the status of an object is "Offline" and hideOfflineUsers is true, an item is not added into the list for it (the *continue* keyword ensures that the loop skips over the subsequent statement that pushes the obj onto the dataProvider):

```
        if (__hideOfflineUsers && obj.status == "Offline") continue;
```

Example 13-10 shows the code for the *clone( )* method from the *PeopleList.as* file.

Example 13-10. The clone( ) method returns a shallow copy of an object

```
function clone (orig) {
  var copy = {};
  for (var p in orig) {
    copy[p] = orig[p];
  }
  return copy;
}
```

Figure 13-5 shows a simple interaction diagram for the PeopleList component. It shows how, when a client connects or disconnects from an application instance, the people shared object is updated on the server, which leads eventually to the PeopleList component receiving an *onSync( )* method call.

If you compare Figure 13-4 with Figure 13-5, you'll see that the PeopleList component receives an *onSync( )* method call when one of five events occurs. The *onSync( )* method in Example 13-9 updates the list based on the current data in both shared

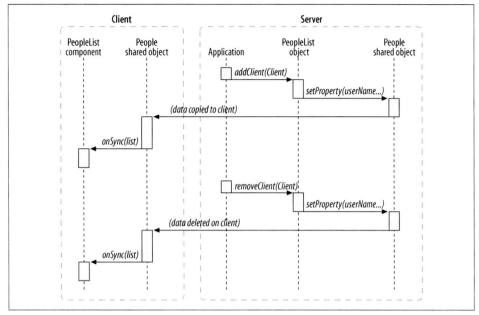

Figure 13-5. How the server-side PeopleList component updates its client-side partner

objects by deleting the contents of the list and rewriting the entire list. For lists of fewer than 50 items, the code in Example 13-9 works well. For larger lists with hundreds or thousands of items, a more efficient approach is required. See Chapter 15 for more information on coding efficient *onSync( )* methods.

Text Chat

A text chat component is an essential part of many applications. Even in the most advanced video conference applications, text chats are almost always available as a reliable low-bandwidth communication tool to fall back on. A very simple text chat application can be built from two text fields, a button, and a shared object. When the user clicks the Send button, the text in the composition field is sent to the server and on to anyone else connected to the same shared object. When new text messages arrive, they are displayed in a larger scrolling message field.

Users who join a text chat midsession also expect to see the conversation that has gone on before they arrived. So text chats need to have some mechanism for storing chat history. Some chats must make available the full text of previous sessions for review. Other common features include sending private messages to just a few individuals, creating smaller breakout private chats, text formatting including selecting fonts and font colors, adding HTML links, and embedding small graphics (or emoticons) within the text. In fact, for something that initially seems so simple, there are endless variations in text chat designs.

The TextChat component described in this section, while relatively basic, is designed to show the essential mechanics of building full-featured text chat components. A shared object is used to send messages to everyone in the chat. Each chat session is recorded as a sequence of remote method calls in data-only streams stored on the server. A record of each chat session, including how many posts each user made, is saved in a persistent shared object. The chat automatically converts text that begins with "http://" or "www." to active HTML links using regular expressions and Server-Side ActionScript, while removing all other HTML markup. The TextChat component can be used either as a global component that every user accesses or in a pop-up window to facilitate breakout or one-to-one chat sessions. This chapter describes designing and building the component. Other chapters, especially Chapter 18 on security, develop the component further to provide different functions to users depending on each user's role.

Text Chat Resources and Messaging

Previous sections of this chapter have described the basic design of each component in terms of the resources it must manage, the user interface it provides, and the services it makes available to other components. For the TextChat component, we'll do the same thing but spend more time on message control and management and the shared object and stream resources the component manages.

TextChat message passing

Each text message is created when someone using a Flash movie types something into a text input field. The text message can be sent to FlashCom via *NetConnection call( )* or *SharedObject.send( )*. If *call( )* is used, the message arrives at a remote method on the server and must be redistributed to each Flash movie that needs to receive it. If *send( )* is used, the message is automatically delivered to every Flash movie connected to the same shared object. Using *send( )*, therefore, appears to be the easiest way to distribute messages. However, in some scenarios, using *send( )* can be less secure than using *call( )*, because the application must trust the client enough to provide write access to the shared object. See Chapter 18 to understand why trusting the client is often not a good idea. The TextChat component described here uses the *call( )* method to send each text message to the server, and a shared object to redistribute the message to each client connected to the shared object. Figure 13-6 is a simple interaction diagram that shows how text messages that originate on one client are distributed to every client.

Figure 13-6 shows how *call( )* is used to pass the message to the server-side TextChat component, which processes it and then sends it back to all the clients by calling *send( )* on the messages shared object. It shows the *call( )* method being used to call a method named *sendMessage( )* on the server-side *Client* object. The actual client method name will be a little more complicated—for example *pfcs/TextChat/main/ sendMessage( )*—because of the component naming scheme used for all the compo-

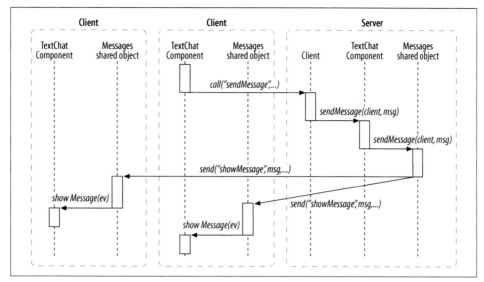

Figure 13-6. How a text message is sent from one client and distributed via a shared object to many clients

nents in this chapter. The client passes a reference to itself and the text message on to the component by calling *sendMessage(client, msg)* on a server-side TextChat component instance. After the TextChat component finishes processing the message, the message is passed as a parameter into a *send( )* call on the messages shared object. Finally, the *showMessage( )* remote method is called on each client's copy of the shared object and passed on to each client-side TextChat component.

TextChat history

Text messages can be saved in shared objects, in streams, and in a database via Flash Remoting calls. The Macromedia Chat communication component uses a shared object to store and retrieve its chat history. If you want to see how it works, have a look in the Library of a movie that uses the Chat component. You'll find the client-side code on the first frame of the component and the server-side code in the *.../Flash Communication Server MX/scriptlib/components/chat.asc* file.

One disadvantage of using a shared object is that, over time, the number of messages can get quite large. When a client is connected to a shared object, a complete copy of the shared object resides in memory. Memory consumption can be minimized using separate shared objects for each chat session that are connected, read, and disconnected as needed. Flash Remoting provides an appealing alternative because individual messages, as well as author, timestamp, and session information, can all be stored in a searchable database. To reduce the number of remoting calls, messages and other information can be stored in a stream or shared object until the end of a chat session. When the session ends, a single database call can save the entire chat history. The TextChat component described here creates a stream for each chat session and maintains a listing of each session in a shared object. When a chat starts, the last session is read from the stream and displayed in the chat. Controlled access for retrieving, displaying, and managing older session histories is described in Chapter 18.

TextChat message parsing

As a convenience to users, text entered into the chat input text field is often parsed for special instructions or text and represented differently in the actual chat window. A classic example is automatically replacing a smiley, such as :-), in the text field with an emoticon. In Flash, showing graphics within lines of text is an overly complex undertaking and is not shown here. Another convenience is converting text that begins with "http://" or "www." into a full HTML link—a feature that is implemented here. We also want to protect users from one another by limiting what HTML tags they can use in the chat. The TextChat component uses regular expressions on the server to parse and manipulate messages before sending them to each client.

In summary, the TextChat component manages a shared object for distributing messages, streams that contain all the messages of each chat session, and a shared object that contains summary information about each session and the location of each stream history.

Text Chat User Interface

The user interface consists of three v2 components: a TextArea, InputText, and Button.

The *TextChat.createChildren( )* method from the *TextChat.as* file in the *PeopleList. zip* archive is listed in Example 13-11. It shows how the three subcomponents are attached to, initialized, and set up to deliver events to the TextChat component.

Example 13-11. Attaching and initializing TextChat subcomponents

```
function createChildren () {
  var depth = 1;
  // Create and set up the messages area.
  createObject("TextArea", "messagesArea", depth++, {_x:0, _y:0});
  messagesArea.html = true;
  messagesArea.editable = false;
  messagesArea.wordWrap = true;
  createObject("TextInput", "messageInput", depth++);
  messageInput.addEventListener("enter", this);
  createObject("Button", "sendButton", depth++, {label:"Send", _width: 70});
  sendButton.addEventListener("click", this);
}
```

When a TextChat component instance is placed on the Stage, it must resize itself and its subcomponents so that they maintain a relative position to one another. The layout of the TextChat component is illustrated in Figure 13-7.

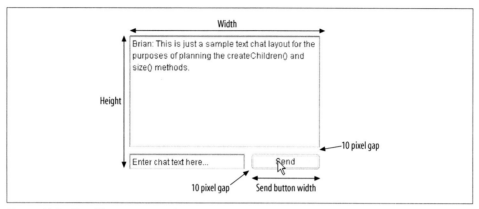

Figure 13-7. TextChat component layout

When resized, the messagesArea TextArea is always positioned in the upper left at (0,0) and has the same width as the entire TextChat component. However, its height must be adjusted to allow for the height of the sendButton and messageInput field as well as a 10-pixel gap. The height of the messagesArea is calculated as:

```
height - sendButton._height – 10
```

The messageInput TextInput component instance must be moved any time the TextChat is resized. Its _x location is always 0 but its _y coordinate is always 10 pixels more than the height of the TextArea above it. Similarly, its width must be calculated to allow room for the sendButton on its right and a 10-pixel gap. The TextInput component height is the same as the sendButton instance. Example 13-12 shows the *size( )* method that is responsible for repositioning and resizing the three subcomponents that make up the client-side *TextChat* user interface.

Example 13-12. The size( ) method repositions and resizes subcomponents
```
function size () {
  super.size();
  messagesArea.setSize(width, height - sendButton._height - 10);
  messageInput.move(0, height - sendButton._height);
  messageInput.setSize(width - sendButton._width - 10, sendButton._height);
  sendButton.move(messageInput.width + 10, messagesArea.height + 10);
}
```

Even though the three v2 UI components are attached to the TextChat component in the *createChildren( )* method, it is often a good idea to place the components in a test movie in order to work with the layout visually—then code the *size( )* method.

Connecting the User Interface and Shared Object

The *createChildren( )* method ensures the TextChat component receives *enter* events from the TextInput component and *click* events from the Button. Example 13-13 shows the code from the *TextChat.as* file that handles these two events.

Example 13-13. The enter( ) and click( ) event handlers

```
function click (ev) {
  enter(ev);
}

function enter (ev) {
  // The static Text.trim( ) method trims leading and trailing whitespace. It is
  // defined in the Text.as file, which is provided on the book's web site.
  var msg = Text.trim(messageInput.text);
  if (msg == "") return;
  messageInput.text = "";
  _nc.call(path + "/sendMessage", null, msg);
}
```

Aside from trimming the message text and clearing the messageInput field, the *enter( )* method sends a remote method request to a *sendMessage( )* method attached to a server-side *Client* object. If the TextChat instance's path is "pfcs/TextChat/main" then the method call is delivered to *client.pfcs.TextChat.main.sendMessage( )*. On the server, the remote method request is passed to a *TextChat* object and its *sendMessage( )* method in much the same way the *Status* object receives *setStatus( )* method calls, as shown in Example 13-6. Example 13-14 shows the server-side *TextChat* class's *addClient( )* method from the *TextChat.asc* file.

Example 13-14. The server-side TextChat addClient( ) method

```
TextChat.prototype.addClient = function (client) {
  if (!this.activeSession) {
    var startString = this.session.getStartString( )
    this.sessions_so.setProperty("currentSession", startString);
    this.activeSession = true;
  }
  this.addObjectPath(client);
  var thisComponent = this;
  client.pfcs[this.className][this.name].sendMessage = function (msg) {
    // Pass the client object and message to the TextChat instance.
    thisComponent.sendMessage(client, msg);
  };
};
```

When *client.pfcs.TextChat.main.sendMessage( )* is called, it just calls the *TextChat. sendMessage( )* method and passes it both a reference to the calling client and the text message. Example 13-15, excerpted from the server-side *TextChat.asc* file, shows the *TextChat.sendMessage( )* method as well as the *fixURL( )* method it calls to wrap

HTML anchor tags around URLs. The server-side *sendMessage( )* method replaces HTML tag brackets with encoded characters in order to remove any tags created by the user and creates HTML links for any URLs it finds using regular expressions. Then, it adds the username of the person who sent the message to the beginning of the message text and sends it to every client participating in the chat using the *send( )* method of the messages shared object.

Example 13-15. The fixURL( ) and sendMessage( ) methods of the server-side TextChat class

```
// Prepend "http://" if one is not found and then create an HTML anchor.
TextChat.prototype.fixURL = function (str) {
  if (str.indexOf("http://") == -1) str = "http://" + str;
  str = '<font color="#0000FF"><u><a href="' + str +
        '" target="_blank">' + str + '</a></u></font>';
  return str;
};

TextChat.prototype.sendMessage = function (client, msg) {
  if (typeof msg != "string") return;
  if (msg == "") return;
  // Replace < with &lt; and > with &gt;
  msg = msg.replace(/</, "&lt;");
  msg = msg.replace(/>/, "&gt;");
  // Turn URLs into links if they start with http:// or www.
  // and also have at least one more dot in them.
  msg = msg.replace(/(http:\/\/|www\.)\S*\.\S*\b/ig, this.fixURL);
  msg = "<b>" + client.pfcs.user.userName + "</b>: " + msg;
  this.messages_so.send("showMessage", msg);
  this.messages_s.send("showMessage", msg, client.pfcs.user.userName, new Date());
  this.session.addContributor(client.pfcs.user.userName);
};
```

 Passing messages from the client-side part of a component to its server-side part is a good practice. The server-side part of the component can securely manage or manipulate the data before distributing it to other clients.

In this case, the server makes sure the message's sender name is correctly identified. The userName is retrieved from the client.user object and added to the message. (See the *main.asc* file in the *PeopleList.zip* archive.)

The message is also stored in a messages stream for later retrieval, and a session object that counts the number of chat messages generated by each user is updated.

When the remote method call named *showMessage( )* arrives at each client, the messagesArea text field is updated by appending the text message as shown in Example 13-16.

Example 13-16. showMessage() is called by the showMessage() method attached to the messages_so shared object

```
function showMessage (ev) {
  messagesArea.text += ev.args[0] + "\n";
  messagesArea.vPosition = messagesArea.maxVPosition;
  messagesArea.redraw( );
}
```

There are two things to note about the simple client-side *showMessage()* method in Example 13-16. The method is called by a shared object that has been set up to broadcast remote method calls to registered listeners by using *SharedObjectFactory*. (See Example 13-2 for more details on *SharedObjectFactory*, and consult Example 13-17 to see how the *TextChat* class sets up the remote method.) An event is passed to *showMessage()* that includes an args property that contains the arguments passed to the remote method. Also, the *redraw()* method is called to force the v2 TextArea component to scroll properly to the end. (A   bug in the two initial releases of the v2 TextArea component causes the scrollbar to bounce back after scrolling to the bottom unless *redraw()* is called.)

Chat History

Let's look at how the user who joins a chat can see the chat history from the previous session and any messages that were sent during the current session before she connected. Example 13-17 shows the client-side *set nc()* setter that is called when a *NetConnection* object is passed to a client-side TextChat component. The method saves a reference to the *NetConnection*, configures shared objects and the stream object it needs, and then connects the shared objects.

Example 13-17. set nc() method is passed a NetConnection object and configures and connects to the server-side TextChat's shared objects and streams

```
public function set nc (nc:NetConnection) {
  __nc = nc;
  // Set up the shared object that will send all new messages.
  messages_so = SharedObjectFactory.getRemote(path + "messages", nc.uri);
  messages_so.addRemoteMethod("showMessage");
  messages_so.addEventListener("showMessage", this);
  messages_so.connect(nc);

  // Set up the NetStream so we can play back the last session's history.
  history_ns = new NetStream(nc);
  history_ns.owner = this;
  history_ns.setBufferTime(1);
  history_ns.onStatus = function (info) {
    if (info.code == "NetStream.Play.Stop") {
      this.hasStopped = true;
    }
    else if (this.hasStopped && info.code == "NetStream.Buffer.Empty") {
      this.owner.showHistory( );
```

```
    }
  };
  history_ns.showMessage = function (msg, userName, dateTime) {
    this.owner.accumulateHistory(msg, userName, dateTime);
  };

  // Can't play it until we get the path to the right stream.
  sessions_so = SharedObjectFactory.getRemote(path + "sessions", nc.uri, true);
  sessions_so.addEventListener("onFirstSync", this);
  sessions_so.connect(nc);
}
```

The setter method uses *SharedObject.addRemoteMethod( )* to add a *showMessage( )* remote method to the messages shared object and then adds itself as a listener for *showMessage( )* remote method calls before connecting:

```
  messages_so.addRemoteMethod("showMessage");
  messages_so.addEventListener("showMessage", this);
```

The *addRemoteMethod( )* and *addEventListener( )* methods are not native methods of the *SharedObject* class. They were added by the *SharedObjectFactory.getRemote( )* method (refer to Example 13-2 and Example 13-3). Calling both methods ensures that the component's *showMessage( )* method is called whenever a new message is received as part of a *showMessage( )* remote method call. The component's *showMessage( )* method is listed in Example 13-16.

The setter method in Example 13-17 also creates a history_ns `NetStream` object and configures it to receive data-only messages by attaching *showMessage( )* and *onStatus( )* methods. The idea is that when the stream is played, each chat message in the history will have been stored as a *showMessage( )* call. When the stream is played, the *showMessage( )* method will be called for every message in the stream. When the server finishes sending the stream to the server, the *onStatus( )* method will be passed an information object with a code value of "NetStream.Play.Stop". So the *onStatus( )* method remembers that the stream has stopped by setting its hasStopped property to true. Even though the server is not sending messages, there may still be some data left in the stream's buffer; so the *onStatus( )* method waits until hasStopped is true and it receives an information object with a code value of "NetStream.Buffer.Empty" before it calls the TextChat component's *showHistory( )* method to show all the messages it has received.

Information about each chat session, such as what stream its history is stored in, is available in a sessions shared object. Since it has to be read only once to find the location of the chat history streams, the TextChat component merely sets itself up to listen for an *onFirstSync* event before connecting the sessions shared object. When the sessions shared object connects, the TextChat component must read it to find the location of two streams. The first location is that of the stream with the last chat session's messages in it. The second stream contains any messages that have been collected during the current chat session. The current session's messages have to be retrieved for clients connecting while a session is in progress.

The sessions shared object contains the stream names for the last session and current session streams in the `lastSession` and `currentSession` properties, as shown in Example 13-18, excerpted from the *TextChat.as* file.

Example 13-18. The onFirstSync( ) method

```
function onFirstSync (ev) {
  var soPath = sessions_so.data.lastSession;
  if (soPath) history_ns.play(path + "/" + soPath, 0, -1, 3);
  var soPath = sessions_so.data.currentSession;
  if (soPath) history_ns.play(resourcePath + "/" + soPath, 0, -1, 2);
}
```

The *onFirstSync( )* method gets the stream names and plays them using the same *NetStream* object, one after the other, as part of a playlist. The 0 and -1 parameter values in the calls to *NetStream.play( )* tell each stream to play from the beginning until the end. Passing a 2 or 3 as a last parameter tells the stream to play all the data messages immediately rather than delivering them synchronized with stream time. Passing in 3 as a last parameter closes any stream that is playing, and passing 2 adds the stream to the playlist without closing any previous stream. See Chapter 5 for more details on playlists.

As each stream plays, the *showMessage( )* method is invoked on the `history_ns` object, which in turn calls the *TextChat.accumulateHistory( )* method, shown in Example 13-19, excerpted from the *TextChat.as* file. Rather than adding each message as it arrives to the `messagesArea` TextArea component, the messages are appended to the `historyBuffer` property of the TextChat. When all the messages have arrived, the *showHistory( )* method is called, which inserts the messages before any live messages that have arrived since the client connected.

Example 13-19. Receiving and displaying the chat history

```
function accumulateHistory (msg, userName, dateTime) {
  var date = dateTime.getFullYear( ) + ":" +
             dateTime.getMonth( ) + ":" +
             dateTime.getDate( );
  if (date != historyDate) {
    historyDate = date;
    historyBuffer += '<p align="center"><b><i>----' +
                     date + '----</i></b></p>\n';
  }
  historyBuffer += msg + "<br>";
}

function showHistory ( ) {
  messagesArea.text = historyBuffer + messagesArea.text;
```

Example 13-19. Receiving and displaying the chat history (continued)

```
    historyBuffer = "";
    history_ns.close();
}
```

That's it for how the client collects and shows the chat messages of the last and current chat sessions. It's time to look at how those messages were saved into streams in the first place. Everything is done on the server. If you look back at the *sendMessage()* method in Example 13-15, you'll see these three lines:

```
    this.messages_so.send("showMessage", msg);
    this.messages_s.send("showMessage", msg, client.user.userName, new Date());
    this.session.addContributor(client.user.userName);
```

After cleaning up the text in the msg variable, the server-side script sends the message back to every client connected to the messages shared object by calling *send()*. It also stores a remote method call in the messages_s stream by calling its *send()* method. So the message, the user who sent it, and the time it was received are all saved as part of the chat history.

Finally, a session object is updated so that it knows that the contributor has just added a message. The session object is an instance of the *TextChatSession* class. Each *TextChatSession* instance contains a path property with the name of its stream file, its startTime and endTime, and a list of contributors to the chat. The session object is used to play back the chat history in the *onFirstSync()* method (see Example 13-18). Note that the contributor information is not used in the code shown here. It could be used by an administrative application collecting TextChat statistics.

Example 13-20 shows the listing of the server-side *TextChatSession* class from the *TextChat.asc* file. It is a simple record class with methods that provide formatted stream names that include date information.

Example 13-20. The TextChatSession class

```
function TextChatSession (path) {
  this.path = path;
  this.startTime = new Date();
  this.endTime = null;
  this.contributors = {};
}

TextChatSession.prototype.getStartString = function () {
  var t = this.startTime;
  return t.getFullYear() + "_" + t.getMonth() + "_" + t.getDate() + "_" +
         t.getHours() + "_" + t.getMinutes() + "_" + t.getSeconds() + "_" +
         t.getMilliseconds();
};

TextChatSession.prototype.getName = function () {
  return this.path + "/" + this.getStartString();
};
```

Example 13-20. The TextChatSession class (continued)

```
TextChatSession.prototype.addContributor = function (userName) {
  if (!this.contributors[userName]) this.contributors[userName] = 1;
  else this.contributors[userName]++;
};

TextChatSession.prototype.endSession = function () {
  this.endTime = new Date();
};
```

Each session object is updated as messages arrive during a chat and is saved into a slot of the session shared object. Each session slot is named after the time when the session started. The session generates a string in the format YYYY_MM_DD_HH_MM_SS_MM in its *getStartString()* method.

Whenever a session ends, the shared object is updated with the new session information, as shown in Example 13-21.

Example 13-21. Closing the chat

```
TextChat.prototype.close = function () {
  this.messages_so.close();
  var startString = this.session.getStartString()
  this.sessions_so.setProperty(startString, this.session);
  this.sessions_so.setProperty("lastSession", startString);
};
```

Finally, the currentSession property is set up when the first client is added to the TextChat, as shown in Example 13-14.

There is a fair bit to follow in the TextChat component's server- and client-side code. To help it all fit into a picture of how the component works, it might be helpful to recall the roles of the three server-side resources the server-side code manages:

- The sessions_so shared object contains every session object. Each session object is stored in a slot named after the session start time. There are two other sessions_so properties: the lastSession property contains the startTime string of the last session, and currentSession contains the startTime string of the current one.

- The messages_so shared object is used only to copy messages from the server to each client.

- The messages_s *Stream* object is used to save each message and is named after the startTime of the session.

We've seen one way to implement a TextChat component with a basic features set. For the sake of brevity, the complete code of the TextChat component is not reproduced here, but it is available on the book's web site in the file *PeopleList.zip*. Also, the TextChat component's security is improved in Chapter 18.

Shared Text

A shared text area acts much like a whiteboard. Any user can add to or edit text so that everyone can see it. However, allowing everyone to make changes at once can lead to anarchy and frustration. So a mechanism is required to control who can add or edit text at one time. The SharedText component described here uses an Edit button to allow a user to take control of the SharedText component. When a user clicks the button, the button is toggled into the on state for the user who clicked it and disabled for everyone else. The text area of the SharedText component becomes editable for only the one user. When the user has finished making changes, he clicks the Send button and everyone sees the update. Figure 13-8 shows the user interface for the SharedText component in its default state. The text field cannot be edited, and the only button enabled is the Edit button. In the default mode, the version stepper control can be used to page through all the previous versions of the text area. Each version is saved in a separate shared object slot so that previous versions of the text can be reviewed.

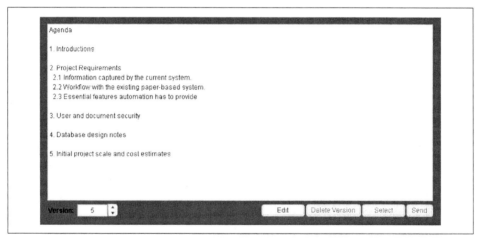

Figure 13-8. SharedText component in its default state

Figure 13-9 shows the SharedText component after the Edit button has been clicked and control of the text area has been granted. The Edit button's label is now Cancel and all the buttons are toggled on. Clicking the Delete Version button deletes the version of the text that is currently displayed and releases control of the shared text area. Dragging the mouse over some text to select it and clicking the Select button displays the same version with selected text for everyone and also releases control of the component. Making changes to the text and clicking the Send button creates a new version of the text and stores it in another slot of the shared object before releasing control.

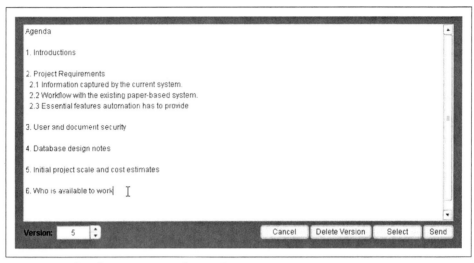

Figure 13-9. SharedText component during editing

The SharedText component manages one resource: a shared object named messages. The shared object contains a variety of slots that are used for different purposes.

The currentUser slot is used as part of the locking mechanism that allows only one user to update the shared text component at a time. If the slot contains an empty string, the shared text component is not being updated by anyone and is therefore available for use. If the currentUser slot contains a username, then only that user has permission to update the shared text component.

There are a length slot and a sequence of numbered slots. The slot name of each numbered slot is actually a string representation of a number. Slot 1, for example, is really named slot "1". The full text of each version of shared text is stored in each numbered slot and the length slot contains the number of text slots. For example, if there is only one version of text, in slot "1", then length will be 1.

Finally, there are slots that, when updated, force each client to display one of the versions of text, scroll to a position within it, and select some of the text. The slot names are: selectCount, selectScroll, selectVersion, endIndex, and startIndex. The selectCount slot represents the number of selections that have been made during the history of the component. When it changes, each client knows to display the text in the slot indicated by the selectVersion property, scroll to the selectScroll position in the TextArea, and bold the text between the startIndex and endIndex characters.

The locking mechanism used in the SharedText component is a cooperative one, because it relies on each client responding to changes in the currentUser slot. When a user clicks the Edit button, a remote method named *edit( )* is called on the server. If the currentUser slot is empty when the call is executed, the client's username is placed in the currentUser slot. The change in the currentUser slot results in an *onSync( )* call on each client, in response to which each client checks whether its username is in the currentUser slot. If so, it activates all the editing buttons and allows the user to update the shared text area. If someone else's username is in the currentUser slot, all the buttons are disabled.

The client that has control can now safely update the other properties of the shared object to add another version of text, select some text, or delete a version of text. When the client updates the shared object, it is detected on the server and the currentUser slot is immediately cleared. In turn, *onSync( )* is called, and each client puts the buttons back into the default state. The initial sequence of events is illustrated in Figure 13-10.

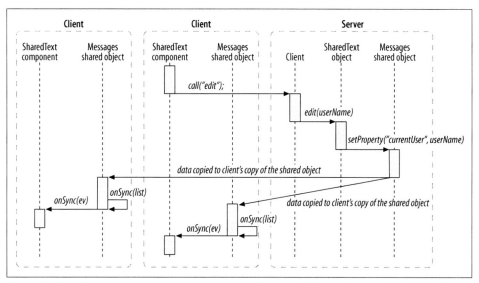

Figure 13-10. The sequence of events required to set the currentUser property and notify each client (two clients are shown)

Example 13-22 lists part of the server-side *SharedText* class definition, which should be placed in a *SharedText.asc* file. Two methods common to other components—*addObjectPath( )* and *removeClient( )*—have been omitted to reduce the size of the listing. They are included in the version on the book's web site.

Example 13-22. The server-side SharedText class

```
/* SharedText constructor is passed its name. The default is "main".
 * All resources exist in the namespace: pfcs/SharedText/name/.
 * Gets and initializes the pfcs/SharedText/name/messages shared object.
 */
function SharedText (name) {
  this.name = name;
  if (!name) this.name = "main";
  this.path = "pfcs/" + this.className + "/" + name;
```

Example 13-22. The server-side SharedText class (continued)

```
  this.so = SharedObject.get(this.path + "/messages", true);
  this.so.ready = false;
  this.so.onSync = function () {
    /* If any change is made in the SO, the client is done,
     * so the current user is set to an empty string.
     * Note: server-side changes always succeed so they
     * do not result in an onSync() call.
     */
    var currentUser = this.getProperty("currentUser");
    if (currentUser != "") this.setProperty("currentUser", "");
  };
  this.so.setProperty("currentUser", "");
  if (typeof this.so.getProperty("length") != "number") {
    this.so.setProperty("length", 0);
  }
}

SharedText.prototype.className = "SharedText";

// addClient() is called whenever a client needs to connect
// to the SharedText component.
SharedText.prototype.addClient = function (client) {
  this.addObjectPath(client);
  var thisComponent = this;
  client.pfcs[this.className][this.name].edit = function () {
    thisComponent.edit(client.pfcs.user.userName);
  };
};

/* edit() is called by a client to get or release control
 * of the SharedText component. The messages shared object's
 * currentUser slot may have one of three values. It can be
 * empty, contain someone else's username, or contain
 * the userName property of the person calling this method.
 */
SharedText.prototype.edit = function (userName) {
  var currentUser = this.so.getProperty("currentUser");
  if (userName == currentUser)
    this.so.setProperty("currentUser", "");
  else if (currentUser != "")
    return;
  else
    this.so.setProperty("currentUser", userName);
};

SharedText.prototype.close = function () {
};
```

When the client requests control of the SharedText component, it calls the server-side *edit( )* method on the client object. In turn, the client's *edit( )* method calls the component's *edit( )* method and passes the user's userName to it. If no one else is actively using the component, the `messages` shared object's `currentUser` property will be an empty string and the method will set it to the `userName` of the user making the request. If the user cancels editing the text area, *edit( )* is called again and the `currentUser` property is set back to an empty string. If another user attempts to get access to the component while it is in use, the function will simply return without doing anything.

The shared object being used here is a persistent one. If the program crashes or the instance unloads without a user releasing control, the `currentUser` property may have a username in it from a previous session. So to start the session off correctly, the `currentUser` property is always set to an empty string. If the session is the first ever, the `length` property is set to contain a 0:

```
this.so.setProperty("currentUser", "");
if (typeof this.so.getProperty("length") != "number") {
  this.so.setProperty("length", 0);
}
```

Control of the shared text area is determined using the string in the `currentUser` property of the `messages` shared object. Now, all that is necessary to make the control of the component work properly is to have the client-side SharedText component send edit requests and respond correctly to changes in the shared object. Example 13-23 shows the client-side *onSync( )* method from *SharedText.as* that responds to shared object changes.

Example 13-23. The client-side SharedText.onSync( ) method

```
function onSync (ev) {
  if (ev.list.length == 0 && messages.data.length > 0) {
    replaceSharedText( );
    updateButtons( );
    return;
  }
  var info;
  for (var i in ev.list) {
    info = ev.list[i];
    if (info.name == "length") {
      replaceSharedText( );
    } else if (info.name == "currentUser") {
      updateButtons( );
    } else if (info.name == "selectCount") {
      showSelection( );
    }
  }
}
```

For brevity, the initialization code for the client-side component that connects to the `messages` shared object is not shown. The complete code is available on the book's web site. The `messages` shared object is persistent and therefore requires some special handling for the case in which a movie connects, disconnects, and then reconnects to the shared object. If the shared object has not changed between the time the movie disconnects and reconnects, the list passed to *onSync( )* will be empty because the local copy of the shared object will already contain the same data that is in the remote shared object. To handle the situation, the *onSync( )* method checks whether the list is empty but there is already data in the shared object. If so, the component is updated to correctly reflect the state of the shared object. Otherwise, the *onSync( )* method calls *replaceSharedText( )* if the number of entries in the shared object has changed, calls *updateButtons( )* if the currentUser has changed, and calls *showSelection( )* if someone has selected text in the text area. The three methods called by *onSync( )* are listed in Example 13-24, Example 13-25, and Example 13-26.

The *updateButtons( )* method listed in Example 13-24 is perhaps the simplest. It enables or disables each button, selects (toggles on) or deselects (toggles off) each button, and changes the label of the Edit button to Edit or Cancel as needed by calling one of three methods. For example, *enableButtons( )* enables each button and highlights them all by setting selected to true. (The *disableButtons( )* and *defaultButtons( )* methods are not shown.) The *updateButtons( )* method checks the currentUser property of the shared object against its own __user property that contains the username used when the person logged in. The method makes sure only the person who has control of the shared text area can edit it.

Example 13-24. The enableButtons( ) and updateButtons( ) methods

```
function enableButtons ( ) {
  editButton.enabled = true;
  editButton.selected = true;
  editButton.label = "Cancel";
  sendButton.enabled = true;
  sendButton.selected = true;
  selectButton.enabled = true;
  selectButton.selected = true;
  deleteButton.enabled = true;
  deleteButton.selected = true;
  sharedTextArea.editable = true;
}

/* Whenever the currentUser property in the shared object
 * changes, the buttons must be updated to correctly reflect
 * this user's permission to edit the TextArea.
 */
function updateButtons( ) {
  var currentUser = messages.data.currentUser;
  if (currentUser == "" && __user) {
    defaultButtons( );
  } else if (currentUser == __user.userName && __user) {
    enableButtons( );
  } else {
    disableButtons( );
  }
}
```

Whenever new text is added to the shared object, its length property is incremented and the *replaceSharedText( )* method, shown in Example 13-25, is called. The method displays the text in the most recently added shared object slot and updates the versionStepper NumericStepper subcomponent to show the current version and to reset the stepper's limits.

Example 13-25. The replaceSharedText( ) method

```
function replaceSharedText (ev) {
  var len = messages.data.length;
  if (len == 0) {
    sharedTextArea.text = "";
    versionStepper.minimum = 0;
    versionStepper.maximum = 0;
    versionStepper.value = 0;
    return;
  }
  sharedTextArea.text = messages.data[len];
  versionStepper.minimum = 1;
  versionStepper.maximum = len;
  versionStepper.value = len;
}
```

The *showSelection( )* method, shown in Example 13-26, displays the version of text the user has selected and highlights a selected region using the <b></b> HTML tag.

Example 13-26. The showSelection( ) method

```
function showSelection ( ) {
  versionStepper.value = messages.data.selectVersion;
  sharedTextArea.html = true;
  // Wrap it in a bold tag.
  var start = messages.data.startIndex;
  var end   = messages.data.endIndex;
  var slot = messages.data.selectVersion;
  var msg = messages.data[slot].substring(0, start) + "<b>";
  msg += messages.data[slot].substring(start, end) + "</b>";
  msg += messages.data[slot].substring(end)
  sharedTextArea.text = msg;
  sharedTextArea.vPosition = messages.data.selectScroll;
  sharedTextArea.redraw( );
  sharedTextArea.html = false;
}
```

Unlike the TextChat component, the SharedText component updates the shared object directly.

Allowing a client to directly update a shared object is less secure than having the client request a change via a remote method call and then having your own server-side code accept or reject the request. However, updating shared objects directly can be more efficient because server-side code does not have to run and therefore tie up the single ActionScript thread for the instance on the server.

The SharedText component described here was originally written for an in-house project that was used by a small number of authenticated users. Improving the security of the component is discussed in Chapter 18.

The *shareText( )* method, shown in Example 13-27, is called when the user clicks the Send button in order to update the shared text area. It creates a new slot in the shared object based on the number of numbered text slots, copies text in the TextArea subcomponent into it, and increases the count (length) of the number of text slots.

Example 13-27. The shareText( ) method adds new text to the messages shared object

```
function shareText (ev) {
  var len = messages.data.length;
  if (messages.data[len] == sharedTextArea.text) {
    return;
  }
  len++;
  messages.setFPS(0);
  messages.data.length = len;
  messages.data[len] = sharedTextArea.text;
  messages.setFPS(12);
  disableButtons( );
}
```

Similarly, the *selectText( )* method, shown in Example 13-28, is called when the Select button is clicked; it selects the text version to display, and any text within it to bold, by directly setting properties of the messages shared object.

Example 13-28. The selectText( ) method

```
function selectText (ev) {
  messages.setFPS(0);
  messages.data.startIndex = startIndex;
  messages.data.endIndex = endIndex;
  messages.data.selectVersion = versionStepper.value;
  messages.data.selectScroll = sharedTextArea.vPosition;
  if (!messages.data.selectCount) messages.data.selectCount = 1;
  else messages.data.selectCount++;
  messages.setFPS(12);
  disableButtons( );
}
```

Finally, the *deleteVersion( )* method, shown in Example 13-29, is called when the Delete Version button is clicked and the user has control of the shared text area. It deletes the text in the version slot the user is currently viewing. Then it adjusts the slot numbers and length property so the version numbers run continuously from beginning to end without interruption.

Example 13-29. The deleteVersion( ) method

```
function deleteVersion (ev) {
  messages.setFPS(0);
  var len = messages.data.length;
  if (len < 1) {
    return;
  }
  for (var i = versionStepper.value; i < len; i++) {
    messages.data[i] = messages.data[i+1];
  }
  delete messages[len];
  messages.data.length = len-1;
  messages.setFPS(12);
  disableButtons( );
}
```

The SharedText component shown here is quite simple. Many more features, such as text formatting and text archiving, could be added. However, this simple component has proven one of the most successful for making online meetings useful—especially the versioning feature. The shared area can be used to keep track of evolving task lists; to share, explain, and change source code; and to edit short memos or notices in advance of publication.

Now that we have the TextChat and SharedText components under our belts, let's look at a more complex video conferencing component.

Video Conference and Video Window

In a video conference application, each user's client publishes a stream that may carry video, audio, and other data. Each client must somehow be made aware of each stream being published by other clients so that they can all be played. The VideoConference component presented here uses a simple stream naming convention. Each stream is created within the component namespace and is named using each user's unique username. For example:

```
pfcs/VideoConference/main/users/blesser/presence
```

where blesser is a username and users is a subdirectory under the component's name, in this case, main. The name of the stream is presence. It also creates a shared object that contains information about the current state of the stream. The shared object has the same name as the stream.

The VideoConference component, shown in Figure 13-11, displays a separate pop-up window that shows video and plays audio for each incoming stream and contains a drop-down menu that shows information about the stream based on the information in the shared object. The VideoConference component also creates a publishing window that allows the user to control his outgoing video and audio and updates the shared object associated with the stream.

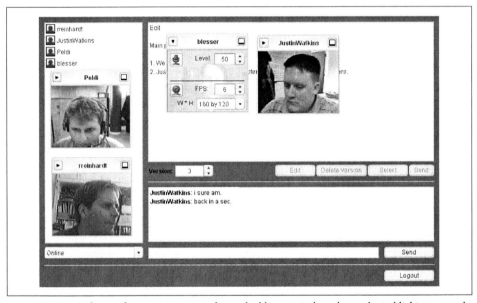

Figure 13-11. Video conference pop-up windows; the blesser window shows the publishing controls in a drop-down list

To create a pop-up window that plays all remote users' streams, the component must know the username of each connected user. The component could create a shared object on the server containing usernames in the same way the PeopleList and PeopleGrid components do. However, since those components already manage a shared object with information about each user, the VideoConference component simply uses the PeopleList or PeopleGrid shared object. When an instance of a VideoConference component exists in a Flash movie, it can be initialized this way:

```
videoConference.userName = application.user.userName;
videoConference.userList = peopleList.peopleList;
videoConference.nc = application.nc;
```

Once the `userName`, `userList`, and `nc` properties are set, the component's *enterConference( )* method from the *VideoConference.as* file, shown in Example 13-30, is called. Among other things, it saves a reference to the people shared object named `__userList` and sets itself up as a listener on it. If the shared object has already connected, *enterConference( )* make sure the *VideoConference.onSync( )* method is called once with a list of information objects—one for each user. See "Listenable Shared Objects" earlier in this chapter for more information on the isConnected property and *onSync( )* message broadcasting.

Example 13-30. The VideoConference component's enterConference( ) method

```
function enterConference (nc, userName, userList) {
  if (nc) __nc = nc;
  if (userName) __userName = userName;
  if (userList) __userList = userList;
  __userList.addEventListener("onSync", this);
  if (__userList.isConnected) {
    var list = [];
    for (var p in __userList.data) {
      list.push({code:"change", name: p});
    }
    onSync({target:__userList, list:list});
  }
}
```

The *VideoConference.onSync( )* method is called by the people shared object. When a client connects to the application instance, the application creates a playback window and provides the username to indicate which user's stream it should play. When a client disconnects, the window is deleted. Example 13-31 shows the *VideoConference.onSync( )* method from the *VideoConference.as* file.

Example 13-31. The onSync( ) method is responsible for creating and deleting video playing and video publishing windows

```
function onSync (ev) {
  var list = ev.list;
  for (var i in list) {
    var name = list[i].name;
    var code = list[i].code;
    // If the code is "delete", remove the window, if it exists.
    if (code == "delete" && windows[name]) {
      windows[name].deletePopUp( );
      delete windows[name];
      vidWinCount--;
    }
    // If the code is "change", add the window if it does not exist already.
    else if (code == "change" && !windows[name]) {
      var x = (vidWinCount % xMaxClips) * vidWidth + 20;
      var y = Math.floor((vidWinCount & xyMaxClips) / xMaxClips) * vidHeight + 20;
      vidWinCount++;
      // If the name is the same as the one the user logged in with,
      // display a VideoWindow and ask it to publish a stream.
      if (name == __userName) {
        displayVideoPublisher(name, x, y);
      }
      // Otherwise display a VideoWindow and have it play a stream.
      else{
        displayVideoPlayer(name, x, y);
```

Example 13-31. The onSync( ) method is responsible for creating and deleting video playing and video publishing windows (continued)

```
      }
    }
  }
}

function displayVideoPublisher(name, x, y) {
  // Create a new VideoWindow pop up.
  var pubWindow = mx.managers.PopUpManager.createPopUp(this,
                                      VideoWindow, false, {_x:x, _y:y});
  // Have it publish a stream.
  pubWindow.publish(__nc, path + "users/" + name + "/presence", name);
  // Remember we opened the window by userName.
  windows[name] = pubWindow;
}

function displayVideoPlayer(name, x, y) {
  var playWindow = mx.managers.PopUpManager.createPopUp(this,
                                      VideoWindow, false, {_x:x, _y:y});
  playWindow.play(__nc, path + "users/" + name + "/presence", name);
  windows[name] = playWindow;
}
```

To avoid the possibility of creating duplicate windows for each user, the VideoConference component maintains an object named windows that keeps a reference to each video window indexed by username. Before deleting a window, the windows object is checked to make sure one exists under the userName that has just been removed from the shared object. Before adding a window, the windows object is checked to make sure a video window does not already exist with the same userName.

Aside from creating, deleting, and determining the initial position of video windows, the VideoConference component does not do much work. Most of the work of setting up camera and microphone objects, publishing and playing streams, and muting video and audio is done by the VideoWindow component.

The VideoWindow component is the most complex component presented in this chapter because it is composed of several movie clips and uses a variety of objects. The *VideoWindow* class is a subclass of the *Window* class provided with Macromedia's v2 components. It is responsible for adding a menu and minimize/maximize button to a pop-up window and handling menu, minimize/maximize, play, publish, and dragging events. When a VideoWindow is created, it adds two SimpleButton components to its titlebar and loads the VideoWindow_Contents movie clip as the window's content. The *init( )* method of the *VideoWindow* class is listed in Example 13-32.

Example 13-32. The init( ) method of the VideoWindow component loads the VideoWindow_ Contents clip and listens for the complete event to discover when it is loaded

```
function init(Void):Void {
  super.init( );
  // Center the title.
  var styleObj = _global.styles.newStyle=new mx.styles.CSSStyleDeclaration( );
  styleObj.fontFamily = "_sans";
  styleObj.fontSize = 12;
  styleObj.fontWeight = "bold";
  styleObj.textAlign = "center";
  titleStyleDeclaration = styleObj;
  // Load the VideoWindow_Contents symbol designed for this window subclass.
  addEventListener("complete", this);
  contentPath = "VideoWindow_Contents";
}

function complete (ev) {
  contentLoaded = true;
  if (pendingStateInit) {
    pendingStateInit = false;
    vControlsState.enterState( );
  }
}
```

The VideoWindow_Content clip contains a stack of three other objects: at the top, a menuPanel clip that contains Buttons and other components used to control stream playback or publishing; a clip that contains an embedded Video object to play video; and on the bottom, an event mask clip that captures mouse events and stops them from affecting components underneath the window. Figure 13-12 shows a VideoWindow with buttons and video playing, as well as the same window with the menuPanel clip visible. The center VideoWindow shows what the menuPanel clip looks like when it contains the components needed to control publishing a stream. The Video Mute button has been clicked to stop publishing video. The VideoWindow on the right of Figure 13-12 shows the playback components in the menuPanel clip. The video clip with the line through it indicates no new video frames are being received.

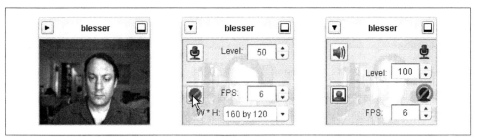

Figure 13-12. Three views of a ViewWindow—with the menu closed (left), with the publishing menu (center), and with the playing menu (right)

When its *play( )* method is called, a VideoWindow delegates all the work to an object it creates to play a stream. When *publish( )* is called, a different object that knows how to publish a stream is called, and the work is delegated to it. Separate objects are used because a window that is publishing a stream needs to create a camera and microphone object, create a specialized menu to control the video and audio being published, and manage menu and shared object events. On the other hand, a playback window must create and manage a different menu and handle different events.

A common way to create an object that can exhibit different behaviors, such as playing or publishing a stream, while keeping code as simple as possible, is to use separate *state objects*. When an object has to behave one way, a state object is used to implement behaviors. When the object has to behave differently, a different state object is used in its place. Each state object implements a different set of behaviors. An excellent and more detailed description of the state pattern is available in the book *Design Patterns* (Addison Wesley).

The VideoWindow component does something similar. It keeps an object in a variable named vControlsState and passes most events and requests to it. When it needs to publish a stream, it creates a *PublishVideoControlsState* object and stores it in vControlsState. When it needs to play a stream, it creates a *PlayVideoControlsState* object and stores it in vControlsState.

When a VideoWindow is first created, it creates a new *VideoControlsState* object this way:

```
vControlsState = new VideoControlsState(this);
```

The *VideoControlsState* class doesn't do much. However, it has two important subclasses that handle playing and publishing. Example 13-33 shows the *VideoWindow.publish( )* method, which is called to have a VideoWindow publish a stream.

Example 13-33. The publish( ) method of the VideoWindow class replaces the current state with an instance of PublishVideoControlsState

```
function publish (nc, streamName, displayName) {
  if (nc) __nc = nc;
  if (streamName) __streamName = streamName;
  if (displayName) title = displayName;
  vControlsState.exitState( );
  vControlsState = new PublishVideoControlsState(this);
  if (contentLoaded) {
    vControlsState.enterState( );
  }
  else {
    pendingStateInit = true;
  }
}
```

Whatever else the window was doing, it stops doing it by calling:

```
vControlsState.exitState( );
```

After the vControlsState object exits, its current state can be replaced with another object:

```
vControlsState = new PublishVideoControlsState(this);
```

The new *PublishControlsState* object is passed a reference (this) to the VideoWindow, so it can find and manipulate any part of the window or its contents. Assuming that the contents of the pop-up window have completed loading, the new state can be started:

```
vControlsState.enterState( );
```

Otherwise, the call to *enterState( )* must be delayed until all the VideoWindow assets are loaded. (See the *complete( )* method in Example 13-32.)

A *PublishVideoControlsState* object does all the real work of publishing a stream, creating a shared object with information about the stream, and providing a control menu in a pop-up window. Its *enterState( )* method will set up the drop-down menu panel with the controls needed to allow the user to control what is published within the stream and then actually start publishing the stream.

If a VideoWindow must play a stream, the *play( )* method, shown in Example 13-34, changes the vControlsState object as well.

Example 13-34. The play( ) method of the VideoWindow class replaces the current state with an instance of PlayVideoControlsState

```
function play(nc, streamName, displayName) {
  if (nc) __nc = nc;
  if (streamName) __streamName = streamName;
  if (displayName) title = displayName;
  vControlsState.exitState( );
  vControlsState = new PlayVideoControlsState(this);
  if (contentLoaded) {
    vControlsState.enterState( );
  }
  else {
    pendingStateInit = true;
  }
}
```

As in the early publishing example, the following two statements cause the window to exit a previous state and prepare to enter the play video state:

```
vControlsState.exitState( );
vControlsState = new PlayVideoControlsState(this);
```

When the contents of the pop-up window are completely loaded, the new state is initialized:

```
vControlsState.enterState( );
```

The *PlayVideoControlsState* and *PublishVideoControlsState* objects initialize themselves when their *enterState( )* methods are called and clean up their resources when *exitState( )* is called. When either object's *enterState( )* method is called, the state attaches the menu controls it needs to initialize the menuPanel movie clip and sets itself up as a listener of their events. It gets the *NetConnection* object from the VideoWindow and uses it to create a *SharedObject* and *NetStream* object before publishing or playing a stream. The shared object is used to provide information about the stream to all the VideoWindows that will play the stream in other clients. It contains information on the height, width, and frames per second of the video and whether the stream is sending audio or video.

Publishing

A partial listing of the *enterState( )* method of the *PublishVideoControlsState* class is provided in Example 13-35. The somewhat lengthy code that creates the components within the menuPanel clip has been removed to keep the listing at a reasonable length.

Example 13-35. An abbreviated listing of the PublishVideoControlsState.enterState( ) method

```
function enterState () {
  super.enterState();
  // Set up user interface elements.
  menuPanel.visible = false;
  // Place components inside the menuPanel and listen for events.
  var depth = 1000;

  // NOTE: CODE REMOVED HERE THAT PLACES COMPONENTS IN THE MENU PANEL.

  // Set up capture sources, the stream, and shared object.
  nc = context.__nc;
  streamName = context.__streamName;
  video = context.content.videoContainer.video;
  var instance = this;

  // Set up the camera.
  cam = Camera.get();
  // If there is no camera, create a fake one that is muted.
  if (!cam) cam = Camera({muted: true});
  cam.onStatus = function (info) {
    instance.setCameraStatus();
  };
  cam.setMode(160, 120, 6);
  menuPanel.fpsStepper.value = 6;
  menuPanel.rComboBox.selectedIndex = 2;
  setCameraStatus();

  // Set up the microphone.
  mic = Microphone.get();
```

*Example 13-35. An abbreviated listing of the PublishVideoControlsState.enterState( )
method (continued)*

```
if (!mic) mic = Microphone({muted: true});
mic.onStatus = function (info) {
  instance.setMicrophoneStatus( );
};
menuPanel.gStepper.value = mic.gain;
setMicrophoneStatus( );

// Set up the stream and attach sources.
if (ns) ns.close( );
ns = new NetStream(nc);
ns.publish(streamName);
ns.attachVideo(cam);
ns.attachAudio(mic);
video.attachVideo(cam);

// Set up the shared object and add data to it after the first sync.
so = SharedObjectFactory.getRemote(streamName, nc.uri);
so.addEventListener("onFirstSync", this); // set initial control values.
so.connect(nc);
}
```

Once the stream is published and the shared object connected, events arrive at the
PublishVideoControlsState object. For example, if the user clicks the Microphone or
Camera button, a click event will be handled by the *click( )* method and either
setMicrophoneStatus( ) or *setCameraStatus( )* will be called to attach or remove audio
or video from the stream. A property of the cam or mic object is used to remember the
state it was left in. The shared object will be updated so that all the clients playing
the stream will be informed of the change in the stream's contents. Example 13-36
shows the *click( )* and *setCameraStatus( )* methods of the *PublishVideoControlsState*
class from the *PublishVideoControlsState.as* file.

*Example 13-36. The PublishVideoControlsState click( ) and setCameraStatus( )
methods*

```
function click (ev) {
  var b = ev.target;
  switch(b) {
    case menuPanel.mButton:
      setMicrophoneStatus( );
      break;
    case menuPanel.vButton:
      setCameraStatus( );
      break;
  }
}

function setCameraStatus ( ) {
  if (cam.muted) {
    menuPanel.vButton.enabled = false;
```

```
    menuPanel.vButton.selected = false;
    so.data.video = "Off";
    cam.wasMuted = true;
  }
  else {
    if (cam.wasMuted) {
      cam.wasMuted = false;
      menuPanel.vButton.selected = true;;
    }
    menuPanel.vButton.enabled = true;
    so.data.video = menuPanel.vButton.selected ? "On" : "Off";
    ns.attachVideo(menuPanel.vButton.selected ? cam : null);
  }
}
```

Now that we've looked at the publishing feature, let's continue with playing the video.

Playing

A partial listing of the *enterState( )* method of the *PlayVideoControlsState* class from the *PlayVideoControlsState.as* file is provided in Example 13-37. The somewhat lengthy code that creates the components within the menuPanel clip has been removed to keep the listing a reasonable length. After adding the controls to menuPanel, *enterState( )* creates a new *NetStream* object and begins to play the stream. It also sets itself up as a listener on the shared object named after the stream so that it can respond to changes.

Example 13-37. An abbreviated listing of the PlayVideoControlsState.enterState( ) method

```
// enterState() sets up this state object.
function enterState ( ) {
  super.enterState( );
  video = context.content.videoContainer.video;
  //  Set up user interface elements.
  menuPanel.visible = false;
  // Place components inside the menuPanel and listen for events.
  var depth = 1000;

  // NOTE: CODE REMOVED HERE THAT PLACES COMPONENTS IN THE MENU PANEL.

  // Set up the stream and shared object.
  nc = context.__nc;
  streamName = context.__streamName;
  if (ns) ns.close( );
  ns = new NetStream(nc);
  ns.play(streamName);
  video.attachVideo(ns);
```

*Example 13-37. An abbreviated listing of the PlayVideoControlsState.enterState( )
method (continued)*

```
  menuPanel.attachAudio(ns);
  soundControl = new Sound(context.content.menuPanel);
  menuPanel.lStepper.value = soundControl.getVolume( );
  so = SharedObjectFactory.getRemote(streamName, nc.uri);
  so.addEventListener("onFirstSync", this); // Set initial control values.
  so.addEventListener("onSync", this);      // Reset state of sound and video.
  so.connect(nc);
}
```

The *onSync( )* method, also from *PlayVideoControlsState.as*, is shown in
Example 13-38. If the audio or video slot of the shared object has changed, the new
value is used to update the appropriate icon in menuPanel. For example, if the video
property contains the string "On", the web cam icon will appear in its normal state.
If the value is "Off", the web cam will appear with a line through it as seen in
Figure 13-12.

Example 13-38. The onSync( ) method of the PlayVideoControlsState class

```
function onSync (ev) {
  var list = ev.list;
  for (var p in list) {
    var info = list[p];
    if (info.code == "clear") continue;
    switch (info.name) {
      case "audio":
        menuPanel.dmStatus.gotoAndPlay(so.data.audio); // "On" or "Off"
        break;
      case "video":
        menuPanel.wcStatus.gotoAndPlay(so.data.video); // "On" or "Off"
        break;
      case "fps":
        menuPanel.fpsStepper.maximum = so.data.fps;
        if (menuPanel.fpsStepper.maximum < menuPanel.fpsStepper.value) {
          menuPanel.fpsStepper.value = menuPanel.fpsStepper.maximum;
        }
        break;
      case "res":
        var w = so.data.res[0];
        var h = so.data.res[1];
        changeResolution(w, h);
        break;
      default:
        trace("Error: Unhandled shared object property. " + streamName);
        for (var prop in info) {
          trace("   >> " + prop + ": " + info[prop]);
        }
    }
  }
}
```

Similarly, when the publisher changes the frame rate of its video, the new value is displayed in menuPanel. When the res slot is changed, the *changeResolution( )* method is called and both the embedded Video object and the entire VideoWindow component are resized to accommodate the new size of the video.

In summary, a people shared object is responsible for letting the VideoConference component know when a user has joined or left the application instance. The user's username is used as a unique identifier to publish her stream from her own client and to play it on all the other clients. A shared object with the same name as the stream is created—one for each user—to provide additional information about the current state of the stream and the data it carries. The actual work of publishing or playing a stream and updating or responding to changes in a shared object is done by a state object in each VideoWindow.

Let's look at one more example, an advanced cousin of the PeopleList component called PeopleGrid.

PeopleGrid

Some application designs require more than can be provided by the PeopleList component presented earlier. You may need to aggregate different information about people into one place, using a number of icons or components to represent the data. For example, you may need icons or components to show the connection status, audio/video capabilities, whether each user has questions about a presentation, or whether each user feels the presentation is moving too quickly or too slowly. When so much information must be aggregated into one place, a DataGrid can be used in place of a List component to present it. The DataGrid component provides a mechanism for creating custom columns that can contain regular text or specialized cell renderers that can display graphics or other components in each cell of the column. Figure 13-13 shows a PeopleGrid component in use; the first column contains status icons and the second column shows the number of questions each user has. The PeopleGrid works much the same way the PeopleList component does but contains a DataGrid instead of a List component.

Figure 13-13. The PeopleGrid component with Status and Questions columns

The PeopleList component discussed earlier had the logic to display an icon from the Status component hardwired into it. However, while it is relatively easy to adapt the PeopleList code to show different icons or to work with another component, it is unrealistic to hardwire the display logic into a DataGrid for any number of components that may need to display information within the grid. Instead, the PeopleGrid provides an *addColumn( )* method for other components to define a column within its DataGrid. For example, Status and Questions components may each export a column to the PeopleGrid. The Questions component may also want to know when one of its icons has been clicked on. It can set itself up as a listener of the PeopleGrid component in order to receive custom events sent by its own cell renderer via the grid.

Example 13-39 shows one way a PeopleGrid component placed on the Stage may be initialized and connected with other components. This code would go in the timeline of your Flash client.

Example 13-39. Timeline code to initialize and connect the PeopleGrid component with other components

```
peopleGrid.hideOfflineUsers = true;
peopleGrid.nc = application.nc;
peopleGrid.name = "main";
peopleGrid.addEventListener("change", application);
peopleGrid.addColumn(status.column);
peopleGrid.addColumn(questions.column);
peopleGrid.addEventListener("showQuestions", questions);
```

In the following statement, the getter method of the status component generates an object that contains all the information the peopleGrid needs to display and update a column within its DataGrid:

```
peopleGrid.addColumn(status.column);
```

Example 13-40 shows the Status component's *get column( )* method from the *Status.as* file in the *PeopleGrid.zip* archive.

Example 13-40. The Status component's get column( ) method

```
public function get column () {
  if (!__status_so && __nc) {
    __status_so = SharedObjectFactory.getRemote(path + "status",__nc.uri);
    __status_so.connect(__nc);
  }
  var col = {
    name: path,
    so: __status_so,
    propertyName: "status",
    dgColumn: new DataGridColumn("status"),
    target: this
  }
  col.dgColumn.cellRenderer = "StatusCellRenderer",
  col.dgColumn.headerRenderer = "StatusHeaderRenderer";
```

Example 13-40. The Status component's get column( ) method (continued)

```
  col.dgColumn.width = 24;
  col.getPropertyValue = function (slot) {
    return slot;
  };
  return col;
}
```

The *get column( )* method creates an object that contains a *DataGridColumn* object that uses the *StatusCellRenderer* class (see Example 13-43) to show custom icons in the column. It also contains a reference to the Status component's shared object so that it can get status data for the *StatusCellRenderer* instance to display. The People-Grid will use the propertyName property and *getPropertyValue( )* method to get the data it needs from an entry in the status shared object and add it to each item in its DataGrid. In this case, the status shared object contains a text value, so it is all that is returned. In other words, a property named status containing a text string like "Online" or "Busy" will be added to each DataGrid item.

Example 13-41 shows the PeopleGrid component's *addColumn( )* method from the *PeopleGrid.as* file in the *PeopleGrid.zip* archive.

Example 13 41. The PeopleGrid component's addColumn( ) method

```
public function addColumn(col) {
  // Add this column to a hash (associative array) by component name.
  columnObjects[col.name] = col;
  grid.addColumnAt(0, col.dgColumn);
  col.so.addEventListener("onSync", this);
  // Forces the Questions column label to show up.
  grid.redraw(true);
}
```

The PeopleGrid contains an object named columnObjects that stores each column it receives from other components for later use and then adds a column onto its Data-Grid. The columnObjects object is used each time an *onSync( )* method is received. Example 13-42 shows the *onSync( )* method of the PeopleGrid and how the columnObjects object is used to correctly update the item in the DataGrid.

Example 13-42. The PeopleGrid component's onSync( ) method handles events from the people shared object and other components' shared objects

```
function onSync (ev) {
  // Get the list's dataProvider and truncate it.
  var dp = grid.dataProvider;
  dp.length = 0;

  // Fill the dataProvider using the Array.push( ) method.
  for (var userName in __people_so.data) {
    // Copy a slot in the people shared object.
    var item = clone(__people_so.data[userName]);
```

```
    // Add the userName as a property so it will appear in the grid.
    item.userName = userName;
    // Check all the columnObjects and add any properties from the
    // shared objects of other components that have columns in the grid.
    for (var col in columnObjects) {
      var c = columnObjects[col];
      // Get the user's slot in the other component's shared object.
      var slot   = c.so.data[userName];
      // If there is one, get the data from the slot and put it
      // in the cloned object.
      if (slot) {
        item[c.propertyName] = c.getPropertyValue(slot);
      }
    }
    // Skip any users with status "Offline".
    if (_hideOfflineUsers && item.status == "Offline") continue;
    dp.push(item);
  }
  dp.dispatchEvent({target:dp, type:"modelChanged", eventName: "updateAll"});
}
```

The *onSync( )* method makes use of a number of objects so we'll describe it step-by-step. The grid property of the component holds a reference to a DataGrid. In order to reduce the time the grid needs to insert, update, and delete items, the DataGrid methods such as *addItem( )* are not used. Instead, grid.dataProvider is retrieved and manipulated directly. The dataProvider object is based on an *Array* object, so we can manipulate it as an array. First, we get the dataProvider from the grid:

```
    var dp = grid.dataProvider;
```

Then we simply dispose of all the items in the dataProvider by resetting the length property of the array to 0:

```
    dp.length = 0;
```

Now, we create a copy of each entry in the people shared object using the *clone( )* method of the PeopleGrid. The copy is necessary because other properties from other shared objects may have to be added to it. If those properties were added to an object in the people shared object, the slot would be updated. Each copy will become an item in the grid:

```
    for (var userName in _people_so.data) {
      // Copy a slot in the people shared object.
      var item = clone(_people_so.data[p]);
      // Add the userName as a property so it will appear in the grid.
      item.userName = userName;

      //... code omitted here that adds other properties to item.
    }
```

Notice that we have to add in a property to the object so the grid will display the username from each entry in the grid's userName column:

```
item.userName = userName;
```

Now that we have an item with all the information from the people shared object in it, we have to add information from any component's shared objects that have columns in the PeopleGrid. We have to go through each column object from each component and use it to copy information from the other component's shared object into the item:

```
for (var col in columnObjects) {
  var c = columnObjects[col];
  // Get the user's slot in the other component's shared object.
  var slot = c.so.data[userName];
  // If there is one, get the data from the slot and put it
  // in the cloned object.
  if (slot) {
    obj[c.propertyName] = c.getPropertyValue(slot);
  }
}
```

For each column, we get the column object:

```
var c = columnObjects[col];
```

Now, we use the username in userName to get the slot for the user in the other component's shared object:

```
var slot = c.so.data[userName];
```

Finally, we can create a new property in the object this way:

```
obj[c.propertyName] = c.getPropertyValue(slot);
```

In the example of the Status component, the propertyName will be status and *getPropertyValue( )* will return a string like "Online". So, if the item originally contained userName, firstName, and lastName properties, each will now also have a status property. As we loop through each component's column object, other properties will be added to the item. If there is a Questions column, for example, a questions property may be added containing the number of questions a user has.

When each item, with all its new properties, is complete, it is added to the data provider for the grid:

```
dp.push(item);
```

Finally, when all the items have been added to the data provider, its *dispatchEvent( )* method is called to tell the grid to display the new data:

```
dp.dispatchEvent({target:dp, type:"modelChanged", eventName: "updateAll"});
```

The *updateAll* event name is required to make the grid redraw itself completely.

The *onSync( )* method, together with the column objects in the `columnObjects` hash, do the key work of aggregating data from the shared objects owned by other components into items that appear in the grid.

The appearance of each component's column in the grid can be customized by having each component provide a cell renderer. A cell renderer is a component that implements the *CellRenderer* API. The code for the *StatusCellRenderer* class is reproduced in Example 13-43. It belongs in a file named *StatusCellRender.as*.

Example 13-43. The StatusCellRenderer code

```
import mx.core.UIComponent

class StatusCellRenderer extends UIComponent {
  var boundingBox_mc:MovieClip;

  function StatusCellRenderer () {
  }

  function setValue(suggested, item, selected) {
   if (!item || !item.status) {
      gotoAndStop("Blank");
      return;
    }
    gotoAndStop(item.status);
  }

  function init () {
    super.init();
    boundingBox_mc._visible = false;
    boundingBox_mc._width = boundingBox_mc._height=0;
  }

  function getPreferredHeight () {
    return 18;
  }

  function getPreferredWidth () {
    return 18;
  }
}
```

Whenever the grid needs to display a cell or update its visual appearance, the renderer's *setValue( )* method is called. In Example 13-43, it sends its playhead to a blank frame if there is no item or item property named status. The `Blank` frame will display in any empty cells or empty rows in the grid. When the item has a `status` property, the renderer sends the playhead to a frame of the same name. Figure 13-14 shows the timeline and Stage of the *StatusCellRenderer* movie clip symbol. You can see from the timeline that the blank frame actually contains a movie clip. It is the boundingBox_mc clip with its _alpha level set to 0. The transparent clip makes sure the grid lays out the cell correctly even when there is nothing to look at.

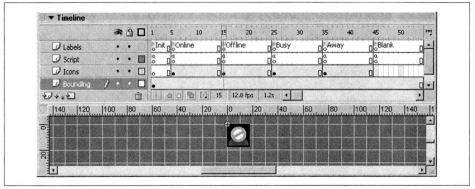

Figure 13-14. The StatusCellRenderer's timeline; the Blank frame includes a boundingBox_mc clip with _alpha set to 0

Sometimes a cell renderer needs to communicate with its component. For example, if you have a Questions component and the user clicks on the questions icon, you may want the Questions component to display a window with that user's questions in it. When a cell renderer is used inside a DataGrid, a property named listOwner is automatically created for it. The listOwner property can be used to have the DataGrid broadcast a message by calling the grid's *dispatchEvent( )* method. For example, if an *onRelease* event occurs, a custom event named *showQuestions* can be generated this way:

```
function onRelease () {
  listOwner.dispatchEvent(
    {type:"showQuestions", target:this, userName:userName, questions:questions}
  );
}
```

We've seen that the Status component is responsible for creating a column object, complete with cell renderer and *getProperty( )* method, that provides a view of the Status component within a column of the DataGrid. Some developers would prefer to implement the Status component so that it doesn't need to know anything about *DataGridColumn* objects. They would argue that unless every possible UI that displays Status would use *DataGridColumns*, the code for the *get column( )* method should be placed in the *PeopleGrid* or in some other class instead.

The problem with putting the code in the PeopleGrid component is that it cannot possibly know how to present every column. The PeopleGrid should allow other components or objects to set up columns with their own cell and header renderers. For example, if you build a new Questions component, to show which user has a question, after the PeopleGrid is complete, you will write a new renderer for it. The developer of the Question component can create the library symbols and so on to provide what the PeopleGrid needs to display Questions in a column. In a sense, the Questions component knows how to display a view of itself in the PeopleGrid. The idea isn't much different than the way the DataGrid expects an application to create cell renderers and column objects that it will use.

Adding the code to generate a column object within each component such as the Status component does increase its size. If it is not used with a PeopleGrid, the increase in code size is not warranted. A solution to this problem would be to move the column generation code out to a separate StatusColumn component.

The PeopleGrid component puts to good use the DataGrid component's ability to show custom content in columns using cell renderers and to broadcast messages using the *dispatchEvent( )* method. There is almost no end to the information other components can pack into a PeopleGrid using the methods described here. As a more complete example, the *PeopleGrid.zip* file on the book's web site includes a Questions component.

Summary

The components presented in this chapter all manage their own stream and shared object resources. For example, the PeopleList component's server-side code is responsible for creating and updating the people shared object. No other component updates it. The SharedText component's messages shared object is updated by the SharedText component's server-side object and is also directly updated by the client-side SharedText component's code. Updates may first occur on the server or in the client; in either case, the component manages its own resources. Separation of component resources is partly achieved by using a naming convention. All the component resource names and remote methods are grouped under a single name, pfcs, followed by the component's class name and then a unique name for the instance of the component. The naming convention was used for streams, shared objects, and remote method naming.

It is easy to look at components as small, self-contained applications. A component can maintain its own data, present it, and allow the user to update it. However, a component can also make its resources available to other components. The shared object of each component contains information about its current state and notifies any listeners of changes in that state through *onSync( )* calls. For example, the PeopleList can present a view of the Status component's data within its listbox. As long as the PeopleList does not update the status shared object, both components can easily be modified and improved separately.

When you design a component, consider designing it so that the current state of the component is kept in a shared object. The information in the shared object should not include large amounts of data that are better managed by streams or a database but should be enough to maintain the component's state. For example, the TextChat component used streams to store messages but kept track of the streams it was working with and other information about the current chat session in a shared object.

Returning to the questions we asked before designing the SimplePeopleList component, let's consider them in a little more detail:

- Are any database, stream, or shared object resources already available to the component? In applications composed almost entirely of communication components, this question can be rephrased as, "What other communication components will be available in the application and what resources will they provide?" Consider, for example, whether a PeopleList or component like it can provide information about users to a component you are planning to build. Ask yourself if a component like the VideoConference component really needs to create a duplicate shared object of users or whether it can use the one from a PeopleList or PeopleGrid? Of course, exceptional circumstances may sometimes require a separate shared object.

- What resources must the component create and manage by itself? This is always the most important question. Don't try to manage too much with one component. Just manage the resources the component needs to get its job done. The TextChat should manage only text messages. The VideoWindow should manage only the stream it is publishing and the shared object that describes the contents of the stream. If a component must do more, consider having it broadcast a message to another component that implements it. For example, suppose you want to allow application-level commands to be issued from within a TextChat. If you want a user to be able to log out by typing **/logout**, have the TextChat component broadcast the message and have another component handle the logout event.

- What user interface components should the component contain? The primary user interface elements should be the primary view of the resources the component manages. However, you may need to have multiple views of data that belongs to one component. We've already seen an example in which the status of each user appears in both the Status component and the PeopleGrid or PeopleList. When you must provide more than one view of a component's data, consider creating a separate object—such as the column object and its *CellRenderer* created by the Status component—to provide the view. In other cases, consider creating an entirely separate component with no data of its own solely to display another component's data in a different way. Resist the temptation to hardcode the presentation of one component into another component that also is responsible for managing its own data. For example, if the PeopleList and Status components are ever refactored or enhanced, having the PeopleList include code that displays the user status could cause conflicts.

- What information must the component make available to other components or objects? Start by considering what the component puts in a shared object. Is the essential information there so that another component can react to changes in a meaningful way? Also, don't forget that, on the client, the v2 components can make use of an event broadcasting mechanism. For example, clicking the Questions icon in a PeopleGrid can send an event back to the Questions component to retrieve and display a user's questions.

Creating components is the first and perhaps most exciting step in creating full-fledged FlashCom applications. They provide a way to partition an application into manageable pieces that can be built and tested separately. And you can use many of the features of Flash and FlashCom to allow your communication components to communicate with one another in familiar ways, such as broadcasting events to one another and providing access—though not control—to one another's shared objects. Building components frees you from worrying about the entire application and allows you to focus on building one part of it at a time. Once you get going with them, it is hard to stop. It is easy to create a long list of possible components and to keep adding features to existing components.

Conclusion

If you've read through the sample components described in this chapter, you should be ready to adapt them to your purposes and even build your own. You may also be wondering about some of the limitations of what you've seen. For example, many of the components have duplicate methods. Consider the *addObjectPath( )* method of every server-side object or the *set name( )* method of all the client-side components. A good way to reduce the redundancy in the samples here would have been to create a base class that contained common methods and properties. You may have also wondered about how scalable some of the components are. Some of the shared object *onSync( )* methods simply discard the contents of a data provider and rebuild it from scratch whenever a single shared object slot changes. For small shared objects, that works well, but for large ones, it may not.

Many other improvements to and uses of components are explored in later chapters. The next chapter describes how to modify and write your own communication components that work with Macromedia's communication component framework. Chapter 15 looks at components in the context of application design, including adding a recording/playback framework as well as improving component performance in response to shared object updates. Chapter 16 looks at multi-instance applications and how components can support multi-instance designs. Finally, Chapter 18 looks at integrating authentication and role-based authorization into components, which could be used with a VideoConference component to allow only the moderator to adjust the microphone gain of another participant.

CHAPTER 14

Understanding the Macromedia Component Framework

You learned how to use communication components in Chapter 2 and have seen a quick description of each API. This chapter goes deeper, and shows you how to modify an existing component and how to create a whole new one. The second part of this chapter will dive into the server-side framework code and discuss its core features and data structures in detail. At the end of the chapter, we will run through most of the framework code, with a line-by-line explanation of many framework files. If you find the technical details overwhelming or uninteresting, feel free to skim sections. Much of the highly technical information is for developers who want to fully understand the Macromedia framework so they can adapt or expand it, or develop their own custom frameworks.

The Component Framework

The Macromedia Communication Component Framework (a.k.a. the Macromedia component framework, or simply, the framework) is a set of server-side files and coding rules that allows developers to build communication components, just like the ones that ship with FlashCom Server, which were described in detail in Chapter 2.

Before looking at the framework's code, it helps to understand why it was built and its general goals. During the beta period for the first release of FlashCom Server, the server was in a good enough shape to be usable; people on the beta program and inside Macromedia could start building real-world applications on top of it.

It quickly became apparent that, whereas the client-side code could be organized to follow old Flash patterns such as components and libraries or just simple movie clips, no such patterns existed on the server side. So FlashCom programmers would not be able to easily create a well-structured, complex application on the server side.

At the same time, during the development of all of the sample applications, we realized that we were building the same people list and chat components in every application, and it would make a lot of sense to encapsulate such common functionality inside client/server components, a new concept at the time.

To solve both of these problems, a couple of the smartest Macromedia engineers (Srinivas Manapragada and Jon Gay, backed by Sarah Allen) sat down in front of a whiteboard and designed the Macromedia component framework and wrote the code in about two weeks.

The framework's goals were multiple and sometimes diametrically opposed to one another:

Modularity
Using the framework, developers should be able to build complex, well-structured applications that follow the common object-oriented programming (OOP) patterns. The server-side code should be easily split into independent libraries.

Extensibility
Creating components on top of the framework should be easy. To meet this goal, each component's APIs should follow the regular Server-Side ActionScript APIs, such as *onConnect( )*, *onDisconnect( )*, *onAppStart( )*, *onAppStop( )*, and so on. The reasoning was that if someone were already able to write a server-side *main.asc* file, he should be able to write a component using the same APIs. In retrospect, this was probably a bad decision, because it made the framework's code much more complex and inaccessible to people who wanted to dive into it, which in turn caused some developers to distrust what the framework was doing (it's hard to trust code that you can't understand). Creating component-specific events and calling them *onUserConnect*, *onUserDisconnect*, and so on would probably have been easy enough for component developers to understand while shaving a lot of complexity off the component framework.

Multiple instances
One should be able to have multiple instances of a component in the same application, such as an application with two or more chat components. To make sure that the various instances would not conflict with one another, a naming scheme was devised so that each *SharedObject* or *NetStream* used by a component would be properly namespaced.

Seamless integration
The framework should be unobtrusive; a developer should be able to code an application without using the framework, then add a communication component and load the framework on the server side (using *load("components.asc");*) without having her existing code break.

Authentication
A developer should be able to create an authenticating component. This goal was pulling in the opposite direction of seamless integration. If a component's *onConnect( )* method can decide whether to accept or reject a client, how can we avoid conflicts with the *onConnect( )* functionality in *main.asc*? The compromise

solution was to add *onConnectAccept( )* and *onConnectReject( )* methods to the `application` object, as discussed later.

Rich API

The framework should have enough APIs to make components easy to develop. Having a framework in place is one thing; having a framework that supports a rich set of commonly needed APIs enables developers to focus on their component's core functionality, rather than on how to fit within the framework.

Figure 14-1 shows the relationships among the core object model, the objects added by the component framework, and the communication components.

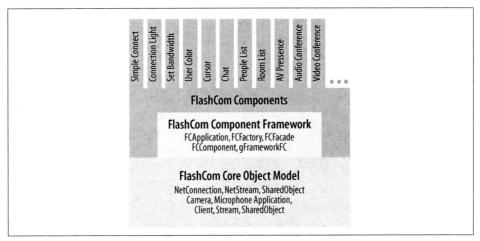

Figure 14-1. The FlashCom component architecture

It is important to note that even though developers build the components on top of the framework, they can continue to use the core objects such as *Streams*, *SharedObjects*, and others. The framework was designed to be as unobtrusive as possible; this allows you to include it in applications that don't have components. An application designer can add in as many or as few components as required, and they may be built-in, third-party, or other custom components.

The framework implements a lot of basic functionality on behalf of the components. We will discuss the framework's features in detail in the second half of this chapter. First, let's take a component apart to learn how it's built.

Under the Hood of the Chat Component

In this section, we look at the code of the Chat component that ships with Flash-Com to understand how it works, and we enhance it with some more functionality.

The Server-Side Code

The server-side code for the Chat component is pretty simple, but it's worth examining. Note that some code has been removed for brevity. Look at *chat.asc* in your *scriptlib/components* folder for the full code.

The code begins with a *try/catch* block, which ensures that the component is defined only once:

```
try {var dummy = FCChat;} catch (e) { // #ifndef FCChat
```

If the *FCChat* class is already defined, we do nothing (assign a reference to the class to a dummy variable); otherwise, we define it. This emulates the #ifndef (if not defined) directive of the C language, which Server-Side ActionScript (SSAS) does not support.

Next, we load *components/component.asc*, the base class for components:

```
load("components/component.asc");
```

This class contains a few methods that make it easier for component developers to focus on the functionality of the component itself, rather than on how to interface it with the rest of the framework.

Next comes the *FCChat* class constructor:

```
FCChat = function (name) {
  this.init(name);

  // Get a non-persistent shared object for sending broadcasts.
  this.message_so = SharedObject.get(this.prefix + "message", false);

  // If persist is true, then get the history back.
  this.history_so = SharedObject.get(this.prefix + "history", this.persist);
  this.history = this.history_so.getProperty("history");
  if (this.history == null)
    this.history = new Array;
};
```

The constructor is a great place to get resources that will be needed by the component during its lifetime. In this case, we get two shared objects whose names begin with the prefix property, which is a unique identifier defined for the component in the superclass when we call *this.init(name)*.

This ensures that multiple copies of the Chat component used in the same application won't conflict (we'll also use the prefix property to route calls from the server to the clients and vice versa).

The message shared object is non-persistent and is used to send new messages to all the clients as they arrive (as we will see in the *sendMessage( )* definition later):

```
this.message_so = SharedObject.get(this.prefix + "message", false);
```

The history shared object is persistent (assuming the persist property is true, its default) and is used to save the chat's history in an array:

```
this.history_so = SharedObject.get(this.prefix + "history", this.persist);
```

The following line defines this component as a subclass of *FCComponent*. (If you're not familiar with prototype-based inheritance, see *ActionScript for Flash MX: The Definitive Guide* (O'Reilly).):

```
FCChat.prototype = new FCComponent("FCChat", FCChat);
```

These lines define some default values for the component:

```
FCChat.prototype.histlen    = 250;        // Maximum history length
FCChat.prototype.persist    = true;       // Whether to save history
FCChat.prototype.allowClear = true;       // Allow clients to clear history
FCChat.prototype.history    = new Array;  // History
FCChat.prototype.message_so = null;       // Message broadcasts
FCChat.prototype.history_so = null;       // History persistence
```

The *onAppStop( )* method is called on our component automatically when the application is about to get unloaded by garbage collection. At that time, a component should flush all its data that's worth saving to disk. The Chat component flushes the chat's history stored in the history shared object:

```
// This is called when the application is about to stop.
FCChat.prototype.onAppStop = function ( ) {
  if (this.persist && this.history_so != null) {
    this.history_so.setProperty("history", this.history);
    this.history_so.flush( );
  }
};
```

The *connect( )* method is the first one called by each client when it connects to the application. In it, we return the history (stored in the component's history property) through a server-to-client call (routed through this.callPrefix), and also call *setUsername( )* on the client:

```
// Methods that a client-side component calls explicitly.
// The first method called by a client component.
FCChat.prototype.connect = function (client) {
  var cglobal = this.getClientGlobalStorage(client);

  if (!cglobal.usercolor) {
    cglobal.usercolor = "0x000000";
  }
  client.call(this.callPrefix + "receiveHistory", null, this.history);
  client.call(this.callPrefix + "setUsername", null, cglobal.username);
};
```

The *close( )* method can be called by a client when the component unloads (*onUnload( )*):

```
// The last method called by a client component.
FCChat.prototype.close = function (client) {
};
```

Note that this is not the same as *onDisconnect( )*, which gets called when the server realizes that the user has disconnected from the application. The *onUnload( )* method gets called on a movie clip when the movie goes to a different frame that doesn't contain it or the movie clip is unloaded with *removeMovieClip( )* or *unload-Movie( )*. In this particular component, we don't need to do anything in the *close( )* handler, but some other components might clean up client-specific variables or flush them to disk.

The *sendMessage( )* method is invoked by a client when it wants to send a new chat message:

```
// Send a message to all others participating in the chat session.
FCChat.prototype.sendMessage = function (client, mesg) {
  var cglobal = this.getClientGlobalStorage(client);
  mesg = this.hiliteURLs(mesg);
  var hexColor = "#" + cglobal.usercolor.substring(2, cglobal.usercolor.length)
  mesg = "<font color=\"" + hexColor + "\"><b>" + cglobal.username + ": </b>" +
        mesg + "</font><br>\n";
  this.history.push(mesg);
  while (this.history.length > this.histlen)
    this.history.shift( );

  this.message_so.send("message", mesg);
};
```

The message to be sent, mesg, is first passed through the *hiliteURLs( )* utility function (not shown), which turns any URLs in the message into hyperlinks (wrapping them in <a> tags).

The code stylizes the text with the color associated with the user who sent the message; this information is stored in cglobal.usercolor (we'll talk more about the client's global storage later). The code prefixes the message with the sender's username and appends the message to the history array. For performance reasons the data is kept in memory in the history array, and is only saved to the history_so shared object, and therefore to disk, only when the application unloads (see *onAppStop( )*, discussed earlier).

The *while* loop limits the lines of chat saved based on histlen.

The *sendMessage( )* method finally uses *SharedObject.send( )* to broadcast the new message to every client connected to the chat.

By now, the chat's server-side architecture should be clear:

- It saves the history in a server-side array (this.history). The data isn't written to disk until the application stops.
- The history is updated by appending each new message as it arrives.
- When a new client connects, the component sends it the current history through a server-to-client *receiveHistory( )* call.

This architecture is bandwidth efficient: one big lump of data (the chat's history) is sent to each client when he first connects, but each client receives only new messages thereafter.

The *clearHistory( )* method allows clients to clear the chat's history:

```
FCChat.prototype.clearHistory = function (client) {
  // If this is client request, check if it is allowed.
  if (client != null && !this.allowClear)
    return false;

  this.history_so.setProperty("history", null);
  this.history_so.flush( );
  delete this.history;
  this.history = new Array;

  // Broadcast a clearHistory command to all clients.
  this.message_so.send("clearHistory");
  return true;
};
```

The *clearHistory( )* method saves null to the history shared object and clears the local history array in memory (this.history). It then sends a *clearHistory* message to all clients, so that they can clear their UI.

The *saveHistory( )* utility method can be called by clients or other server-side scripts to force a flush to disk of the chat's history:

```
FCChat.prototype.saveHistory = function ( ) {
  this.history_so.setProperty("history", this.history);
  this.history_so.flush( );
};
```

The last thing the code does is trace out that it loaded the Chat component successfully:

```
trace("Chat loaded successfully.");
```

In the following sections, we modify this basic Chat component to allow for some special inline commands, such as "/clear" and "/kick".

The Client-Side Code

The Chat component's client-side code was written in ActionScript 1.0 (remember that the communication components were built for Flash MX). Again, some comments and code have been removed for brevity. You can find the full code by looking in the *Actions* layer of the Chat component (drag the component to your *.fla* file's Stage and double-click the *Chat* symbol in the Library to see it).

The code defines the *FCChatClass* class, which implements the Chat component, as a subclass of *MovieClip*, and registers its class with the symbol named *FCChatSymbol*:

```
#initclip
function FCChatClass () {
  this.init();
}

FCChatClass.prototype = new MovieClip();
Object.registerClass("FCChatSymbol", FCChatClass);

FCChatClass.prototype.init = function () {
  this.name = (this._name == null ? "_DEFAULT_" : this._name);
  this.prefix = "FCChat." + this.name + ".";

  this.enterListener = new Object();
  this.enterListener.owner = this;
  this.enterListener.enterPressed = false;
  this.enterListener.onChanged = function () {
    enterChar = this.owner.message_txt.text.charAt(Selection.getEndIndex()-1);
    if (enterChar == String.fromCharCode(Key.ENTER)) {
      this.owner.message_txt.text = this.owner.message_txt.text.substring(0,
                                    this.owner.message_txt.text.length-1);
      this.owner.sendMessage();
    }
  };
  this.message_txt.addListener(this.enterListener);
  this.username = null;
};
```

The *FCChatClass* constructor defines two properties, name and prefix, that will be needed for receiving calls from the server side. As we will see, these property's values are unique, because Flash requires components' instance names to be unique.

The constructor also defines a keyboard listener to which to send messages when a user presses the Enter key.

The component *onUnload( )* event handler calls the *close( )* method when the component is unloaded:

```
FCChatClass.prototype.onUnload = function () {
  this.close();
};
```

The *setUsername( )* method is called by the server side in the *connect( )* call (see earlier code). It tells us what our username is, and we show or hide assets depending on its value (this is to prevent lurkers from participating in the discussion):

```
FCChatClass.prototype.setUsername = function (newName) {
  this.username = newName;
  this.sendButton._visible = (newName != null);
  this.message_txt._visible = (newName != null);
  this.inputBg_mc._visible = (newName != null);
};
```

The *connect( )* method is the first one that must be called on any communication component. If you use the SimpleConnect component, it will call *connect( )* on each component instance you specify; otherwise, you'll have to call *connect( )* manually:

```
FCChatClass.prototype.connect = function (nc) {
  this.history_txt.htmlText = "";

  this.nc = nc;

  if (this.nc.FCChat == null)
    this.nc.FCChat = {};
  this.nc.FCChat[this.name] = this;

  this.so = SharedObject.getRemote(this.prefix + "message", this.nc.uri, false);
  this.so.owner = this;
  this.so.message = function (mesg) { this.owner.receiveMessage(mesg); };
  this.so.clearHistory = function (mesg) { this.owner.receiveHistory([]); };
  this.so.connect(this.nc);

  // Need to call connect() on our server-side counterpart first.
  this.nc.call(this.prefix + "connect", null);
};
```

The nc parameter passed to *connect( )* is a reference to the application's main *Net-Connection*. The *connect( )* method first creates a way for server-to-client calls to get to the client by setting:

```
this.nc.FCChat[this.name] = this;
```

As we saw in Chapter 9, attaching an object reference to a *NetConnection* object causes server-to-client calls to that object's path ("*FCChat/instanceName/method-Name*") to be automatically routed to that object.

The *connect( )* method also subscribes to the message shared object and defines the *message( )* and *clearHistory( )* methods on it.

Finally, the client-side *connect( )* method calls *connect( )* on its server-side counterpart. If this is the first client to call this method, it causes the server-side part of the Chat component to be instantiated. (This is known as *lazy instantiation* because component instances aren't created on the server until the client side tries to call the server side. The fancy code that makes lazy instantiation possible is discussed later under "How Components Are Registered and Instantiated.") If, instead, some other client has already connected to the application, this call will simply result in a client-to-server call to the *connect( )* method, which we discussed earlier.

The *close( )* method is called by either the client movie's ActionScript or the *onUnload( )* method. This method cleans up memory and calls the server side to notify it that this client is going away:

```
FCChatClass.prototype.close = function () {
  var fullName = "FCChat." + this.name;
```

```
// Let our server-side counterpart know that we are going away.
this.nc.call(this.prefix + "close", null);

this.so.owner = null;
delete this.so.owner;
delete this.so.message;
this.so.close();
this.so = null;

this.nc.FCChat[this.name] = null;
this.nc = null;
};
```

The *clearHistory( )* method can be called by your ActionScript code when you want
to clear the history:

```
FCChatClass.prototype.clearHistory = function () {
  this.nc.call(this.prefix + "clearHistory", null);
};
```

Invoking the client-side *clearHistory( )* method calls the server-side *clearHistory( )*
method, which triggers a *clearHistory* message on the message shared object, which
in turn results in a *receiveHistory( )* call on each client, which finally clears the history from the text field:

```
FCChatClass.prototype.receiveHistory = function (h) {
  var history;
  for (var i = 0; i < h.length; i++)
    history += h[i];

  this.history_txt.htmlText = history;
  this.history_txt.scroll = this.history_txt.maxscroll;
};
```

The *receiveHistory( )* method is called by the server side's *connect( )* method (and by
the *clearHistory( )* method of message_so). In it, we simply turn the array into a long
string and copy it into the text field.

The *receiveMessage( )* method gets called by the message shared object whenever a
new message arrives. In it, we simply append the new message to the text field:

```
FCChatClass.prototype.receiveMessage = function (mesg) {
  this.history_txt.htmlText += mesg;
  this.history_txt.scroll = this.history_txt.maxscroll;
};
```

The *sendMessage( )* method sends a new message to the server for broadcasting:

```
FCChatClass.prototype.sendMessage = function (mesg) {
  this.nc.call("FCChat." + this.name + ".sendMessage", null,
               this.message_txt.text);
  this.message_txt.text = "";
};
```

Like all components, the *FCChatClass* class defines a *setSize( )* method (not shown), which simply resizes the component to the specified width and height. The last four lines of the client-side class definition, beyond the #endinitclip directive, set the component to its default state:

```
#endinitclip

// Disable the Send button.
this.sendButton._visible = (this.username != null);
this.message_txt._visible = (this.username != null);
this.inputBg_mc._visible = (this.username != null);

this.setSize(this._width,this._height);
```

Enhancing the Chat: Creating MyChat

You'll commonly tweak the behavior of a component to suit an application's needs. Because of how the Macromedia components were built, this is a pretty straightforward but also error-prone process. To make a copy of the Chat component on which to base MyChat, you will need to do the following:

On the client side:

1. Drag an instance of the Chat component from the Components panel to the Stage.
2. Rename its symbol name in the Library from Chat to MyChat.
3. Set its linkage ID in the Symbol Properties dialog box to *MyChatSymbol*.
4. Open its timeline, and open the Actions panel. In the code, replace every occurrence of "FCChat" with "MyChat".
5. If you want your component to appear alongside the other communication components in the Components panel, open *Communication Component.fla* and drag your MyChat component to the *.fla* file's Library. (You may need to restart Flash to see the new components.)

On the server side:

1. Make a copy of *chat.asc*, and call it *mychat.asc*.
2. Open *mychat.asc* and replace every occurrence of "FCChat" with "MyChat".
3. If you want your new MyChat component to be loaded with all the other components when *components.asc* is loaded, open the *components.asc* file from your *scriptlib* folder and add a line to it that says *load("components/mychat.asc");*.

Now you can safely edit the client-side and server-side code to suit your needs (you may want to create a simple test movie that contains your new MyChat component to make sure everything still works).

Changing MyChat: Turning Off the Chat History

Now that we have a custom MyChat component as embodied in *mychat.asc*, we can simplify it so that it, for example, doesn't save the chat's history. With this change, users will not receive the transcript of the prior conversation when they first log on; instead, they'll receive only messages sent after they have logged on. The easiest way to remove such functionality is to delete every reference to the history array from the server-side code, so it looks like this:

```
try {var dummy = MyChat;} catch (e) { // #ifndef MyChat
  load("components/component.asc");

  MyChat = function (name) {
    this.init(name);
    this.message_so = SharedObject.get(this.prefix + "message", false);
  };

  MyChat.prototype = new FCComponent("MyChat",MyChat);
  MyChat.prototype.message_so = null;

  // This is called when the application is about to stop.
  MyChat.prototype.onAppStop = function () {
  };

  // The first method called by a client component.
  MyChat.prototype.connect = function (client) {
    var cglobal = this.getClientGlobalStorage(client);
    if (!cglobal.usercolor) {
      cglobal.usercolor = "0x000000";
    }
    client.call(this.callPrefix + "setUsername", null, cglobal.username);
  };

  // The last method called by a client component.
  MyChat.prototype.close = function (client) {
  };

  // Send a message to all others participating in the chat session.
  MyChat.prototype.sendMessage = function (client, mesg) {
    var cglobal = this.getClientGlobalStorage(client);
    mesg = this.hiliteURLs(mesg);
    var hexColor = "#" + cglobal.usercolor.substring(2, cglobal.usercolor.length)
    mesg = "<font color=\"" + hexColor + "\"><b>" + cglobal.username + ": </b>" +
           mesg + "</font><br>\n";
    this.message_so.send("message", mesg);
  };

  // Highlight the urls in a message.
  MyChat.prototype.hiliteURLs = function (msg) {
    // Code removed, look at the original chat.asc.
    return hilited;
  };
```

```
    trace("MyChat loaded successfully.");
  } // #endif
```

Note how the code is much smaller and cleaner (but also less powerful!). We will use this code as a starting point to make more changes to MyChat in subsequent sections. Somewhat surprisingly, there wasn't any client-side code worth removing for this change.

Enhancing MyChat: Adding Special Commands

Suppose we want to modify MyChat to support special commands such as "/clear" or "/kick", to clear the chat or kick somebody out of the room.

All the changes can be made within the *sendMessage( )* method in the *mychat.asc* file, by adding the code to the following listing where it says "ADD MODIFICATIONS HERE!!!!":

```
// Send a message to all others participating in the chat session.
MyChat.prototype.sendMessage = function (client, mesg) {
  var cglobal = this.getClientGlobalStorage(client);

  // ADD MODIFICATIONS HERE!!!!

  mesg = this.hiliteURLs(mesg);
  var hexColor = "#" + cglobal.usercolor.substring(2, cglobal.usercolor.length)
  mesg = "<font color=\"" + hexColor + "\"><b>" + cglobal.username + ": </b>" +
        mesg + "</font><br>\n";
  this.message_so.send("message", mesg);
};
```

A very simple enhancement is to prevent users from sending empty messages:

```
if (mesg == "") { return; }
```

This code allows the special command "/clear" to clear the chat's transcript:

```
if (mesg == "/clear") {
  trace("clear called!");
  this.message_so.send("clearHistory");
  return;
}
```

So whenever any client sends the message "/clear", the chat history is cleared for everyone connected.

Another special message could be "/ip", which could list all the IPs of users connected to the application:

```
// List every user's IP address.
if (mesg == "/ips") {
  var allips = "<font color=\"#AAAAAA\"><b>People's IPs:</b>";
  for (var i = 0; i < application.clients.length; i++) {
    var name = this.getClientGlobalStorage(application.clients[i]).username;
    allips += "<br><b>" + name + "</b>: " + application.clients[i].ip;
```

```
      }
      allips += "</font><br>\n";
      client.call(this.callPrefix + "receiveMessage", null, allips);
      return;
    }
```

The script goes through the `application.clients` array and gets the `username` and `ip` of each client, to create a big string (`allips`). It sends that string back to the client that sent the "/ip" message, as a regular chat message.

Now that a user has a list of people's IPs, you could let her kick someone out by supporting a "/kick *ip*" command, like this:

```
    // Kick a user (by IP address).
    if (mesg.substr(0,5) == "/kick") {
      var ipToKick = mesg.substr(mesg.indexOf(" ") + 1);
      for (var i = 0; i < application.clients.length; i++) {
        if (application.clients[i].ip == ipToKick) {
          trace("Disconnecting " + application.clients[i]);
          var name = this.getClientGlobalStorage(application.clients[i]).username;
          this.message_so.send("message", "<font color=\"#AAAAAA\"><i>" + name +
                               " (" + ipToKick + ") was kicked</i></font>");
          application.disconnect(application.clients[i]);
          break;
        }
      }
      return;
    }
```

The code loops through the `application.clients` array. If the `ip` property matches the address specified in the message, the code disconnects that client and sends a message to all clients notifying them that the user was kicked out.

Another simple command that we could add support for is "/help", which lists all the commands supported by MyChat:

```
    if ((mesg == "/help")||(mesg == "/?")) {
      var helpStr = "<font color=\"#AAAAAA\"><b>Available Commands:</b>";
      helpStr += "<br>  /clear";
      helpStr += "<br>  /help";
      helpStr += "<br>  /ips";
      helpStr += "<br>  /kick ip";

      helpStr += "</font><br>\n";
      client.call(this.callPrefix + "receiveMessage", null, helpStr);
      return;
    }
```

Note that the "/help" command doesn't run any server-side code, so it could be moved entirely to the client side (just before sending the message). You can add other commands, such as "/private name" (to initiate a private conversation with the named user) or "/ban ip" (to bar users from the specified IP address from connecting), in an analogous way.

Creating a Simple Component from Scratch: SharedTextInput

The communication components that ship with FlashCom are all complex, high-level components that do much more than a simple UI component such as a Button or a CheckBox. They could be considered small applications that include other UI components to perform client/server operations that were packaged as components because they could be used in many different end user applications.

Their complexity, coupled with the lack of documentation, made it almost impossible for programmers who just started looking at FlashCom to understand how each communication component worked and to learn from its code. To make things clearer, this section creates a communication component derived from a regular component but enhanced to have multiuser functionality through FlashCom.

The base component is a TextInput field, but we want to make its contents (text) shared among all users. We will call the new component SharedTextInput. Whenever a user types in the SharedTextInput component, everybody else connected to the application sees what the user is typing in real time. They can then type over what the original user has typed to change it, and everyone will see the changes.

As you will see, this component is very easy to write and understand. It's also flexible and easy to extend, in the sense that it can be used in a wide variety of applications and even included in other components (we will see an example of such a "container" component in the next section, when we build SharedAddressForm).

The .fla File

Building the *.fla* for the SharedTextInput component is really easy:

1. Create a new movie clip.
2. Set it to Export for ActionScript in the Symbol Properties dialog box.
3. Specify the AS 2.0 Class name *SharedTextInput* in the Symbol Properties dialog box.
4. Create a two-frame timeline for the component, such as you would do in all other components: a *stop( );* action and a BoundingBox (call it m_boundingBox) in frame 1 and an instance of TextInput in frame 2. If you are not familiar with building components, refer to Chapter 13.

After writing the client-side code, you could turn your component into a SWC, as described in Chapter 13, or leave it as a movie clip to use in your applications.

The Client-Side Class File

For the sake of code readability and simplicity, we will write the *SharedTextInput* class in ActionScript 2.0 but make it extend *MovieClip* instead of *UIComponent*. This is intended to ease the transition for developers still learning the UI components v2 architecture. If you understand the v2 architecture, it should be a breeze for you to make *SharedTextInput* extend *UIComponent* or even *TextInput* itself.

Example 14-1 shows the code for *SharedTextInput.as*. It's followed by a detailed description of each section.

Example 14-1. The client-side code for the SharedTextInput class

```
import mx.controls.TextInput;

class SharedTextInput extends MovieClip {
  private var m_boundingBox:MovieClip;    // On the Stage
  private var m_text:TextInput;           // Attached at _level0
  private var m_name:String;
  private var m_prefix:String;
  private var m_nc:NetConnection;
  private var m_so:SharedObject;

  function SharedTextInput (Void) {
    m_name = _name;
    if ((m_name == null) || (m_name == ""))
      m_name = "_DEFAULT_";
    m_prefix = "SharedTextInput." + m_name + ".";

    m_boundingBox.removeMovieClip(); //Hide the bounding box
    // Declare a change listener for the TextInput field
    var l = new Object();
    l.mc = this;
    l.change = function (p_eventObj) {
      this.mc.m_so.data.text = this.mc.m_text.text;
    };
    this.attachMovie("TextInput", "m_text", 0);
    m_text.setSize(100, 22);
    m_text.addEventListener("change", l);
  }

  function onUnload (Void):Void {
    this.close();
  }

  function connect (p_nc:NetConnection):Void {
    // Save a reference to the NetConnection passed in (for convenience).
    m_nc = p_nc;
    // Attach a reference to ourselves to the NetConnection
    // so that server-to-client calls can be routed to this instance
    // using the same naming scheme we used for m_prefix.
    if (m_nc.SharedTextInput == null)
      m_nc.SharedTextInput = new Object();
```

Example 14-1. The client-side code for the SharedTextInput class (continued)

```
    m_nc.SharedTextInput[m_name] = this;

    // Get the shared object that contains the text
    m_so = SharedObject.getRemote(m_prefix + "text", m_nc.uri, false);
    m_so.mc = this;
    m_so.onSync = function (p_list) {
      for (var i = 0; i < p_list.length; i++) {
        // Update the UI only if the change came from someone else
        if ((p_list[i].name == "text") && (p_list[i].code != "success")) {
          this.mc.m_text.text = this.data.text;
          break;
        }
      }
    };
    m_so.connect(m_nc);
    // Call the server side of SharedTextInput
    m_nc.call(m_prefix + "connect", null);
  }

  function close (Void):Void {
    // Clean up
    m_nc.call(m_prefix + "close", null);
    m_nc.SharedTextInput[m_name] = null;
    m_nc = null;
  }
  function setSize (p_w:Number, p_h:Number):Void {
    m_text.setSize(p_w, p_h);
  }
}
```

The *SharedTextInput* class code imports *TextInput* because we are going to embed an instance of it in our component. The class then defines some private variables needed. The class constructor first creates the m_name and m_prefix variables, inferring them from the instance name (_name) of the SharedTextInput component, which is chosen by the developer who uses this component. The m_prefix has to follow the naming conventions of the framework:

```
    ClassName + "." + instanceName + "."
```

As you will see, this prefix is used for remote method invocations and resources namespacing (this prevents conflicts if two SharedTextInput components share the Stage at the same time).

Next, the constructor removes the m_boundingBox clip from the Stage and attaches a TextInput component instance, calling it m_text. The constructor also defines an event listener (1), which stores the text from the TextInput component in the m_so shared object (which triggers an *onSync* event for all the users connected to it, including the client that sets the value).

The class defines an *onUnload( )* method that calls *close( )* if the SharedTextInput component is removed from the Stage (allowing the component to clean up after itself). The class also defines a *connect( )* method, which is required by the framework. This is the function that tells us which *NetConnection* instance to use for our shared objects and streams; it is called automatically by the SimpleConnect component or manually by each application that wants to use communication components.

In the *connect( )* method, we save a reference to the *NetConnection* passed in (for convenience), and we add a reference to ourselves (the *SharedTextInput* instance) to it as follows:

```
m_nc.SharedTextInput[m_name] = this;
```

This is done so that server-to-client calls can be routed to the *SharedTextInput* instance using the same naming scheme we used for m_prefix, namely:

```
ClassName + "." + instanceName + "." + methodName
```

Every component should attach a reference to itself to the *NetConnection* object at the beginning of its *connect( )* function if it wants to receive calls from its server-side code.

The *connect( )* method then gets an RSO (notice how we use m_prefix in its name, to avoid collisions) and defines an *onSync( )* method on it:

```
m_so = SharedObject.getRemote(m_prefix + "text", m_nc.uri, false);
m_so.onSync = function (p_list) {
...
```

The *onSync( )* method should be fairly simple to understand by now. It loops through the updated slots in the shared object; if the value that changed is "text" and it was updated by someone else—the code is "change" or "delete" but not "success"—we update the text in the m_text TextInput area. If you didn't exclude the "success" case, the text field would update twice as you're typing, making the component pretty horrible to type in (try it for yourself).

Finally, the *connect( )* method performs a client-to-server call to our server-side *connect( )* method (always using the prefix):

```
m_nc.call(m_prefix + "connect", null);
```

Calling *connect( )* on the server-side part of the component is required by the framework (that's how the server-side component instance is created!).

The class's *close( )* method simply cleans up by telling the server-side code that the user instance is leaving and freeing memory resources. The *close( )* method can be called by the host application or by the *onUnload( )* method we defined earlier.

The last method of the class is *setSize( )*, which is also required by the framework, and simply resizes the component to the requested dimensions.

This small class contains most of the logic for the component. To reiterate its strategy for multiuser interaction:

1. Whenever someone types in the m_text TextInput component, a change event is trapped (by 1).
2. The content of m_text is stored in the "text" slot of a shared object.
3. Changes trigger an *onSync* event in all the clients connected.
4. If the client is not the one that triggered the change, the new value of "text" is copied to the text property of m_text, updating it.

That wasn't so hard, was it? On to the server-side code.

The Server-Side Code

The server-side code lives in the *SharedTextInput.asc* file, which gets included in applications that use the component.

The server-side code shown in Example 14-2 is even shorter than its client-side counterpart.

Example 14-2. The server-side implementation of the SharedTextInput class

```
try {var dummy = SharedTextInput;} catch (e) { // #ifndef SharedTextInput
  load("components/component.asc");

  SharedTextInput = function (p_name) {
    this.init(p_name);

    this.so = SharedObject.get(this.prefix + "text", false);
    this.so.owner = this;
    this.so.onSync = function (p_list) {
      // This triggers an onPropertyChange event to those who are listening.
      this.owner.text = this.getProperty("text");
    };
  };

  // All named instances are held in the instances associative array.
  // SharedText extends FCComponent.
  SharedTextInput.prototype = new FCComponent("SharedTextInput", SharedTextInput);

  // The first method called by a client component.
  SharedTextInput.prototype.connect = function (p_client) {
  };

  SharedTextInput.prototype.setText = function (p_text) {
    this.so.setProperty("text", p_text);
    // This will not trigger an onSync event, which is good,
    // because, otherwise, we could cause an infinite loop.
```

Example 14-2. The server-side implementation of the SharedTextInput class (continued)

```
  };
  trace("SharedTextInput loaded successfully.");
} // #endif
```

After the usual "fake #ifndef" statement (implemented with the *try/catch* statement), the code defines the class constructor. The constructor calls *init(p_name)*, which triggers code in *FCComponent*, the base class that all server-side communication components extend. This runs some initialization code to set up event and method routing. It also defines the prefix property on this class, which we use in the next section. The code gets a reference to the shared object used by this component (the same one that we got on the client-side code) and defines an *onSync( )* handler on it:

```
    this.so = SharedObject.get(this.prefix + "text", false);
    this.so.onSync = function (p_list) {
    ...
```

The *onSync( )* handler merely updates the text property of the component instance with the content of the "text" slot of the shared object. As we will see later, this is all that's needed to send an event to all listening classes. This *onSync( )* handler is triggered whenever any client makes a change to the TextInput component.

The code specifies that the *SharedTextInput* class extends *FCComponent* (because SSAS doesn't support the extends keyword, we establish inheritance using the prototype property, as was common in client-side ActionScript 1.0 development):

```
    SharedTextInput.prototype = new FCComponent("SharedTextInput", SharedTextInput);
```

The empty *connect( )* method allows the lazy instantiation of this component.

Finally, the class defines a *setText( )* method, which is a public API for the server-side code of this component (we'll see how it's used in a real-world example in the next section). For now, notice it simply sets the value of the shared object to what's passed in as a parameter. The fact that using *setProperty( )* on the server side doesn't trigger server-side *onSync* events is a lifesaver here; otherwise, we might end up in an infinite loop.

The final *trace( )* statement tells the world that the server-side code loaded successfully.

This code is very simple, and yet it throws an event whenever the text is changed by anyone, and it has a public API for setting the text from the server side. As you will see in the next section, this makes the component extremely flexible.

A Sample Application That Uses SharedTextInput

Now that we have the component all ready to go—client-side *.fla*, client-side *.as* class code, and server-side *.asc* code—we need to put it to the test!

To do so, we'll create a simple application that could be used by a math teacher. Figure 14-2 shows what the application is going to look like.

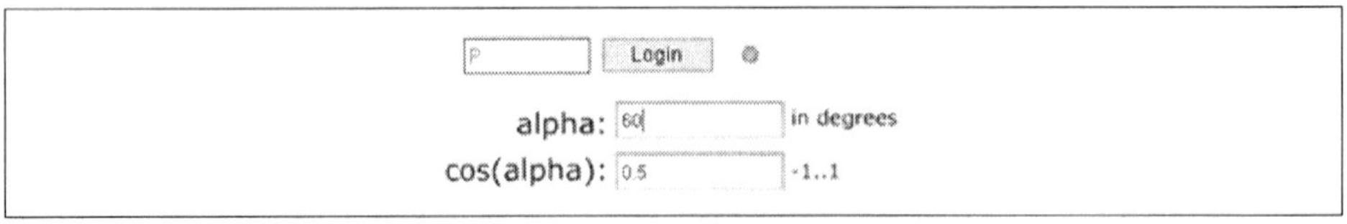

Figure 14-2. A simple application using SharedTextInput

Basically, we have two SharedTextInput components on the Stage, one to hold the value of an angle (alpha), and another to hold the value of the cosine of alpha. Whenever anybody changes the value of alpha, the cosine is updated, and vice versa. Imagine a math teacher changing the value of alpha, knowing that all his students are seeing what he's typing, and allowing his students to test it themselves, with everyone else seeing the changes in real time.

Let's see how to create such an application.

After creating all the text labels needed, drag two instances of SharedTextInput to the Stage, and name them m_alpha and m_cosAlpha using the Properties panel.

Drag a SimpleConnect component to the Stage and connect m_alpha and m_cosAlpha to it by specifying their instance names in SimpleConnect's Communication Components parameter list.

Create a server-side application folder named *cosAlphaTest*, and write the code in Example 14-3 into a *main.asc* file placed in that folder.

Example 14-3. The main.asc file for the cosAlphaTest application

```
load("components.asc");
load("SharedTextInput.asc");

// This example shows how to create an application that uses
// two instances of the SharedTextInput component to do some math.
function toDeg (p_rad) { return p_rad*180/Math.PI; }
function toRad (p_deg) { return p_deg*Math.PI/180; }

l = new Object();
l.onPropertyChange = function (p_eventSource, p_eventData) {
  if (p_eventData.name != "text")
    return;

  if (p_eventSource.name == "m_alpha") {
    var alpha = toRad(p_eventData.newValue/1);
    SharedTextInput.instances["m_cosAlpha"].setText(Math.cos(alpha));
  }
  else {
    var cosAlpha = p_eventData.newValue/1;
    SharedTextInput.instances["m_alpha"].setText(toDeg(Math.acos(cosAlpha)));
```

Example 14-3. The main.asc file for the cosAlphaTest application (continued)

```
  }
};
SharedTextInput.addListener("text",l);
```

Copy *SharedTextInput.asc* to the *cosAlphaTest* application folder or to your *scriptlib* folder.

Update your SimpleConnect parameters to tell it to connect to the *cosAlphaTest* application, and you should be ready to test your application.

Let's look at the *main.asc* code in Example 14-3. First, it loads *components.asc* to load the framework, including the SimpleConnect component. It then loads *Shared-TextInput.asc* (the code for the server-side *SharedInputText* class from Example 14-2).

After defining a couple of utility functions to transform radians to degrees, we create a class-wide listener object for the *SharedTextInput* class. Whenever the text property of any of the instances of SharedTextInput is updated, the framework invokes the *onPropertyChange( )* method of the listener. The *onPropertyChange( )* method first makes sure that the property that was changed is "text" and ignores changes made to any other property. It then looks at the name (p_eventSource.name) of the SharedTextInput instance that triggered the *onPropertyChange* event. If the change was in the m_alpha SharedTextInput instance, we transform the value to radians and use the public *setText( )* method of the m_cosAlpha SharedTextInput instance to set its value to *Math.cos(alpha)*. This will update the m_text TextInput component of all clients connected to the application, through the *onSync* event generated by *setText( )* with *setProperty( )*.

Still with us? Good.

The *else* branch in the *onPropertyChange( )* handler is symmetrical to the preceding *if* branch. It takes the value typed in m_cosAlpha, calculates its arc cosine, and saves it in m_alpha.

 Make sure you have the FlashCom Server 1.5.2 updater. In prior versions, a bug in the event dispatching mechanism of the framework prevented class-wide events from being dispatched. (The author discovered the bug when writing this section of this book, and was able to fix in time for 1.5.2.)

Test the Flash movie. Whenever anybody types in the m_alpha SharedTextInput field, everybody sees the changes to it. Furthermore, because of the "wiring" on the server side, the contents of m_cosAlpha are also updated for all users of the application.

This is a simple application (very little code), but it shows how to use multiple components in the same application and link them together, using the communication component framework's event dispatching system and using components' server-side methods (such as *setText( )*).

The next section shows how to create a container component, which includes multiple copies of SharedTextInput to do its job.

Creating a Container Component: SharedAddressForm

The previous section described how to turn a simple UI component into a multiuser communication component using shared objects and event broadcasting. Using very similar code, you can turn other existing UI components into communication components. Once that is done, building multiuser, real-time online forms and a wide variety of other applications becomes very easy.

Some sections of forms appear in many different applications—you've seen them all over the Internet—things like a set of fields for a user's address, billing information, and shipping information.

In this section, we will create a SharedAddressForm component, which is just a container of a few labels and instances of SharedTextInput.

The main goal of this section is to show you how to include communication components inside of other components, which we call "containers."

The .fla File

By now, you should be familiar with all the steps involved in creating a new component. Just place a few labels on the Stage ("Name", "Address", "City", etc.) and don't forget to include an instance of SharedTextInput in frame 2 of your component (we will attach and place all the instances programmatically). At the end, your component should look something like Figure 14-3.

Once you have set the linkage name for the class to *SharedAddressForm*, you're ready to create the *SharedAddressForm.as* class file, which implements the client-side behavior.

The Client-Side Code

As before, the *SharedAddressForm* class extends *MovieClip* for the sake of simplicity. Example 14-4 shows the code for the *SharedAddressForm.as* file (the client-side *SharedAddressForm* class).

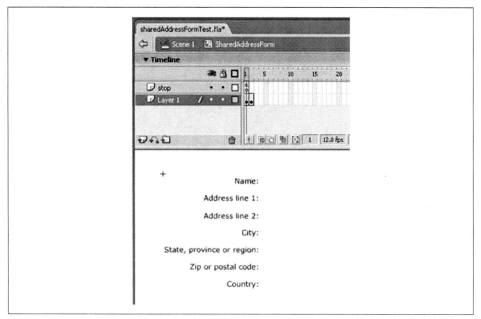

Figure 14-3. The .fla file for the SharedAddressForm component

Example 14-4. The client-side code for the SharedAddressForm class

```
import SharedTextInput;

class SharedAddressForm extends MovieClip {
  private var m_name:String;
  private var m_prefix:String;

  function SharedAddressForm (Void) {
    m_name = _name;
    if ((m_name == null) || (m_name == ""))
      m_name = "_DEFAULT_";
    m_prefix = "SharedAddressForm." + m_name + ".";

    attachMovie("SharedTextInput", m_name + "_name_st", 0, {_x:164, _y:0});
    this[m_name + "_name_st"].setSize(178, 22);

    attachMovie("SharedTextInput", m_name + "_address1_st", 1, {_x:164, _y:27.5});
    this[m_name + "_address1_st"].setSize(178, 22);

    attachMovie("SharedTextInput", m_name + "_address2_st", 2, {_x:164, _y:55});
    this[m_name + "_address2_st"].setSize(178, 22);

    attachMovie("SharedTextInput", m_name + "_city_st", 3, {_x:164, _y:82.5});
    this[m_name + "_city_st"].setSize(178, 22);

    attachMovie("SharedTextInput", m_name + "_state_st", 4, {_x:164, _y:110});
    this[m_name + "_state_st"].setSize(104, 22);
```

```
    attachMovie("SharedTextInput", m_name + "_zip_st", 5, {_x:164, _y:137.5});
    this[m_name + "_zip_st"].setSize(104, 22);

    attachMovie("SharedTextInput", m_name + "_country_st", 6, {_x:164, _y:165});
    this[m_name + "_country_st"].setSize(178, 22);
  }

  function onUnload (Void):Void {
    this.close();
  }

  function connect (p_nc:NetConnection):Void {
    this[m_name + "_name_st"].connect(p_nc);
    this[m_name + "_address1_st"].connect(p_nc);
    this[m_name + "_address2_st"].connect(p_nc);
    this[m_name + "_city_st"].connect(p_nc);
    this[m_name + "_state_st"].connect(p_nc);
    this[m_name + "_zip_st"].connect(p_nc);
    this[m_name + "_country_st"].connect(p_nc);

    p_nc.call(m_prefix + "connect", null);
  }

  function close (Void):Void {
    this[m_name + "_name_st"].close();
    this[m_name + "_address1_st"].close();
    this[m_name + "_address2_st"].close();
    this[m_name + "_city_st"].close();
    this[m_name + "_state_st"].close();
    this[m_name + "_zip_st"].close();
    this[m_name + "_country_st"].close();
  }

  function setSize (p_w:Number, p_h:Number):Void {
    // do nothing
  }
}
```

First, the *SharedAddressForm* class imports the *SharedTextInput* class (so make sure that *SharedTextInput.as* is in the classpath, which can be modified under Edit → Preferences → ActionScript → Language → ActionScript 2.0 Settings → Classpath). The class then defines two variables that we're going to need (the usual m_name and m_prefix).

In the class constructor, we determine the values for m_name and m_prefix and attach the SharedTextInput component instances that we need. Notice how we prefix their instance names with m_name, such as:

```
    attachMovie("SharedTextInput", m_name + "_name_st", 0, {_x:164, _y:0});
```

This makes each instance unique, so that you can have two SharedAddressForm components on the Stage without conflict. The only drawback of this is that to address an asset, you need to use the this["..."] notation, as we do in the different *setSize( )* calls:

```
this[m_name + "_name_st"].setSize(178, 22);
```

After the usual *onUnload( )* method, we define the *connect( )* method, which simply calls *connect( )* on all the child SharedTextInput component instances, and calls *connect( )* on its server-side counterpart to instantiate it lazily.

The *close( )* function simply invokes *close( )* on all the SharedTextInput children of the component. The *setSize( )* function, for simplicity, doesn't do anything in this example.

You can see why we call this a container component—all it does is attach some children and pass the calls (*connect( )*, *close( )*) along to them when needed. SharedAddressForm doesn't have any shared objects or other resources of its own; it lets the different SharedTextInput components get their own.

The Server-Side Code

The server-side code for the *SharedAddressForm* class, shown in Example 14-5, is the simplest server-side communication component script you can imagine. This code belongs in a file named *SharedAddressForm.asc*, which should be loaded for any server-side application that uses the component.

Example 14-5. The server-side implementation of the SharedAddressForm class

```
try {var dummy = SharedAddressForm;} catch (e) { // #ifndef SharedAddressForm
  load("components/component.asc");
  load("SharedTextInput.asc");

  SharedAddressForm = function (p_name) {
    this.init(p_name);
  };

  SharedAddressForm.prototype = new FCComponent("SharedAddressForm",
                               SharedAddressForm);

  // This will instantiate this class.
  SharedAddressForm.prototype.connect = function (p_client) {
    // trace("SharedAddressForm.connect!");
  };

  trace("SharedAddressForm loaded successfully.");
} // #endif
```

The *SharedAddressForm* class loads *SharedTextInput.asc*, just as we imported the *SharedTextInput* class on the client side. The *SharedAddressForm* class defines minimal constructor and *connect( )* functions. As you can see, this component's server-side implementation doesn't do much, but it's set up to make the client-side companion work properly.

Using the SharedAddressForm Component

Using the SharedAddressForm component is really easy. Your server-side code should include the following *load( )* commands:

```
load("components.asc");
load("SharedAddressForm.asc");
```

Then, simply drag an instance of the SharedAddressForm component onto your Stage in the Flash movie client. Set its instance name and connect it to SimpleConnect (or call *connect( )* on it manually), and you're good to go.

One last interesting note: if you look at the shared objects through the Communication Application Inspector, you'll see the name of the TextInput shared objects being prefixed with the name of the SharedAddressForm instance you put on the Stage. This is expected and assures us that the two instances of SharedAddressForm on stage at the same time will not conflict.

Creating an Authenticating Component

One feature of the framework is the ability for each component to accept or reject a connection. The framework then tallies all the components' decisions and dispatches an *onConnectAccept* or *onConnectReject* event accordingly (a client is accepted only if all the components accept its connection).

Although this is a powerful feature, creating a component that takes advantage of it is not trivial.

In this section, we are going to create such a component, using Flash Remoting on the server side to connect to a simple ColdFusion component (CFC), which performs the authentication against a users database.

We will also create a client-side application to show how to use the authenticating component alongside other communication components, such as Chat and PeopleList.

Think of the authenticating component as a simplified version of SimpleConnect that requires the user to type in a password to log in.

The Tester Application: AuthConnectTest

The application we are about to build has two states: a login screen and a chat screen.

The login screen contains only an instance of the authenticating component, which we will call AuthConnect, as seen in Figure 14-4.

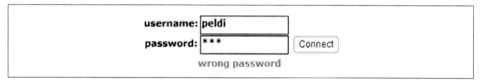

Figure 14-4. The simple UI of the AuthConnect component

If the user provides a proper username/password pair, he will be taken to the chat screen, as shown in Figure 14-5.

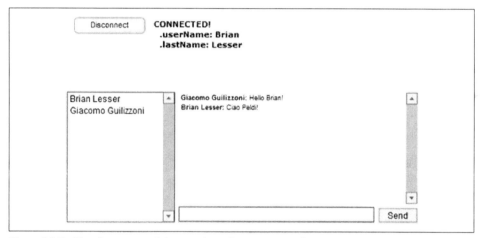

Figure 14-5. The chat screen of the sample authenticating application

Before diving into the details of how the AuthConnect component is built, let's look at how it is used in the sample application, which we will call *AuthConnectTest*.

The client side of AuthConnectTest

The client-side *.fla* for the *AuthConnectTest* application is very simple. It contains only one frame and the following assets on the Stage:

m_authConnect
> An instance of the AuthConnect component

m_disconnect_pb
> A Button instance

m_people
> An instance of the PeopleList component that ships with FlashCom

m_chat
> An instance of the Chat component that ships with FlashCom

m_txt

A dynamic text field used for debugging

The only code on the frame is a single directive:

```
#include "AuthConnectTest.as"
```

The *AuthConnectTest.as* code is pretty simple, as shown in Example 14-6.

Example 14-6. The AuthConnectTest.as source code included in the client .fla

```
var l = new Object( );
l.connected = function (p_evtObj:Object):Void {
  showScreen("chat");
  m_txt.text = "CONNECTED!";
  for (var i in p_evtObj.userData)
    m_txt.text += newline + "  ." + i + ": " + p_evtObj.userData[i];
  m_chat.connect(m_authConnect.nc);    // Connect the Chat component
  m_people.connect(m_authConnect.nc);  // Connect the PeopleList component
};
l.disconnected = function (p_evtObj:Object):Void {
  showScreen("login");
};
m_authConnect.addEventListener("connected", l);
m_authConnect.addEventListener("disconnected", l);
m_authConnect.setUp("localhost", "authConnectTest");

l.click = function (p_evtObj:Object):Void {
  showScreen("login");
  m_chat.close( );
  m_people.close( );
  m_authConnect.nc.close( );
};
m_disconnect_pb.addEventListener("click", l);

function showScreen (p_screen:String):Void {
  m_authConnect._visible = (p_screen == "login");
  m_disconnect_pb._visible = m_txt._visible = (p_screen == "chat");
  m_chat._visible = m_people._visible = (p_screen == "chat");
}

showScreen("login");
```

The preceding code defines a listener object (l) and defines some event handlers on it. As we will see, AuthConnect dispatches two events: *connected* and *disconnected*.

When the *connected( )* handler is called, it:

- Shows the chat screen (using the *showScreen( )* function defined at the end of the code)
- Fills the m_txt text field with the user data that the AuthConnect component includes in the event object

- Connects the Chat and the PeopleList components to the main NetConnection using the standard *connect( )* method provided by all communication components that ship with FlashCom

Notice how we use `m_authConnect.nc` to refer to the movie's NetConnection. As we will see, the AuthConnect component provides a getter function for the `nc` property.

Conversely, the *disconnected( )* handler returns the user to the login screen. The AuthConnect component dispatches a *disconnected* event if there is a network glitch or the application gets reloaded on the server side.

After setting up the two event handlers with `m_authConnect`, we call its public *setUp( )* method. As we will see later, the method takes two parameters: the name of the FlashCom Server to which to connect and the name of the application instance to connect to on that server.

The code also defines a *click( )* method on the same multipurpose listener object, so that when users click on the Disconnect button, they are taken back to the login screen. The *click( )* handler also calls the standard *close( )* method on the Chat and PeopleList components, so that they can run their "cleanup" code. Last, the *click( )* handler calls *close( )* on the movie's NetConnection directly.

After adding the *click( )* event listener to the Disconnect button, we define the *showScreen( )* utility function, which shows and hides assets on the Stage depending on the application's state. Calling *showScreen("login")* starts the application in the login state.

Nothing advanced here. Now let's look at the server-side part of this application.

The server side of AuthConnectTest

The *main.asc* code found in the *AuthConnectTest* application folder is also relatively simple, as shown in Example 14-7.

Example 14-7. The main.asc file for the AuthConnectTest application

```
// framework.asc is discussed later in this chapter.
load("framework.asc");
// AuthConnect.asc is available on the book's web site.
load("AuthConnect.asc");
load("components/chat.asc");
load("components/people.asc");

AuthConnect.instances["GateKeeper"].setUp("localhost:8500", "cfdocs.authenticate",
    "authenticateUser");

application.onConnect = function (p_client, p_username, p_pwd) {
  trace("main.asc onConnect(" + p_username + ", " + p_pwd + ")");
  application.acceptConnection(p_client);
};
```

Example 14-7. The main.asc file for the AuthConnectTest application (continued)

```
application.onDisconnect = function (p_client) {
  trace("main.asc onDisconnect!");
};
```

As seen in the preceding code, the *AuthConnectTest* application first loads the *frame-work.asc*, then the server-side code of the AuthConnect component, *AuthConnect.asc*. As we will see later, the code creates a singleton instance of the AuthConnect component named "GateKeeper". (For those not familiar with the term, *singleton* refers to an object that is the only instance of its class. It takes its name from the well-known Singleton design pattern.)

The *AuthConnect* class performs authentication. Normally communication components are instantiated when a client calls a method on them. But an authentication component must be created in advance of any clients connecting. So we use the static *AuthConnect.create( )* method to create a singleton instance:

```
AuthConnect.create("GateKeeper");    // Create the singleton
```

The *AuthConnect* class uses an instances array—which is a built-in part of the Macromedia component framework—to access and use the singleton instance. Because the instances array is an associative array, "GateKeeper" must be referred to in quotes:

```
AuthConnect.instances["GateKeeper"].methodName( )
```

The code also calls the *setUp( )* method on the "GateKeeper" instance, passing it three parameters: the name of the ColdFusion server to which to connect, the name of the CFC to use as a remoting service, and the name of the function contained within the CFC to invoke:

```
AuthConnect.instances["GateKeeper"].setUp("localhost:8500", "cfdocs.authenticate",
    "authenticateUser");
```

The application also loads the Chat and PeopleList components, *chat.asc* and *people.asc*.

The simple *onConnect( )* and *onDisconnect( )* functions are there just to show that the component doesn't interfere with other logic that you might need to put in the application's *main.asc*.

Looking at the tester application code gave us a little insight into the interface of the AuthConnect component and how it can be used within a larger application.

It is time now to look into the three parts that make up the component: the client-side script (*AuthConnect.as*), the FlashCom server-side script (*AuthConnect.asc*), and the ColdFusion component used for database authentication (*authenticate.cfc*).

The Client Side of AuthConnect

As you have seen in Figure 14-4, the UI for the AuthConnect component is extremely simple. It contains a username input text field (named m_username_txt), a password input text field (named m_password_txt), a Connect button (m_connect_pb), and a feedback dynamic text field (m_feedback_txt).

The following methods, events, and properties allow application elements to communicate with the AuthConnect component:

setUp( ) method
> Tells the component what server and what application it should try to connect to.

connected event
> The component dispatches this event after the user specifies a valid username and password.

disconnected event
> The component dispatches this event if the connection is closed.

nc *property*
> Points to the NetConnection used by AuthConnect.

The client-side AuthConnect code is a regular ActionScript 2.0 class, augmented with the *EventDispatcher* class. The code in Example 14-8 belongs in a file named *AuthConnect.as*.

Example 14-8. The AuthConnect.as client-side class definition

```
import mx.controls.Button;
import mx.events.EventDispatcher;

class AuthConnect extends MovieClip {
  // EventDispatcher needs these
  var addEventListener:Function;
  var removeEventListener:Function;
  var dispatchEvent:Function;
  var dispatchQueue:Function;

  // Assets
  private var m_username_txt, m_password_txt, m_feedback_txt:TextField;
  private var m_connect_pb:Button;

  // Private vars
  private var m_nc:NetConnection;
  private var m_serverName:String, m_appName:String;
  private var m_prefix:String;

  function AuthConnect (Void) {
    m_prefix = "AuthConnect.GateKeeper.";  // Hardcoded name
```

Example 14-8. The AuthConnect.as client-side class definition (continued)

```
    EventDispatcher.initialize(this);

    attachMovie("Button", "m_connect_pb", 0);
    m_connect_pb._x = 199.3;
    m_connect_pb._y = 25.4;
    m_connect_pb.label = "Connect";
    m_connect_pb.setSize(60,22);

    m_connect_pb.addEventListener("click", this);

    m_nc = new NetConnection( );
    m_nc["owner"] = this;
    m_nc.onStatus = function (p_info:Object):Void {
      trace("nc.onStatus:" + p_info.code);
      if (p_info.code == "NetConnection.Connect.Success")
        this.owner.getUserData( );
      else if (p_info.code == "NetConnection.Connect.Rejected") {
        this.owner.m_feedback_txt.text = p_info.application.message;
      }
      else if (p_info.code == "NetConnection.Connect.Closed") {
        this.owner.dispatchEvent({type:"disconnected"});
      }
    };
  }

  // nc getter
  function get nc ( ):NetConnection {
    return m_nc;
  }

  function setUp (p_serverName:String, p_appName:String) {
    m_serverName = p_serverName;
    m_appName = p_appName;
  }

  // m_connect_pb Button handler
  private function click (p_evt:Object):Void {
    m_feedback_txt.text = "";
    m_nc.connect("rtmp://" + m_serverName + "/" + m_appName,
               m_username_txt.text, m_password_txt.text);
  }

  private function getUserData (Void):Void {
    var res = new Object( );
    res.owner = this;
    res.onResult = function (p_val:Object):Void {
      this.owner.dispatchEvent({type:"connected", userData:p_val});
    };
    m_nc.call(m_prefix + "getUserData", res);
  }
}
```

After importing *Button* and *EventDispatcher*, we define our class as a subclass of *MovieClip* (for simplicity; we could just as well have extended *UIComponent*). We then define a few self-explanatory variables that we are going to need.

In the constructor, we define the m_prefix property. As we will see later, this component is different than other communication components, in that it is first instantiated on the server side and has a well-defined name, independent of what the client-side developer names the AuthConnect component instance on stage. This name is always "GateKeeper".

The rest of the constructor code sets up the Connect button and the NetConnection. When the Connect button is clicked, the *AuthConnect.click( )* method is called. When the connection is accepted, the *AuthConnect.getUserData( )* method is called. If the connection is rejected due to a bad username and/or password, the error message is displayed in the m_feedback_txt text field. If the connection is closed, a *disconnected* event is dispatched.

The next definition is for the getter function for nc. This allows other components to reach within AuthConnect and control the NetConnection directly. As you have seen in the tester application, the Disconnect button uses m_authConnect.nc to disconnect from the server.

Then, we define the *setup( )* method, which saves the server name and the application name into local variables, used by the *click( )* method to connect to the server.

The last method defined is *getUserData( )*, which queries the server side of the Auth-Connect component for more information about the user who just logged in. This information is then attached to the *connected* event that gets dispatched, in the userData field of the event object. Notice how we use m_prefix to route the client-to-server call to the component's server-side instance.

The Server Side of AuthConnect

The server-side code for the AuthConnect component is the trickiest. Consider the following code carefully. It is presented in excerpts with commentary here, but the entire listing is available in a single file (*AuthConnect.asc*) on the book's web site.

As before, we use *try/catch* to ensure that the component's class will be defined only once. Then, we load *netservices.asc*, which is required for Flash Remoting on the server side.

We define our *AuthConnect* class as a subclass of *FCComponent* and call the *init( )* method provided by the framework in its constructor. The constructor also defines an activeUsers associative array, which we use to maintain a list of users who are currently logged in to the application. We also use this array to reject users who are already logged in:

```
try {var dummy = AuthConnect;} catch (e) { // #ifndef AuthConnect
    load("netservices.asc");
```

```
load("components/component.asc");

AuthConnect = function (p_name) {
  this.init(p_name);
  this.activeUsers = new Object();
};

AuthConnect.prototype = new FCComponent("AuthConnect", AuthConnect);

AuthConnect.onConnect = function (p_client, p_username, p_pwd) {
  AuthConnect.instances["GateKeeper"].checkConnect(p_client, p_username, p_pwd);
  // Don't return a value, defer accept or reject to doAccept() and doReject().
};
// The code is continued in the following excerpts.
```

Because of how the component framework is created, we have to define the *onConnect( )* function as a static member of the *AuthConnect* class (that is, it is a class method attached directly to AuthConnect and not an instance method attached to AuthConnect.prototype). For those not familiar with the term, in this context, a *member* is simply a method or property associated with a class or instance.

In *onConnect( )*, we simply defer the decision to accept or reject the user to the *checkConnect( )* function of this class's "GateKeeper" singleton instance.

By not returning either true or false, we leave the client in a pending state. Its fate will be decided asynchronously by the authenticating ColdFusion component.

First, we need to make some assumptions in the ColdFusion component used to authenticate clients. We expect the CFC to return an object of the following form:

- The return object has a code property. A code equal to 0 means a successful connection. Any other code means that the username and password pair is not allowed in the application.

- If the code is 0, we expect the result object to contain a data object, which contains more data for the user who just authenticated successfully. The only required field for the data object is username.

- If the code is not equal to 0, we expect the result object to contain a msg property, which is a string that explains the error condition (such as "unknown user", "wrong password", etc.).

Next we define *AuthConnect.checkConnect( )*, which uses such a CFC to decide whether to accept or reject the connection:

```
AuthConnect.prototype.checkConnect = function (p_client, p_username, p_pwd) {
  var res = new Object();
  res.client = p_client;
  res.owner = this;
  res[this.remotingFunctionName + "_Result"] = function (p_val) {
    if (p_val.code == 0) {
      if (this.owner.activeUsers[p_val.data.username]) {
```

```
         AuthConnect.doReject(this.client, {message:"already logged in"});
      }
      else {
        var cGlobal = this.owner.getClientGlobalStorage(this.client);
        // Used by other components like Chat
        cGlobal.username = p_val.data.username + " " + p_val.data.lastName;
        cGlobal.userData = p_val.data;
        this.owner.activeUsers[p_val.data.username] = true;
        AuthConnect.doAccept(this.client);
      }
    }
    else {
      AuthConnect.doReject(this.client, {message:p_val.msg});
    }
  };
  res[this.remotingFunctionName + "_Status"] = function (p_info) {
    if (p_info.message == undefined)
      p_info.message = "Authenticating Error";
    AuthConnect.doReject(this.client, p_info);
  };
  var service = this.conn.getService(this.remotingServiceName, res);
  service[this.remotingFunctionName](p_username, p_pwd);
  // Don't return until the result arrives from the remoting call.
};
```

We create a callback object, res, and define two handlers on it: the this.
remotingFunctionName+"_Result" handler catches the successful results from the
remoting call, while the this.remotingFunctionName+"_Status" handler is invoked by
Flash Remoting if the call fails. We will see that this.remotingFunctionName is
defined in the *setup( )* method of this component.

In the _Result handler, we check the return object's code property. If the code is 0,
the CFC authenticated the user. If the user is already logged into the application, we
reject the client's connection (using *AuthConnect.doReject( )*, described next). Otherwise, we save the client's user data in the client's global storage (discussed later
under "The Framework's Memory Management") and accept the connection (using
AuthConnect.doAccept( ), described shortly).

If the code returned is not 0, we simply reject the connection, passing the error message directly to the client.

If the _Status handler gets called, the CFC has detected a problem. In this case, we
are forced to reject the connection. Notice how we pass the error object straight to
the client, so that the UI can show some descriptive error to the user.

Last, *checkConnect( )* performs the actual Flash Remoting call, passing the username
and password as parameters.

Now let's look at the *doAccept( )* and *doReject( )* methods, which follow the preceding code:

```
// Called by the remoting result object
AuthConnect.doAccept = function (p_client) {
  gFrameworkFC.application.requestAcceptConnection(p_client, this);
};
AuthConnect.doReject = function (p_client, p_errObj) {
  p_client.__ERROBJ__ = p_errObj;
  gFrameworkFC.application.requestRejectConnection(p_client, this);
};
```

First of all, notice that *doAccept( )* and *doReject( )* are defined as static (i.e., class) methods of the *AuthConnect* class, attached directly to AuthConnect, not AuthConnect. prototype. This is also dictated by the component framework. Simply calling *application.acceptConnection( )* or *application.rejectConnection( )* from within *checkConnection( )* wouldn't have worked; the framework expects static methods to run equivalent code.

That's precisely what *doAccept( )* and *doReject( )* do: they call either *requestAcceptConnection( )* or *requestRejectConnection( )* on the framework. This will put an end to the "pending" condition of the client and either accept or reject the connection. After these calls (and assuming no other authenticating component is running at the same time), the *NetConnection.onStatus( )* handler is invoked on the client side. The *onStatus( )* handler receives an info object with a code property of either "NetConnection.Connect.Success" or "NetConnection.Connect.Rejected".

The remainder of the component's code is pretty simple:

```
// This is called when a client disconnects.
AuthConnect.prototype.onDisconnect = function (p_client) {
  // Remove from table
  var name = this.getClientGlobalStorage(p_client).userData.username;
  this.activeUsers[name] = false;
  // Need to call this at the end since we are overriding the base onDisconnect().
  this.releaseLocalStorage(p_client);
};

// Called by each client upon successful connect.
AuthConnect.prototype.getUserData = function (p_client) {
  return this.getClientGlobalStorage(p_client).userData;
};
```

The *onDisconnect( )* method is called automatically by the framework whenever a user disconnects. We clear the user's slot in the activeUsers table and call *releaseLocalStorage( )*, just as any well-behaved communication component should do.

The *getUserData( )* method is the first one called by the client side, as soon as a user is accepted, to get more information about the user.

With us so far? Let's look at the remaining elements, which complete the *AuthConnect.asc* file listing.

The last method we define is the *setUp( )* method we called in the *main.asc*. In it, we create a remoting connection to the ColdFusion Flash Remoting gateway of choice, and we save the CFC's name and function name so that we can use them in *check-Connect( )*.

The last thing we do before ending the *catch* directive is create a singleton server-side instance of this class, with the name "GateKeeper". This bypasses the lazy instantiation provided by the framework, and gives us a way to address the component immediately, whether for calling *setUp( )* on it or to respond to *onConnect( )* invocations.

```
AuthConnect.prototype.setUp = function (p_remotingServerName,
                  p_remotingServiceName, p_remotingFunctionName) {
  this.conn = NetServices.createGatewayConnection("http://" +
              p_remotingServerName + "/flashservices/gateway");
  this.remotingServiceName = p_remotingServiceName;
  this.remotingFunctionName = p_remotingFunctionName;
};
AuthConnect.create("GateKeeper");  // Create the singleton
trace("AuthConnect loaded successfully.");
} // #endif
```

A Sample CFC to Use with AuthConnect

The last piece of the puzzle is the ColdFusion component that does the authentication. Creating a full-fledged CFC that queries a database to do authentication is beyond the scope of this chapter, but the following code could be used as a starting point and for testing. See Chapter 12 for ColdFusion code that performs such a database query and authentication:

```
<cfcomponent>
  <cffunction name="authenticateUser" access="remote" returnType="struct">
    <cfargument name="p_username" type="string" default="" required="true">
    <cfargument name="p_password" type="string" default="" required="true">

    // Do your database query here to validate the user's credential.
    // Hardcoding two users for testing.
    <cfif #p_username# IS "peldi">
      <cfif #p_password# IS "pwd">
        <cfset res["code"]=0>
        <cfset userData=StructNew( )>
        <cfset userData["username"]="Giacomo">
        <cfset userData["lastName"]="Guilizzoni">
        <cfset res["data"]=userData>
      <cfelse>
        <cfset res["code"]=-2>
        <cfset res["msg"]="Wrong Password">
      </cfif>
    <cfelseif #p_username# IS "brian">
      <cfif #p_password# IS "pwd">
        <cfset res["code"]=0>
        <cfset userData=StructNew( )>
```

```
        <cfset userData["username"]="Brian">
        <cfset userData["lastName"]="Lesser">
        <cfset res["data"]=userData>
     <cfelse>
        <cfset res["code"]=-2>
        <cfset res["msg"]="Wrong Password">
     </cfif>
   <cfelse>
     <cfset res["code"]=-1>
     <cfset res["msg"]="Unknown user">
   </cfif>
   <cfreturn #res#>
 </cffunction>
</cfcomponent>
```

The code is fairly self-explanatory. If the username is "peldi" or "brian" and the password is "pwd", it authenticates the client and returns the data for the user.

We realize that the authentication process described in this section may be a little hard to understand at first. We encourage you to read the rest of the chapter and come back to it if you need to.

As always, the code provided for the AuthConnect component should be considered as nothing more than a starting point. One obvious improvement would be to decouple the remoting call from the *AuthConnect.asc*, so that you can use remoting, a server-side-only shared object, or any other method for authenticating.

Integrating Components with Your Existing Applications

In the previous sections, you learned how communication components work, how to modify existing ones, and how to create new ones.

In this section, we talk about how to integrate communication components into applications that are not fully "componentized" (i.e., applications that have some code in the *main.asc* or in other libraries that are not communication components).

The onConnectAccept and onConnectReject Events

One of the features of the framework is the ability for developers to create authenticating components, such as the one covered in this chapter. This feature allows each component to have a vote as to whether a client's connection should be accepted or rejected. The framework automatically tallies each component's decision and allows a client to connect only if all the components decided to allow the connection.

If you are not using the framework, you can execute code right after calling *application.acceptConnection( )* or *application.rejectConnection( )*. However, if using the framework, because the decision is now shared among all the components that are

---

586 | Chapter 14: Understanding the Macromedia Component Framework

loaded, code following acceptance/rejection of the connection needs to be moved to two new event handlers introduced by the framework: *application.onConnectAccept()* and *application.onConnectReject()*.

Here's an example of an *onConnect()* handler defined in an application's *main.asc* file, as it would appear if not using the framework:

```
application.onConnect = function (newClient, arg1, arg2) {
  // ...some code here.
  if (someCondition == true) {
    // Accept the connection.
    this.acceptConnection(newClient);

    // Code to execute upon acceptance.
  }
  else {
    // Reject the connection.
    this.rejectConnection(newClient);

    // Code to execute upon rejection.
  }
};
```

When the application includes the framework, however, it introduces explicit *onConnectAccept* and *onConnectReject* events. Hence, the preceding code would change to:

```
load("components.asc");

application.onConnect = function (newClient, arg1, arg2) {
  if (someCondition == true)
    this.acceptConnection(newClient);  // Vote to accept the connection.
  else
    this.rejectConnection(newClient);  // Vote to reject the connection.

  // No additional code here; instead,
  // use the functions described below.
};

application.onConnectAccept = function (newClient, arg1, arg2) {
  // Code to execute upon acceptance.
};

application.onConnectReject = function (newClient, arg1, arg2) {
  // Code to execute upon rejection.
};
```

Authentication issues should not affect most applications. You need to modify only applications that explicitly have logic that follows an explicit *acceptConnection()* or *rejectConnection()* call. Such logic should be moved to *onConnectAccept()* or *onConnectReject()*, as shown in the preceding example.

Referencing a Component Instance in main.asc

Another common thing to do when using communication components is to call methods on their server-side code. The most common example is when you want to clear the chat history in a Chat component's instance. The *clearHistory( )* method is available only on the server side, so we need a way to call it from within our *main.asc* file.

Let's assume the Chat instance name is chat1_mc. This is how you'd call *clearHistory( )* on it from *main.asc*:

```
FCChat.instances.chat1_mc.clearHistory();
```

 Each server-side class maintains an instances property from which you can access all server-side instances of the class.

For example, the *FCChat* class has a static property named instances that contains all the server-side class instances. They are named after what you called the component on the client side. So in our case, we use chat1_mc. Once you have addressed the server-side class instance (FCChat.instances.chat1_mc), all you have to do is call the *clearHistory( )* method on it.

As we will see later, this follows the naming scheme that is such an important part of the framework.

Server-Side Events

Starting with FlashCom 1.5 (and updated with some bug fixes in updater 1.5.2), the Macromedia component framework was enhanced to provide a simple event mechanism.

The event mechanism supports both a *throw* model and a *watch* model. With the throw mechanism, components can dispatch events for other scripts to catch. In the watch mechanism, events are not thrown by a component. Rather, each component modifies its own property values and other scripts (components or not) can listen to changes to such properties.

Here's an example of the watch model. The following is a simple component, which we will call ComponentA:

```
try {var dummy = ComponentA;} catch (e) { // #ifndef ComponentA
  load("components/component.asc");

ComponentA = function (p_name) {
  this.init(p_name);
  this.currentValue = 0;
  this.theInt = setInterval(this, "updateProperty", 5000);
};
```

```
ComponentA.prototype = new FCComponent("ComponentA", ComponentA);

// The first method called by a client component.
ComponentA.prototype.connect = function (p_client) {
};

ComponentA.prototype.updateProperty = function () {
  this.currentValue++;
};

trace("ComponentA loaded successfully.");
} // #endif
```

This very simple component has a property named currentValue, which is incremented every 5 seconds by a simple interval.

Now imagine that there are two instances of ComponentA—named instance1_mc and instance2_mc—on the Stage of a sample application.

Now imagine that a *main.asc* script wants to be notified whenever currentValue of instance1_mc gets updated. In other words, the script would like to catch the event represented by the property change of currentValue. Here's how you could write your *main.asc*:

```
load("components.asc");
load("ComponentA.asc");

var listenerObj = new Object();
listenerObj.onPropertyChange = function (p_eventSource, p_eventData) {
  trace("onPropertyChange: " + p_eventSource.name + "."
      + p_eventData.name + " is now "
      + p_eventData.newValue + " (was "
      + p_eventData.oldValue + ")");
};

ComponentA.instances.instance1_mc.addListener("currentValue", listenerObj);
```

First we load the component; then we set up an event catcher (listener) object, with an *onPropertyChange( )* method defined on it. Finally, we tell the framework that we want to listen to changes of the property called "currentValue" on the instance1_mc instance of the *ComponentA* class (note the uses of the static instances property).

Now whenever currentValue is updated, the *onPropertyChange( )* method of listenerObj will be triggered, with two parameters. The first, p_eventSource, is a reference to the component instance instance1_mc, so that you could call methods on it or check other properties of it.

The second, more interesting parameter is an object with three properties:

name

> The name of the property that changed (you can use the same listener object for more than one property)

oldValue
> The old value of the property that changed

newValue
> The new value of the property that changed

What if you wanted to listen to changes of currentValue in both instances of ComponentA?

You could do this to listen to both the instance1_mc and instance2_mc instances:

```
ComponentA.instances.instance1_mc.addListener("currentValue", listenerObj);
ComponentA.instances.instance2_mc.addListener("currentValue", listenerObj);
```

Or you could use another syntax provided by the framework. The following triggers *onPropertyChange( )* on listenerObj whenever the currentValue property changes in any instance of ComponentA. This is also handy when you don't know the names of the instances of a certain component (when this syntax is used, listenerObj is known as a "class-wide listener"):

```
ComponentA.addListener("currentValue", listenerObj);
```

The framework also provides the *sendUserEvent( )* method so you can throw your own custom events, as shown here, instead of just automatically triggering *onPropertyChange( )* on the listener objects:

```
chat1.onMyFooEvent = gOnEvent;
chat1.onMyBarEvent = gOnEvent;
cursor1.addListener("MyFooEvent", chat1);
FCCursor.addListener("MyBarEvent", chat1);

cursor1.sendUserEvent("MyFooEvent", "Hello Foo");
FCCursor.sendUserEvent("MyBarEvent", "Hello Bar");
```

These two mechanisms for throwing and catching events should be powerful enough to be used within your scripts or your other components. Nonetheless, more and more Flash developers are standardizing on the *EventDispatcher* class (*mx.events. EventDispatcher*), a client-side class introduced with the v2 UI components architecture. The class is small, clean, and elegant. An explanation of the *EventDispatcher* class is out of the context of this book, but you can find a lot of documentation about it online. Example 14-9 provides a port of the *EventDispatcher* class to Server-Side ActionScript for you to use in your server-side code. Note that the "@param" syntax used in some of the comments is used by JavaDoc to automatically generate documentation.

Example 14-9. Server-side port of the EventDispatcher class

```
/* EventDispatcher
 * ported to ASC by Giacomo 'Peldi' Guilizzoni - http://www.peldi.com/blog/
 */
EventDispatcher = function () {
};
```

Example 14-9. Server-side port of the EventDispatcher class (continued)

```
// Internal function for removing listeners
EventDispatcher.prototype._removeEventListener = function (queue, event, handler) {
  if (queue != undefined) {
    var l = queue.length;
    var i;
    for (i = 0; i < l; i++) {
      var o = queue[i];
      if (o == handler) {
        queue.splice(i, 1);
        return;
      }
    }
  }
};
// Make it static by attaching it directly to EventDispatcher
EventDispatcher._removeEventListener =
  EventDispatcher.prototype._removeEventListener;

/* Add listening and dispatching methods to an object
 * @param object - the object to receive the methods
 */
EventDispatcher.prototype.initialize = function (object) {
  // This part of the original client-side EventDispatcher code is not used in SSAS.
  /* Creating the instance at the bottom instead
  if (_fEventDispatcher == undefined) {
    _fEventDispatcher = new EventDispatcher();
  }*/
  object.addEventListener = _fEventDispatcher.addEventListener;
  object.removeEventListener = _fEventDispatcher.removeEventListener;
  object.dispatchEvent = _fEventDispatcher.dispatchEvent;
  object.dispatchQueue = _fEventDispatcher.dispatchQueue;
};

// Make it static
EventDispatcher.initialize = EventDispatcher.prototype.initialize;

// Internal function for dispatching events
EventDispatcher.prototype.dispatchQueue = function (queueObj, eventObj) {
  var queueName = "__q_" + eventObj.type;
  var queue = queueObj[queueName];
  if (queue != undefined) {
    var i;
    // Loop it as an object so it resists people removing listeners during
    // dispatching
    for (i in queue) {
      var o = queue[i];
      var oType = typeof(o);

      // A handler can be a function, object, or movie clip
      if (oType == "object" || oType == "movieclip") {
        // This is a backdoor implementation that
        // is not compliant with the standard
```

Example 14-9. Server-side port of the EventDispatcher class (continued)

```
        if (o.handleEvent == undefined) {
          o[eventObj.type](eventObj);
        }
        else {   // This is the DOM3 way
          o.handleEvent(eventObj);
        }
      }
      else {    // It is a function
        o.apply(queueObj, [eventObj]);
      }
    }
  }
};

/* Dispatch the event to all listeners
 * @param eventObj - an instance of Event or one of its subclasses
 *                   describing the event
 */
EventDispatcher.prototype.dispatchEvent = function (eventObj) {
  if (eventObj.target == undefined)
    eventObj.target = this;

  if (this[eventObj.type + "Handler"] != undefined)
    this[eventObj.type + "Handler"](eventObj);

  // Dispatch to objects that are registered as listeners for this object.
  this.dispatchQueue(this, eventObj);
};

/* Add a listener for a particular event
 * @param event - the name of the event ("click", "change", etc.)
 * @param handler - the function or object that should be called
 */
EventDispatcher.prototype.addEventListener = function (event, handler) {
  var queueName = "__q_" + event;
  if (this[queueName] == undefined) {
    this[queueName] = new Array();
  }
  // Not supported in SSAS so comment it out. We don't need it.
  //_global.ASSetPropFlags(this, queueName,1);

  EventDispatcher._removeEventListener(this[queueName], event, handler);
  this[queueName].push(handler);
};

/* Remove a listener for a particular event
 * @param event - the name of the event ("click", "change", etc.)
 * @param handler - the function or object that should be called
 */
EventDispatcher.prototype.removeEventListener = function (event, handler) {
  var queueName = "__q_" + event;
  EventDispatcher._removeEventListener(this[queueName], event, handler);
```

Example 14-9. Server-side port of the EventDispatcher class (continued)

```
};

_fEventDispatcher = new EventDispatcher();
```

Understanding the Framework

The component framework comprises nearly 600 lines of code (not counting the components' code), which was never documented. It's no wonder some developers decided to shy away from it and develop their own framework!

As we've seen throughout the chapter, to load one or more external *.asc* files, use the *load( )* command in your application, such as *main.asc*:

```
load("components.asc");
```

An *.asc* file can load other *.asc* files. For example, loading *components.asc* is really just a shortcut to loading *framework.asc* and many other components cited within it. You can load the framework and only those components you want (such as the Chat), as follows:

```
load("framework.asc");
load("components/chat.asc");
```

The Framework's Files

Let's look at the files that make up the server-side framework. For a detailed description of each file, refer to "The Framework's Code," later in this chapter. Here's a brief description of all the files that make up the server-side framework:

components.asc

> A very simple file that loads the *framework.asc* and every communication component that ships with FlashCom. You can add a *load( )* statement to automatically load your own custom components as well. Loading *components.asc* is easy but is overkill if you need only one or two components.

framework.asc

> This constitutes the framework itself and is where the global gFrameworkFC singleton—one of two main pillars of the component framework—is defined. The gFrameworkFC stores references to each component's instances, along with the components' clientGlobals memory space, as discussed later. This file automatically loads *application.asc* and *facade.asc* as well.

application.asc

> This file is necessary for the framework. This is where the framework hijacks the application object to enhance it with some framework-specific functionality.

facade.asc

> This file is in charge of method routing and lazy instantiation of server-side components. This is the second pillar of the framework.

component.asc

> This is the base class for all server-side components (and should not be confused with *component.asc* mentioned earlier). It defines some common variables (such as `prefix` and `callPrefix`) and handles event dispatching for intracomponent communications.

The Framework's Data Structures

Before diving into the framework's code, it helps to understand three fundamental aspects of the framework:

- Everything is based on a naming scheme.
- The `gFrameworkFC.components` data structure stores references to component classes, indexed by component type.
- Every client-to-server call has to go through the server-side *Client* object and is therefore attached to `Client.prototype` or one of its subproperties.

Keeping these in mind will make the code much easier to understand.

Everything is based on a naming scheme

A key decision in the creation of the framework was to come up with a naming scheme that would uniquely identify component classes, instances, and methods. The result was this general format for naming:

```
ComponentClassTypeName.ComponentInstanceName.ComponentMethodName
```

So, for example, to call the *sendMessage( )* method on the instance named `chat1_mc` of the FCChat component, the naming scheme is:

```
FCChat.chat1_mc.sendMessage()
```

As you will see, this naming scheme is the basis of most of the architectural decisions made during the creation of the framework.

The gFrameworkFC.components data structure

Understanding how component references are stored within the framework is key to understanding its code. As an example, let's see how a reference to an instance of the FCChat component named `chat1_mc` is stored in the framework. Here we navigate down the dot-delimited data structure in a progression:

`gFrameworkFC`

> The global framework singleton.

```
gFrameworkFC.components
```
An array indexed by component type.

```
gFrameworkFC.components.FCChat
```
A reference to the *FCChat* class (extended from *FCComponent*).

```
gFrameworkFC.components.FCChat.instances
```
An array of references to instances of the *FCChat* class.

```
gFrameworkFC.components.FCChat.instances.chat1_mc
```
A single instance of the *FCChat* class named chat1_mc. This is what you can invoke methods on.

As you can see, gFrameworkFC stores the class type name first, then the instance name, and then the method name. So, for example, if you want to call *clearHistory( )* on our sample chat1_mc instance from your *main.asc* code, you could use:

```
gFrameworkFC.components.FCChat.instances.chat1_mc.clearHistory( )
```

Of course, typically you'll have a shorter, more convenient reference to a given instance:

```
var chat1 = gFrameworkFC.components.FCChat.instances.chat1_mc;
chat1.clearHistory( );
```

This is just a general purpose way to access any instance to demonstrate how instances are stored in gFrameworkFC.

The Client.prototype data structures

Because of how FlashCom Server is built, every client-to-server call has to go through the server-side *Client* object. Because of this, the component framework needs to define a way to route components' calls from the *Client* object to the appropriate component's class instance. Such routing is established in *facade.asc*, based on the naming scheme described earlier. The end result is a collection of objects attached to the *Client* object, described as follows:

```
Client.prototype
```
The *Client* object's prototype, through which all client-to-server calls automatically pass. Through some fancy "__resolve" mechanism (we'll look at this later when we analyze *facade.asc),* the following other data structures are attached to it.

```
Client.prototype.FCChat
```
An instance of *FCFactory*, a class that generates class instances and saves them in gFrameworkFC.components.FCChat.instances.

```
Client.prototype.FCChat.chat1_mc
```
An instance of *FCFacade*, a class that grabs method invocations and attaches a reference to the *Client* object as the first parameter to them before delivering them to the appropriate class instance.

In this case, the names of the variables attached to the Client object can be misleading. For instance, Client.prototype.FCChat is an instance of the *FCFactory* class (not of the *FCChat* class, as you might think at first). Similarly, Client.prototype.FCChat. chat1_mc, is an instance of *FCFacade*.

We will analyze the code that generates these data structures and wires them together when we discuss *facade.asc*.

The Framework's Memory Management

Another important part of the framework is its set of APIs that supports data structures for the components. During the lifetime of a component instance, it typically needs to manipulate and access different kinds of data, classified as follows:

Globals
> Shared across all component instances, regardless of their type, and all users. Any item placed under, or made a member of, gFrameworksFC qualifies as a global.

Client globals
> Distinct for each client but shared across all components. These require special support from the framework. Components extending the base *FCComponent* class inherit the *getClientGlobalStorage( )* method through which the client global area may be accessed. An example of a property that should be a client global is userColor, which is unique for each user but is used by every component in the application.

Component globals
> Shared across all component instances of a given type. Achieved by attaching the items to the component's constructor function (class) object. As such, there is no need for any special support from the framework. These are basically static variables on the component class. An example of a component global could be currentSpeaker, a variable accessed by all the instances of a component, but attached to the class directly, not to the instances of the class.

Client locals
> These are unique to each component instance for each connected client. Like client globals, these require special support from the framework; all components extending the base *FCComponent* class inherit the *getClientLocalStorage( )* method that you can use to access the client local area.

Component locals
> These are unique to a given component instance and are simply the member variables of a component instance.

How Components Are Registered and Instantiated

Component registration occurs when the application loads. For example, the *chat.asc* component loads *component.asc*, which takes care of the registration of the component with the framework (calling *registerComponent( )* on *framework.asc*).

Registration consists of two parts:

- Adding the component as a listener to the gFrameworkFC.application broadcaster
- Saving the class name in the gFrameworkFC.components array so that the method name resolution mechanism can find it

Server-side components are usually instantiated *lazily*, meaning only as needed. When the client-side portion of a component calls into its server-side portion, the framework determines whether the call is valid, instantiates the server-side portion if necessary, and dispatches the call appropriately. Although this is the default component behavior, you can turn it off on a per-component basis. Bypassing lazy instantiation is useful for components that must use singletons with well-known names (such as the "GateKeeper" instance of *AuthConnect* described earlier in this chapter).

The Framework's Method Routing

The framework's built-in method routing mechanism enables the client-side portion of a component instance to call its server-side portion in a reliable manner. Conceptually, the framework intercepts remote calls arriving at the *Client* object (on the server), inspects the name of the call, and looks up and routes it to the appropriate server-side component instance, instantiating it if necessary. The actual implementation of this process is based on the "__resolve" mechanism (discussed later under "Analyzing facade.asc") and is optimized so that the lookup happens no more than once for any given component method. Server-to-client calls are a little simpler and are implemented by inserting an object chain on the *NetConnection* object. For example, if foo1 is an instance of the Foo component, nc.Foo.foo1 is set up to point to foo1 (where nc is the *NetConnection* object).

The Framework's Code

To finish our overview of the Macromedia component framework, we analyze the details of the files that make up the framework.

To be able to fully follow the next sections, either print out the framework files from your FlashCom Server's *scriptlib* installation folder or open them up in a text editor and look at them on your monitor.

Analyzing components.asc

The *components.asc* file is the simplest of the framework's files. It simply provides a shortcut to load the framework and all the components that ship with FlashCom Server. Its name is easy to remember, and it allows developers to write just one line of server-side code to build a wide variety of applications that use the framework:

```
load("components.asc");
```

Its code consists of numerous *load( )* commands followed by a *trace( )* to indicate it is done.

Analyzing framework.asc

The *framework.asc* file, which is loaded automatically by *components.asc*, creates the global framework singleton object, named gFrameworkFC. This object stores references to all the component instances and other memory management methods for the components to use.

Let's look at the code. First, we create the gFrameworkFC object.

The next function, *__toarray__( )*, is a utility function that simply converts the arguments object into an array and returns the array.

Next, the *framework.asc* loads two other *.asc* files that we'll discuss later:

```
load("application.asc");
load("facade.asc");
```

The framework also provides a unique ID to each client connected to the application, by incrementing a counter (nextClientID) each time a client connects.

Next, the code defines gFrameworkFC.clientGlobals as a new object. It is an associative array with indexes of client.__ID__, which is the unique ID that the framework assigns to each client. Each slot of gFrameworkFC.clientGlobals is also an object that contains client global variables. An example of a client global is the client's chosen userColor or username. These values change for each client but are global to all components. The *getClientGlobals( )* function defined in *framework.asc* simply returns the appropriate slot of gFrameworkFC.clientGlobals given a reference to a client object.

Next, *framework.asc* defines gFrameworkFC.components. This property is also an associative array, with indexes represented by component class names. It contains a slot for each component type, and each slot contains a reference to that component's class.

The next function in *framework.asc* is *registerComponent( )*, which is called by each component to tell the framework that "a new component type is in town!" (you'll see how *component.asc*, the base class, calls this during *init( )*).

The *registerComponent( )* function takes two parameters, a string containing the name of the component class (for example, "FCChat") and a reference to the actual component class, such as FCChat without the quotes. This function's main job is to save the reference to the component class in gFrameworkFC.components.

Next, *registerComponent( )* sets up the component class as a listener to gFrameworkFC.application, which is a wrapper for the application object, defined in *application.asc*, which we discuss later. For now, the *addListener( )* call means that whenever Flash-Com gets an event on the application object (such as *onAppStart* or *onConnect*), it dispatches it to this component's class as well.

Finally, *registerComponent( )* defines *onAppStop( )* and *onDisconnect( )* handlers on the component class itself as static methods (note the absence of .prototype). These methods dispatch the *onAppStop* or *onDisconnect* messages to all the component's instances. Because *onAppStop( )* can return false to prevent the application from stopping, the *onAppStop( )* static method returns the logical AND (&&) of the results from each instance's *onAppStop( )* handler. Therefore, if any *onAppStop( )* handler returns false, the application is not stopped. (If all *onAppStop( )* handlers return true, it means "OK, go ahead and garbage collect this application.")

This mechanism means you should not define a static *onDisconnect( )* or *onAppStop( )* method on your class, because it will be overridden. Instead, define them on the class's prototype, and they will get called on each instance at the appropriate times.

That concludes the discussion of *framework.asc*. Now let's look at how *application.asc* enhances the framework with gFrameworkFC.application, and what it is.

Analyzing application.asc

The *application.asc* file is probably the most complex piece of the framework, so let's look at it in detail. This file defines how the framework traps the default events that the application singleton receives from FlashCom and dispatches them to the different components. The *application.asc* file is loaded automatically by *framework.asc*, which is in turn loaded by *components.asc*.

The goal of *application.asc* is to hijack the application object and wrap it in another object, which is a subclass of application. We'll see what this means later.

For now, let's look at the first two-thirds of the code in *application.asc*, which holds no surprises.

First, *application.asc* creates a reference to the application object and saves it in gFrameworkFC.application. Now repeat this mantra at least three times before you go on: "When I see gFrameworkFC.application in the following code, I will just think of it as a shortcut to the good old application object that I know and love."

Done? Great. Let's move on.

The next thing *application.asc* does is:

```
application = null;
```

Don't panic: you didn't just break FlashCom Server. The application property was just a reference, a shortcut that was automatically created for us by FlashCom. We can safely delete this reference without the memory it points to being garbage collected because we stored another reference to the application object in gFrameworkFC.application, remember?

Next, *application.asc* simply enhances the application reference stored in gFrameworkFC.application with some methods and properties that are useful to the framework. This is no different than doing the following in your *main.asc*:

```
application.onConnect = function ( ) {...};
application.myVariable = 3;
```

except *application.asc* uses gFrameworkFC.application instead of application (which, again, points to the same FlashCom object).

Next, *application.asc* adds some event-listening mechanisms with nextListenerID, a listeners associative array (indexed by ID), and *addListener( )* and *removeListener( )* methods. This creates the gFrameworkFC.application.listeners associative array, which we loop through whenever we need to dispatch an event to interested listener objects.

As we have seen in *framework.asc*, each component class calls *addListener( )* in its constructor (when it calls *init( )* on the base class, which in turn calls *registerComponent( )* on gFrameworkFC). This assures that each component class receives all the events that gFrameworkFC.application dispatches to it.

Next, *application.asc* defines the standard *onAppStart( )* and *onAppStop( )* handlers, which FlashCom calls on application (now saved in gFrameworkFC.application) automatically.

The *application.asc* file's implementation of *onAppStart( )* loops through all the listeners and invokes *onAppStart( )* on them, if they have it defined. We need to test for the existence of *onAppStart( )* on the component class because Server-Side ActionScript will complain with a runtime error if you call a method on a class that doesn't define it (client-side ActionScript 2.0 can perform compile-time checking for non-dynamic classes, but I wish it had similar runtime checking).

The *onAppStop( )* handler is very similar to *onAppStart( )*, in that it loops through all the listeners and calls *onAppStop( )* on them, tallying the results before returning. The interesting part here is that, as we have seen in *framework.asc*, the *onAppStop( )* method attached to a component class also loops through all its component instances.

So imagine you have two instances of the Chat component, chat1_mc and chat2_mc, in your movie. On the server side, this means that both gFrameworkFC.components. FCChat.instances.chat1_mc and gFrameworkFC.components.FCChat.instances.chat2_mc are defined.

So when FlashCom calls *onAppStop( )* on gFrameworkFC.application, the handler will call *onAppStop( )* on FCChat, which in turn will call *onAppStop( )* on chat1_mc and chat2_mc.

The next method defined on the gFrameworkFC.application object is *onDisconnect( )*. This method also has a "double-loop" effect, calling *onDisconnect( )* on all the component classes, with each class calling *onDisconnect( )* on all of its instances. Then, *onDisconnect( )* cleans up the clientGlobals for the client that just disconnected, to clean up memory.

The next method defined in *application.asc*, *onStatus( )*, simply invokes *onStatus( )* on all registered components that have it defined. The *onStatus( )* method defined here is invoked when FlashCom calls *onStatus( )* on the application object (this is very similar to *gFrameworkFC.application.onAppStart( )*, seen earlier).

The next method defined in *application.asc*, *gFrameworkFC.application.onConnect( )*, is more complex. FlashCom calls it automatically whenever a new client connects. Remember that FlashCom doesn't accept or reject a client until *application.acceptClient( )* or *application.rejectClient( )* is called. This allows developers to perform authentication asynchronously, for example by connecting to a database through Flash Remoting (as seen earlier with the AuthConnect component). Also, *application.acceptClient( )* and *application.rejectClient( )* can be called by any method in your application, not just *onConnect( )* (it's not like *onAppStop( )*, in which the return value of the function tells FlashCom what to do).

With these concepts clear in our minds, we can look at the *gFrameworkFC.application.onConnect( )* handler.

First it assigns an unique ID (client.__ID__) to the client that just connected. Then it creates the clientGlobals object on gFrameworkFC to hold this client's global variables (username, userColor, and whatever component developers want to store in it).

The code also assigns a __RESPONSE__ object to the client object that just connected. This is an associative array indexed by the listener ID of each component class. Basically, this is a table of what each component has decided to do with this client: each slot can have one of four values:

true
    Indicates the component has accepted the client
false
    Indicates the component wants to reject the client

Indicates the component is still undecided, maybe because it's running some asynchronous authentication code

undefined

Indicates the component doesn't have an *onConnect( )* handler

 The *onConnect( )* code in *application.asc* was not cleaned up as much as it could have been. You can safely ignore *var response*, as it's never used anywhere else. You should also ignore the client._PROCESSING_ property; Server-Side ActionScript is single-threaded and *onConnect( )* is synchronous, so at the end of its execution, _PROCESSING_ is always false.

Next, the code saves the arguments to *onConnect( )* into the client._ARGUMENTS_ array (using the private *gFrameworkFC._toArray_( )* method to convert them from an object). Then, the code loops through all the components registered with the framework and calls *onConnect( )* on them, if they have it defined.

Note that gFrameworkFC does not define a static *onConnect( )* method on the component class, so you'll have to define it on the class (and not on the class's prototype) yourself if you want to have one.

If a component does not define an *onConnect( )* handler, its result is assumed to be true, which makes sense. The way the framework does it, though, is a bit tricky. If the component doesn't have *onConnect( )* defined, the loop's *continue* statement will leave an empty slot in the client._RESPONSE_ table. (This works because, when *dispatchConnectionStatus( )* loops through the client._RESPONSE_ table with a *for...in* loop, it skips slots that have never been defined, but not slots that have been set to null.)

If a component's *onConnect( )* handler returns synchronously (with true, false, or null), the value is saved in the client._RESPONSE_ table slot for that component, with this code:

```
if (client._RESPONSE_[this.listeners[i]._LID_] == null)
  client._RESPONSE_[this.listeners[i]._LID_] = null;

if (status != null)
  client._RESPONSE_[this.listeners[i]._LID_] = status;
```

The first test sets the default value to null (and creates the slot in the table at the same time). The second test sets the value to true or false if a component's *onConnect( )* handler returned a value.

Finally, *onConnect( )* calls *dispatchConnectStatus( )* for that client, which tallies all the responses and decides what to do.

The next two methods are defined for those authenticating components that want to accept or reject a client asynchronously. Such components must define an *onConnect( )* method with an empty *return;* statement at the end, with no return value. This will set the corresponding slot in the client._RESPONSE_ table to null, to indicate that a result is pending (in *dispatchConnectStatus( )*, described later).

When the component has decided whether to allow the connection (because the database has returned a value after attempting to authenticate the user), it can notify the framework of its decision by invoking *requestAcceptConnection( )* or *requestRejectConnection( )*.

Each method updates the client._RESPONSE_ table with the required result and calls *dispatchConnectStatus( )* to ask the framework to count all the responses again.

We will see later that these two methods are wrapped in *acceptClient( )* and *rejectClient( )*, methods that every component developer already knows how to use.

The *dispatchConnectStatus( )* method is how the framework counts all the components' responses to the *onConnect* request for a specific client. Basically, it checks whether there are any components that are still deciding what to do by looking at the value of each slot in the client._RESPONSE_ table. If there are still pending components, the method returns without doing anything (small thing: the code here could be optimized by returning as soon as a pending status is found, instead of counting all the other responses). When every component has made a decision, if even a single one has decided to reject the client, the connection is rejected by calling *dispatchConnectReject( )*. Otherwise, the client is accepted by calling *dispatchConnectAccept( )*.

The last two methods that *application.asc* attaches to the gFrameworkFC.application object (remember, it's still a reference to the good old application object that you know and love) are *dispatchConnectAccept( )* and *dispatchConnectReject( )*. They are wrappers around the *application.acceptConnection( )* and *application.rejectConnection( )* methods, but do a little more.

The *dispatchConnectAccept( )* method calls *this.acceptConnection(client)*, which accepts the connection. Next, it loops through the component instances and calls *onConnectAccept( )* on each one. (The *onConnectAccept( )* method was introduced by the framework to allow for authenticating components, as described earlier in this chapter.)

The *dispatchConnectReject( )* method is very similar but has the ability to pass an error message (whatever is stored in client._ERROBJ_) back to the client. The error is passed to *NetConnection.onStatus( )* as a property of the info object passed in as a parameter (info.application.message). Later, we will see how client._ERROBJ_ is populated.

That concludes all the handlers that *application.asc* defines on gFrameworkFC. application. If you repeated the mantra as you were reading the code, you were (hopefully) able to follow so far.

The last part of *application.asc* is where the real magic happens. Let's look at the rest of the code from the bottom up.

The last real line of *application.asc* is:

```
application = new FCApplication();
```

This is not bad. We create a reference, named application, pointing to an instance of the *FCApplication* class. Any method invoked on application should be a method defined for the *FCApplication* class. Nothing too strange here. We've done it a million times.

Now let's look at the line that precedes it:

```
FCApplication.prototype = gFrameworkFC.application;
```

Don't panic. This is simply prototype-based inheritance as is necessary in Server-Side ActionScript to establish a subclass. It simply establishes the *FCApplication* class as a subclass of gFrameworkFC.application; as such, the subclass inherits all the methods and properties defined on the superclass.

 This inheritance means that all the handlers, methods, and properties that are defined on gFrameworkFC.application are available to instances of the *FCApplication* class.

Let's not forget that FlashCom automatically invokes handlers on the object that's saved in gFrameworkFC.application. By performing this subclassing and instantiation, any application that defines *application.onAppStart( )* and *application.onAppStop( )* handlers defines them only on the instance of the *FCApplication* class named application, not on the object that FlashCom Server calls (which is, once again, gFrameworkFC.application).

Why do this? We explain it with the last bit of magic, which is the constructor for the *FCApplication* class:

```
// FCApplication class inherits and wraps the actual application object.
FCApplication = function () {
  // Hide the following members.
  this.addListener = null;
  this.removeListener = null;
  this.requestAcceptConnection = null;
  this.requestRejectConnection = null;

  // Set up ourselves as a listener on the actual application object.
  gFrameworkFC.application.addListener(this);

  // Clear all the events.
```

```
      this.onConnect = null;
      this.onConnectAccept = null;
      this.onConnectReject = null;
      this.onDisconnect = null;
      this.onAppStart = null;
      this.onAppStop = null;
      this.onStatus = null;

      // Define acceptConnection( ) and rejectConnection( )
      // to request the actual application object.
      this.acceptConnection = function (client) {
        gFrameworkFC.application.requestAcceptConnection(client, this);
      };

      this.rejectConnection = function (client, errObj) {
        client.__ERROBJ__ = errObj;
        gFrameworkFC.application.requestRejectConnection(client, this);
      };
    };
```

Let's look at this gem: it hides some methods, calls *addListener( )*, clears some other methods, and then defines the *acceptConnection( )* and *rejectConnection( )* methods.

Let's look at the *addListener( )* call first:

```
gFrameworkFC.application.addListener(this);
```

Look familiar? It's the same exact call shown in *registerComponent( )* in *framework.asc*! So what are we doing here? We are adding a special kind of listener to gFrameworkFC. application—one that's not a component.

 This particular type of listener will receive *onAppStart*, *onAppStop*, *onConnect*, *onDisconnect*, and *onAppStop* events just as all the other components will. However, it is not a component class, but rather what the developer thinks is the "application" object (see the hijacking?). This allows a developer to write a *main.asc* in the same way regardless of whether he is using the communication component framework.

The code hides methods of the *FCApplication* class that we don't want developers to use (the private ones that we inherited from gFrameworkFC.application), and we clear those other inherited events that we don't want developers to call (such as *onConnect* and *onConnectAccept*), as developers will override them in their *main.asc* file.

The last thing the *FCApplication* constructor does is define *acceptConnection( )* and *rejectConnection( )* as wrappers for *gFrameworkFC.application.requestAcceptConnection( )* and *requestRejectConnection( )*, as described earlier.

The *application.asc* file (especially the last part of it) was without a doubt the most complex part of the framework's files. If you followed this section, the rest should be fairly easy. Understanding its intricacies will allow you to build efficient components that don't break the framework's model.

Analyzing facade.asc

The second file loaded by *framework.asc* after *application.asc* is *facade.asc* (read it "façade", *a la Francais*).

This file can also seem pretty complex, unless you understand how the *_resolve()* method works.

Server-Side ActionScript automatically invokes the *_resolve()* method on an object whenever other code attempts to access a property or method that can't be found on that object.

It's easier to understand with an example. Suppose you have a class named *MyClass*, defined as follows:

```
function MyClass () {
}
MyClass.testMethod = function () {
  trace("testMethod called");
};
```

Now suppose you have an instance of *MyClass* named myInstance:

```
myInstance = new MyClass();
```

If your code invokes *testMethod()* on myInstance, you'll see the *trace()* output as expected:

```
myInstance.testMethod();
```

However, if you try to invoke a non-existent method:

```
myInstance.someBogusMethod();
```

the Server-Side ActionScript interpreter will throw a runtime error, telling you that "someBogusMethod" is not defined on myInstance (client-side ActionScript fails silently instead of throwing an error).

Now let's imagine that you wanted to inoculate your code against such runtime errors. Server-Side ActionScript gives you a way to trap such problems, with *_resolve()*.

You can define a *_resolve()* method like this:

```
MyClass._resolve = function (p_name) {
  trace("ERROR. This class does not have a member or a function called " + p_name);
};
```

If *_resolve()* doesn't return a value, the interpreter still throws a runtime error, but at least you will see your trace message first.

To prevent the interpreter from throwing a runtime error, have your *_resolve()* method return data of the type that the invoker expected.

In the earlier "someBogusMethod" example, you could write a _resolve( ) handler like this:

```
MyClass._resolve = function (p_name) {
  this[p_name] = function () { trace(this.name + " was created on the fly!"); };
  this[p_name].name = p_name;
  return this[p_name];
};
```

Basically, the interpreter expected to run a function, and _resolve( ) returns us a function reference, so all is fine. Running:

```
myInstance.someBogusMethod( );
```

would now result in this trace:

```
someBogusMethod created on the fly!
```

Not the most useful function, but no runtime error!

Now let's imagine that someBogusFunction( ) is called again on myInstance.

Because in _resolve( ) we saved the function in this.someBogusMethod (with this[p_name]), the _resolve( ) method doesn't even get triggered any more. Now the someBogusFunction( ) method is defined on myInstance, so there's no reason to call _resolve( ) again. This is sometimes referred to as "caching" of the new method. Nifty, eh?

Now you know how to create functions on the fly. You could also create full-fledged objects or simple variables on the fly, as well. And that's exactly what facade.asc does, over and over again.

OK, now that we know how _resolve( ) works, we are ready to tackle facade.asc.

The facade.asc file's job is to set up client-to-server objects that route methods from the client-side code of a component to its server-side code. This is done following the naming scheme described earlier in this chapter:

```
ComponentTypeName.ComponentInstanceName.MethodName
```

To route methods from the client to the server, first we define a _resolve( ) handler on the Client.prototype object. This method is triggered every time a client-to-server call does not correspond to a function attached to the Client.prototype object. Such is the case the first time a client-to-server call on a component is made (those have the form "FCChat.chat1_mc.connect").

The _resolve( ) handler in the facade.asc file checks whether there exists a component in gFrameworkFC.components of type ctype (in our example "FCChat"). Notice how _resolve( ) runs as soon as the interpreter tries to understand "FCChat", effectively splitting the string for us, and then passes only "FCChat" as a parameter of _resolve( ). If there is such a component, the code creates a new FCFactory object (defined later) and caches it on the Client.prototype for next time. Otherwise, the _resolve( ) method doesn't return anything, which generates a server-side error, which in turn generates a "NetConnection.Call.Failed" *onStatus* event on the client side.

In our example, the data structures described so far are:

Client
> Defined by FlashCom Server

Client.FCChat
> An instance of the *FCFactory* class

Let's look at the *FCFactory* class defined in *facade.asc*. It also has a *_resolve( )* method. This is invoked right after the *FCFactory* is created in *Client.prototype._resolve( )* but, this time, with the second part of the call string as a parameter ("chat1_mc" in our example).

This time around, the code checks whether an instance of the class (*FCChat*, in our case) named cname (chat1_mc) has already been created and saved in FCChat. instances.chat1_mc. If not, the code needs to instantiate a new instance.

Before it attempts to create an instance, the code needs to check whether the component allows dynamic instantiation (cclass.dynamic != true). If so, the code creates a new instance of the class, which calls *init( )* on itself (on the base class), which in turn calls *registerComponent( )*, which we have seen earlier. The code also stores a reference to the new instance in the cclass.instances table (FCChat.instances. chat1_mc in our example). So, the next time a call is made on this instance, this part of the code will be skipped and the class won't be instantiated again.

At the end, the code creates an *FCFacade* for the instance (described later), caches it in the *FCFactory* for next time, and returns it.

In addition to Client and Client.FCChat described earlier, the newly defined data structures are:

Client.FCChat.chat1_mc
> An instance of the *FCFacade* class

FCChat.instances.chat1_mc
> A reference to the chat1_mc instance of the *FCChat* class

In our example, the Client.FCChat.chat1_mc instance of the *FCFacade* class is addressed every time a client-side component makes a method call that starts with FCChat.chat1_mc. Let's see what the *FCFacade* class defined in *facade.asc* does.

You guessed it—it has a *_resolve( )* method to trap the third part of the string, the method name (in our example "connect").

First, the *FCFacade* class makes sure that the component exists in gFrameworkFC. components (gFrameworkFC.components.FCChat). Then it makes sure that the instance exists (FCChat.instances.chat1_mc). If this is the case (it would be strange if it wasn't, since the *FCFacade* has been created by the framework itself), we go on.

This is the last of the tricky parts of the framework code. It defines a function with this code:

```
var f = function () {
  var args = [this.client].concat(gFrameworkFC.__toarray__(arguments));
  var cinst = gFrameworkFC.components[this.ctype].instances[this.cname];
  return cinst[name].apply(cinst, args);
};
```

The first line creates an array of arguments that has a reference to the client that called the method as the first argument.

The second line finds the instance (gFrameworkFC.components.FCChat.instances. chat1_mc, in our example).

The third line calls the method (*connect( )* in our case), using the *apply( )* call to pass in the arguments. It also returns the same value returned by the component's method, in case it had one.

Then with this instruction:

```
// Cache and return the above function.
return this[name] = f;
```

the code caches a reference to this new "wrapper" method so that _resolve( ) will not get called next time the method is invoked.

In addition to Client, Client.FCChat, Client.FCChat.chat1_mc, and FCChat. instances.chat1_mc described earlier, the newly defined data structure is:

Client.FCChat.chat1_mc.connect

A little wrapper function that inserts a reference to the calling client as a first parameter and then calls *FCChat.instances.chat1_mc.connect( )*

The beauty of all the caching is that the next time the "*FCChat.chat1_mc.connect*" is called by the client, none of the _resolve( ) handlers will run! We will directly call the little wrapper function that will call the method on the component's server-side code.

Also note that we create only the server-side functions that are needed by a particular client application (we create them only if they are invoked). This makes the server-side framework very efficient, memory-wise.

So that was *facade.asc*. Pretty nifty, huh? Hopefully this section demystified what _resolve( ) does and inspired you to use it for your own method-routing needs.

Analyzing component.asc

The last piece of the puzzle is *component.asc*, the base class for all server-side components. It lives in the *scriptlib/components* folder, and it provides some functionality that's common to all components (as any good base class should).

Most of its code is about event dispatching and trapping for intracomponent communication, which we described earlier in this chapter.

First, it loads the *framework.asc*, just in case you forgot.

Then there is the constructor. This code is run as soon as a component is loaded. As discussed previously, it uses prototype-based inheritance to make the component a subclass of *FCComponent*:

```
FCChat.prototype = new FCComponent("FCChat", FCChat);
```

The *FCComponent* constructor also creates a static object (FCChat.instances) and defines a few static methods on the derived class, such as *create( )*, used to create an instance of the component on the server side.

The next section of code in *component.asc* allows for component-wide listeners (we described those earlier). For example, if you write the following, listObj will be notified whenever the foo property of any *FCChat* instance changes:

```
FCChat.addListener("foo", listObj);
```

The derivedType.__LISTENERS__ table and *addListener( )* and *removeListener( )* methods implement this listening mechanism and are pretty simple to understand. The important thing to know is that the FCChat.__LISTENERS__ is an associative array indexed by property names, with each slot containing an associative array of references to component instances indexed by the component prefix.

For example, if you want to notify chat1_mc that foo has changed in FooComponent, you would look in FooComponent.__LISTENERS__["foo"]["FCChat.chat1_mc"] and find a reference to the chat1_mc object, so that you could call *onPropertyChanged( )* on it.

The *sendUserEvent( )* handler that follows in *component.asc* is easy to understand once you know the data structure.

Finally, the *FCComponent* class calls *gFrameworkFC.registerComponent( )*, which we described earlier in this chapter.

Note that the constructor for your component's class hasn't run yet. It runs only when *facade.asc* creates an instance of it, because it wants to deliver a client-to-server method call to it, and the instance doesn't exist yet. Remember that component instances are created "lazily" on the server—when your client-side code tries to call the server side, and not before.

Next, *component.asc* defines some methods on FCComponent.prototype. These methods will be inherited as-is by the component classes, which all derive from the *FCComponent* class.

The code defines an *FCComponent.prototype.init( )* method, which is called by all well-behaved components at the beginning of their constructor's code. The *init( )* method just saves some variables, such as name, prefix, and callPrefix, which can be used by component authors to namespace shared objects and net streams, or to make server-to-client calls.

Next, *component.asc* defines four utility methods that component developers can use:

getClientID( )
> Returns the unique ID that the framework automatically assigns to each client that connects.

getClientGlobalStorage( )
> Used for data management, it returns references to objects that component developers can use to store client-specific global information. A client global is different for each client but the same for each component (think of username or userColor).

getClientLocalStorage( )
> Used for data management, it returns references to objects that component developers can use to store client-specific local information. A client local is like a local variable for a component instance, but it's attached to the client object.

releaseLocalStorage( )
> Cleans up the client local variables. If your component overrides the default *onDisconnect( )*, your component should call this function explicitly to avoid memory leaks in your application.

The next few functions all have to do with event notifications: the static *onWatch( )* function and the *addListener( )*, *removeListener( )*, and *sendUserEvent( )* methods. They all use the __LISTENER__ data structure described earlier.

The only tricky thing is the call to:

```
this.watch(prop, FCComponent.onWatch);
```

This is how Server-Side ActionScript sets up a *watch* on a particular variable (i.e., a way to get notified when changes to its value occur). The major caveat is that there can be only one watcher for each property.

Conclusion

This concludes our discussion of the Macromedia component framework. Hopefully this chapter gave you some insight on how the framework was constructed and made it seem less inaccessible.

For more tips on how to develop your own client- and server-side framework, see Chapters 13 and 15. Building a good framework is a work of art and takes many iterations, but once it is settled, it can become the foundation of many different applications.

CHAPTER 15

Application Design Patterns and Best Practices

This chapter describes some of the best practices available to application developers. In it, we summarize and extend material from previous chapters and introduce some new ideas. While not quite a design pattern catalog, this chapter does attempt to provide you with useful design options, patterns, and best practices that will help you build better applications.

Shared Object Management

Object-oriented programmers are used to designing a set of custom classes to work together to get some job done. Each class defines objects that have their own responsibilities and collaborate with other types of objects. The state of all the objects represents the current state of an application. When I first came across shared objects, I wasn't sure how to approach working with them. They are clearly designed to share application state across Flash movies, but I encountered problems when I tried to imagine giving each shared object separate responsibilities. You can't extend the *SharedObject* class the way you can extend other classes like *Object* or *MovieClip*. For example, you can't get this to work:

```
class VideoConferenceManager extends SharedObject {
  //...
}
```

As I've already pointed out in Chapter 8, you can't extend the *SharedObject* class, because the only way to get a remote shared object is to use the *SharedObject.getRemote()* method:

```
remote_so = SharedObject.getRemote("UsersData", nc.uri);
```

Once I get a shared object, I can customize it by dynamically adding methods and private properties to it. But I wanted to design classes of interacting objects.

Eventually, I realized that shared objects could be treated like distributed associative arrays that are managed by other objects. When it comes to designing applications with shared objects, the challenge is writing classes that manage shared objects to get your job done.

To make a shared object part of an application, it should be controlled or contained by another object. The controlling object provides the custom behavior needed by the application and often hides the shared object within it. The object that contains or controls a shared object can treat the shared object as an internal data collection that it is solely responsible for managing. In general, one, and only one, object within each client should be responsible for updating a shared object or sending messages using it. When server-side scripting is involved, one object on the server should be responsible for managing server-side updates. However, in some cases, more than one object may need to access data in a shared object or receive notifications when a remote method is called on the shared object. In this section, I review some techniques for working with shared objects and deal with some difficult problems such as populating List and DataGrid components with shared object data. When I'm done, I hope you'll be as comfortable designing applications that use shared objects as you are using arrays and movie clips.

One-to-One Owner/SharedObject Relationships

Let's start with the simplest case: we'll give a single object responsibility for updating and responding to updates on a shared object as the *SharedBall* class did in Chapter 8. In this more general example, a client-side object can create a shared object, customize it by adding properties and methods to the shared object itself (not the data property of the shared object), and then connect it. We often refer to the object that customizes its shared object as the shared object's *owner*. Here is a short skeletal example of a demonstration *Owner* class:

```
class Owner {
  var nc:NetConnection;
  var so:SharedObject;

  function Owner (p_nc) {
    nc = p_nc;
    so = SharedObject.getRemote("soName", nc.uri, false);
    so.owner = this;
    so.onSync = function (list) {
      this.owner.onSync(list);
    };
    so.onStatus = function (status) {
      this.owner.onStatus(status);
    };
    so.connect(nc);
  }
```

```
function onSync (list) {
  trace("onSync called with list length: " + list.length);
}

function onStatus (status) {
  trace("onStatus called with status code: " + status.code);
}
}
```

The *Owner* object makes sure it receives *onSync( )* and *onStatus( )* method calls by adding an owner property to the shared object that refers back to itself (using the keyword this). Then it adds *onSync( )* and *onStatus( )* methods to the shared object, which use the owner property to call the owner's *onSync( )* and *onStatus( )* methods. In other words, no real work is done within the shared object. It simply passes on status and synchronization information to its owner for processing. The owner object will also be responsible for updating the shared object, but that is not shown in the preceding example.

The example uses a temporary shared object. Since a temporary shared object cannot be updated until it has been synchronized by the server, the owner needs to know when the shared object is first synchronized. It is not difficult to extend the shared object to call a method on the owner object to indicate the shared object is ready to be updated. In the following example, the shared object is modified to call the owner's *onConnect( )* method when the shared object is synchronized for the first time (additions to the preceding example are shown in bold):

```
class Owner {
  var nc:NetConnection;
  var so:SharedObject;

  function Owner (p_nc) {
    nc = p_nc;
    so = SharedObject.getRemote("soName", nc.uri, false);
    so.isConnected = false;
    so.owner = this;
    so.onSync = function (list) {
      if (!this.isConnected) {
        this.isConnected = true;
        this.owner.onConnect();
      }
      this.owner.onSync(list);
    };
    so.onStatus = function (status) {
      this.owner.onStatus(status);
    };
    so.connect(nc);
  }

  function onConnect (list) {
    trace("onConnect called.");
  }
```

```
function onSync (list) {
  trace("onSync called with list length: " + list.length);
}

function onStatus (status) {
  trace("onStatus called with status code: " + status.code);
}
}
```

The owner object knows it is safe to update the shared object as soon as the *onConnect( )* method is called. For example, it may enable components so that a user can start updating a shared object when it receives the *onConnect( )* call:

```
function onConnect( ) {
  deleteButton.enabled = true;
  updateButton.enabled = true;
}
```

The owner's *onSync( )* method will also be called when the shared object is synchronized for the first time.

Often no further customization of the shared object is necessary. And that's what we want! Now, we are free to define the responsibilities of our *Owner* class or its subclasses, without having to further customize the shared object the owner contains.

The owner object in each client can update its shared object and will be notified when the shared object is updated by other clients. If the owner object must interpret the information objects in the list array passed into the shared object's *onSync( )* method, it will do so in its own *onSync( )* method.

Developers working with shared objects often must write *onSync( )* methods that loop though each information object in the array passed into *onSync( )*. Returning to the *SharedBall* example in Chapter 8, each information object had to be examined to see if another movie had moved the ball. Here's a short snippet from Example 8-4:

```
for (var i in list) {
  if (list[i].code == "change" || list[i].code == "reject") {
    this.owner.onChange( );
    break;
  }
}
```

If you have to do something often enough, such as writing code to loop through a list, it's only natural to try to find a way out of writing yet another loop. Some developers, therefore, would rather not have the owner object implement its own *onSync()* method. They would prefer the shared object's *onSync( )* method do the work of looping through the list of information objects and pass each information object to the owner for further processing. Since the code property of each information object is almost always the first thing to be checked in an *onSync( )* method, it's easy to imagine calling owner methods named after possible code values: "change", "success", "reject", "delete", and "clear". In some cases, this practice can increase the number of function calls required to handle changes and make it harder to update List and DataGrid components efficiently. However, it has the advantage of providing slot-level notifications of changes to the owner object.

The following example shows one of many possible ways to notify an owner object of shared object changes:

```
so.onSync = function (list) {
  if (!this.isConnected) {
    this.isConnected = true;
    this.owner.onConnect( );
  }
  var len = list.length;
  for (var i = 0; i < len; i++) {
    var code = list[i].code;
    switch (code) {
      case "change":
        this.owner.onSlotChanged(list[i]);
        break;
      case "success":
        this.owner.onSlotChanged(list[i]);
        break;
      case "reject":
        this.owner.onSlotChanged(list[i]);
        break;
      case "delete":
        this.owner.onSlotDeleted(list[i]);
        break;
      case "clear":
        this.owner.onClearSlots( );
        break;
    }
  }
};
```

As in the earlier example, the shared object's *onSync( )* method still calls the owner's *onConnect( )* method to notify it that the shared object is ready to be updated. Instead of just passing the list on to the owner's *onSync( )* method, each information object in the list is checked from beginning to end based on its code property. Depending on the code value, one of three methods is called. The first and most frequently called method is *onSlotChanged( )*, which is called if a slot has been created or updated by another client. It is also called if a slot change made by the owner succeeded or was rejected. Owner objects that don't want to handle certain codes like "reject" or "success" can still check the information object passed to their *onSlotChanged( )* method. The *onSlotDeleted( )* method is called when a slot is deleted. The *onClearSlots( )* method is called when the server clears (in other words, deletes) all the slots in the shared object. It is essential to pass on and handle "clear" events when persistent shared objects are used that have a resyncDepth value other than the default of -1. Otherwise, the entire contents of the shared object may be deleted without the owner object receiving any notification.

Connecting and reconnecting

A potential weakness of all the examples shown so far is that they assume the owner object will connect to the server and to the shared object only once. If the client disconnects and then reconnects to the server, the shared object also has to be reconnected. If the owner object is disposed of and a new owner object is created, the examples presented so far will work without problem. Each time an owner object is instantiated, it is passed a connected *NetConnection* object that it uses to connect its shared object. But if an owner object cannot be disposed of and re-created, the initialization code for the shared object should be moved out of its constructor. There are lots of ways to inform the owner object that an application has reconnected. One simple way is to call a method and pass it a connected *NetConnection* object as indicated in bold:

```
class Owner {
  var __nc:NetConnection;
  var so:SharedObject;

  function Owner() {
  }

  function set nc (nc:NetConnection) {
    __nc = nc;
    so = SharedObject.getRemote("soName", nc.uri, false);
    so.isConnected = false;
    so.owner = this;
    so.onSync = function (list) {
      if (!this.isConnected) {
        this.isConnected = true;
        this.owner.onConnect();
      }
      this.owner.onSync(list);
    };
    so.onStatus = function (status) {
      this.owner.onStatus(status);
    };
    so.connect(nc);
  }

  function onConnect () {
    // The SO is ready for use. Enable GUI objects if necessary.
  }

  function onSync (list) {
    // Handle shared object updates here.
  }

  function onStatus (status) {
```

```
      // Handle shared object errors here.
   }
}
```

In the preceding ActionScript 2.0 example, a setter method is used. The *set nc( )* method must be called whenever a *NetConnection* object is connected or re-created so that the owner object can correctly initialize and connect its shared object using the *NetConnection*.

In all the examples we've seen so far, each shared object is customized only enough so that it passes on synchronization and status messages to its owner. The owner can be any class we like with any responsibilities we care to give it. Unfortunately, the owner object still has to do the work of setting up its shared object. Soon we'll see how to reduce the setup work that the owner has to do to a minimum.

One-to-Many Owner/Listeners Relationships

Since shared object data has to be sent across the network every time a shared object is updated, you should minimize data duplication as much as possible. For example, if a PeopleGrid component manages a people shared object, other components should not have to duplicate some or all of the data already available in the People-Grid's shared object. Somehow, they should be able to get the data—and notifications of changes to the data—from the people shared object, too.

In other words, while one object should be responsible for updating a shared object, we want to allow more than one object to receive updates as the shared object is changed. In short, we want the *SharedObject* to become an event broadcaster. A number of techniques have been used to make objects into event broadcasters in Flash. You can use the *ASBroadcaster* object, write your own custom code, or, as of Flash MX 2004, use the *mx.events.EventDispatcher* mixin class. (A *mixin class* adds methods and properties to other objects dynamically.) In Server-Side ActionScript (SSAS), you have to write your own broadcaster code. Chapter 13 makes extensive use of the *EventDispatcher* option. The *SharedObjectFactory* class listed in Example 13-2 uses *EventDispatcher* to turn shared objects into event broadcasters. It can be used in the owner/shared object one-to-one scenario. And it can be used to allow more than one object to receive events and remote method calls from a shared object. In each case, it is essential that one and only one object in each client uses the *SharedObjectFactory* class to get a reference to a shared object. Other objects that need access to synchronization messages and remote methods must get a reference to the shared object from their owners and add themselves as listeners. Looking back at Chapter 13, here's how the VideoConference component gets access to the people_so shared object maintained by a PeopleGrid component:

```
peopleGrid.nc = application.nc;
videoConference.userName = application.user.userName;
videoConference.people_so = peopleGrid.people_so;
videoConference.nc = application.nc;
```

The PeopleGrid sets up the shared object using the *SharedObjectFactory* class:

```
_people_so = SharedObjectFactory.getRemote(path + "people", nc.uri);
_people_so.addEventListener("onSync", this);
_people_so.connect(_nc);
```

When the VideoConference component gets a reference to the people_so shared object, it only has to set itself up as a listener in order to receive any new *onSync* events:

```
_people_so.addEventListener("onSync", this);
```

However, in some cases, it is possible that the listener will set itself up to listen to the shared object too late to receive some of the first *onSync( )* calls or remote method calls. In that case, each listener can check whether the shared object has already been connected by checking its isConnected property and initialize itself accordingly:

```
if (_people_so.isConnected) {
  var list = [];
  for (var p in _people_so.data) {
    list.push({code:"change", name: p});
  }
  onSync({target:_people_so, list:list});
}
```

The isConnected property is added by the *SharedObjectFactory* class and is maintained by the modified *connect( )* and *close( )* methods that it attaches to each shared object before returning it for use. In other words, the *SharedObjectFactory* class returns an already customized shared object that should not be further modified. See Example 13-3 for the listing of a test program that exercises all the features of a shared object returned from the *SharedObjectFactory* class. The earlier caution about connecting and reconnecting owner objects applies to shared objects as well. The isConnected property will not be reset if a *NetConnection* closes. Your application must have the component call *connect( )* on the shared object again when the *NetConnection* is reestablished.

 To keep your code as simple as possible, use one and only one technique for getting and customizing shared objects. If you are using Flash MX 2004 or Flash Pro, consider using *SharedObjectFactory* exclusively to get every shared object regardless of how you intend to use each one.

What should you do if you need to broadcast synchronization events in ActionScript 1.0? There are a number of possibilities. An extremely simple approach is to modify SharedObject.prototype. Example 15-1 shows one way to customize the *SharedObject* prototype so that you can still use *getRemote( )* to get a shared object you could use normally or as a broadcaster after calling its *init( )* method.

Example 15-1. Customizing the SharedObject class

```
SharedObject.prototype._onSyncConnect = function (list) {
  this.notify("onSyncConnect", list);
  this.onSync = this._onSync;
  this.onSync(list);
};
SharedObject.prototype._onSync = function (list) {
  this.notify("onSync", list);
};
SharedObject.prototype.init = function () {
  this._mcListeners = {};
  // Must have unique _name property.
  this.onSync = this._onSyncConnect;
};
SharedObject.prototype.notify = function (method, list) {
  for (var p in this._mcListeners) {
    var mc = this._mcListeners[p];
    if (mc[method]) {
      mc[method](this, list);
    }
  }
};
SharedObject.prototype.addListener = function (mc) {
  this._mcListeners[mc._name] = mc;
};
SharedObject.prototype.removeListener = function (mc) {
  delete this._mcListeners[mc._name];
};
```

The code in Example 15-1 relies on the _mcListeners object to keep track of each listener using its _name property. If each listener does not have a unique _name property, the code will not work. If there is any chance that listeners will not have a unique _name property, consider using the server-side port of the *EventDispatcher* class provided in Example 14-9.

However, if each listener has a unique property, a modified version of Example 15-1 can be used to provide an event broadcast mechanism. For example, if each object has a unique path property, just change _name to path in Example 15-1 to create a server-side version of the script.

Using the *SharedObjectFactory* class, or something similar you create, simplifies writing classes that contain their own shared objects. Look at how little work the People-Grid had to do to set up the people shared object:

```
_people_so = SharedObjectFactory.getRemote(path + "people", nc.uri);
_people_so.addEventListener("onSync", this);
_people_so.connect(_nc);
```

Compare that to the 14 or more lines of code in some of the earlier examples. Even better, using *SharedObjectFactory* means each shared object will be customized in the same way and make available one well-defined set of events.

Delegating Updates

Many components have to manage a lot of objects. For example, a PeopleCursors component has to manage a separate cursor for each user. In situations like that, it is often a good idea to have an owner of a shared object delegate the responsibility of updating the shared object to other objects under its control. The PeopleCursors component and similar components are a good candidate for delegation. For example, the PeopleCursors component allows each user to show everyone else where his cursor is. Each user can either hide or show his cursor at any time, and his username will appear below it. Also, not only should his cursor be visible to everyone else, but also the same movie clip representation of his cursor should follow around his system cursor so he has some indication of what other people are seeing.

How to design such a component? Assuming the changing position of each cursor is to be stored in a shared object, you have to immediately choose if you are going to create a shared object for each cursor or use one shared object for all of them. In some cases, it is simpler to use one shared object for all the cursors. If you don't, you need some mechanism for discovering the existence of each separate shared object before connecting to it. Often that requires the use of another shared object with the name of each user in it. The VideoConference component in Chapter 13 makes use of both the people shared object and a shared object for each stream.

The PeopleCursors component must manage a cursors shared object and any number of PersonalCursor movie clips. It must also provide a button that allows each user to show or hide her cursor. When a user toggles the button on, an entry in the cursors shared object must be created for her cursor, containing its current position. When the button is toggled off, the entry must be deleted. When an entry appears in the cursors shared object, a movie clip representing that cursor must be created in each PeopleCursors component. When an entry is deleted, the movie clip must also be deleted. The name of each slot in the cursors shared object will be the username of the person who has made her cursor visible as will the name of the movie clip that follows her cursor.

Two questions naturally arise from this scheme. Should the owner object running in each client be responsible for getting the current mouse position and updating the position of its user's mouse, or should updates be the job of the PersonalCursor movie clip that represents the user? Furthermore, should each PersonalCursor movie clip be a listener on the cursors shared object so that it knows where it should move when its slot is updated, or should the PeopleCursors component listen and then tell each clip where to move?

In truth, either of these options can work. However, for simplicity and performance, it is better to delegate to the PersonalCursor clip the job of updating the shared object and have the PeopleCursors component listen for cursor position changes. Here's why: The PeopleCursors component is really a coordinator. Its job should be to create the context for the PersonalCursor clips to work and then create or destroy

PersonalCursor clips as needed. The PeopleCursors component connects to the cursors shared object and must listen for synchronization events so it knows what PersonalCursor clips to create and delete. Also, when the user clicks the Show/Hide Cursor button, the PeopleCursors component is responsible for creating the user's PersonalCursor clip.

On the other hand, the PersonalCursor clips should be able to create and respond to cursor-level events like moving around the Stage. So from a division of responsibilities perspective, there is nothing wrong with the owner delegating update responsibilities to another object under its control. But then why not allow each cursor to listen directly to the shared object so it can move around in response to changes in its position within the shared object? The answer is that it is inefficient. If many cursors are moving at the same time, a long list may be returned to the *onSync( )* method containing many information objects that represent changes. It is not efficient for each PersonalCursor to do a linear search in the list to see if it has changed. It is much more efficient to have the owner check the list once and tell any PersonalCursor clips that have to move where to go.

Example 15-2 shows the complete listing for the PeopleCursors component. This client-side ActionScript 2.0 class should be stored in *PeopleCursors.as*.

Example 15 2. The PeopleCursors component

```
import mx.controls.Button;
import com.oreilly.pfcs.SharedObjectFactory;

class com.oreilly.pfcs.framework.components.PeopleCursors extends
        com.oreilly.pfcs.framework.PFCSComponent {

    // Connect component class and symbol.
    var className:String = "PeopleCursors";
    static var symbolName:String = "PeopleCursors";
    static var symbolOwner:Object = PeopleCursors;

    // Default path.
    var path:String = "pfcs/PeopleCursors/main/";

    // Subcomponents and movie clips.
    var showHideButton:Button;
    var boundingBox_mc:MovieClip;

    var __cursors_so:SharedObject;
    var __nc:NetConnection;
    var __user:Object;
    // cursors object holds references to movie clips that represent
    // each visible user cursor.
    var cursors = {};
    var depth:Number = 100;

    // Constructor function calls UIComponent's constructor.
```

Example 15-2. The PeopleCursors component (continued)

```
function PeopleCursors( ) {
  super( );
}

// init() is called before createChildren() and before onLoad() if it exists.
// In this case, we just call UIComponent.init() and hide the bounding box.
function init( ) {
  super.init( );
  boundingBox_mc._visible = false;
  boundingBox_mc._width = boundingBox_mc._height=0;
  cursors = {};
}

// No drawing is required, as the button is the entire GUI for this
// component. It just needs to resize.
function draw( ) {
  size( );
}

function size( ) {
  super.size( );
  // Uncomment the following line to have the button change width.
  // showHideButton.setSize(width, 22);
}

function createChildren( ) {
  var depth = 1;
  createObject("Button", "showHideButton", depth++, {_x:0, _y:0});
  showHideButton.enabled = false;
  showHideButton.toggle = true;
  showHideButton.selected = false;
  showHideButton.addEventListener("click", this);
  showHideButton.label = "Show Cursor";
}

function click (ev) {
  if (showHideButton.selected) {
    // Create the clip.
    showHideButton.label = "Hide Cursor";
    addCursor(__user.userName, true);
  }
  else {
    // Delete the clip.
    showHideButton.label = "Show Cursor";
    removeCursor(__user.userName);
  }
}

// The PeopleCursors.nc() setter method uses the nc
// to get the cursors remote shared object.
public function set nc (nc:NetConnection) {
  if (!nc) {
```

Example 15-2. The PeopleCursors component (continued)

```
    return;
  }
  __nc = nc;
  if (!nc.isConnected) {
    trace("PeopleCursors Error: nc must be connected before use.");
    return;
  }
  __user = _global.pfcs.getUser( );
  // First get a reference to the cursor list (cursors) shared object.
  __cursors_so = SharedObjectFactory.getRemote(path + "cursors", nc.uri);
  // Register the PeopleCursors instance as a listener of onSync events.
  __cursors_so.addEventListener("onSync", this);
  __cursors_so.setFps(3);
  // Connect it.
  __cursors_so.connect(__nc);
}

function onFirstSync( ) {
  showHideButton.enabled = true;
}

/* onSync( ) receives events from the cursors shared object and
 * responds by adding new cursors, deleting cursors, or asking
 * cursors to update themselves. The cursors update the cursors
 * shared object directly when they are moved.
 */
function onSync (ev) {
  var list = ev.list;
  var len = list.length;
  for (var i = 0; i < len; i++) {
    var code = list[i].code;
    var name = list[i].name;
    switch (code) {
      case "success":          // Tell this user's cursor to update itself.
        cursors[name].update( );
        break;
      case "change":           // Someone else's cursor has moved or been created.
        if (!cursors[name]) {
          addCursor(name, false);
        }
        cursors[name].update( );
        break;
      case "delete":           // Someone else's cursor has been deleted.
        if (cursors[name]) {
          removeCursor(name);
        }
        break;
      case "clear":            // The temporary shared object is available.
        onFirstSync( );
        break;
    }
  }
}
```

Example 15-2. The PeopleCursors component (continued)

```
}
// addCursor() attaches a PersonalCursor movie clip to this component.
function addCursor (name, homeInstance) {
  cursors[name] = attachMovie("PersonalCursor", name, depth++,
                          {homeInstance:homeInstance,
                           userName:name, so:__cursors_so,
                           xOffset:Math.floor(_x), yOffset:Math.floor(_y)});
}
// removeCursor() removes a PersonalCursor movie clip from this component.
function removeCursor (name) {
  var myCursor = cursors[name];
  myCursor.deleteClip();
  delete cursors[name];
}

// Clean up.
function close() {
  __cursors_so.removeEventListener("onSync", this);
}
}
```

When the user clicks the showHideButton, his cursor must be either created or destroyed. If you look at the *click()* method, you can see that the button's selected property is used to keep track of the show or hide state and that *addCursor()* and *removeCursor()* are called to actually add and delete the cursor. The *addCursor()* method takes two parameters: name and homeInstance. If the Boolean homeInstance is true, this slot represents the current user's cursor, so his PersonalCursor component assumes responsibility for following his cursor and updating the shared object with its position. It will use the name passed into it as the slot name to update. Note that a reference to the shared object is passed into each cursor but is really used by only the homeInstance cursor. When someone else's PersonalCursor is created, an entry for it is created in the cursors shared object. Have a look at the *onSync()* method in Example 15-2. The PeopleCursors component keeps track of each of its PersonalCursor movie clips by name in a cursors object. In the switch statement, the "change" case first checks if a clip exists for a slot that has changed. If not, it creates a cursor, passing false as the homeInstance parameter. In either case, it calls the *update()* method of the clip directly.

Example 15-3 lists the complete client-side ActionScript 2.0 code stored in *PersonalCursor.as* for the PersonalCursor component.

Example 15-3. The PersonalCursor class

```
class com.oreilly.pfcs.framework.components.PersonalCursor extends MovieClip {

  // Connect component class and symbol.
  var className:String = "PersonalCursor";
  static var symbolName:String = "PersonalCursor";
  static var symbolOwner:Object = PersonalCursor;
```

Example 15-3. The PersonalCursor class (continued)

```
// initObject variables.
var homeInstance:Boolean; // Indicates if this is the user's cursor.
var userName:String;      // The user's username and slot name for this cursor.
var so:SharedObject;      // Shared object to update with the cursor's position.
var xOffset:Number        // Parent clip's x position.
var yOffset:Number        // Parent clip's y position.
// Note: If the parent clip is resized or moved, the xOffset and yOffset values
//       must be updated. Resizing is not provided in this version.

// Subcomponents and movie clips.
var userName_txt:TextField;

function PersonalCursor ( ) {
  super( );
}

function onLoad ( ) {
  userName_txt.text = userName;
  if (homeInstance) {
    onMouseMove = function ( ) {
      so.data[userName] = {x: _root._xmouse - xOffset,
                           y: _root._ymouse - yOffset};
    };
  }
}

function update( ) {
  var cursor = so.data[userName];
  _x = cursor.x;
  _y = cursor.y;
}

function deleteClip( ) {
  onMouseMove = null;
  delete so.data[userName];
  this.removeMovieClip( );
}

function setOffsets(x, y) {
  xOffset = x;
  yOffset = y;
}
}
```

There are additional advantages to the division of responsibility demonstrated in
Example 15-2 and Example 15-3. If the cursor's behavior must change, it can be
coded in the *PersonalCursor* class without touching the *PeopleCursors* class code at
all. In fact, I'll do exactly that in Chapter 17 in order to compensate for network
latency.

Slot Owners

In the *PeopleCursors* example, each user has only one cursor. What do you do for a chess game in which each user must control many different pieces? In fact, in many computer games, more than one clip may be under the control of each user. In these cases, the idea of delegating updates can be taken further. Each clip can be designed to update its own slot in a shared object with information such as its current position on the game board. The key to making it work is making sure each clip knows the name of the correct slot to update in the shared object. In the *PeopleCursors* example, the username was used as a slot name and passed into the object. The same idea can be extended using other slot name conventions. For example, in chess, the username and piece name can be concatenated together to provide a unique name for a piece's slot in the shared object. (This assumes that each piece is named uniquely, such as "pawn1", "pawn2", etc.) For example, using an underscore as a separator, the format could be *userName_pieceName*. The key to doing efficient updates is to have the owner of the shared object maintain an object in which it can look up each piece's movie clip using its slot name, just as the PeopleCursors component could get each personal cursor by name from its internal cursors object:

```
var name = list[i].name
cursors[name].update( );
```

In other words, each movie clip is saved in an object by name. The name must be the same as the name of the slot the movie clip updates in the shared object. When a change occurs in the shared object, the owner looks up the movie clip by its slot name in the object and calls a method on the movie clip.

Update Sequence Options

When a user does something such as move a piece on a game board or click a button that will result in a shared object update, should you show her the results of her action immediately? Or, should you wait until the update is accepted by the server and *onSync( )* has been called on her copy of the shared object? Getting the update sequence right can have a big impact on the usability of a component.

In the PeopleCursors example, the user's PersonalCursor does not update its position on the Stage in response to changes in the current mouse position—it updates only its slot in the shared object. Each PersonalCursor waits for the PeopleCursors object to receive notification in its *onSync( )* method and tell it to move. See the "success" *case* clause in Example 15-2. The resulting delay is intentionally provided to give the user a sense that what she does is not immediately reflected for all the other users. In games, where any delay is undesirable, waiting for the shared object to synchronize is a bad idea. In fact, updating the clip when its position is synchronized may be entirely unnecessary. There are really only three update sequences that are possible when a user makes a change that must be reflected in a shared object:

• Show the update locally without waiting for the shared object to change.

- Wait for the shared object to report the change was successful before showing the change.
- Show the change immediately and again when the shared object synchronizes.

The PersonalCursor component implements the second option. The *SharedBall* class listed in Example 8-4 uses the first option. When the mouse is dragging the ball, the ball's *onMouseMove( )* method checks the x and y values to make sure they aren't off the Stage and then updates both the position of the ball clip and the shared object:

```
this.so.data[this.xSlot] = this._x = x;
this.so.data[this.ySlot] = this._y = y;
```

When the position updates are accepted by the server, the *onSync( )* method is called with a list containing an information object with code set to "success". The *SharedBall* class simply ignores "success" messages. It updates its position only when someone else moves the ball and *onSync( )* is passed a list containing an information object with a code value of "change" or "reject". A "reject" code indicates the user's attempt to move the ball was rejected by the server in favor of another client's position update.

You might think that there is never a reason to update the visible state of an application before and after the changes are synchronized in the shared object. Samuel Wan posted a nice sample application that makes good use of the third option. The ScratchPad component, made available as part of his Flash Forward 2003 NY sample files, updates the screen while the user draws on the scratch pad. When the drawing is complete, the graphic is removed from the Stage and the graphic information is sent to the server where it is stored in a shared object. When the shared object synchronizes, the original drawing is redrawn on the Stage. From the user's perspective, the two-step update sequence is a good choice. The user can draw and see immediately what the drawing looks like but is also made aware of the delay between releasing the mouse and everyone else seeing the drawing. The source files are available at:

http://www.samuelwan.com/information/archives/000157.html

Example 17-6 demonstrates a fourth option, which is attempting to anticipate an object's future position based on its current speed and direction of movement, but we save that discussion for Chapter 17.

Interval Update Checks

The ScratchPad component waits until the user has completely drawn a shape before sending the drawing information to the server, whereas the PersonalCursor component updates the shared object whenever the cursor moves. Sometimes, something in between immediate updates and waiting for the user to finish is required. A good example is a shared Input Text field. The field may be part of a form that multiple users can each contribute to filling in. Each shared Input Text field cannot be updated every time a user types a character, because that will reposition the cursor and make the text field unusable to anyone trying to edit or add text to it. But the text field does have to be updated as users add to it. A solution to the problem is to wait a period of time such as 3 seconds after the user edits the field before performing the update. Example 15-4 lists some sample code that uses a three-second delay whenever the text_txt field on the Stage is changed.

Example 15-4. Updating a shared object after a 3-second delay

```
so = SharedObject.getRemote("SharedText", nc.uri, false);
so.mc = this;
so.onSync = function (list) {
  this.mc.text_txt.text = this.data.text;
};
so.connect(nc);

var KeyListener = new Object();
KeyListener.mc = this;
KeyListener.onChanged = function ( ) {
  clearInterval(this.intervalID);
  this.intervalID = setInterval(this, "updateModel", 3000);
};
KeyListener.updateModel = function ( ) {
  clearInterval(this.intervalID);
  delete this.intervalID;
  this.mc.so.data.text = this.mc.text_txt.text;
};
text_txt.addListener(KeyListener);
```

Each time the field is changed, the timer is cleared and reset to 3 seconds. If the user changes the text in the input field before 3 seconds are up, the interval is deleted and re-created, effectively moving the update 3 seconds into the future.

Getting the sequence of updates and responses right is very important for the user experience in multiuser applications. Make sure you choose a sequence that helps your users understand what is happening and makes it easier for them to work with the component or objects you create.

Populating Lists and DataGrids

A common problem when working with shared objects is to find a simple and efficient way to update a List or DataGrid component with data stored in a shared object. Some techniques work up to a point but fail miserably if pressed too far. For example, a StreamList component may seem to work fine for lists of fewer than 100 items. But when the StreamList has to list several thousand items, it may bog down your entire application. Unfortunately, there is no one, ideal, simple, and efficient algorithm for updating lists and grids. The simplest methods are not as efficient as the more complex update strategies. The following section is designed to provide you with everything you need to know about adding items to the v2 list components, how to get shared object data into those list items, and how to choose the right update strategy for your application.

The v2 UI List and DataGrid components require access to a DataProvider object that stores the individual items to be displayed in the list or grid. The DataProvider is usually an array with some additional methods such as *addItemAt( )* or *removeItemAt( )* added to it. Each item in the DataProvider is accessed by number. By contrast, shared objects access data by slot name, so it is not possible to use a shared object's data object as a DataProvider. Somehow, shared object data must be placed in a DataProvider before it can appear in a List or DataGrid. By default, each List and DataGrid comes with its own DataProvider. Each provides methods to add items to their DataProvider. For example, you can add an item to a List very simply:

```
myList.addItem("This text will appear in the list");
```

The *addItem( )* method creates an item object with a label property containing the text passed into *addItem( )*. You can optionally pass a second parameter, which is stored as the data property of the item:

```
myList.addItem("blesser", {firstName:"Brian", lastName:"Lesser"});
```

Each time *myList.addItem( )* is called, the new item is appended to myList's DataProvider. You can also create the item object yourself without a data property if you like:

```
myList.addItem({label:"blesser", firstName:"Brian", lastName:Lesser});
```

You can get the currently selected item back from a List this way with the selectedItem property:

```
var item = myList.selectedItem
```

And you can retrieve any item from the List's internal DataProvider by index number:

```
var item = myList.getItemAt(2);
```

A DataGrid component has no concept of a label, so only the last form of the *addItem( )* method can be used. Every property of the item whose property name matches a grid column name is displayed in the grid.

Now that we've surveyed all the usual ways to get an item into a List or DataGrid, let's look at getting shared object data into those items.

Example 8-3, reproduced in part here, contained a shared object *onSync( )* method that used the *removeAll( )* and *addItem( )* methods to populate a people list with shared object data:

```
this.userList_so.onSync = function (list) {
  this.owner.peopleList_lb.removeAll( );
  for (var p in this.data) {
    this.owner.peopleList_lb.addItem(p, this.data[p]);
  }
};
```

In the preceding example, whenever the shared object is updated, the entire contents of the peopleList_lb list is deleted using *removeAll( )*. Then, each slot of the shared object is added as an item into the list using a *for...in* loop. In Example 8-3, the property name of each slot is copied into the label property of each item in the list, and the contents of each slot become the data property of each item. In other words, the data property of each list item is just a reference to the contents of a shared object slot. Assuming the data in the slot is an object, then it is not copied into the people list's DataProvider—only a reference to it is placed in the DataProvider. Using a reference saves space, as the entire object in the shared object slot is not duplicated. After each *onSync( )* call, the peopleList_lb list will always accurately reflect the contents of the userList_so shared object. Although Example 8-3 is extremely simple and works reliably, it is terribly inefficient and should not be used (a better approach is presented in Example 13-1). One reason it is inefficient is because the entire contents of the DataProvider are deleted and rebuilt even if only one slot in a hundred has changed. We'll improve on it later. First, we have to deal with a little problem you should avoid.

The __ID__ update problem

If we modify the *addItem( )* method call so that we just pass in the slot value, we can create an endless loop of useless shared object updates that will cripple our application:

```
this.owner.peopleList_lb.addItem(this.data[p]); // Never do this!
```

To see why, we have to assume that each shared object slot has an object within it. For example, a slot may hold an object that contains information about users, similar to the following anonymous object:

```
{userName:"blesser", firstName:"Brian", lastName:"Lesser"}
```

In theory, passing the contents of a shared object slot into the *addItem( )* method should be similar to the earlier example of passing in an anonymous object:

```
myList.addItem({label:"blesser", firstName:"Brian", lastName:Lesser});
```

The only difference is that there is no label property in the object stored in the shared object slot. Without a label property, the item will not show up in the visual display of the List component. But this is easy to fix. Just tell the List component to use a different property name (username) to label list items, as follows:

```
myList.labelField = "userName";
```

Now let's get to the real problem: when an item is added to the DataProvider, the DataProvider adds a hidden __ID__ property to each item. The __ID__ property contains a unique number that the List or DataGrid uses to uniquely identify each item even when the DataProvider is sorted. Now, remember that in our example, the item is also an object in a shared object slot. When the DataProvider adds the __ID__ property, the contents of the shared object slot appear to have changed, so the contents are sent to the server and *onSync( )* is called. Since the __ID__ property is hidden immediately after being created, the property is not actually sent to the server, but the damage is done—a never-ending flurry of useless updates occur, wasting bandwidth and often bringing your Flash movie to its knees.

One solution to the problem is to go back to adding the label and data separately in *addItem( )*. Another option is to copy the information in each shared object slot into a new object in each item. For example:

```
this.userList_so.onSync = function (list) {
  this.owner.peopleList_lb.removeAll( );
  for (var p in this.data) {
    var slot = this.data[p];
    this.owner.peopleList_lb.addItem(
      {label:p, firstName:slot.firstName, lastName:slot.lastName} );
  }
};
```

Although copying data from the slot into an anonymous object solves the problem, it is a waste of memory because it duplicates all the data in the slot. The original update from Example 8-3 is better in that at least it sets the data property of the item to point at the slot so that not everything has to be duplicated:

```
this.owner.peopleList_lb.addItem(p, this.data[p]);
```

Unfortunately, there is no such thing as an item.data property when a DataGrid is in use. You cannot do this:

```
myDataGrid.addItem(p, this.data[p]); // Does not work!
```

The safe way to add items to a DataGrid is to copy the data from the shared object slot into another object that is added to the DataGrid. For example:

```
myDataGrid.addItem(
  {userName:"blesser", firstName:slot.firstName, lastName:slot.lastName}
);
```

Or, as an alternative, a *clone( )* method that performs a shallow (i.e., non-recursive) copy is often used:

```
function clone(obj) {
  var copy = {};
  for (var p in obj) {
    copy[p] = obj[p];
  }
  return copy;
}
```

which may simplify things a little in the *onSync( )* method:

```
myDataGrid.addItem(clone(this.data[p]));
```

To sum up, whenever you store objects in shared object slots, you have to be careful about how you get data from each shared object slot into each list item. You should not simply add the object in the shared object slot to the list as an item! If you are using a DataGrid, you should copy the object's data from the slot into each item. If you are using a List, you can assign the contents of the slot to the data property or copy the data into each item.

There is one way the contents of a shared object slot can be added directly to a List or DataGrid. The technique is a little esoteric, but it has the advantage of saving memory by avoiding duplication of data. If every object in every shared object slot already has a unique __ID__ property, the DataProvider will simply use it, and there will be no flurry of unwanted updates. To make a scheme like that work, every object in a shared object slot has to be assigned a unique number. Since __ID__ numbers are created in Flash starting at 0, you can avoid conflicts by creating __ID__ numbers on the server starting at a very high number and working down. If all this seems like a bit much, don't worry. If you just copy the data from your shared object slots into the items you are adding into a DataGrid, it will waste space but you will not have to redesign everything you have done on the server.

Improving List and DataGrid update performance

Now that we've dealt with the vagaries of getting data from shared object slots into list items, let's see how to do it more efficiently. Using the *removeAll( )* and *addItem( )* methods of a List or DataGrid carries with it a lot of overhead that can seriously reduce a movie's performance. Each method not only updates the DataProvider but also makes a redraw request. The List and DataGrid components don't actually waste time redrawing themselves each time they get a redraw request, but making and handling each request takes time. A much more efficient way to update a List or DataGrid is to get its DataProvider and manipulate it directly. Then, only when the DataProvider is up-to-date do you ask the List or DataGrid to redraw. The following code snippet—already discussed in Chapter 13—shows one way to update the DataProvider of a List:

```
function onSync (ev) {
  var dp = list.dataProvider;        // Get the list's dataProvider.
  dp.splice(0);                      // Delete all its items.
  for (var p in userList.data) {     // Loop through the shared object.
    dp.push({label:p, data:userList.data[p]});  // Add items to the dataProvider.
  }
  // Tell the dataProvider to send a modelChanged message to the List
  // so the list will redraw itself.
  dp.dispatchEvent({target: dp, type:"modelChanged"});
}
```

By updating the DataProvider directly and calling the *dispatchEvent( )* method of the DataProvider only after all the updates are complete, the time to update the List can be reduced to as little as one-tenth the time it would take using List methods. For some test results of different update methods, see:

http://flash-communications.net/technotes/mappingSharedObjectsToArrays/index. html

When updating a DataGrid's DataProvider, the object passed into *dispatchEvent( )* must include an eventName property value of "updateAll" or the grid will not redraw:

```
dp.dispatchEvent({target:dp, type:"modelChanged", eventName: "updateAll"});
```

Even though manipulating the DataProvider directly can produce as much as a ten-fold increase in performance, sometimes even that is not enough. It can take a long time to copy all the properties of a shared object with hundreds or even a few thousand items into a DataProvider. When only a few properties have changed in a shared object, copying so many slots is wasteful.

The alternative is to make use of the list array passed into *onSync( )* that identifies the slots in the shared object that have been changed or deleted. The list array contains information objects, each with a name and code property. The name is the name of the shared object slot, and the code says what has happened to the slot. Ideally, we would walk through the list and, if a code other than "delete" were found, check whether there was an item in the DataProvider representing the slot that has changed. If the DataProvider already had an item for the slot, we would update it with the current contents of the slot. If an item corresponding to the slot didn't exist, we would add one. An item for a deleted slot that did exist in the DataProvider would be found and deleted.

Unfortunately, finding an item in a DataProvider that corresponds to a slot requires doing a linear search—checking the items one at a time—until the right item is found. Usually, each item is checked to see if one of its properties matches the unique name of a shared object slot. Another problem is that a linear search is itself time-consuming, and searching the DataProvider for each information object in the list passed into *onSync( )* would mean performing multiple linear searches for one *onSync( )* call.

If the DataProvider is always sorted on the slot name in each item, a binary search could be used, but keeping the DataProvider sorted is time-consuming and unusual.

 The best approach is to search the DataProvider only once after each *onSync( )* call. As each item in the DataProvider is retrieved, it must be checked against each information item in the list. If a match is found—that is, the item corresponds to the slot an information object has a code for—then the item can be updated or deleted.

But the list passed into *onSync( )* is an array and we don't want to do a linear search of it each time an item is examined. So before searching through the DataProvider, the information items in the list are placed in an object from which they can be retrieved by slot name. Example 15-5 lists three functions that together provide a much more efficient way to update the DataProvider of a DataGrid. The example code is based on some important assumptions:

- The *SharedObjectFactory* class was used to get the shared object, and the *onSync( )* method belongs to a component that has registered itself as an event listener on the shared object.
- Each slot of the shared object contains a simple object. There are no nested data structures in a slot such as objects inside objects or arrays of objects.
- The name of each slot is the unique key that will identify each item in the DataProvider.
- The slot name is also a username that uniquely identifies each user.
- A userName property must be added to each item in the DataProvider and will always match one slot's name.

These assumptions will not always be true, so the code presented here may have to be carefully adapted to your own needs. However, in cases in which small changes are regularly made on large shared objects, the performance improvement is worth it! The code has been extensively commented to help explain what each part does so you can adapt it to your own needs.

Example 15-5. Efficiently updating a DataGrid's DataProvider

```
/* clone( ) makes a shallow copy of an object. It will not copy nested
 * data structures such as objects within objects. It clones objects in
 * shared object slots so that the copies can be updated without automatically
 * updating the shared object. Copies are required when merging data from other
 * objects or when a DataProvider adds an __ID__ property. If an __ID__
 * property already exists but is hidden, it is also copied.
 */
function clone(obj) {
  var copy = {};
  // Copy the visible properties of the object.
  for (var p in obj) {
    copy[p] = obj[p];
  }
  // Add in the hidden __ID__ property if it exists.
  if (obj.__ID__ != undefined) copy.__ID__ = obj.__ID__;
  return copy;
}

// Deletes all the items in a dataProvider and repopulates it
// with new items copied from data in each slot of a shared object.
function rebuildProvider (ev) {
  // Get a reference to the originating shared object.
  var so = ev.target;
```

Example 15-5. Efficiently updating a DataGrid's DataProvider (continued)

```
  // Get the list's dataProvider and truncate it.
  var dp = grid.dataProvider;
  dp.length = 0;

  // Fill the dataProvider using Array.push().
  for (var slotName in so.data) {
    dp.push(clone(so.data[slotName]));
  }
  dp.dispatchEvent({target:dp, type:"modelChanged", eventName: "updateAll"});
}

// onSync() receives events from the shared object that this
// object is an event listener on.
function onSync (ev) {
  // Get the list's dataProvider.
  var dp = grid.dataProvider;

  // If all the contents of the shared object have been cleared (deleted)
  // or the dataProvider has fewer than 20 items in it, then it is as efficient
  // (or better) to truncate the provider and copy all the slots into it.
  if (ev.list[0].code == "clear" || dp.length < 20) {
    rebuildProvider(ev);
    return;
  }

  // Build an object of the information items in the list, so we can
  // look up each one by slot name efficiently.
  var list = ev.list;
  var nameLookup = {};
  for (var i in list) {
    var info = list[i];
    nameLookup[info.name] = info;
  }

  var so = ev.target;
  // Visit each item in the dataProvider to see if its userName property
  // matches a slot name that was in the list passed into onSync(), and
  // either update or delete the item that matches.
  for (var i = 0; i < dp.length; i++) {
    var slotName = dp[i].userName;     // Get the userName property of the item.
    var info = nameLookup[slotName];   // Look it up in the nameLookup object.
    if (info) {                        // If it's in the nameLookup.
      // If the info object code is "delete" remove it from the array.
      if (info.code == "delete") {
        dp.splice(i, 1);               // Delete the item from the list.
        i--;                           // Decrement i to adjust for splice().
      }
      // Otherwise the info object code is "change", "success", or "reject",
      // so update the array by replacing the item in it.
      else {
        dp[i] = clone(so.data[slotName]);
      }
```

Example 15-5. Efficiently updating a DataGrid's DataProvider (continued)

```
      // Delete this entry in the nameLookup object so that after examining
      // every item in the dataProvider, we are left only with entries that
      // don't correspond to any item in the dataProvider.
      delete nameLookup[slotName];
    } // end if (info)
  }/  / end for loop

  // Any new records that are left in the nameLookup object that have
  // changed must be added into the dataProvider.
  for (var slotName in nameLookup) {
    dp.push(clone(so.data[slotName]));
  }

  // Tell the list that the model has changed and to redraw itself now.
  dp.dispatchEvent({target: dp, type:"modelChanged"});
}
```

For most applications, the strategy first used in Example 13-1—getting the DataProvider, deleting everything in it, pushing new items into it, and only then having the DataProvider ask the List or DataGrid to redraw itself—works well enough. More important, the code is simple and easy to adapt to a wide variety of requirements. If your List or DataGrid is unlikely to hold more than 50 items, that approach may be your best choice. But if you need to display a List or DataGrid with hundreds of items, you should use something like the technique shown in Example 15-5.

I hope I've answered all your burning questions regarding working efficiently with shared objects and integrating them into well-designed applications.

Moving Code to the Server

We all want to build scalable, efficient, and easy-to-maintain applications. In this section, we try to convince you that moving application logic to the server-side is the best way to accomplish that goal.

Flash programmers who first start working with FlashCom may not immediately see the value for splitting up code—especially objects—so that part runs in the client and part on the server. In fact, the FlashCom API gives so much power to a Flash client that it may appear there isn't any reason to write Server-Side ActionScript beyond controlling connections. However, the longer you work with FlashCom, the more you recognize the importance of server-side code. Server-side scripts are often safer from a security standpoint and help to simplify designs and code; you should consider them the backbone of your applications.

A few classic examples of things to do on the server side are:

- Increment a counter (for example, to assign a unique ID to each user).
- Keep track of the number of users connected.

- Write to shared objects.
- Set shared objects' default values.
- Secure your application from rogue clients.
- Side-step the Flash Player security sandbox.

Here is an example server-side script that keeps track of the number of users connected:

```
application.onAppStart = function () {
  this.numUsers_so = SharedObject.get("numUsers", false);
  this.numUsers_so.setProperty("users", 0);
  this.numUsers_so.setProperty("guests", 0);
  this.nextID = 0;
};
application.onConnect = function (client, isGuest) {
  client.id = "user_" + this.nextID++;
  client.isGuest = isGuest;
  trace("accepting client " + client.id);
  application.acceptConnection(client);
  client.call("setID", null, client.id);
  if (isGuest)
    this.numUsers_so.setProperty("guests",
            this.numUsers_so.getProperty("guests") + 1);
  else
    this.numUsers_so.setProperty("users",
            this.numUsers_so.getProperty("users") + 1);
};
application.onDisconnect = function (client) {
  trace("client " + client.id + " left");
  if (client.isGuest)
    this.numUsers_so.setProperty("guests",
            this.numUsers_so.getProperty("guests")-1);
  else
    this.numUsers_so.setProperty("users",
            this.numUsers_so.getProperty("users")-1);
};
```

And here is the simple, companion script on the client side:

```
nc = new NetConnection();
nc.setID = function (myID) {
  _global.myID = myID;
  setUp();
};
function connectAsUser () {
  nc.connect("rtmp:/test", false);
}
function connectAsGuest () {
  nc.connect("rtmp:/test", true);
}
function setUp () {
  so = SharedObject.getRemote("numUsers", nc.uri, false);
  so.onSync = function (list) {
```

```
    trace("There are " + this.data.users +
        " users and " + this.data.guests + " guests connected");
  };
  so.connect(nc);
}
```

Notice how the client side never makes changes to the numUsers shared object; it just listens to it via the *onSync( )* handler. All the changes are done on the server side, where *onConnect( )* and *onDisconnect( )* methods get called for you at the appropriate times.

There are other cases in which having code on the server side is the right thing to do.

Any time you are about to write code that makes changes to a shared object on the client side, ask yourself: are multiple clients going to run this same code? Could there be a *race condition*, a situation in which one client's update interferes with another's update? (Concurrency and synchronization problems are covered in more detail in Chapter 17.) For example, say you have an Edit button that allows users to gain unique control over a shared whiteboard or note. A typical implementation is to have a property in a shared object called inUseBy, which is null if nobody's editing the whiteboard or contains the user ID of a user who clicked on the Edit button. You could do this on the client side:

```
// Called by the Edit button on click.
function doEdit () {
  this.so.data.inUseBy = _global.myID;
}
// With something like this in the onSync( ) definition.
this.so.data.onSync = function (p_list) {
  for (var i in p_list) {
    if (p_list[i].name == "inUseBy") {
      if (this.data.inUseBy == undefined) {
        edit_pb.setEnabled(true);
        status_txt.text = "Click Edit to edit the Whiteboard ";
      } else if (this.data.inUseBy == _global.myID) {
        edit_pb.setLabel("done");
        status_txt.text = "Click Done when finished";
        startEditMode( );
      } else {
        edit_pb.setEnabled(false);
        status_txt.text = "Whiteboard being edited by " + this.data.inUseBy;
      }
    }
  }
};
```

What happens if inUseBy is null and two users click on the Edit button at around the same time? Both users will try to set the value of inUseBy to their ID, but one of the changes will be rejected. For the user who got rejected, it will look as if clicking on the button didn't do anything. Depending on timing, both changes might be accepted! In that case, it will look as if a client is stealing control of the whiteboard from the other, which makes your application look untrustworthy.

A much better approach is to move the shared object update to the server side. Now the client-side code calls the server-side *editWB( )* method instead of performing the update directly:

```
// Called by the Edit button on click
function doEdit () {
  nc.call("editWB", null, _global.myID);
}
// with the same onSync() as in the previous example.
```

Here is the implementation for the *editWB( )* method on the server, which updates the shared object:

```
Client.prototype.editWB = function (p_id)
{
  var isBeingUsed = (this.so.getProperty("inUseBy") != undefined);
  if (isBeingUsed)
    return;
  this.so.setProperty("inUseBy", p_id);
};
```

The *setProperty( )* call triggers the *onSync( )* handler on all clients, just like before.

Because the server side is single-threaded, we now know that only one execution of *editWB( )* will be run at a time, with other requests being queued up by the server. So we can safely add a check to avoid the "stealing" that can occur inadvertently if the clients are allowed to update the shared object directly.

Here is another example to demonstrate why and when to move a shared object update to the server. Sometimes you want to make changes to a shared object based on the result object received by another shared object's *onSync( )* method. For example, suppose your application has different layouts, and each layout can have different components visible or hidden. The current layout ID is saved in a layouts_so shared object, and all the data about your components on the Stage is saved in a components_so shared object.

It's tempting, at first, to update the components_so on the client side:

```
function changeLayout (p_newLayoutID) {
  layouts_so.data.layoutID = p_newLayoutID;
}
layouts_so.onSync = function (p_list) {
  switch (this.data.layoutID) {
    case "discussion":
      components_so.data.chat = true;
      components_so.data.video = true;
      break;
    case "video-only":
      components_so.data.chat = false;
      components_so.data.video = true;
```

```
      break;
    case "chat-only":
      components_so.data.chat = true;
      components_so.data.video = false;
      break;
  }
};
components_so.onSync = function (p_list) {
  for (var i in p_list) {
    _root[p_list[i].name+"_mc"]._visible = this.data[i];
  }
};
```

On second thought, it means that all the clients will try to make the same changes to the components_so shared object whenever the layout is changed. This is a waste of resources; we'd prefer to change the components_so contents only once.

Once again, the server side comes to the rescue. You can choose between two ways to perform the update on the server side. You could add an *onSync( )* handler to layouts_so on the server side as well and make changes to components_so from there. Unfortunately, server-side *onSync( )* handlers don't get triggered by server-side *setProperty( )* calls, so you'd have to manually generate an *onSync* event every time you change layouts_so in your server-side code. The other option (preferred and simpler) is to move the change to the layouts_so shared object to the server side as well, just as we did in the previous example. Here's what the revised version look likes on the client side:

```
function changeLayout (p_newLayoutID) {
  nc.call("changeLayout", null, p_newLayoutID);
}
layouts_so.onSync = function (p_list) {
  trace("Now in layout " + this.data.layoutID);
};
components_so.onSync = function (p_list) {
  for (var i in p_list) {
    _root[p_list[i].name+"_mc"]._visible = this.data[i];
  }
};
```

And here's the revised server-side code:

```
Client.prototype.changeLayout = function (p_id) {
  application.layouts_so.setProperty("layoutID", p_id);
  application.components_so.lock();
  switch (p_id) {
    case "discussion":
      application.components_so.setProperty("chat", true);
      application.components_so.setProperty("video", true);
      break;
    case "video-only":
      application.components_so.setProperty("chat", false);
      application.components_so.setProperty("video", true);
      break;
```

```
    case "chat-only":
      application.components_so.setProperty("chat", true);
      application.components_so.setProperty("video", false);
      break;
  }
  application.components_so.unlock( );
};
```

Did you notice the code follows the façade design pattern? (If not, don't fret; it's covered in the next section.) One call makes changes to two shared objects, which triggers two different *onSync( )* handlers on all clients.

The important part is that all the changes to components_so are done only once.

As you have seen, the server side is a centralized location in which to put the most critical parts of your scripts. The more you write client-to-server code in FlashCom, the more you'll get a feel for what should go where. You'll probably find yourself writing code on the client first, only to realize later that it should really go on the server. The good thing is that the language is very similar, and porting is pretty quick.

Building Façades on the Server

As your application grows, so does the number of classes and components that it uses. In many situations, to complete an operation, you will have to affect multiple components at the same time. On these occasions, the *façade pattern* comes to the rescue. *Design Patterns* (Addison Wesley) defines *façade* as a way to "provide a unified interface to a set of interfaces in a subsystem. Façade defines a higher level interface that makes the subsystem easier to use." In other words, it provides a unified frontend to a set of functionality that would normally be sparse. Here's a very simple example.

On the client side, we have a Chat component and a Notes component. We also have a Clear All button. When this button is clicked, the following call is made to the server side:

```
nc.call("clearAll", null);
```

The server-side script is something like this:

```
Client.prototype.clearAll = function ( ) {
  var chat_so = SharedObject.get("chat", true);
  chat_so.setProperty("history", "");

  var notes_so = SharedObject.get("notes", true);
  notes_so.setProperty("note", "");
};
```

In a more realistic example, the function would call the appropriate method on each component it wants to clear, like this:

```
Client.prototype.clearAll = function () {
  application.components.chat.clearHistory();
  application.components.note.clear();
};
```

The effect is the same: one single call on the server-side, *clearAll( )*, triggers seemingly unrelated *onSync( )* calls on each client (one for the chat and one for the notes).

The important aspect of this pattern is the trickle-down effect of making a single call.

For a much more complex example of the façade pattern, look at how the server-side part of each communication component is instantiated lazily (i.e., only when the first client-to-server call is made on it; the code is in your *scriptlib/facade.asc* file; see Chapter 14). Whenever a client-to-server call is first made on an uninstantiated component (say, with a call to *FCChat.chat_mc.connect( )*), it gets trapped by a *_resolve( )* method, which creates an instance of a class (gFramework.components.FCChat, of type *FCFactory*), which in turn creates an instance of another class (gFramework. components.FCChat.instances.chat_mc, of type *FCFacade*) which finally instantiates the component class and calls the method on it.

Once again, a simple client-to-server call triggered a blur of activity on the server side, with code touching a bunch of different classes behind the scenes.

 So any time you find yourself modifying multiple shared objects or making calls to multiple parts of your application to achieve a single goal, wrapping the operation in a façade function on the server side is often a good idea.

Server-Side Client Queues

The concept of queuing up clients comes in handy when building applications that authenticate users through a call to a database or whenever your server-side code needs to perform an asynchronous operation, the results of which affect the clients connected to the application.

Consider a multi-instance application, for example. When building a complex Flash-Com application, it's common to use different application instances to partition users into different "rooms." Each of these rooms will have some information that differentiates it from other rooms, such as a room name or a room password.

These room properties are usually kept in a database, which maps application instance names to the room-specific properties and features. The database could simply be a shared object in a separate "manager" application instance (look at the lobby/rooms application in Chapter 9 for an example) or in a database system connected to FlashCom through server-side Flash Remoting.

Either way, retrieving these properties from the database requires an asynchronous operation, such as a server-to-server call or a Flash Remoting call.

Now imagine that clients need to have this information in order to function properly (for example, the room UI needs to display the room name at the top of the users' screens).

The most logical thing to do is to put the code that retrieves these properties in the *onAppStart( )* handler of your application, like this:

```
application.onAppStart = function () {
  // Perform the Remoting or server-to-server call here
  nc = new NetConnection();
  nc.connect("rtmp://someserver/someapp");
  nc.onStatus = function (p_info) {
    if (p_info.code == "NetConnection.Connect.Success") {
      application.roomInfoHandler = new GetRoomInfoHandler();
      this.call("getRoomInfo", application.roomInfoHandler);
    }
  };
};
```

The problem is that *onAppStart( )* is not run until the first client connects, and it is run just before the *onConnect( )* handler for that client. So this is what's going to happen:

1. Client connects to a room instance that's not yet running.

2. *application.onAppStart( )* runs, and the server-to-server (or Remoting) connection is started.

3. *application.onConnect( )* runs, and room properties are still unknown.

4. Some time elapses.

5. Room properties arrive.

So, what can we do in the *onConnect( )* handler? We have two options:

- If the room properties are not vital, we can simply accept the client connection (through *application.acceptConnection( )*) and notify the client of the room properties when they arrive, through a server-to-client call. The client might be able to use a subset of the application functionality while the room properties are unknown.

- If the room properties are very important for the client (for example, if it's the password that users need to provide in order to enter a room), we need to put the client "on hold" until the room properties are returned asynchronously.

Now imagine that 100 people connect right around the same time—as is possible for a large lecture or if, for example, your application has some automatic reconnecting code and a server briefly goes down—all while the initial asynchronous call to get the room properties is still pending.

In this case, you need a client queue, which can be implemented as simply as this (you can place *GetRoomInfoHandler( )* at the top of *main.asc* as shown here or in its own file):

```
// getRoomInfo result handler.
function GetRoomInfoHandler () {
  this.queue = new Array();     // Create queue
}
GetRoomInfoHandler.prototype.onResult = function (p_val) {
  // Save results.
  application.roomName = p_val.name;
  application.roomPwd = p_val.pwd;

  // Set flag.
  application.roomIsReady = true;

  // Flush queue.
  for (var i = 0; i < this.queue.length; i++) {
    application.acceptClientWithRoomReady(this.queue[i]);
  }

  // Clean up queue.
  this.queue = new Array();
};

GetRoomInfoHandler.prototype.addToQueue = function (p_client) {
  this.queue.push(p_client);
};
//-

application.onAppStart = function () {
  // Perform the Remoting or server-to-server call here.
  nc = new NetConnection();
  nc.connect("rtmp://someserver/someapp");
  nc.onStatus = function (p_info) {
    if (p_info.code == "NetConnection.Connect.Success") {
      application.roomIsReady = false;
      application.roomInfoHandler = new GetRoomInfoHandler();
      this.call("getRoomInfo", application.roomInfoHandler);
    }
  };
};

application.onConnect = function (p_client) {
  if (application.roomIsReady)
    application.acceptClientWithRoomReady(p_client);
  else
    application.roomInfoHandler.addToQueue(p_client);
};

application.acceptClientWithRoomReady = function (p_client) {
  application.acceptConnection(p_client);
  p_client.call("setRoomInfo", null, {name:this.roomName});
};
```

The code is pretty self-explanatory: we create a result handler for our server-to-server call, with an added *addToQueue( )* method, which adds a client to the pending queue. We also use a global `application.roomIsReady` flag, which is used in *onConnect( )* to decide whether to add a client to the queue or accept it right away. Also, we move the *application.acceptConnection( )* call to an *acceptClientWithRoomReady( )* method, which notifies the newly accepted client of the room properties right after accepting it (note that, for added security, we don't pass the room password to the client).

As we have seen, a queue can be nothing more than a simple array attached to the result handler of the asynchronous call.

This concludes the "tips-and-tricks" section of this chapter. The next section covers a frequently requested feature that is complicated to implement, so you may want to go get some coffee now!

A Framework for Recording and Playing Back Componentized Applications

One of the coolest things you can build with FlashCom is an application that's completely recordable and replayable: you can record every event that happens as people use the application and play back these events at a later time, and your application will "drive itself"! Imagine the applications in usability studies, for instance: place a tester in front of your application and start recording every mouse click or even every mouse position. Play the session back and you will learn wonders about how your users actually use your application!

As seen in Chapter 5, the *NetStream.send( )* method allows you to save data events in a NetStream, which are then thrown during the stream playback.

This feature allows you to build applications and components that are recordable and replayable. As an added bonus, because you're recording only "change events," the recorded file is usually an order of magnitude smaller than the ones created by competing technologies, which essentially record a screen capture of the application and play it back as a regular AVI movie.

This feature is often overlooked, and even less often implemented in applications, because it's not easy to implement. In this section, we will create a framework that makes it easier to build components that are recordable and replayable. Our hope is that by the end of this section you'll be able to understand how to leverage the *NetStream.send( )* API fully and be inspired to build components that make use of the framework described, or even improve upon the framework itself!

What's Covered in This Section

To illustrate how to build recordable and replayable applications, we will build a simple application made of a single component (a shared TextField), and enhance it to make it recordable and replayable.

We will start by creating a simple PTextField component, which is simply an Input Text field shared among all users.

Then, we will design a recording and playback framework (referred to from now on as the *R&P Manager*), enhance PTextField to use it, and finally go over the nitty-gritty details of the implementation of the R&P Manager.

For the sake of brevity, the component we create is extremely simple. For a better example of creating full-fledged components, refer to Chapter 13.

The PTextField Component

Before we do anything else, let's build a very simple PTextField component. After introducing the R&P Manager, we will enhance this component to be recordable and replayable.

We will create five files, two for the component itself and three for a simple application that uses it (think of it as a unit test):

tester.fla
> The tester client-side Flash movie

tester.as
> The script for the tester movie

main.asc
> The server-side application script for the tester movie

PTextField.as
> The client-side portion of our component

PTextField.asc
> The server-side portion of our component

The tester.fla file

Create a Flash MX 2004 *.fla* file with a single frame and two layers named *Actions* and *Assets*.

In the first frame of the *Actions* layer, open the Actions panel and enter the following code:

```
#include "tester.as"
```

Create a new movie clip symbol named *PTextField*, select the Export for Action-Script option, and leave the Export in First Frame option selected (you can change that in your real application later). Enter **PTextField** as the Linkage name and also as the AS 2.0 Class identifier. Within this movie clip symbol, create an Input Text field with the instance name m_text_txt.

Go back to the main timeline and drag an instance of your newly created PTextField component to the *Assets* layer, and give it the instance name pTextField_mc.

Save the movie as *tester.fla* and move on to the writing the code.

The tester.as file

The *tester.as* file holds the external ActionScript for a simple unit test for the component. Here's the entire code:

```
function setUp (Void):Void {
  // Set up components.
  pTextField_mc.connect("c0", nc);
}

nc = new NetConnection( );
nc.onStatus = function (p_info:Object):Void {
  if (p_info.code == "NetConnection.Connect.Success")
    setUp( );
};
nc.connect("rtmp:/pRecorderTest/pRecorder");
```

You should be able to write this code with your eyes closed by now. All we do is create a NetConnection and call a *setUp( )* function if everything goes right.

The only thing to notice is that in the *setUp( )* function we call a *connect( )* method on the component, passing it an ID and a reference to the main NetConnection. The component will use the ID to namespace its shared object, save a reference to the NetConnection, and connect its shared objects to the NetConnection.

For the sake of brevity, in this example we are going to have only one instance of the PTextField component, and we are going to hardcode its name and ID ("c0"). In a real-world application, you might have a much more flexible and automatic way to create and connect components (maybe with something like a SimpleConnect component). Refer to Chapter 13 for more info.

The main.asc file

The last part of the tester application is a simple server-side script, *main.asc*, whose only job is to set up the server-side code for our component:

```
load("PTextField.asc");
application.onAppStart = function () {
  this.pTextField_mc = new PTextField("c0");
};
```

Place this *main.asc* file in a folder named *pRecorderTest* in the FlashCom *applications* directory.

The *main.asc* file loads the component's code (*PTextField.asc*) and creates an instance of it as soon as the application is launched. Notice once again that we assign the "c0" ID to it manually.

This concludes our simple unit test. Now let's look at the code for the PTextField component in detail.

The PTextField.as file

This is the client-side code for the PTextField component. It's a pretty simple AS 2.0 class and must be stored in a file named *PTextField.as*:

```
class PTextField extends MovieClip {
  // Private vars.
  private var m_nc:NetConnection;
  private var m_so:SharedObject;
  private var m_id:String;

  // Text instance on the Stage.
  private var m_text_txt;

  // Empty constructor.
  function PTextField (Void) {
  }

  public function connect (p_id:String, p_nc:NetConnection):Void {
    m_id = p_id;
    m_nc = p_nc;

    var keyListener = new Object();
    keyListener.mc = this;
    keyListener.onChanged = function () {
      this.mc.m_so.data.text = this.mc.m_text_txt.text;
    };
    m_text_txt.addListener(keyListener);

    m_so = SharedObject.getRemote(m_id + "_text", p_nc.uri, false);
    m_so.owner = this;
    m_so.onSync = function (p_list:Array):Void {
      this.owner.m_text_txt.text = this.data.text;
    };
    m_so.connect(m_nc);
  }
}
```

As you probably imagined, all we need to do is to create a shared object that stores the content of the Input Text field. Notice how we use the unique ID as a namespace for the shared object name (m_id + "_text"), so that if two instances of the component were created, they wouldn't conflict.

The logic is extremely simple. The Input Text field has an *onChanged( )* listener attached to it, which updates the shared object, which triggers *onSync* events on all connected clients, which in turn update the contents of their text fields.

The PTextField.asc file

The server-side code for this component, stored in the *PTextField.asc* file, is even simpler (it doesn't really do anything):

```
PTextField = function (p_id) {
  this.m_id = p_id;
};
```

When we make this component recordable, we will see why we need a server-side script at all.

Save this server-side file alongside *main.asc* in the *pRecorderTest* folder under your FlashCom *applications* folder.

Store the client-side *.fla* and *.as* files wherever you want (on your web server's root, for example). Compile the *.fla* and open two instances of the resulting *.swf* to test it. Entering text in one *.swf* should update the text in both movies.

Voila, you have created a nice and simple componentized shared text application.

Now to the fun part!

The Recording and Playback Framework APIs

In the "Publishing and Playing ActionScript Data" section of Chapter 5, you learned how streams can be used to store remote method invocation requests, which will be triggered at the right time when the recorded stream is played back. This feature is the centerpiece of this whole example. Here's how it can be used to create a framework for recording and replaying any application:

- Your application is made of a main script and a set of components.
- Your application creates a singleton R&P Manager, which is in charge of recording events to a "master stream" and trapping those events when the stream is played back. This R&P Manager is also in charge of recording events for other components (through an API it exposes to them) and routing the events to playback components during playback.

Figure 15-1 shows how the pieces interact when recording an event generated by the component to the master stream.

During playback of the master stream, the R&P Manager traps the events and passes them to whoever is interested in them (with *dispatchEvent( )*). A replayable component will listen to those events and update the UI accordingly.

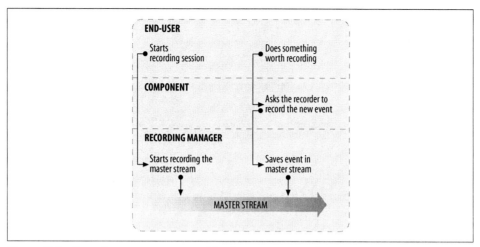

Figure 15-1. Recording an event generated by the component to the master stream

The next issue is that there can be multiple clients connected to a single application instance, and they might see different pieces of the UI at the same point in time (imagine a presenter having more controls than a viewer). So the question is, whose view should we record? Whose experience should we re-create when we play back the session?

The best solution is to do all recording on the server side. No matter who generates events, they will arrive at the server-side scripts in the same way, and there is only one server-side code thread for each application instance, which makes it a prime candidate for a centralized operation such as recording all events that happen in the application (regardless of who generated them).

As we will see, most of the playback code is going to be on the client side.

> So the strategy to remember is "record on the server side, play back on the client side."

Before we start building the R&P Manager classes, let's think of the APIs needed for all the pieces to fit together. We will worry with the actual implementation later.

We will create two new files and modify three existing files:

PRecorder.asc
: The server-side part of our R&P Manager

PRecorder.as
: The client-side file that provides the playback API

tester.fla

The existing tester client-side Flash movie, left as an exercise for the reader to update

tester.as

The existing script for the tester movie, which we'll enhance shortly

main.asc

The existing server-side application script, which we'll enhance shortly

The recording APIs

Here's the set of APIs that the R&P Manager will offer for recording events to the master stream (my preference is to put the APIs at the top of my scripts, in this case *PRecorder.asc*, the server-side part of our R&P Manager):

```
/**
 * PRecorder
 *
 * Public Properties
 *   .isRecording [Boolean]
 *
 * Public Methods
 *   .recordEvent(p_id:String, p_eventName:String, p_args:Array):Void
 *     // Records event p_eventName for component p_id with arguments p_args
 *
 *   Throws:
 *     "onRecordingEvent"
 *       status: "start" | "stop"
 */
```

The R&P Manager keeps an isRecording flag, which can be checked by components to see whether a master stream is being recorded.

There is only one method that can be called by the server-side code of components: *recordEvent( )*. Its parameters are the ID of the component generating the event, a custom name for the event, and an array of arguments. All this info will be saved in the master stream.

The R&P Manager is also an *EventDispatcher*, throwing an *onRecordingEvent* event to all listeners whenever a recording starts or stops.

We will see later how these functions (along with some other private functions) are implemented to create *PRecorder.asc*.

The playback APIs

The playback APIs are on the client side (at the top of the *PRecorder.as* file):

```
/**
 * PRecorder.as
 *
 *   .startRecording(p_name:String):Void
```

```
 *   .stopRecording(Void):Void
 *
 *   .startPlayback(p_name:String):Void
 *     // starts playback of the recording called p_name
 *   .pausePlayback(p_pause:Boolean):Void
 *     // true for pausing, false for resume playing
 *   .stopPlayback(Void):Void
 *   .seekPlayback(p_time:Number):Void
 *
 * Throws:
 *   "onPlaybackEvent"
 *     status: "start" | "stop" | "pause" | "seek"
 *   "onPlaybackCustomEvent"
 *     id: id of the component that threw this event
 *     name: "eventName"
 *     args: Array of event parameters
 */
```

The *startRecording( )* and *stopRecording( )* methods tell the R&P Manager to start and stop recording a master stream named p_name.

The *startPlayback( )*, *pausePlayback( )*, *stopPlayback( )*, and *seekPlayback( )* methods allow users to control the playback of the master stream.

The way the R&P Manager notifies components of playback events is through the regular *dispatchEvent( )* method of *EventDispatcher*. Two types of events can be thrown:

onPlaybackEvent
  Notifies listeners of events happening on the master stream (start, stop, pause, and seek)

onPlaybackCustomEvent
  Notifies listeners of a custom event being triggered (a custom event is one recorded by some component using the *recordEvent( )* method on the server side)

We will see later how these functions (along with some other private functions) are implemented to create *PRecorder.as*.

Updating the Tester Application

Now that we have the skeleton of an R&P Manager, we need to update the unit test application to make use of it.

Client-side code

On the client side, we'll need to create a VCR-style recording and replaying UI which calls *startRecording( )*, *stopRecording( )*, *startPlayback( )*, *pausePlayback( )*, *stopPlayback( )*, and *seekPlayback( )* on the R&P Manager. Building this UI is a pure Flash exercise and doesn't have any educational value in the context of FlashCom Server.

So we'll leave that up to you to build (or look on the book's web site for a premade component that does the trick, under *RnPSample.zip*). Either way, we'll omit that code in this section.

Open your *tester.as* file and add an import statement to the very top of the script and change your *setUp( )* function as follows (changes from previous version shown in bold):

```
import PRecorder;
function setUp(Void):Void {
  _global.pRecorder = new PRecorder(nc);
  //Set up components.
  pTextField_mc.connect("c0", nc);
  pTextField_mc.setRecorder(_global.pRecorder);
}
// Remainder of script is unchanged
```

Essentially we create the singleton R&P Manager and save it as _global.pRecorder.

Then, after connecting our PTextField component, we tell it that this application has an R&P Manager, through a new *setRecorder( )* method (see later for what it does in the component code).

Server-side code

Very similarly to the client-side code, we instantiate the R&P Manager on the server side. Modify your *main.asc* as follows (changes from previous version shown in bold):

```
load("PRecorder.asc"); // It creates the singleton application.pRecorder
load("PTextField.asc");
application.onAppStart = function () {
  this.pTextField_mc = new PTextField("c0");
  this.pTextField_mc.setRecorder(this.pRecorder);
};
```

As per the preceding script, we also call *setRecorder( )* on the server-side part of our component.

Making PTextField Recordable

Now that we have some APIs and the enhanced unit tester in place, we can make the PTextField component recordable.

Our strategy is very simple: whenever the text input changes, we record its new value as a recording event.

As we have seen, all recording is done on the server side. If you go back and look at *PTextField.asc*, you'll see that the server-side code doesn't know when the Input Text field is changed. Because the multiuser communication is done through a shared object, we can define a server-side *onSync( )* handler on the same shared object to

---

effectively trap any change to the Input Text field, regardless of who generated the change.

We want to do this only if the component is being recorded, so it makes sense to define the *onSync( )* handler in the *setRecorder( )* method definition. Add this code to the *PTextField.asc* file:

```
PTextField.prototype.setRecorder = function (p_recorder) {
  this.m_recorder = p_recorder;
  this.m_recorder.addEventListener("onRecordingEvent", this);

  // Use the SO on the server side for recording only.
  this.m_so = SharedObject.get(this.m_id + "_text", false);
  this.m_so.owner = this;
  this.m_so.onSync = function (p_list) {
    if (this.owner.m_isRecording)
      this.owner.m_recorder.recordEvent(this.owner.m_id,
            "textChanged", [this.getProperty("text")]);
  };
};
```

First, the code adds the *PTextField* component as a listener to the global R&P Manager (which will trigger the *onRecordingEvent( )* method whenever a master stream starts or stops being recorded).

Then the code gets a reference to the shared object and defines an *onSync( )* for it. The *onSync( )* handler checks whether the component is being recorded and, if so, asks the global R&P Manager to record a *textChanged* event containing the text for us.

The next thing to do is define an *onRecordingEvent( )* method, which will be triggered by the R&P Manager. Add this code to *PTextField.asc* as well:

```
PTextField.prototype.onRecordingEvent = function (p_eventObj) {
  this.m_isRecording = (p_eventObj.value == "start");
  if (this.m_isRecording)
    this.m_so.onSync(); // Generate an onSync event.
};
```

This function sets the m_isRecording flag depending on the event being triggered (value can be "start" or "stop").

Also note how we generate an artificial *onSync* event whenever a recording is started, to record the initial state of the Input Text field.

That's all that's needed to make PTextField recordable. Now let's look at how to make it replayable.

Making PTextField Replayable

All the code necessary to make PTextField replayable is added to the client-side *PTextField.as* file.

First of all, add a private variable to store a reference to the global R&P Manager:

```
private var m_recorder:PRecorder;
```

Then, we define a *setRecorder( )* method, which, as we saw, is invoked by the unit-test application. This method saves a reference to the global R&P Manager and registers the PTextField component as a listener to the R&P Manager's *onPlaybackEvent* and *onPlaybackCustomEvent* events:

```
public function setRecorder (p_recorder:PRecorder):Void {
  m_recorder = p_recorder;
  m_recorder.addEventListener("onPlaybackEvent", this);
  m_recorder.addEventListener("onPlaybackCustomEvent", this);
}
```

In the *onPlaybackEvent( )* handler definition, we change the look of the Input Text field so that it has a border and is selectable only if we're not playing back a session:

```
public function onPlaybackEvent (p_eventObj:Object):Void {
  m_text_txt.border = (p_eventObj.status == "stop");
  m_text_txt.selectable = (p_eventObj.status == "stop");
}
```

The *onPlaybackCustomEvent( )* handler definition is very simple: if the id of the custom event is our same ID, we trap the event and set the text of the Input Text field to be the first argument (which, as we saw, is the recorded text). This ensures that the PTextField component instance updates only if the event was recorded for it (as opposed to being recorded for another instance of the same component):

```
public function onPlaybackCustomEvent (p_eventObj:Object):Void {
  if (p_eventObj.id == m_id)
    m_text_txt.text = p_eventObj.args[0];
}
```

Notice how every component that listens to *onPlaybackCustomEvent* receives a notification for every custom event. This is very flexible and allows you to build two different components that listen to the same recorded events or to split a component into a recordable component and a replayable component. All the filtering is done through the component's unique ID, which acts as a namespace.

With the unit tester and the component in place, let's complete the framework.

The Recording and Playback Framework Implementation

Now that we have all the pieces in place, we need to actually build the R&P Manager files (*PRecorder.as* and *PRecorder.asc*).

The client-side framework (PRecorder.as)

The client-side code of the R&P Manager is fairly long, but not very complex. Here's the entire code, which belongs in *PRecorder.as*, with comments on the most interesting parts. I've broken it up into sections to make it digestible:

```
import mx.events.EventDispatcher;

class PRecorder extends Object {
  // EventDispatcher needs these
  var addEventListener:Function;
  var removeEventListener:Function;
  var dispatchEvent:Function;
  var dispatchQueue:Function;

  // Private vars
  private var m_nc:NetConnection;
  private var m_ns:NetStream;
  private var m_name:String;

  // Constructor
  function PRecorder (p_nc:NetConnection) {
    EventDispatcher.initialize(this);
    m_nc = p_nc;
  }

  public function startRecording (p_name:String):Void {
    m_ns = new NetStream(m_nc);
    m_ns.publish(p_name, "record");
    m_nc.call("pRecorder/startRecording", null, p_name);
  }

  public function stopRecording (Void):Void {
    m_nc.call("pRecorder/stopRecording", null);
  }
```

The preceding code creates a new NetStream and publishes it from the client that
clicked the Record button. It doesn't really matter which client is the publisher of the
stream, because all the contents of the master stream are inserted by the server side.

The code also calls the private *startRecording( )* method on the server side of the
R&P Manager, which just tells the server side to start recording.

The next method is the longest, but the bulk of it is the *NetStream.onStatus( )* definition which dispatches a *playbackEvent* with status "stop" when we have reached the
end of the stream. Notice that it also defines a single handler, *customEvent( )*, for all
custom events. All we do in it is dispatch an *onPlaybackCustomEvent* that will be
trapped by all the replayable components:

```
public function startPlayback (p_name:String):Void {
  m_name = p_name;
  m_ns.close(); // Stop the master stream in case it was already playing
  m_ns = new NetStream(m_nc);
  m_ns.owner = this;

  // Handle and dispatch custom events.
  m_ns.customEvent = function (p_id:String, p_eventName:String, p_args:Array) {
    this.owner.dispatchEvent({type:"onPlaybackCustomEvent",
                              id:p_id, name:p_eventName, args:p_args});
```

```
    };

    m_ns.onStatus = function (p_info) {
      switch (p_info.code) {
        case "NetStream.Play.Start":
          this.stopped = false;
          break;
        case "NetStream.Play.Stop":
          if (this.bufferLength == 0) {
            this.close();
            this.owner.dispatchEvent({type:"onPlaybackEvent", status:"stop"});
          }
          this.stopped = true;
          break;
        case "NetStream.Buffer.Empty":
          if (this.stopped) {
            this.close();
            this.owner.dispatchEvent({type:"onPlaybackEvent", status:"stop"});
          }
          break;
      }
    };

    m_ns.play(p_name);
    dispatchEvent({type:"onPlaybackEvent", status:"start", streamName:p_name});
}
```

Pretty long, but not complex, and it works like a charm. Notice how it broadcasts the appropriate *onPlaybackEvent* events to all the listening replayable components when appropriate.

The next methods are self-explanatory:

```
public function pausePlayback (p_pause:Boolean):Void {
  m_ns.pause(p_pause);
  dispatchEvent({type:"onPlaybackEvent", status:"pause", paused:p_pause});
}

public function stopPlayback (Void):Void {
  m_ns.close();
  dispatchEvent({type:"onPlaybackEvent", status:"stop"});
}

public function seekPlayback (p_time:Number):Void {
  m_ns.play(m_name, 0, p_time, 3);  // 3 means "play all events at once"
  dispatchEvent({type:"onPlaybackEvent", status:"seek", time:p_time});
}
}
```

The only thing worth noticing is the use of the number 3 in the arguments passed to *play( )* in the *seekPlayback( )* definition. This instructs the stream to play all the events between 0 and the time specified at once, when we do a seek in the master stream. Without this feature, seeking through a playback wouldn't be possible, as the only other way to receive all the events between time 0 and the time specified would be to play the stream, in real time (which is not a seek at all!). See Chapter 5 for more info on this feature.

The server-side code (PRecorder.asc)

The last remaining file is the server-side code of the R&P Manager. Here's all the code for *PRecorder.asc*, with comments. It starts by loading *EventDispatcher.asc*, a server-side port of the client-side *EventDispatcher* class, which can be found in Example 14-9:

```
load("EventDispatcher.asc");
PRecorder = function () {
  EventDispatcher.initialize(this);
  this.nextID = 0;
};
```

We saw how *PTextField.asc* uses the *recordEvent( )* method to record a custom event to the master stream. All it does is use the server-side *NetStream.send( )* method:

```
// Public
PRecorder.prototype.recordEvent = function (p_id, p_eventName, p_args) {
  this.m_ns.send("customEvent", p_id, p_eventName, p_args);
};
```

This private *startRecording( )* method is called by the client-side *PRecorder.as* file and is used by the server side to get hold of the *Stream* object and to notify the server-side portion of each recordable component that a recording is starting:

```
// Private (called by PRecorder.as)
PRecorder.prototype.startRecording = function (p_name) {
  this.isRecording = true;
  this.m_ns = Stream.get(p_name);
  this.dispatchEvent({type:"onRecordingEvent", value:"start", streamName:p_name});
};
```

The next method is self-explanatory:

```
// Private (called by PRecorder.as)
PRecorder.prototype.stopRecording = function () {
  this.isRecording = false;
  this.m_ns.record(false);
  this.dispatchEvent({type:"onRecordingEvent", value:"stop"});
};
```

The last two lines create the server-side singleton and attach a reference to it on the global application object. It also attaches a reference to itself to the Client. prototype object, so that the client-side *PRecorder.as* code can call methods on it just by doing *call("pRecorder/methodname")*:

```
// Create singleton R&P Manager
application.pRecorder = new PRecorder();
// Attach to Client.prototype
Client.prototype.pRecorder = application.pRecorder;
```

And that's it. You are now armed with the essential information you need to create applications that can record and play back all sorts of events—from chat and video conference sessions to multicamera live events. Now, try to imagine an application that couldn't benefit from this feature.

Components and Component Frameworks

Perhaps the best piece of advice this book can provide is to recommend you use, extend, and write communication components. Components provide a way to build complex applications in manageable chunks and can be designed following something resembling the classic Model-View-Controller (MVC) design pattern.

Each component:

- Will generate events that a controller-like object can preprocess
- Will have a model—often a shared object—and the code that enforces business rules on it
- Will have a view that consists of subcomponents that respond to changes in the model

By developing components with both client- and server-side parts, components can leverage the resources of both.

However, components cannot be designed ad hoc. They should have naming conventions, a way to instantiate them on both the client and server, and a standard way to hook them together. In fact, the word "component" normally refers to a piece of software designed to work without alteration within a component container of some type. The container is sometimes referred to as a *component framework*. A component specification and framework may define:

- A naming convention designed to avoid collisions between components and their resources. Namespace rules avoid collisions between different types and instances of the same type of component.
- A message-passing or event system for intercomponent messaging and life cycle management—for example, notifying a component when a user connects to an application.
- Component base classes that simplify writing new components and that can already perform common tasks. In the Flash v2 UI component framework, the *UIComponent* class is a good example.
- A framework or context that components work within and can rely on to perform certain services. Often it is the component framework that will deliver application-level events that components must respond to.

Along with FlashCom, Macromedia released a set of components and a component framework that are the subject of Chapter 14. The design of the communication components and component framework were driven by one overriding goal: adding a component to an application had to be simple. All that is required to have a component work is to drag an instance to the Stage in Flash, give it a name, and connect it to a SimpleConnect component. In other words, little or no server-side coding is required.

As a consequence, the server-side part of each component is automatically created whenever a client-side component connects. For some applications, automatic generation of server-side objects (so-called lazy instantiation) is a great feature. But in other applications, it represents a potential security problem. Another consequence of Macromedia's design choices is that all the server-side component class files are loaded by the framework in case they are needed—whether they are used or not.

No authentication mechanism or hooks were provided with the component system and little in the way of user management and control. See Chapter 14 for how to authenticate users and Chapter 18 for some ways to implement role-based access controls. And unfortunately, the namespace design of the components was not extended to define a URI namespace for component resources. Component resources are created in the root folder of the application instance, making it impossible to protect other resources in subfolders using the `client.readAccess` and `client.writeAccess` properties.

Yet Another Component Framework?

Any developer faced with the need to create any but the simplest FlashCom application has to decide whether to use Macromedia's components and component framework or strike out in a different direction. Chapter 13 presented a set of FlashCom components that used little more than the v2 UI components provided with Flash. If you read through Chapter 13, you will have seen a number of redundancies in some of the components and other things that could have been improved. The remainder of this chapter describes a very simple and lightweight component framework that was designed as an outgrowth of the work shown in Chapter 13. Naturally, the complete framework is available as a download from the book's web site.

The design goals of this PFCS framework are:

- Remove redundancy from the Chapter 13 components and move common functions into a base class (*PFCSComponent*) that can be used to develop new component objects on the client and server.

- Provide a foundation for user authentication, user management, and better server-side security on the client and server that is leveraged in later chapters of the book.

- Keep it simple—add to the base classes and framework only features that are needed to reduce redundancy and improve user management and security.

- Assume a developer using the framework is fully capable of server-side coding, including loading only the class files that are needed and writing some code to name and instantiate component instances on the server.

The PFCSComponent Base Classes

The *PFCSComponent* base classes are designed to simplify creating the client- and server-side objects that work together to create a communication component. The *PFCSComponent.as* file can be found in the */com/oreilly/pfcs/framework* directory in any Zip archive on the book's web site that uses the PFCS framework; the *PFCSComponent.asc* file can be found in the *scriptlib/pfcs* directory. Both classes are designed to support the naming conventions of the components and the management of each component's remote methods. On the server, the *PFCSComponent* class also provides a simple storage mechanism for client-specific data that the component needs to manage.

The client-side *PFCSComponent* base class is the simpler of the two *PFCSComponent* classes, so let's look at it first. It implements the namespace-related methods that set and get a component's name and update its path. For example, the default name for a component is main. The full path of the component will be in the *pfcs/ClassName/ main* format. If a component is named something other than main, setting its name will also update its full path. For example, to name a TextChat component instance breakout1, set the name this way:

```
myTextChat.name = breakout1;
```

The internal path will be updated to *pfcs/TextChat/breakout1*.

Whenever the server-side part of a component must call a client-side remote method, the method must be attached to the *NetConnection* object the client is using to communicate to the server. To avoid collisions between remote methods belonging to different components, each method follows the namespace of the components. For example, if a ConnectionTester component named main had to attach an *echoRequest( )* method to the *NetConnection* object it was using, it would attach it as follows:

```
var proxy = getProxy(nc);
proxy.echoRequest() = function () {
  return;
};
```

The effect is the same as if it had done the following:

```
addObjectPath(__nc);
__nc.pfcs.ConnectionTester.main.echoRequest() = function () {
  return;
};
```

The main object in the object path *__nc.pfcs.ConnectionTester.main* is the component's proxy object. The component places whatever remote methods it must define

---

on its proxy. The *getProxy( )* method takes care of making sure the proxy object exists and returning it to the component. Example 15-6 lists the code for the client-side *PFCSComponent* class, stored in *PFCSComponent.as*.

Example 15-6. The code for the client-side PFCSComponent class

```
class com.oreilly.pfcs.framework.PFCSComponent extends mx.core.UIComponent {
  // Connect component class and symbol.
  var className:String = "PFCSComponent";
  static var symbolName:String = "PFCSComponent";
  static var symbolOwner:Object = PFCSComponent;

  // Variables.
  var __user:Object;
  var __nc:NetConnection;
  var instance;

  // Default path and name.
  var path:String;
  var __name:String = "main";

  // Constructor--call the superclass constructor.
  function PFCSComponent() {
    super();
  }

  function init() {
    instance = this;
    super.init();
  }

  function set name (name:String) {
    if (!name) name = "main";
    __name = name;
    path = "pfcs/" + className + "/" + __name + "/";
  }

  function get name() {
    return __name;
  }

  public function set nc (nc:NetConnection) {
    __nc = nc;
  }

  public function set user (user:Object) {
    __user = user;
  }

  /* addObjectPath() adds an object path to the NetConnection object based on
   * the path property and returns the last object added. If the path is
   * pfcs.PFCSComponent.main, the nc will have the nested object
   * nc.pfcs.PFCSComponent.main, which will be returned.
```

```
 * The main object is a proxy for the component
 * where remote methods arrive and are passed on to the component.
 */
function addObjectPath (nc) {
  var pathArray = path.split("/");
  var obj = nc;
  var name;
  for (var i = 0; i < pathArray.length; i++) {
    name = pathArray[i];
    if (!name) continue;
    if (!obj[name]) {
      obj[name] = {};
    }
    obj = obj[name];
  }
  return obj;
}


// removeObjectPath() removes the proxy object in the object path
// and the class name object if it has no other subobjects.
function removeObjectPath (nc) {
  var classObject = nc.pfcs[this.className];
  delete classObject[this.name];
  var deleteClassObject = true;
  for (var p in classObject) {
    deleteClassObject = false;
    break;
  }
  if (deleteClassObject) {
    delete nc.pfcs[this.className];
  }
}

function getProxy (nc) {
  var proxy = nc.pfcs[className][name];
  if (!proxy) {
    // trace("No proxy, so making one.");
    proxy = addObjectPath(nc);
  }
  return proxy;
}
}
```

The PeopleCursors component listed in Example 15-2 extends PFCSComponent and so does not need to replicate the *set name( )* method to create a path. The *ConnectionTester* class shown in Example 17-1 provides an example of using the *getProxy( )* method.

The server-side PFCSComponent does a little more work. In addition to creating the path string when its name is set and providing a *getProxy( )* method, it also provides methods that can be used to update each client's access control strings. Chapter 18 describes how each component can control access to its *SharedObject* and *Stream* resources using the *addAccessPath( )* and *removeAccessPath( )* methods. Unlike the client-side part of each component, the server-side component's name is passed into its constructor and the *getProxy( )* method is passed a client object instead of a *Net-Connection*. Example 15-7 lists the complete code for the server-side *PFCSComponent* class, stored in *PFCSComponent.asc*.

Example 15-7. The code for the server-side PFCSComponent class

```
// Base class for the server-side object part of a communication component.
function PFCSComponent (name) {
  if (this.className == "PFCSComponent") {
    return; // Return when overwriting a subclass's prototype.
  }
  if (!name) name = "main";
  this.name = name;
  this.path = "pfcs/" + this.className + "/" + name;
  trace("PFCSComponent(" + this.name + ")> className: " + this.className);
}

p = PFCSComponent.prototype;
p.className = "PFCSComponent";

/* addObjectPath( ) adds an object path to the client object based on
 * the path property and returns the last object added. If the path is
 * pfcs.PFCSComponent.main, the client will have objects:
 * client.pfcs.PFCSComponent.main and main will be returned.
 * The main object is a proxy for the component
 * where remote methods arrive and are passed on to the component.
 */
p.addObjectPath = function (client) {
  var pathArray = this.path.split("/");
  var obj = client;
  var name;
  for (var i = 0; i < pathArray.length; i++) {
    name = pathArray[i];
    if (!obj[name]) {
      obj[name] = {};
    }
    obj = obj[name];
  }
  return obj;
};

// removeObjectPath( ) removes the proxy object in the object path
// and the class name object if it has no other subobjects.
p.removeObjectPath = function (client) {
  var classObject = client.pfcs[this.className];
  delete classObject[this.name];
  var deleteClassObject = true;
  for (var p in classObject) {
    deleteClassObject = true;
```

```
    break;
  }
  if (deleteClassObject) {
    delete client.pfcs[this.className];
  }
};

// getAccessArray( ) returns the access string broken down into elements
// within an array. Used by addAccessPath( ) and removeAccessPath( ).
p.getAccessArray = function (client, accessStringName) {
  var accessString = client[accessStringName];
  if (accessString.length > 0)
    return accessString.split(";");
  else
    return [];
};

// addAccessPath( ) adds a path to the semicolon-delimited string in the client.
// Valid values for accessStringName are "readAccess" and "writeAccess".
p.addAccessPath = function (client, accessStringName, path) {
  var pathArray = this.getAccessArray(client, accessStringName);
  pathArray.push(path);
  client[accessStringName] = pathArray.join(";");
};

// removeAccessPath( ) deletes a path from the semicolon-delimited string in the
// client. Valid values for accessStringName are "readAccess" and "writeAccess".
p.removeAccessPath = function (client, accessStringName, path) {
  var pathArray = this.getAccessArray(client, accessStringName);
  var len = pathArray.length;
  for (var i = 0; i < len; i++) {
    if (pathArray[i] == path) {
        pathArray.splice(i, 1); // remove the element
        break;
    }
  }
  client[accessStringName] = pathArray.join(";");
};
```

Inheriting from the *PFCSComponent* base class on the server requires a little more work in Server-Side ActionScript than in client-side ActionScript 2.0 because the former uses prototype-based inheritance and does not support the more formal class and extends keywords. Example 15-8 shows the complete listing of the server-side part of the *PeopleCursors.asc* file.

Example 15-8. The server-side part of the PeopleCursors.asc file

```
function PeopleCursors (name) {
  PFCSComponent.apply(this, [name]);
  this.so = SharedObject.get(this.path + "/cursors");
}
```

```
// PeopleCursors inherits from (is a subclass of) PFCSComponent.
PeopleCursors.prototype = new PFCSComponent();
PeopleCursors.prototype.constructor = PeopleCursors;
PeopleCursors.prototype.className = "PeopleCursors";

PeopleCursors.prototype.addClient = function (client) {
  // Let all clients read and write the shared object.
  this.addAccessPath(client, "readAccess", this.path);
  this.addAccessPath(client, "writeAccess", this.path);
};

PeopleCursors.prototype.removeClient = function (client) {
  // Make sure this user's cursor is deleted when the client
  // disconnects or no longer is using this component.
  var user = pfcs.getUser(client);
  this.so.setProperty(user.userName, null);
  // Remove all the access strings that were added for this component.
  this.removeAccessPath(client, "readAccess", this.path);
  this.removeAccessPath(client, "writeAccess", this.path);
};

PeopleCursors.prototype.close = function () {
  this.so.close();
};
```

Since there is no *super* operator in Server-Side ActionScript, the *PFCSComponent* constructor function is called directly and applied to the object being instantiated in the *PeopleCursors( )* constructor in place of calling *super( )*. In place of the class declaration and extends keyword in AS 2.0, the prototype object is overwritten with a *PFCSComponent* object to establish inheritance:

```
PeopleCursors.prototype = new PFCSComponent();
```

When the prototype is replaced, its constructor property is automatically set to *PFCSComponent*. To set it back to the correct constructor function, the constructor property has to be updated as follows:

```
PeopleCursors.prototype.constructor = PeopleCursors;
```

Otherwise, the code is much like what was shown in Chapter 13. Every server-side component is expected to implement an *addClient( )*, *removeClient( )*, and *close( )* method. The *addClient( )* method is the component's opportunity to make the component work for the client. If necessary, a slot for the client in a shared object can be created, remote methods can be added to the client, and client-specific data can be added to the component's proxy on the client. The *addClient( )* method is also where the client's access rights to component resources are determined and limited access is granted. The *removeClient( )* method removes anything added to the client including access to component resources. The *close( )* method is used to clean up component resources before the component is disposed of.

I've spent a fair amount of time explaining the *PFCSComponent* base classes and how to extend them, because most of the work that goes into developing a component is done in the process of extending the base classes. But components don't live in a vacuum. The *PFCSFramework* classes provide some essential services you'll need to use, as described in the next section.

The PFCSFramework Classes

On the client side, the *PFCSFramework* and *Auth* classes are responsible for managing the login and connection events on behalf of the application and providing information about the user to any component that needs it. The actual login and authentication process is done by an *Auth* object. Example 15-9 is a small snippet of code from the main timeline of a test movie that uses the PFCS framework. It imports the two classes required by the framework—the *PFCSFramework* class and an authentication class.

Example 15-9. Timeline code of a test movie that uses the PFCS framework

```
import com.oreilly.pfcs.framework.PFCSFramework;
import com.oreilly.pfcs.framework.auth.TicketAuth;

_global.pfcs = new PFCSFramework(this);
auth:TicketAuth = new TicketAuth("http://localhost:8500/flashservices/gateway",
                                 "pfcs.conference.user");
pfcs.setAuth(auth);
pfcs.setURI("rtmp:/conference/room1");
gotoAndStop("Login");
```

The preceding code initializes the framework, sets its authentication object and the URI of the application instance, and then moves the playhead to a Login frame. From now on, any component or form that needs to use the framework will call a method on the global pfcs object. Example 15-9 uses an authentication object that uses a web application to get a ticket before using the ticket to log in to FlashCom. Other authentication objects can also be used. Ticketing is discussed in Chapter 18.

When the login form is filled in and the user is ready to log in, the form will call:

```
    pfcs.doLogin(this, userName, password);
```

which will connect to a web application to get a ticket and then to a FlashCom instance (using the ticket for authentication). The entire *PFCSFramework.as* file is not listed here, but here is a list of often-used methods:

pfcs.getUser( )
Returns the current user object that includes any personal information about the user returned from the authentication database

pfcs.getUserName( )
Returns the user's username

pfcs.getUserRoles( )

    Returns an object; each property name is a user role

pfcs.inRole("roleName")

    Returns true if the user is in the role

pfcs. inRoles(role_1, role_2 [, role_n])

    Returns true if the user is in any of the named roles

pfcs.doLogin(loginForm, userName, password)

    Starts the login process

pfcs.doLogout( )

    Disconnects from the web application (if there is one) and FlashCom

pfcs.getNC( )

    Gets a *NetConnection* object that components can use to connect with

On the server, all the framework files are found in the *scriptlib/pfcs* or *scriptlib/pfcs/components* directories. Example 15-10 shows the beginning of a *main.asc* file that uses the framework and abbreviated parts of the rest of the file.

Example 15-10. Part of a main.asc file that uses the framework

```
load("pfcs/PFCSFramework.asc");
load("pfcs/Auth.asc");
load("pfcs/components/PeopleGrid.asc");
load("pfcs/components/SharedText.asc");
load("pfcs/components/TextChat.asc");
load("pfcs/components/PeopleCursors.asc");

application.onAppStart = function ( ) {
  // Create a global pfcs object to manage clients.
  pfcs = new PFCSFramework( );
  // Create an authentication object to authenticate clients.
  auth = new Auth('conference');
  // Create a main component manager and tell it what components to create.
  cManager = new PFCSComponentManager("main");
  cManager.addComponent(PeopleGrid);
  cManager.addComponent(SharedText);
  cManager.addComponent(TextChat);
  cManager.addComponent(PeopleCursors);
};

application.onConnect = function (client, userName, password) {
  return auth.authenticate(client, userName, password);
};

application.onAuthenticate = function (client, result) {
  // Code removed...
  // Control access and bandwidth based on one of the user's roles.
  client.readAccess = "";    // Deny all readAccess to start.
  client.writeAccess = "";   // Deny all writeAccess to start.
```

Example 15-10. Part of a main.asc file that uses the framework (continued)

```
  // Store the client in the pfcs.clients object by username.
  pfcs.addClient(client, result);

  cManager.addClient(client);

  // Accept the client's connection request.
  application.acceptConnection(client);
};

application.onDisconnect = function (client) {
  cManager.removeClient(client);
  pfcs.removeClient(client)
};

application.onAppStop = function () {
  cManager.close();
};
```

The authentication part of the code is explained in Chapter 18. Instead of passing each component's *addClient( )* method a client reference, as in Chapter 13, a component manager does the work of setting up and initializing each component it manages. Component managers allow you to group components together logically. The idea is that sets of components for things like a breakout session can be handled separately by another component manager. Every component can call any of the following methods on the global pfcs object:

pfcs.addClient(client, user)
> Allows the framework to manage the client and associate the user object's information with the client

pfcs.getUser(client)
> Returns the current user object associated with the client

pfcs.getUserName(client)
> Returns the username for the user associated with the client

pfcs.getUserRoles(client)
> Returns an object where the user's role names are property names

pfcs.getClient(userName)
> Returns a user's client

pfcs.clientInRole(client, "roleName")
> Returns true if the client matches the specified role

pfcs.clientInRoles = function (client, role_1, role_2, [role_n])
> Returns true if the client matches any of the specified roles

The complete source files for the framework are available from the book's web site. It is designed to be a minimal framework that you can experiment with, adapt, and extend to suit your own needs. It is not cast in stone, so please experiment with it! We'll make extensive use of it in the following chapters.

Conclusion

From the diversity of topics discussed in this chapter, you can get a feel for the breadth and depth of FlashCom application development. If you are new to Flash-Com programming, don't allow yourself to be overwhelmed by the technical details at this point. Regardless of your level of programming experience, your approach to FlashCom application architecture will evolve over time as you develop your own favorite techniques. Every application's requirements are different, but you'll eventually master a set of best practices that you can apply to almost any situation. We hope that this chapter has saved you some time along that journey. Be sure to revisit this chapter as you delve deeper into FlashCom programming. A subtopic within this chapter that seemed too difficult or obscure the first time you read it may well help solve a future dilemma.

This was the first chapter of the book that dealt largely with the architectural decisions you'll need to make as you design an application. Instead of being spoon-fed an existing solution, you were asked to contemplate appropriate design choices. But its demands will help you build upon the firm foundation of knowledge you gained in earlier chapters. Soon you will be able to develop your own components and frameworks. Testing and experience will tell you which approaches are more likely to work for the task at hand. Don't be afraid to make mistakes or ask the community at large for advice.

The remaining chapters offer additional advice and an opportunity for more practice applying your skills. They cover important topics that affect almost every FlashCom application: scalability, performance, bandwidth management, and security.

CHAPTER 16
Building Scalable Applications

Most production applications require more than one application instance. For example, a chat room system may have several lobby application instances running at the same time, as well as many chat room instances. In fact, instances of an application may be running on more than one server. Some of the good reasons to partition an application across multiple instances on one or more servers are as follows:

Performance
> Each instance has a single ActionScript thread, which can constitute a bottleneck. Using multiple instances allows for multiple simultaneous threads.

Separation of resources
> Clients that need common access to the same shared objects and streams can be grouped into separate instances.

Scalability
> As the number of clients increases, a single server may not be able to handle the load. Adding CPUs, RAM, and network cards to a single server increases its capacity to handle more clients, but only up to a point. Placing separate instances on different servers allows applications to scale to accommodate as many clients as necessary.

Failover
> When an instance or server fails, instances on another server can take over so that clients can reconnect and continue working.

A multi-instance application should still appear as one seamless application to the user. For example, a multiroom chat system can provide a global user list that shows who is online despite the fact that users are connected to different instances (perhaps on different servers). Where multiple lobbies are used, a user connected to one lobby should be able to invite users connected to other lobby instances to connect to a chat instance.

This chapter introduces some of the problems of coordinating multiple instances that make up an application, scaling applications across multiple servers, and providing failover. It provides some guidance on how to approach building multi-instance applications and gives some examples. However, it does not present a single *n*-tiered architecture as is common for web-based applications. One reason a single architecture is not presented is that there are so many different types of FlashCom applications. Another reason is that shared objects and streams can be directly updated by one master instance only. Custom ActionScript is required to provide access to streams and shared objects to other instances.

Some of the hosting companies cited in the Preface offer scalable, fault-tolerant FlashCom application hosting of their own on-demand and live streaming applications. However, it is very difficult for hosting companies to offer scalable and fault-tolerant standard hosting packages for customer-written applications because each application will have different requirements. Some vendors are willing to negotiate custom agreements for multiserver hosting.

Coordinating Instances

Achieving a unified application experience often involves controlling what instance each user connects to and making users aware of what other people are doing in other instances. The broad categories of applications are (1) those in which each instance can pretty much manage itself—often with help from an application server and database—and (2) those in which instances must cooperate with one another in real time. An example of the first type of application is a video conference application in which one person manages a room instance and controls who is invited to visit it. A list of invitees held in a database is often all that is needed to invite users and control access.

An example of the second type of application is an online gaming system in which users enter one of a series of lobbies depending on their interests or how busy each lobby is. From there, they can see what game rooms are available and agree to move to one that contains a game of interest to them, such as chess. Another example in which real-time coordination is required is a help desk waiting room in which users wait in a queue to get into a help operator's room for assistance. Each operator may need to see who is in the queue and even select some users out of order based on information each user provides or information about ongoing problems.

There are three common ways to make multiple instances appear as one application:

- Allow instances to manage themselves based on information in a database.
- Create network connections between instances so that they can share information in real time with one another.
- Have the instances poll an application server and database for real-time coordination.

Managing Independent Instances

For some applications, an application server working with a database can provide all the logic required to manage a set of application instances that do not need to interact directly with one another. In traditional teleconferencing applications, the essential part of setting up and using a conference is scheduling each meeting, establishing a connection between each conference site, and getting participants into the meeting room on time. A web-based conferencing system may not have to do much more. A meeting time must be set and an application instance name reserved for that time. Participants must be invited to the meeting—often by email—and sent a URL they can use to connect to the conference. Finally, only people invited to the meeting should be aware of the instance (room) and be able to connect.

The work of defining instance names and the user records for the people who will connect to them, distributing a unique URL to users, and controlling access can be done with a web application and database. FlashCom and Flash are not required for the setup phase. FlashCom (and Flash) are required only when each user actually connects to the conference room instance. For example, each user may receive a unique URL that includes a room name as extra path information. The .swf loaded from the page must know the RTMP address of the correct room to connect to. If the web application part of a conferencing system has generated the URL for a specific room, it can translate the extra path information into HTML FlashVars attributes that can be used to embed the RTMP address right in the page.

Another scheme is to have the .swf file access an XML file with the RTMP connection information. The room instances do not even need to be on the same server. A web application can schedule the use of room instances across multiple FlashCom Servers based on the total number of simultaneous participants. For example, each meeting that starts within a certain time window can be allocated to the server with the fewest number of scheduled users. An even more sophisticated system can be used that assigns users a load figure based on the user role they are assigned when they connect. Users with roles that will place a lot of demand on the server will get a higher load number and users who demand less, a lower number. The web application can use the user's load rating to spread application instances across multiple servers in a way that more accurately balances the load across machines.

This chapter does not discuss further the web applications that are responsible for setting up and controlling multiple but independent instances. However, Example 18-11 includes an example of using FlashVars and a discussion of how to restrict access to specific resources, such as restricting room instances to certain users. See the section called "Access Control Tables" in that chapter.

Interinstance Communications

The only way for instances to share information in real time is for one instance to create a network connection to another instance. As described in Chapter 4, a *Net-Connection* object can be used to connect two FlashCom application instances in the same way a Flash movie uses a *NetConnection* to connect to an instance. The methods and *NetConnection* information objects are almost identical.

When one instance attempts to connect to another, it is treated as if it were a Flash client, so we can refer to it as a *client instance*. There are no restrictions on how many or what type of instance can connect to another one, other than the physical capacity of the server to support network connections. However, each instance-to-instance connection is counted by the FlashCom license manager, as discussed in the Preface. Instances of an application can connect to an instance of the same application on the same server, to a different application on the same server, or to applications on a different server.

Once a network connection has been established between instances, the client instance can use its *NetConnection* object, much as a Flash client can, to connect to resources that belong to the instance to which it is connected. The *NetConnection* object can be used by the client instance to play streams, connect to shared objects, and call remote methods that belong to the other instance. The instance that owns a shared object or stream is referred to as a *master instance*.

Proxies

After a client instance connects to a master instance, it can get a reference to the master instance's shared objects and play the master instance's streams. Flash clients connected to a client instance see the master instance's shared objects and streams as though they belong to the client instance. Because the client instance is making the master instance's resources available to its clients, the shared object and streams are referred to as *proxies*. See Chapters 5, 8, and 9 for more details on proxied streams, shared objects, and remote methods. From the Flash client's point of view, it simply uses a shared object, stream, or remote method belonging to the client instance to which it is connected. It has no way of knowing that the resource belongs to another instance.

Interinstance connections and proxies make possible a number of applications. For example, a chat room system can be built in which every visitor, regardless of whether she is connected to a room or the lobby, can know where all the other users in the system are.

Figure 16-1 illustrates a simple example of a lobby and chat room system.

Each Flash client connects to only one instance at a time. A user is either in the lobby or in a chat room. When each chat room instance is created, it opens a *NetConnection* to the lobby and proxies any resources it needs to make available to its clients.

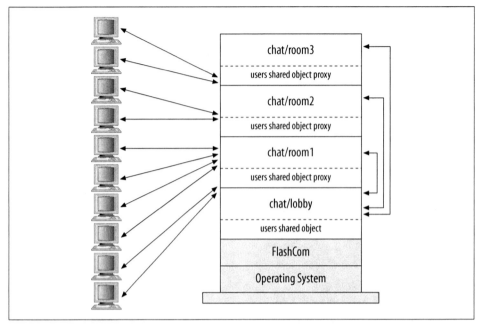

Figure 16-1. A lobby and chat room system in which each room instance connects to the master lobby instance

A lobby instance can maintain a users shared object that each room updates as users connect and disconnect from each room. Since each slot contains user and room information, the shared object contains all the necessary information to determine where each user is within the system. If each client (chat) instance makes a proxy of the global user list available to its clients, every user will be able to see where everyone else is within the system. Sample code and a basic example of a lobby chat room system with a global user list is available at:

http://flash-communications.net/technotes/flashLobby/index.html

Of course, the scheme illustrated in Figure 16-1 has limits. If too many clients connect to the lobby instance, lobby performance will suffer. So a variation on having a single lobby with multiple chat rooms is to introduce multiple lobbies as illustrated in Figure 16-2.

Figure 16-2 illustrates a better performing and more flexible chat system. Clients first connect to one of many lobby instances. Each lobby instance connects to a single master instance. The master instance does not accept Flash client connections. Its only purpose is to provide each lobby with common resources such as a users shared object. Each lobby updates the users shared object when clients connect and disconnect. While a client is connected to the chat system, it never closes its connection to a lobby. The lobby provides each client with a proxy to the users shared object and any other resources it needs. For example, if a user connected to one lobby wants to

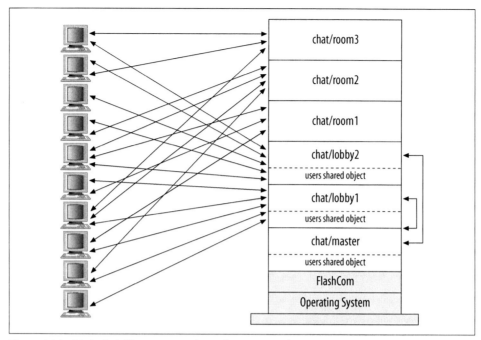

Figure 16-2. Multiple lobbies connected together via a single master instance

invite someone connected to another lobby to chat, a message to the other user can be routed through the master instance.

When clients connect to a chat room, they create additional *NetConnection* objects—one for each chat room. Chat rooms do not need to connect back to a lobby or the master instance. Each client can tell its lobby what rooms it is connected to if that information must be made available to other clients.

Coding a multi-lobby system is not nearly as complicated as it may appear. As long as the code for the master instance, lobby, and chat rooms can be kept separate, it is not too difficult. A good practice is to use different *.asc* files within a single application to create instances with different behaviors.

For example, we can create five files in an *applications/chatSystem* subdirectory:

main.asc
    Loads the other files depending on the RTMP address

master.asc
    Responsible for creating global objects for the lobbies

lobby.asc
    Connects to the master instance and proxies its resources

room.asc
    Provides resources for each chat room

error.asc
   Rejects client connections with invalid RTMP addresses

The *main.asc* file can load one of the other files by examining its own application.
name property:

```
switch (application.name.split("/")[1]) {
  case "lobby":
    load("lobby.asc");
    break;
  case "room":
    load("room.asc");
    break;
  case "master":
    load("master.asc");
    break;
  default: load("error.asc");
}
```

Loading the correct *.asc* file relies on the use of RTMP addresses with the following
format:

   `rtmp://host.domain.com/chatSystem/typeOfInstance/instanceName`

For example, when each lobby starts, it will request a connection to the master
instance at:

   `rtmp://host.domain.com/chatSystem/master`

When a client connects to a lobby, it will connect to an instance with an address
such as:

   `rtmp://host.domain.com/chatSystem/lobby/lobby21`

When a client connects to a chat room, it will use an address such as:

   `rtmp://host.domain.com/chatSystem/room/room42`

In each case, the *main.asc* file checks the *typeOfInstance* portion of the RTMP
address to determine which *.asc* file to load.

After each file is loaded and initialized, it can start accepting connections. The master instance needs to authenticate and accept connections from lobby instances only. It does not have to contain any code to accept connections from Flash clients. The lobby must open a connection to the master instance when it starts and need accept connections only from Flash clients. Room instances have only to authenticate and accept connections from Flash clients. Finally, the room and lobby instances have only to support the features expected from a room or lobby, but not both in the same instance.

Example 16-1 shows the contents of the *master.asc* file, which makes use of the PFCS framework discussed in the preceding chapter.

Example 16-1. The master.asc file

```
load("pfcs/Text.asc");          //Part of PFCS framework
load("pfcs/PFCSComponent.asc");  //Part of PFCS framework
load("ActiveChatUsers_Root.asc");//See Example 16-3

validIPs = {};
validIPs["141.117"] = true;
validIPs["209.29.148"] = true;
validIPs["192.168.0.23"] = true;
validIPs["127.0.0.1"] = true;

application.onAppStart = function () {
  this.hostIdentifier = "k38djskl3o9";
  this.clientHash = {};
  activeUsers = new ActiveChatUsers_Root("main");
};

application.onConnect = function (client, instanceName, hostIdentifier) {
  // The static Text.trim() method trims leading and trailing whitespace. It is
  // defined in the Text.as file, which is provided on the book's web site.
  instanceName   = Text.trim(instanceName);
  hostIdentifier = Text.trim(hostIdentifier);
  // Make sure the strings have something that might be useful in them.
  if (!instanceName || !hostIdentifier) {
    application.rejectConnection(client,
        {msg:"Empty or missing user instanceName or hostIdentifier."});
    return false;
  }

  // Check the IP address of the client instance.
  var ip = client.ip
  var validAddress = false;
  do {
    if (validIPs[ip]) {
      validAddress = true;
      break;
    }
    ip = ip.substring(0, ip.lastIndexOf("."));
  } while (ip.length > 0);

  if (!validAddress) {
    application.rejectConnection(client, {msg:"Access Denied."});
    return false;
  }

  // Check the host identifier.
  if (hostIdentifier != this.hostIdentifier) {
    application.rejectConnection(client, {msg:"Access Denied."});
    return false;
  }

  client.pfcs = {
    user:{userName:client.ip + "/" + instanceName}
```

Example 16-1. The master.asc file (continued)

```
    }

    this.clientHash[client.pfcs.user.userName] = client;
    client.writeAccess = "";
    client.readAccess = "";
    activeUsers.addClient(client);
    return true;
}

application.onDisconnect = function (client) {
    var userName = client.pfcs.user.userName;
    delete this.clientHash[userName];
    activeUsers.removeClient(client);
};
```

Most of the code is designed to test whether a lobby instance is really connecting; the code is explained in detail in Chapter 18. An activeUsers object is created, which is responsible for creating a global users list. As each lobby connects, it is represented by a *Client* object within the *onConnect( )* method. Each client object is passed to the *activeUsers.addClient( )* method so that the activeUsers object can provide it access to the global users list.

Example 16-2 shows the contents of the *lobby.asc* file. It should look similar to the code discussed in Chapters 13 and 15, with the exception of the Auth component that is used to authenticate each Flash client. See Chapter 18 for information on the Auth component.

Example 16-2. The lobby.asc file

```
load("pfcs/PFCSEventDispatcher.asc");
load("pfcs/PFCSFramework.asc");
load("pfcs/Auth.asc");
load("pfcs/PFCSComponent.asc");
load("pfcs/NetConnectionFactory.asc");
load("pfcs/SharedObjectFactory.asc");
load("ActiveChatUsers_Leaf.asc");//See Example 16-4

application.onAppStart = function () {
    pfcs = new PFCSFramework();
    // Tack on a NetConnection.
    pfcs.nc = NetConnectionFactory.get();
    // The connect() call includes a host password as the last parameter
    pfcs.nc.connect("rtmp://localhost/chatSystem/master",
                    application.name, "k38djskl3o9");
    // Create an authentication object to authenticate clients.
    auth = new Auth('lobbyAuth');
    // Create a main Component Manager.
    cManager = new PFCSComponentManager("main");
    cManager.addComponent(ActiveChatUsers_Leaf);
};
```

Example 16-2. The lobby.asc file (continued)

```
// username and password are actually ticketID and ticket.
application.onConnect = function (client, userName, password) {
  return auth.authenticate(client, userName, password);
};

application.onAuthenticate = function (client, result) {
  // Make sure the authenticated user has not already logged in.
  if (pfcs.clients[result.USERNAME]) {
    application.rejectConnection(client, {msg:"You are already logged in."});
    return;
  }

  var noRoles = true;
  for (var p in result.ROLES) {
    var obj = result.ROLES[p];
    if (typeof obj == "function") continue;
    noRoles = false;
    break;
  }

  if (noRoles) {
    application.rejectConnection(client, {msg:"Access Denied."});
    return;
  }

  // Control access and bandwidth based on one of the user's roles.
  client.readAccess = "";    // Deny all readAccess to start.
  client.writeAccess = "";   // Deny all writeAccess to start.

  // addClient() extracts data, including the userName, from the result
  // object and stores it in the client in the client.pfcs.user object.
  // Store the client in the pfcs.clients object by userName.
  pfcs.addClient(client, result);

  // If any components are still waiting, enqueue the client.
  if (pfcs.getPendingComponents()) {
    pfcs.addPendingClient(client);
  }
  else {
    // Add the client to each component.
    cManager.addClient(client);
    // Accept the client's connection request.
    application.acceptConnection(client);
  }
};

application.onDisconnect = function (client) {
  cManager.removeClient(client);
  pfcs.removeClient(client)
};

application.onAppStop = function () {
```

Example 16-2. The lobby.asc file (continued)

```
  cManager.close();
};
```

Aside from the code to handle Flash clients, the lobby connects to the master instance as follows:

```
  pfcs.nc = NetConnectionFactory.get();
  pfcs.nc.connect("rtmp://localhost/chatSystem/master",
                  application.name, "k38djskl3o9");
```

The *NetConnectionFactory.get( )* method returns a modified *NetConnection* object that the lobby uses to connect to the master instance. Any component that needs to know if the nc NetConnection is connected can set itself up as a listener on nc. In a full production environment, additional instance-level error handling should be provided in case the connection cannot be established.

In many cases, a client connection cannot be accepted until every component is fully initialized. When a component relies on a *NetConnection* to connect to another instance, the initialization may take some time while the connection is established and shared objects connected. Consequently, the *onConnect( )* method places arriving Flash clients in the PFCS framework's pending client queue if any components are not ready:

```
  // If any components are still waiting, enqueue the client.
  if (pfcs.getPendingComponents()) {
    pfcs.addPendingClient(client);
  }
  else {
    // Add the client to each component.
    cManager.addClient(client);
    // Accept the client's connection request.
    application.acceptConnection(client);
  }
```

The preceding two *.asc* files are not long and complex, because much of the work of providing resources to clients is done by the PFCS framework and ActiveChatUsers component. The ActiveChatUsers component is similar to the PeopleList component used in earlier chapters but displays users connected to all lobby instances in one list. The complete code is available on the book's web site.

To further simplify coding, each file loads its own version of each communication component. As an example, let's look at creating the activeUsers shared object. The ActiveChatUsers component in the client includes a DataGrid to display the names of every user on the system. It connects to the activeUsers proxied shared object in the lobby instance. Within the lobby instance, an *ActiveChatUsers* object creates the proxy for the client to connect to by connecting to the master instance's activeUsers shared object. Finally, the *ActiveChatUsers* object in the master instance creates the global users list shared object. Figure 16-3 illustrates the relationship between instances and component objects.

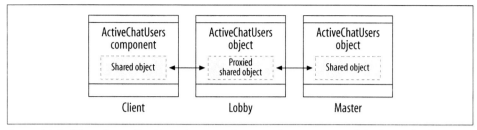

Figure 16-3. Three ActiveChatUser objects working together to proxy and display in the client a shared object that belongs to the master instance

To make writing a component that has to be distributed across two separate instances (the lobby and master) simpler, create separate files—one for the master and one for the lobby:

ActiveChatUsers_Root.asc
    Contains the code that implements the component in the master

ActiveChatUsers_Leaf.asc
    Contains the code required to implement the component in the lobby

We chose filenames ending in "_Root" and "_Leaf" rather than "master" and "proxy" to reflect the typical upside-down tree structure of a FlashCom broadcast network, as seen in Figure 16-6. Root nodes represent a single master instance or server, and leaf nodes represent the instance or server to which Flash clients connect.

Example 16-3 shows the code from the *ActiveChatUsers_Root.asc* file that is loaded into the master instance by the *master.asc* code shown in Example 16-1.

Example 16-3. The ActiveChatUsers_Root class definition

```
function ActiveChatUsers_Root (name) {
  // Set this component's path.
  PFCSComponent.apply(this, [name]);

  // Create the shared object that the leaf instances will proxy with
  // user information.
  this.activeUsers_so = SharedObject.get("pfcs/ActiveChatUsers/main/activeUsers",
                                         false);
}

// Inherit from PFCSComponent.
ActiveChatUsers_Root.prototype = new PFCSComponent();
ActiveChatUsers_Root.prototype.constructor = ActiveChatUsers_Root;
p = ActiveChatUsers_Root.prototype;
p.className = "ActiveChatUsers_Root";

p.addClient = function (client) {
  // We assume a valid ActiveChatUsers_Leaf is connecting.
  // Give read and write access to the path.
  this.addAccessPath(client, "readAccess", "pfcs/ActiveChatUsers/main");
```

Example 16-3. The ActiveChatUsers_Root class definition (continued)

```
    this.addAccessPath(client, "writeAccess", "pfcs/ActiveChatUsers/main");
};

p.removeClient = function (client) {
  this.removeAccessPath(client, "readAccess", "pfcs/ActiveChatUsers/main");
  this.removeAccessPath(client, "writeAccess", "pfcs/ActiveChatUsers/main");
};

p.close = function () {
};
```

The code uses the *PFCSComponent* base class and *PFCSFramework* introduced in Chapter 15. The *master.asc* file shown in Example 16-1, which implements the master instance, loads the *ActiveChatUsers_Root.asc* file and creates an object this way:

```
    load("ActiveChatUsers_Root.asc");
    activeUsers = new ActiveChatUsers_Root("main");
```

Afterward, every lobby that connects to the master instance is passed to the activeUsers object:

```
    activeUsers.addClient(client);
```

Example 16-4 lists the code for the *ActiveChatUsers_Leaf* class, which is stored in *ActiveChatUsers_Leaf.asc* and instantiated in the lobby. When the leaf instance is first created, it gets the nc object from the pfcs framework object and makes itself a listener on it. If the *NetConnection* is already established, the *onConnect( )* method is called to set up the activeUsers shared object. Otherwise, the *onConnect( )* method is called when the connection is established.

Example 16-4. The leaf object defined in ActiveChatUsers_Leaf.asc

```
function ActiveChatUsers_Leaf (name) {
  // Set this component's path.
  PFCSComponent.apply(this, [name]);
  this.nc = pfcs.nc;
  this.nc.addEventListener("onConnect", this);
  if (this.nc.isConnected) {
    this.onConnect();
  }
  pfcs.addPendingComponent(this);
}

// Inherit from PFCSComponent.
ActiveChatUsers_Leaf.prototype = new PFCSComponent();
p = ActiveChatUsers_Leaf.prototype;
p.constructor = ActiveChatUsers_Leaf;
p.className = "ActiveChatUsers_Leaf";

p.addClient = function (client) {
  // Provide read-only access for Flash clients.
  this.addAccessPath(client, "readAccess", "/pfcs/ActiveChatUsers/main");
```

```
  // Add the client to the shared object.
  this.activeUsers_so.setProperty(pfcs.getUserName(client),
                                  {rn: application.name, t:new Date()});
};

p.removeClient = function (client) {
  // Remove read-only access from Flash clients.
  this.removeAccessPath(client, "readAccess", "/pfcs/ActiveChatUsers/main");
  this.activeUsers_so.setProperty(client.pfcs.user.userName, null);
};

p.onConnect = function (ev) {
  this.activeUsers_so = SharedObjectFactory.getRemote(
                        "pfcs/ActiveChatUsers/main/activeUsers",
                        false, this.nc);
  this.activeUsers_so.addEventListener("onFirstSync", this);
};

p.onFirstSync = function (ev) {
  // Tell the framework we are ready!
  pfcs.removePendingComponent(this);
};

p.close = function () {
};
```

When the ActiveChatUsers_Leaf component has received its first *onFirstSync( )* call, it is fully initialized and tells the pfcs framework it is ready. If it is the last component to report it is ready, the pfcs framework will accept the connection of any pending clients.

Finally, the *ActiveChatUsers_Leaf* object is responsible for updating the activeUsers shared object each time a client connects to or disconnects from the lobby. When *addClient( )* is called, it adds a slot for the client in the activeUsers shared object. When the client disconnects, it deletes the slot in the shared object.

The code in Example 16-3 and Example 16-4 provides across multiple lobbies an activeUsers proxied shared object that contains a slot representing every user connected to all the lobbies. Other components can be designed to perform similar tasks, such as sending messages between any two clients. Or, in a large conference scenario in which each instance represents a separate conference room, other information, such as who is currently speaking in each room or a list of viewable streams from other rooms, can be distributed across instances.

A global users list with information about a hundred-thousand active users will require a large number of frequent updates and may consume a few megabytes of memory in every client that connects to it. Memory consumption on the server may be extreme, and the time and bandwidth required to send thousands of records to each client may be considered too much. For systems with several thousand simultaneous users or more, user searches and size-limited friend lists are more appropriate than simply providing a massive global list of every connected user.

Scalability and Load Balancing

A FlashCom application designed to run on one server usually must be redesigned and rewritten to run across multiple servers. In other words, there is no automatic clustering technology available for FlashCom Servers. The primary reason each application must be designed for multiple servers is that only one instance can directly update resources such as shared objects. Any clustering technology would have to provide a way to share instance state across machines.

Designing an application to scale across multiple servers can be relatively simple or quite complex, depending on the type of application. Let's look at the three general categories of applications: media-on-demand, live one-way broadcasting, and *n*-way communication applications.

Media-on-Demand

Media-on-demand applications provide access to content that is uploaded to one or more FlashCom Servers or to a filesystem accessible to each server. The content is prepared in advance and may be video, audio, and/or data delivered by playing prerecorded streams. Applications such as a library of video tutorials, promotional video on a high-traffic site, or synchronized video/slide presentations are all examples. Media-on-demand applications are the simplest to build. Content such as *.swf* and *.flv* files can be uploaded either separately to each server or to one common high-speed storage system connected to each FlashCom Server by an internal high-speed network.

Figure 16-4 shows one possible configuration for on-demand media distribution.

The major challenge in building an on-demand application is determining which clients connect to which server. Since the same content is available on every server—Chapter 12 shows how to use ColdFusion to automatically mirror streams across multiple servers—the goal is to try to balance the load on each server by controlling which server each client connects to. Ideally, the relative load on every server should be almost identical. For example, if several servers are used—some with four CPUs and 4 GB RAM and some with two CPUs and 2 GB RAM—the percentage of memory and CPU cycles used on each machine should be the same. More clients would be serviced by the more powerful machines so that each machine is utilized at a similar proportion of its capacity to serve streams. There are a number of ways to assign clients to servers, such as allowing the client to pick a server at random, having a web application direct a client to a specific server, or using a network load-balancing device.

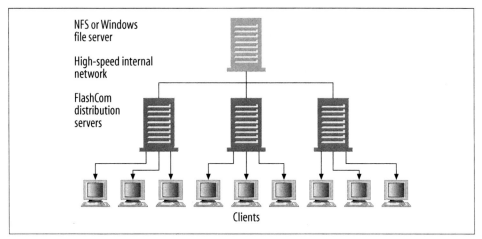

Figure 16-4. Media-on-demand distribution servers and file server

We explore each of these options in turn in subsequent sections.

Client-side server selection

Possibly the simplest way to select a server is to have the client select a random number within a range of integers and compose a server name from it. For example, if five servers named *fcs1.ryerson.ca* through *fcs5.ryerson.ca* are available, then a server can be selected by getting a random number between 1 and 5:

```
serverName = "fcs" + Math.floor(Math.random( )* 5 + 1) + ".ryerson.ca";
```

The *Math.random( )* method produces pseudorandom numbers that are evenly distributed. If each server has the same capacity, a large number of clients will be reasonably well distributed across servers. If a server is down, each client can randomly select a name from the remaining servers and try again. If the distribution servers have different network, CPU, or memory capacity, a capacity rating can be assigned to each server and a weighting system used to select a server.

One problem with generating server names in code is that the code must be updated when new servers are brought online or retired. A simple enhancement is to have the client load an XML file containing the name and capacity of every server in production. Example 16-5 lists such a simple *serverList.xml* file.

Example 16-5. The serverList.xml file

```
<serverList>
  <server name="fcs1.ryerson.ca" capacity="20" />
  <server name="fcs2.ryerson.ca" capacity="20" />
  <server name="fcs3.ryerson.ca" capacity="10" />
  <server name="fcs4.ryerson.ca" capacity="10" />
  <server name="fcs5.ryerson.ca" capacity="15" />
</serverList>
```

Each capacity value is an integer greater than 0. To randomly select a server weighted by the capacity values, the capacities can be summed and a pseudorandom number between 0 and the total capacity selected. Table 16-1 shows one way a capacity range can be calculated for each server based on the capacity value and the cumulative sum of capacities.

Table 16-1. Weighting server selection by capacity

Server name	Capacity	Sum	Sum -1	Range
fcs1.ryerson.ca	20	20	19	0–19
fcs2.ryerson.ca	20	40	39	20–39
fcs3.ryerson.ca	10	50	49	40–49
fcs4.ryerson.ca	10	60	59	50–59
fcs5.ryerson.ca	15	75	74	60–74

A pseudorandom number between 0 and 74, inclusive, can be used to select a server. When a large number of clients connect, the weighting will be closely in proportion to the capacity of each server. Example 16-6 shows one way to select a server name from a *serverList.xml* file.

Example 16-6. Sample code to output the name of a server selected from the server List.xml file

```
request = new XML( );
request.ignoreWhite = true;
request.onLoad = function (success) {
  if (success) {
    var capacityArray = [];
    var sumCapacity = 0;
    var serverName;
    // Get an array of <server> tags.
    var servers = this.firstChild.childNodes;
    var len = servers.length;
    // Get the capacity of each server and build an array of sum capacities.
    for (var i = 0; i < len; i++) {
      var serverInfo = servers[i].attributes;
      sumCapacity += parseInt(serverInfo.capacity);
      capacityArray.push(sumCapacity - 1);
    }
    // Get a random number from 0 to sumCapacity -1.
    var selector = Math.floor(Math.random( ) * sumCapacity);
    // Find the selector in the capacity array.
    for (var i = 0; i < len; i++) {
      if (selector <= capacityArray[i]) {
        serverName = servers[i].attributes.name;
        break;
      }
    }
  }
  else {
```

Example 16-6. Sample code to output the name of a server selected from the server
List.xml file (continued)

```
   // Hardcoded fallback: assume we have servers numbered 1 to 5.
   serverName = "fcs" + Math.floor(Math.random( )* 5 + 1) + ".ryerson.ca";
 }
 // Trace out the server name selected.
 trace("Server name: " + serverName);
};
request.load("serverList.xml");
```

Software server selection

Server-side software can perform something similar to the calculation made in the client-side code in Example 16-6. Each client can request a server name from a web application. The web application can provide a name using code similar to Example 16-6 or, in more sophisticated systems, can look at the actual load on each server in real time and ask each client to connect to the least-busy server. The load on the server can be determined by calling the Admin Service's *getServerStats( )* method, which returns CPU and memory usage information, as described in Chapter 10. Alternatively, a non-FlashCom application may be available to monitor server load.

Network-level server selection

Load-balancing devices that can provide efficient server selection on a network are available from various vendors. A load-balancing device can be configured to listen at one IP address and redirect traffic to one of many servers on other IP addresses. For example, a DNS entry for *fcs.mydomain.ca* might resolve to one IP address. The load balancer is set up to receive IP traffic for that address and is programmed with information about the servers at the other addresses. Figure 16-5 provides a simple illustration of a load balancer and the servers connected to it.

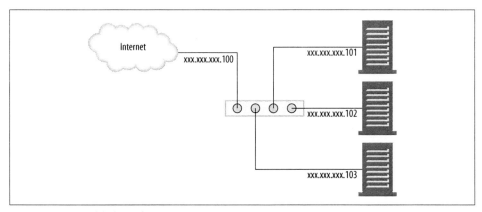

Figure 16-5. Load-balanced servers

Every client attempts to connect to the address xxx.xxx.xxx.100. Each client's connect request is redirected to a server at another address. Load balancers provide different options for determining what server to redirect to and can perform regular health checks on servers so that, if one is not available, clients will be redirected to the other servers. One option is to have the load balancer assign each client connection request to the server with the fewest number of current connections. Another is to hash the client's IP address or to use weighted hashing. Finally, a weighted percentage can also be used.

Regardless of the method used, media-on-demand applications are unaffected if a client connects to one server to play a stream and later to another server to play another stream. That is, because there is no application state, it doesn't matter whether the physical server providing the media changes during the application's lifetime (provided it doesn't change in the middle of playing a given data stream, which would require the second server to pick up where the first server left off).

One-Way Live Delivery

One-way delivery of live audio, video, and/or data is similar to media-on-demand applications except that the same live stream and supporting shared objects must be made available across multiple servers in real time.

A simple example of a one-way live application running on several servers is a live video streaming application that uses a broadcast tree of servers. The root server collects the incoming live video streams and sends them to other servers, which then send the streams on to each client. It is relatively simple to build out a broadcast tree to handle any number of clients.

Figure 16-6 illustrates a simple broadcast tree that could be used to deliver live audio and video streams to more clients than could normally be handled by a single server.

For example, if testing shows that each distribution server can handle only 1200 streams, for safety you might decide to allow no more than 900 streams per server. If a live event requires the delivery of a total of 2700 streams, then three leaf servers are needed. Figure 16-6 illustrates this scenario—each client plays only one of the three streams in the illustration.

The root server in Figure 16-6 serves only nine streams. In this example, a root/leaf scheme can be scaled out to 900 leaf servers before an intermediate layer of servers would have to be added in between the root and leaf servers.

The primary difference between one-way live delivery and media-on-demand is that each instance on a leaf server must connect to a root server instance. The leaf instance creates proxy shared objects or streams of any resources that must be made available to its clients. A broadcast tree can be described by levels starting from the source clients that connect to the root server and then working down the tree until

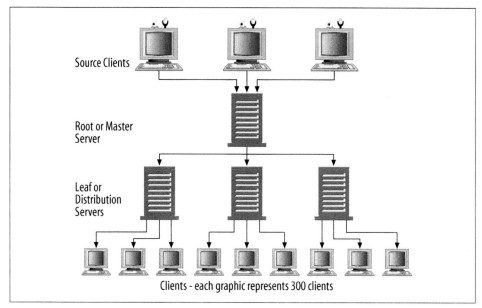

Source Clients

Root or Master
Server

Leaf or
Distribution
Servers

Clients - each graphic represents 300 clients

Figure 16-6. A broadcast tree with one root server and three leaf servers

reaching the destination clients. The software running at each level in the tree has different responsibilities. Let's look at each level from top to bottom.

Source clients

The source clients are designed to be used by the camera/microphone operators and allow the operator to log into the root server application. The client is designed to provide convenient controls to control camera and microphone sources and to publish one or more streams at a controlled bit rate.

Root server application instance

The root server application allows connections from the source clients who authenticate to the server and from intermediate or leaf FlashCom Servers. Streams and shared objects in the root application are available to intermediate or leaf server applications.

Intermediate server instances

Intermediate server instances are used to increase the height of the broadcast tree when extremely large numbers of streams must be served. They connect to the root server or another intermediate server one level higher in the tree and allow connections from leaf or lower-level intermediate servers. They proxy higher-level resources so that they are available lower down in the broadcast tree.

Leaf server application instances

Leaf server instances connect to the server above them in the broadcast tree. In smaller trees, they connect to the root. Once connected, the leaf application creates a proxy of every shared object and stream that must be made available to the destination clients. If authentication is required before streams can be viewed, the leaf instance implements user/viewer authentication.

Destination clients

The destination clients are the ones designed to view the stream or streams delivered via the leaf servers in the broadcast tree and are often simple viewer movies that allow the user to select one of a number of streams for viewing.

The same server selection options are available for one-way live applications as work with on-demand applications. Because servers are interchangeable, a client can connect to any server at any time and will be able to function correctly.

n-Way Live Communications

Applications that are not one-way are the most challenging to scale and require different approaches to server selection. *n*-way applications can consume greater server and network resources than one-way applications and require extra work to manage instances correctly.

Figure 16-7 shows 12 clients connected to a single server. In a one-way application, the server may have to send only one stream to each client for a total of 12 streams. However, in an *n*-way video conference application, each client may send 1 stream and receive 11 streams—one for each of the other clients. The server must therefore send or receive 12 streams per client for a total of 144 streams. That's 12 times more than a one-way application!

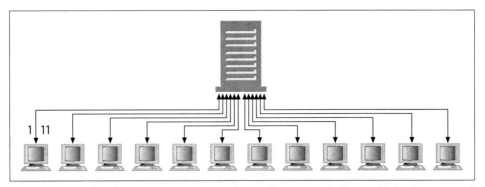

Figure 16-7. Twelve clients participating in a video conference—each client publishes 1 stream and subscribes to 11 streams

---

Figure 16-8 shows the same clients connected to one of three distribution or leaf servers that are in turn connected together by one master or root server.

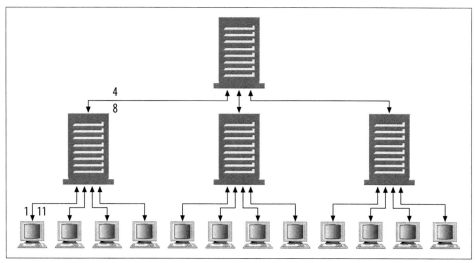

Figure 16-8. A video conference spread across three leaf servers and one root server

Again, each client publishes 1 stream and receives 11 streams—one for every other client in the conference. Each leaf server must send four streams to the root server— one for each client connected to the leaf server. It must receive from the root server eight streams—one for every client connected to a remote leaf server. So, each leaf server must handle:

- Four streams arriving from its clients
- Eight streams arriving from the top-level server
- Four streams going out to the top-level server
- Forty-four streams going to its clients (11 each)

In total, each leaf server must handle 60 streams. That is a 58% reduction from the single-server scenario of 144 streams.

To make the arrangement illustrated in Figure 16-8 work, the root server normally contains the master instance for the application and the leaf servers' host instances that proxy the resources in the master instance. The arrangement is similar to the application illustrated in Figure 16-2, in which separate lobbies connected to a master instance to share its resources.

Unlike a one-way broadcast tree that can be increased in size indefinitely, the number of streams that must traverse the root server increases with the number of clients. Of course, clients involved in an *n*-way application will likely run out of bandwidth from trying to receive so many streams before the number of streams exceeds the server's capacity. In practice, *n*-way applications rarely send more than six simultaneous video streams to each client.

Let's return to the application illustrated in Figure 16-2 and assume that an application has to maintain lobby and room instances spread across multiple servers. Whenever a client connects to a lobby, a slot in the master instance's activeUsers shared object is updated with the client's location and time of arrival. Every client has an ActiveChatUsers component that shows every user connected to the application. As already mentioned, this scheme is scalable only up to a point. A user will not want to scroll through thousands of usernames to find someone. Worse, each added slot in the activeUsers shared object takes up memory in the master instance and in every proxied shared object in the leaf instances. At some point, memory consumption will incapacitate the servers.

The solution is to redesign the application so that it shows only a subset of clients to each user while still maintaining information about what clients are connected. The master instance can be replaced with a database server. Lobby instances in each leaf server will poll a database for information in the friend list of the clients connected to it. The database replaces the master instance. Polling—which is not an ideal solution—must be used in FlashCom 1.5.2 and earlier because Flash Remoting is a request/response protocol.

Another complexity in the lobbies/rooms application is that while a client could, in theory, connect to any lobby on any server, it must connect to the correct instance on one server in order to participate in a room. Rooms are single instances and are not necessarily spread across servers. In that case, each client must connect directly to a particular leaf server.

By default, hardware load-balancing devices usually hide the IP address of the real servers they are load balancing. For applications in which clients must connect directly to an individual host, the IP address of each server must be directly reachable. If your hardware load balancer does not support direct access, software-based load balancing should be implemented instead.

Redundancy and Failover

Servers, firewalls, packet shapers, and networks are all capable of failing to work when your clients are using them. Few clients are really happy about coming back later when the problem is fixed. To increase the probability that a client can continue working, redundant servers, firewalls, and network connections can be provided so that the client can reconnect—or fail over—to the redundant hardware.

Providing redundancy and failover for *n*-way FlashCom applications presents some special challenges. In a one-way application, if a client loses a connection to a server and cannot reestablish it, it simply tries to connect to another server. If it is playing a recorded stream, it can play the same stream from another server and seek to where it left off. If a live stream is being played, it just begins playing the stream at its current location as soon as the connection is established. Similar strategies can be used with conference rooms, but they require a little more care.

When a conference room is allocated on a single-leaf server, a fallback RTMP address on another FlashCom Server can also be allocated. If the instance goes down for some reason, clients connected to it can automatically attempt to connect to the alternate instance. If each FlashCom Server is connected to a centralized filesystem and has an identical FlashCom installation on it with the same drive mappings (or same mount points), the alternate instance can read the same files, including shared objects and streams that were available to the original. However, under no circumstances can two instances be allowed to access the same shared object files or update the same stream files at the same time. In other words, either all the clients are disconnected from the original instance and connected to the alternate instance or none should be moved. When an instance or entire server goes down, the client's *NetConnection* object will eventually receive an information object with a code value of "NetConnection.Connect.Closed". Unfortunately, such a code can also mean that the client's network connection was dropped temporarily and that many other clients are still happily connected to the instance. So when a client loses a connection to an instance before a meeting is over, it should attempt to contact the same instance again before trying the alternative server. To avoid any possibility of clients ending up in separate instances, the alternative instance can attempt to contact the original instance and refuse the client access if the latter is still available. This level of interinstance coordination requires careful planning and coding.

When multiple lobbies are using one master instance, failure of a lobby may be easy to handle. The client simply reconnects to another lobby on another server. However, if a master instance goes down, an alternative must be available that can start up and take over. The new master will have to re-create the state of the old master by asking each lobby to update it. Keeping a master instance and another instance in sync so that the other can take over as the master without having to rebuild its state is difficult because a proxied shared object cannot simply be promoted to become a master shared object. One scheme is to use persistent shared objects that are frequently flushed to disk by the master instance. The shared objects are stored on a separate storage file server. If a master server fails, a new master is allocated and reads the persistent shared object from the storage file server. Another scheme is to replicate updates by sending every shared object slot change from the master instance to a shadow copy of the master instance. If the master instance fails, the shadow copy becomes the master instance.

Conclusion

Just as there are different types of FlashCom applications, there are different approaches to building multi-instance applications that are scalable and fault-tolerant. Media-on-demand, live one-way broadcasting, and n-way communication applications all provide different challenges. Applications that require real-time instance coordination are more challenging to design and build than those that do not. Component-based applications are a good way to partition multi-instance applications. The components introduced in Chapters 13 through 15 have client- and server-side parts that work together. In a multi-instance application, a good practice is to further divide components so that their server-side parts know how to communicate with one another. In a simple broadcast tree, a stream list component might have four parts—one each for a source client, root server, leaf server, and destination client. Writing each part of the component separately simplifies multi-instance development.

This chapter has dealt with building multi-instance and multiserver applications that don't bog down as the number of client connections increases. Unfortunately, adding instances and servers won't help application performance over slow network connections. The next chapter describes what you can do to provide a good application experience despite network limitations.

CHAPTER 17

Network Performance, Latency, and Concurrency

In many science fiction stories, people talk with each other across astronomical distances as though they were in the same room. The technology never gets in the way. Computer networks do not work that way. They have real physical limitations. Software developers who ignore the problems of building network-enabled communication applications risk alienating their users. Let's consider some examples.

A university professor holds an online seminar with students at a number of remote locations. One student logs in using a dial-up modem over a low-quality telephone line. By default, the application attempts to send the student video and audio from each of the other participants and to have the student send video and audio to everyone else. The result is immensely frustrating to everyone. The student's connection is so saturated with video and audio data that nothing seems to work. Phone calls asking the student to turn off video do not help.

A pair of friends decides to play an online car racing game. Near the end of the game, as the two approach the finish line, each can see that the other is lurching forward and back well behind him. Each of the two players seems to cross the finish line well ahead of the other. One of them is happy to be declared the winner while the other is outraged at losing after appearing to win the race by a safe margin.

In both cases, the software is likely to be abandoned because the users' perception is that it simply does not work. And the users are right. The software was written without taking into account the limitations of computer networks. This chapter is about tailoring applications to work on the real Internet and describes strategies for adapting to different bandwidths and latency. But it cannot suggest solutions for every problem. Some games are simply unplayable unless latency is below a certain threshold and live high-resolution video conferences simply will not work at slow modem speeds.

Latency

Network latency is the time it takes for a packet of information to travel across a network (or networks) from sender to receiver. On a high-speed local network, it may take only a millisecond (ms; one-thousandth of a second) for a single packet of information to travel from sender to receiver. An organization with network nodes spread over a few kilometers and a high-speed backbone should still provide latency of less than 10 ms. Organizations with a high-speed connection into an Internet service provider (ISP) may achieve latencies of 15 to 50 ms when reaching well-connected national sites, as well as some international sites. On the other hand, home users will often experience latencies in the 40 ms to 500 ms range when accessing the same sites on the Internet. Network congestion can increase latency dramatically. The routers in a congested network will drop packets they cannot handle. FlashCom uses the TCP protocol, which automatically resends dropped packets. If packets are repeatedly dropped and resent, latency can increase dramatically.

While everyone who has ever used the Internet has experienced network latency, the delay in delivering packets across the Internet is not the only cause of slow response times. A busy FlashCom application instance will queue remote method calls and deal with them one at a time. If there is a long delay between the time someone sends a message in a text chat and the time it takes her message to appear in the chat message area, it may be because of a slow network connection, a busy application instance, or both.

Measuring Latency

Latency is normally measured by sending information from the sender to the receiver and having the receiver immediately return it. The round-trip time is calculated when the information is returned and divided by 2 to get an approximation of the latency. The idea of bouncing a packet of information off the receiver and measuring the time it takes to return is somewhat analogous to sonar. So when Mike Muuss wrote a program that sent an Internet Control Message Protocol (ICMP) ECHO_REQUEST packet and measured the time until an IP/ICMP ECHO_REPLY packet was returned to measure latency, he named it *ping*. *Ping* is still a tremendously useful diagnostic tool, provided the system you are pinging is not on a network that refuses to forward ICMP packets. *Ping* gives a good point-in-time measure of basic network performance at the packet level. Most computers, including Windows machines, have a *ping* program you can run at the command prompt. Just type **ping** followed by a space and the hostname or IP address of the machine you want to ping. For example, pinging *flash-communications.net* as follows from my home machine, which has a DSL connection, typically reports latency of 65 ms:

```
C:\>ping flash-communications.net

Pinging flash-communications.net [209.29.148.179] with 32 bytes of data:
```

```
Reply from 209.29.148.179: bytes=32 time=60ms TTL=118
Reply from 209.29.148.179: bytes=32 time=70ms TTL=118
Reply from 209.29.148.179: bytes=32 time=60ms TTL=118
Reply from 209.29.148.179: bytes=32 time=71ms TTL=118

Ping statistics for 209.29.148.179:
    Packets: Sent = 4, Received = 4, Lost = 0 (0% loss),
Approximate round trip times in milli-seconds:
    Minimum = 60ms, Maximum =  71ms, Average =  65ms
```

From my high-speed office connection, the same command produces dramatically faster results (latency below 10 ms is reported as 0 ms):

```
C:\>ping flash-communications.net

Pinging flash-communications.net [209.29.148.179] with 32 bytes of data:

Reply from 209.29.148.179: bytes=32 time<10ms TTL=117
Reply from 209.29.148.179: bytes=32 time<10ms TTL=117
Reply from 209.29.148.179: bytes=32 time<10ms TTL=117
Reply from 209.29.148.179: bytes=32 time<10ms TTL=117

Ping statistics for 209.29.148.179:
    Packets: Sent = 4, Received = 4, Lost = 0 (0% loss),
Approximate round trip times in milli-seconds:
    Minimum = 0ms, Maximum =  0ms, Average =  0ms
```

There are two ways to construct a similar test using Flash and FlashCom to provide latency information to an application. One way is to have the client bounce a message off FlashCom or vice versa, by calling a remote method. For example, a Flash movie can get the current time, call a remote method on the server that does nothing but return, and then get the current time again after the remote method returns. The difference in time between when the remote method invocation was sent and when its *onResult( )* handler is called is the round-trip time.

The other way to test latency is available only on the server. The *Client.ping( )* method will send a message to the client, which the client will immediately return. Some time after the message is returned, the *Client.getStats( )* method can be called to retrieve the round-trip time.

Example 17-1 is part of the definition of the client-side ConnectionTester component available from the book's web site. The abbreviated listing shows the pingResponder object that is created in the constructor, the *set nc( )* method in which the component is passed an already connected *NetConnection* object, and the *onEchoReply( )* method that is called when the *onEchoReply( )* method being invoked on the server returns. For the full listing, see the *ConnectionTester.as* file in the *example17-1.zip* archive.

Example 17-1. Partial listing of the client-side ConnectionTester class

```
function ConnectionTester ( ) {
  super( );
  // Ping responder.
  pingResponder = {owner:this};
  pingResponder.onResult = function ( ) {
    var receiveTime = new Date( );
    this.owner.onEchoReply(this.sendTime, receiveTime);
  };
  pingResponder.onStatus = function (status) {
    trace("ping responder.onStatus: " + status);
  };
}

public function set nc (nc:NetConnection) {
  __nc = nc;
  buffer = [];
  pingResponder.sendTime = new Date( );
  __nc.call(path + "echoRequest", pingResponder);
}

function onEchoReply (sendTime, receiveTime) {
  var deltaTime = receiveTime - sendTime;
  buffer.push(deltaTime);
  pingCount++;

  if (pingCount < totalPingCount) {
    pingResponder.sendTime = new Date( );
    __nc.call(path + "echoRequest", pingResponder);
  }
  else {
    var sum = 0;
    writeln("Pinged " + pingCount + " times.");
    for (var i = 0; i < buffer.length; i++) {
      writeln("Ping #" + i + " rtt: " + buffer[i]);
      sum += buffer[i];
    }
    writeln("Average ping rtt: " + (sum/buffer.length));
  }
}
```

If the full component path is *pfcs/ConnectionTester/main*, then the actual remote method being called is *pfcs/ConnectionTester/main/echoRequest( )*. The pingResponder object is passed into the *call( )* method. When the remote method returns, the *pingResponder.onResult( )* method will be called. It will get the current time and then call the component's *onEchoReply( )* method where the round-trip time is calculated.

The remote method is attached to the client on the server in the *addClient( )* method of the server-side *ConnectionTester* class, as shown in Example 17-2.

Example 17-2. The addClient( ) method of the server-side ConnectionTester component

```
ConnectionTester.prototype.addClient = function (client) {
  var proxy = this.getProxy(client);
  proxy.echoRequest = function () {
    return;
  };
};
```

The *getProxy( )* method returns the main object on the client as though it had been obtained this way:

```
    var proxy = client.pfcs.ConnectionTester.main;
```

The net result is the creation of a method at:

```
    client.pfcs.ConnectionTester.main.echoRequest
```

The *echoRequest( )* method simply returns without performing any other action. Example 17-1 just reports the ping results in a TextArea.

Example 17-3 shows the *pingClient( )* function of the server-side *ConnectionTester* class. It is meant to be called repeatedly using *setInterval( )*; it both gets the round-trip time for the last ping and sends a new ping to the client using *client.ping( )*. The results are simply output using a *trace( )* call.

Example 17-3. The server-side ConnectionTester.pingClient( ) method

```
ConnectionTester.prototype.pingClient = function (client) {
  var proxy = this.getProxy(client);
  if (typeof proxy.pingCount == "undefined" || proxy.pingCount == 0) {
    proxy.pingCount = 0;
    proxy.buffer = [];
  }
  else {
    proxy.pingCount++
  }
  if (proxy.pingCount > 0) {
    var stats = client.getStats();
    proxy.buffer.push( stats.ping_rtt );
  }
  if (proxy.pingCount > 20) {
    clearInterval(proxy.intervalID );
    var sum = 0;
    for (var i = 0; i < proxy.buffer.length; i++) {
      sum += proxy.buffer[i];
      trace("ping_rtt: " + proxy.buffer[i]);
    }
    trace("Average: " + (sum/proxy.buffer.length));
  }
  client.ping();
};
```

The following statements can be executed within any method of the *Connection-Tester* class and will start pinging the client by repeatedly calling the component's *pingClient( )* method:

```
var proxy = this.getProxy(client);
delete proxy.pingCount = 0;
proxy.intervalID = setInterval(this, "pingClient", 500, client);
```

I ran some tests in different scenarios to measure the round-trip time using various approaches. The results are shown in Table 17-1.

Table 17-1. Round-trip times for packet transmission

Test description	Min. round-trip	Max. round-trip	Avg. round-trip
Pinged a remote FlashCom test machine from home using the ping program	70 ms	81 ms	72 ms
Called a remote method on FlashCom from a Flash client	70 ms	90 ms	76 ms
Used FlashCom to call a remote method on the same Flash client	62 ms	125 ms	78 ms
Used *client.ping( )*	68 ms	132 ms	76 ms

The command-line *ping* program is doing its best to measure the round-trip time using ICMP packets, and the test program is doing the best it can to measure the round-trip time using TCP packets. The *client.ping( )* method is also using TCP packets, but unlike the remote method test, its packets are sent by FlashCom to the client with the highest possible priority. The test program also incurs the extra overhead of calling a remote method on a FlashCom Server. During the test, I made sure the test FlashCom Server was not doing anything else—a highly unrealistic scenario.

In real applications, you will have to choose how you want to determine latency. Remote methods are queued for each application instance on the server. If an application instance is handling a lot of remote method calls, there may be a significant delay while other calls are invoked. So a remote method test is a good way to measure the response time for queued processes such as the *call( )* method or *NetStream.send( )* and *SharedObject.send( )*. For something closer to the latency that will be experienced by streams, use a *client.ping( )* test, as it should not suffer from message queuing delays.

If you run a large number of tests in which you compare the results of an ICMP packet–based ping test against a TCP-based remote method test, you may notice that you get slightly lower average times with a narrower range of individual round-trip times from the ICMP-based test. One reason for this is that ICMP is used to deliver messages about network status and is an unreliable protocol. "Unreliable" just means that not every packet must be delivered. TCP is a reliable protocol designed to carry data between hosts. TCP is reliable because any packets that are dropped in transit are resent. Messages that contain packets that have been resent will be delayed longer than messages composed entirely of packets that that did not have to be resent. So a TCP-based test will often contain a number of round-trip values that are much higher than the average.

There is a problem with trace output in the App Inspector (*app_inspector.swf*). The output may appear out of sequence. When debugging, output appearing out of sequence can be a real problem. Often it is necessary to include a millisecond timestamp in each message to see the real sequence of events. For example:

```
trace((new Date()).getTime() +
              " client disconnected.");
```

Clock Synchronization

Sometimes we want to do more than calculate an average latency. For example, in some computer games, the clocks of each client must be closely synchronized with the time on the server. Of course, Flash cannot reset the client's clock, but a test can be used to determine the difference in UTC time in milliseconds between the two clocks. Once the difference is known, the server time can always be estimated using the client's clock and the difference between the two clocks.

A test to determine the difference in time between the client's and server's clocks is similar to performing a latency test using remote methods. In a case in which Flash is used to call a remote method on FlashCom, the primary steps are:

1. Get the current time and save it.
2. Request the current time from the server by calling a remote method.
3. The server receives the remote method call, and gets and returns the current time.
4. When the client-side result handler is called, the client time is taken again and stored.

As a result, there are three times: sent time, server time, and received time. The latency is calculated as:

```
latency = (receivedTime - sentTime)/2;
```

Ideally, the four steps should be repeated five or more times with pauses of a few seconds between receiving a response from the server and sending another request. With five or more latency values, received times, and server times, a simple way to calculate the difference between clocks is to average all the times and then calculate:

```
clientServerDelta = avgServerTime - avgReceivedTime + avgLatency;
```

However, there is a problem with using simple averages, because there may be a small number of latency values that have been inflated by TCP packet resends. Exclude them from the averages with the following technique:

1. Sort all the latency values.
2. Select the median value.
3. Multiply the median value by 1.5 to determine an upper-limit value.
4. Remove all data with latencies higher than the upper limit from the data set.

As an alternative, the standard deviation of the latency values can be calculated, and all samples above one standard deviation from the median can be removed.

Once any out-of-range latency values have been discarded, the client-to-server delta can be calculated using the remaining averages. The ConnectionTester component contains an implementation of this technique that can be used when a client first connects. Even better would be to check latency periodically as long as the connection to FlashCom is open.

The algorithm is based on an article by Zachary Booth Simpson named "A Stream-based Time Synchronization Technique For Networked Computer Games," available at:

   http://www.mine-control.com/zack/timesync/timesync.html

A related article, "Minimizing Latency in Real-Time Strategy Games" by Jim Greer and Zachary Booth Simpson, is available in *Game Programming Gems 3* (Charles River Media).

In later sections of this chapter, I'll return to some techniques for minimizing some of the problems latency can cause.

Bandwidth

Bandwidth is often described as the carrying capacity of the network between two nodes. It is usually measured in bits per second, and the usual multiples of kilo (K) or mega (M) are often used. The multiples when referring to bits per second in a network refer to 1000 and 1,000,000 bits, respectively. A kilobit (1 Kb) is 1000 binary digits and a megabit (1 Mb) is 1000 kilobits or 1,000,000 bits.

Programmers often prefer to work with bytes instead of bits because bytes are the typical unit of data stored and retrieved in a computer. Since each byte contains 8 bits, a kilobit is equal to 125 bytes. To translate from bits to bytes, divide by 8; to go from bytes to bits, multiply by 8. However, byte prefixes such as kilo and mega refer to powers of 2. So 1 kilobyte (KB) contains 1024 bytes or 8192 bits. To translate between bits and kilobytes or megabytes is therefore a little more complicated. One method is to take the number of bits and divide by 8 to find the number of bytes. Divide the result by 1024 to get kilobytes. To get megabytes, divide kilobytes by 1024. Table 17-2 shows some common bandwidth values for an ideal connection.

The actual throughput of a network connection can be much less than, but will never match, the ideal figure in Table 17-2. And a given connection's throughput can vary significantly over time due to changing network and usage conditions. Some of the many factors affecting actual throughput are described at *http://www.symantec.com/smallbiz/library/need.html*.

Table 17-2. Bandwidth

Connection type	Ideal kilobits/sec (Kbps)	Ideal kilobytes/sec (KB/sec)
56 Kbps modem	56	6.8
1 Mbps ADSL	1000 downstream; 300 upstream	122.1 downstream; 37 upstream
1 Mbps SDSL	1000	122.1
3 Mbps DSL	3000	366.2
10 Mbps LAN	10,000	1220.7 (1.19 MB/sec)
100 Mbps LAN	100,000	122207.0 (11.92 MB/sec)

Network equipment and communication systems are described by the highest bandwidth they can achieve under ideal conditions. For example, a 100 Mbps network card in full-duplex mode is supposed to be able to simultaneously send and receive 100 megabits of data per second. In everyday use, the network card will not be able to achieve its full 100 Mbps rating due to the limitations of the computer it is installed in and network overhead. However, a more serious constraint is that the same computer with a 100 Mbps network card may be connected via ADSL (asymmetric DSL) to an ISP that provides only 1 Mbps downstream bandwidth and 300 Kbps upstream bandwidth. Even these figures are optimistic. Noise on the lines that connect the computer to the ISP's network may reduce bandwidth to much lower levels. It is not uncommon that a home with a 1 Mbps downstream connection will achieve only 400 Kbps or less downstream bandwidth.

Things get worse if the networks available between one computer (node) and another one on the Internet are congested. One node may realize throughput of 320 Kbps when downloading data from one server but a much lower throughput when connecting to another server. The slowest part of the network will determine the overall throughput. Another factor to consider is that available bandwidth changes over time—sometimes quite rapidly—as networks become more or less congested. A network connection to an ISP that often achieves 300 Kbps can easily fluctuate over a few minutes between 40 Kbps and 100 Kbps.

Adapting to Bandwidth

Let's consider a scenario in which four participants—each on an ADSL connection with 400 Kbps downstream bandwidth and 150 Kbps upstream—are participating in a video conference. Each participant's camera is set to the default values of a 160 x 120 frame size, 15 fps, and a bandwidth limit of 16 KB/sec. Each microphone is set to its default 8 kHz sampling rate. If each person were constantly moving in front of the camera and always speaking, each could produce more than 16 KB of video data and send more than 2 KB of audio data per second. However, on average, a less-animated participant might produce about 16 KB of audio and video data combined. In other words, each person will send 132 Kbps to the server. Each participant's connection may be able to send that much data but must also receive the three streams from the other participants. With four participants, each will need to receive about 396 Kbps. This is barely manageable with their current bandwidth. Even if two more ADSL users join the video conference, all will not be lost. Each of the six participants will need to receive 5 times 132 Kbps or about 660 Kbps. Since each has only 400 Kbps downstream bandwidth, FlashCom will drop the number of video frames it sends to each participant as necessary in order to maintain audio quality. Also, many applications allow users to turn off some or all video streams if video quality deteriorates.

Now consider what happens when someone using a dial-up modem attempts to join the video conference. Even with a 56 Kbps modem, most dial-up users will get no more than 30 Kbps downstream and upstream bandwidth. Not nearly enough to send or receive a single 132 Kbps stream containing both audio and video. A single, audio-only stream will consume 2 KB/sec (16 Kbps), more than half of the user's upstream bandwidth. The user with a 56 Kbps modem has no hope of receiving four audio streams, which require 16 Kbps each or 64 Kbps total, twice the modem's realistic throughput. In this case, the only hope for a good user experience is to cut off all video and attempt to reduce the amount of audio coming from each participant who is not speaking. We've already seen in Chapters 5 and 6 how to control sending and receiving audio and video. But how do we know what capacity each client has?

Measuring Bandwidth

On the server, each *Client* object's *getStats( )* method can be used to determine the number of bytes received from the client and the number of bytes sent out to the client since the client connected. Table 17-3 describes the information returned by *getStats( )*. Provided enough data has been sent or received, the information returned by *getStats( )* also includes the outbound and inbound bandwidth of the client.

Using *setInterval( )* on the server, it is possible to regularly monitor the bandwidth consumption of the client over time, as shown in Example 17-4.

Table 17-3. The properties of the information object returned by the client object's getStats( ) method

Information object property	Description
audio_queue_bytes	The number of bytes currently in the outgoing audio queue.
audio_queue_msgs	The number of messages in the outgoing audio queue.
bw_in	The current client-to-server bandwidth being used in bytes/sec.
bw_out	The current server-to-client bandwidth being used in bytes/sec. Note: the value is calculated based on data delivered to the TCP stack and not data actually delivered to the client.
bytes_in	The number of bytes received from the client since it connected.
bytes_out	The number of bytes sent to the client since it connected.
data_queue_bytes	The number of bytes currently in the outgoing data queue.
data_queue_msgs	The number of data messages in the outgoing data queue.
dropped_audio_bytes	The number of audio bytes that could not be sent to the client.
dropped_audio_msgs	The number of audio messages that could not be sent to the client.
dropped_video_bytes	The number of video bytes that could not be sent to the client.
dropped_video_msgs	The number of video messages that could not be sent to the client.
msg_dropped	Total number of outgoing messages that have not been sent to the client including audio, video, shared object, and data messages.
msg_in	Total number of messages received from the client since it connected.
msg_out	Total number of messages sent to the client since it connected.
ping_rtt	The round-trip time (in milliseconds) to send an empty message to the client and get it back.
so_queue_bytes	The number of bytes in the outgoing shared object queue.
so_queue_msgs	The number of messages in the outgoing shared object queue.
tunnel_bytes_in	Total number of bytes received from the client through the tunnel.
tunnel_bytes_out	Total number of bytes sent to the client through the tunnel.
tunnel_idle_requests	Current number of idle requests.
tunnel_idle_responses	Current number of idle responses.
tunnel_requests	Current number of tunnel requests.
tunnel_responses	Current number of tunnel responses.
video_queue_bytes	Current length of the outgoing video queue for this client in bytes.
video_queue_msgs	Current number of video messages in the outgoing queue.

In theory, the easiest way to check the actual client's bandwidth consumption is to use *setInterval( )* on the server to regularly call *getStats( )* and extract the bw_in and bw_out properties from the returned info object. The bandwidth values are updated at least after every 3 seconds, so a testing interval of 3 seconds is ideal. However, as of FlashCom version 1.5.2, the values returned are not correct if the actual bandwidth in or out drops to zero.

You can get a good calculation of the bandwidth being used over any time interval by using the bytes_in and bytes_out properties.

If you want to know the bandwidth used since the last time you checked, you can calculate it by keeping track of the number of milliseconds between tests and the change in the bytes_in and bytes_out properties. Example 17-4 traces out some basic bandwidth statistics every 2 seconds.

Example 17-4. Monitoring throughput over time

```
Client.prototype.checkBandwidth = function () {
  var stats = this.getStats();

  var now = (new Date()).getTime();
  var elapsedTime = now - this.lastTime;    // Elapsed time in milliseconds.
  var deltaBytesOut = stats.bytes_out - this.lastBytesOut;
  var deltaBytesIn  = stats.bytes_in  - this.lastBytesIn;

  msg = "Bandwidth stats for client: " + this.ip + ":\n";
  msg += (deltaBytesOut/elapsedTime)* 1000 + " downstream bytes per second.\n";
  msg += (deltaBytesIn /elapsedTime)* 1000 + " upstream bytes per second.\n";

  this.lastBytesOut = stats.bytes_out;
  this.lastBytesIn  = stats.bytes_in;
  this.lastTime = now;

  trace(msg);
};

application.onConnect = function (client) {
  // Remember the initial time and bytes in and out.
  client.lastTime = (new Date).getTime();
  var stats = client.getStats();
  client.lastBytesOut = stats.bytes_out;
  client.lastBytesIn  = stats.bytes_in;
  // Test the bandwidth every 2 seconds.
  client.bwIntervalID = setInterval(client, "checkBandwidth", 2000);
  return true;
};

application.onDisconnect = function (client) {
  clearInterval(client.bwIntervalID);
};
```

While this code is somewhat useful for testing purposes, bandwidth detection and monitoring are more productively built into a component or object that can be used as needed. For example, see the server-side code of Macromedia's ConnectionLight component in the *.../scriptlib/components/connectionlight.asc* file. The *client.ping( )* method sends the client bandwidth statistics at a set interval.

Monitoring the bandwidth used by a client can be useful if you know the amount of data a client is trying to send or receive. For example, if a client is attempting to send

16 KB/sec of audio and video data but is actually sending only 4 KB/sec, then it should stop trying to send any video. However, while you can test the activity level of both the *Camera* and *Microphone* objects to determine if they are sending data, you cannot tell exactly how much data each is attempting to send.

Testing the maximum bandwidth available to a client may often be necessary. One approach to determining each client's bandwidth is to have the client and server attempt to send each other a large amount of data during a short test period and then measure the actual data sent and received during that time. Since the FlashCom Server and Flash Player will attempt to adapt to bandwidth limitations by dropping video frames and audio messages, it is difficult to use live audio or video to test bandwidth. What is needed is a reliable way to send a known amount of test data. Fortunately, ActionScript data is never dropped. It can be sent as a remote method invocation using the *send( )* method of a shared object or stream or with the *call( )* method of a *NetConnection* object. Since each client may have to be tested at a different time, the *call( )* method is normally used (there is no point in broadcasting test data to more than one client at a time).

Macromedia has made available at least two different bandwidth measurement methods. The first one, the *bwcheck* utility, is available as two files named *bwcheck.as* and *bwcheck.asc*. They measure both downstream (server-to-client) bandwidth and upstream (client-to-server) bandwidth. The source files are available at:

> *http://www.peldi.com/archives/2004/01/automatically_c.html*

The FLVPlayer project uses bandwidth detection code that is optimized to return the downstream bandwidth to the Flash Player in less time than the *bwcheck* utility. You can download the FLVPlayer source here:

> *http://www.peldi.com/blog/archives/2004/05/fvplayer_new_r.html*

Look at the *main.asc* file in the FLVPlayer distribution, especially the *calculateClientBw( )* function.

Both the *bwcheck* utility and FLVPlayer use a similar technique to measure bandwidth. The basic steps are:

1. Determine latency.
2. Get the current time and the current number of bytes in or out for the client.
3. Send a sequence of messages containing a large text string or array of random numbers from client to server or server to client, but test in only one direction at a time.
4. After a certain amount of time or when all the messages have been received, get the current time and the current number of bytes in or out for the client.
5. Calculate the number of bytes in or out during the test period.
6. Calculate the test duration and subtract the latency time.
7. Divide the number of bytes by the adjusted time to get bytes/sec.

There are a number of challenges in making the test work. In *bwcheck* and the initial version of FLVPlayer, a text string is used. For example, to create a text string that is 1 KB (1024 bytes) in length, you can use:

```
sampleData = "12345678";
for (var i = 0; i < 7; i++) sampleData += sampleData;
```

The data sent cannot be too small or too large. If the data is too small, the time it takes to send it will be not much different than the results of a simple latency test. For example, if the round-trip time for a few bytes of data over a connection is 70 ms, and it takes only 70 ms to send a 1 KB string, then it is impossible to measure bandwidth because the larger sample size had no measurable effect on transmission time. Even if the string took 80 ms and the round-trip latency was 70 ms, the 10 ms difference is statistically insignificant.

Round-trip measurements are always used because after the data is sent, the only way to know it has arrived at the other end is to wait for an acknowledgment from the receiver.

The test string has to be large enough that it takes much longer than the latency round-trip time to transmit it and get back an acknowledgment of receipt. However, if the string is too large, the test will take too long and risk alienating the user. The problem is compounded by the fact that a bandwidth test has to work for high-bandwidth low-latency connections, high-bandwidth high-latency connections, low-bandwidth connections, and everything in between.

The initial FLVPlayer dealt with the problem by sending strings in separate messages of constantly increasing size. Each string is twice the size of the previous one. It will not send more than six messages in less than 2 seconds. The test is over and the results are calculated after acknowledgment of receipt of the last string is received.

The most recent version of FLVPlayer repeatedly sends a 16 KB array of random numbers instead of strings. It was changed because the older tests with repeating string patterns produced inflated bandwidth numbers under some circumstances. Some modems and virtual private networks (VPNs) automatically compress data before sending it over the network. The earlier string patterns were highly compressed compared with typical compression rates for audio and video streams. In my own initial tests, sending an array of random numbers improves, but does not completely remove, the problem of inflated bandwidth numbers when compression is used. FlashCom bandwidth testing methods have been evolving since the first *bwcheck* code was released and can be expected to improve further over time.

The latency and bandwidth tests in the *bwcheck* and FLVPlayer code employ slightly different measurement algorithms and are not designed as a general purpose component. Even if they were, they would have to be adapted to provide the type of information required by different applications.

If someone has already written a bandwidth tester, why do you need to know the technical details? So you can write your own of course! This isn't merely an exercise in geekdom. Your specific configuration will typically allow or require a more specific test than the generic ones publicly available.

For my purposes, I created a ConnectionTester component. The source is available on the book's web site. It is a derivation of the algorithm used in FLVPlayer's *main.asc* file. Instead of setting the maximum number of messages at an arbitrary number and time limit, ConnectionTester sends increasingly large messages until the total test time exceeds twice the latency round-trip time. Then, four more increasingly large messages are sent. When receipt of the last message is acknowledged, the bandwidth is calculated. The ConnectionTester tests both downstream and upstream bandwidth, latency, and the difference in milliseconds between the client and server's clocks. The information is both sent back to the client and stored in a shared object. The *ConnectionTester* class does very little of the actual testing. Instead, it coordinates the work of three other objects: *DownstreamBWTester*, *UpstreamBWTester*, and *RMILatencyTester*. Example 17-5 lists the source for the *DownstreamBWTester* class.

Example 17-5. The DownstreamBWTester class

```
function DownstreamBWTester (owner, client, rtt) {
  this.owner = owner;
  this.client = client;
  this.rtt = rtt;
  this.minMessageDelta = rtt * 2 + 10;
  this.messageCount = 0;
  this.maxMessages = 4;
  this.validMessages = 0;
  this.sendCount = 0 ;
  // Create a 512 byte length string.
  this.sampleData = "12345678";
  for (var i = 0; i < 6; i++) {
    this.sampleData += this.sampleData;
  }

  this.startStats = client.getStats( );
  this.startStats.startTime = (new Date).getTime( );

  this.sendData( ); // 1K
  this.sendData( ); // 2K
  this.sendData( ); // 4K
}

DownstreamBWTester.prototype.sendData = function ( ) {
  this.sendCount++;
  this.sampleData += this.sampleData;
  this.client.call(this.owner.path + "/echoRequest", this, this.sampleData);
};
```

Example 17-5. The DownstreamBWTester class (continued)

```
DownstreamBWTester.prototype.onResult = function (info) {
  var receiveTime = (new Date).getTime( );
  this.messageCount++;
  var delta = receiveTime - this.startStats.startTime;
  var pendingMessageCount = this.sendCount - this.messageCount;
  if (delta > this.minMessageDelta) {
    this.validMessages++;
    var requiredMessages = this.maxMessages - this.validMessages;
    if (requiredMessages > pendingMessageCount) {
      this.sendData( );
    }
  }
  else if (pendingMessageCount < 3) this.sendData( );

  if (this.sendCount - this.messageCount == 0) {
    var endStats = this.client.getStats( );
    var startStats = this.startStats;
    var deltaBytes = endStats.bytes_out - startStats.bytes_out;
    var deltaTime = receiveTime - startStats.startTime - this.rtt;
    var bytesPerSecond = 1000 * deltaBytes/deltaTime;
    this.owner.onDownstreamBW(this.client, bytesPerSecond);
  }
};
```

A *DownstreamBWTester* instance is created by the ConnectionTester component when it needs to test a client's downstream bandwidth:

```
var proxy = this.getProxy(client);
proxy.downstreamBWTester = new DownstreamBWTester(this, client, rtt);
```

At the beginning of the test, the *client.getStats( )* method is used to get the amount of data the client has already been sent before the test started:

```
this.startStats = client.getStats( );
this.startStats.startTime = (new Date).getTime( );
```

When the test is over, *client.getStats( )* is called again to get the total amount of data the client has been sent since connecting. The difference in bytes out between the beginning and end of the test is calculated, as is the elapsed test time:

```
var endStats = this.client.getStats( );
var startStats = this.startStats;
var deltaBytes = endStats.bytes_out - startStats.bytes_out;
var deltaTime = receiveTime - startStats.startTime - this.rtt;
```

Since the time difference is calculated in milliseconds, we multiply the bytes/ms by 1000 to gets bytes/sec:

```
var bytesPerSecond = 1000 * deltaBytes/deltaTime;
```

You can tweak my ConnectionTester's parameters to suit your needs or use it as the basis for a custom latency and bandwidth measuring component of your own. The current version uses a repeating string pattern. Future versions will use different test data to reduce the effects of modem and VPN compression and will be available from the book's web site.

Latency, Bandwidth, and Performance

Latency is the minimum time to deliver each packet and is unrelated to the capacity or bandwidth of the network. However, as a network becomes congested, it will drop more and more packets—each of which will have to be resent—so that the average time to deliver packets will increase. Therefore, when designing and tuning applications for performance, both latency and bandwidth need to be accounted for. There is no point in sending messages more frequently than the network's ability to deliver them, and there is no point in trying to send more data than the network can handle. In fact, both are counterproductive.

 You should minimize the total number of messages that every client sends or receives and their size. Send the minimum data necessary and batch messages together when possible.

Sending too many, too large messages via *send( )* and *call( )* will fill up each application's message queue and slow down the responsiveness of an application instance's ActionScript thread. Frequently sending many small messages will increase the total overhead of the network and server and therefore reduce performance. Sending a batch of messages less frequently will improve performance. A good example of minimizing the load on the network and server is the way the *PFCSLogger* class, introduced in Chapter 11, caches log messages and then sends them in batches rather than sending each one immediately. A number of techniques can be of use in increasing performance by reducing the frequency and size of data being sent.

Latency and SharedObject updates

The frequency of *SharedObject* updates can often be decreased even further than described in the section "Updates and Frame Rates" in Chapter 8. Consider an application that must work well for users with latencies of up to 200 ms. Since an acknowledgment is required for each shared object update, 400 ms is the effective frame rate. That's just 2.5 fps! So it makes sense to set the frame rate on shared objects to 3 or 4 fps (using *SharedObject.setFps( )*) to reduce the number of messages that will be sent, even when local updates to the shared object are more frequent. For some things, like updates in business data, slower frame rates may be fine. For other purposes, such as sending real-time presence information or positioning a visible entity in a game, it will produce distracting and spasmodic motion that visibly lags behind the current state of the game. However, there are techniques that can smooth motion when updates are infrequent, and even ways to extrapolate motion between updates that often make reducing update frequency practical and, therefore, improve overall application performance.

To illustrate smoothing and extrapolating motion between updates, I'll use the PersonalCursors component first introduced in Chapter 15 as a demonstration platform. When a user moves his cursor, an *onMouseMove* event is generated. When the mouse is moving, events may occur as often as every 5 milliseconds. For the owner of the local cursor, the hardware cursor will move smoothly on the screen. However, if the mouse position in a shared object is updated at only 3 or 4 fps, remote users will see the cursor jerk and jump discontinuously. One solution is to slow the remote cursor down! If some additional delay can be tolerated, a series of intermediate steps between its previous position and the current position in the shared object can be calculated so that the mouse moves smoothly between steps.

My version, the full version of which is available on the book's web site, is based on a presentation at the 2004 Flash in the Can Festival by Brian Robbins of Fuel Industries. The sample files from his presentation are available at:

> *http://www.dubane.com/cons*

Example 17-6 shows the source code for the *update( )* method of my *InterpolatedPersonalCursor* movie clip subclass that implements a very simple motion-smoothing algorithm.

Example 17-6. InterpolatedPersonalCursor.update( ) method

```
function update ( ) {
  var requiresUpdate = false;
  var cursor = so.data[userName];
  var delta_x = cursor.x - _x;
  if (Math.abs(delta_x) > maxTravel) {
    if (delta_x > 0) _x += maxTravel;
    else _x -= maxTravel;
    requiresUpdate = true;
  }
  else {
    _x = cursor.x;
  }
  var delta_y = cursor.y - _y;
  if (Math.abs(delta_y) > maxTravel) {
    if (delta_y > 0) _y += maxTravel;
    else _y -= maxTravel;
    requiresUpdate = true;
  }
  else {
    _y = cursor.y;
  }
  if (requiresUpdate) {
    if (!onEnterFrame) onEnterFrame = enterFrameHandler;
  }
  else {
    onEnterFrame = null;
  }
}
```

The *update( )* method is called whenever the position of the cursor it represents has been updated in the so shared object. The movie clip is allowed to travel no more than the number of pixels specified by maxTravel. If that means the clip will not reach its position in the shared object, it arranges to have *update( )* called for every *onEnterFrame* event until it reaches the position specified in the shared object.

When *update( )* is called, the distance between the x coordinate in the shared object and the current _x position of the movie clip is calculated:

```
var delta_x = cursor.x - _x;
```

If the absolute value of the distance is greater than maxTravel, the movie clip is moved maxTravel pixels to the left or right. Otherwise, it is moved directly to the x coordinate in the shared object:

```
if (Math.abs(delta_x) > maxTravel) {
  if (delta_x > 0) _x += maxTravel;
  else _x -= maxTravel;
  requiresUpdate = true;
}
else {
  _x = cursor.x;
}
```

The same process is repeated for the y coordinate. If either value has been constrained to move only maxTravel pixels, an *onEnterFrame( )* handler that simply calls *update( )* again on the next frame is set up:

```
if (requiresUpdate) {
  if (!onEnterFrame) onEnterFrame = enterFrameHandler;
}
else {
  onEnterFrame = null;
}
```

When the next frame is reached, the movie clip will again be moved no more than maxTravel pixels. When the clip is moved to its coordinates in the shared object, the onEnterFrame property is set to null and the position of the cursor movie clip will not be updated again until the coordinates in the cursor's slot in the shared object change. For the PersonalCursors component, the additional delay is not a problem because the user also sees a movie clip of her cursor following her hardware cursor and so has a good idea what other people are seeing. Other more sophisticated animation algorithms can be used to smooth motion. See Robert Penner's easing equations available at:

http://robertpenner.com

In multiuser computer games, lag is the enemy of every game developer. Instead of delaying visible changes between updates, an approach is required to try to predict an entity's position before the next update arrives. In Flash, that means each movie clip that represents a moving game entity must be repositioned when each *onEnterFrame* event occurs. Each entity must continue moving rather than stop to wait for the next update to arrive. If the prediction of movement is slightly off, the entity's position can be corrected when the next update arrives. Extrapolating the position of entities in between updates is often done using a *dead reckoning algorithm*. Dead reckoning was originally employed to improve military simulations. Jesse Aronson's article at Gamasutra provides a good overview of dead reckoning (free membership required):

> *http://www.gamasutra.com/features/19970919/aronson_01.htm*

Dead reckoning works best for game entities such as tanks and aircraft that behave according to a set of predictable physical rules. For example, while a jet can change direction, it cannot suddenly stop in midair and reverse direction. A simple version of dead reckoning works to minimize the number of updates sent on the network this way:

1. The current position, velocity, acceleration, orientation, and other attributes of an entity under the control of a user are sent to all the other game or simulation clients.

2. When the information arrives at each client, the entity's position is moved to the position specified in the message.

3. At regular intervals, the change in time between the last position update and the current time is calculated, and each entity's position is extrapolated based on the entity's orientation, velocity, and acceleration. Then, the entity is moved to the extrapolated position. As time proceeds, each entity's position is continually extrapolated until another update arrives.

4. An owner of an entity receives back its own messages about its entity and also uses them to extrapolate its position. When the owner changes the direction of his entity, the extrapolated position and the real position will diverge. When they diverge by a certain threshold, the system sends a new message with updated position and movement information to every client.

In other words, dead reckoning is designed to send updates only when the real entity's position is significantly different from its extrapolated position.

Shared object updates work a little differently. If a slot in a shared object is constantly changed, the shared object will attempt to send updates at the regular interval defined by its frame rate. However, it is not difficult to adapt dead reckoning to work with shared objects with a fixed update interval. One technique is to regularly update the shared object with position and velocity information. To return to the PersonalCursors component as an example, whenever an *onMouseMove* event is received, the shared object is updated with the mouse's _x and _y position and its velocity in x and y. When the mouse stops moving, each velocity value will be set to zero. When other clients receive updates, they will move a cursor movie clip to the position defined in the update. On every subsequent frame, they will use the position and velocity as well as the time elapsed since the last update to extrapolate a position for the cursor and move it accordingly. Example 17-7 shows the source code for the *DeadReckoningPersonalCursor* class.

Example 17-7. The DeadReckoningPersonalCursor class definition

```
class com.oreilly.pfcs.framework.components.DeadReckoningPersonalCursor
    extends MovieClip {

  // Connect component class and symbol.
  var className:String = "DeadReckoningPersonalCursor";
  static var symbolName:String = "DeadReckoningPersonalCursor";
  static var symbolOwner:Object = DeadReckoningPersonalCursor;

  // initObject variables.
  var homeInstance:Boolean; // Indicates if this is the user's cursor.
  var userName:String;      // The user's userName and slot name for this cursor.
  var so:SharedObject;      // Shared object to update with the cursor's position.

  var lastPos:Object;           // Previous position of the mouse.
  var lastTime:Number;          // Last time the mouse position was determined.
  var lastUpdateTime:Number = 0; // Last time the shared object changed.
  var intervalID;               // To get a mouse position after it stops.

  // Subcomponents and movie clips.
  var userName_txt:TextField;

  function DeadReckoningPersonalCursor () {
    super();
    // If this instance belongs to the user.
    if (homeInstance) {
      lastTime = getTimer();
      onMouseMove = onMouseMoveHandler;
      onEnterFrame = homeEnterFrameHandler;
      // Set initial position in the shared object:
      var cursorRecord = {x: _root._xmouse - _parent._x,
                          y: _root._ymouse - _parent._y,
                          vx: 0, vy: 0, ax: 0, ay: 0}
      lastPos = cursorRecord;
      so.data[userName] = cursorRecord;
    }
    else {
      onEnterFrame = enterFrameHandler;
    }
  }

  function onLoad () {
    userName_txt.text = userName;
  }

  function onMouseMoveHandler () {
    clearInterval( intervalID );
    var now = getTimer();
```

```
    var dt = now - lastTime;
    if (dt < 2) return;
    lastTime = now;
    var current = {x: _root._xmouse - _parent._x,
                   y: _root._ymouse - _parent._y,
                   vx: 0, vy: 0, ax: 0, ay: 0}
    if (!lastPos) return;
    current.vx = (current.x -lastPos.x)/dt;
    current.vy = (current.y -lastPos.y)/dt;
    current.ax = (current.vx -lastPos.vx)/dt;
    current.ay = (current.vy -lastPos.vy)/dt;
    lastPos = current;
    so.data[userName] = current;
    intervalID = setInterval( this, "onMouseMove", dt*2 );
  }

  function homeEnterFrameHandler ( ) {
   _x = _root._xmouse - _parent._x;
   _y = _root._ymouse - _parent._y;
  }

  function enterFrameHandler ( ) {
    var now = getTimer( );
    var dt = now - lastUpdateTime;
    if (dt < 5) return;
    var lastUpdate = so.data[userName];
    if (!lastUpdate) return;
    if ((Math.abs(lastUpdate.vx) < 0.1) && (Math.abs(lastUpdate.vy) < 0.1)) {
      _x = lastUpdate.x;
      _y = lastUpdate.y
    }
    else {
      _x = lastUpdate.x + lastUpdate.vx * dt ;
      _y = lastUpdate.y + lastUpdate.vy * dt;
    }
  }

  function update ( ) {
    var cursorRecord = so.data[userName];
   _x = cursorRecord.x;
   _y = cursorRecord.y;
    lastUpdateTime = getTimer( );
  }

  function deleteClip ( ) {
    Mouse.removeListener(this);
    delete so.data[userName];
    this.removeMovieClip( );
  }
}
```

The *onMouseMoveHandler( )* method is assigned to the *onMouseMove( )* method of the clip if it is the owner's instance. Whenever the mouse moves, it determines its current local position within its parent clip, calculates its velocity and acceleration, and places all the information in an object inside its shared object slot. The property names are _x and _y for position, vx and vy for velocity, and ax and ay for acceleration. Putting all the properties in a single object increases bandwidth because the entire object is sent when any property changes. However, we assume that most properties are changing simultaneously; even if they are not, updating them in one bunch at low frame rates such as 3 fps seems reasonable. You are welcome to customize the component to transmit the properties in separate slots rather than combined into one object.

The code also starts a timer, so the *onMouseMove( )* method will be called again after the mouse stops. Otherwise, the cursor would keep moving indefinitely, as it is assumed to continue along an extrapolated path.

The *update( )* method is called whenever the shared object is updated and moves the movie clip cursor to the position specified in the shared object. It also remembers the time of the last update.

The *enterFrameHandler( )* is designed to be assigned to the *onEnterFrame( )* method if the clip represents a cursor that is not owned by the current user. For each *onEnterFrame* event, the elapsed time since the last shared object update is calculated:

```
var now = getTimer( );
var dt = now - lastUpdateTime;
```

If enough time has elapsed since the last shared object update, it extrapolates a new position for the clip and moves it with these two statements:

```
_x = lastUpdate.x + lastUpdate.vx * dt ;
_y = lastUpdate.y + lastUpdate.vy * dt;
```

The statements do not use acceleration. However, depending on the application, acceleration can also be used:

```
var halfdtdt = 0.5 * dt * dt;
_x = lastUpdate.x + lastUpdate.vx * dt + lastUpdate.ax * halfdtdt;
_y = lastUpdate.y + lastUpdate.vy * dt + lastUpdate.ay * halfdtdt;
```

If you try out the *DeadReckoningPersonalCursor* class, you will see that, when you move the mouse relatively slowly and without very sudden changes in direction, the remote versions of the cursor will follow it remarkably well and with a much better feeling of simultaneity. On the other hand, if you move the cursor quickly and with sharp changes in direction, the remote cursor will often noticeably diverge from the real cursor's position. When the real cursor changes direction sharply, the difference is most noticeable as the remote cursor overshoots the inflection point and then snaps back to the correct position. Large errors are a problem with rapidly changing entities but, in some cases, can be compensated for by enforcing other rules on each entity. For example, a vehicle should not be able to "overshoot" and move through an impenetrable wall or drive at the same speed on the shoulder of a road as it can on a paved road.

Regardless of dead reckoning's accuracy, the updates that travel from the owner's client to the server and on to everyone else's clients still arrive some time after they were sent, so each entity still lags behind its owner's copy. We'll return to this problem in the next section.

Concurrency

When multiple computers must work together at the same time, all sorts of interference problems can arise. Shared object updates are a simple example. Unless an application is designed carefully, there is always the danger that one client will overwrite another client's data in a shared object. While there is a slot-level locking mechanism, there is no intrinsic mechanism for locking shared object slots for a controlled period of time.

In the database field, interference problems are well understood and often easily dealt with using the database's ability to lock records, maintain a multiversion consistency model, and to commit or roll back transactions. In real-time multiuser applications, the tools available to deal with interference problems are often not quite so advanced. Consequently, FlashCom developers need to be aware of the potential for problems and how to deal with them. Unfortunately, the subject of concurrency is a large one and cannot be covered in detail here. A good reference is the chapter on concurrency in recent editions of C. J. Date's book *An Introduction to Database Systems* (Addison Wesley). This section reviews a number of problems you may run into when developing FlashCom-enabled applications and some common ways to deal with them.

Serializing Requests and the ActionScript Thread

In all versions of FlashCom (up to and including 1.5.2), each application instance has one and only one ActionScript thread. For applications that use Server-Side ActionScript extensively throughout the instance's life, the single thread can be a performance bottleneck. So, some caution is required in designing applications in regard to how much server-side code must regularly be invoked.

 In general, server-side code should be designed to run as quickly as possible and not spend a long time regularly performing complex calculations such as collision detection. However, being limited to a single thread is also a valuable resource for dealing with all sorts of concurrency problems.

Every *call( )* and *send( )* message is queued on the server if it cannot be handled immediately. If Server-Side ActionScript is invoked by a *call( )* or *send( )* message, each message is dealt with sequentially. There is no possibility that while one message is being processed by server-side code that another message can interfere with it. As already noted in Chapters 13 and 15, calling server-side code to get an exclusive lock on a resource is an excellent use of the *call( )* method. Whenever a locking mechanism is needed or a particular order of operation must be enforced on individual clients, each client should call a server-side method using *call( )*. The server-side script can then set values in a shared object to make every client aware of the correct state of the application or create an internal queue of events or objects to be processed in order.

Some caution is required with shared objects.

Shared object updates occur asynchronously so that, even while server-side code is executing, the values in a shared object can change.

The shared object data visible to a server-side script is not a snapshot in time. If calculations such as banking transactions must be performed using multiple slots, the only option is to make it impossible for clients to update the shared object directly. When sophisticated data management is required, a much better strategy is to have a database do the difficult work of managing transactions and use a shared object as a read-only way to make clients aware of the state of any part of the database that must be visible to clients.

Asynchronous Callbacks

Of course, calling an application server to reach a database takes time, so the Server-Side ActionScript thread cannot wait for the response. Instead, when a result is returned from the application server, the response is queued until the ActionScript thread can deal with it. In several cases, server-side scripts can take an action but will not get a result immediately. For example:

- Using a NetConnection to connect to another instance
- Calling a remote method on another instance
- Calling a remote method on a client
- Calling a remote method on a service using Flash Remoting
- Playing a stream
- Updating another instance's shared object

In every case in which a server-side script initiates a request, it will not get a response back immediately. In many cases, that means the thread must put the work it was doing on hold until it receives a response. A classic example of this type of problem is when a client attempts to connect and must be authenticated. The authentication step usually requires calling an application server using Flash Remoting. No further processing of the client is possible until the remote method returns. So the server-side code places the *Client* object in a queue and returns `null` from *onConnect( )*, leaving the client in a pending state. When the result is returned, the server-side script must pick up where it left off. It retrieves the client from the queue and accepts or rejects the connection.

When multiple remote methods must be called, extra caution is required. For example, when an application instance must both call a remote method in order to initialize itself and also call a remote method to authenticate each client, there is no guarantee that the calls will return in the same order they were made. The initialization information may return before or after the authentication information. The strategy you develop for dealing with this kind of problem will depend on whether one call is dependent on the other. In this scenario, if the initialization information is required before an authentication call can be made, clients should be placed in a queue until initialization is complete. Then each client can be authenticated. To simplify processing, the client can be moved from the initialization queue into a pending authentication queue. If authentication can be performed before initialization, the client should be placed in a pending authentication queue and authenticated. When the authentication call returns, if the initialization call has not returned, the client can be placed into an initialization queue. The *lobby.asc* code in Example 16-2 showed how authentication can be performed before initialization of the instance is complete (see the *onAuthenticate( )* method). Queuing clients during authentication is discussed in detail in Chapter 18.

Latency and Application State

The individual latency of clients connected to an instance can vary dramatically. A client on the same local network as the server may have very fast response times while a distant client on a remote network may not. For many applications, this doesn't really matter. However, for some games, auctions, certain online testing scenarios, and other applications, it does. Consider a simple quiz game in which a question is asked and the first person to indicate she has the answer gets the first try at answering. Each user clicks a button to indicate she wants to answer the question, and the Flash client uses the *call( )* method to send a message to the server. The low-latency client has a distinct advantage over the high-latency client. For example, if the local client has a latency of 5 ms and the remote client a latency of 500 ms, the remote client must click the button half a second earlier in order to be judged first.

One way to deal with this sort of problem is to have each client timestamp her request. Provided a clock offset has been determined, as described earlier under "Clock Synchronization," a good approximation of the server time when each user clicked the button can be determined. Another solution is to have the client track the time between when the question was received and the button clicked and send that elapsed time to the server. In either case, when the first message arrives, the server-side script can set an interval equal to roughly one-and-a-half times the largest client latency. When the interval is over, the server can look at each time-corrected or delay-time message and choose the winner. The added delay can often be disguised by updating all the clients with partial information as soon as the first message arrives. For example, a sound can play and the button controls of each player can be disabled in response to the first message. When the winner is determined, the clients are sent another message so they know who will try to answer the question.

In other games, such as multiplayer Minesweeper, it is more important for each user to know that a square has been uncovered as soon as possible rather than who uncovered it. The process of providing feedback in two steps can be simplified to avoid an interval step. When a message first arrives that a user has chosen to uncover a square, the user's ID and corrected server time can be stored in a shared object slot representing the square. If another message arrives for the same square, its corrected server time can be compared with the server time in the shared object slot. If the message was sent earlier, the slot is updated with the more recent user ID and time. Users playing the game will likely be too busy trying to figure out what square to turn over to worry about who owns each square.

The same problem—users with low latency having an advantage over users with high latency—also occurs when the server sends information to clients. For example, during an auction, someone with a low-latency connection will see or hear auction information before users with slower connections. If a live stream containing audio or video is used, very little can be done about it. However, data-only messages can be timestamped and sent out to each client with calculated delays so that each client receives a message at roughly the same time. Similarly, all messages can be timestamped and sent out immediately but displayed after a calculated delay on each client. In either case, the effect will be to slow down the auction to accommodate the user with the highest latency.

The solutions presented here assume that the client *.swf* has not been tampered with. That is, that the user is compliant or does not have the technical skill to crack the system. They should not be considered secure mechanisms for ensuring fairness.

Latency problems can compound one another. If no latency compensation is provided in an auction, users with low-latency connections will be provided information earlier and their bids will arrive sooner. Figure 17-1 shows the interaction of two clients and a server. The length of the arrows is not meaningful, but their slope is. Time is measured on the vertical axis increasing downward, so the more horizontal an arrow appears, the less the latency.

Client 1 has lower latency than Client 2 so messages arrive from the server sooner and take less time to deliver to the server. The illustration shows that Client 1 can work with a server message longer than Client 2 and still beat Client 2.

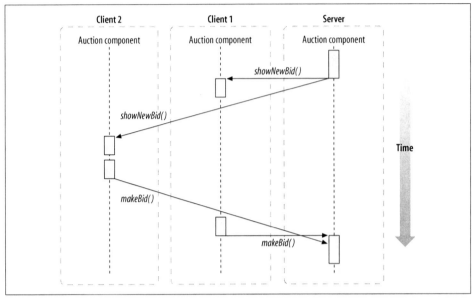

Figure 17-1. The low-latency client provides more time for the user to think than does the high-latency client

In other words, latency effects can add up. If Client 1 has a 5 ms latency and Client 2 has a 500 ms latency, then Client 1 has almost a full second advantage.

Living in the Future

Another technique for dealing with latency is to use *predictive time management*. Whenever it is possible to predict that an event will occur, a message including a timestamp of when the event will happen can be sent out in advance of the actual event. For example, if a projectile is fired, its trajectory can be calculated in advance, but it may not be possible to determine if another entity can redirect or stop its motion. At some point when it is determined that nothing can interfere with its travel, an event message containing the time and location of impact can be broadcast in advance so that every client will display the event at very nearly the same time.

When events cannot be predicted because of unpredictable user intervention, some other techniques are still available. In some cases, events can be deliberately desynchronized. In a game of Pong, the player who returns the ball can be presented with a slower version of the ball moving toward the opposing player's paddle. The opposing player is presented with a slightly faster version. When the opposing player returns the ball, the message of the return can reach the first player as he sees the ball contact his opponenet's paddle.

Using simple dead reckoning, you can sometimes use the calculated server time of each event—rather than the time the update is received—to position each entity. As a consequence, every clip position will always be an extrapolation. In simulations or games in which sudden changes are not possible, extrapolation based on a common clock is possible, and often desirable.

Conclusion

Although a full discussion of concurrency issues in game play or online transactions such as auctions is beyond the scope of this book, I hope this chapter has introduced you to many of the issues involved. For further study, see the following resources:

Dead Reckoning: Latency Hiding for Networked Games by Jesse Aronson:

> *http://www.gamasutra.com/features/19970919/aronson_01.htm*

Encapsulating Network Latency Compensators in VRML by Benjamin G. Worthington and David J. Roberts:

> *http://www.isrg.reading.ac.uk/common/publications/00347.pdf*

David Mills' Network Time Synchronization Project:

> *http://www.eecis.udel.edu/~mills/ntp.html*

See also the Network and Multiplayer sections in the *Game Programming Gems* series of books (numbers 3 through 5) from Charles River Media.

The next and final chapter discusses an equally important topic in ensuring the fairness and integrity of any online application, security.

CHAPTER 18

Securing Applications

If you have ever looked at the access logs of a web server or firewall, you've likely seen firsthand how dangerous a place the public Internet is. Chances are that any access log will show repeated attempts to attack your system. Logs are proof that there are people who will try to crash or get control of your server, delete your files, use your server to anonymously relay spam, cheat at online games, steal your personal or corporate information, harass you, and in general make life as miserable for you as they can. Attacks come in a variety of forms and are often launched using sophisticated software. FlashCom Server has no special immunity from attack. There are reports of people discovering their FlashCom Server being used by someone without their permission. The perpetrators had not been granted any special access to the server. Parasites, as they have been called, discovered the address of a valid application instance on someone else's server, wrote their own *.swf* files—often called rogue clients—to connect to it, and created their own applications. Some descriptions of the problem have been written up on the Chattyfig FlashComm mailing list and on Peldi's blog:

> *http://chattyfig.figleaf.com/mailman/htdig/flashcomm/2003-November/*
> *http://chattyfig.figleaf.com/mailman/htdig/flashcomm/2004-January/013138.html*
> *http://chattyfig.figleaf.com/mailman/htdig/flashcomm/2004-January/013056.html*
> *http://www.peldi.com/blog/archives/2003/07/protecting_your.html*

 In its default configuration, the FlashCom Server is not secure enough to be used for application delivery on the public Internet.

A few simple changes in the server's configuration files buy a significant improvement in protection. But if you create applications using Macromedia's components without adding a layer of authentication, you are asking for trouble. The server needs to be configured for security, and your applications must be written with security in mind.

This chapter focuses on designing secure FlashCom applications and is not intended to provide detailed setup and configuration information for security, nor is it intended as a complete course on network security. However, some recommendations and advice are provided throughout the chapter. See also the resources for further reading cited near the end of the chapter.

If you are responsible for setting up a FlashCom Server that will be reachable from the Internet, you should also consult the following resources provided by Macromedia:

> *http://www.macromedia.com/devnet/mx/flashcom/articles/security_overview.html*
> *http://www.macromedia.com/devnet/mx/flashcom/articles/security_setup.html*
> *http://www.macromedia.com/devnet/mx/flashcom/articles/firewalls_proxy06.html*
> *http://download.macromedia.com/pub/flashcom/documentation/*
> *FlashCom_Installing.pdf*
> *http://download.macromedia.com/pub/flashcom/documentation/*
> *FlashCom_Managing.pdf*

If you don't have the time, knowledge, or resources available to set up a secure server, consider one of the hosting options cited in the Preface.

In keeping with O'Reilly's attempt to reclaim the word *hacker* for its positive connotations (see the *Hacks* series), we refer to programmers attempting to compromise your security as *attackers*, not hackers.

The Three A's: Authentication, Authorization, and Accounting

Applications should be designed from the beginning for security. If you try to bolt security on after you have moved into production, you will likely fail to really secure the application. If you do secure it, the cost may be much higher than if you had designed for security from the beginning (but not as costly as foregoing security altogether!). In simple terms, a secure application is designed to control who can do what and provides an accounting of what the application was asked to do and what it actually did. The three features essential to a secure application that we will discuss are authentication, authorization, and accounting.

Authentication is the process in which a user (or process) identifies herself and proves she is who she claims to be by providing information available only to her. The most common authentication mechanism on the Internet today is to log into a system using a username and password. Under some circumstances, passwords may be stolen as they are transmitted across networks, and badly chosen passwords can be guessed. There are other stronger authentication systems that employ certificates and encryption. We'll look at some of the problems of username/password authentication schemes and what you can do about them later.

Authorization is the process that grants controlled access to resources to a user or process based on who the user is—determined during the authentication process—and what she is entitled to do. Authorization can take different forms. For example, a user may be authorized to connect to an application instance but not permitted to draw on a whiteboard within it. Users are often grouped together and assigned *roles*. What they are permitted to do often depends on the role they are given in relation to a particular resource.

Accounting, or *logging*, is the way you discover if your application and users are doing what they are supposed to. It allows you to discover when someone is trying to break into your system or misuse it. It is every bit as important as authentication and authorization but is perhaps the most often ignored of the three *A*'s. Accounting can reveal unusual usage patterns, which may indicate that a password was stolen, that attackers have found a vulnerability in your system, or a previously well-behaved user (or ex-employee) has had a change of heart.

Authentication

When a client attempts to connect to the server, FlashCom:

1. Accepts the connection at the network level
2. Reads the information passed by the client when *connect( )* was called
3. Places the client in a pending state from which it cannot send or receive data
4. Calls the *application.onConnect( )* method

The information passed into the *onConnect( )* method is used by a FlashCom application to authenticate the person using the client. One way to authenticate a user is to create a *.swf* that will pass the user's username and password in the *connect( )* call:

```
nc.connect("rtmp:/ch18Samples/simpleAuthDemo", userName, password);
```

Shortly, we'll address the fact that passing the username and password via RTMP isn't a great idea, because RTMP sends the data as plain text allowing passwords to be stolen. We'll discuss RTMPS in a minute. First, let's just see how a FlashCom application can authenticate a user.

When an application receives the username and password, it can look them up in a database or directory server. If the username and password match, the client connection is accepted, and the client is removed from the pending state. If the username and password don't match, the connection to the FlashCom Server is broken after sending a message to the client. The message can include a custom property, in this case msg:

```
application.rejectConnection(client, {msg: "Invalid Credentials!"});
```

Chapters 11 and 14 contain examples of simple username and password authentication.

Other credentials—for example, an access token or ticket—may be used. In addition to user- or system-supplied credentials, connection information should be checked. For example, the IP address of the connecting *.swf* may have to match a list of valid addresses, and the URL of the connecting *.swf* may have to match a specific address or partial address.

The entire process is based on the idea that only the user knows, and therefore can provide, her secret password. Anything that increases the possibility that her password can become known by someone else reduces the level of security of the system. Of course, if the user tells her password to someone else, the password has been fatally compromised. Some passwords are better than others because they are harder to guess, so password policies are often used to require the use of stronger and frequently changed passwords. Maintaining good password policies is an essential part of keeping credentials secure. However, there are some unique challenges in keeping credentials secret while Flash connects to FlashCom.

Network or Packet Sniffing

As of FlashCom 1.5.2, the RTMP protocol does not provide any level of encryption. RTMP information in a connection is encoded into AMF, MPEG, Nelly Moser, or other data formats. All these formats were designed to be efficiently decoded into ActionScript data, video, or audio. If an attacker can gain access to the network traffic being communicated between a *.swf* client and FlashCom, all the RTMP information can be decoded, including the username and password transmitted during the connection process. Therefore, before a username and password authentication scheme is used, the network connection must be secured against eavesdropping; otherwise, another more secure authentication method must be found.

Not all networks are equal in resisting eavesdropping. For example, a well-controlled switched network within a single organization may make it extremely difficult to intercept data flowing between clients and the server within the same network. If a FlashCom application is used only within the organization's network, passing a username and password when connecting via RTMP is acceptable. However, you should never simply assume without checking that an organization's network is secure. There may be wireless areas or other risks that are not immediately obvious.

Organizations often deploy a virtual private network (VPN) to secure access to their core networked resources within their own physical network and out onto the Internet. VPNs work by providing an encrypted tunnel that all information between the client and core services in the organization travels within. The security of VPNs is generally very good—including the authentication process, which normally involves the use of certificates in addition to usernames and passwords before a VPN connection is accepted. If connections to the FlashCom Server will always pass through a VPN, simple username and password authentication is also acceptable. In fact, it may be possible to create a system in which VPN users do not have to log in a second time to a FlashCom application after authenticating to the VPN. Instead, when a client attempts to connect, a FlashCom application can query the VPN system to identify each user connecting via the VPN. See the "Web applications and portals" section later in this chapter.

Another way to secure network traffic is to have each Flash client request an RTMPS connection. An RTMPS connection is similar to a tunneled RTMPT connection, except that tunneling is done using SSL. FlashCom 1.5.2 and earlier do not support SSL, so you must use additional hardware or software to decrypt tunneled traffic before it reaches FlashCom. More information on tunneling and using RTMPS is available at:

> http://www.macromedia.com/devnet/mx/flashcom/articles/firewalls_proxy.html

For many, if not most, FlashCom applications, there is no guarantee that connections will occur across secured networks. In these cases, passing usernames and passwords across RTMP is strongly discouraged. Fortunately, many organizations already have the resources in place to provide protection for usernames and passwords. All that is needed is a web server and application server that support SSL, a database, and a Flash Remoting gateway.

The remainder of this section explores alternatives to username and password authentication over RTMP.

One-Time Ticket Systems

One way to protect a username and password is never to send them directly to Flash-Com. In summary, a *ticket* can be used only once and only within a narrow time period to authenticate the user.

The sequence for a so-called *ticketing system* is as follows:

1. The Flash movie passes the username and password via SSL to a web server.
2. The web server hands the authentication request to an application server that looks up the username and password.
3. If the user's credentials are valid, the server returns a single-use ticket to the Flash movie.
4. The ticket acts like a one-time pass to connect to FlashCom. The Flash movie connects to FlashCom and passes the ticket—instead of the username and password—in the *connect( )* call.
5. The FlashCom application checks with the application server that the ticket is valid and accepts the connection if it is.

The advantage of a ticketing system is that the username and password are passed over the encrypted SSL connection only. From then on, a ticket replaces the username and password as a way to authenticate a user.

The ticket is a long but unique string of characters that is used only once. An attacker who sniffs the ticket in transit to the server never sees the user's username or password and cannot use the same ticket later to connect to FlashCom, because a ticket can be used only once.

To use a web server that supports SSL to authenticate users, the following systems must be in place:

- An SSL-equipped web server that can pass requests to the application server
- A Flash Remoting gateway such as the one included with ColdFusion (see Chapter 12)
- An application server that can query the authentication database
- An authentication database such as a directory system or relational database
- The Flash Communication Server

The interaction diagram in Figure 18-1 shows step-by-step how the client gets a single-use ticket.

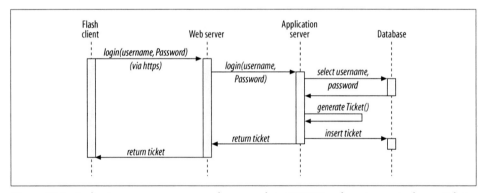

Figure 18-1. A client passes a username and password via HTTPS and receives a single-use ticket. Separately, the ticket is stored in a server-side database for later authentication.

In Figure 18-1, the same database is used to check the user's username and password and to store the user's ticket after it has been generated. When a directory server is used, the user's credentials are checked against the directory server, but a separate database is required to store, retrieve, and delete tickets.

The client in Figure 18-1 is the Flash movie talking to the web server (don't mistake it for a normal browser connection).

Once the Flash client has a ticket, it can use the ticket to connect to a FlashCom application instance. The instance must check the ticket before accepting the client. Figure 18-2 shows step-by-step how the client connects to FlashCom using a ticket.

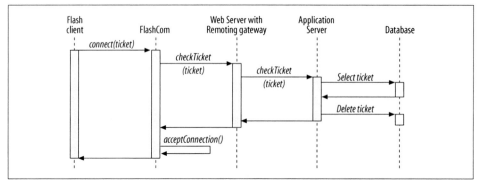

Figure 18-2. The client passes the ticket when connecting to FlashCom. If the ticket is valid, the client is allowed to connect. The ticket is deleted.

When the web/application server responds to FlashCom's request to check a ticket, it sends all the user information the FlashCom application needs, including things like the user's name and application roles. The user information is normally stored in the authentication database but may include information the user provided when logging in.

To illustrate one way to create a single-use ticket system, the book's web site provides sample files that use ColdFusion as an application server. The application uses two tables: a user table named PFCS_USER that contains usernames and passwords and a table named PFCS_TICKET that holds tickets. Table 18-1 shows the PFCS_USER table structure.

Table 18-1. PFCS_USER table

Attribute name	Datatype	Notes
userName	varchar(100)	Primary key
firstName	varchar(100)	
lastName	varchar(100)	
email	varchar(255)	
password	varchar(255)	Should be encrypted

The PFCS_USER table structure could have been different. Instead of a userName attribute being the primary key, a sequence number (or autoincrementing number) is often used. If there is any possibility that a person's username will change, a sequence number is recommended. The password should also be encrypted.

It is a poor security practice to store unencrypted passwords in a database. To check the submitted password, encrypt it with the same algorithm used to encrypt the original password stored in the database and compare the two, as demonstrated a bit later under "Generating a ticket and returning user information."

This means that if a user forgets his password, you can't send him back his original (because you store only the encrypted version); instead, send the user a new, temporary password and ask him to change it after he logs in successfully.

Table 18-2 shows the structure for the PFCS_TICKET table.

Table 18-2. PFCS_TICKET table

Attribute name	Datatype	Notes
ticketID	char(35)	Primary key created using CreateUUID( ), which produces a unique 35-character string. If using char, the string length must exactly match what the hash produces.
userName	varchar(100)	Foreign key on PFCS_USER(userName); see Table 18-1.
ticket	char(32)	A pseudo-randomly generated string that has been hashed using MD5. If using char, the string length must exactly match what the hash produces.
ip	varchar(30)	IP address of the Flash client.
issueDateTime	Date	MS SQL requires you declare the datatype as DateTime instead of Date.
staleDateTime	Date	MS SQL requires you declare the datatype as DateTime instead of Date.

It is possible to generate tickets that are guaranteed to be unique and so, in theory, a ticket could act as the primary key of the PFCS_TICKET table. However, in this example, a separate ticketID is used as a primary key. The ticketID could be generated using a sequence number, but for added security, ColdFusion's *CreateUUID( )* function is used because it generates a unique sequence of characters that is much harder to guess than a sequence number. Generating the ticket is described later. The IP address of the Flash client is stored as a further check that the same client that provided credentials initially is the one connecting to FlashCom with a ticket. Finally, the issueDateTime and staleDateTime dates define the range of time for which the ticket is valid. In most systems, the issueDateTime is not needed, because if the current time is greater than the staleDateTime, the ticket is no longer valid. If a ticket is preallocated—for example, to be used once during a meeting—the issueDateTime may be useful, so we have kept it in the implementation.

Requesting a ticket

A Flash client can request a ticket by passing the user's username and password over an SSL connection to any script capable of authenticating the user and storing and returning a ticket. With ColdFusion, a CFML page can be used. However, since a Flash Remoting gateway is required so that FlashCom can communicate with an application server, a ColdFusion component is used. Example 18-1 shows the complete listing from a simple test client. It uses the newer Flash Remoting classes for ActionScript 2.0.

Example 18-1. Flash ticket authentication code

```
import mx.remoting.Service;
import mx.remoting.PendingCall;
import mx.rpc.RelayResponder;
import mx.rpc.ResultEvent;
import mx.rpc.FaultEvent;
import mx.controls.*;

// Create a _global.pfcs.user object to hold the username and password.
_global.pfcs = {user:{userName:"", password:""}};

// Create a Remoting ServiceProxy that points to the user.cfc file.
// user.cfc has a getTicket(userName, password) method and is located in the
// pfcs/ch18/ticketAuth subdirectory of the web server's document root directory.
authService = new Service(
  "https://flash-communications.net/flashservices/gateway",
  null,
  "pfcs.ch18.ticketAuth.user",
  null,
  new RelayResponder(this, "onAuthResult", "onAuthFault") );

// onAuthResult( ) handles a result event from the getTicket( ) call.
function onAuthResult (ev) {
  var result = ev.result;
  if (result.SUCCESS != 1) {
    showConnectionError("Invalid Credentials.", ">>> Authentication Alert!!! <<<");
    return;
  }
  nc.pendingConnection = true;
  nc.connect("rtmp:/ch18Samples/ticketAuthDemo", result.TICKETID, result.TICKET);
}

// onAuthFault( ) handles fault events that occur after calling getTicket( ).
function onAuthFault (ev) {
  showConnectionError("Error connecting to authentication server or database.",
          ">>> Authentication Alert!!! <<<");
}

// Create and initialize the NetConnection object.
nc = new NetConnection( );
nc.pendingConnection = false;
nc.onStatus = function (info) {
  switch (info.code) {
    case "NetConnection.Connect.Success":
      _root.gotoAndPlay("Main");
      break;
    case "NetConnection.Connect.Rejected":
      showConnectionError("Invalid Credentials.", info.code);
      break;
```

Example 18-1. Flash ticket authentication code (continued)

```
  case "NetConnection.Connect.Closed":
    if (this.pendingConnection)
      showConnectionError("Server closed the connection.", info.code);
    break;
  case "NetConnection.Connect.Failed":
    showConnectionError("Unable to reach communication server.", info.code);
    break;
  }
};

function showConnectionError (message, title) {
  Alert.show(message, title);
  nc.pendingConnection = false;
  enableLoginForm(true);
}

// doLogin( ) is called when a user submits her username and password.
function doLogin (userName, password) {
  enableLoginForm(false);
  pfcs.user.userName = userName;
  pfcs.user.password = password;
  authService.getTicket({userName:userName, password:password});
}

// doLogout( ) is called when a user clicks the logout button.
function doLogout ( ) {
  nc.pendingConnection = false;
  nc.close( );
  _root.gotoAndPlay("Login");
}
```

The preceding script creates a service object, authService, that refers to the *users.cfc* ColdFusion component:

```
authService = new Service(
  "https://flash-communications.net/flashservices/gateway",
  null,
  "pfcs.ch18.ticketAuth.user",
  null,
  new RelayResponder(this, "onAuthResult", "onAuthFault") );
```

The CFC contains the *getTicket( )* method the client will call and is located in the *pfcs/ch18/ticketAuth* subdirectory of the web server's document root directory. The *RelayResponder* instance is used to route *onResult( )* calls to the *onAuthResult( )* function on the main timeline (this) and to route *onFault( )* calls to the *onAuthFault( )* function.

When the *doLogin( )* function is called, the authService object is used to call the *getTicket( )* method of the *user.cfc*:

```
authService.getTicket({userName:userName, password:password});
```

If all goes well, the *onAuthResult( )* method is called and passed a result event that contains a result object:

```
function onAuthResult (ev) {
  var result = ev.result;
  if (result.SUCCESS != 1) {
    showConnectionError("Invalid Credentials.", ">>> Authentication Alert!!! <<<");
    return;
  }
  nc.pendingConnection = true;
  nc.connect("rtmp:/ch18Samples/ticketAuthDemo", result.TICKETID, result.TICKET);
}
```

If the result object's SUCCESS property equals 1, login was successful and the result object will also contain TICKETID and TICKET properties. Otherwise, the username and password passed to *getTicket( )* were either invalid or some other problem occurred. If *user.cfc* is not reachable or an unhandled exception occurs, *onAuthFault( )* is called.

Generating a ticket and returning user information

Example 18-2 shows the *getTicket( )* function from the *user.cfc* file. It creates the ticket to return to the user after accepting the username and password as inputs.

Example 18-2. The getTicket( ) function from user.cfc

```
<cffunction name="getTicket" access="remote" returnType="struct" output="false">
  <cfargument name="userName" type="string" required="true">
  <cfargument name="password" type="string" required="true">
  <cfset result=StructNew( ) />
  <cfset result.success = 0 />

  <cftry>
    <cfquery datasource="pfcs" name="userQuery">
      SELECT userName, firstName, lastName, email
      FROM PFCS_USER
      WHERE userName = <cfqueryparam
                        cfsqltype="cf_sql_varchar"
                         value="#userName#">
    AND password = '#Hash(password)#'
    </cfquery>

    <cfif userQuery.RecordCount neq 1>
      <cfreturn result>
    </cfif>

    <cfset ticketID = CreateUUID( ) />
    <cfset ticket = Int(Rand()* 1000000000000) & TimeFormat(Now( ), "hms")>
    <cfset ticket = Hash(ticket)>

    <cfquery datasource="pfcs" name="insertTicket">
      INSERT into PFCS_TICKET
      (ticketID, ticket, userName, ip, issueDateTime, staleDateTime)
```

Example 18-2. The getTicket( ) function from user.cfc (continued)

```
      VALUES
      ('#ticketID#', '#ToString(ticket)#',
       '#userQuery.userName#', '#CGI.REMOTE_ADDR#',
       #CreateODBCDateTime(Now( ))#,
       #CreateODBCDateTime( DateAdd( "n", 5, Now( ) ) )#)
    </cfquery>

    <cfset result.success = 1 />
    <cfset result.userName = userQuery.userName />
    <cfset result.firstName = userQuery.firstName />
    <cfset result.lastName = userQuery.lastName />
    <cfset result.email = userQuery.email />
    <cfset result.ticket = ticket />
    <cfset result.ticketID = ticketID />

    <cfcatch type="Any">
       <cfreturn result />
    </cfcatch>
  </cftry>
  <cfreturn result />
</cffunction>
```

In the preceding CFML script, setting required to true in the <cfargument> tags
ensures that the function will not execute unless both the userName and password are
passed in. The <cfset> tags generate a result struct (or object) with an initial success
property set to 0.

> Even though struct property names, such as success, are lowercase in
> the CFML code, when the struct is passed back to Flash or FlashCom,
> all the property names are uppercase, such as SUCCESS, and must be
> referred to that way.

Then the username and password are looked up in the user table using a SELECT
statement:

```
SELECT userName, firstName, lastName, email
FROM PFCS_USER
WHERE
userName = <cfqueryparam cfsqltype="cf_sql_varchar" value="#userName#">
AND password = '#Hash(password)#'
```

The <cfqueryparam> tag is used to ensure that an attacker cannot use an SQL injection attack, in which an attempt is made to execute an SQL command in place of
passing a plain username. Regardless of what text is passed in the userName variable—including SQL fragments—it is treated only as a string to compare against
userName values in the database.

In the SELECT statement, a simple WHERE clause, as follows:

```
WHERE userName = '#userName#'
```

should never be used, because it is not secure against SQL injection attacks. If you do not hash passwords (i.e., you store them in your database in plain text, which is not recommended), use the `<cfqueryparam>` tag as follows to avoid SQL insertion attacks:

```
AND password = <cfqueryparam
        cfsqltype="cf_sql_varchar" value="#password#">
```

The password clause of the SELECT statement warrants explanation:

```
AND password = '#Hash(password)#'
```

The plain text password passed to the *getTicket( )* method is passed to the *Hash( )* function before being compared to passwords in the database. The *Hash( )* function performs an MD5 one-way hash of the plain password into a string of text that cannot be decoded to retrieve the original password. For example, if the text string "bigSecret" is passed into the *Hash( )* function, it returns a 128-bit value formatted as a 32-character string of hexadecimal characters, such as 975F81B906D47185D164EA64163834C3.

Some MD5 functions return lowercase letters *A* through *F*. For example, "bigSecret" may hash to 975f81b906d47185d164ea64163834c3. Use the same hash function to hash a password before saving it into a database and before looking a password up. To avoid problems, make sure every function used to hash a password produces the same letter case in the result.

The *Hash( )* function is used in this example because passwords are not stored in the database in plain text; instead, the database stores a hash of the original password. Because hashes are one-way (the original string can't be retrieved from the hashed value) and it is computationally infeasible to produce two strings that hash to the same value (making it infeasible to guess a second string whose hash matches that of the password), hashes can serve in place of the actual password without revealing it. When a user provides a password, the server hashes the submitted password and checks whether it matches the hashed one in the database. If it does, the server can assume the user provided the correct password.

Since the password submitted to the *getTicket( )* function is hashed to a 32-character string, no SQL insertion attack can be used in the `password` variable. If you do not hash passwords because you are storing them in your database in plain text (not recommended), then you must use the `<cfqueryparam>` tag to avoid insertion attacks.

If the `userName` and hashed `password` inputs do not match the username and password—which was hashed when stored—of one and only one record in the database, the result object is returned with a `success` value of 0 (indicating invalid credentials).

If the user's credentials do match, a ticket and ticketID are generated:

```
<cfset ticketID = CreateUUID( ) />
<cfset ticket = Int(Rand()* 1000000000000) & TimeFormat(Now( ), "hms")>
<cfset ticket = Hash(ticket)>
```

The *CreateUUID( )* function generates a 35-character string representation of a 128-bit number. The string is guaranteed to be unique and is based on the system time, the IEEE 802 Host ID, and a random number. It is used as the primary key in the PFCS_TICKET table. The ticket itself is created initially as a random integer between 0 and 1,000,000,000,000, concatenated with the current time, and then MD5 hashed.

Then a new record is inserted into the PFCS_TICKET table with the new ticketID and ticket values:

```
INSERT into PFCS_TICKET
(ticketID, ticket, userName, ip, issueDateTime, staleDateTime)
VALUES
('#ticketID#', '#ToString(ticket)#', '#userQuery.userName#',
 '#CGI.REMOTE_ADDR#',
 #CreateODBCDateTime(Now())#, #CreateODBCDateTime( DateAdd( "n", 5, Now( ) ) )#)
```

The CGI object and its REMOTE_ADDR property are used to retrieve the IP address of the Flash client. Checking the IP address is not foolproof—it can be spoofed. However, it is good practice to make sure that the IP address used when the ticket was generated matches the IP address of the client when it connects to FlashCom.

The *Now( )* function returns the current date/time in ColdFusion, and the *DateAdd( )* function adds time to a date/time object to produce a new date/time. In this case, the date/time produced is 5 minutes from now. If the client does not present the ticket to FlashCom in less than 5 minutes, the ticket will be considered stale and therefore invalid. A typical record in the PFCS_TICKET table is illustrated in Table 18-3.

Table 18-3. Record in the PFCS_TICKET table

Field name	Contents
ticketID	3ACFC25F-103A-8D7D-0C0E9751EC07F8E7
ticket	367F0308AFF69B898D3A034D37C75CF0
userName	blesser
ip	127.0.0.1
issueDateTime	6/18/2004 10:50:20 PM
staleDateTime	6/18/2004 10:55:20 PM

Provided all goes well—the user's credentials were found in the database and a new ticket record was stored—the result object is updated with information about the user, the ticketID, and ticket values, and the success property is set to 1.

Before going on to describe how the client uses the ticket and ticketID to log into FlashCom, it is worth looking at directory server queries.

Authenticating against directory servers

In many organizations, usernames and passwords are stored in directory servers and can be checked against the directory server instead of looking them up in a database. The simplest and most secure way is often to use the user's credentials to bind (connect to) the directory server and search for his own entry in it. Example 18-3 shows a ColdFusion <cfldap> tag that could be used to replace the SELECT statement in Example 18-2.

Example 18-3. Using <cfldap> to look up a user's directory entry

```
<cfldap
  action="Query"
  name="userQuery"
  server="ldap1.flash-communications.net"
  attributes="uid, cn, mail, sn"
  start="ou=people, o=flash-communications.net, o=flash-communications"
  filter="uid=#userName#"
  username="uid=#userName#,
          ou=people, o=flash-communications.net, o=flash-communications"
  password="#password#"
/>
```

Example 18-3 performs a query named userQuery against an LDAP server named *ldap1.flash-communications.net* (that server doesn't exist so don't try the actual tag as shown). The query requests the user ID (uid), common name (cn), email address (mail), and surname (sn) attributes of the user's entry in the directory. The starting point for the search is a node in the directory tree. In this case, the search begins in the organizational unit (ou) named "people", which is a child of the "flash-communications.net" and "flash-communications" organization (o) nodes. The search filter states that the uid must match the username property. The filter does not need to include the password because the user is authenticated while binding to the directory. If the user's password is invalid, the bind attempt will be rejected and no search will take place. The username and password attributes of the <cfldap> tag are used to authenticate against and bind to the directory. However, the username cannot simply be passed to the directory. It must be specified in a way that matches a uid attribute in the directory. In this case, the uid is an attribute of an entry in the "people" ou. The username is therefore set as follows:

```
"uid=#userName#, ou=people, o=flash-communications.net, o=flash-communications"
```

Example 18-3 illustrates only one directory query. It assumes all user records are in the "people" organizational unit. Every directory server can have its own unique schema and access controls that may require a very different set of search criteria. Consult with the administrators of a directory before attempting to connect to one.

Although we've changed authentication schemes from a database to a directory server, the results of our ColdFusion CFC *getTicket( )* method don't change as far as the Flash client can tell. So even if using a directory server for authentication, the *getTicket( )* method still returns a result object with `ticketID` and `ticket` properties to the Flash client, in this case to the *onAuthResult( )* method.

Connecting to FlashCom with a ticket

Once the client's *onAuthResult( )* method receives a ticket, it can attempt to connect to FlashCom as follows (note that it passes the ticket ID and ticket instead of a username and password as credentials):

```
nc.connect("rtmp:/ch18Samples/ticketAuthDemo", result.TICKETID, result.TICKET);
```

In the example, the `TICKETID` and `TICKET` properties are passed as separate parameters in the *connect( )* call. They could also be passed as properties of a credentials object. However they are passed to the application, the important point is that no user information such as the username or password is passed. An attacker that has successfully sniffed the network traffic between the Flash client and FlashCom will see only two long hashed strings similar to those shown in Table 18-3. There is a low risk that an attacker can intercept the ticket and impersonate the user (if the ticket hasn't been presented yet) as discussed later under "One-time ticket systems summary."

Barring such diversions, let's see how the ticket is authenticated by a FlashCom application.

Checking the ticket and returning user information

When a FlashCom application receives the connection request, it has to check the ticketID and ticket values before allowing the connection:

```
this.authService.checkTicket(new AuthResponder(this, pendingID),
  {ticketID:ticketID,
   ticket:ticket,
   ip:client.ip,
   hostIdentifier:"k38djskl3o9"});
```

Shortly, we'll show how FlashCom can use Flash Remoting to call the *checkTicket( )* method of the same *user.cfc* that includes the *getTicket( )* method. However, *checkTicket( )* might easily be part of another CFC or even on another server that is not reachable from the Internet. Example 18-4 shows the *user.cfc* file's *checkTicket( )* function in its entirety, which we'll discuss after you've perused the code. We'll have a look at the Server-Side ActionScript that calls it later.

Example 18-4. The checkTicket( ) function in user.cfc

```
<cffunction name="checkTicket" access="remote" returnType="struct" output="false">
  <cfargument name="ticketID" type="string" required="true">
  <cfargument name="ticket" type="string" required="true">
```

Example 18-4. The checkTicket( ) function in user.cfc (continued)

```
<cfargument name="ip" type="string" required="true">
<cfargument name="hostIdentifier" type="string" required="true">

<cfset result=StructNew( ) />
<cfset result.success = 0 />
//Check that the user agent begins with "FlashCom"
<cfif (FindNoCase("FlashCom", CGI.HTTP_USER_AGENT) neq 1)>
  <cfreturn result />
</cfif>

//Perform a combined IP check and host password lookup
<cfset ipList=StructNew( )>
<cfset ipList["127.0.0.1"] = "k38djskl3o9">
<cfset ipList["172.28.253.102"] = "cmvhw1sOlv">
<cfset ipList["192.168.0.1"] = "Okn59sxnd">

<cfif (ipList[CGI.REMOTE_ADDR] neq hostIdentifier)>
  <cfreturn result />
</cfif>

<cftry>
  <cfset rightNow = CreateODBCDateTime( Now( ) ) >

  <cfquery datasource="pfcs" name="userTicketQuery">
    SELECT u.userName, u.firstName, u.lastName, u.email
    FROM PFCS_USER u, PFCS_TICKET t
    WHERE
      t.ticketID = <cfqueryparam cfsqltype="cf_sql_varchar" value="#ticketID#">
      AND t.ticket = <cfqueryparam cfsqltype="cf_sql_varchar" value="#ticket#">
      AND t.ip = <cfqueryparam cfsqltype="cf_sql_varchar" value="#ip#">
      AND (#rightNow# BETWEEN t.issueDateTime AND t.staleDateTime)
      AND u.userName = t.userName
  </cfquery>

  <cfif userTicketQuery.RecordCount neq 1>
    <cfreturn result />
  </cfif>

  <cfquery datasource="pfcs" name="deleteTicket">
    DELETE FROM PFCS_TICKET
    WHERE
      ticketID = <cfqueryparam cfsqltype="cf_sql_varchar" value="#ticketID#">
      AND ticket = <cfqueryparam cfsqltype="cf_sql_varchar" value="#ticket#">
  </cfquery>

  <cfset result.success = 1 />
  <cfset result.userName = userTicketQuery.userName />
  <cfset result.firstName = userTicketQuery.firstName />
  <cfset result.lastName = userTicketQuery.lastName />
  <cfset result.email = userTicketQuery.email />

  <cfcatch type="Any">
```

Example 18-4. The checkTicket( ) function in user.cfc (continued)

```
      //Uncomment the next line for debugging purposes
      //cfset result.error = cfcatch.detail /
      <cfreturn result />
    </cfcatch>
  </cftry>
  <cfreturn result />
</cffunction>
```

Before checking the database to see if the ticket is valid, the *checkTicket( )* function performs some simple checks to reduce the possibility that something other than an authorized FlashCom Server is attempting to call it. First, it checks the user agent string sent by FlashCom using the CGI.HTTP_USER_AGENT property. FlashCom always provides a string similar to "FlashCom/1.5.2", so we simply check that the string begins with "FlashCom". The CGI.HTTP_USER_AGENT property can be spoofed, but it is an easy and good thing to check.

Then the script does a combined IP check and host password lookup. It retrieves the IP address via the CGI.REMOTE_ADDR property and compares the hostIdentifier argument against the host identifier in the ipList. The hostIdentifier is not the domain name of each FlashCom Server. It is a password-like string such as "k38djskl3o9". If the IP address is not in the ipList or the hostIdentifier does not match the text in the ipList for the IP address specified by CGI.REMOTE_ADDR, the function simply returns. Hardcoding a password—which is effectively what the hostIdentifier is—is not a best practice and an attacker can also spoof an IP address. However, all three measures raise the bar on what an attacker must do to call the *checkTicket( )* function successfully.

To provide better security, the *checkTicket( )* function can be moved to a script hosted on a secured Flash Remoting server behind a firewall that can be reached only by permitted hosts. Even then, these simple checks are valuable in case an allowed host is briefly compromised.

Assuming the caller has passed our security checks, the function gets the current time and looks up the ticket in the database using a SELECT statement:

```
SELECT u.userName, u.firstName, u.lastName, u.email
FROM PFCS_USER u, PFCS_TICKET t
WHERE
t.ticketID = <cfqueryparam cfsqltype="cf_sql_varchar" value="#ticketID#">
AND t.ticket = <cfqueryparam cfsqltype="cf_sql_varchar" value="#ticket#">
AND t.ip = <cfqueryparam cfsqltype="cf_sql_varchar" value="#ip#">
AND (#rightNow# BETWEEN t.issueDateTime AND t.staleDateTime)
AND u.userName = t.userName
```

The query is run against two tables so that some personal information can be retrieved from the PFCS_USER table at the same time as the ticket is checked in the PFCS_TICKET table. For convenience, short aliases for the tables, u and t, are created and used throughout the statement to make it clear which table each attribute belongs to:

```
FROM PFCS_USER u, PFCS_TICKET t
```

The two tables are joined on their userName columns:

```
AND u.userName = t.userName
```

Since there will be only one matching user record in the PFCS_USER table and one matching ticket entry in the PFCS_TICKET table, a successful query will return only one record. If the ticket, ticketID, and IP address are not all found in a record, no records will be returned. The query also makes sure the ticket is not stale by verifying that the current time is between the time the ticket was issued and the time it is set to expire:

```
AND (#rightNow# BETWEEN t.issueDateTime AND t.staleDateTime)
```

If the query is successful, the result object is updated with user information, given a success property of 1, and returned to FlashCom. Again, the user's personal information was never sent unencrypted to the client but is now available both to the client via the earlier call to *getTicket( )* and to FlashCom via the call to *checkTicket( )*.

Authentication in FlashCom

It's time to have a look at how FlashCom calls the *checkTicket( )* method and handles the results from it. Instead of providing a simple demonstration script, I'll cover how to use an authentication object, which makes authentication easier to manage in real-world FlashCom applications. Example 18-5 shows the *main.asc* file that uses an *Auth* class (not shown but available on the book's web site) to create an object capable of authenticating clients.

Example 18-5. A main.asc script with Auth class and onAuthenticate( ) method

```
load("Auth.asc");

application.onAppStart = function () {
  // Create a global pfcs object with a clients object to
  // store client objects by userName.
  pfcs = {clients:{}};
  // Create an authentication object to authenticate clients.
  // In this case we specify ticket authentication.
  auth = new Auth("ticketAuth");
};

application.onConnect = function (client, ticketID, ticket) {
  return auth.authenticate(client, ticketID, ticket);
};

application.onAuthenticate = function (client, result) {
  // Make sure the authenticated user has not already logged in.
  if (pfcs.clients[result.USERNAME]) {
```

```
    application.rejectConnection(client, {msg:"You are already logged in."});
    return;
  }

  // Set up the client's user record.
  client.pfcs = {user:{}};
  var user = client.pfcs.user;
  user.userName = result.USERNAME;
  user.firstName = result.FIRSTNAME;
  user.lastname = result.LASTNAME;
  user.email = result.EMAIL;

  // Store the client in the pfcs.clients object by userName.
  pfcs.clients[user.userName] = client;

  // Accept the client's connection request.
  application.acceptConnection(client);
};

application.onDisconnect = function (client) {
  var userName = client.pfcs.user.userName;
  delete pfcs.clients[userName];
  trace("Deleted pfcs clients entry for " + userName);
};
```

When the preceding *main.asc* script loads, it also loads the *Auth.asc* file that contains the definition for the *Auth* class. In the *onAppStart( )* method, an *Auth* object is created, and the constructor is passed the string "ticketAuth". Behind the scenes, the *Auth* object will load configuration information to customize its *authenticate( )* method to perform ticket-based authentication. The class can also load other authentication methods, which we'll look at later.

When a client attempts to connect to the FlashCom application, the application's *onConnect( )* method is called. In this example, *onConnect( )* simply calls *Auth. authenticate( )* and passes back its return value. Therefore, if *authenticate( )* returns false, the client connection is immediately refused.

If it returns null, the client is placed in a pending state. If the *Auth* object cannot authenticate the client later, it will simply reject the client's connection. However, if the client is authenticated, the *application.onAuthenticate( )* method is called and the result object returned to it. Any application logic required to further check or initialize an accepted client is performed in the *onAuthenticate( )* method. The *onAuthenticate( )* method is not intrinsic to the application object. It is added dynamically to it in the *main.asc* file.

In Example 18-5, the global pfcs.clients object is checked to make sure the user has not already logged in. If not, the client is added to the pfcs.clients object and the user's personal information is added to the client object before her connection is accepted. When the client disconnects, she is removed from the pfcs.clients object.

Example 18-6 shows the *authenticate( )*, *onAuthResult( )*, and *onAuthStatus( )* methods of the *Auth* object used when "ticketAuth" is passed to the *Auth* constructor. This code is loaded by the *Auth.asc* file from the *ticketAuth/authMethod.asc* file.

Example 18-6. The authenticate( ), onAuthStatus( ), and onAuthResult( ) methods when "ticketAuth" has been specified

```
Auth.prototype.name = "ticketAuth";

Auth.prototype.authenticate = function (client, ticketID, ticket) {
  // The static Text.trim( ) method trims leading and trailing whitespace. It is
  // defined in the Text.as file, which is provided on the book's web site.
  ticketID = Text.trim(ticketID);
  ticket = Text.trim(ticket);
  if (!ticketID || !ticket) {
    application.rejectConnection(client,
        {msg:"Empty or missing user name or ticket."});
    return false;
  }

  var pendingID = this.freeID++;
  this.pendingClients[pendingID] = client;

  this.authService.checkTicket(new AuthResponder(this, pendingID),
    {ticketID:ticketID,
     ticket:ticket,
     ip:client.ip,
     hostIdentifier:this.hostIdentifier});
  return null;
};

Auth.prototype.onAuthStatus = function (pendingID, status) {
  var client = this.removePendingClient(pendingID);
  if (status.description) msg = status.description;
  else msg = "Error: Can't reach authentication service.\n";
  if (!client) return;
  application.rejectConnection(client, {msg: msg});
};

Auth.prototype.onAuthResult = function (pendingID, result) {
  var client = this.removePendingClient(pendingID);
  if (!client) return;
  if (result.SUCCESS != 1) {
    application.rejectConnection(client, {msg: "Invalid Credentials"});
  }
  else {
    if (application.onAuthenticate) application.onAuthenticate(client, result);
  }
};
```

Before calling *authService.checkTicket( )*, the *authenticate( )* method places the client in a pendingClients object where it can be retrieved later by its pendingID. When it calls the *checkTicket( )* function, it creates a new *AuthResponder* object and passes it a reference to itself and the pendingID. The responder's *onResult( )* method (not shown) will be called if *checkTicket( )* returns a result, and its *onStatus( )* method (also not shown) will be called if there is an unhandled error. The *onResult( )* method will use the reference to the auth object to call the *Auth.onAuthResult( )* method and the responder's *onStatus( )* method will call the *Auth.onAuthStatus( )* method. Both *Auth* methods are passed the pendingID of the client.

The *authenticate( )* method returns null unless it finds something immediately wrong with the ticketID or ticket. The value it returns is also returned by the *application.onConnect( )* method. If null is returned, the client is kept in a pending state by FlashCom while it waits for the call to return and the *Auth* object to decide whether to accept the client or not.

The server-side *onAuthResult( )* method is similar to the Flash client's *onAuthResult( )* method in Example 18-1. If the result.SUCCESS property is not 1, it rejects the client's connection attempt. If it is 1, it calls the *application.onAuthenticate( )* method and passes it a reference to the client and the result from the *checkTicket( )* call.

The *onAuthResult( )* and *onAuthStatus( )* methods have to retrieve the client object from the pendingClients object. They use the *removePendingClient( )* method, shown in Example 18-7, to do so.

Example 18-7. The Auth.removePendingClient( ) method

```
Auth.prototype.removePendingClient = function (pendingID) {
  var client = this.pendingClients[pendingID];
  delete this.pendingClients[pendingID];
  return client;
};
```

The rest of the *Auth* class and the *AuthResponder* code is not shown but is available from the book's web site. The code is organized with the *Auth.asc* file in the application's home directory. Subdirectories hold the various authentication methods. Each subdirectory, for example the *ticketAuth* subdirectory, also holds a *config.asc* file that contains information about the host and authentication service. Example 18-8 lists a *ticketAuth/config.asc* file.

Example 18-8. An authentication method config.asc file

```
// DO NOT EDIT THIS LINE.
Auth.current = Auth.instances[Auth.instances.length - 1];

// Edit the following lines so that you correctly set the remoting host
// and remoting service name you need to access for authentication.
// For example:
// Auth.current.gatewayURL = "http://myHost.myDomain.com/flashservices/gateway/";
// Auth.current.serviceName = "my.path.to.a.service";

// OK TO EDIT FROM HERE ON.
```

Example 18-8. An authentication method config.asc file (continued)

```
Auth.current.gatewayURL  = "http://localhost:8500/flashservices/gateway/";
Auth.current.serviceName = "pfcs.ch18.ticketAuth.user";
Auth.current.hostIdentifier = "k38djskl3o9";
```

One-time ticket systems summary

One-time ticket systems provide excellent protection for sensitive information such as usernames and passwords by using an HTTPS-enabled web application. If you have a ticketing system in place, you can also send other sensitive data such as financial information via HTTPS rather than through FlashCom. However, ticket systems like the one described here are not perfect. They can still be compromised by a sophisticated man-in-the-middle attack if an attacker is able not only to sniff but also intercept the ticket and then forward it to FlashCom from his own client. To put the risk in perspective, an attack of that nature is very difficult to do on today's networks.

One-Time Hash Systems

Under some circumstances, an SSL-enabled web server may not be available. In that case, a one-time hashing scheme can be used. In practice, it is somewhat less secure and more limited than using an SSL-enabled web application and ticketing system. One-time hashing relies on the client receiving a unique string of text called a *challenge*. The client combines the challenge text with the user's password, performs a one-way hash of the combined text, and returns the hash to the server. The server performs the same operation—combining the user's password and the challenge text and hashing it. If the hash sent by the client matches the server's version of the hash, the client is allowed to connect. On its own, a one-time hash system cannot protect the user's username during the connection process or things like financial information the way SSL can, but it can protect the user's password. Every time the user authenticates, a different challenge message is sent and, therefore, the resulting hash that is sent back is also different. There are different one-time hash schemes. Another name for them is *challenge-response authentication*. The Challenge Handshake Authentication Protocol (CHAP) described in RFC 1994 is a good example.

We've already used a one-way hash function named *Hash( )* in ColdFusion that implements the MD5 algorithm. Another one-way hash algorithm is named SHA1. Instead of a 128-bit value, it produces a 160-bit value and is considered stronger than MD5 (the longer the hash result, the harder to reverse it). If the text "bigSecret" is hashed with an SHA1 function, the text string 6b9b36293b36e4c410ad0b5a-51bc9eb8af1be63b is returned. It is a 40-character hexadecimal representation of the hashed value.

The challenge string is required because the client must send a different hashed string every time it tries to connect. If it sent the same string each time, someone sniffing the network would not learn the original password but would be able to log into the system using the hashed text. The fact that the challenge phrase is sent in plain text and could be intercepted poses a potential problem. The same challenge phrase should not be issued more than once to a client. If an attacker gets a challenge phrase that is associated with a particular user login, she may be able to retrieve the correct hash and send it. Random numbers are used as challenge strings, so the scheme described in this chapter is good but not perfect.

A drawback to using a one-time hashing system with FlashCom is that it requires a Flash client to request a challenge string, receive it, and then send back the hash of the challenge string and password. FlashCom does not permit a three-step conversation to occur between a client and FlashCom until after a client has been accepted. When a client connects to FlashCom, the values passed into the *connect( )* method are available to the server, but Flash cannot receive challenge text and send a response without the connection being accepted.

There are two ways around the problem. One approach is to use a web application to provide a challenge phrase and then have the client try to connect to FlashCom using that phrase. An alternative is for FlashCom to provide the challenge phrase. Once the challenge phrase is obtained from FlashCom or a web application—we don't deal directly with the web application portion here—the remainder of the problem is the same.

In the latter scenario, the client attempts to connect to FlashCom twice. The first time it passes FlashCom the user's username and is rejected. When FlashCom rejects the connection, it passes back the challenge phrase in the object specified as the second parameter to the *application.rejectConnection( )* method:

```
application.rejectConnection(client, {challenge:"challengeText"});
```

When the client's connection is rejected, it can get the challenge phrase from the application property of the info object passed back to the *onStatus( )* method of the client's *NetConnection* object:

```
nc.onStatus = function (info) {
  challengeString = info.application.challenge;
  // Perform a hash of the challenge text and attempt a reconnection.
}
```

Then it can attempt to connect to FlashCom again with a hash of the challenge text (challengeString in this example) and the user's password.

To demonstrate a working one-time hash system, we'll use the "connect to Flash-Com twice" approach and the SHA1 algorithm. However, because passwords are MD5-hashed before being stored in the sample application's database, we'll also be using MD5. However, there is a small problem: neither Flash nor FlashCom provide built-in MD5 or SHA1 hash functions. Fortunately, Paul Johnston has made available JavaScript implementations of both MD5 and SHA1 under BSD licensing. For the sample introduced here, I've ported his scripts to ActionScript 2.0 for use in Flash and ActionScript 1.0 for use with FlashCom. The source is not shown here but is available from the book's web site.

Connecting twice with Flash

To simplify the process of attempting to connect to FlashCom to get the challenge text and then connecting on the second try, two *NetConnection* objects can be used. One is responsible for the first connection attempt that will be rejected (but will obtain the challenge text) and the other for the second attempt that may be accepted. Example 18-9 includes code that creates both challenge_nc and main_nc *NetConnection* objects.

Example 18-9. Using two NetConnection objects to log into FlashCom

```
import mx.controls.*;
import SHA1;
import MD5;

// Create a _global.pfcs.user object to hold the username and password.
_global.pfcs = {user:{userName:"", password:"", cpHash:""}};

sha1 = new SHA1( );
md5 = new MD5( );

// Create the NetConnection object we will use to connect to FlashCom
// the second time.
main_nc = new NetConnection( );
main_nc.pendingConnection = false;
main_nc.onStatus = function (info) {
  switch (info.code) {
    case "NetConnection.Connect.Success":
      _root.gotoAndPlay("Main");
      break;
    case "NetConnection.Connect.Rejected":
      this.pendingConnection = false;
      showConnectionError(info.application.msg, info.code);
      break;
    case "NetConnection.Connect.Closed":
      if (this.pendingConnection) {
        showConnectionError(info.application.msg, info.code);
      }
      break;
    case "NetConnection.Connect.Failed":
      showConnectionError("Can't connect to the server.", info.code);
      break;
  }
};
```

Example 18-9. Using two NetConnection objects to log into FlashCom (continued)

```
// Create the NetConnection object we will use to connect the first time
// in order to get the challenge text. If the connection is rejected and
// the challenge text is returned, the main_nc object will be used
// to attempt the second connection.
challenge_nc = new NetConnection( );
challenge_nc.pendingConnection = false;
challenge_nc.onStatus = function (info) {
  switch (info.code) {
    case "NetConnection.Connect.Success":
      showConnectionError("Application Error.", info.code);
      break;
    case "NetConnection.Connect.Rejected":
      this.pendingConnection = false;
      var challenge = info.application.CHALLENGE;
      if (challenge) {
        var id = info.application.ID;
        var hashedPassword = md5.hex_md5(pfcs.user.password).toUpperCase( );
        var finalHash = sha1.hex_sha1(hashedPassword + challenge);
        main_nc.connect("rtmp:/ch18Samples/chapAuthDemo", id, finalHash);
      }
      else {
        showConnectionError(info.application.msg, info.code);
      }
      break;
    case "NetConnection.Connect.Closed":
      if (this.pendingConnection) {
        showConnectionError(info.application.msg, info.code);
      }
      break;
    case "NetConnection.Connect.Failed":
      showConnectionError("Can't connect to the server.", info.code);
      break;
  }
};

// showConnectionError( ) displays an alert and reenables the login form.
function showConnectionError (message, title) {
  Alert.show(message, title);
  challenge_nc.pendingConnection = false;
  enableLoginForm(true);
}

// doLogin( ) is called when a user submits his username and password.
function doLogin (userName, password) {
  enableLoginForm(false);
  pfcs.user.userName = userName;
  pfcs.user.password = password;
  challenge_nc.pendingConnection = true;
  challenge_nc.connect("rtmp:/ch18Samples/chapAuthDemo", userName);
}

// doLogout( ) is called when a user clicks the logout button.
```

Example 18-9. Using two NetConnection objects to log into FlashCom (continued)

```
function doLogout ( ) {
  main_nc.pendingConnection = false;
  main_nc.close( );
  _root.gotoAndPlay("Login");
}
```

When the user attempts to log in, the challenge_nc *NetConnection* object is used to pass the user's username to FlashCom:

```
challenge_nc.connect("rtmp:/ch18Samples/chapAuthDemo", userName);
```

The FlashCom Server will check whether the username is valid. If it is, FlashCom will reject the connection but will also return an application object containing a challenge ID and challenge text. The challenge ID is not strictly necessary, but is used in this example to look up the challenge text. The application object is checked within the challenge_nc object's *onStatus( )* method, an excerpt of which is shown here:

```
case "NetConnection.Connect.Rejected":
  this.pendingConnection = false;
  var challenge = info.application.CHALLENGE;
  if (challenge) {
    var id = info.application.ID;
    var hashedPassword = md5.hex_md5(pfcs.user.password).toUpperCase( );
    var finalHash = sha1.hex_sha1(hashedPassword + challenge);
    main_nc.connect("rtmp:/ch18Samples/chapAuthDemo", id, finalHash);
  }
  else {
    showConnectionError(info.application.msg, info.code);
  }
  break;
```

If there is no info.application.CHALLENGE property, then the username was not found and a login error is reported to the user. However, if a CHALLENGE property is returned, the following steps are taken:

1. The plain text password is hashed using an MD5 hash so that it matches the hashed password in the authentication database. Omit this step if you are storing passwords in your authentication database in plain text (not recommended).

2. The hashed password and challenge text are concatenated together into a single string of text.

3. The concatenated password and challenge text are hashed using the SHA1 algorithm.

4. The main_nc *NetConnection* object is passed the challenge ID and the final hash from Step 3 and used to attempt to connect to FlashCom a second time.

Here are the three lines of code that perform the four aforementioned steps:

```
var hashedPassword = md5.hex_md5(pfcs.user.password).toUpperCase( );
var finalHash = sha1.hex_sha1(hashedPassword + challenge);
main_nc.connect("rtmp:/ch18Samples/chapAuthDemo", id, finalHash);
```

After these lines execute, the *main_nc.onStatus( )* method will be called and we will know whether we are allowed to connect.

If you are storing passwords in your authentication database in plain text (not recommended), omit Step 1 and change the code to:

```
var finalHash = sha1.hex_sha1(pfcs.user.password + challenge);
main_nc.connect("rtmp:/ch18Samples/chapAuthDemo", id, finalHash);
```

Managing connection attempts in FlashCom

The *main.asc* file for our two-connection-attempts example is not shown but is almost identical to the *main.asc* file shown in Example 18-5. The only difference is that a different authentication method is used by the *Auth* object:

```
auth = new Auth("chapAuth");
```

The *chapAuth* subdirectory contains a *config.asc* and an *authMethod.asc* file. Example 18-10 lists most of the *authMethod.asc* file. The entire file can be downloaded from the book's web site.

Example 18-10. An excerpt of the chapAuth/authMethod.asc file

```
Auth.prototype.name = "chapAuth";
load("SHA1.asc");

Auth.prototype.authenticate = function (client, id, hash) {
  id = Text.trim(id);
  hash = Text.trim(hash);

  if (!id && !hash) {
    application.rejectConnection(client,
        {msg:"Empty or missing user name or hash."});
    return false;
  }

  var pendingID = this.freeID++;
  this.pendingClients[pendingID] = client;

  if (id && !hash) {
    // Assume client has passed a username and requires a challenge phrase
    // in return.
    this.authService.setChallenge(new AuthResponder(this, pendingID),
        {userName:id,ip:client.ip,hostIdentifier:this.hostIdentifier})
  }
  else {
    // Assume the client is presenting a challengeID and hash
    // and remember the hash the client provided.
    client.__hash = hash;
    this.authService.getChallenge(new AuthResponder(this, pendingID),
        {id:id,ip:client.ip,hostIdentifier:this.hostIdentifier})
  }
  return null;
```

Example 18-10. An excerpt of the chapAuth/authMethod.asc file (continued)

```
};

Auth.prototype.onAuthResult = function (pendingID, result) {
  var client = this.removePendingClient(pendingID);
  if (!client) return;
  if (result.SUCCESS != 1) {
    application.rejectConnection(client, {msg: "Invalid Credentials"});
    return;
  }
  if (result.CHALLENGE) {
    application.rejectConnection(client, result);
    return;
  }
  if (result.USERNAME) {
    var hash = client._hash;
    delete client.hash;

    if (hash == SHA1.hex_sha1(result.PASSWORD + result.TICKET)) {
      if (application.onAuthenticate)
        application.onAuthenticate(client, result);
      return;
    }
  }
  application.rejectConnection(client, {msg: "Invalid Credentials"});
};
```

The *authenticate( )* method in the preceding code is called from within the *application.onConnect( )* method whenever a client tries to connect. If both parameters are missing, the connection is simply rejected after placing an error message in the application object, as shown in this excerpt:

```
if (!id && !hash) {
  application.rejectConnection(client,
    {msg:"Empty or missing user name or hash."});
  return false;
```

However, if only the id parameter has been passed in, then we assume the client has passed in a username and is requesting a challenge. In that case, the *setChallenge( )* method of *user.cfc* is called. If the username passed to it is valid, it creates a new ID and challenge, stores them (along with the username and IP address) in a database, and returns the id and challenge properties in a result object. If the username is not valid, nothing is stored and a SUCCESS property of 0 is returned. For convenience, the PFCS_TICKET table shown in Table 18-2 is used to store the challenge text and ID. The challenge is stored in the ticket column and challenge ID in the ticketID column.

If both an id and hash are passed into the *authenticate( )* method, the hash is stored as a property of the client object so it can be retrieved later. The *user.cfc*'s *getChallenge( )* method is called with the id. The *getChallenge( )* method will also return a result object. If the challenge text was found, the result.SUCCESS property will be 1.

Before *setChallenge( )* and *getChallenge( )* are called, the client is placed in a pending state. When *setChallenge( )* or *getChallenge( )* returns, the *onAuthResult( )* method will be called. It retrieves the pending client and looks at the result object to determine which method is returning. If the SUCCESS property is not 1, it simply rejects the client connection attempt and returns an error message. However, if a CHALLENGE property is returned, it rejects the connection and returns the result object that includes the challenge ID and challenge text to the client. Finally, if the result. USERNAME property is present, then a result record has been returned that contains the challenge ID, challenge text, personal user information, and, most importantly, the user's password:

```
var hash = client.__hash;
delete client.hash;

if (hash == SHA1.hex_sha1(result.PASSWORD + result.TICKET)) {
  if (application.onAuthenticate)
    application.onAuthenticate(client, result);
  return;
}
```

All that is necessary when the challenge text is returned by the *getChallenge( )* function is to combine it with the password retrieved from the database, hash it with SHA1, and compare it to the hash submitted by the client. If the two hashes match, the client has authenticated.

The *setChallenge( )* and *getChallenge( )* functions are not reproduced here but can be found on the book's web site.

Single Sign-On

Unless you need to provide significantly different levels of security within a portal or Internet application, there is no reason to force users to log in more than once per session. For example, if you need to add a communication feature such as video chat to an existing web application, why make the user log in a second time to chat? If a user is already logged in to a web application, the application should be able to get her username or user ID from her session information and generate a single-use ticket that Flash can use to connect to FlashCom. The same is true of portals.

Web applications and portals

There are a number of ways to implement single sign-on systems. Many web applications and portals use different authentication schemes and make user information available in different ways. It is not possible to review them all here. Instead, here is a simple example that uses a ColdFusion page that both loads a *.swf* file and provides it with a single-use ticket, ticketID, and other information it can use to connect to FlashCom. The page is protected by an *Application.cfm* page (not shown here) that forces a user to log in before the page can be displayed. See "Role-Based Authorization" later in this chapter for more information on *Application.cfm* files.

The page shown in Example 18-11 uses the FLASHVARS parameter to create ticketID, ticket, and userName variables on the main timeline of a movie called *webPortalTicketTestClient.swf*.

Example 18-11. The main.cfm page

```
<html>
<head>
<title>webPortalTicketTestClient</title>
</head>
<body bgcolor="#ffffff">

<cfquery datasource="pfcs" name="userQuery">
  SELECT userName, firstName, lastName, email
  FROM PFCS_USER
  WHERE userName = '#GetAuthUser( )#'
</cfquery>

<cfif userQuery.RecordCount eq 1>
  <cfset ticketID = CreateUUID( ) />
  <cfset ticket = Int(Rand()* 1000000000000) & TimeFormat(Now( ), "hms")>
  <cfset ticket = Hash(ticket)>

  <cfquery datasource="pfcs" name="insertTicket">
    INSERT into PFCS_TICKET
    (ticketID, ticket, userName, ip, issueDateTime, staleDateTime)
    VALUES
    ('#ticketID#', '#ToString(ticket)#', '#userQuery.userName#',
     '#CGI.REMOTE_ADDR#', #CreateODBCDateTime(Now( ))#,
     #CreateODBCDateTime( DateAdd( "n", 5, Now( ) ) )#)
  </cfquery>
  <cfset flashVars="userName=#GetAuthUser( )#" />
  <cfset flashVars="#flashVars#&firstName=#userQuery.firstName#" />
  <cfset flashVars="#flashVars#&lastName=#userQuery.lastName#" />
  <cfset flashVars="#flashVars#&email=#userQuery.email#" />
  <cfset flashVars="#flashVars#&ticket=#ticket#" />
  <cfset flashVars="#flashVars#&ticketID=#ticketID#" />
</cfif>

<object classid="clsid:d27cdb6e-ae6d-11cf-96b8-444553540000"
        codebase="http://fpdownload.macromedia.com/pub/shockwave/cabs/flash/
swflash.cab#version=7,0,0,0"
        width="550" height="400" id="webPortalTicketTestClient"
        align="middle">
<param name="allowScriptAccess" value="sameDomain" />
<param name="movie" value="webPortalTicketTestClient.swf" />
<param name="quality" value="high" />
<cfoutput><param name="FLASHVARS" value="#flashVars#" /></cfoutput>
<cfoutput>
<embed src="webPortalTicketTestClient.swf"
```

Example 18-11. The main.cfm page (continued)

```
        quality="high"
        width="550" height="400"
        name="webPortalTicketTestClient" align="middle"
        allowScriptAccess="sameDomain"
        type="application/x-shockwave-flash"
        pluginspage="http://www.macromedia.com/go/getflashplayer"
        FLASHVARS="#flashVars#" />
</cfoutput>
</object>

</body>
</html>
```

The page uses a SELECT statement to retrieve the user's personal information such as first and last name:

```
SELECT userName, firstName, lastName, email
FROM PFCS_USER
WHERE userName = '#GetAuthUser()#'
```

The ColdFusion function *GetAuthUser( )* returns the username of the person logged in to the ColdFusion session.

The script creates a ticketID and ticket and inserts a row into the PFCS_TICKET table using identical code to Example 18-2. Then, the information is assembled into a URL-encoded query string named FLASHVARS, which is used in the <param> and <embed> tags so that the data will be loaded into the Flash movie. For example, here is the <param> tag:

```
<cfoutput><param name="FLASHVARS" value="#flashVars#" /></cfoutput>
<cfoutput>
```

Since the CFML page provides the Flash movie all the information it needs to connect and authenticate to FlashCom, the page does not have to show the user a login screen. Instead, it simply connects. Example 18-12 shows a short client-side Action-Script excerpt that uses the ticket and ticketID timeline variables created by the FLASHVARS parameter to connect to FlashCom:

Example 18-12. Connecting to FlashCom using a ticket and ticketID supplied by a FlashVars parameter

```
import mx.controls.*;

// Create and initialize the NetConnection object.
nc = new NetConnection();
nc.pendingConnection = false;
nc.onStatus = function (info) {
  switch (info.code) {
    case "NetConnection.Connect.Success":
      _root.gotoAndPlay("Main");
      break;
```

```
    case "NetConnection.Connect.Rejected":
      showConnectionError("Invalid Credentials.", info.code);
      break;
    case "NetConnection.Connect.Closed":
      if (this.pendingConnection)
        showConnectionError("Invalid Credentials.", info.code);
      break;
    case "NetConnection.Connect.Failed":
      showConnectionError("Unable to reach communication server.", info.code);
      break;
  }
};

nc.connect("rtmp:/ch18Samples/ticketAuthDemo", ticketID, ticket);

function showConnectionError (message, title) {
  Alert.show(message, title);
  nc.pendingConnection = false;
  _root.gotoAndPlay("Error");
}
```

In Example 18-12, the *.swf* connects to the same FlashCom application as Example 18-1 did. The application calls the same method via Flash Remoting to check the ticket and accept the client's connection. See Example 18-2 and Example 18-3.

Flash Remoting with FlashCom logins

Sometimes a Flash movie must log in directly to an application server using Flash Remoting and also connect to FlashCom. In that case, an approach similar to Example 18-1 through Example 18-3 can be used to generate a ticket. The services should be available only to clients that have logged into the Remoting application. Once a Flash movie has logged in, it should be able to call a service's *getTicket( )* function without having to send another username and password. The *getTicket( )* method should be able to get the client's username from the application server without the client having to send it again. If ColdFusion is being used, *GetAuthUser( )* can be used to get the user's username. An example of protecting ColdFusion components with an *Application.cfm* file and logging clients into an application is provided under "Role-Based Authorization" later in this chapter.

Checking Connection Information

When a client attempts to connect to FlashCom, information about the client is made available via properties of the client object. The most important of these are the IP address of the client, the URL from which the *.swf* was loaded, and the agent or name of the Player or software trying to connect. For example, when a Flash movie is loaded into the Flash Player in my machine from:

http://flash-communications.net/technotes/clientInformation/index.html

the following properties of the `client` object are displayed:

```
ip: 64.231.161.59
agent: WIN 7,0,14,0
referrer: http://flash-communications.net/technotes/clientInformation/
clientInformation.swf
protocol: rtmp
```

The IP address is the address my ISP provided for my machine today, the agent indicates the version of the Flash Player and platform it is running on, and the referrer shows the location from which the *.swf* was loaded into the Flash Player. If another FlashCom application connects to the application, it might receive the following information:

```
ip: 64.231.161.59
agent: FlashCom/1.5.2
referrer: rtmp://_defaultVHost_:1935/getClientInfo/_definst_
protocol: rtmp
```

In this case, the agent reflects the fact that a FlashCom Server, not the Flash Player, is connecting. The referrer is the name of the FlashCom application and instance running in the default virtual host (Vhost) on my machine. While it is possible for an attacker to spoof information sent to FlashCom, it is important to check the information anyway. There are two ways to check the information. One is to use Flash-Com's configuration files to define access rules, and the other is to write code to check the client's connection information in each application. In general, you should use the server's *.xml* files to define adaptor- and Vhost-level rules wherever you can and only do checks that are required by applications in your scripts. The blanket protection provided by configuring the server is better than relying on each script to control access.

The `<Allow>`, `<Deny>`, and `<Order>` tags in the *Adaptor.xml* file can be used to control access to an adaptor by full or partial IP address or domain name. (They have no direct relationship to the `<Allow>`, `<Deny>`, and `<Order>` tags in the *Server.xml* file discussed in Chapter 10. Those are used to limit access to the Admin Service application only.) The `<Allow>` tag (and under some circumstances the `<DNSSuffix>` tag) in a *Vhost.xml* file can perform referrer checks based on allowed domain names. Information on configuring the server using these XML tags is available in the *Managing Flash Communication Server* document available from Macromedia at:

http://www.macromedia.com/support/flashcom/documentation.html

An introduction to using the tags with some examples is also available on Macromedia's site:

http://www.macromedia.com/devnet/mx/flashcom/articles/firewalls_proxy06.html

Unfortunately, not every organization that offers a FlashCom hosting service will custom configure the *Adaptor.xml* and *Vhost.xml* files for you or allow you to configure them yourself. In that case, you must write code to check the client connection information yourself.

IP checks

IP checks are not difficult to code. IP addresses are returned as dot-delimited strings. They can be split and joined as needed, or string searches or pattern matching can be performed on them. For example, if you want to allow any client to connect from within Ryerson University's class B address, you need to make sure that every client's address begins with 141.117. You can check with a simple string search:

```
if (client.ip.indexOf("141.117.") != 0) {
  application.rejectConnection(client, {msg:"Access Denied."});
  return false;
}
```

If you have to check only one address this way, using a string search works well. However, if you need to check multiple addresses, consider using an object as an associative array:

```
validIPs = {};
validIPs["141.117.35.14"] = true;
validIPs["141.117.35.15"] = true;
validIPs["141.117.35.16"] = true;
```

To check a client when it tries to connect, look up its IP address in the object:

```
if (!validIPs[client.ip]) {
  application.rejectConnection(client, {msg:"Access Denied."});
  return false;
}
```

To check based on a partial IP address is not much more difficult:

```
validIPs = {};
validIPs["141.117.35"] = true;
validIPs["141.117.27"] = true;
validIPs["141.117.72"] = true;
```

You can extract a partial address using the *substring( )* and *indexOf( )* methods:

```
var partialIP = client.ip.substring(0,client.ip.lastIndexOf("."));

if (!validIPs[partialIP]) {
  application.rejectConnection(client, {msg:"Access Denied."});
  return false;
}
```

Or you can use the *split( )* and *join( )* methods:

```
var partialIP = client.ip.split(".");  // Split the string into an array.
partialIP.length = 3;                   // Keep the first three elements.
partialIP = partialIP.join(".");        // Reassemble the string into a partial IP.
```

If the IP addresses are of varying lengths, a little more work is required:

```
validIPs = {};
validIPs["141.117"] = true;
validIPs["209.29.148"] = true;
validIPs["192.168.0.23"] = true;
```

The full IP address, as well as partial versions of it, has to be tested. For example, you can test it by looking up the IP and, if it does not match, removing a token and trying again until there are no tokens left in the IP:

```
var ip = client.ip
var validAddress = false;
do {
  if (validIPs[ip]) {
    validAddress = true;
    break;
  }
  ip = ip.substring(0, ip.lastIndexOf("."));
} while(ip.length > 0);

if (!validAddress) {
  application.rejectConnection(client, {msg:"Access Denied."});
  return false;
}
```

One thing you cannot code in Server-Side ActionScript that the server's configuration tags can do is a reverse lookup to try to match an IP address against an allowed domain name. However, you could make a reverse lookup available via an application server and Flash Remoting.

Checking the client's IP address is especially valuable when you need to distinguish between Flash clients and other application instances connecting to the same instance. Normally, you will have a list of FlashCom Server addresses:

```
fcsIPs = {};
fcsIPs["141.117.101.222"] = true;
fcsIPs["141.117.27.180"] = true;
```

that are easy to check:

```
if (fcsIPs[client.ip]) {
  return(flashcomAuth.authenticate(client, credentials));
}
else {
  return(clientAuth.authenticate(client, credentials));
}
```

Referrer checks

Imagine the scenario in which someone decompiles one of your .swf files. In the code, he finds the RTMP address of an application on your server. Rather than paying for his own server and bandwidth, he writes his own Flash movie that connects to your application in order to create his own chat or video streaming application.

Then he distributes his movie on the Internet. As this has actually happened, you should be asking yourself what would stop someone from using your application as his own. The first and best protection is to force users to log in, whenever possible. But not all applications—such as streaming on-demand—should require logins.

Another way to stop someone from using your application is to check the referring address the Flash Player sends FlashCom when it connects. This assures that the *.swf* file was served from a known location, such as your server and not someone else's.

The best and safest place to do referrer checking is using the <Allow> tag in each *Vhost.xml* file. However, you can script referrer checks as easily as IP checks. For example, to check against a list of valid *.swf* locations, build a list of URLs:

```
referrerList = {};
referrerList["http://flash-communications.net/technotes/test.swf"] = true;
referrerList["http://echo.ryerson.ca/textPublisher/main.swf"] = true;
referrerList["http://echo.ryerson.ca/onDemand/streamPlayer.swf"] = true;
```

Then check each client's referrer property:

```
if (!referrerList[client.referrer]) {
  application.rejectConnection(client, {msg:"Access Denied."});
  return false;
}
```

If the referrerList contains URLs for the hosts, you can use *split( )* and *join( )* again:

```
referrerList = {};
referrerList["http://flash-communications.net"] = true;
referrerList["http://www.ryerson.ca"] = true;
referrerList["http://echo.ryerson.ca"] = true;
```

For example, in an *onConnect( )* method:

```
var partialReferrer = client.referrer.split("/");
partialReferrer.length = 3;
partialReferrer = partialReferrer.join("/");

if (!referrerList[partialReferrer]) {
  application.rejectConnection(client, {msg:"Access Denied."});
  return false;
}
```

If necessary, you can also extract the hostname from the referrer property:

```
var hostName = client.referrer.split("/")[2];
```

While it is possible to write a program that will send false referrer information to a server, it is extremely difficult or impossible to distribute a Flash movie that will trick a Flash Player into sending false referrer information. (It is possible, of course, to create a custom Player, as the *.swf* format is publicly available, but the attacker would need to get his Player distributed to potential users.) So, while you should never assume you are receiving correct referrer information, you should implement referrer checking to reduce the chances that someone is going to hijack your server and bandwidth. The "Role-Based Authorization" section later in this chapter includes other things you can do to prevent your server and bandwidth from being hijacked by someone else's applications.

Another problem that has been reported is a site including a *.swf* or framing a page containing a *.swf* that belongs to another site without permission. For example, a "parasite" might claim to offer free chat without investing in a FlashCom Server. Such a site would simply include a *.swf* belonging to someone else in a web page using a full URL:

```
<param name="movie" value="http://host.anotherDomain.com/freeChat.swf" />
```

A referrer check within FlashCom will not catch the problem because the *.swf* file is being served from the correct server. One strategy for discouraging parasites is to have the web server do a referrer check on the page loading the *.swf* file. If it is not an HTML page from the correct domain, the request is refused. See, for example, Fernando Flórez's post that describes using an Apache *.htaccess* file to protect a *.swf* with a URL rewrite rule:

   http://blog.function.com/en/archives/000209.php

If your HTML page containing the *.swf* is framed, a web server referrer check on the *.swf* will not help. JavaScript can be used to detect framing and to escape from it in some cases. However, there is no foolproof way to stop someone from including content from another site. Non-technical means such as complaining to a hosting service or litigation may be necessary. However, when appropriate, the entire problem can be avoided by requiring each user to authenticate before accessing content.

For other suggestions on avoiding misappropriation of *.swf* content, see the chapter on security in *Flash Hacks* (O'Reilly).

Agent checks

Another, more common way to distinguish between an application instance and client connecting to an application is to check the client.agent property. For example:

```
if (client.agent.indexOf("FlashCom") == 0) {
  return(flashcomAuth.authenticate(client, credentials));
}
else {
  return(clientAuth.authenticate(client, credentials));
}
```

Each authentication object should also check the IP address and other information to make sure another application instance, rather than an attacker sending false user agent information, is really connecting.

Some Warnings and Caveats

Even though the front matter of this book provides the usual warnings that exclude the publisher and author from liability, I want to provide an extra note of caution here.

 The code in this chapter has been tested, and much of it has been used in production environments. However, you should be very cautious before deploying the code shown here in a live environment.

The code, some of which is intended for demonstration, may have undiscovered bugs (check the book's errata page for the latest corrections). Or you may introduce bugs or other security holes in adapting it to your environment. It is also possible that your web server, application server, or FlashCom Server itself has hidden security flaws. Before going into production, you must test and retest your system for security problems.

Flash Remoting

As of FlashCom 1.5.2, the only way for FlashCom to communicate directly with an application server is via a Flash Remoting gateway. However, Macromedia's gateway cannot control what web services a client can connect to using the gateway. It is true that you can protect ColdFusion CFC files using an *Application.cfm* file, but the gateway itself does not provide any security controls. Fortunately, Alon Salant of Carbon Five created a servlet filter called FlashGatekeeper. Information on Flash-Gatekeeper is available from:

> *http://carbonfive.sourceforge.net/flashgatekeeper*

Anonymous connections

From a security perspective, allowing anonymous connections is dangerous. You have no idea who is connecting, and the people who connect without logging in know this. Worse, some users assume because they have not logged in to an application that they can do anything they want without fear of being identified or held responsible. And, unfortunately, they are often right. Some anonymous users are also capable of so poisoning conversations in lobbies and chat sessions that most users will simply leave and never return. In fact, applications in which users are allowed to interact or send information to the server should not allow anonymous connections. In other words, anonymous users should be quarantined.

Authorization

Authentication tells you who is connecting, not whether you should accept their connection. Even if you allow someone to connect, you may not want to grant access to all the functions and resources available in an application. Authorization—controlling who can do what—is every bit as important as authentication in creating secure applications. We need to look at two parts of authorization in relation to FlashCom applications. The first is deciding whether a user or process will be allowed to establish a connection to an application instance. The second is controlling access to functions and resources in the instance.

Deciding if someone is allowed to connect and what he can do when you accept his connection is usually determined using one of two schemes. The first and simplest is to use application-wide, role-based authorization. Every user is assigned one or more roles within the application such as administrator, moderator, presenter, or participant. If a user doesn't have at least one role, she can't connect to an application instance. The roles assigned to each user also determine what the user can do within the application. The second and more complex way to control access is to use an *access control table*. Each record in the table associates a user or group of users with a resource or group of resources and defines the type of access they have to the resource. Access control records—or something like them—are required in larger, more complex applications such as a conferencing system in which access to different conference rooms must be controlled on a room-by-room basis.

Role-Based Authorization

It is possible for a user to have more than one role within an application. To accommodate multiple roles for each user, a user roles tables is often created within a database. For demonstration purposes, Table 18-4 and Table 18-5 show the structure of two database tables that define each role and the roles each user has.

Table 18-4. PFCS_ROLE table

Attribute name	Datatype	Notes
roleName	varchar(100)	Primary key

Table 18-5. PFCS_USERROLES table

Attribute name	Datatype	Notes
roleName	varchar(100)	Together these two attributes are the primary key of this table. The roleName attribute refers to the PFCS_ROLE table's roleName.
userName	varchar(100)	The userName attribute refers to the PFCS_USER.userName attribute.

The PFCS_ROLE table defines the allowed role names for the application that will appear in the roleName column of the PFCS_USERROLES table. The role names will depend on the roles that need to be defined for an application. The PFCS_USERROLES table defines the roles that each user plays within the application. The database does not define what the roles mean. The application code uses each user's role names to determine what resources and features to provide to them.

For example, suppose that the application is a simple conference application run by a university. Authentication might be done against the university's directory server but only people registered, presenting, or organizing the conference will have access to the application. In that case, we might define four roles and assign them to users in the database as illustrated in Table 18-6 and Table 18-7.

Table 18-6. Sample role names for a conference application

roleName
administrator
presenter
participant
cameraOperator

Notice that in Table 18-7 a single user can appear in more than one record if he has more than one role. User "blesser" is both an administrator and a presenter. User "joey" is both a cameraOperator and a presenter.

Table 18-7. Sample rows in the PFCS_USERROLES table

userName	roleName
blesser	administrator
blesser	presenter
justin	participant
joey	cameraOperator
joey	presenter
rreinhardt	presenter
peldi	participant

When a user connects to an application instance employing role-based authorization, we need to know her role(s) in order to decide if the connection should be allowed. Then we need to grant access only to the resources each user needs according to her role(s). For example, we want participants to be able to view session streams only, whereas camera operators need to be able to connect and send session streams as well as view them. Presenters may need to read and write to a personal area in a *presentations* directory. For example, */presentations/peldi* would be user "peldi's" private area for storing and playing back streams.

So the first thing we have to do is get each user's role names from the database when he authenticates and then have a look at them. If the same database contains all the user and user role information, a simple SELECT statement can retrieve a query that can be used to build a result record to return to the application. If a separate directory system is in place, a two-step process is used. The user is authenticated against the directory service and then a SELECT is run on the database to retrieve the user's roles. In either case, the result is returned to the application server and FlashCom. There are many ways to get user and role information and return it. The sample database and code shown here is just one option.

If a Flash client is using a number of services via a Remoting gateway, the services may also have to provide different functions and information depending on the user's roles. In other words, both the application server and FlashCom will need to authenticate and get the roles for each client. Using ColdFusion, the easiest way to protect both sets of services (components) is to place an *Application.cfm* file in the same directory or in one above them in the directory tree.

Example 18-13 lists a complete *Application.cfm* file designed to force clients to authenticate before calling services and to establish the client's username and role. The script also allows FlashCom application instances to log in. When an application instance connects, it passes its application.name as a username and its hostIdentifier as a password. Flash clients pass the user's username and a plain text password.

Example 18-13. An Application.cfm that authenticates FlashCom and Flash client requests to the services it protects

```
<cfsetting showdebugoutput="no" />
<cfapplication name="Conference" />
<cfset dbName="pfcs" />

<cfset ipList=StructNew( ) />
<cfset ipList["127.0.0.1"] = "k38djskl3o9" />
<cfset ipList["172.28.253.102"] = "cmvhw1sOlv" />
<cfset ipList["192.168.0.1"] = "Okn59sxnd" />

<cflogin>
  <cfif not isDefined("cflogin")>
    <cfabort showerror="Invalid credentials." />
  </cfif>

  //Deal with Flash Communication Server instance connections
  <cfif (FindNoCase("FlashCom", CGI.HTTP_USER_AGENT) eq 1)>
    <cfif (ipList[CGI.REMOTE_ADDR] neq cflogin.password)>
      <cfabort showerror="Invalid credentials.." />
    <cfelse>
      <cfloginuser name="#cflogin.name#" password="FlashCom" roles="FlashCom"/>
    </cfif>

  //Deal with Flash client connections
  <cfelse>
  <cftry>
    <cfquery name="authenticate" datasource="#dbName#">
      SELECT u.userName, ur.roleName
      FROM PFCS_USER u, PFCS_USERROLES ur
      WHERE
      u.userName = <cfqueryparam value="#cflogin.name#">
```

```
      AND password = <cfqueryparam value="#Hash(cflogin.password)#">
      AND u.userName = ur.userName
   </cfquery>
   <cfif authenticate.recordCount eq 0>
     <cfabort showerror="Invalid credentials..." />
   </cfif>
   <cfset roles="" />
   <cfloop query="authenticate" >
     <cfset roles = ListAppend(roles, "#authenticate.roleName#") />
   </cfloop>
   <cfloginuser name="#cflogin.name#"
                password="#cflogin.password#"
                roles="#roles#" />
 <cfcatch type="Any">
   <cfthrow message = "Invalid credentials...." >
 </cfcatch>
 </cftry>
 </cfif>
</cflogin>
```

When a Flash client attempts to access a service protected by this *Application.cfm* file, it must pass the username and password using *NetConnect.setCredentials( )*. For example, using Flash Remoting for AS 2.0, a service proxy is created:

```
authService = new Service(
  "https://flash-communications.net/flashservices/gateway",
  null,
  "pfcs.ch18.conference.user",
  null,
  null);
```

When the user logs in, the NetConnection's credentials are set, and then the service's *getTicket( )* method is called:

```
authService.connection.setCredentials(pfcs.user.userName, pfcs.user.password);
var temp_pc:PendingCall = authService.getTicket({userName:pfcs.user.userName});
temp_pc.responder = new RelayResponder(this,"onAuthResult","onAuthFault");
```

The request to call a function on pfcs.ch18.conference.user is intercepted by the *Application.cfm* script, and the credentials set in the client are available as properties in the <cflogin> struct. The SELECT statement looks them up in the PFCS_USER table but also retrieves the user's roles, if any, from the PFCS_USERROLES table:

```
SELECT u.userName, ur.roleName
FROM PFCS_USER u, PFCS_USERROLES ur
WHERE
u.userName = <cfqueryparam value="#cflogin.name#">
AND password = <cfqueryparam value="#Hash(cflogin.password)#">
AND u.userName = ur.userName
```

If there are no PFCS_USERROLES rows for the user, no records are returned and the client will not be allowed to log in. ColdFusion stores user roles in a comma-delimited string (also called a *list* in ColdFusion), so a `<cfloop>` tag is used to loop through all the records returned by the query and build up the string:

```
<cfset roles="" />
<cfloop query="authenticate" >
  <cfset roles = ListAppend(roles, "#authenticate.roleName#") />
</cfloop>
```

When the roles are collected in a string, the `<cflogin>` tag is used to log the client in to the ColdFusion application and the service's function will be called:

```
<cfloginuser name="#cflogin.name#" password="#cflogin.password#" roles="#roles#" />
```

If the login does not succeed, the service's function will not be called. The *getTicket( )* function does not need to authenticate the client. It only has to create a ticket and store it in the database. When the application instance needs to check the ticket, it calls the enhanced *checkTicket( )* function shown in Example 18-14 (compare it with the original in Example 18-4). To stop Flash clients that have logged in from calling *checkTicket( )*, hostIdentifier and agent checks are still done.

Example 18-14. The checkTicket( ) function, enhanced to support roles

```
<cffunction name="checkTicket" access="remote" returnType="struct" output="false">
  <cfargument name="ticketID" type="string" required="true">
  <cfargument name="ticket" type="string" required="true">
  <cfargument name="ip" type="string" required="true">
  <cfargument name="hostIdentifier" type="string" required="true">

  <cfset result=StructNew( ) />
  <cfset result.success = 0 />

  <cfif (FindNoCase("FlashCom", CGI.HTTP_USER_AGENT) neq 1)>
    <cfset result.error="user agent error." >
    <cfreturn result />
  </cfif>

  <cfset ipList=StructNew( )>
  <cfset ipList["127.0.0.1"] = "k38djskl3o9">
  <cfset ipList["172.28.253.102"] = "cmvhw1s0lv">
  <cfset ipList["192.168.0.1"] = "0kn59sxnd">

  <cfif (ipList[CGI.REMOTE_ADDR] neq hostIdentifier)>
    <cfset result.error="host identifier error." >
    <cfreturn result />
  </cfif>

  <cftry>
   <cfset rightNow = CreateODBCDateTime( Now( ) ) >

    <cfquery datasource="#dbName#" name="userTicketQuery">
      SELECT u.userName, u.firstName, u.lastName, u.email, ur.roleName
```

```
      FROM PFCS_USER u, PFCS_TICKET t, PFCS_USERROLES ur
      WHERE t.ticketID = <cfqueryparam cfsqltype="cf_sql_varchar"
                                        value="#ticketID#">
      AND t.ticket = <cfqueryparam cfsqltype="cf_sql_varchar" value="#ticket#">
      AND t.ip = <cfqueryparam cfsqltype="cf_sql_varchar" value="#ip#">
      AND (#rightNow# BETWEEN t.issueDateTime AND t.staleDateTime)
      AND u.userName = t.userName
      AND u.userName = ur.userName
   </cfquery>

   <cfif userTicketQuery.RecordCount eq 0>
     <cfset result.error="record of zero." >
     <cfreturn result />
   </cfif>

   <cfquery datasource="#dbName#" name="deleteTicket">
     DELETE FROM PFCS_TICKET
     WHERE ticketID = <cfqueryparam cfsqltype="cf_sql_varchar"
                                    value="#ticketID#">
     AND ticket = <cfqueryparam cfsqltype="cf_sql_varchar" value="#ticket#">
   </cfquery>

   <cfset result.success = 1 />
   <cfset result.userName = userTicketQuery.userName />
   <cfset result.firstName = userTicketQuery.firstName />
   <cfset result.lastName = userTicketQuery.lastName />
   <cfset result.email = userTicketQuery.email />
   <cfset result.roles=StructNew( ) />
   <cfloop query="userTicketQuery">
     <cfset result.roles["#userTicketQuery.roleName#"] = true />
   </cfloop>

   <cfcatch type="Any">
     //Uncomment the next line for debugging purposes
     <cfset result.error = cfcatch.detail />
     <cfreturn result />
   </cfcatch>
  </cftry>
  <cfreturn result />
</cffunction>

<cffunction name="silentLogout"
            access="remote" returnType="string" output="false" >
  <cflogout />
  <cfreturn "OK" />
</cffunction>

<cffunction name="logout" access="remote" returnType="string" output="false" >
  <cflogout />
  <cfreturn "OK" />
</cffunction>
```

The code performs a join on three tables to get the user's personal information, ticket information, and role names in one SELECT statement. In ActionScript, it is more convenient to have each role as a property of an object, so the code creates a struct with a property for each role within the result struct:

```
<cfset result.roles=StructNew( ) />
<cfloop query="userTicketQuery">
  <cfset result.roles["#userTicketQuery.roleName#"] = true />
</cfloop>
```

Finally, Example 18-15 shows the *onAuthenticate( )* method that is called when a client uses a ticket to connect to an application instance. Compare it to the original in Example 18-5.

Example 18-15. The onAuthenticate( ) method, enhanced to support roles

```
application.onAuthenticate = function (client, result) {
  // Make sure the authenticated user has not already logged in.
  if (pfcs.clients[result.username]) {
    application.rejectConnection(client, {msg:"You are already logged in."});
    return;
  }

  // Exclude client's with no roles from connecting.
  var noRoles = true;
  for (var p in result.ROLES) {
    noRoles = false;
    break;
  }

  if (noRoles) {
    application.rejectConnection(client, {msg:"Access Denied."});
    return;
  }

  // Set up the client's user record.
  client.pfcs = {user:{}};
  var user = client.pfcs.user;
  user.userName = result.USERNAME;
  user.firstName = result.FIRSTNAME;
  user.lastname = result.LASTNAME;
  user.email = result.EMAIL;
  user.roles = result.ROLES;

  // Store the client in the pfcs.clients object by userName.
  pfcs.clients[user.userName] = client;

  // Control access and bandwidth based on one and only one of the
  // user's roles.
  client.readAccess = "";   // Deny all readAccess to start.
  client.writeAccess = "";  // Deny all writeAccess to start.

  if (user.roles["administrator"]) {
```

Example 18-15. The onAuthenticate( ) method, enhanced to support roles (continued)

```
    client.readAccess = "/";
     client.writeAccess = "/";
  }
  else if (user.roles["presenter"]) {
    client.readAccess = "/sessions;/presentations/" + user.userName;
    client.writeAccess = "/presentations/" + user.userName;
    client.setBandwidthLimit(250000, 100000);
  }
  else if (user.roles["cameraOperator"]) {
    client.readAccess = "/sessions";
    client.writeAccess = "/sessions";
    client.setBandwidthLimit(250000, 500000);
  }
  else if (user.roles["participant"]) {
    client.readAccess = "/sessions";
    client.setBandwidthLimit(250000, 8000);
  }

  // Accept the client's connection request.
  application.acceptConnection(client);
};
```

Much of the code should look familiar. The result object that includes the user's personal information is passed into *onAuthenticate( )*. The result object also contains a roles object that can be checked for certain roles. For example, if the user has the role "administrator", full access to read and write any resource within the instance is granted, and no bandwidth limits are adjusted:

```
    if (user.roles["administrator"]) {
      client.readAccess = "/";
      client.writeAccess = "/";
    }
```

On the other hand, if the user role is "participant", then no write access is provided at all and the client-to-server bandwidth limit is reduced to constrain how much data the client can send to the server:

```
    else if (user.roles["participant"]) {
      client.readAccess = "/sessions";
      client.setBandwidthLimit(250000, 8000);
    }
```

Functions within an application instance may have to check if a user has a certain role before performing certain tasks. In Example 18-15, the roles object is stored in the client object as the client.pfcs.user.roles object. The role can be looked up directly, or a simple global function can be used to find out if a client has a certain role:

```
    function clientInRole(client, role) {
      if (client.pfcs.user.roles[role]) {
        return true;
```

```
    }
    return false;
}
```

Component-level authorization

In component-based applications, each component is responsible for managing its own streams, shared objects, and remote methods. When a client is added to or connects to a component, the component should look at the user's roles and decide what resources to make available to the client. The best way to control access is to deny all access to each client when it attempts to connect to the application and then have each component grant access only to resources within its own namespace. For example, after turning off read and write access, the client's readAccess and writeAccess strings will be empty. If a TextChat component allows read and write access to some of its resources, it will add paths to them. A SharedText component will do the same. As each component grants access, the readAccess and writeAccess properties of the client will grow into long semicolon-delimited strings.

Table 18-8 shows the readAccess and writeAccess strings a user with an administrator role might have in an application. For readability, line breaks have been added after each semicolon. Table 18-9 shows the access strings for someone with the role of participant.

Table 18-8. Access strings for an administrator

Client property	Value
readAccess	pfcs/PeopleGrid/main;
	pfcs/SharedText/main;
	pfcs/TextChat/main/currentSession;
	pfcs/TextChat/main/sessionArchive
writeAccess	pfcs/PeopleGrid/main

Table 18-9. Access strings for a participant

Client property	Value
readAccess	pfcs/PeopleGrid/main;
	pfcs/SharedText/main;
	pfcs/TextChat/main/currentSession
writeAccess	(None)

Note that even the administrator does not have root-level access. Each part of each access string gives access either to a component's unique namespace or to an area within it. For example, both users have read access to the *pfcs.PeopleGrid.main* URI containing the people shared object. However, no one has access to the *pfcs/TextChat/main* URI. The participant has access to the *pfcs/TextChat/main/currentSession* URI, and the administrator has access to both the *pfcs/TextChat/main/currentSession* and *pfcs/TextChat/main/sessionArchive* URIs. The administrator has write access to one URI and the participant has no write access—for participants, `writeAccess` is an empty string.

In other words, everyone can read the `people` shared object so that the client-side PeopleGrid component can display its contents. However, no client can update the `people` shared object directly. The server-side PeopleGrid component is responsible for updating its shared object. Even a malicious user or attacker with a hacked (modified) Flash client cannot update the shared object directly. Similarly, every TextChat user has read access to the *pfcs/TextChat/main/currentSession* URI so that her client can receive messages from the `pfcs/TextChat/main/currentSession/messages` shared object. TextChat messages are sent to the server using *NetConnection.call( )* and are checked before being sent to all clients.

Implementing component-level authorization

To illustrate one of many ways to implement component-level authorization, I'll use the components first introduced in Chapter 13 and the simple PFCS component framework introduced in Chapter 15. The server-side object part of each component is based on the *PFCSComponent* class. Example 18-16 shows the methods related to controlling read and write access to streams and shared objects.

Example 18-16. PFCSComponent access control methods

```
PFCSComponent.prototype.addAccessPath = function (client, accessStringName, path) {
  var pathArray = this.getAccessArray(client, accessStringName);
  pathArray.push(path);
  client[accessStringName] = pathArray.join(";");
};

PFCSComponent.prototype.removeAccessPath = function (client,
                                                accessStringName, path) {
  var pathArray = this.getAccessArray(client, accessStringName);
  var len = pathArray.length;
  for (var i = 0; i < len; i++) {
    if (pathArray[i] == path) {
      pathArray.splice(i, 1);    // Remove the element
      break;
    }
  }
  client[accessStringName] = pathArray.join(";");
};

PFCSComponent.prototype.getAccessArray = function (client, accessStringName) {
  var accessString = client[accessStringName];
  if (accessString.length > 0)
    return accessString.split(";");
  else
    return [];
};
```

The access control methods do the work of adding or deleting a string from either the client.readAccess or client.writeAccess string. Now, let's have a look at how a PeopleGrid component makes use of the *addAccessPath( )* and *removeAccessPath( )* methods. Since the class is small, Example 18-17 is a complete listing.

Example 18-17. The server-side PeopleGrid class

```
function PeopleGrid (name) {
  PFCSComponent.apply(this, [name]);
  this.so = SharedObject.get(this.path + "/people");
}

PeopleGrid.prototype = new PFCSComponent( );
PeopleGrid.prototype.constructor = PeopleGrid;
PeopleGrid.prototype.className = "PeopleGrid";

PeopleGrid.prototype.addClient = function (client) {
  var user = pfcs.getUser(client);
  this.so.setProperty(user.userName, user);
  // Let all clients read the shared object.
  this.addAccessPath(client, "readAccess", this.path);
  // Only administrators can write to the shared object.
  if (pfcs.clientInRole(client, "administrator")) {
     this.addAccessPath(client, "writeAccess", this.path);
  }
};

PeopleGrid.prototype.removeClient = function (client) {
  var user = pfcs.getUser(client);
  this.so.setProperty(user.userName, null);
  // Remove all the access strings that were added for this component.
  this.removeAccessPath(client, "readAccess", this.path);
  if (pfcs.clientInRole(client, "administrator")) {
    this.removeAccessPath(client, "writeAccess", this.path);
  }
};

PeopleGrid.prototype.close = function ( ) {
  this.so.close( );
};
```

When a client is registered with a component on the server, the component's *addClient( )* method is called just as illustrated in Chapters 13 and 15. In Example 18-17, the component gets information from the PFCS framework and the user's roles and then calls its own *addAccessPath( )* method to add access strings as illustrated in Table 18-8 and Table 18-9. When the client is removed from the chat, the *removeClient( )* method is called and the component uses the *removeAccessPath( )* method to deny access to the client.

Granting temporary access

In some cases, you may want to grant only temporary access to a resource. For example, in the SharedText example in Chapter 13, a voluntary locking system was used to control which client could update the component's shared object. One way to enforce locking, rather than having it based on cooperating clients, would be to abandon having each client update the shared object directly. Every client would use *NetConnection.call( )* to request updates. If the server received an update request from a client that did not have the shared text area locked, the server would ignore the update request.

In many cases, using *NetConnection.call( )* to send data that is checked over by the server is the best and most secure approach. However, if the client is able to add, delete, and update items, then it is possible to grant temporary access to each client without imposing the potential performance penalty of handling all the data in Server-Side ActionScript.

Example 18-18 shows the server-side *SharedText.edit( )* method. It is very similar to the one described in Chapter 13 with the difference that the *addAccessPath( )* and *removeAccessPath( )* methods are used to provide one, and only one, client with write access to the shared object.

Example 18-18. The SharedText.edit( ) method with access control

```
SharedText.prototype.edit  = function (userName) {
  var client = pfcs.getClient(userName);
  var currentUser = this.so.getProperty("currentUser");
  if (userName == currentUser) {
    this.so.setProperty("currentUser", "");
    this.removeAccessPath(client, "writeAccess", this.path);
  }
  else if (currentUser != "")
    return;
  else {
    this.addAccessPath(client, "writeAccess", this.path);
    this.so.setProperty("currentUser", userName);
  }
};
```

Role-Based Remote Method Access

Any method attached to the server-side `client` object or `Client.prototype` is a potential security problem because it can be called directly by the Flash movie using *NetConnection.call( )*. For example, it might seem like a good design idea to attach, to a client, a *User* object that includes all the methods an application needs for manipulating user information:

```
client.user = new User(result);
```

However, there is always the danger that the Flash client will call a method that it shouldn't on the client object. For example, if the *User* object has a method to promote the user to another role, you wouldn't want a malicious user to promote himself to administrator using a hacked Flash client:

```
nc.call("user.promoteRole", null, "administrator");
```

Even when you do want a Flash client to be able to call a method on the server-side client object, you must make sure a malicious user cannot do more than he should be allowed to. For example, in a chat application, you don't want the user to be able to use a hacked Flash client to pretend to be someone else during a chat session.

A good way to minimize security threats with remote methods is to attach only proxy methods to each server-side client object individually when the client connects, based on the client's user roles. Each proxy method calls a component method and passes on information about the client. The component method validates the information and then acts on it.

In component-based applications, each component should be responsible for attaching to the client object a proxy object that contains methods for only that component. That way, each component has its own object on the client object, which it can manage without interfering with other components. The *addObjectPath( )* method of the server-side *PFCSComponent* class is designed to add a proxy object to the client based on the unique path of each component. For example, a SharedText component named main would use the *addObjectPath( )* method to add the pfcs. SharedText.main object path to the client object. The client.pfcs.SharedText.main object is the SharedText component's proxy object. When the client no longer needs the SharedText component, the component can use the *removeObjectPath( )* method to delete the proxy object from client. Example 18-19 shows both the *addClient( )* and *removeClient( )* methods of a SharedText component, which is based on *PFCSComponent* and therefore inherits the *addObjectPath( )* and *removeObjectPath( )* methods.

Example 18-19. The server-side addClient( ) and removeClient( ) methods of the SharedText component

```
SharedText.prototype.addClient = function (client) {
  // Add remote methods to the client.
  this.addObjectPath(client);
  // Any client can ask to edit the messages shared object.
  var thisComponent = this;
  client.pfcs[this.className][this.name].edit = function () {
    thisComponent.edit(pfcs.getUserName(client));
  };
  // Only some clients can delete the current user on the messages
  // shared object.
  if (pfcs.clientInRoles(client, "administrator", "moderator", "presenter")) {
    client.pfcs[this.className][this.name].unlock = function () {
      thisComponent.unlock(pfcs.getUserName(client));
```

Example 18-19. The server-side addClient( ) and removeClient( ) methods of the SharedText component (continued)

```
    };
  }
  // Any client can read the messages shared object.
  this.addAccessPath(client, "readAccess", this.path);
  // Write access is granted only when a client has access permission.
};

SharedText.prototype.removeClient = function (client) {
  // Remove remote methods.
  this.removeObjectPath(client);
  // Remove access.
  this.removeAccessPath(client, "readAccess", this.path);
  this.removeAccessPath(client, "writeAccess", this.path);
  // Release user's lock on the messages shared object stored in this.so.
  var currentUser = this.so.getProperty("currentUser");
  if (client.pfcs.user.userName == currentUser) {
    this.so.setProperty("currentUser", "");
  }
};
```

In the preceding *addClient( )* method, every client is provided with an *edit( )* method so that it can request access to the shared text area:

```
var thisComponent = this;
client.pfcs[this.className][this.name].edit = function () {
  thisComponent.edit(pfcs.getUserName(client));
};
```

The method itself is only a proxy for the real method of the component. All it does is call the component's *edit( )* method, pass it the username retrieved from the global pfcs object. If the user is in certain roles, the *unlock( )* method is also added to the client:

```
if (pfcs.clientInRoles(client, "administrator", "moderator", "presenter")) {
  client.pfcs[this.className][this.name].unlock = function () {
    thisComponent.unlock(pfcs.getUserName(client));
  };
}
```

The *unlock( )* method is designed to solve a problem you may have noticed with the SharedText component presented in Chapter 13. A user is supposed to click the Edit button to stop anyone else from using the shared text area while she prepares to update it. A malicious user could simply lock the component and refuse to release it for the entire session. One solution is to provide trusted users, such as administrators or moderators, the ability to unlock the shared text area, overriding other users if necessary. Example 18-20 shows the server-side *unlock( )* method.

Example 18-20. The unlock( ) method of the server-side SharedText component

```
SharedText.prototype.unlock = function (userName) {
  var currentUser = this.so.getProperty("currentUser");
  if (currentUser) {
    this.removeAccessPath(pfcs.getClient(currentUser), "writeAccess", this.path);
    this.so.setProperty("currentUser", "");
  }
};
```

On the client, only an administrator or other privileged user will see an Unlock button, which can be used to release control of the shared text area. Here is the code in the client-side SharedText component that displays the Unlock button to privileged users only:

```
if (_global.pfcs.inRoles("administrator", "moderator", "presenter")) {
  createObject("Button", "unlockButton", depth++);
  unlockButton.label = "Unlock";
  unlockButton.setSize(80, 22);
  unlockButton.addEventListener("click", this);
}
```

The important point is that even if an attacker hacks the code in a *.swf* to show the hidden button and clicks it, the *unlock( )* method on the server cannot be called by non-privileged users.

Fine-Grained Access Controls

Sometimes URI-level access controls are not fine-grained enough for an application. In a typical scenario, a number of streams will have been saved in one directory on the server, and you want to provide access to only some of them. Fortunately, the server-side *Stream* object can be used to create a stream at an accessible URI and play a stream in an inaccessible URI. The *Stream* object's *get( )* and *play( )* methods are all that are needed:

```
ns = Stream.get("public/broadcast");
ns.play("private/announcement27");
```

Now, any connected client that does not have read access to the *private* directory but does have read access to the *public* directory can play the stream this way:

```
ns = new NetStream(nc);
ns.play("public/broadcast");
```

Sometimes, we want to make the stream available to only one user and not broadcast it to everyone. In that case, we can give each client read access to his own directory based on his username or user ID and use the server-side *Stream* object to play the stream for one client only:

```
ns = Stream.get("users/blesser/announcement");
ns.play("private/announcement27");
```

Only a client with read access to the *users/blesser* directory will be able to subscribe to the stream.

A similar mechanism for providing access to individual shared objects in the same directory is not available. However, shared objects are less likely to require individual access controls. When write access to individual shared objects or shared object slots must be controlled, remote methods can be used to control updates on the server. However, individual shared object and stream-level access controls would be a welcome enhancement to a future version of FlashCom.

As a practical application of using the *Stream* object for fine-grained access control, we'll improve on the TextChat component introduced in Chapter 13. The TextChat component records every text message to a stream. All the messages of each chat session are recorded in a separate stream file.

When a user connects, the client has to show each user any messages she missed earlier in the current session. To establish a little more context, the component also shows the messages from the previous session. Since the messages are stored in streams, the client creates a *NetConnection* object and plays the last session and current session's streams to get the messages. In the previous version of TextChat, all the other streams are still there in a directory with read access. Anyone who can connect to the application can—with the right *.swf*—play any chat session stream. If it is important to protect the stream archives so that only the last and current stream can be played, we need to reorganize the directory structure of the older TextChat component so that there is a readable URI space for TextChat users and another one that is not readable. The two URIs we'll use are:

```
pfcs/TextChat/main/currentSession
pfcs/TextChat/main/sessionArchive
```

where main is the name of a TextChat instance. In the *addClient( )* method, we control access to the two namespaces this way:

```
this.archivePath = this.path + "/sessionArchive";
this.currentPath = this.path + "/currentSession";

this.addAccessPath(client, "readAccess", this.currentPath);
if (pfcs.clientInRoles(client, "administrator", "moderator", "presenter")) {
  this.addAccessPath(client, "readAccess", this.archivePath);
}
```

Now that we have protected the archive, we need to make the last and current session streams available. When a client needs to play the two streams, it calls a remote method named *getHistory( )* on the component. Example 18-21 lists the server-side *getHistory( )* method from the *TextChat.asc* file.

Example 18-21. The server-side TextChat.getHistory( ) method

```
TextChat.prototype.getHistory = function (client) {
  var proxy = client.pfcs[this.className][this.name];
```

Example 18-21. The server-side TextChat.getHistory( ) method (continued)

```
  // Stream path the user can read.
  var ns = Stream.get(this.currentPath + "/" + pfcs.getUserName(client));
  proxy.ns = ns;
  ns.onStatus = function (info) {
    if (info.code == "NetStream.Play.Stop") {
      this.send("endHistory");
      delete proxy.ns;
    }
  };

  // Play streams the user could not otherwise read.
  var lastSession = this.sessions_so.getProperty("lastSession");
  if (lastSession) {
    lastSession = this.archivePath + "/" + lastSession;
    ns.play(lastSession, 0, -1, 2);
  }
  var currentSession = this.sessions_so.getProperty("currentSession");
  if (currentSession) {
    currentSession = this.archivePath + "/" + currentSession;
    ns.play(currentSession, 0, -1, 2);
  }
};
```

The *Stream* object ns plays the recorded streams as a new live stream. Since each client needs to play the stream from the beginning, the component publishes it to a different URI for each client. The URI is the current path with the user's username tacked on the end:

```
    var ns = Stream.get(this.currentPath + "/" + pfcs.getUserName(client));
```

When the server-side *ns.onStatus( )* method receives an information object with a code value of "NetStream.Play.Stop" it sends a message to indicate that the stream is over:

```
    this.send("endHistory");
```

Example 18-22 shows the client-side code from the TextChat component that sets up a *NetStream* object, calls the server-side *getHistory( )* method, and plays the stream. That work can't begin until a connected *NetConnection* is available, so we perform the operation in the *set nc( )* method (by which time the connection is available).

Example 18-22. The client-side TextChat component setter method for nc

```
public function set nc (nc:NetConnection) {
  _nc = nc;
  var currentPath = path + "currentSession";
  // Set up the NetStream so we can play back the last session's history.
  history_ns = new NetStream(nc);
  history_ns.owner = this;
  history_ns.setBufferTime(10);
  history_ns.endHistory = function () {
```

```
    this.owner.showHistory();
  };
  history_ns.showMessage = function (msg, userName, dateTime) {
    this.owner.accumulateHistory(msg, userName, dateTime);
  };
  history_ns.play(currentPath + "/" + _global.pfcs.getUserName(), -2, -1, 3);
  // Set up the shared object that will send out all new messages.
  messages_so = SharedObjectFactory.getRemote(currentPath + "/messages", nc.uri);
  messages_so.addRemoteMethod("showMessage");
  messages_so.addEventListener("showMessage", this);
  // Wait until the messages shared object is sync'ed before
  // we ask for the history.
  messages_so.addEventListener("onFirstSync", this);
  messages_so.connect(nc);
}

function onFirstSync (ev) {
  __nc.call(path + "getHistory", null);
}
```

Using proxies to provide fine-grained access control to streams has one drawback. Recorded streams are played as though they are live. So, for example, it is not possible to seek within the stream using the client's *NetStream* object. If it is necessary to seek within a stream, the client must call server-side methods to have the server-side *Stream* play the stream from the correct point.

Access Control Tables

Even moderately complex applications often need something more than application-wide user roles to control access to instances and their resources. For example, a multiroom conferencing system needs to allow some users into some rooms and not others. In one room, a user may have the role of moderator and in another that of participant. In other words, we need to associate a user role with a resource such as a room. A common and powerful approach is to use *access control tables*. Each entry in an access control table should have three parts: the name of the resource, the access rule describing what can and cannot be done with the resource, and the ID of a user or user group that is being granted access.

As a practical example, we imagine a course seminar system. One seminar room is provided for each course section. Users in a course section could be given access to seminar rooms as shown in Table 18-10. The resourceName column represents the application instance name of each seminar room.

Table 18-10. The PFCS_ACCESSCONTROL access control table

groupName	roleName	resourceName
CPS001Section001	participant	seminar/room1

Table 18-10. The PFCS_ACCESSCONTROL access control table (continued)

groupName	roleName	resourceName
CPS001Section002	participant	seminar/room2
CPS001Professor	presenter	seminar/room1
CPS001Professor	presenter	seminar/room2
CPS001Assistant	moderator	seminar/room1
CPS001Assistant	moderator	seminar/room2

When user groups are used in an access control table, a user group table must be available to associate users with those groups. Table 18-11 shows some sample records from a user groups table.

Table 18-11. The PFCS_USERGROUPS table with sample entries

userName	groupName
blesser	CPS001Section001
peldi	CPS001Professor
peldi	CPS003Assistant
joey	CPS001Professor
justin	CPS001Section002
dave	CPS004Professor
rreinhardt	CPS001Section001

When someone logs into our web-based seminar application, a simple database search can retrieve the seminar rooms to which the user is entitled to connect:

```
SELECT ac.resourceName, ac.roleName
FROM PFCS_ACCESSCONTROL ac, PFCS_USERGROUPS ug
WHERE
ug.groupName = ac.groupName
AND ug.userName = <cfqueryparam cfsqltype="cf_sql_varchar" value="#userName#">
```

Similarly, to check whether a user is entitled to a resource when he tries to connect to a seminar room, the seminar instance can authenticate and get the user's role using a three-way join on the user, user groups, and access control tables. The resource name can be the instance name in the application.name property:

```
SELECT u.firstName, u.lastName, u.email, ac.roleName
FROM PFCS_ACCESSCONTROL ac, PFCS_USERGROUPS ug
WHERE
ug.groupName = ac.groupName
ug.userName = u.userName
AND ug.userName = <cfqueryparam value="#userName#">
AND u.password = <cfqueryparam value="#password#">
AND ac.resourceName = <cfqueryparam value="#resourceName#">
```

Given the data in Table 18-11, if user "dave" tries to connect to the CPS001Section001 instance, his connection will be refused. If user "blesser" attempts to connect to the same room instance, he will have the participant role, whereas user "peldi" will have the presenter role.

Anonymous Access Restrictions

Anonymous users present special problems. Users who are not forced to log in should never be allowed to write anything to the server or communicate directly with other users. They should be provided only controlled, read-only access to the resources you want them to have. Even then, some special precautions are necessary to avoid denial-of-service (DoS) attacks. Anonymous users are especially challenging for a number of reasons. There are always people who, if they believe they cannot be identified, will persistently harass and drive away other users, cheat at online games, try to disable your server, and post hate propaganda, spam, or pornography.

Only marginally better are users who can acquire a free account using nothing more than an email address (especially a bogus email address). They are virtually anonymous, as it is extremely difficult if not impossible, short of taking expensive legal action, to identify a user. If someone breaks your acceptable use rules, you can disable his account, but he can just sign up for another one using another free email account. You should be extremely cautious about providing write access of any kind or the ability to interact with other users to users with free self-registering accounts. Consider, as a warning, the experience of popular bloggers who allowed anonymous readers to post comments. Many have been so inundated with spam that, after trying various filtering options, they have simply given up accepting comments. Text comments are generally very small, so accepting thousands of them over a day or two may not slow down a web server.

 Accepting video and audio streams is quite different from accepting text messages. Video and audio can consume huge amounts of bandwidth and disk space, and the server has to do a lot more work to manage streams. Don't accept video and audio streams from anonymous users unless it is in a very controlled environment, such as a kiosk at a museum or trade show. Even at a trade show, you should consider requiring the user to swipe his magnetic trade show badge, if applicable, to gain access.

Accounting

Designing and implementing moderately complex software that works reliably while satisfying its design goals can be difficult. Designing and building secure software is significantly more difficult. An error or omission in the design or implementation of software may provide avenues that can be exploited by cheaters and attackers.

Unfortunately, designing, building, and testing for security will not necessarily make an application completely secure. Just as there are functional bugs in software, there are usually security flaws. Unlike most software bugs, which may be reported with great passion by your customers, cheaters and attackers are unlikely to tell you about the security flaws they discover in your software.

Accounting provides an electronic "paper trail" to detect and diagnose security flaws. An essential component of a secure application is that it automatically provides a complete accounting of every significant thing it was asked to do and every action it took in response. In particular, the application software, in conjunction with the server it is running on, should provide detailed information about:

- Attempts to compromise the security of the system—for example, attempts to log in by guessing passwords or to deny service to legitimate users by flooding the server with data or connection attempts
- Successful intrusions by attackers
- Misuse and abuse of the system by legitimate users or cheaters

A thorough accounting of what your software is really doing and how it is being used requires logging server- and application-level events, as well as regular examination and rotation of the logs that are generated.

 Recording logs doesn't help if you never check them for suspicious activity (either manually or automatically). Furthermore, logs can be modified to hide the trail of an attacker, so make sure your log files themselves are secured.

Server-Level Logging

Before we look at FlashCom's logging facilities, you should consider acquiring intrusion detection software such as Tripwire (*http://www.tripwire.com*). Tripwire and similar products monitor changes in the software installed on a server and will immediately provide an alarm when the software is changed. It doesn't matter if the change is caused by a remote attacker or by an administrator's mistake. Detecting a successful intrusion or unauthorized software change from the beginning can help administrators limit or prevent further damage and bring systems back more quickly to the state they are supposed to be in.

Once you have intrusion detection, you need to make sure you can access Flash-Com's server logs. On a Windows server, FlashCom updates the operating system's Application Log with information about startup and shutdown events and, more importantly, about bad connection attempts. You can use the Windows Event Viewer to review the Application Log by going to Start → Control Panel → Administrative Tools → Event Viewer. Select Application Log to see application events. If your system has been port scanned or attacked, you will see error messages such as this one:

```
Bad network data; terminating connection : (IP: xxx.xxx.xxx.xxx, App: FlashComAdmin
(TCAdminAdaptor)) : 02 00 02 00 00 00 02 00 00 00 00 00 00 00 00 00 00 00 00 00 00 00
00 00 00 00 00 00 00 00 00 00 00 00 00 00 00 00 00 00 00 N e s s u s - T e s t - U s e
r 00 00 00 00 00 00 00 00 00 00 00 00 00 00 00 10 X X X X X X X X X X X X X X X X X X
X X 00 00 00 00 00 00 00 00 00 00 00 14 0 0 0 0 0 0 a 0 00 00 00 00 00 00 00 00 00 00 00
00 00 00 00 00 00 00   18 81 B8 , 08 03 01 06 0A 09 01 01 00 00 00 00 00 00 00 00 00
00 s q u e l d a   1 . 0 00 00 00 00 00 00 00 00 00 00 00 00 00 00 00 00 00 00 00
```

I've shortened the listing and removed the actual IP address, but the entry was the result of a port scan by Ryerson University's security staff on a university FlashCom server. You should discuss with your system administrator how to monitor and archive FlashCom error messages. To prevent FlashCom from having to handle a very large number of invalid connection attempts, you may be forced to temporarily block access at the network level to IP addresses that persistently make a large volume of invalid connection attempts.

Other messages include failures to log in to the administrative server (I've removed the actual IP address):

```
Failed login attempt from xxx.xxx.xxx.xxx at 10/08/2004 5:20:25 PM.
```

Also, if a client attempts to connect to an application that does not exist, the log will show the message:

```
Connection rejected by server. Reason : [ Server.Reject ] :
  (_defaultRoot_, _defaultVHost_) : Application (noApp) is not defined..
```

Access logs

Once you are sure you can monitor server-level events and bad connection attempts, you have to decide if you want to turn on access logging for each virtual host. If you decide to enable access logging, follow the directions in Chapter 10 or available from Macromedia in the section on the *Vhost.xml* file in *Managing Flash Communication Server* at:

http://www.macromedia.com/support/flashcom/documentation.html

Over time, the access log file can grow in size so it should be regularly rotated (files older than a determined age must be moved to an archive). Otherwise, the filesystem will eventually fill up with log data and the server will stop working. You can ask the system administrator running the server to use a log rotation script or a utility available from Macromedia:

http://www.macromedia.com/support/flashcom/ts/documents/flashcom_logging.htm

The access log file (or simply access log) contains a series of *onLog( )* method calls and the information object that was passed into each call. To read the file, which is

---

stored as a stream named *access.flv*, it must be played by a *Stream* or *NetStream* object with a predefined *onLog( )* method. See Chapter 10 and Example 10-13 for more details.

Here is a sample entry from an access log on my local development server:

```
id: 72121824
referrer: file:///F|/Flash/OreillyBook/chapter13/PeopleGrid/peopleGrid.swf
uri: rtmp:/peopleGrid/_definst_
pid: 1784
time: Mon Apr 19 10:59:15 GMT-0400 2004
description: Connect
code: NetStream.Admin.Access
level: information
tunnel: false
```

The description field indicates whether the client connected or disconnected. The time, the name of the application instance (uri), and the address of the referring *.swf* (referrer) are also available. Unfortunately, the security value of the information is limited because the IP addresses of the client and agent are not provided. However, the log is useful for monitoring the total number of connections across a virtual host to every application instance, as well as the address of each *.swf* that connected. The id field is a unique identifier for each client. To determine how long each client was connected, match the client id for a "Disconnect" description against the record with the same id and a "Connect" description.

Bandwidth logs

Macromedia provides a sample bandwidth-logging application, named *Flogger*:

   http://www.macromedia.com/support/flashcom/ts/documents/flashcom_logging.htm

The application is installed like any other application by creating an *applications* subdirectory named *Flogger* and installing a Server-Side ActionScript file (*Flogger.asc*) in it. An updated but unsupported version of Flogger (version 1.1) was announced here:

   http://www.markme.com/mesh/archives/000774.cfm

The *Flogger* application was designed primarily as a sample application, but it is useful as a starting point for developing your own application for monitoring bandwidth consumption of virtual hosts and by applications. However, you should expect to spend some time modifying it to meet your own needs before relying on it in a production environment.

Flogger generates a new bandwidth log file every day and updates it every minute. Each log file is an *.flv* file with a filename in the following format:

```
BandwidthInfo_yyyy_mm_dd.flv.
```

For example:

```
BandwidthInfo_2003_07_26.flv.
```

A Flash client is provided that can read bandwidth log files by connecting to the *Flogger* application and playing each recorded stream. The stream contains stored remote method calls and an information object passed into each call. An *onServer-Stats( )* method information object contains the following properties:

```
bytes_in
bytes_out
total_connects
total_disconnects
connected
memory_Usage
cpu_Usage
time
```

See the Server Management API, discussed in Chapter 10, for information on how to interpret each field. The `time` property is the time the log entry was added. The stream also contains *onAppStats( )* method calls with information objects that contain the following properties:

```
bytes_in
bytes_out
accepted
rejected
connected
time
appName
vhostName
```

Collecting FlashCom Server logs

Both the access and bandwidth-logging applications come with Flash movies that can read the stream files they create. However, in many cases, a better approach is to read, analyze, and archive log files at regular intervals using a separate administrative or logging server. If any of the primary FlashCom Servers are compromised and their logs erased, the administrative server will have protected copies of the logs. An administrative server should also issue alerts when significant events occur so that a system administrator can take action as necessary.

Many medium- and large-scale organizations already have secured logging or administrative servers. A FlashCom Server installation can be added to the system to run custom-written logging applications. The custom applications connect to and read the log files of the primary FlashCom Servers at regular intervals. Figure 18-3 shows an administrative FlashCom Server protected behind a firewall.

The administrative server can connect to the primary FlashCom Servers but cannot be reached from the Internet due to the firewall.

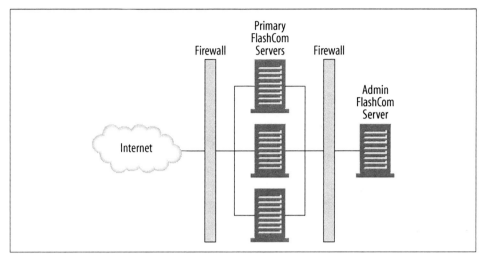

Figure 18-3. An administrative FlashCom Server for logging purposes behind a firewall

Later releases of FlashCom (after 1.5.2) may generate text or other types of log files that can be handled in more traditional ways. In that case, a separate logging server to securely store and analyze logs is still a good idea. Also, the code in *Flogger.asc* and *admin.asc* files is an excellent starting point for designing and building custom logging and monitoring applications.

Application-Level Logging

Server-level logging may not tell you when someone is using an automated program to try to guess user passwords or catch someone trying to cheat in an online game. To deal with those and other problems, you need to analyze your application to determine what events are significant enough to log and learn how to analyze logs to find problems. When an event occurs, both the event and the server's response should be captured. For example, every application should log each login attempt, how the attempt was handled, and why.

Built-in application logging is available in FlashCom and is described in Chapter 10. When it is enabled, a separate *.flv* file that contains the output of every *trace( )* statement is created for every application instance. No log rotation system is available, so one has to be developed to rotate and archive each *.flv*. The code in Chapter 12 for finding and reporting all the *.flv* files in a directory using ColdFusion is a good starting point for a log rotation and archiving function if necessary.

Another and more flexible approach is to use the PFCSLogger component described in Chapter 12. Although it requires access to an application server via Flash Remoting, it is an excellent way to create useful logs in a central location.

Finally, in some cases, there may be legal or other requirements to record everything, including all the audio/video sent to the server by every user. In that case, the recording framework introduced in Chapter 15 can be used in conjunction with a regular logging and archiving system to record and archive everything.

 One important security feature offered by FlashCom is worth noting. Audio and video streams served by FlashCom are never recorded in the user's cache. This affords an extra measure of security for copyrighted materials. Flash video played without FlashCom (either embedded or progressive video) is cached on the end user's hard drive and is therefore more susceptible to copyright infringement.

Suggestions and References

Security is a large subject that has only been touched upon here. Setting up and hardening a FlashCom Server are an important part of providing secure applications, but outside the scope of this chapter. You should make sure that whoever is hosting your applications has worked through Macromedia's security recommendations and hardened their servers. Pay special attention to whether a referrer check has been put in place; if not, you need to code one in every application.

The following list of references should be consulted as needed to help you administer or secure FlashCom and FlashCom applications:

- The CERT Coordination Center (CERT/CC) is a center of Internet security expertise, located at the Software Engineering Institute at Carnegie Mellon:

    http://www.cert.org

- The full Macromedia Flash Communication Server MX documentation is available online. Be sure to read *Managing Flash Communication Server*—especially the section on Configuring Flash Communication Server:

    http://www.macromedia.com/support/flashcom/documentation.html

- David Simmons provides a FlashCom security overview at:

    http://www.macromedia.com/devnet/mx/flashcom/articles/ security_overview.html

- Mike Chambers' security white paper (PDF; 496 KB) is also good background reading:

    http://www.macromedia.com/devnet/mx/flash/whitepapers/security.pdf

- TechNote 16631: HTTP Tunneling Protocols:

    http://www.macromedia.com/support/flashcom/ts/documents/ http_tunneling.htm

- Macromedia Flash Communication Server MX 1.5 Release Notes:

    http://www.macromedia.com/support/flashcom/releasenotes/ mx/rn_mx_15.html

- TechNote 16448: Securing Macromedia Flash Communication Server:

  http://www.macromedia.com/support/flashcom/ts/documents/securing_flashcom.htm

- TechNote 18537: Updates to the SimpleConnect component:

  http://www.macromedia.com/support/flashcom/ts/documents/simpleconnect_update.htm

- Stunnel, a universal SSL wrapper that allows you to encrypt arbitrary TCP connections inside SSL:

  http://www.stunnel.org

- The OpenSSL project:

  http://www.openssl.org

- The SSL 3.0 specification:

  http://wp.netscape.com/eng/ssl3

- Branden Hall's Flash security article:

  http://www.macromedia.com/desdev/mx/flash/extreme/extreme003.html

- Paul Johnston's JavaScript SHA1 and MD5 code:

  http://pajhome.org.uk/crypt/md5/index.html

- The BSD license:

  http://www.opensource.org/licenses/bsd-license.php

- Macromedia's security zone:

  http://www.macromedia.com/v1/developer/securityzone

- Macromedia's Des/Dev security page:

  http://www.macromedia.com/desdev/security

- Tunneling Macromedia Flash Communications through firewalls and proxy servers:

  http://www.macromedia.com/devnet/mx/flashcom/articles/firewalls_proxy.html

- PPP Challenge Handshake Authentication Protocol (CHAP), RFC 1994:

  http://www.ietf.org/rfc/rfc1994.txt?number=1994

- FlashCom logging:

  http://www.macromedia.com/support/flashcom/ts/documents/flashcom_logging.htm

- Flogger 1.1 is available at:

  http://www.markme.com/mesh/archives/000774.cfm

Conclusion

That brings us to not only the end of the chapter but also the end of the book.

We hope that this book has provided you with the information and ideas you were looking for. Programming FlashCom is a big subject, so I also hope this book continues to be valuable to you as you work with and explore all the things you can do with Flash and FlashCom.

Good luck, and drop by *http://www.flash-communications.net* to let us know what you've come up with.

About the Authors

Brian Lesser

Brian Lesser is the lead author of *Programming Flash Communication Server*. He works in Ryerson University's Computing and Communications Services, where he has the ungainly title of Assistant Director, Teaching and Technology Support. Brian's background is in imaging and information systems. Before Ryerson, he worked in the National Archives of Canada Photograph Conservation Lab and the Xerox Research Centre of Canada Thin Film Science Lab. He has been captivated with Flash and FlashCom, and their potential in education, since FlashCom was first released. Many of his early experiments and tutorials are still available on Ryerson's FlashCom development server: *http://echo.ryerson.ca*. When he can find time, Brian enjoys teaching a multimedia programming course or two in Ryerson's School of Image Arts.

Giacomo "Peldi" Guilizzoni

Giacomo Guilizzoni (aka, Peldi-dot-com) is a software engineer working on Macro-media Breeze Live, possibly the most complex Rich Internet Application powered by the Flash Communication Server ever built. He has been involved in the FlashCom community since the very beginning and to this day maintains the only FlashCom-centered blog on the Web, at *http://www.peldi.com/blog*. Peldi wrote Chapters 9 and 14 of *Programming Flash Communication Server* and coauthored Chapter 15 with Brian Lesser.

Joey Lott

Joey Lott has worked extensively with Flash and Flash-related technologies such as Flash Communication Server. He's authored several books (including the *Action-Script Cookbook*) and movie-based training titles. You can read more about Joey's

Flash and Internet-related work at *http://www.person13.com*. Joey wrote Chapters 6 and 12 of *Programming Flash Communication Server*.

Robert Reinhardt

Robert Reinhardt, partner at [theMAKERS] (*http://www.theMakers.com*), is internationally regarded as an expert on multimedia application development, particularly in Macromedia Flash. Robert is the lead author of several books, notably the *Flash Bible* and the *Flash ActionScript Bible* series (Wiley). His books have sold more than 200,000 copies and have been translated into 13 languages. Robert develops multimedia training for educational facilities and businesses in Canada and the United States. He also maintains FlashSupport.com, a resource for Flash designers and developers. Robert wrote Chapters 2 and 7 of *Programming Flash Communication Server*.

Justin Watkins

Justin Watkins is the senior multimedia programmer for Career Education Corporation's Online Education Group. Justin leads a team of Flash programmers and developers to produce synchronous and asynchronous applications that thousands of online students use daily. Justin is one of the lead developers on the open source PHP alternative for Flash Remoting, AMFPHP (*http://www.amfphp.org*). Justin also has contributed articles to devmx (*http://www.devmx.com*), a community-based web site for Macromedia developers. Justin wrote Chapters 10 and 11 of *Programming Flash Communication Server*.

Index

We'd like to hear your suggestions for improving our indexes. Send email to *index@oreilly.com*.

P

packet sniffing, 729

packet transmission, round-trip times for, 702

parameters, passing objects as, 377

passwords (see authentication, username/password)

pause( ) method, 173

Paused.Notify code string, 201

Pegg, Nigel, 473

Peldi (blog), 726

PendingAdminCall object, 392

Penner, Robert (web site), 715

people list components, 474–485

PeopleCursors component, 621, 622

PeopleCursors.asc file, server-side part, 666

PeopleGrid class, server side, 775

PeopleGrid component, 538–545
  addColumn( ) method, 540
  initializing, 539
  onSync( ) method, 540

PeopleGrid.zip, 474

PeopleList class, definition from PeopleList.asc file, 503

PeopleList component, 7, 35, 49
  adding user status input and display, 489–507
  fc_lurker, 50
  onSync( ) method, 505
  passing status shared object to, 504
  process overview, 49
  UI components
    ListBox, 49
    ScrollBar, 49

PeopleList.as file, clone( ) method, 506

PeopleList.asc file, server-side PeopleList class definition from, 503

peopleList_mc, 106

PeopleList.zip, 474

performance, 181, 672
  bandwidth and, 161

performance problems, 161

persistent shared objects, 303–315
  clearing, 309
  flush( ) method, 313
  resynchronization depth, 313
  synchronizing, 305–309

PersonalCursor class, 625

PFCS_ACCESSCONTROL access control table, 782

PFCSComponent base classes, 662–668

PFCSComponent class
  access control methods, 774
  client-side, 663

pfcs.doLogin( ) method, 669

pfcs.doLogout( ) method, 669

PFCSFramework class, timeline code of test movie that uses, 668

PFCSFramework classes, 668–671

pfcs.getNC( ) method, 669

pfcs.getUser( ) method, 668

pfcs.getUserName( ) method, 668

pfcs.getUserRoles( ) method, 669

pfcs.inRole( ) method, 669

pfcs.inRoles( ) method, 669

PFCS_ROLE table structure, 765

PFCS_TICKET table, record, 739

PFCS_TICKET table structure, 733

PFCS_USER table structure, 732

PFCS_USERGROUPS table with sample entries, 783

PFCS_USERROLES table structure, 765

PFSCFramework.as file
  methods
    pfcs. inRoles( ), 669
    pfcs.doLogin( ), 669
    pfcs.doLogout( ), 669
    pfcs.getNC( ), 669
    pfcs.getUser( ), 668
    pfcs.getUserName( ), 668
    pfcs.getUserRoles( ), 669
    pfcs.inRole( ), 669

Ping, 698

ping( ) method, 138

ping( ) method (Server Management API), 397

ping_rtt property (information object), 707

pixel-based fonts designed for Flash movies web site, 271

play( ) method, 10, 150
  VideoWindow class, 533

playback events, 168

playback of streams, 198

PlayBackDirector class, 178, 200
  partial listing, 178

Play.Failed (see NetStream object, Play.Failed)

playing ActionScript data, 192–197

playing streams, 166–183

playlists
  creating, 167
  server-side, 186

Register Proxy, 375
Reinhardt, Robert, xvi
RelayResponder class, 418
reloadApp( ) method (Server Management
        API), 396
remote method invocation (RMI), 336
    when to use, 296
remote methods, 14, 336–380
    application.registerProxy( ), 375
    broadcasting calls with send( ), 326–328
    call( ) and send( ) together, 374
    call( ) method, 337
    Client.method versus
        Client.prototype.method, 342
    defining a full-blown result handler
        object, 341
    defining on NetStream object, 193
    handling a return value, 339
    invoking, 14
    limiting how much data is sent to or
        received from each client, 338
    making calls without waiting for
        connect( ), 368
    multiple clients, 14
    passing objects as parameters, 377
    passing variable numbers of
        arguments, 367
    resolving complex method names, 370
    returning results, 14
    reusing result objects, 369
    routing remote calls through a common
        function, 371
    send( ) method, 337
    server-to-server calls, debugging, 364
    using a façade method on the
        server-side, 373
remote procedure call (RPC), 336
remote shared objects (see RSOs)
remoting NetConnection, 409
removeApp( ) method (Server Management
        API), 393
replaceSharedText( ) method
        (SharedText), 525
requests, making with send( )
        method, 193–197
__resolve( ) method, 373
resource name collisions, 117
Resource.Limit.Exceeded message, 112
resources, 114–117
restartVHost( ) method (Server Management
        API), 397
result objects, 369

resyncDepth property, 314
reverse lookup, 761
RMI (remote method invocation), 336
Robbins, Brian, 714
Roberts, David J., 725
role-based remote method access, 776–779
room application, 347–363
RoomList component, 35, 54–57
    client-side component parameters, 56
    process overview, 56
    standard user experience, 55
    UI components
        ListBox, 55
        PushButton, 55
        ScrollBar, 55
R&P Manager (see Recording and Playback
        Framework)
RSOs (remote shared objects)
    connecting instance with server, 283
    getting and using, 283–287
    onSync( ) method and, 284
    persistent, 310–312
    private versus shared data, 286
    reading data from, 285
    writing properties to data
        property of, 285
    (see also shared objects)
RTMP (Real-Time Messaging Protocol), 4,
        7–9
    live streams and, 161
    paths, 263
    tunneling, 16
RTMPS
    connection, 730
    Flash Player and, 79
RTMPT, 16

S

Salant, Alon, 764
scalability, 672
scalability and load balancing, 686–695
scalable applications, building, 672–696
.scr files, 304, 312
Screen Recording codec, 242
script files
    dynamically loading, 143
    using load to include, 140–143
scripting application instances, 113–118
scriptlib directory, 141
<ScriptLibPath> tag, 141

Stream.record( ) method, 188
streams, 149–205
    buffering, 162, 171
    calling remote method, 156
    chaining, 188
    chaining between application instances
        running on separate FlashCom
        servers, 151
    chaining from one server to another, 188
    checking length, 341
    creating playlists, 167
    deleting, 189–192
    detecting end of, 172
    enhancements and limitations, 203
    getting a recorded streams length, 184
    getting length of list of, 184
    interface for selecting and switching, 271
    managing bandwidth, 180–183
    MP3 files, 170
    NetStream subclass subscribing to
        recorded, 176
    pausing and unpausing, 174
    playback, 198
    playback events, 168
    playing, 166–183
        live or recorded, 166
    publishing, 158–166
    publishing live, 153–155
    reading ID3 tags and playing MP3 audio
        using one stream, 170
    recording, 188
        buffering, 162
    retrieving length of stream from server
        using a client-side script, 185
    seeking within, 172
    subscribing to live, 155–157
    switching, 187
    uploading prerecorded, 170
streams directory, 116
<Streams> tag, Vhost.xml, 171
strong typing and NetStream class, 204
Stunnel, SSL wrapper, 791
subscriber, 149
subscriber/publisher example, 151
subscribing to live streams, 155–157
subscribing to recorded streams, 176
super operator, 120
superclass, calling constructor and methods
    in SSAS, 120
surveillance application, 233–236
SWC file, 484

.swf files (see movies)
swfFile property (PresentationSWF), 51
switchStream( ) method, defining for client
        object, 187
synchronization limitations, 204
synchronized presentations, 197–200
    adding synchronized slides, 200
    closed captions, 198
SynchronizedEventsManager class, 200

T

temporary access, 776
Test Movie command, 73
test movies, 94
test scripts, organizing, 144
testing server-side scripts, 143–145
TestSOListener class, 487
text
    bolding section of, 197
    formatting in text field, 196
TextChat class, fixURL( ) and
        sendMessage( ) methods, 513
TextChat component, 507–518
    chat history, 514–518
    client-side setter method for nc, 781
    history, 509
    message parsing, 510
    message passing, 508
    messages_s Stream object, 518
    messages_so shared object, 518
    resources and messaging, 508
    scroll bug, 514
    sessions_so shared object, 518
    UI, 510–511
        connecting to shared object, 512–514
TextChat subcomponents
    attaching and initializing, 510
TextChat.as file, enter( ) and click( )
        event handlers, 512
TextChat.asc file, server-side
        TextChat class addClient( )
        method, 512
TextChat.createChildren( ) method, 510
TextChat.getHistory( ) method,
        server-side, 780
TextChatSession class, 517
TextInput component, 22, 24
three-client conference, 182
threshold property, 39
threshold property (ConnectionLight), 47
throw model, 588

Colophon

Our look is the result of reader comments, our own experimentation, and feedback from distribution channels. Distinctive covers complement our distinctive approach to technical topics, breathing personality and life into potentially dry subjects.

The animal on the cover of *Programming Flash Communication Server* is the brown bear (*Ursus arctos*). The range of the brown bear is the widest among all species of bears. They are found in localized populations in Eastern and Western Europe, across Northern Asia, and in Japan. In North America, brown bears are found in Western Canada as well as Alaska, Wyoming, Montana, Idaho, and Washington. Although once abundant on the central plains of the United States, they have since been exterminated.

The brown bear is usually dark brown in color but can vary from a light cream color to almost black. If the tips of the guard hairs are white, they give the bear a grizzled appearance, hence the name grizzly bear, applied to the smaller of the two North American subspecies. Brown bears are distinguished by the characteristic muscle hump over their shoulders, which gives their front legs extra strength. Fully grown brown bears can weigh anywhere between 300 and 1,400 pounds, with males being characteristically larger than females. Even at this size, the brown bear can reach speeds of about 35 miles per hour for short intervals.

Brown bears live alone, except when females are accompanied by their cubs. During the fall they eat up to 90 pounds of food a day, including a diet of grasses, fruits, bulbs and roots, insects, fish, and small animals, to fatten up for the four to seven months of winter hibernation. The bear's normal heart rate of about 40 beats a minute drops during hibernation to as low as 8 beats a minute. Although brown bears can be awakened easily during their long sleep, the female bear doesn't wake up when her two cubs are born midwinter. The chipmunk-size bears crawl into a position where they settle in to nurse until spring. By the time the mother bear wakes up, her cubs are strong enough to follow her out of the den.

Adam Witwer was the production editor, and Norma Emory was the copyeditor for *Programming Flash Communication Server*. Sada Preisch proofread the text. Sanders Kleinfeld and Emily Quill provided quality control. Julie Hawks wrote the index.

Emma Colby designed the cover of this book, based on a series design by Edie Freedman. The cover image is a 19th-century engraving from the Dover Pictorial Archive. Emma Colby produced the cover layout with Adobe InDesign CS using Adobe's ITC Garamond font.

David Futato designed the interior layout. This book was converted by Joe Wizda to FrameMaker 5.5.6 with a format conversion tool created by Erik Ray, Jason McIntosh, Neil Walls, and Mike Sierra that uses Perl and XML technologies. The text font is Linotype Birka; the heading font is Adobe Myriad Condensed; and the code font is LucasFont's TheSans Mono Condensed. The illustrations that appear in the book were produced by Robert Romano, Jessamyn Read, and Lesley Borash using Macromedia FreeHand MX and Adobe Photoshop CS. The tip and warning icons were drawn by Christopher Bing. This colophon was written by Lydia Onofrei.

CPSIA information can be obtained at www.ICGtesting.com
265326BV00005B/94/P

9 780596 005047